Oil and Sovereignty

OIL AND SOVEREIGNTY

Petro-Knowledge and Energy Policy in the United States and Western Europe in the 1970s

Rüdiger Graf

Translated by Alex Skinner

berghahn
NEW YORK • OXFORD
www.berghahnbooks.com

First published in 2018 by
Berghahn Books
www.berghahnbooks.com

English-language edition
© 2018, 2026 Berghahn Books
First paperback edition published in 2026

German-language edition
© 2014 Walter de Gruyter GmbH Berlin Boston
Originally published in German as Öl und Souveränität: Petroknowledge und Energiepolitik in den USA und Westeuropa in den 1970er Jahren

The translation of this work was funded by Geisteswissenschaften International – Translation Funding for Work in the Humanities and Social Sciences from Germany, a joint initiative of the Fritz Thyssen Foundation, the German Federal Foreign Office, the collecting society VG WORT and the Börsenverein des Deutschen Buchhandels (German Publishers & Booksellers Association).

All rights reserved. Except for the quotation of short passages for the purposes of criticism and review, no part of this book may be reproduced in any form or by any means, electronic or mechanical, including photocopying, recording, or any information storage and retrieval system now known or to be invented, without written permission of the publisher.

Library of Congress Cataloging-in-Publication Data
Names: Graf, Rüdiger, 1975– author.
Title: Oil and Sovereignty: Petro-Knowledge and Energy Policy in the United States and Western Europe in the 1970s / by Rüdiger Graf; translated by Alex Skinner.
Other titles: Öl und Souveränität. English
Description: First Edition. | New York: Berghahn Books, [2018] | Includes bibliographical references and index.
Identifiers: LCCN 2017057759 (print) | LCCN 2018004381 (ebook) | ISBN 9781785338076 (Ebook) | ISBN 9781785338069 (hardback: alk. paper)
Subjects: LCSH: Petroleum industry and trade—Political aspects—United States—History—20th century. | Petroleum industry and trade—Political aspects—Europe, Western—History—20th century. | Energy policy—United States—History—20th century. | Energy policy—Europe, Western—History—20th century.
Classification: LCC HD9565 (ebook) | LCC HD9565 .G724 2018 (print) | DDC 338.2/72809409046—dc23
LC record available at https://lccn.loc.gov/2017057759

British Library Cataloguing in Publication Data
A catalogue record for this book is available from the British Library

EU GPSR Authorized Representative
LOGOS EUROPE, 9 rue Nicolas Poussin, 17000, LA ROCHELLE, France
Email: Contact@logoseurope.eu

ISBN 978-1-78533-806-9 hardback
ISBN 978-1-83695-368-5 paperback
ISBN 978-1-83695-369-2 epub
ISBN 978-1-78533-807-6 web pdf

https://doi.org/10.3167/9781785338069

Contents

List of Illustrations		vi
Acknowledgements		vii
Abbreviations		x
Introduction	Sovereignty and Petro-Knowledge	1
Chapter 1	The World of Oil in the 1950s and 1960s	19
Chapter 2	Shortages, Forecasts, Prevention: Supplying the Western World with Oil	51
Chapter 3	The Global Communication of the 'Arab Oil Weapon'	88
Chapter 4	The Politics of Sovereignty in the Energy Crisis: The United States	123
Chapter 5	West Germany within the World of Oil	203
Chapter 6	Oil Conferences: Global Interdependence and National Sovereignty	286
Chapter 7	Petro-Knowledge, the Perception of Limits and Sovereignty: Creating the Oil Crisis	332
Conclusion	Sovereignty in Crisis and the Oil Crisis in Contemporary History	387
Bibliography		396
Index		447

Illustrations

Figure 0.1. Halliburton advertisement, in 'Petroleum Panorama: Commemorating 100 Years of Petroleum Progress', *Oil and Gas Journal* 57(5) (1959), inside front cover.   2

Figure 1.1. Ferdinand Mayer, *Erdöl-Weltatlas* (Hamburg/Braunschweig, 1966). © Westermann, Bildungshaus Schulbuchverlage, Braunschweig.   27

Figure 3.1. 'Yamani leaves Kennedy Airport, 3 December 1973', *New York Daily News*. © Getty Images.   109

Figure 7.1. George A. Lincoln, 'Energy Security: New Dimension for US Policy', *Air Force Magazine* 56(11) (1973), 49–55, here 51.   352

Acknowledgements

This book was first published in German in 2014 as *Öl und Souveränität: Petroknowledge und Energiepolitik in den USA und Westeuropa in den 1970er Jahren*. Its translation was made possible by the 'Geisteswissenschaften International' translation prize awarded by the German Publishers and Booksellers Association (Börsenverein des Deutschen Buchhandels), which I was fortunate enough to receive in 2016. I have shortened the text slightly for the translation and included references to a number of significant new publications. But I concluded the bulk of the research in 2012 when I completed the first version of the manuscript while working at Ruhr-University Bochum. My thanks go to the Bochum Faculty of History and particularly to Constantin Goschler for his many years of support and innumerable useful suggestions, which have helped make the book what it is today. The staff at the Chair of Contemporary History have made Bochum both an interesting and pleasant place to work. A number of my colleagues in Bochum have contributed to the present work in various ways, particularly Benjamin Herzog, Martin Kohlrausch, Helmut Maier, Walther Sperling, Xenia von Tippelskirch and Cornel Zwierlein.

The present study was made possible – or at least much easier – by several scholarships for which I am deeply grateful. A three-month travel grant from the Max Weber Foundation (Max Weber Stiftung – Deutsche Geisteswissenschaftliche Institute im Ausland) enabled me to visit the German Historical Institutes in Washington, Paris and London. It also allowed me to carry out research at the Library of Congress, the Bibliothèque Nationale de France, the British Library, the National Archives – College Park, the Nixon Presidential Library, the Lafayette-College Libraries and Archives, the Archives Nationales de France, the Institut Français du Pétrole and the National Archives of the United Kingdom. My acceptance into the Junges Kolleg programme of the North Rhine-Westphalian Academy of Sciences, Humanities and the Arts (Nordrhein-Westfälische

Akademie der Wissenschaften und der Künste) provided me with financial room for manoeuvre. This allowed me to carry out research at the Staatsbibliothek zu Berlin – Preußischer Kulturbesitz, the German Federal Archives (Bundesarchiv Koblenz) and the Political Archive of the Federal Foreign Office (Politisches Archiv des Auswärtigen Amts) in Berlin. For archival support I thank Diane Shaw, Marc Hanisch and Rüdiger von Dehn and I am grateful to William Hogan and Hans-Stefan Kruse for allowing me to interview them.

In the academic year 2010–11, as a John F. Kennedy Memorial Fellow, I was able to carry out further research at the Minda de Gunzburg Center for European Studies at Harvard University. There I developed the conceptual framework of the present study and wrote the first chapters. I benefited not just from the inexhaustible holdings of the Widener Library, but also from many lectures and from conversations with David Engerman, Arthur Goldhammer, Stanley Hoffmann, Hans-Helmut Kotz, Christina May, John Munro, Uta Poiger, Warren Rosenblum, Quinn Slobodian, Jan Teorell and Andrew Zimmerman. A second sabbatical in 2011–12 at the Historisches Kolleg in Munich allowed me to complete the first version of the manuscript. I would like to express my sincere gratitude to the Historisches Kolleg and the Gerda Henkel Foundation (Gerda Henkel Stiftung), which provided a research grant. The peaceful atmosphere at the Kolleg, situated between the Bavarian State Library (Bayerische Staatsbibliothek) and the Englischer Garten, provided excellent conditions for the concluding phase of the writing, during which I received valuable support from Kolleg staff – especially Franz Quirin Meyer. My thanks go to Karl-Ulrich Gelberg and the other fellows, above all Friedrich Lenger, as well as Martina Steber, Roman Köster, Nicolai Hannig and Sebastian Ullrich for stimulating insights and for making this such a pleasant time.

It took several years to write this book, incurring a tremendous debt of gratitude. It is often impossible to reconstruct precisely when and where particular ideas arose. For their criticisms and critical questions, I thank the organizers and participants at research colloquia in Freiburg, Cologne, Gießen, Augsburg, Potsdam, Berlin, Bochum, Cambridge/Mass., Munich, Gießen, Jena, London, Trier, Zurich and Göttingen, where I had the opportunity to present my work. During a semester in Göttingen, Bernd Weisbrod, Habbo Knoch and their colleagues provided me with useful suggestions. I presented various parts of my work at conferences in San Diego, Washington, Berlin, Bonn, Padua, Hamburg, Göttingen, Freiburg, Bern and Edmonton, at the Historikertage in 2010 in Berlin and 2012 in Mainz, at conferences I organized in collaboration with Hannah Ahlheim, Cornel Zwierlein and Frank Bösch in Bochum and at the Centre for Contemporary History in Potsdam. I thank them and the participants for their support, questions and criticisms. My thanks also go to Andreas Wirsching and Magnus Brechtken for enabling publication of the original German text in the *Quellen und Darstellungen zur Zeitgeschichte* series and to Gabriele Jaroschka of Walter de Gruyter Verlag for her dedicated supervision of the book. I am delighted that Berghahn Books has agreed to publish an English translation. I am grateful to Konrad H. Jarausch for setting things up, Marion Berghahn for agreeing to publish the book, and Chris Chappell and Amanda Horn for their fine stewardship. It was a pleasure to work with Alex Skinner, who provided the translation. My thanks to Peter Mercer for formatting the bibliographic information for the English publication, and for being such a reliable source of research support over the last few years.

The idea of writing a book on the oil crisis arose in 2006 over lunch with Matthias Pohlig in the inner courtyard of Humboldt-Universität, and I am grateful to him for that conversation and many others during this book's gestation. Moritz Föllmer and Philipp Müller have read virtually everything I have written over the last few years, their always friendly but firm criticisms leading to marked improvements. In the absence of their support and without the critical readings of various parts of the manuscript by Marcus Böick, Aimee Genell, Constantin Goschler, Martin Kohlrausch, Kim Christian Priemel, Annelie Ramsbrock, Christiane Reinecke, Ulrike Schaper, Quinn Slobodian and Janosch Steuwer, the book might well have been finished sooner – but it might not have been completed at all. It has certainly benefited greatly from their input.

Rüdiger Graf, Berlin, August 2017

ABBREVIATIONS

AA	Auswärtiges Amt (Federal Foreign Office)
AAPG	American Association of Petroleum Geologists
AdsD	Archiv der Sozialen Demokratie (Archive of Social Democracy)
AIME	American Institute of Mining and Metallurgical Engineers
AIOC	Anglo-Iranian Oil Company
ANF	Archives Nationales de France
API	American Petroleum Institute
Aramco	Arabian-American Oil Company
AUGE	Arbeitsgruppe Umwelt, Gesellschaft, Energie (Working Group on Environment, Society and Energy)
BArch	Bundesarchiv (German Federal Archives)
BDI	Bundesverband der Deutschen Industrie (Federation of German Industries)
BM	Bundesminister (federal minister)
BMWF	Bundesministerium für Wissenschaft und Forschung (Federal Ministry of Science and Research)
BMWi	Bundesministerium für Wirtschaft (Federal Ministry of Economics)
BP	British Petroleum
CBS	Columbia Broadcasting Systems
CDU	Christlich Demokratische Union Deutschlands (Christian Democratic Union of Germany)
CFP	Compagnie Française des Pétroles

Abbreviations

CIA	Central Intelligence Agency
CIEC	Conference on International Economic Cooperation
Comecon	Council for Mutual Economic Assistance
CSCE	Conference on Security and Cooperation in Europe
CSU	Christlich-Soziale Union in Bayern (Christian Social Union in Bavaria)
DEMINEX	Deutsche Mineralölexplorationsgesellschaft mbH (German Petroleum Exploration Company)
DIW	Deutsches Institut für Wirtschaftsforschung, Berlin (German Institute for Economic Research)
DNSA	Digital National Security Archive
EC	European Communities
ECSC	European Coal and Steel Community
EEC	European Economic Community
EPC	European Political Cooperation
ERP	European Recovery Program
Euratom	European Atomic Energy Community
EWI	Energiewirtschaftliches Institut an der Universität Köln (Institute of Energy Economics, Cologne)
FDP	Freie Demokratische Partei (Liberal Democratic Party)
FES	Friedrich Ebert Stiftung (Friedrich Ebert Foundation)
IEA	International Energy Agency
IEP	International Energy Programme
LCL	Lafayette College Libraries
MEES	*Middle East Economic Survey*
MIT	Massachusetts Institute of Technology
mph	miles per hour
NARA	National Archives and Records Administration
NA UK	National Archives of the United Kingdom
NBC	National Broadcasting System
NSSM	National Security Study Memorandum
OAPEC	Organization of Arab Petroleum Exporting Countries
OECD	Organization for Economic Cooperation and Development

OEEC	Organization for European Economic Cooperation
OPEC	Organization of Petroleum Exporting Countries
PIES	Project Independence Evaluation System
PLO	Palestinian Liberation Organization
RWI	Rheinisch-Westfälisches Institut für Wirtschaftsforschung (Rhineland-Westphalia Institute for Economic Research)
SKE	Steinkohleeinheiten (coal units)
Socal	Standard Oil of California
SPD	Sozialdemokratische Partei Deutschlands (Social-Democratic Party of Germany)
SPE	Society of Petroleum Engineers
StS	Staatssekretär (undersecretary)
UNCTAD	United Nations Conference on Trade and Development
UNEP	United Nations Environment Programme
UNIDO	United Nations Industrial Development Organization
USD	United States Dollar
USGS	United States Geological Survey
USSR	Union of Soviet Socialist Republics
WAES	Workshop on Alternative Energy Strategies

Introduction

SOVEREIGNTY AND PETRO-KNOWLEDGE

> *When I no longer know where your power ends and mine begins; . . . when the more I try to force you to depend on me, the more I depend on you; when world politics becomes a test of vulnerability, and degrees of vulnerability are not identical with power supplies, who can feel secure?*
> —Stanley Hoffmann, *Primacy or World Order*

In 1959, when the renowned *Oil and Gas Journal* brought out a special issue marking the one hundredth anniversary of oil production in the United States, every significant company with a stake in the sector took out major advertisements. Halliburton's contribution reflected the oil industry's characteristic self-confidence, which was anchored in the increasing economic and social significance, in the mid twentieth century and beyond, of the natural resource it processed. Grouped around a depiction of the first legendary oil well, the Drake Well in Titusville, Pennsylvania, were images of civilizational achievements, from the ancient wonders of the world to modern ships, aeroplanes, trains and cars, a refinery, a factory and a farm, the goal being to highlight oil's elementary significance to the emergence of modern civilization.

The text of the advertisement reinforced the visual message that oil helped create civilization and was of constitutive importance to the Western world:

> The needs of civilized man have increased throughout the ages based on desires of increasing populations to live better. Oil and its energy making components have been and will continue to be part of this progressive program of civilization which guarantees function and preservation of this ideology. On this theme the future of democracy will forever depend. Halliburton's extensive research and development programs are devoted to this progressing civilization.[1]

Figure 0.1. Halliburton advertisement, in 'Petroleum Panorama: Commemorating 100 Years of Petroleum Progress', *Oil and Gas Journal* 57(5) (1959), inside front cover.

Just under two decades later, in 1977, physicist and environmental activist Amory Lovins constructed a fundamentally different relationship between energy use and economic, social and political systems. He distinguished between a 'soft energy path' centred on the decentralized use of renewable sources such as wind, sun and water, and a 'hard energy path', which he believed to be the current trajectory of Western societies. The latter, he explained, was based mainly on fossil fuels and increasingly on nuclear energy and was producing unwelcome economic, social and political effects:

> The hard path ... demands strongly interventionist central control, bypasses traditional market mechanisms, concentrates political and economic power, encourages urbanization, persistently distorts political structures and social priorities, increases bureaucratization and alienation, compromises professional ethics, is probably inimical to greater distributional equity within and among nations, inequitably divorces costs from benefits, enhances vulnerability and the paramilitarization of civilian life, introduces major economic and social risk, ... and nurtures – even requires – elitist technocracy whose exercise erodes the legitimacy of democratic government.[2]

In the eighteen years lying between these two quotations, the international oil economy, along with energy policy structures and strategies, changed dramatically in Western Europe and the United States. Ideas about oil and energy and debates on these topics in the scientific, political and public spheres also changed as part of this process. Chiefly as a result of accelerating shifts in the oil market in the early 1970s, a set of problems and discursive frameworks emerged that continue to exercise an effect to this day. But this was by no means a linear development away from the notion of a brave new world of oil to an acknowledgement of the negative domestic and international consequences of the increasing use of fossil hydrocarbons, as the quotations from Halliburton and Lovins might seem to imply. Instead, the oil industry's claim to have created modern civilization and buttressed Western democracy on the one hand, and the environmental movement's critique of fossil fuels on the other, mark out the two poles of the political and social debate on oil and energy from the 1970s to the present.[3]

Yet despite all their differences, energy companies and environmental activists shared the same basic assumption: that the growing use of fossil fuels was constitutive of the development of modern, industrial, affluent societies. From the 1960s onwards, both viewed the modern world essentially as a world of oil. The exceptional economic boom of the postwar decades, the 'Golden Age' (Eric Hobsbawm) or 'Trente Glorieuses' (Jean Fourastié), which ended in the mid 1970s, was based in large part on the unlimited availability of cheap fossil fuels.[4] The most significant development was the rapidly mounting use of oil, which increasingly came from the Middle East and superseded coal as the most important primary energy source in the Western industrialized countries. Within the discourse of national security and the critique of oil, both of which identify a close connection between the growing dependency on oil and the United States' military engagements, oil is considered the leading basic commodity of modern industrialized societies.[5] In the absence of an adequate supply of this substance, it is commonly argued, the economy would collapse and the entire social structure would face challenges that might threaten the stability of the political order. In the days of the Cold War, this nexus seemed all the more dramatic inasmuch as the legitimacy of Western democracies was essentially derived from increasing affluence, which was in part facilitated by the rapidly growing consumption of energy and oil.

Irrespective of whether oil, modern economic and social forms and the legitimacy of Western democratic institutions were truly linked in this way, those who believed they were saw the first oil crisis of 1973–74 as a fundamental challenge to political legitimacy and sovereignty in the United States, Western Europe and Japan.[6] During the 1960s, resource-rich 'Third World' countries, and above all the oil-producing countries that had united in the Organization of Petroleum Exporting Countries (OPEC), had already made increasingly strident calls for the right to exercise permanent sovereignty over the natural resources in their territories. Even after their political independence, these resources were still being extracted by companies headquartered in the United States and Western Europe on the basis of concessions dating back to the colonial era. When negotiations between the producing countries and the oil firms on an oil price hike collapsed in October 1973, the former unilaterally sent prices soaring, and before long the cost of oil had quadrupled. At the same time, the Arab producing countries in the Organization of Arab Petroleum Exporting Countries (OAPEC) announced production cutbacks and imposed an embargo on the United States and the Netherlands. Their objective was to support the Arab side in the Yom Kippur War with Israel and compel Western countries to adopt a more pro-Arab position.

The course pursued by OPEC and OAPEC destroyed the complex communicative and interactive routines of the global oil economy and challenged the sovereignty of the Western industrialized nations on a fundamental level. While the producing countries acquired rights of sovereignty and coordinated their production policies, the sovereignty enjoyed by the governments of Western industrialized nations appeared to be under threat. The oil crisis showed what energy experts and attentive observers had been concluding since the late 1960s: the Western European, North

American and Japanese political systems rested on a foundation that they themselves could not guarantee, namely the cheap and unlimited availability of low-priced energy sources, chiefly oil. In what follows, I investigate the measures and strategies adopted by political actors in Western Europe and the United States in response to this challenge to national sovereignty and their political authority, that is, to the legitimate exercise of sovereignty.

Sovereignty

The concept of sovereignty has always been an ambiguous one.[7] As Jean Bodin framed it from a constitutional law perspective, it initially referred to the 'ultimate decision making authority within a state and the complete independence of this state from the external world', a concept that was supposed to supersede the older forms of legitimate authority (such as that of the estates).[8] In the nineteenth century, partly through attempts to get to grips with the colonial Other, the concept of sovereignty attained the status of a European norm, prompting Lassa Francis Lawrence Oppenheim to declare that, in addition to territory and people, a sovereign government was one of the state's key components: 'There must ... be a sovereign government. Sovereignty is supreme authority, an authority which is independent of any other earthly authority. Sovereignty in the strict and narrowest sense of the term includes, therefore, independence all around, within and without the borders of the country'.[9] In the twentieth century, as large-scale imperial structures collapsed or dissolved as a result of the world wars, and the United Nations was founded as an organization of sovereign states, the principle of sovereignty attained universal validity. Having been granted no rights of sovereignty in the course of European expansion, the colonized peoples obtained them in the process of decolonization, though only while recognizing international law.[10] But its rules immediately placed new limits on their sovereignty, forcing them to adhere to the treaties through which Western firms extracted the raw materials within their territory. In the 1960s, the decolonized countries of the so-called Third World thus began to demand 'permanent sovereignty over natural resources'.[11]

In the final third of the twentieth century, however, it was not just the countries of the Third World that faced restrictions on their sovereignty. Around 1970, in Western Europe and the United States, influential economists and political scientists increasingly identified an erosion of national sovereignty and questioned whether the idea of supreme and absolute authority over a given territory could still capture the present-day structures and problems of statehood.[12] First, as a result of far-reaching economic globalization – 'interdependence' as it was generally referred to at the time – economic structures appeared to have emerged that were largely beyond the control of individual states, while simultaneously having a potentially enormous impact upon them. For economic historian Charles Kindleberger, as early as 1969 the nation state could no longer be taken seriously as an economic unit. And in light of the existence of powerful multinational companies, economist Raymond Vernon stated: 'Suddenly, it seems, the sovereign states are feeling naked. Concepts such as national sovereignty and national economic strength appear curiously drained of meaning'.[13] Second, transnational organizations and international treaty systems appeared to curb nation states' scope for action, as argued by Robert Keohane and Joseph Nye.[14] The global politics of human rights and the United Nations, for example, increasingly came into conflict with national claims to sovereignty.[15] At the same time, the treaties of the European Communities were a much-discussed example of the voluntary surrender of national sovereignty through supranational structures.[16]

In the early 1970s, however, highlighting the example of West Germany, conservative constitutional law expert Ernst Forsthoff questioned the sovereignty of Western democracies in an even more fundamental sense. The 'state of the industrial society' could no longer be called sovereign in the classical sense because it had lost the 'right of, or de facto capacity for, decision-making within the existential conflicts'.[17] As this student of Carl Schmitt elaborated, this was because 'the hard core of the present-day social whole is no longer the state but industrial society, and this hard core is typified by the watchwords full employment and economic growth'.[18] As he saw it, the legitimacy of the state – especially that of West Germany – was entirely dependent on the economic performance of industrial society and would inevitably erode when the economy ceased its by then customary steady growth. In 1972, another constitutional law scholar, Ernst-Wolfgang Böckenförde, highlighted an 'increasing tendency to identify state with economy', the state alone being incapable of carrying out its additional responsibilities, namely ensuring social security, increasing affluence and guaranteeing social progress. Instead, the crucial factor was economic growth, for which the state could only try to provide a general framework.[19] So Böckenförde's dictum, already formulated by 1967 and much quoted ever since, that the 'liberal, secular state' is dependent on prerequisites that this state 'itself [cannot] guarantee', applied not just to the spheres of religion and morality that he had in mind.[20] In the oil crisis, it appeared as if it was also true of the state's energetic base and its potential to pursue economic policies.

Against the background of this theoretical debate on sovereignty, leading politicians in Western Europe and the United States perceived the actions of OPEC and OAPEC as a threat to their political sovereignty. Many agreed with British opposition leader Harold Wilson when he claimed, in November 1973, that the policies being pursued by the producing countries represented the greatest threat to British sovereignty since the Danish invasion more than a millennium ago.[21] So in the present work I do not apply the concept of sovereignty to events ex post; contemporaries were already using it to interpret them. The oil crisis itself influenced the debate on sovereignty, which received new impetus in the 1990s after the end of the Cold War and remains ongoing.[22] In the following chapters, I aim to establish the exact nature of the challenge posed by the oil crisis to political sovereignty, while simultaneously locating this challenge within the history of sovereignty. This throws up a fundamental problem. While I historicize the debates on sovereignty and seek to assess the impact of the oil crisis upon them, I have to work with a concept of sovereignty that is itself located within this discursive tradition. This requires me to begin by elaborating the different strands of the concept of sovereignty, in order to resolve or explicate this ambivalence in the conclusion.

In what follows, I understand sovereignty not as an attribute that a state may or may not have, but as a claim that may be asserted, questioned, attacked and defended.[23] In other words, sovereignty is constituted through social and communicative processes: to be sovereign means to be recognized as such by others, and the establishment of sovereignty is closely bound up with its demonstration. So sovereignty rests not just on the effective exercise of power over a particular territory and the securing of this authority against the external world, but also on its communication, as practised, in the second half of the twentieth century, through globally networked media ensembles.[24] We can expand on this dual character of the concept of sovereignty with respect to its internal and external dimensions by drawing on the insights of Stephen D. Krasner. He distinguishes four aspects of the concept of sovereignty, which may be but are not necessarily linked: 'international legal sovereignty', that is, mutual recognition within the system of states; 'Westphalian sovereignty', the exclusion of external influences from one's own territory; 'domestic sovereignty', the capacity to exercise political authority in a given territory; and 'interdependence sovereignty', the ability to regulate the flow of ideas, goods and people across borders.[25]

In what sense, then, did the actions of OPEC and OAPEC threaten sovereignty in Western Europe and the United States? So-called Westphalian sovereignty was never at issue. It was interdependence sovereignty that faced a challenge, though not in the sense of the ability to keep certain goods, people or ideas out of a given territory by securing its borders, but in the sense of the capacity to guarantee an adequate flow of a particular good, in this case oil, across borders. OAPEC also attacked the Western democracies' international sovereignty by trying to compel them to adopt a particular foreign policy position through production cutbacks and the embargo. The basis of this threat was that sustained supply shortages might impair states' domestic political sovereignty and imperil their governments, if not their political systems as a whole.

Petro-Knowledge

The oil economy and the politics of oil formed a complex, global system of interaction and communication within which numerous actors had varying options to influence the flow of oil – the oil firms, particularly the large multinational companies, the governments of the producing countries, international organizations such as OPEC, OAPEC, the Organization for Economic Cooperation and Development (OECD) and the European Communities (EC), governments, but also individual governmental institutions or other authorities in the consuming countries, scientists and oil experts of various disciplines and, ultimately, individual consumers of oil and energy. Their interaction and communication were governed by routines and habitual practices that had been established over many years. In October 1973, OPEC and OAPEC challenged and destroyed these routines. A new sense of uncertainty prevailed as key actors were unable to easily anticipate or make assumptions about others' conduct as well as their own responses to it. In the absence of new routines, this doubly contingent state of affairs inevitably generates great insecurity among all those involved.[26] The scope for action is crucially dependent on how much one knows, or believes one knows, about other actors and topics of shared concern.

At the time, contingency, uncertainty and ignorance reinforced the impression that the changes in the international oil economy and national energy policies touched on fundamental issues of political sovereignty, legitimacy and authority. At the moment of crisis, in the United States, West Germany, Western Europe and Japan, democratically legitimatized governments and their civil services seemed to lack oil-related knowledge, casting doubt on their capacity to take effective action. When Democratic Senator Henry M. Jackson opened a hearing of the US Senate Committee on Government Operations concerning the oil crisis in January 1974 with the following words, he expressed a sentiment widely felt in the public sphere and governmental circles in the United States and Western Europe:

> The first conclusion that we have drawn from the first three days of hearings is that we still do not have the facts we need to make sound national economic and energy policy. We know we have an energy shortage but we do not know how big the shortage is or how bad it will get. We don't have accurate or reliable figures on stocks, on demand, on costs, on imports, or virtually anything else. Today, no one, I repeat no one, has access to accurate current information on energy reserves or resources.[27]

Statements like this were underpinned by a scientized conception of policymaking. The idea was that political decisions ought to be based on knowledge, understood as justified, true belief, generated in the correct – and this generally meant scientific – way.[28] Specifically, the knowledge at issue in the oil crisis was that concerning the future availability of oil, referred to hereafter, following political scientist Timothy Mitchell, as 'petro-knowledge'.[29] Mitchell uses the term to refer to a form of Keynesian economic knowledge after the Second World War, which he claims to have been based on the unlimited availability of cheap energy sources, and oil in particular, though he fails to adequately reflect on this epistemic foundation. In what follows, meanwhile, the term is extended to include all forms of expert knowledge about oil. When Western democracies' supply of oil and energy began to look shaky in the early 1970s, and above all during the oil crisis, the political and public demand for oil-related knowledge skyrocketed. Petro-knowledge became almost as inflationary as so-called petrodollars, thereby changing its importance to policymaking.[30]

In the early 1970s, Western European and US politicians found themselves confronted with a new problem in the field of energy, one they had previously spent little time considering. In response, by drawing on supposedly solid expert knowledge, they aspired to enhance their capacity for effective political action while at the same time demonstrating it publicly. Initially, during the period of acute crisis, the main focus was on highly specific questions, such as how much oil would be lacking on a daily basis or what energy-saving measures might offset this deficit without impairing economic development. Beyond this, over the medium and long term the key goal was to determine likely energy needs and, by attending to the composition and origin of primary energy, ensure that the supply of energy would be sufficient, secure and as cheap as possible. The development of official governmental expertise in the United States, or the recourse to the expertise of research institutes and think tanks that was solicited or offered, was thus intended to safeguard energy sovereignty. At the same time, the public demonstration that the government was acting on the basis of the best possible expertise was meant to help secure its legitimacy vis-à-vis the general population as well as its standing in relation to the multinational oil companies and the producing countries.

Petro-knowledge neither grows on trees nor is it as fluid and transitory as many theoretical discussions of the concept of knowledge might lead us to believe. In fact, it emerged in very specific places: among the petroleum engineers involved in its extraction and production, within petroleum geology and the discipline of economics, but also in the social and political sciences. Beyond practices in the oilfields and manufacturing sector, its emergence was closely bound up with specific disciplines, making classical assumptions about the diffusion and popularization of scientific knowledge quite plausible in this context. Ultimately, in the twentieth century, petro-knowledge became so highly differentiated that even experts in one discipline could often receive the findings of other disciplines only as popularized by the media.[31] If for no other reason, petro-knowledge was far from disinterested because it was produced mainly in the major oil companies' research departments and was thus directly bound up with economic processes.[32] The economization of petro-knowledge continued in the 1960s and 1970s as oil's importance to modern economies and societies increased. But at the same time, it was politicized, as an increasing number of political and social scientists began to contemplate the importance of oil and the securing of energy supplies and sought to insert their expertise into the political decision-making process.[33] At the time, the various economic and political interests involved in the production of petro-knowledge prompted some contemporaries to question whether political strategies could truly be underpinned by objective data. In what follows, I neither uncritically embrace the notion of knowledge-based policymaking nor do I seek to unmask it as ideological.[34] Instead, my goal is to determine the significance and instrumentalization of petro-knowledge in the strategies pursued by Western industrial countries as they strove to bolster their political sovereignty.

In addition to the production and use of energy-related knowledge, domestic and foreign policy measures were pursued in an effort to guarantee governments' capacity for effective action and secure their sovereignty. Attempts were made to centralize energy policy or institutionalize it on a higher level, while simultaneously expanding the executive's capacity to take emergency measures to safeguard energy supplies. Historically, political competences relating to coal, oil and nuclear power were dispersed among various governmental agencies. But what now emerged was an independent political field with a comprehensive focus on energy, one that has become increasingly significant up to the present day.[35] This book is interested both in these changes and in the specific energy policy measures intended to ensure 'energy security'. Essentially, this security could be enhanced either by diversifying sources of energy, diversifying countries of origin or introducing energy-saving measures. But because it takes a long time to restructure energy industries, in the acute phase of the oil crisis only energy-saving measures held the prospect of short-term improvements. All governments therefore called on citizens to save energy or implemented compulsory energy-saving measures, further increasing the public visibility of the oil crisis. These sparked both discussions in the media and direct processes of communication between governing and governed, highlighting what happens to a highly mobile and technological society when energy threatens to become scarce.

The oil embargo and the regime of production cutbacks were in part attempts by the producing countries to force Western Europe, the United States and Japan to adopt more pro-Arab policies, so foreign policy or international relations was another field in which the latter felt compelled to safeguard their sovereignty. Here, especially, we can see the analytical strength of the concept of sovereignty, as it enables us to get to grips with the interplay of foreign and domestic political strategies. Energy savings in a given country were meant to enhance its negotiating position vis-à-vis the producing countries; the restructuring of energy policy was intended to get across the message that the latter would only damage themselves, because over the medium term Western Europe and the United States would reduce oil imports from the Middle East. In negotiations with the producing countries, the governments of the consuming countries tried to eliminate or at least alleviate production restrictions and limit oil price rises. At the same time, however, along with other consuming countries, they looked for possible ways of enhancing their position within the global oil economy or restructuring the world of oil as a whole. In the context of the oil crisis, the world of oil or its order hitherto had lost their taken-for-granted status and now differing visions of a new order jostled with one another. While the French government called for a dialogue to include producing, developing and industrial countries under the aegis of the UN, the United States and the other Western European countries sought to establish an organization of the leading consuming countries, and this came to fruition in the shape of the International Energy Agency.

Structure of the Present Work

Because oil reserves are distributed unequally across the world, and for the most part oil is not processed and consumed in the same places where it is extracted, in the twentieth century the oil economy took the form of a worldwide lattice of interconnections. The moment at which changes in the flow of oil crossed a certain threshold, they were felt throughout the entire system. And the oil crisis too was a global phenomenon. Only the countries of the Eastern Bloc, which were essentially self-sufficient in oil and energy due to the Soviet Union's oil reserves, were initially spared any direct impact. In fact, over the medium term they profited from the increased cost of energy and the Western Europeans' interest in importing oil and gas, only to be hit all the harder by plunging oil prices in the 1980s.[36] Given the global structure of the oil economy, studies that restrict themselves to a single country are necessarily deficient.[37] At the same time, it would be illusory to seek to achieve a complete global picture or even a globally balanced one. Because the present work examines the Western industrialized countries' strategies for enhancing their political sovereignty, one focal point must inevitably be the United States. The US was the homeland of industrial oil production, the largest producing and consuming country until the early 1970s, the hegemonic power within the Western alliance and home to five of the seven largest oil companies. To achieve a more balanced picture, a second key focus will be on West Germany, which lacked major oil reserves and was home to no significant oil companies. When it came to energy and foreign policy, West Germany was integrated into the international and supranational structures of the European Communities, so I also consider its European partners, particularly the United Kingdom and France. In addition to these national case studies, I take a close look at the interaction and communication within international organizations such as the OECD and the UN, which sought to give structure to the world of oil. From a global perspective, the present work's greatest shortcoming is probably its merely second-hand view of the producing countries and their policies. I examine the conduct of OPEC and OAPEC first through the media in which their representatives expressed their views and, second, in light of the diplomatic reports produced by Western governments. However, in what follows, my goal is not to grasp the world of oil as a whole but to understand Western Europe's and the United States' place and self-placement, or assertion of sovereignty, within this world, phenomena that underwent rapid change in the first half of the 1970s as a result of the producing countries' policies.

The key sources for the present work are records and official government publications from the United States and West Germany and to a lesser extent the United Kingdom and France, published and unpublished scholarly studies on the issue of energy from these countries, and media reports on the oil and energy crisis, mostly in daily newspapers and on television. Methodologically, I attempt to link the history of energy policy in the 1970s with a history of knowledge about oil and energy in the second half of the twentieth century. By scrutinizing the significance of petro-knowledge in the oil crisis while simultaneously investigating its transformation by that crisis, I seek to contribute to the history of the scientification of the political sphere.[38] At the same time, due to its temporal anchorage in the 1970s, the present study finds itself amid a booming field of research, one dominated so far by a narrative that was already being spun by contemporaries. According to this perspective, the 1970s was an important period of transformation in the history of the Western industrial societies. It is believed to be a time when a shift occurred, away from the exceptional postwar economic boom towards the crisis of the present era, away from full employment towards mass unemployment and all its attendant problems, away from an industrial society towards a 'post-industrial society', away from a time of seemingly unlimited possibilities towards an acknowledgement of limits, away from euphoric hopes towards dark fears of decline, and away from the idea of economic and social planning by rational experts towards pragmatic crisis management.[39] In many of these contexts, the oil crisis of 1973–74 is identified as a key factor or even just as a particularly significant indication of changing times, but only rarely is the crisis itself made an object of investigation.[40]

A closer examination of the oil crisis only partially confirms the standard narrative. In some respects it adds nuance to it, and in others again calls it fundamentally into question. So in what follows the oil crisis serves as a means of getting to grips with key changes that occurred in the Western democracies in the 1970s. While oil and energy are central to the present study, my goal is only partly to write a history of the oil and energy crisis or, more generally, of the politics of energy in Western Europe and the United States in the 1970s. In analogy to the micro-historians' determination to carry out research *in* rather than *about* villages, I instead aim, in light of the oil crisis, to investigate fundamental problems of Western industrial societies. Though these problems did not arise in the 1970s, it was during this era that they became clearly evident, taking on concrete forms in the context of the energy crisis. What I am essentially concerned with here are strategies for asserting sovereignty under conditions of global economic entanglement; to put it another way, I seek to illuminate national governments' ability to communicate and ensure both their capacity for effective political action and their legitimacy under conditions of contingency, uncertainty and a highly differentiated ensemble of mass media. I also discuss the plannability and controllability of the political process by experts and the closely related issues of the 'governability' of modern democracies and the role of the state in the economy. The oil crisis turned a whole range of problems – from energy security through the Middle East conflict to economic globalization and issues of global 'governance' – into key political issues, so exploring its history means grappling with the genesis of the present.

To understand what the governments of Western Europe and the United States did during the oil crisis, the present work begins by reconstructing the world of oil in the 1950s and 1960s (chapter 1). By 'world of oil', I mean both the specific practices of production, processing and consumption and, by extension, the economic, social and political world shaped by these practices. What were the key structures and who were the main actors? What was the significance of oil and oil products to the increasing prosperity of Western Europe and the United States in the years of the economic boom? And which knowledge systems grew up around the international oil economy? I then examine the expectations that determined the responses of experts, within and outside of governments, to the actions taken by OPEC and OAPEC (chapter 2). By whom and in what form was a set of circumstances such as the oil crisis expected, and what preparatory measures did Western governments take? Here the standard narrative – that the oil crisis of 1973–74 suddenly descended upon the Western industrialized countries, which only then became aware of their dependency and began to reorganize their energy sectors – emerges as false. With the help of the OECD's Oil Committee, the governments of all member states had already considered their growing vulnerability to supply disruptions and sought to identify countervailing measures. Nonetheless, it was the skilfully communicated, so-called 'Arab oil weapon', that is, the effectively asserted claims to sovereignty put forward by the OPEC and OAPEC countries, that first created a global constellation of contingency and uncertainty, one in which energy was suddenly on everybody's lips and was catapulted up the list of political priorities (chapter 3). It was not until the world of oil fell into disarray that the reshaping of energy policies really took off.

The following two chapters (4 and 5) concentrate on the strategies pursued by the US and West German governments to enhance political sovereignty as a result of the oil crisis, strategies that led to a reorganization of the energy sectors and continue to influence energy policies to this day. I analyse the establishment of energy as a political field, the national communication of sovereignty vis-à-vis the general population and the significance of an oil- and energy-related expertise or expert personnel in this process. In addition to national efforts, I examine international strategies intended to assert and safeguard a given country's sovereignty through public and diplomatic communication with both the producing countries and other consuming countries. West Germany was integrated into a European framework of political cooperation so I also pay attention to its European partners, particularly France, the United Kingdom and the Netherlands.

I then further expand the international perspective, investigating the conferences at which governments, in the wake of the oil crisis, sought to reorder the world of oil (chapter 6). In light of the complex global interdependencies so dramatically illuminated by the oil crisis, most governments argued that national sovereignty could no longer be safeguarded in isolation but only through international cooperation. Yet it would be too simple merely to reproduce the contemporary opposition between national and international strategies. In fact, these were not mutually exclusive but in many ways intertwined. To conclude, I investigate the discursive changes that went hand in hand with developments in oil and energy policy in the first half of the 1970s (chapter 7). On the one hand, I explore to what extent, on the international and domestic level, key actors perceived the new conditions governing the national politics of sovereignty. On the other, I scrutinize how the view of the oil crisis that prevails today emerged within these discussions on oil and energy – namely the notion that it was a significant turning point in the history of the Western industrialized nations and perhaps beyond. The goal here is not to recapitulate contemporary interpretations but to assess their impact on the politics of energy in subsequent years and thus on our own thinking about energy and sovereignty in the present.[41]

Notes

1. Halliburton advertisement, in 'Petroleum Panorama: Commemorating 100 Years of Petroleum Progress', *Oil and Gas Journal* 57(5) (1959), inside front cover.

2. Amory B. Lovins, *Soft Energy Paths: Toward a Durable Peace* (Harmondsworth, 1977), 148.

3. Commonly, oil price increases and oil disasters trigger broad debates on the future of fossil fuels. See: 'Over a Barrel: The Truth about Oil', ABC News, 2009; *The End of Suburbia: Oil Depletion and the Collapse of the American Dream*, film, dir. Gregory Greene (Canada, 2004); 'The Hunt for Black Gold', TV series, dir. Jeff Pohlman (United States, 2008); *A Crude Awakening: The Oil Crash*, film, dir. Basil Gelpke and Ray McCormack (Switzerland, 2007); *Gasland*, film, dir. Josh Fox (United States, 2010).

4. John A. Hassan and Alan Duncan, 'The Role of Energy Supplies during Western Europe's Golden Age, 1950–1972', *Journal of European Economic History* 18 (1989), 479–508; John G. Clark, *The Political Economy of World Energy: A Twentieth-Century Perspective* (New York, 1990); Christian Pfister, 'Das "1950er Syndrom": Zusammenfassung und Synthese', in Christian Pfister and Peter Bär (eds), *Das 1950er Syndrom: Der Weg in die Konsumgesellschaft*, 2nd ed. (Bern, 1996), 21–48; Vaclav Smil, *Energy in World History* (Boulder, CO, 1994); Vaclav Smil, 'Energy in the Twentieth Century: Resources, Conversions, Costs, Uses, and Consequences', *Annual Review of Energy and the Environment* 25 (2000), 21–51.

5. Michael T. Klare, *Blood and Oil: The Dangers and Consequences of America's Growing Dependency on Imported Petroleum* (New York, 2005); Ian Rutledge, *Addicted to Oil: America's Relentless Drive for Energy Security* (London, 2005); Jay E. Hakes, *A Declaration of Energy Independence: How Freedom from Foreign Oil Can Improve National Security, Our Economy, and the Environment* (Hoboken, NJ, 2008); Thomas Seifert and Klaus Werner, *Schwarzbuch Öl: Eine*

Geschichte von Gier, Krieg, Macht und Geld (Vienna, 2005); Daniel Yergin, *The Prize: The Epic Quest for Oil, Money, and Power* (New York, 1991).

6. Timothy Mitchell sees a constitutive link between hydrocarbon-based energy systems and democratic political orders, with coal facilitating modern forms of political participation while oil has imperilled and destroyed them. Timothy Mitchell, *Carbon Democracy: Political Power in the Age of Oil* (London/New York, 2011), 6: 'The leading industrialised countries are also oil states'.

7. Reinhart Koselleck, 'Staat und Souveränität', in Otto Brunner, Werner Conze and Reinhart Koselleck (eds), *Geschichtliche Grundbegriffe*, vol. 6 (Stuttgart, 1990), 1–154, here 98–154; Dieter Grimm, *Souveränität: Herkunft und Zukunft eines Schlüsselbegriffs* (Berlin, 2009); F.H. Hinsley, *Sovereignty* (London, 1966).

8. Koselleck, 'Staat und Souveränität', 1; Hinsley, *Sovereignty*, 25; Grimm, *Souveränität*, 16–34.

9. L. Oppenheim, *International Law: A Treatise*, vol. 1, *Peace* (New York/Bombay, 1905), 101. On the significance of the colonial context, see Andreas Osiander, 'Sovereignty, International Relations, and the Westphalian Myth', *International Organization* 55(2) (2001), 251–87; Martti Koskenniemi, *The Gentle Civilizer of Nations: The Rise and Fall of International Law, 1870–1960* (Cambridge, 2002).

10. Antony Anghie, *Imperialism, Sovereignty and the Making of International Law* (Cambridge, 2005), 5.

11. Ibid., 196–243, esp. 213; see chapter 6.

12. Niels P. Petersson and Wolfgang M. Schröder, 'Souveränität und politische Legitimation: Analysen zum "geschlossenen" und zum "offenen" Staat', in Georg Jochum (ed.), *Legitimationsgrundlagen einer europäischen Verfassung: Von der Volkssouveränität zur Völkersouveränität* (Berlin, 2007), 103–50, here 105. Daniel Philpott, *Revolutions in Sovereignty: How Ideas Shaped Modern International Relations* (Princeton, NJ, 2001), sees decolonization as a second 'sovereignty revolution' following the first, which occurred at the end of the Thirty Years' War.

13. Raymond Vernon, *Sovereignty at Bay: The Multinational Spread of US Enterprises* (London, 1971), 3; Charles Poor Kindleberger, *American Business Abroad: Six Lectures on Direct Investment* (New Haven, CT, 1969), 207; see also David A. Lake, 'The New Sovereignty in International Relations', *International Studies Review* 5 (2003), 303–23.

14. Joseph S. Nye, Jr., and Robert O. Keohane, 'Transnational Relations and World Politics: A Conclusion', *International Organization* 25(3) (1971), 721–48.

15. Samuel Moyn, *The Last Utopia: Human Rights in History* (Cambridge, MA, 2010).

16. On the issue of sovereignty, see the debate on the 'saving of the European nation states' through integration. Alan S. Milward, in collaboration with George Brennan and Federico Romero, *The European Rescue of the Nation-State* (Berkeley, 1992); see also James J. Sheehan, 'The Problem of Sovereignty in European History', *American Historical Review* 111(1) (2006), 1–15; Kiran Klaus Patel, 'Europäische Integrationsgeschichte auf dem Weg zur doppelten Neuorientierung: Ein Forschungsbericht', *Archiv für Sozialgeschichte* 50 (2010), 595–642.

17. Ernst Forsthoff, *Der Staat der Industriegesellschaft: Dargestellt am Beispiel der Bundesrepublik Deutschland* (Munich, 1971), 12, 17.

18. Ibid., 164; in a similar vein, see the report for the Trilateral Commission on the crisis of democracy by Michel Crozier, Jōji Watanuki and Samuel P. Huntington, *The Crisis of Democracy: Report on the Governability of Democracies to the Trilateral Commission* (New York, 1975).

19. Ernst-Wolfgang Böckenförde, 'Die Bedeutung der Unterscheidung von Staat und Gesellschaft im demokratischen Sozialstaat der Gegenwart [1972]', in *Staat, Gesellschaft, Freiheit: Studien zur Staatstheorie und zum Verfassungsrecht* (Frankfurt am Main, 1976), 185–220, here 206.

20. Ernst-Wolfgang Böckenförde, 'Die Entstehung des Staates als Vorgang der Säkularisation [1967]', in *Staat, Gesellschaft, Freiheit*, 42–64, here 60.

21. [Karl-Günther v.] Hase, Bericht über den Besuch Abdessalams und Yamanis in London, 30.11.1973, Politisches Archiv des Auswärtigen Amts, Berlin (henceforth PA AA), B 35 (Referat 310), 104992.
22. Joseph A. Camilleri and Jim Falk, *The End of Sovereignty? The Politics of a Shrinking and Fragmenting World* (Aldershot, 1992); Saskia Sassen, *Losing Control? Sovereignty in an Age of Globalization* (New York, 1996); Manuel Fröhlich, 'Lesarten der Souveränität', *Neue Politische Literatur* 50(4) (2005), 19–42; David J. Eaton (ed.), 'The End of Sovereignty? A Transatlantic Perspective', Transatlantic Policy Consortium Colloquium, Hamburg, 2006; Trudy Jacobsen, C.J.G. Sampford and Ramesh Chandra Thakur (eds), *Re-envisioning Sovereignty: The End of Westphalia?* (Aldershot, 2008); Grimm, *Souveränität*.
23. Hinsley, *Sovereignty*; Camilleri and Falk, *The End of Sovereignty?*, 11; Sheehan, 'The Problem of Sovereignty in European History'; Michael Stolleis, 'Die Idee des souveränen Staates', in *Entstehen und Wandel verfassungsrechtlichen Denkens (Der Staat, Beiheft 11)* (Berlin, 1995), 63–85.
24. Thomas J. Biersteker and Cynthia Weber, 'The Social Construction of State Sovereignty', in Thomas J. Biersteker and Cynthia Weber (eds), *State Sovereignty as Social Construct* (Cambridge, 1996), 1–21.
25. Stephen D. Krasner, *Sovereignty: Organized Hypocrisy* (Princeton, NJ/Chichester, 1999) 3.
26. Niklas Luhmann, *Soziale Systeme: Grundriß einer allgemeinen Theorie* (Frankfurt am Main, 2001), 148–90.
27. US Congress. Senate. Committee on Government Operations, *The Federal Energy Office: Hearings before the Permanent Subcommittee on Investigations* (Washington, DC, 1974), 597. See also Martin Greenberger, *Caught Unawares: The Energy Decade in Retrospect* (Cambridge, MA, 1983).
28. It is in this sense that the concept of knowledge is used throughout the present work, with its justification always relating to contemporary conditions and with no intention of affirming these claims to knowledge from a present-day perspective.
29. Timothy Mitchell, 'Carbon Democracy', *Economy and Society* 38(3) (2007), 399–432, here 417; Mitchell, 'The Resources of Economics: Making the 1973 Oil Crisis', *Journal of Cultural Economy* 3(2) (2010), 189–204; Mitchell, *Carbon Democracy*, 139.
30. Ibrahim Oweiss, 'Petro-Money: Problems and Prospects', in G. C. Wiegand (ed.), *Inflation and Monetary Crisis* (Washington, DC, 1975), 84–90.
31. Gerhard Bischoff, Werner Gocht (eds), *Das Energiehandbuch* (Braunschweig, 1970).
32. On the transformation of scholarship under the conditions of industrial big science in the twentieth century, see Steven Shapin, *The Scientific Life: A Moral History of a Late Modern Vocation* (Chicago, 2008).
33. Rüdiger Graf, 'Expert Estimates of Oil-Reserves and the Transformation of "Petroknowledge" in the Western World from the 1950s to the 1970s', in Frank Uekötter and Uwe Lübken (eds), *Managing the Unknown: Essays on Environmental Ignorance* (New York, 2014), 140–67.
34. The latter project is pursued by Aaron B. Wildavsky and Ellen Tenenbaum, *The Politics of Mistrust: Estimating American Oil and Gas Resources* (Beverly Hills, CA, 1981), 133–35, 228.
35. Peter Z. Grossman, *US Energy Policy and the Pursuit of Failure* (Cambridge, 2013), 67.
36. Stephen Kotkin, 'The Kiss of Debt: The East Bloc Goes Borrowing', in Niall Ferguson (ed.), *The Shock of the Global: The 1970s in Perspective* (Cambridge, MA, 2010), 80–93.
37. Jens Hohensee, *Der erste Ölpreisschock 1973/74: Die politischen und gesellschaftlichen Auswirkungen der arabischen Erdölpolitik auf die Bundesrepublik Deutschland und Westeuropa* (Stuttgart, 1996); Meg Jacobs, *Panic at the Pump: The Energy Crisis and the Transformation of American Politics in the 1970s* (New York, 2016).
38. Lutz Raphael, 'Die Verwissenschaftlichung des Sozialen als methodische und konzeptionelle Herausforderung für eine Sozialgeschichte des 20. Jahrhunderts', *Geschichte und Ge-*

sellschaft 22 (1996), 165–93; Jakob Vogel, 'Von der Wissenschafts- zur Wissensgeschichte: Für eine Historisierung der "Wissensgesellschaft"', *Geschichte und Gesellschaft* 30(4) (2004), 639–60; Margit Szöllösi-Janze, 'Wissensgesellschaft in Deutschland: Überlegungen zur Neubestimmung der deutschen Zeitgeschichte über Verwissenschaftlichungsprozesse', *Geschichte und Gesellschaft* 30 (2004), 277–313.

39. 'Die siebziger Jahre', *Archiv für Sozialgeschichte* 44 (2004); Eric J. Hobsbawm, *The Age of Extremes: The Short Twentieth Century 1914–1991* (London, 1995), 248–86; Tony Judt, *Postwar: A History of Europe since 1945* (New York, 2005); Thomas Raithel, Andreas Rödder and Andreas Wirsching (eds), *Auf dem Weg in eine neue Moderne? Die Bundesrepublik Deutschland in den siebziger und achtziger Jahren* (Munich, 2009); Anselm Doering-Manteuffel and Lutz Raphael, *Nach dem Boom: Perspektiven auf die Zeitgeschichte seit 1970* (Göttingen, 2008); Konrad H. Jarausch (ed.), *Das Ende der Zuversicht? Die siebziger Jahre als Geschichte* (Göttingen, 2008); Ferguson, *The Shock of the Global*; Daniel T. Rodgers, *Age of Fracture* (Cambridge, MA, 2011), 9; Elke Seefried, *Zukünfte: Eine Geschichte der Zukunftsforschung in den 1960er und 1970er Jahren* (Munich, 2015). Now and then contemporaries repeat their earlier assessments thirty years later as historical analysis; see Hans Maier, 'Fortschrittsoptimismus oder Kulturpessimismus? Die Bundesrepublik Deutschland in den 70er und 80er Jahren', *Vierteljahrshefte für Zeitgeschichte* 56 (2008), 1–17.

40. But see Hohensee, *Der erste Ölpreisschock 1973/74*, who tries to reconstruct government action on the basis of published sources and therefore fails to obtain an accurate picture either of such action or of public discourse. From a political science perspective, Fiona Venn, *The Oil Crisis* (London, 2002), asks in what respects the oil crisis was a turning point. There is a greater number of studies on specific countries; see, for example, Karen R. Merrill, *The Oil Crisis of 1973–1974: A Brief History with Documents* (Boston/New York, 2007), though she merely provides a very short introduction; Duco Hellema, Cees Wiebes and Toby Witte, *The Netherlands and the Oil Crisis: Business as Usual* (Amsterdam, 2004), concentrate on the Netherlands. Jacobs, *Panic at the Pump*, which is chiefly concerned with the impact of the energy crises on US domestic politics and the transformation of the right, appeared after the German publication of the present study.

41. Rüdiger Graf and Kim Christian Priemel, 'Zeitgeschichte in der Welt der Sozialwissenschaften. Legitimität und Originalität einer Disziplin', *Vierteljahrshefte für Zeitgeschichte* 59(4) (2011), 1–30.

Chapter 1

THE WORLD OF OIL
IN THE 1950s AND 1960s

Oil Abundance and Western Society

Human societies have always transformed the energy stored in their environment in pursuit of various objectives. Since the 1970s, this has tempted anthropologists and historians to construct entire civilizational histories in terms of energy use.[1] Fundamentally impossible though it may be to explain economic, political and social developments solely with reference to a society's energy system, we can distinguish a number of energy regimes in light of the energy sources dominant in economy and society. For thousands of years, human societies had mainly used renewables such as wood, water and wind, but the Industrial Revolution changed this fundamentally through the increased use of fossil energy sources. The burning of coal and oil produced unprecedented quantities of energy, facilitating processes of economic expansion and growth as well as engendering novel forms of settlement and social organization.[2] Coal was the energy source for the steam engine and thus the primary fuel of the nineteenth century, but it was increasingly overtaken by oil over the course of the twentieth century. The steam engine was superseded by the combustion engine and gas turbine as leading technologies, and these enabled a new intensity of global economic exchange and, as a result, stimulated an ever greater demand for oil.[3] The key period of expansion in the use of oil and thus in the oil industry itself came after the Second World War: 'The numbers – oil production, reserves, consumption – all pointed to one thing: bigger and bigger scale. In every aspect the oil industry became elephantine',[4] as Daniel Yergin concluded in his award-winning history of oil. This remains true in the early twenty-first century. In 2012, petroleum was central to the activities of eight of the world's ten richest companies.[5]

Some figures can help bring out the spectacular growth in the oil economy in the twentieth century. In 1900, around 21 million tonnes of oil were being produced in twelve countries; in 1965 it was 1,505 million tonnes in fifty-four countries.[6] Between 1949 and 1972, in other words during the postwar economic boom, global energy use tripled, and oil made up the largest share of this increase. In the United States, where the oil economy had already been far advanced before the war, oil use tripled and in Western Europe it increased fifteen times over.[7] Between 1920 and 1960, oil and gas as a share of total energy use increased from 17.7 to 73 per cent in the United States, and in the postwar era the countries of Western Europe recapitulated this shift to varying degrees.[8] Coal still played a major role in the economic reconstruction of the postwar period, but towards the end of the 1950s the economic parameters shifted in favour of oil, which became cheaper in real terms and especially in comparison to coal.[9] From the mid 1950s until 1972, coal as a share of total energy production in Western Europe sank from around 75 to 22 per cent, while in the same period oil's share increased from around 23 to 60 per cent.[10] In France, almost all the rapid increases in energy use of the 1960s were based on the growing consumption of oil, and in West Germany too, during the same period, oil overtook coal as the most important primary energy source. In 1957, oil still made up only 11 per cent of the West German energy supply, but this had grown to more than 55 per cent by 1973.[11] The economic boom in Western Europe during the first few postwar decades was based on energy-intensive industries whose growth was facilitated by an abundance of cheap energy. While this did not trigger processes of economic growth in Western Europe, Japan and the United States, it undoubtedly fuelled them.[12]

In the second half of the twentieth century, due to its many practical advantages over coal, oil became the leading energy source in Western Europe, the United States and Japan. First, per unit of weight, oil provides almost one and a half times as much combustion energy as coal.[13] Second, due to its liquid state, it is easier to extract and transport, giving rise to more flexible structures of transportation. While the transportation routes of coal start off thick and culminate in branches, those of oil look more like a decentralized web.[14] Third, in the 1950s, its less labour-intensive extraction not only made oil cheaper than coal, but also reduced the influence of workers and unions on energy production.[15] Finally, oil burns more cleanly than coal, so in view of mounting concerns about air pollution in the 1960s, oil's relative environment-friendliness was another argument in its favour.[16] Nonetheless, oil's rise to dominance was no natural necessity. It required economic and political decisions.[17] The financial aid provided by the Marshall Plan, for example, facilitated the first steps towards the expansion of the oil economy in Western Europe. Ten per cent of European Recovery Program (ERP) funds were spent on oil – more than for any other commodity – and ERP money thus paid for more than half the oil delivered by US firms to Marshall Plan countries between 1948 and 1951, securing an important market for the American oil industry.[18] In Japan, it was not until 1959–60 that the government decided to shift the Japanese economy away from expensive indigenous coal towards cheaper imported oil, triggering accelerated economic growth.[19]

The expansion of the oil economy led to massive social changes in Western Europe and the United States while at the same time being propelled by them. As economic growth produced increased prosperity for broad swathes of society in the first three decades after the Second World War, oil products largely determined the forms taken by this increasing affluence.[20] The number of automobiles in the United States increased from 45 million in 1949 to 119 million in 1972. In the rest of the world, the increase was from just under 19 to 161 million over the same period.[21] Automobilization altered patterns of residence, living and work, and in the 1950s and 1960s, the 'car-friendly city' became a core paradigm of urban planning. In the United States in particular, the rise of the car inaugurated a trend towards suburbanization that created residential structures in which the car was indispensable. In 1946, there were eight shopping centres in the United States but more than twenty thousand in 1980, the size of two-thirds of all retail sales.[22] This development did not occur on the same scale in Western Europe but here too – though later and with regional differences – supermarkets and shopping centres proliferated that were easiest to reach by car.[23] Very similar patterns pertained to the equipping of private households with technological appliances, which massively increased their need for electricity. In the United States, from 1920 to 1970, the demand for electricity doubled roughly every decade and – in addition to the car – the washing machine, television, dishwasher, air conditioner and other appliances were soon among the standard fittings of an increasing number of households.[24]

Cars, electric household appliances and thus an ever more energy-intensive lifestyle increasingly defined the character of modern existence and were central to the so-called 'American Way of Life'. Over the course of the twentieth century, energy and electrical appliances played a crucial role at the world exhibitions – and well beyond them. In the Western European countries, exhibitions featuring American household appliances quite consciously sought to get Europeans excited about the American lifestyle.²⁵ Rather than a private matter, in the Cold War context energy-intensive consumption was highly politicized, as evident in the famous Kitchen Debate between US vice president Richard Nixon and Nikita S. Khrushchev on the occasion of an American exhibition in Moscow in 1959.²⁶ One of the key issues thrown up by the competition between communism and capitalism was which system was better suited to providing the general population with consumer goods. In light of their surging economic growth, the Western democracies and market economies held out the prospect of equally rapid increases in prosperity, and their ability to convince people of their superiority increasingly depended on their capacity to meet the expectations they had raised. In this context, oil not only played a key role as provider of energy in the form of heating oil, petrol and electricity, but also as the feedstock of the chemical industry, which supplied countless products that defined the world of consumption and goods in the second half of the twentieth century.²⁷ Even agriculture was fundamentally transformed by oil, because mechanization facilitated the cultivation of larger areas by a smaller number of people. These areas could, moreover, be farmed more intensively through the use of oil-based artificial fertilizers.²⁸

In view of the crucial significance of oil in so many fields of twentieth-century economic and social life, it may seem reasonable to refer to a 'century of oil'. From this perspective, at least in the postwar era, Western societies appear to have become 'hydrocarbon societies', and the average citizen 'hydrocarbon man':

> Today we are so dependent on oil, and oil is so embedded in our daily doings, that we hardly stop to comprehend its pervasive significance. It is oil that makes possible where we live, how we live, how we commute to work, how we travel – even where we conduct our courtships. It is the lifeblood of suburban communities. Oil (and natural gas) are the essential components in the fertilizer on which world agriculture depends; oil makes it possible to transport food to the totally non-self-sufficient megacities of the world. Oil also provides the plastics and chemicals that are the bricks and mortar of contemporary civilization, a civilization that would collapse if the world's oil wells suddenly went dry.²⁹

The metaphor of oil as the 'lifeblood of modern economies', also used by Yergin, has long been particularly suggestive. This is due in large part to the fluid physical state common to both. The analogy crops up again, from an opposing perspective, in the slogan 'no blood for oil'.³⁰ But the suggestive rhetoric must not be allowed to gloss over the reductionism inherent in statements such as Yergin's, quoted above, in which one aspect of society – albeit an important one – becomes a metonym for society as a whole.³¹ The world of the 1950s and 1960s was much more than just a world of oil and cannot be reduced to the trade in oil, but it was still partly a world of oil.

How was this world structured? Who created and organized it? And which knowledge systems developed around it in the postwar period?

Global Structures of the Oil Economy

Petroleum is a fluid mix of various carbohydrates, which may also contain nitrogen, oxygen and sulphur compounds, and is found in subterranean deposits of porous rock. Drilling into these oil reservoirs causes the oil to rise to the surface as a result of the pressure in the deposit, or alternatively it may be extracted through mechanical procedures.[32] Petroleum deposits are distributed unequally across the world and the difficulty of exploiting them depends on geographical position, depth and soil composition. To a limited degree, oil that had risen to the surface of the earth without human intervention was used for millennia for various purposes, but commercial oil production began in the United States in the second half of the nineteenth century. The oil industry is generally considered to have come into existence when Edwin L. Drake drilled the first successful well for the Seneca Oil Company in Titusville, Pennsylvania in 1859, triggering the first oil boom. The United States thus became the homeland of the oil industry. In every year between 1903 and 1962, it produced more than half the oil extracted worldwide. It remained the largest producing country until the mid 1970s and the largest consumer of oil during the entire twentieth century.

Though the use of oil was essentially limited to lamp oil and lubricants before the invention of the combustion engine, the oil industry developed rapidly. It was initially dominated by John D. Rockefeller's Standard Oil Company, which was broken up into a number of smaller regional firms in 1911 as a result of the Sherman Antitrust Act. Of these, Standard Oil of New Jersey (later Exxon), Standard Oil of New York (later Mobil) and Standard Oil of California (later Socal and Chevron) subsequently developed into large oil companies with a global presence.[33] In addition, the United States was home to two more of the seven largest oil companies that dominated the global oil economy, in the shape of Texaco and Gulf Oil.[34] Like the Anglo-Persian/Iranian Oil Company (from 1954 British Petroleum) and Royal Dutch Shell, a Dutch-British firm, these were vertically integrated companies, active across the world, that sought to control the extraction of oil and its processing in refineries as well as the sale of oil products – particularly petrol, through their own network of petrol stations.[35]

But the rise of the oil industry, within the context of mass mechanization, did not proceed without difficulties or regulatory efforts emanating from the political sphere. From its beginnings, the oil economy was haunted by intermittent fears of the oil reserves' imminent exhaustion. From 1908 onwards, the United States Geological Survey (USGS) estimated the remaining oil reserves on the territory of the United States and often came to sceptical conclusions.[36] Following the First World War, in which oil had played a crucial role in ensuring victory, David White, chief geologist at the USGS, estimated the amount of extractable oil remaining on US territory at around seven billion barrels. If no other fields were discovered, he predicted, production would already begin to fall in the next three to five years: 'An unprecedented crisis in our country may call for action without precedent'.[37] In response to the conservative estimates being made by the USGS and building on the experience of the National Petroleum War Service Committee, at the end of the war US oil companies founded the American Petroleum Institute (API).[38] This was intended to facilitate the exchange of information between the large internationally active oil companies, the so-called majors, and the smaller, often regionally based firms, known as the independents, while at the same time representing the interests of the oil industry vis-à-vis the government. The data gathered by the API on the extraction, processing and use of oil became the most important source of information on the state of the US oil economy.

As it turned out, however, the difficulties facing the American oil industry in the interwar period were not due to the feared lack of oil, but rather to its abundance, which prompted two significant interventions in the oil economy: the regulation of indigenous production and restrictions on imports. Following spectacular oil finds in Oklahoma in 1927 and Texas in 1931, during the world economic crisis a veritable oil glut ensued, triggering ruinous competition and a dramatic drop in prices. In response, the oil industry declared its willingness to regulate production, a task to be entrusted to the Texas Railroad Commission. Henceforth, this body laid down production quotas for US oilfields in order to stabilize prices and exploit the fields more effectively than would have been possible in the case of more rapid extraction.[39] The regulatory work of the Texas Railroad Commission, which ensured that, as late as the 1960s, some oil wells in Texas were allowed to produce only seven days per month, was highly successful. In combination with the oil import restrictions introduced in 1959, known as the Mandatory Oil Import Program, which was implemented for reasons of national security and to protect the independents, this regulatory framework determined the price of oil in the United States and generated a reserve production capacity, which could be brought into play in case of shortages and thus influence the oil price worldwide.[40] It was only when the Texas Railroad Commission eliminated production restrictions in March 1971 – in light of increased oil consumption in the United States – that it ceased to be the most important player on the international oil market.⁴¹ Hitherto, the US oil industry had been well served both by regulation and the so-called 'depletion allowance', which excepted a portion of its profits from taxation. This is especially evident if we contrast this set-up with the development of oil production in regions where conditions were far less favourable.⁴²

Due to the unequal distribution of oil reserves across the world and the fact that most of them are located in regions in which the oil is not consumed, the oil firms developed a global system, encompassing production in often remote regions, transportation in oil tankers or through pipelines, processing in refineries, and distribution through filling stations and tanker lorries. The emergence of this global system was facilitated by the low cost of transporting oil and the largely interchangeable character of the oil extracted in different regions.⁴³ The global oil economy was a complex phenomenon, and oil firms, national governments and international organizations all sought to comprehend it through statistical surveys.⁴⁴ In addition to specialist journals such as the US *Oil and Gas Journal* (from 1902) or, in West Germany, *Öl. Zeitschrift für die Mineralölwirtschaft* (from 1963), both of which monitored and analysed developments in the world of oil, there emerged a number of periodicals that collated oil-related news from across the world. In condensed form, these presented the global world of oil to the top brass of the oil industry and government officials concerned with oil policies. By 1934, the London-based *Petroleum Press Service* was already being published monthly in English, French, Spanish, German, Arabic and Japanese. Despite its title, the news and data collated from 1957 onwards on a weekly basis by the *Middle East Economic Survey* (MEES), published by the Middle East Research and Publishing Center in Beirut, were not limited to the oil economy of the Middle East. Also based in Beirut was the *Petroleum Intelligence Weekly*, established in 1961 by Wanda Jablonski. The latter two publications were probably the world's leading organs of information and communication concerning the oil economy.

As a rule, statistical surveys of oil reserves, transportation, production and consumption were initially produced within firms before being aggregated on the national level. Globally, after the Second World War it became common to divide the world of oil into various regions. A distinction was generally made between the western hemisphere of the Americas, which was sometimes further divided into North and South America, Western Europe, the Eastern Bloc, the Near or Middle East (depending on how it was conceptualized), Africa and Southeast Asia, which included Australia. Diagrams served to clarify the content of often highly complex statistics (depending on the degree of aggregation), or data were plotted on regional or world maps in order to visualize the geographical structure and global character of the oil economy. Typical here is the visualization strategy deployed by the *Erdöl-Weltatlas* (World Atlas of Oil), commissioned by Esso AG in the mid 1960s in order to 'get to grips, on the basis of uniform criteria, with the countless facts about this vast industry, which have long defied simple summation, using the tools of thematic cartography, and [present them] in a readily graspable form' for business, schools and universities.[45]

In Figure 1.1, the pyramids represent output, the columns refinery capacity and the arrows the quantity of oil transported between regions. The map reveals a rough balance between output and refinery capacity in both the Eastern Bloc and South America. Meanwhile, Western Europe and Southeast Asia – above all Japan – were highly dependent on imports, while the Near and Middle East had the production capacity to supply Western Europe and Japan with oil. The latter regions also imported oil from Africa, where it had been produced since the early 1960s, chiefly in Algeria and Libya and later also in Nigeria, Gabon and Angola. The United States had also begun to import substantial quantities of oil after the Second World War, but obtained it chiefly from South America. In 1965, the latter continent was home to the largest oil-exporting country in the world, Venezuela, which had only just been ousted by the Soviet Union as the second-largest producing country after the United States.[46] While the snapshot provided by the map in the *Erdöl-Weltatlas* already gives some indication of the significance of the Near and Middle East as a producing region, it fails to convey contemporaries' expectation that the focus of oil production would shift from the western hemisphere to the Gulf region. According to the *Erdöl-Weltatlas*, 60 per cent of worldwide oil reserves were located in this area, and the book indicated its potential as a producing region by highlighting the following figures: 'While the number of oil wells has already reached the one million mark in the United States and around 624,000 are producing, Middle Eastern output, which made up more than a quarter of global production in 1965, comes from just under 2,000 wells'.[47] In this part of the world, then, oil could be produced more easily and at a lower cost.

The significance of the Near and Middle East to the oil economy became increasingly apparent after the First World War. When David White delivered his gloomy forecast on the future of US oil production in 1920, he divided the world up into just two major regions, namely 'regions closed to American oil companies or open only under discriminating restrictions' and 'open door territories'. The former mainly comprised the European colonial empires or areas in which European oil firms possessed exclusive production licences. The white area adorned with question marks on White's map, which was not covered by this bipartite classification, included the former Ottoman Empire and the Arabian Peninsula. In the 1920s, conflict

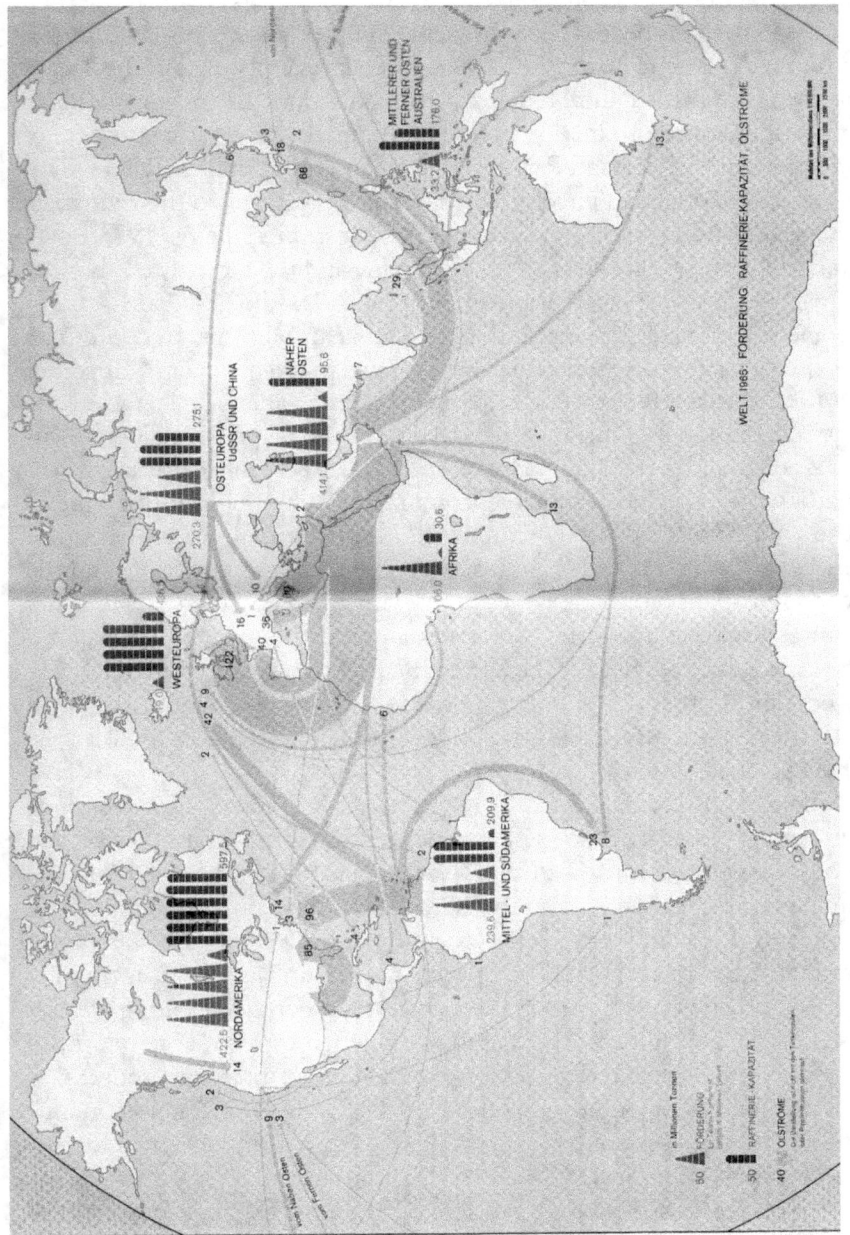

Figure 1.1. Ferdinand Mayer, *Erdöl-Weltatlas* (Hamburg/Braunschweig, 1966). © Westermann, Bildungshaus Schulbuchverlage, Braunschweig.

over the control of this region flared up between the major international oil companies, which were supported by their national governments. Although the extent of the oil reserves there was as yet unknown, at the time many oil experts suspected the presence of ample deposits. In 1920, at the San Remo Conference (whose decisions were later embodied in the Treaty of Sèvres), the British and French governments came to an agreement on France's share of oil production in Iraq and agreed on the future division of production on the Arabian Peninsula between France and the UK. US oil firms and the American government saw this as a threat to their interests in the region.[48] In response to massive American pressure, in 1928 Royal Dutch/Shell, the Anglo-Persian Oil Company and the recently established Compagnie Française des Pétroles (CFP) agreed with the Near East Development Company, an association of American oil firms, to coordinate their activities in the region, which they circled in red on a map.[49] Together with the Achnacarry Agreement, concluded the same year between the major international oil firms, which was intended to prevent global overproduction by means of quotas, the so-called Red Line Agreement laid the ground for Western companies' profitable exploitation of the oilfields in the Gulf region by largely eliminating the potentially negative consequences of competition.[50] Not least, this reduced competition allowed firms to negotiate profitable concessions with the local rulers. As in other countries, these concessions essentially granted them exclusive exploration rights for a specified period. While the firms bore the commercial risks and committed themselves to payments to the various governments with which they had negotiated licences, they could do as they wished with the carbohydrate deposits.[51]

If the *Erdöl-Weltatlas* argued in 1965 that, as a result of growing crude oil imports, 'the oil-consuming countries in Western Europe [had] given the oil-producing countries in the Near East, Africa and South America the chance to develop and strengthen their own economic power', this certainly fit the oil industry's self-perception in the West, but it was at best a partial truth.[52] In economics, the problems of countries whose economies are based chiefly on the exploitation of a single natural resource are discussed under the rubric of the 'paradox of plenty' or, from a more critical perspective, the 'resource curse'. An abundance of natural resources, as one group of authors argue, impedes the development of other economic sectors that might generate more sustainable growth, and fosters undemocratic political structures.[53] Saudi Arabia, the most important producing country in the Gulf region, is considered the best example of a 'petro-' or 'rentier state'. The Arabian-American Oil Company (Aramco), a subsidiary of Socal, Exxon, Texaco and Mobil, began producing there in the 1940s. By threatening to nationalize the country's oil, in 1950 King Saud, following Venezuela's example, managed to obtain for his country a 50 per cent share in the profits accruing from Aramco's oil production – in light of which the US government offered Aramco matching tax relief – but he gained no influence over output or pricing. The revenues, however, stabilized the monarchical rule of the house of Saud, not least by facilitating the development of modern armed forces. None of this appeared in the glossy, lavishly produced bimonthly house journal *Aramco World*. Here the company's activities in Saudi Arabia were instead presented as a model of non-colonial development aid geared towards the interests of the country and the local population. In richly illustrated articles, *Aramco World* gave readers an understanding of the history, art and culture of the Arabian Peninsula while depicting a world of harmonious labour relations, in which people of different cultures worked together to advance progress across the world.[54] Technological development was identified as the engine of progress, and was presented in richly illustrated articles on exploration methods, production techniques and oil tankers.[55] Ultimately, though, the basis for progress was human ingenuity, which Aramco purported to foster and cultivate. The firm was supposedly improving the educational prospects of the local population, by sending its Arab employees to American universities or American experts to the country to provide educational opportunities.[56] *Aramco World* had nothing to say about its concurrent export to Saudi Arabia of racial segregation or its bolstering of an undemocratic political system.[57]

Before the discovery of oil in the Arabian Peninsula, production in the Gulf region began in Persia in the early twentieth century. There it was carried out on the basis of an exclusive licence obtained by the Anglo-Persian Oil Company, later known as the Anglo-Iranian Oil Company (AIOC) and subsequently BP.[58] Unlike the US oil firms, the AIOC, much of which was owned by the British state, denied the Iranian government a 50 per cent share of profits, as oil production in Iran was the largest British investment abroad and thus crucial to the mother country's foreign trade balance.[59] This attitude was one of the main factors in the growing influence of forces in Iran that regarded the activities and rights of the AIOC as an excessive restriction on national sovereignty, and ultimately led to the nationalization of the company's property by popular prime minister Mohammad Mossadegh in 1951.[60] In response, the AIOC and the British government initially attempted to prevent the sale of Iranian oil and the employment of foreign engineers, and they largely succeeded due to contemporary market conditions and the fact that the Iranian government could not control the transportation and distribution of oil. Not satisfied with this, in 1953, in collaboration with the CIA, the British secret services orchestrated a coup to topple Mossadegh and subsequently backed the

Shah, decisively clarifying the limits of Iranian sovereignty.[61] The successful coup certainly safeguarded Western influence in Iran for another quarter of a century, but simultaneously undermined the country's democratic development. The memory of this coup played an important role in the Iranian Revolution and beyond. To this day, together with similar conduct in other settings, such as Syria, it has fuelled deep scepticism about US involvement in the region.[62]

Though most producing countries managed to achieve 50 per cent revenue shares, events like those in Iran demonstrated their lack of control over the commodities sector, their dependency on oil and the multinational companies and thus their limited sovereignty. Prompted by another oil price cut by the international oil companies, in 1960 Venezuela, Iran, Iraq, Kuwait and Saudi Arabia came together to form the Organization of Petroleum Exporting Countries (OPEC), in order to enhance their negotiating position vis-à-vis the oil companies and Western governments.[63] OPEC proceeded on the premise that while oil revenues were essential to the development of the producing countries' economies, one day they would run dry. By coordinating their actions, the producing countries aimed to prevent the oil companies from continuing to unilaterally set the oil price and also sought to annul the most recent price reductions. As with the Texas Railroad Commission, prices were to be influenced by production cutbacks: 'Members shall study and formulate a system to ensure the stabilization of prices by, among other means, the regulation of production'.[64] After initial difficulties, over the course of the 1960s OPEC became ever more powerful and admitted Libya, Indonesia, the United Arab Emirates and Algeria as new members.[65] In 1968, OPEC then embraced a more ambitious agenda, invoking the 'inalienable right of all countries to exercise permanent sovereignty over their natural resources in the interest of their national development' in its Declaratory Statement. Over the long term, the goal was for member countries to control their oil production themselves: 'Member Governments shall endeavour, as far as feasible, to explore for and develop their hydrocarbon resources directly. The capital, specialists and the promotion of marketing outlets for such direct developments may be complemented when necessary from alternate sources on a commercial basis'.[66] In other words, the governments of the OPEC countries attempted to gain sovereignty over the natural resources within their territories by ceding certain sovereign powers, such as the right to impose production quotas, to a new international organization of which they were members but which they could not control unilaterally.

In the same year that OPEC issued the Declaratory Statement, Saudi Arabia, Libya and Kuwait founded the Organization of Arab Petroleum Exporting Countries (OAPEC).[67] This was their response to the failed embargo during the Six-Day War, and an attempt to more closely coordinate and harmonize their oil policies. The architect of OAPEC was the Saudi Arabian oil minister Sheikh Zaki Yamani, who also composed the OPEC Declaratory Statement. Initially, one of his key goals was to organize the three most conservative producing countries to oppose the demands, being made by the more radical Arab countries, to deploy oil as a means of exerting pressure on the West.[68] It was not until after the Libyan Revolution and the admission of Algeria, Iraq, Syria and Egypt that the character of the organization changed, as it was now dominated by countries that were calling for the rapid nationalization of Western oil firms and the gearing of production policies to political interests.[69]

From the 1960s, however, even the conservative Saudi Arabian government cautiously tried to overcome its dependency on the oil firms, first, though with little success, by attempting to develop the economy beyond the oil sector and, second, seeking to achieve greater control over production and pricing.[70] But this process of enhancing sovereignty, which I will be looking at in detail in what follows – though from a Western European and American perspective – can be understood only to a limited degree as a conflict between the Western and Arab worlds. If for no other reason, such a perspective falls short simply because petro-knowledge was transnational, or at the very least spanned the boundaries between Saudi Arabia and the United States. When Saudi Arabia nationalized Aramco in the mid 1970s, initially 60 per cent and then all of it, after Algeria, Libya and Iraq had done much the same with the oil companies based there, three key individuals played an outstanding role: Prince Saud bin Faisal, who had studied at Princeton, Sheikh Zaki Yamani, who had completed his law degree at Harvard, and the manager of the state oil company Petromin, who had been educated at Berkeley.[71] So the picture of knowledge transfer between the United States and Saudi Arabia and the other countries where American firms produced oil, as presented in *Aramco World*, was not entirely divorced from reality.

'I'm an Oilman' – (Self-)Images of the Oil Economy

In 1927, Upton Sinclair, who had become famous when his 1906 novel sparked off a scandal over conditions in the Chicago slaughterhouses, turned his attention to the oil economy. His novel *Oil!* begins by depicting an oil boom in a small town in Southern California. Oil having been discovered on a particular property, the town is inundated by investors and adventurers, seeking to lease real estate from its owners and erect oil derricks. According to American law, everyone had the right to make use of the natural resources on his land, even if this resulted in the extraction of the oil beneath the neighbouring property.[72] In Sinclair's narrative, several neighbours join forces to improve their negotiating position, and meet the well-known oil entrepreneur Arnold J. Ross, who wishes to lease their properties. When a dispute flares up between those present over how the expected revenues should be divided up, Ross rises to make a short speech. He had turned up late, he begins, because he had had to attend to another oil well that was producing four thousand barrels and earning him five thousand dollars a day. In addition, he was in the process of drilling two more wells and owned another sixteen, which were already producing oil:

> So, ladies and gentlemen, if I say I'm an oilman, you got to agree. . . . Out of all the fellers that beg you for a chance to drill your land, maybe one in twenty will be oilmen; the rest will be speculators, fellers trying to get between you and the oilmen . . . Even if you find one that has money, and means to drill, he'll maybe know nothin' about drillin' . . . I do my own drillin', and the fellers that work for me are fellers I know. I make it my business to be there and to see to their work. I don't lose my tools in the hole, and spend months a-fishin'; I don't botch the cementin' off, and let water into the hole and ruin the whole lease . . . I can load a rig onto trucks, and have them here in a week.[73]

This speech wins over the residents, who are impressed by the image of the 'oilman', who presents himself as a successful, hands-on businessman, one who also has an excellent knowledge and mastery of the elaborate technical procedures and hard physical realities of his business. In this depiction, Sinclair captured one of the oil industry's central tropes.

Oil entrepreneurs – who oversaw the work in the fields – may have become a rarity given the industry's growth, division of labour and increasing complexity in the twentieth century, but for a long time it was far from unusual in oil companies for individuals to move from engineering into management.[74] Did the industry's key protagonists have anything in common, and if so, what were the main characteristics of the 'oilmen'? The individuals who determined the shape of the international oil economy in the twentieth century moulded not only the world of oil but also how it was perceived, and a key role in the oil industry's ascent was played by the engineers working in the oilfields. This is because, in the nineteenth century, the body of knowledge necessary to successfully exploit oil reserves and the techniques of oil production initially emerged in the practical context of the oilfields. The oilmen of the nineteenth century had varying educational histories and acquired their vital know-how through the practical work of oil exploration and production. It was not until the early twentieth century that the profession of petroleum engineer emerged: in 1914, the American Institute of Mining and Metallurgical Engineers (AIME) established an oil subdivision and at around the same time a number of universities, in states where oil had been discovered, began to offer courses in petroleum engineering.[75] The demand for petroleum engineers and geologists grew rapidly in the 1920s, at a time when the industry was beset by concerns about the future of the oil supply and an exploration boom was underway. But it was only in the years of oil abundance that the discipline really took off.

The Society of Petroleum Engineers (SPE), which emerged from the AIME subdivision mentioned above, started life with 2,000 members in 1938; there were 5,000 in 1950, 12,500 in 1958 and 15,000 in 1960.[76] In parallel to this, the membership of the American Association of Petroleum Geologists (AAPG), founded in 1917, rose from 122 to more than 15,000 in the early 1970s.[77] Petroleum engineers were almost exclusively male, mostly white, Anglo-Saxon and Protestant and came overwhelmingly from the rural regions of the United States in which oil had been found.[78] In the mid 1960s, a third of SPE members had studied at just three universities: Ohio University, the University of Texas and Texas A&M University. Three-quarters of members had degrees from universities in oil-producing US states.[79] In many cases, fathers had worked in the oil industry, and after studying, their sons returned to the oilfields where they had grown up.[80] Despite this initially local anchorage, the aspirations of the oil engineers and geologists were global in nature: the logo of the American Association of Petroleum Geologists consisted of a globe encircled by the acronym AAPG.[81] The Society of Petroleum Engineers initially adopted the AIME's logo, which featured an oil derrick surrounded by the organization's name, but in the 1980s it too opted for a world map, which formed the background to the letters SPE.[82]

Among petroleum engineers, their discipline's origins in oilfields – often located in inhospitable regions – coupled with the oil industry's spectacular ascent in the twentieth century, fostered a tough, manly habitus, a faith in progress, a strong belief in the power of technology and a pronounced professional consciousness. A fictional 1966 job advertisement conveys the oil industry's contemporary self-image and how it was viewed from outside: 'Wanted: Earth scientist with rugged physique, excellent health, strong nerves and inquiring mind. For outdoor job involving constant travel, exacting work, irregular hours. Those afraid of snakes, jungle fevers, foreigners, frostbite, sunstroke and solitude need not apply'.[83] Only those who could respond to this ad from the bottom of their hearts, the author went on, would be promising candidates for exploratory work, which entailed great physical and mental challenges and was currently being pursued by 25,000 oil firm employees on every continent. During the same period, petroleum geologists were describing themselves as the most crucial scientists in an essential industry, even adopting Winston Churchill's famous phrase: 'Never have so many owed so much to so few'.[84] As Merrill W. Haas, president of the American Association of Petroleum Geologists, put it in 1966, 'our "American Way of Life", the envy of most nations in the world is based largely on the energy and the products of the petroleum industry which are derived from your [the geologists'] success. It is almost impossible to separate the good things of our life, which often make life worth living, from the petroleum industry'.[85]

A few years earlier, the oil industry in the United States had celebrated its centenary, and to mark the occasion in 1959 the *Oil and Gas Journal* published a special issue that traced the development of the industry, exploration, drilling technology, extraction, transportation and processing. The history of oil, as stated in the introduction, which set the tone for the entire issue, was the 'greatest romance' in economic history: 'It is the story of a discovery which more radically reshaped human affairs and more completely affected human behavior than any other event of the past 100 years. This discovery transformed vision into reality, annihilated distance, and made personal comfort commonplace'.[86] This had occurred thanks to the greatest industrial pioneers of American history, who had displayed ingenuity, courage and acumen: 'Because of them a new empire grew out of swamps and deserts and creek bottoms and wastelands'.[87] An advertisement taken out by Sun Oil also asserted that a 'special breed' of 'determined men' had turned oil into a 'public servant', thus improving the quality of life in the United States.[88] The Lone Star Steel Company, one of the many steel firms that produced equipment for oil wells, created a new logo featuring the figure of 'Joe Roughneck', a robust, helmet-wearing worker with a plaster on his face. For the Lone Star Steel Company, the term 'roughneck', a colloquialism applied to men who did hard physical labour in dangerous surroundings, particularly in oil production, captured the habitus of every employee in the oil industry, 'whether he's in the field or whether he has come up through the ranks to head of his company'.[89] Suppliers in the steel industry strove to outdo one another in describing the toughness and reliability of their products, which were often linked with the characteristics of the workers in the oilfields.[90] The entire imagery of the advertisements in the *Oil and Gas Journal* and *Journal of Petroleum Technology*, as well as the photographs and illustrations accompanying articles such as 'It Takes Men to Drill Wells', underline the archaically manly, tough and rustic habitus cultivated in the oil industry.[91] From time to time, this image finds its way into historical narratives of oil, where, for example, Daniel Yergin envisages the heroes and adventurers of the oil economy engaged in a struggle over the 'prize' of oil.[92] Another significant element always inherent in the term 'to drill', which describes the most important activity in oil exploration and production, was of course its sexual connotation.

Many of the advertisements emphasized, first, the global character of the oil economy or of the activities pursued by companies involved in it and, second, the significance of oil to the emergence of modern civilization. Halliburton's advertisement, quoted at the beginning of the present work, constructed an entire history of civilization extending from the wonders of the ancient world to the modern oil economy, which was allegedly crucial to the existence of modern society and Western democracies (see Figure 0.1).[93] To this end, Halliburton was purportedly active across the world, as signalled by its logo, which showed the company's exploration vehicles encircling a globe. An advertisement taken out by Rogers Geophysical Companies also involved a globe, which was adorned with pins in various locations. These were supposed to highlight that 'Rogers crews go everywhere'.[94] Texaco conveyed the same message through a photograph of a man in diving gear jumping into the sea. If he managed to find oil, this might turn out to be a 'million dollar dive'. But Texaco's true goal, the ad leads us to understand, is not financial profit. Instead the firm's investments in oil exploration are presented as a service to the community: 'On five continents Texaco oil explorers are using aerial surveys, artificial earthquakes, soil analysis and other methods to locate more oil to satisfy an ever-increasing world demand'.[95] Shell's advertisement put greater emphasis on the significance of oil to modern life and American citizens' everyday existence. Photo montages placed an oil engineer, chemist, diver and secretary in everyday scenes featuring a family around the dinner table, trains, cars and agriculture, pointing up the connection between their work and every sphere of American life. Together, the advertisement underlined, oil industry employees provided three-quarters of the United States' energy supply. 'Without them there would be . . . not much of a world.'[96]

From the 1960s up to the present, these two tendencies have been fundamental to oil industry advertising. First, the firms' global efforts to tap new sources of oil and energy are described and visually orchestrated through photographs of oil wells, technological apparatus and engineers. These generate a sense of global economic interlinkages (with respect to oil). Second, they show filling stations, cars and oil-based products in order to highlight the universality of oil in every domain of existence and identify the world of oil with modern life.[97] Furthermore, from the 1950s onwards, glossy company magazines such as *Aramco World* or Esso's trimonthly *Pétrole Progrès* depicted a brave new world of oil. Here filling stations became icons of modern architecture and focal points of the automotive lifestyle, while top-quality photographs and illustrations presented oil wells, processing plants and various means of transport as essential components of industrial landscapes, which had their own aesthetics while facilitating modern, mechanized lifestyles.[98] Without oil, the recurring message proclaimed, the world, as people had come to know and appreciate it over the preceding decades, would have been quite impossible.

Popular culture often embraced and intensified these visual portrayals of a modern, oil-based life even as it criticized them. In his film *Mon Oncle*, for example, Jacques Tati contrasted modern life, pervaded by mechanization and automobilization, with the image of a traditional and more authentic France. It is no coincidence that the brother of Tati's hero, Monsieur Hulot, buys the latest model of car, lives in a fully automated house and works in a plastics factory.[99] Given the sums and creative potential invested in it, the visual advertising of the oil industry seems likely to have made a major impact, but it did not go uncontested. From the early days of oil production, images of erupting oil wells (so-called 'gushers'), oil fires, and cities or landscapes scarred by oil production symbolized the downside of the oil economy. When the *Torrey Canyon* oil tanker ran aground off the coast of Cornwall in 1967, oil critics' arsenal of imagery incorporated the oil slick and oil-smeared seabirds as icons of the human violation of nature. Up to the present, there has been no lack of opportunities to replenish this arsenal in light of subsequent oil tanker disasters such as the *Exxon Valdez* in 1989 and the *Deepwater Horizon* drilling rig explosion of 2010.[100]

The oil firms' public relations were not limited to advertisements, TV commercials and company magazines, but also entailed the provision and processing of otherwise difficult-to-access information on the oil economy for political representatives and a broad public. This is also the background against which we can best understand Esso AG's above-mentioned *Erdöl-Weltatlas*, first published in 1966, with new editions appearing in 1976 and 1982 and a reworked edition for an English-speaking readership published in 1977.[101] Produced by an educational publisher, it was specifically geared towards pupils and university students, who were presented, at the end of the first edition, with a vision of the quasi-utopian future prospects of the oil economy and the world created by it. In light of the more than five thousand petroleum-based products and the intensive research being pursued by the major international oil companies, this account evoked 'virtually unlimited possibilities'. Particularly promising, it maintained, was the development of a fuel cell driven by oil and air, which would surpass the efficiency of all known ways of producing energy and whose consequences would be revolutionary: 'One day, no matter how scorching the sun, taking a walk will be a pleasantly cool experience. Pocket air-conditioners no larger than a transistor radio will ensure the desired temperature, with dresses and suits made of oil-based plastics providing the necessary insulation to prevent the coolness – or, in winter, the heat – from escaping'. Readers are also informed that plastics are opening up entirely new possibilities for architects, petroleum is helping to feed the world's growing population, and 'oil researchers' are already working on 'methods for influencing weather and climate'. The publication states that while not all of these forecasts can be taken entirely seriously, one thing is certain: 'petroleum will continue to be the raw material of progress'.[102] The brochures of the American Petroleum Institute, which were intended to provide secondary school teachers of various subjects with 'solid', 'up-to-date' information on oil and the oil industry within the framework of the industry's 'Petroleum School Program', contained very similar oil utopias.[103] The brochure 'Facts about Oil' outlined a brief history of the oil industry and methods of exploration, production and processing before concluding by underlining the utility of various oil-based products. Fifty years ago, the authors argued, these were rather basic, but now the entire economy and every domain of life was pervaded by three thousand oil-based goods and a further three thousand products manufactured by the petrochemical industry. Due to its multifaceted qualities, oil opened up undreamt-of potential for product development. In many cases, plastic could replace wood and metal, a protein gleaned from oil could be used to feed animals, and the API brochure also referred to the energy cells and possible techniques for influencing the weather. The authors also thought it worth mentioning that, in future, oil-based growth inhibitors would render mowing the lawn a once-a-year affair.[104] The brochure ended with an optimistic, progress-affirming vision of the year 2000, when much that seemed modern would be obsolete – as long as the oil industry did its job and provided enough oil and energy.

Was this technology-based, optimistic belief in progress the product of the major oil companies' PR departments or did it also reflect the attitudes of oil industry engineers and geologists? When it comes to the development of exploration and production methods, Kenneth Deffeyes at least argues that until the 1960s only ingrained optimists with a high degree of frustration tolerance could pursue a career in the oil industry:

> Internally, the oil industry has an unusual psychology. Exploring for oil is an inherently discouraging activity. Nine out of 10 exploration wells are dry holes. Only one in a hundred exploration wells discovers an important oilfield. Darwinian selection is involved: only the incurable optimists stay. They tell each other stories about a Texas county that started with 30 dry holes yet the next was a major discovery.[105]

This may be a case of kitchen sink psychology, and it is an open question whether such attitudes do not in fact prevail in many professions involving technological innovation. In any case, the fact is that in the 1950s and 1960s mainstream oil geologists and engineers were decidedly optimistic when it came to their own abilities and the oil business's resulting developmental potential. They might, of course, have felt vindicated by their industry's spectacular ascent.

Petro-Knowledge or the Future Availability of Oil

Despite periodic prophecies of the imminent exhaustion of oil reserves – as typical, for example, of the 1920s and the period immediately after the Second World War – the number of oil reserves grew continuously over the course of the twentieth century.[106] In the 1950s and 1960s, in the oil industry and beyond, there was a widespread assumption that this would continue into the foreseeable future, despite the fundamentally finite nature of the Earth's oil reserves. An article in *Petroleum Panorama* made a distinction between 'two opposing camps' that had accompanied oil production from the very beginning: 'the pessimists who have constantly predicted that "we are running out of oil", versus the optimists who have just as consistently held that we will continue to find more than enough new oil to replace that which is being produced'.[107] In the 1950s and 1960s, however, most petroleum engineers and geologists believed that oil reserves would continue to expand, not least because their research would generate new methods of locating and extracting oil. While things could not go on like this forever, 'the professional oil finder feels that it [the turning point] is yet many decades away'.[108] Where did this feeling come from? And what underlay assumptions about the size of oil reserves and their future availability?

Counterintuitive though it may seem, to a great degree natural resources such as oil reserves are constructs. In the experts' assessments, the key variable was not the physical amount of oil in the ground but rather its future availability, which depends not just on its quantity but also on the technological and economic conditions of production. There can be no certain knowledge about these conditions, only more or less plausible assumptions.[109] The quantity of oil in the ground, initially estimated by petroleum geologists for specific fields with the aid of complex methods, differs significantly from the quantity of oil extractable from them, a difference reflected in the terms 'resource' and 'reserve'. Vincent E. McKelvey, appointed chief geologist at the United States Geological Survey in the 1970s, thus explained that determining oil reserves depended on two factors, 'the existence, quality, and magnitude of individual deposits' and 'the feasibility of their recovery under existing prices and technology. . . . Reserves are defined to include only identified deposits presently producible at a profit, and undiscovered and subeconomic material are referred to as resources'.[110] So estimates of oil reserves changed not just because new fields were discovered, but also as a result of improvements in the technologies of exploitation and shifting economic parameters.

Petroleum geologists initially focused on discovering individual fields and assessing their size, prompting them to develop a toolkit that they steadily improved over the course of the twentieth century. Initially the approach of choice was surface exploration, but from the 1930s onwards, seismic methods gained in importance, significantly increasing the success rate of oil drilling in the 1960s.[111] With improved methods and increased exploration, a succession of new fields were discovered in the mid twentieth century. But there were additional structural reasons why oil reserves grew substantially. First, oilfields are generally tapped gradually, so their true size emerges only in the course of their exploitation. Second, given the high costs associated with drilling, geologists tend to make rather cautious estimates of the size of individual fields to avoid being blamed for bad investments.[112] Third, in the mid twentieth century, newly developed methods of reservoir engineering dramatically improved the exploitation of individual fields.[113] Finally, the technological development of offshore production after the Second World War opened up major regions for exploitation.[114] For petroleum geologists and engineers in the 1950s and 1960s, then, there were many good reasons to share the assessment that 'the world petroleum future is one of large and rising consumption with adequate supply'.[115]

But the true magnitude of worldwide oil reserves was notoriously difficult to assess. There were many uncertainties even with respect to a single oilfield and more still on the regional level. So assumptions about oil reserves were always contested and existed within a 'sea of irrationality' and 'fog of mistrust'.[116] From 1935 onwards, a committee of the American Petroleum Institute, consisting of a permanent secretary for statistics and twelve honorary staff responsible for various regions, estimated the oil reserves in the territory of the United States. But the committee limited itself to 'proved reserves', that is, the 'volumes of crude oil which geological and engineering information indicates, beyond reasonable doubt, to be recoverable in the future from an oil reservoir under existing economic and operating conditions'.[117] So, strictly speaking, the figures produced by the API were not estimates of the total amount of oil that would eventually be produced in the United States, but only of the oil producible given the current state of exploration and under existing technological and economic conditions. As a result, many geologists and engineers considered the figures inadequate. In a 1965 study for the think tank Resources for the Future Inc., for example, Wallace F. Lovejoy and Paul T. Homan argued that the API's estimates failed to reflect the industry's well-founded expectations. Instead, they asserted, what was needed were 'estimates, however rough, of the quantities of reserves that can be expected under different economic and technological conditions'.[118] On top of US oil reserves of 31 billion barrels, as estimated by the API in late 1964, one could, according to these authors, add 25 to 35 billion barrels arising from the expansion of known fields over the course of exploitation. Improved secondary extraction, through such methods as liquid injections, they claimed, would generate another 16 billion barrels. If one also factored in likely improvements in exploration and production techniques, the quantity of oil still to be produced in the United States was probably between 300 and 400 million barrels, in other words, more than ten times the 'proved reserves' identified by the API.[119] In the 1960s, the US Geological Survey and other authors attempted to deduce, in light of existing wells' success rate, the prospects of those in promising rock formations and, on this basis, the quantity of extractable oil, a procedure whose uncertainty is obviously due to the definition of the term 'promising'.[120] The more estimates moved away from 'proved reserves', the more uncertain they became, due to multiplying uncertainties regarding the size of as yet undiscovered fields and the 'recovery factor'.[121] In the 1960s, estimates of oil reserves in the territory of the United States thus tended to diverge by between 150 and 600 billion barrels – very substantially indeed.[122]

From the late 1950s onwards, Marion King Hubbert put forward a fundamental critique of resource optimism, though initially his theory of 'peak oil' failed to gain mainstream acceptance and had to wait until the 1970s to find more supporters, before ultimately going on to found a veritable movement in the 1990s.[123] Hubbert had studied geology, mathematics and physics, and he initially taught geophysics at Columbia University in New York before taking up a post at Shell Research Laboratories in Houston, Texas, a prime example of industrial big science, during the Second World War.[124] Hubbert was already a strident but renowned geologist when he gave a lecture in 1956 at a meeting of the American Petroleum Institute in San Antonio, in which he forecast that US oil production would reach its peak in the second half of the 1960s. Down to the last minute, the company headquarters had tried to prevent him from delivering his lecture, which contradicted both Shell's official statements and the majority views of his expert colleagues.[125] Hubbert took seriously the idea of the fundamental finiteness of natural resources and argued that production, plotted on a time axis, will inevitably produce a bell curve, which begins at zero, passes through one peak or a number of peaks and then finishes at zero, whether because the resource has been exhausted or because its production ends for other reasons.[126] His crucial innovation was to correlate two curves, namely that of oil production in the United States, which hitherto pointed more or less straight upwards and which his colleagues simply extended in this direction, and that of the estimates of proven reserves produced by the API. The second curve passed its peak in 1956. Since only oil that was discovered could be produced, Hubbert concluded that the two curves must run in parallel at an interval of ten and a half years, so that oil production in the United States would reach its peak in 1966/67 – a forecast he later corrected to 1970.[127] Using the same method, Hubbert estimated that world oil production would reach its peak around the year 2000.[128]

Despite its high degree of intuitive plausibility, Hubbert's forecast was 'just barely within the envelope of acceptable scientific methods. It was as much an inspired guess as it was hard-core science'.[129] Consequently, his colleagues' criticisms were harsh. Given their own intensive research and exploration activities, they saw no reason to believe that the production curve put forward by Hubbert would pass through just one rather than several peaks.[130] Hubbert's prediction threatened them in part because it was based only on publicly available data and made oil reserve estimates accessible to other groups of experts than just geologists and engineers.[131] Hubbert moved to the US Geological Survey in 1965, but more optimistic forecasts held sway there and he was unable to gain acceptance for his method.[132] It was not until US oil production did in fact reach a peak in the early 1970s, a time when his forecasts were beginning to chime with widespread concerns about the limits of growth, that Hubbert gained more supporters. Ideas Hubbert had formulated in 1962 now resonated with a much larger audience: 'No physical quantity, whether the human population, the rate of energy consumption, or the rate of production of a material resource such as a metal, can continue to increase at a fixed exponential rate without soon exceeding all physical bounds'.[133]

Another factor in the increasing controversy over oil reserve estimates in the 1960s and 1970s was their origin: they no longer came solely from geologists and engineers but increasingly from other disciplines as well, engendering an increasingly competitive discursive environment.[134] In the 1960s, as oil became more and more important to the economic and social order – and ultimately to the political systems – of Western Europe and the United States, political scientists, economists and social scientists began to address issues of oil supply and the future availability of oil. While the economy of exhaustible resources had previously been a fairly marginal topic in the discipline of economics, economists now began to pay it much more attention, though the true breakthrough of energy economics had to wait until the 1970s.[135] From an economic perspective, the issue of oil's future availability was less one of material, geological realities than one of price. A number of factors were responsible for prices and these were the province of economists rather than geologists or engineers. At the same time, political and social scientists regarded consumer behaviour, the political framework of the oil market and political conditions in the producing countries as crucial factors in the future availability of oil in Western Europe and the United States. Here experts in Middle Eastern Studies, which developed in the United States in parallel to the increasing importance of the Middle East as a producing region, offered up their insights.[136] So in the oil crisis of 1973–74, conflict flared between oil experts from a range of academic disciplines, who addressed the future availability of oil in different ways from their differing vantage points as they struggled to attain interpretive sovereignty and political influence. Furthermore, from the late 1960s onwards, due to the politicization and economization of oil, a growing number of ever more senior government officials dedicated themselves to the security of the oil supply, drawing either on external expertise or producing their own knowledge and interpretations, which will be scrutinized in chapters 4 and 5.

Notes

1. Rüdiger Graf, 'Von der Energievergessenheit zur theoretischen Metonymie: Energie als Medium der Gesellschaftsbeschreibung im 20. Jahrhundert', in Hendrik Ehrhardt and Thomas Kroll (eds), *Energie in der modernen Gesellschaft: Zeithistorische Perspektiven* (Göttingen, 2012), 73–92.

2. Rolf Peter Sieferle, *Der unterirdische Wald: Energiekrise und industrielle Revolution* (Munich, 1982), 60–63; Smil, *Energy in World History*, 157; Mitchell, *Carbon Democracy*; Silvana Bartoletto, 'Patterns of Energy Transitions: The Long-Term Role of Energy in the Economic Growth of Europe', in Nina Möllers and Karin Zachmann (eds), *Past and Present Energy Societies: How Energy Connects Politics, Technologies and Cultures* (Bielefeld, 2012), 305–30.

3. Vaclav Smil, *Two Prime Movers of Globalization: The History and Impact of Diesel Engines and Gas Turbines* (Cambridge, MA, 2010), 17.

4. Yergin, *The Prize*, 542.

5. 'Die umsatzstärksten Unternehmen der Welt', *Frankfurter Allgemeine Zeitung*, 4 July 2012; Royal Dutch Shell (1), Exxon Mobil (3), Sinopec (4), BP (5), PetroChina (6), Chevron (7), Total (9) and ConocoPhilipps (10). After market capitalization, however, in 2012 only Exxon Mobil, PetroChina and Royal Dutch Shell were still among the ten largest companies.

6. Ferdinand Mayer, *Erdöl-Weltatlas* (Hamburg/Braunschweig, 1966), 5.

7. The increase was even greater in Japan, where oil consumption had been negligible in the late 1940s. Yergin, *The Prize*, 541; Smil, 'Energy in the Twentieth Century', 22–25; Smil, *Energy in World History*, 157–218.

8. David E. Nye, *Consuming Power: A Social History of American Energies* (Cambridge, MA, 1998), 198; see also Clark, *The Political Economy of World Energy*, 117–36.

9. Christian Pfister, 'Das "1950er Syndrom": Die umweltgeschichtliche Epochenschwelle zwischen Industriegesellschaft und Konsumgesellschaft', in Christian Pfister and Peter Bär (eds), *Das 1950er Syndrom: Der Weg in die Konsumgesellschaft*, 2nd ed. (Bern, 1996), 51–96, here 69; Hassan and Duncan, 'The Role of Energy Supplies'.

10. Martin Chick, *Electricity and Energy Policy in Britain, France and the United States since 1945* (Cheltenham, 2007), 7.

11. Commissariat Général du plan. Commission de l'Énergie et des Matières Premières du VIIIe Plan, *Rapport sur les bilans de la politique énergétique de 1973 à 1978* (Paris, 1979),

5–8; 'Unterrichtung durch die Bundesregierung: Die Energiepolitik der Bundesregierung', in *Deutscher Bundestag. Drucksachen. 7. Wahlperiode 1972–1976.* No. 1057, 3 October 1973; see also Hans-Dieter Schilling and Rainer Hildebrandt, *Primärenergie, elektrische Energie: Die Entwicklung des Verbrauchs an Primärenergieträgern und an elektrischer Energie in der Welt, in den USA und in Deutschland seit 1860 bzw. 1925* (Essen, 1977).

12. Hansjörg Siegenthaler, 'Zur These des "1950er Syndroms": Die wirtschaftliche Entwicklung der Schweiz nach 1945 und die Bewegung relativer Energiepreise', in Christian Pfister and Peter Bär (eds), *Das 1950er Syndrom: Der Weg in die Konsumgesellschaft*, 2nd ed. (Bern, 1996), 97–103, here 99; see also André Nouschi, *La France et le pétrole: de 1924 à nos jours* (Paris, 2001), 10f.; Bernard C. Beaudreau, *Energy and the Rise and Fall of Political Economy* (Westport, CT, 1999).

13. Bischoff and Gocht, *Das Energiehandbuch*, xii.

14. Mitchell, *Carbon Democracy*, 38: 'Whereas the movement of coal tended to follow dendritic networks, with branches at each end but a single main channel, creating potential choke points at several junctures, oil followed along networks that often had the properties of a grid, like an electricity network, where there is more than one possible path and the flow of energy can switch to avoid blockages or overcome breakdowns'. Nonetheless, there were critical bottlenecks such as the Suez Canal.

15. Despite its overstatements, see Timothy Mitchell, 'Hydrocarbon Utopia', in Michael D. Gording, Gyan Prakash and Helen Tilley (eds), *Utopia/Dystopia: Conditions of Historical Possibility* (Princeton, NJ, 2010), 117–47.

16. Yergin, *The Prize*, 543.

17. Raymond G. Stokes, *Opting for Oil: The Political Economy of Technological Change in the West German Chemical Industry, 1945–1961* (Cambridge, MA, 1994).

18. David S. Painter, 'Oil and the Marshall Plan', *Business History Review* 58 (1984), 359–83, here 362; Mitchell, *Carbon Democracy*, 29f.

19. Laura E. Hein, *Fueling Growth: The Energy Revolution and Economic Policy in Postwar Japan* (Cambridge, MA, 1990), 160, 316.

20. On the general social history of the boom, see Hartmut Kaelble (ed.), *Der Boom 1948–1973: Gesellschaftliche und wirtschaftliche Folgen in der Bundesrepublik Deutschland und in Europa* (Opladen, 1992); Göran Therborn, *Die Gesellschaften Europas 1945–2000* (Frankfurt am Main, 2000); Hartmut Kaelble, *Sozialgeschichte Europas: 1945 bis zur Gegenwart* (Munich, 2007); and for a brief account, see Constantin Goschler and Rüdiger Graf, *Europäische Zeitgeschichte seit 1945* (Berlin, 2010), 73–82, 105–18.

21. Yergin, *The Prize*, 542; see also the instructive diagrams in Smil, *Energy in World History*.

22. Yergin, *The Prize*, 551. For an in-depth look at the emergence of 'post-urban society', see Nye, *Consuming Power*, 187–207; on the ideal of the car-friendly city, see Hans B. Reichow, *Die autogerechte Stadt: Ein Weg aus dem Verkehrs-Chaos* (Ravensburg, 1959); and for a general account of the history of transport, see Ralf Roth and Karl Schlögel (eds), *Neue Wege in ein neues Europa: Geschichte und Verkehr im 20. Jahrhundert* (Frankfurt/New York, 2009).

23. Victoria de Grazia, *Irresistible Empire: America's Advance through Twentieth-Century Europe* (Cambridge, MA, 2005), 377–404.

24. Nye, *Consuming Power*, 198; on Europe, see the introductory text by Goschler and Graf, *Europäische Zeitgeschichte seit 1945*, 105–14; on the history of electricity and household appliances, see Horst A. Wessel, *Das elektrische Jahrhundert. Entwicklung und Wirkungen der Elektrizität im 20. Jahrhundert: Ergebnisse einer Tagung des VDE-Ausschusses 'Geschichte der Elektrotechnik' und des Umspannwerkes Recklinghausen-Museum Strom und Leben, am 24.–25. Oktober 2001 in Recklinghausen* (Essen, 2002); Sophie Gerber, Nina Lorkowski and Nina Möllers, *Kabelsalat: Energiekonsum im Haushalt* [On the occasion of the exhibition 'Kabelsalat: Energiekonsum im Haushalt' at the Deutschen Museum, Munich, 13 January–15 April 2012] (Munich, 2012); Silvia Schmitz, *Energiegeschichten* (Lamspringe, 2007); Theo Horstmann and Regina Weber (eds), *'Hier wirkt Elektrizität': Werbung für Strom 1890 bis 2012* (Essen, 2012).

25. Nina Möllers, 'Electrifying the World: Representations of Energy and Modern Life at World's Fairs, 1893–1982', in Nina Möllers and Karin Zachmann (eds), *Past and Present Energy Societies: How Energy Connects Politics, Technologies and Cultures* (Bielefeld, 2012), 45–78; Greg Castillo, 'Domesticating the Cold War: Household Consumption as Propaganda in Marshall Plan Germany', *Journal of Contemporary History* 40(2) (2005), 261–88.

26. Zoe A. Kusmierz, '"The Glitter of Your Kitchen Pans". The Kitchen, Home Appliances, and Politics at the American National Exhibition in Moscow, 1959', in Sebastian M. Herrmann (ed.), *Ambivalent Americanizations: Popular and Consumer Culture in Central and Eastern Europe* (Heidelberg, 2008), 253–72; Ruth Oldenziel and Karin Zachmann (eds), *Cold War Kitchen: Americanization, Technology, and European Users* (Cambridge, MA, 2009).

27. See the breakdown in Mayer, *Erdöl-Weltatlas*, 134f.

28. Nye, *Consuming Power*, 187–94.

29. Yergin, *The Prize*, 14f.

30. For examples of the use of this metaphor, see John C. Campbell, Guy de Carmoy and Shinichi Kondo, *Energy: A Strategy for International Action. A Report of the Task Force on the Political and International Implications of the Energy Crisis to the Executive Committee of the Trilateral Commission* (Washington, DC, 1974), 9; Albert J. Fritsch and Ralph Gitomer, *Major Oil: What Citizens Should Know about the Eight Major Oil Companies* (Washington, DC, 1974), 5; Toby Craig Jones, *Desert Kingdom: How Oil and Water Forged Modern Saudi Arabia* (Cambridge, MA, 2010), 236; Klare, *Blood and Oil*; US Senate. Committee on Energy and Natural Resources, *The Geopolitics of Oil: Staff Report* (Washington, DC, 1980), 2; Hans J. Morgenthau, 'The New Diplomacy Movement: International Commentary', *Encounter* (August 1974), 52–57, here 57; Erich Schieweck, 'Die kommende Welterdöl- und Energiekrise', *Glückauf. Zeitschrift für Technik und Wirtschaft des Bergbaus* 108(9) (1972), 343–55, here 344; Horst Wagenfuehr, *Report zur Energiekrise: Fakten, Vorschläge und futurologische Aspekte* (Tübingen, 1973), 4; Ahmed Zaki Yamani, 'Oil: Towards a New Producer–Consumer Relationship', *World Today* 30(11) (1974), 479–86, here 479.

31. Graf, 'Von der Energievergessenheit zur theoretischen Metonymie'. On the relationship between energy consumption on the one hand and technology and society on the other, see Vaclav Smil, *Transforming the Twentieth Century: Technical Innovations and Their Consequences* (Oxford/New York, 2006), 8–12.

32. Lester Charles Uren, *Petroleum Production Engineering: Oil Field Exploitation*, 3rd ed. (New York/Toronto/London, 1953), 1; see also Eugene Stebinger, 'Petroleum in the Ground', in Wallace E. Pratt and Dorothy Good (eds), *World Geography of Petroleum* (Princeton, NJ, 1950), 1–24; W. Rühl, 'Erdöl und Erdgas', in Bischoff and Gocht, *Das Energiehandbuch*, 95–150.

33. Yergin, *The Prize*, 110; Rainer Karlsch and Raymond G. Stokes, *'Faktor Öl': Die Mineralölwirtschaft in Deutschland 1859–1974* (Munich, 2003), 53f.

34. Mayer, *Erdöl-Weltatlas*, 74f.

35. For the classic account, see Anthony Sampson, *The Seven Sisters: The Great Oil Companies and the World They Made* (London, 1975); for a contemporary take, see BP AG, *Buch vom Erdöl: Eine Einführung in die Erdölindustrie* (Hamburg, 1959), 431–45. At least for Shell and BP, comprehensive histories have been published. See James Bamberg, *The History of the British Petroleum Company*, 3 vols (Cambridge, 1983–2000); Stephen Howarth, Joost Jonker and Joost Dankers, *The History of Royal Dutch Shell*, 4 vols (Oxford, 2007); on Exxon, see Joseph A. Pratt, *Exxon: Transforming Energy, 1973–2005* (Austin, TX, 2013).

36. Wildavsky and Tenenbaum, *The Politics of Mistrust*, 60–66.

37. David White, 'The Petroleum Resources of the World', *Annals of the American Academy of Political and Social Science* 89 (May 1920), 111–34, here 111, 134.

38. American Petroleum Institute, *Petroleum: Facts and Figures* (New York, 1928).

39. August W. Giebelhaus, *Business and Government in the Oil Industry: A Case Study of Sun Oil, 1876–1945* (Greenwich, CT, 1980), 199–202; Edward Constant, 'State Management of Petroleum Resources: Texas, 1910–1940', in George H. Daniels and Mark H. Rose (eds),

Energy and Transport: Historical Perspectives on Policy Issues (Beverly Hills, CA, 1982), 157–75; Constant, 'Cause or Consequence: Science, Technology, and Regulatory Change in the Oil Business in Texas, 1930–1975', *Technology and Culture* 30 (1989), 426–55; William R. Childs, *The Texas Railroad Commission: Understanding Regulation in America to the Mid-Twentieth Century* (College Station, TX, 2005).

40. Grossman, *US Energy Policy*, 90–93; Mayer, *Erdöl-Weltatlas*, 120; Vaclav Smil, *Energy at the Crossroads: Global Perspectives and Uncertainties* (Cambridge, MA, 2003), 150; Morris Albert Adelman, 'My Education in Mineral (Especially Oil) Economics', *Annual Review of Energy and the Environment* 22 (1997), 13–46, here 16; see also chapter 2.

41. Kenneth S. Deffeyes, *Hubbert's Peak: The Impending World Oil Shortage*, vol. 2 (Princeton, NJ, 2003).

42. Grossman, *US Energy Policy*, 86; Jacobs, *Panic at the Pump*, 83f.; Alison Fleig Frank, *Oil Empire: Visions of Prosperity in Austrian Galicia* (Cambridge, MA, 2005), 18; on the importance of state regulation, see also Paul Sabin, *Crude Politics: The California Oil Market, 1900–1940* (Berkeley, CA, 2005), xiv–xv.

43. William D. Nordhaus, 'Energy: Friend or Enemy', *New York Review of Books*, 27 October 2011, 29–31.

44. See, for example, BP, *Statistical Review of the World Oil Industry* (1956ff.); Comité professionnel du pétrole, *Elements statistiques – áctivité de l'industrie pétrolière* (1955ff.); OECD *Statistiques pétrolières – approvisionnement et consommation* (1961ff.).

45. Mayer, *Erdöl-Weltatlas*, 5.

46. Ibid., 90 and passim.

47. Ibid., 37.

48. 'Memorandum of Agreement at San Remo, April 24, 1920', in *Papers Relating to the Foreign Relations of the United States: 1920*, vol. 2 (Washington, DC, 1935), 655–58; see Dietrich Eichholtz and Titus Kockel, *Von Krieg zu Krieg: Zwei Studien zur deutschen Erdölpolitik in der Zwischenkriegszeit* (Leipzig, 2008), 26–42.

49. Yergin, *The Prize*, 204 and passim; Anand Toprani, 'The French Connection: A New Perspective on the End of the Red Line Agreement, 1945–1948', *Diplomatic History* 36(2) (2012), 261–99.

50. Helmut Mejcher, *Die Politik und das Öl im Nahen Osten*, vol. 1, *Der Kampf der Mächte und Konzerne vor dem Zweiten Weltkrieg* (Stuttgart, 1980); Yergin, *The Prize*, 260–65.

51. Francisco R. Parra, *Oil Politics: A Modern History of Petroleum* (London/New York, 2004), 9.

52. Mayer, *Erdöl-Weltatlas*, 9.

53. For a classic account, see Terry Lynn Karl, *The Paradox of Plenty: Oil Booms and Petro-States* (Berkeley, CA, 1997), 16: 'The institutional molding brought about by dependence on petrodollars is so overwhelming in oil-exporting countries that their states can appropriately be labeled petro-states'. For a contrasting view, see Massoud Karshenas, *Oil, State and Industrialization in Iran* (Cambridge, 1990).

54. See, for example, the reports on the construction of the Transarabian Pipeline: Daniel Da Cruz, 'The Long Steel Shortcut', *Aramco World* 15(5) (1964), 16–25; or on the hard but good life on a mobile oil rig, where workers of various nationalities enjoyed 'excellent' free food: W. Vernon Tjetjen, 'Rig Ahoy!', *Aramco World* 16(2) (1965), 2–7.

55. William Tracy, 'Island of Steel', *Aramco World* 17(3) (1966), 1–7; Paul F. Hoye (ed.), 'Tankers: A Special Issue', *Aramco World* 17(4) (1966); John Sabini, 'Sea Island Four', *Aramco World* 24(2) (1973), 6–7.

56. Charles E. Wilkins, 'Learn, Remember and Know', *Aramco World* 15(6) (1964), 27–28, here 28: 'far from home, hard at work ... Saudi Arab students on campuses and in classrooms throughout America'; William Tracy, 'A Path to Progress', *Aramco World* 16(1) (1965), 18–23, here 18f: 'in the classrooms of the Industrial Training Centers, Aramco workers find ... a path to progress'; Brainerd S. Bates, 'The Crimson Tide', *Aramco World* 23(2) (1972), 12–14.

57. Robert Vitalis, 'Black Gold, White Crude: An Essay on American Exceptionalism, Hierarchy, and Hegemony in the Gulf', *Diplomatic History* 26(2) (2002), 185–213; Vitalis, *America's Kingdom: Mythmaking on the Saudi Oil Frontier* (Stanford, CA, 2007), 18–23; Douglas J. Little, 'Gideon's Band: America and the Middle East since 1945', in Michael J. Hogan (ed.), *America in the World: The Historiography of American Foreign Relations since 1941* (Cambridge, 1995), 462–500; by way of contrast, *Aramco World* celebrated the moderate industrial progress of the Arab countries, for example, in Editors, 'Introduction. Special Issue: Made in . . . the Arab East', *Aramco World* 25(3) (1974), 3.

58. For an in-depth account, see Yergin, *The Prize*, 134–49.

59. Steve Marsh, 'HMG, AIOC and the Anglo-Iranian Oil Crisis: In Defence of Anglo-Iranian', *Diplomacy & Statecraft* 12(4) (2001), 143–74.

60. Helmut Mejcher, *Die Politik und das Öl im Nahen Osten*, vol. 2, *Die Teilung der Welt 1938–1950* (Stuttgart, 1990), 322–36; Mostafa Elm, 'Iran's Oil Crisis of 1951–1953: New Documents and Old Realities', *Harvard Middle Eastern and Islamic Review* 2(2) (1995), 46–61; Stephen Kinzer, *All the Shah's Men: The Hidden Story of the CIA's Coup in Iran* (New York, 2003).

61. Douglas Little, 'Mission Impossible: The CIA and the Cult of Covert Action in the Middle East', *Diplomatic History* 28 (2004), 663–701, here 667f.; Kinzer, *All the Shah's Men*.

62. Little, 'Mission Impossible', 664; David R. Farber, *Taken Hostage: The Iran Hostage Crisis and America's First Encounter with Radical Islam* (Princeton, NJ, 2005), and for a local voice, see Mostafa T. Zahrani, 'The Coup that Changed the Middle East: Mossadeq v. the CIA in Retrospect', *World Policy Journal* 19(2) (2002), 93–99; on Syria, see Douglas Little, 'Cold War and Covert Action: The United States and Syria, 1945–1958', *Middle East Journal* 44 (1990), 55–75.

63. Ian Skeet, *OPEC Twenty-Five Years of Prices and Politics* (Cambridge, 1988), 1: 'For Opec the equivalent of the murder of Archduke Ferdinand at Sarajevo was the decision by Esso to reduce the posted price of Arabian light crude by 14 cents a barrel in August 1960'.

64. 'Resolutions of the First OPEC Conference Baghdad, September 10–14, 1960', in Organization of the Petroleum Exporting Countries, *Official Resolutions and Press Releases: 1960–1980* (Oxford, 1980), 1–3, here 1; Deffeyes, *Hubbert's Peak*, 5.

65. Parra, *Oil Politics*, 89–110; Skeet, *OPEC Twenty-Five Years of Prices and Politics*, 1; Abdulaziz Al-Sowayegh, *Arab Petropolitics* (London, 1984); Albert L. Danielsen, *The Evolution of OPEC* (New York, 1982).

66. 'Resolutions of the Sixteenth OPEC Conference, Vienna, June 24–25, 1968', in OPEC, *Official Resolutions and Press Releases: 1960–1980*, 80–83.

67. 'Organization of Arab Petroleum Exporting Countries', in *The Middle East and North Africa: 1972–73*, 19th ed. (London, 1972), 118; 'Organization of Arab Petroleum Exporting Countries', in *The Middle East and North Africa: 1974–75*, 21st ed. (London, 1974), 145f.; Abdelkader Maachou, *OAPEC: An International Organization for Economic Cooperation and an Instrument for Regional Integration* (Paris, 1982).

68. Emb. Kuwait to Dept. of State: Memo: The Organization of Arab Petroleum Exporting Countries. Development and Status, 23 January 1969, National Archives and Records Administration, College Park/MD (henceforth NARA), RG 59, Box 1369 PET 6 Nigeria to PET 3 OECD.

69. Al-Sowayegh, *Arab Petropolitics*.

70. Jones, *Desert Kingdom*, 54–89.

71. Federal Energy Administration, *The Relationship of Oil Companies and Foreign Governments* (Washington, DC, 1975), 159f.

72. On the problems involved in oil production in residential areas, see Sarah S. Elkind, 'Oil in the City: The Fall and Rise of Oil Drilling in Los Angeles', *Journal of American History* 99(1) (2012), 82–90.

73. Upton Sinclair, *Oil!* (New York, 1927), 37.

74. Wayne E. Swearingen, 'So You Want To Be a Manager', *Journal of Petroleum Technology* 19(1) (1967), 11–14.

75. Earl Kipp, 'The Evolution of Petroleum Engineering as Applied to Oilfield Operations', *Journal of Petroleum Technology* 23 (January 1971), 107–14, here 107; on the definition of the discipline of 'petroleum engineering', see Benjamin Cole Craft and Murray F. Hawkins, *Applied Petroleum Reservoir Engineering* (Englewood Cliffs, NJ, 1959).

76. Edward Constant, 'Science in Society: Petroleum Engineers and the Oil Fraternity in Texas 1925–65', *Social Studies of Science* 19 (1989), 439–72, here 451f.; Kipp, 'The Evolution of Petroleum Engineering', 113. In 2012, the Society of Petroleum Engineers had more than 100,000 members worldwide; see http://www.spe.org/index.php (accessed 26 June 2012); on the definition and early history of the profession, see also D.V. Carter (ed.), *The History of Petroleum Engineering* (Dallas, 1961).

77. Norman C. Smith, 'AAPG Is a Long Time and a Lot of People', *Bulletin of the American Association of Petroleum Geologists* 56 (1972), 680.

78. Constant, 'Science in Society', 454f.

79. Ibid., 451.

80. Ibid., 459: 'Overall, nearly a third of all petroleum engineers had parents directly engaged in the oil business, nearly a third of all small business parents were in the oil business and almost three out of five blue collar parents worked in the oil industry'.

81. John E. Kilkenny, 'The President's Page: AAPG is Global', *Bulletin of the American Association of Petroleum Geologists* 59 (1975), 1–2, here 1: 'Undoubtedly, the individual who designed our pin envisioned that the practice of petroleum geology would be worldwide and that AAPG would be international in scope'.

82. From 1992–93 onwards, therefore, after numerous branches had been founded in other countries, the SPE called itself the 'International Society of Petroleum Engineers', adding an 'I' to its logo.

83. Daniel Da Cruz, 'How They Find Oil', *Aramco World* 17(1) (1966), 1–11, here 3.

84. Merrill W. Haas, 'The President's Page', *Bulletin of the American Association of Petroleum Geologists* 50 (1966), 1–2, here 1.

85. Ibid., 2; see also John D. Haun, 'The President's Page: Why Teach Petroleum Geology?', *Bulletin of the American Association of Petroleum Geologists* 53 (1969), 249–50, here 249: 'Petroleum and mineral resources form the basis of our modern civilization'.

86. Petroleum Panorama, *Commemorating 100 Years of Petroleum Progress* (Tulsa, OK, 1959), iv; a very similar analysis is provided by James A. Clark, 'The Energy Revolution', in Carter, *The History of Petroleum Engineering*, 1–14.

87. Petroleum Panorama, *Commemorating*, iv.

88. Ibid., A-128.

89. Ibid., A-66.

90. Ibid., A-105f.: 'Steel and Oil ... two giants of industry ... independently great, yet greatly dependent upon each other. ... The vital, pulsing force that is OIL is a treasure that must be found, wrenched from earth, processed and transported'. This required 'dependable, hard-working "tools" that will get the job done'.

91. 'It Takes Men to Drill Wells', *Petroleum Panorama: Commemorating 100 Years of Petroleum Progress; The Oil and Gas Journal* 57(5) (1959), 10–11; see esp. Halliburton's advertisements, generally placed at the beginning and end of the *Journal of Petroleum Technology*, for example 15(10) (1963), 1092 and 19(7) (1967), 978.

92. Yergin, *The Prize*, passim. Specialists in the extinguishing of burning oil wells are located high up the hierarchy of masculinity. Deffeyes, *Hubbert's Peak*, 101: 'Big alpha males are macho, bullfighters have machismo, machissimo is reserved for oil well fire fighters'.

93. Petroleum Panorama, *Commemorating*, inside front cover.

94. Ibid., B-37.

95. Ibid., B-34.

96. Ibid., A-114.

97. This continues into the present era. See, for example, Chevron's commercial 'Untapped Energy' from 2007, which has gained notoriety within the environmental movement as it blames Chevron for massive environmental destruction and human rights violations in the Amazon region; http://www.youtube.com/watch?v=nJZgGb_8pQw (accessed 27 June 2012).

98. *Pétrole Progrès : Revue Trimestrielle* (1950ff.).

99. *Mon Oncle*, film, dir. Jacques Tati (France, 1958).

100. Kathryn Morse 'There Will Be Birds: Images of Oil Disasters in the Nineteenth and Twentieth Centuries', *The Journal of American History* 99(1) (2012), 124–34; John Sheail, 'Torrey Canyon: The Political Dimension', *Journal of Contemporary History* 42 (2007), 485–504.

101. Mayer, *Erdöl-Weltatlas*; Mayer, *Weltatlas Erdöl und Erdgas*, 2nd ed. (Braunschweig, 1976); Mayer, *Petro-Atlas*, 3rd ed. (Braunschweig, 1982); John C. McCaslin (ed.), *International Petroleum Encyclopedia* (Tulsa, OK, 1977).

102. Mayer, *Erdöl-Weltatlas*, 135.

103. American Petroleum Institute, *Facts about Oil* (n.p., 1971).

104. Ibid., 37f.

105. Deffeyes, *Hubbert's Peak*, 7–8. Deffeyes studied geology at Princeton in the 1950s and later worked for Shell in Texas.

106. Gilbert Jenkins, 'World Oil Reserves Reporting 1948–1996: Political, Economic and Subjective Influences', *OPEC Review* 21 (1997), 89–111.

107. 'Reserves – Tomorrow's Storehouse', *Petroleum Panorama: Commemorating 100 Years of Petroleum Progress; The Oil and Gas Journal* 57(5) (1959), 30–32, here B-30. In many ways, this is still the case; see Clifford Krauss 'There Will Be Fuel: New Oil and Gas Sources Abound, But They Come with Costs', *New York Times*, 17 November 2010; Paul Sabin, *The Bet: Paul Ehrlich, Julian Simon, and Our Gamble over Earth's Future* (New Haven, 2013).

108. 'Reserves – Tomorrow's Storehouse', B-32; Tyler Priest, 'Hubbert's Peak: The Great Debate over the End of Oil', *Historical Studies in the Natural Sciences* 44(1) (2014), 37–79, here 46f.

109. On this and what follows, see also Rüdiger Graf, 'Ressourcenkonflikte als Wissenskonflikte: Ölreserven und Petroknowledge in Wissenschaft und Politik', *Geschichte in Wissenschaft und Unterricht* 63(9–10) (2012), 582–99; and see Graf, 'Expert Estimates of Oil-Reserves'.

110. Vincent E. McKelvey, 'Concepts of Reserves and Resources', in John D. Haun (ed.), *Methods of Estimating the Volume of Undiscovered Oil and Gas Resources* (Tulsa, OK, 1975), 11–14, here 11; see also F. Blondel and S.G. Lasky, 'Mineral Reserves and Mineral Resources', *Economic Geology* 51(7) (1956), 686–97, and for a more conceptually nuanced account, see G.J.S. Govett and M.H. Govett, 'The Concept and Measurement of Mineral Reserves and Resources', *Resources Policy* 1 (September 1974), 46–55.

111. See the catalogue of contemporary methods in C. Hewitt Dix, *Seismic Prospecting for Oil* (New York, 1952), 6–16; on the development and success of these methods, see Deffeyes, *Hubbert's Peak*, 70–87.

112. Deffeyes, *Hubbert's Peak*, 6.

113. Craft and Hawkins, *Applied Petroleum Reservoir Engineering*; Carl E. Reistle, 'Reservoir Engineering', in Carter, *The History of Petroleum Engineering*, 811–46; T.V. Moore, 'Reservoir Engineering Begins Second 25 Years', *The Oil and Gas Journal* 54(29) (1955), 148; J.G. Richardson and H.L. Stone, 'A Quarter Century of Progress in the Application of Reservoir Engineering', *Journal of Petroleum Technology* 25 (December 1973), 1371–79; Ferdinand E. Banks, *The Political Economy of World Energy: An Introductory Textbook* (New Jersey, 2007); Jenkins, 'World Oil Reserves Reporting 1948–1996'.

114. Kipp, 'The Evolution of Petroleum Engineering', 113; Lewis G. Weeks, 'World Offshore Petroleum Resources', *Bulletin of the American Association of Petroleum Geologists* 49

(1965), 1680–93; M.S. Kraemer, 'Producing Operations of the Future', *Journal of Petroleum Technology* 23 (1971), 27–32.

115. H.A. Nedom, 'Planning the Energy Years', *Journal of Petroleum Technology* 23 (January 1971), 13–15, here 13; Thomas C. Frick, 'Fossil Fuel Resources in the United States', *Journal of Petroleum Technology* 18 (February 1966), 155–75.

116. Wildavsky and Tenenbaum, *Politics of Mistrust*, 12.

117. Morris Muskat, 'The Proved Crude Oil Reserves of the US', *Journal of Petroleum Technology* 15(9) (1963), 915–21, here 917.

118. Wallace F. Lovejoy and Paul T. Homan, *Methods of Estimating Reserves of Crude Oil, Natural Gas, and Natural Gas Liquids* (Baltimore, 1965), 4.

119. Ibid., 104f.; see also, with very similar calculations, Sam H. Schurr and Bruce C. Netschert, *Energy in the American Economy, 1850–1975: An Economic Study of Its History and Prospects* (Baltimore, 1960), 9–12; and on the 'conservatism' of reserve estimates, see United Nations. Department of Economic and Social Affairs, *Petroleum in the 1970s: Report of the Ad Hoc Panel of Experts on Projections of Demand and Supply of Crude Petroleum and Products, United Nations Headquarters, 9–18 March 1971* (New York, 1974), 2.

120. Alfred Zapp, *Future Petroleum Producing Capacity of the United States: Contributions to Economic Geology. A Discussion of the Nature of Certain Petroleum Statistics and Estimates and their Meaningfulness in Appraising the Outlook for Future Supply* (Washington, DC, 1962) (United States Geological Survey Bulletin, 1142-H); William W. Mallory, 'Accelerated National Oil and Gas Resource Appraisal (ANOGRE)', in John D. Haun (ed.), *Methods of Estimating the Volume of Undiscovered Oil and Gas Resources* (Tulsa, OK, 1975), 23–30; Priest, 'Hubbert's Peak', 57.

121. Dix, *Seismic Prospecting for Oil*, 51.

122. Gary Bowden, 'The Social Construction of Validity in Estimates of US Crude Oil Reserves', *Social Studies of Science* 15 (1985), 207–40, here 211. Between 1965 and 1975, the highest oil reserve estimate for the United States was ten times the lowest. Earl Cook, 'Undiscovered or Undeveloped Crude Oil "Resources" and National Energy Strategies', in John D. Haun (ed.), *Methods of Estimating the Volume of Undiscovered Oil and Gas Resources* (Tulsa, OK, 1975), 97–106, here 97.

123. On Hubbert, see esp. Deffeyes, *Hubbert's Peak*, 1; Priest, 'Hubbert's Peak'; on the renaissance of Hubbert's ideas on the global level since the 1990s, see R.A. Kerr, 'The Next Oil Crisis Looms Large and Perhaps Close', *Science* 281(5380) (1998), 1128–31; C.B. Hatfield, 'Oil Back on the Global Agenda', *Nature* 387 (1997), 121; Colin J. Campbell, *The Coming Oil Crisis* (Essex, 1997); Campbell, *Oil Crisis* (Brentwood, 2005); Yves Cochet, *Pétrole apocalypse* (Paris, 2005); on the movement, see also the Association for the Study of Peak Oil and Gas: http://aspousa.org/ (accessed 29 June 2012).

124. Shapin, *The Scientific Life*, 93–164.

125. Deffeyes, *Hubbert's Peak*, 3.

126. Marion King Hubbert, *Energy Resources: A Report to the Committee on Natural Resources of the National Academy of Sciences – National Research Council* (Washington, DC, 1962) (National Academy of Sciences – National Research Council Publications, 1000 d), 34.

127. Ibid., 50.

128. Ibid., 75.

129. Deffeyes, *Hubbert's Peak*, 6.

130. J.M. Ryan, 'Limitations of Statistical Methods for Predicting Petroleum and Natural Gas Availability', *Journal of Petroleum Technology* 18 (March 1966), 281–84, here 282.

131. Lewis G. Weeks, 'Estimation of Petroleum Resources: Commentary', *Bulletin of the American Association of Petroleum Geologists* 50 (1966), 2008–10; Anibal R. Martinez, 'Estimation of Petroleum Resources', *Bulletin of the American Association of Petroleum Geologists* 50 (1966), 2001–08.

132. Priest, 'Hubbert's Peak', 57.

133. Hubbert, *Energy Resources*, 125.
134. Graf, 'Expert Estimates of Oil-Reserves'.
135. As a classic text that long defined the discipline's concerns, see Harold Hotelling, 'The Economics of Exhaustible Resources', *Journal of Political Economy* 39 (April 1931), 137–75.
136. Martin Kramer, *Ivory Towers on Sand: The Failure of Middle Eastern Studies in America* (Washington, DC, 2001), 12; on the influence of Middle East experts on the formulation of US foreign policy, see also Matthew F. Jacobs, *Imagining the Middle East: The Building of an American Foreign Policy, 1918–1967* (Chapel Hill, 2011).

Chapter 2

SHORTAGES, FORECASTS, PREVENTION
Supplying the Western World with Oil

Historians and political scientists long considered the oil crisis a turning point, one that suddenly confronted both politicians and a broad public in Western Europe and the United States with their dependence on oil supplies from the Near and Middle East.[1] In the 1970s, however, a number of authors still recalled that oil experts had long expected such an event and that governments had taken precautions. But in subsequent decades this was largely forgotten.[2] This happened, first, because the spectacular series of events that constituted the oil crisis overshadowed earlier developments, offering themselves up as the focal points of fundamental change. Second, many contemporary actors described the oil crisis as sudden, and impossible to predict, in order to divert attention away from their own failures and their responsibility for the energy problems of the 1970s.

In order to assess the common interpretation that the oil crisis was unexpected or even unforeseeable, in what follows I reconstruct the oil-related structures of expectation entertained by the governments of Western Europe and the United States. When, if at all, was dependence on oil imports perceived as dangerous, and by whom? Which countermeasures were called for and implemented? These questions are important to understanding the oil crisis because anticipated supply problems prompted the implementation of precautionary measures that later influenced Western governments' response to the embargo and production cutbacks. As we will see, when it comes to the shift in Western energy policies, the crucial date was not October 1973 but January 1970. On the Oil Committee of the Organization for Economic Cooperation and Development (OECD), the member states' oil experts perceived a novel threat to Western Europe's oil supply. They disseminated this perception throughout their respective governments and advocated the restructuring of energy sectors. So changes in energy policy were instigated by the proceedings of a transnational expert body, and we have to take these deliberations into account if we want to understand Western responses to the actions of OPEC and OAPEC and the oil crisis of 1973–74.

Diagnoses and Preventative Measures in the OECD

The governments of many industrialized countries began to restructure their energy policies in the early 1970s. For the most part, they had created oil stockpiles that could be deployed in case of supply shortages, and if necessary they had the legal authority to impose consumption restrictions and other measures affecting oil and energy. The similarity of these structures and policies, and their synchronous introduction, was no mere coincidence: governments had not acted independently, simultaneously generating the same risk assessments and opting for the same defensive measures. In the second half of the twentieth century, rather than monadic, monolithic blocs, in many respects governments, states and administrations were enmeshed across national boundaries through a variety of institutions and forums.[3] International organizations, along with intergovernmental and nongovernmental actors, played an important role in shaping international relations and the international order – while also helping to mould national policymaking.[4]

In the 1960s and 1970s, exchange within the framework of the OECD – successor to the Organization for European Economic Cooperation (OEEC), founded in 1948, which was intended to foster the reconstruction of (Western) Europe – influenced the energy policies of the major consuming countries. Through the OECD, from 1961 onwards, the Western European countries, the United States and Canada, joined by Japan in 1964, sought to secure and increase economic growth, raise living standards, stabilize currencies and, very generally, develop the global economy.[5] Unlike other international organizations, the OECD had no means of sanctioning its members to ensure compliance with its decisions, which were non-binding. It nonetheless exercised a remarkable influence on the policies of its member states, by offering forums in the shape of committees on various policy fields, where experts from various ministries exchanged views. This exchange, in which the staff of the Paris-based OECD secretariat also participated, forged common languages for specific policy fields and problem areas, while standardized statistics were produced that facilitated comparison between different economic regions and societies.[6] This gave rise to the development of transnational networks of experts or 'epistemic communities' that perceived key problems in much the same way, used the same methods of analysis and agreed on possible solutions.[7] Their regular meetings, along with so-called 'peer reviews' of the various national policies, generated a certain degree of pressure, which fed back into the member states' ministries and could instigate policy changes.

In the ten years from 1956 to 1966, oil consumption in the OEEC countries, or later the European members of the OECD, grew by a factor of 3.5, from 113.1 to 385 million tonnes, while the import quota grew from 90 to 95 per cent and the share of imports from the Middle East grew from 70 to 83 per cent.[8] Because economic growth and increasing living standards – the OECD's key concerns – were based in significant part on growing oil consumption, the oil supply became an important subject in its deliberations. Since the foundation of the OEEC, the investigation of developments in the oil sector had been entrusted to the Oil Committee, which brought together oil experts from the member states.[9] In view of increased oil imports, the significance of oil to economic development and the predominantly Middle Eastern origin of the oil consumed in Western Europe, there was a perception within the OEEC that the risk of supply disruptions was rapidly increasing.[10] This seemed to be confirmed in 1956, when Egyptian president Gamal Abdel Nasser closed the Suez Canal, the transportation corridor for around 70 per cent of Europe's Middle Eastern oil imports, after the United Kingdom and France opted for a military response to the nationalization of the Suez Canal Company. Since it took oil tankers – whose carrying capacity was in any case limited – significantly longer to travel around the Cape of Good Hope, a lack of oil was soon making itself felt in Europe, a lack that could be offset only through additional supplies from the United States.[11]

The Suez crisis kicked off the debate on how to prevent supply shortfalls. In its subsequent investigation, the OEEC Oil Committee concluded that this need not be a singular event: 'Arbitrary action by one or many of the producing or transit countries could seriously affect the supply of oil which Europe would expect to import from the Middle East'.[12] In view of this uncertainty, the Oil Committee called for the OECD countries to implement national precautionary measures to boost their capacity to endure future supply bottlenecks. In the 1960s, along with the High Level Group Oil, made up only of the major consuming countries, the Committee took steps to coordinate these measures. It thus emerged as a key hub in which government officials dedicated to energy policy from the various countries came together to exchange information and discuss strategies. To make effective provision for crises, they needed the most accurate possible forecasts of future developments in the international oil market. By collating relevant data, the Oil Committee standardized the perception and description of the structures, and problems, characteristic of the international economy of oil and energy.

The Oil Committee did not limit itself to diagnosis. It also drew up action plans. In the early 1960s, to bolster OECD countries' capacity to cope with future supply shortages, of the kind triggered by the closure of the Suez Canal, at the behest of the Oil Committee the OECD Council proposed that member states take action in five key areas.[13] First, they should build up adequate oil stockpiles to offset temporary supply shortfalls. In view of rapidly growing consumption, the quantity of desired stockpiles was not fixed, but should equate to eighty days' normal oil consumption. Second, attempts should be made to diversify countries of origin and supply routes, and to increase overall oil tanker capacity.[14] Third, the Council proposed the establishment of advisory bodies in the member states, to be made up of representatives of the government and oil industry, in order to facilitate rapid coordination of supply in emergencies. Fourth, it urged member state governments to put in place legal provisions enabling them 'to introduce prompt and effective reductions in consumption of petroleum products if an oil supply emergency should occur'.[15] So the executive's capacity for effective action was to be strengthened to deal with a new type of emergency. Furthermore, the Council stipulated that in the case of a new supply bottleneck, 90 to 95 per cent of available oil in Europe was to be distributed in proportion to the European OECD countries' needs hitherto, while 5 to 10 per cent would be allocated to countries in particular difficulty on an ad hoc basis.[16]

Despite this comprehensive catalogue of measures in response to feared supply shortfalls, in the early 1960s the Oil Committee and the oil industry were fundamentally sanguine about the OEEC countries' future oil supply. In Western Europe, the Committee believed, the demand for oil would undoubtedly grow in coming years, but 'on the present evidence of proven reserves and the likely level of "ultimate recovery", there is no doubt that the world's oil reserves are sufficient to meet all foreseeable demands'.[17] While economic growth in the industrialized countries would rapidly increase oil consumption, the oil price would remain stable or fall due to even more rapidly growing oil reserves. As long as the oil companies made adequate efforts in exploration and production, this development would continue. 'The proved reserves and ultimate resources of oil throughout the world should not justify predictions of scarcity', concluded the Oil Committee's 1964 report.[18] At most, the Committee believed, political factors might restrict the flow of cheap oil. But because a functioning oil market was ultimately in the best interests of all those involved in the oil economy, the Committee assumed that the worst that could happen would be brief supply disruptions, for which OECD governments would be well prepared as a result of the measures it had proposed.[19]

The Oil Committee did not limit itself to providing national governments with advice, but also monitored their activities and the implementation of its recommendations. When it ascertained in 1962 that oil stockpiles in most countries lay well below the target of eighty days' worth, it proposed periodic checks of member countries' precautionary measures to the OECD Council.[20] Annual questionnaires and the resulting reports on the state of members' crisis planning put pressure on the relevant ministries and helped to synchronize national oil policies. In 1963, for example, all OECD countries learned that the Netherlands, Ireland, Italy and Denmark had as yet failed to produce regulations facilitating consumption restrictions in case of emergency, and that Luxembourg, Sweden and Switzerland still lacked advisory bodies made up of industry representatives.[21] Even in the absence of binding decisions or the ability to impose sanctions, this pressure, or the good arguments put forward by the expert groups, helped to standardize member states' energy strategies.[22]

Despite the fundamental confidence with which the experts of the Oil Committee viewed the future, they perceived a residual risk of supply disruptions. The High Level Group Oil, meanwhile, was increasingly keen to produce more precise estimates of future trends in oil consumption and more accurately assess the impact of possible supply disruptions. Under the chairmanship of the British delegation – which took its work on oil policy within the OECD framework particularly seriously as long as the UK was outside the European Economic Community – hypothetical scenarios were thus developed outlining the impact of the loss of one, two or three producing countries.[23] One of the key tasks here was to further harmonize assessments of the future of the oil economy and its risks, which still differed between the various countries.[24] In December 1966, the High Level Group Oil thus produced a report on the prospects for oil supply and demand until 1970–75, which was accepted by the Oil Policy Committee in April 1967 and then, in May, passed on to the OECD Council.[25] The High Level Group wanted to answer three questions in this report. Is there a sufficient physical quantity of oil reserves to satisfy future demand? What other factors might limit the reliability and durability of supply? What precautionary measures might be implemented in this regard? However, the experts were only confident enough to produce forecasts for the next five years. They argued that only short-term forecasts of this kind could provide an accurate basis for policymaking. On this view, energy policy must be based neither on an assessment of contemporary conditions, because they are subject to rapid change, nor on long-term forecasts of a notoriously uncertain character.[26]

Essentially, the High Level Group echoed the views of mainstream geological experts, declaring that there would be no physical limits to oil consumption in the foreseeable future. Worldwide, the Group stated, there were more than fifty billion tonnes of proved reserves, sufficient for thirty years at current production rates.[27] But, its report emphasized, these figures reflected only the current state of oil exploration. The quantity of oil reserves would certainly be several times larger if one factored in technological improvements in locating and exploiting oil deposits that were bound to occur in future. Merely factoring in the exploitation of known fields and of the oil present in tar sands and oil shale resulted in more generous oil reserve estimates. So the crucial aspect of oil supply in the OECD concerned neither physical quantity nor costs, 'but whether exploration and development work can continue at an adequate rate to maintain the increasing production and supply capacity required'.[28] The report also recognized that deliberate acts by producing countries, political unrest or industrial disputes might cause supply cutbacks in the near future. While the oil experts of the OECD self-critically described their ability to evaluate this ultimately political question as rather limited, they nonetheless made a number of general points concerning the security of supply. Because the significance of transit countries had diminished while the number of producing countries had increased, and given that supply disruptions ultimately did economic harm to the producing countries themselves, the experts averred that the risk of deliberate action to disrupt supply had grown smaller. It could not, however, be ruled out completely.[29] After discussing a number of possible supply shortfalls, the report concluded, without explicitly mentioning OPEC, that the risk of a 'monopoly oil exporting bloc emerging and exercising undue pressure' was 'not so great as to be a major factor in energy planning'.[30] The precautionary steps that had already been taken, such as the establishment of oil stockpiles and the diversification of energy sources, was believed to have reduced this risk still further. In addition, US surplus production capacity was bolstering supply security in the OECD countries, offering an alternative source of oil in case of shortages.

During the Six-Day War of early June 1967, just over six weeks after the Oil Committee had approved the report, the Arab producing countries announced an oil embargo and the Suez Canal was blocked once again.[31] Nonetheless, or perhaps because of this, the report was subject to intensive discussion in the OECD Council: 'Recent events in the Middle East made the report even more interesting. Some of the relatively optimistic forecasts it contained had been proved wrong but these were based on assumptions that did not always prove true, as for instance the continuance of oil supplies from North Africa in the event of a breakdown of supplies from the Middle East'.[32] In West Germany too, awareness of oil issues was growing, and the OECD report was now presented directly to the chancellor – along with a brief summary of its contents.³³ In the wake of the embargo, the OECD Oil Committee criticized the member states for ignoring its guidelines and failing to increase their oil stockpiles since 1962, and thus falling short of the OECD's suggested target of eighty days' worth. The American delegates declared their willingness to support the Europeans, but expressed exasperation at their inactivity and called for the establishment of an International Industry Advisory Board with responsibility for crisis coordination.³⁴ The excitement soon died down, however, because the embargo was poorly thought out and did not last long. By August, the oil supply was back at normal levels and oil consumption suffered no more than a short-term dip in the third quarter of 1967. While the shortfall had been offset in significant part through increased US production, the OECD Oil Committee struck a self-congratulatory tone in its report on the 1967 oil embargo: the precautionary measures it had developed had helped to ensure that the OECD countries easily withstood it.³⁵ In addition to the national advisory bodies, the embargo triggered the establishment of an international advisory board including representatives of fifteen of the oil firms most important to the OECD.

Due to the ease with which the OECD countries had survived the embargo of 1967, in 1970 the Oil Committee and the High Level Group produced a risk assessment that differed little from the one published three years earlier: 'Broadly, the conclusions are that there is no reason to fear physical shortage of oil in the period up to 1975 – or, indeed, to 1980; that barring political interventions, there is unlikely to be any major rise in costs'.³⁶ Furthermore, the supply structure of the OECD countries, the flexibility of the oil industry, technological developments and further diversification of source countries gave grounds for hope that individual OECD countries' vulnerability to supply disruptions would diminish further in future. Despite this fundamentally optimistic assessment, from the late 1960s onwards a growing number of critics believed – in light of past oil supply crises – that a more effective embargo might occur in the near future. In 1969, the Oil Committee thus proposed the appointment of a mathematician and computer expert, with relevant knowledge of the oil economy, to produce models simulating supply and demand in the OECD.³⁷ There were also intensive discussions about the mechanisms needed to ensure effective crisis management and the level of likely growth in consumption.³⁸

In early 1970, however, these debates were placed on a new foundation. The US delegation to the High Level Group Oil declared that, due to growing oil consumption in the United States, from 1975 onwards the Europeans would no longer be able to fall back on US stockpiles in case of crisis. This seemed to pose a threat as delegates thought another crisis in the Near or Middle East quite possible.[39] Nonetheless, after the meeting the Americans initially had the impression that their announcement had been received calmly, which may have been partly due to the fact that they had given the British and Dutch delegations advance warning of it. The German and other delegates, conversely, seemed surprised, and believed that only a lack of time had prevented proper discussion of the issue.[40] Outside the UK, which was expecting the advent of North Sea oil in 1975, the loss of American surplus production capacity, which had helped to overcome previous supply crises, was disquieting news for European energy experts.[41] It finally made it clear to the members of the High Level Group that Europeans were now at risk from future Middle Eastern supply disruptions. In response to repeated German inquiries and requests for clarification, the State Department pointed out that the US had highlighted this problem on previous occasions, which was in any case no secret to any attentive energy expert. The West German delegates agreed with this, but it was the Americans' official declaration in January 1970 that triggered more intensive German efforts to establish mechanisms to cope with future crises and prompted changes in national energy policy.[42] It seemed all the more urgent to enhance security of supply as the revolution in Libya had reinforced Europeans' concerns about politically motivated disruptions.[43]

In any case, European unease was severe enough that the State Department had the problem of reserve production capacities placed on the agenda of the next meeting of the High Level Group in late May, where it issued a new statement of its position in an attempt to steer a course between 'promising too much' and 'appearing indifferent'.[44] Nonetheless, the US delegates perceived the atmosphere at this meeting as 'one of very general concern if not yet alarm over oil supply prospects'. This, they believed, was because the Western European and Japanese delegates were still greatly worried about the effects of a disruption of oil supplies from Libya and the Middle East.[45] The Europeans calmed down when the United States assured them of its ongoing commitment to covering Europe's oil needs. The West German delegation at least was satisfied with the US statement, though the basic problem remained the same.[46] This was confirmed by a lecture delivered by Wilson M. Laird, director of the Office of Oil and Gas in the US Department of the Interior, in September 1970, which circulated among the oil experts of the OECD in manuscript form. With the help of diagrams, Laird showed once again that the additional production capacity that had been generated by the US oil industry's efforts to self-regulate – in order to stabilize the oil price – was no more. His conclusions were clear-cut: 'I would like to say a few words about US capability to help out on oil shortages. We can take care of our own military needs by re-adjustments (not without problems), but spare crude capacity is considerably below 1967'.[47]

Apart from the loss of the US safety buffer, however, in the early 1970s the Oil Policy Committee also saw positive signs, because it modelled future supply crises as variants of previous ones. It believed that the situation in the oil tanker market, which had exacerbated previous crises, had eased markedly, while nuclear energy and gas were covering a growing proportion of energy needs.[48] Nonetheless, the Committee recognized the disquieting fact that all previous forecasts had fundamentally underestimated two factors. First, the increase in oil consumption in consuming countries: even if OECD experts corrected predictions that had been overtaken by reality, their new forecasts always lagged behind real growth rates.[49] Second, they had not reckoned with the enhanced power of OPEC, which was in significant part itself a consequence of the rapid growth in demand. Until the early 1970s, Oil Committee reports did not even mention OPEC as a factor, but now it suddenly loomed large as a result of the international oil market's transformation from a seller's to a buyer's market, to use the contemporary phrase. In early 1971, reporting from a meeting of the High Level Group Oil, energy expert at the West German Ministry of Economics Ulf Lantzke informed his senior colleague, undersecretary Detlev Karsten Rohwedder, and minister for economic affairs Hans Friderichs, that 'in view of OPEC's strong position', every country was aware that it 'would have to make significant price concessions in the coming negotiations in order to avoid oil supply disruptions and thus serious economic upheavals'.[50] Under Libyan leadership, in negotiations with the oil companies in Tripoli in February 1971 and Tehran in April, OPEC did in fact secure an increased share of oil industry profits and price increases.[51] After this agreement, at the latest, it finally sank in that 'OPEC was not a joke', to quote State Department oil expert James Akins.[52]

In addition to the issue of which precautionary measures would help to ensure energy security, the discussions in the High Level Group and Oil Committee now revolved around whether the oil firms ought to be supported in their negotiations with the producing countries, and whether the consuming countries ought to try to achieve a joint strategy or proceed separately. Conflicts emerged on every issue due to diverging national interests. The various actors agreed that energy security had become the number one energy policy issue and also agreed on the reasons for this: 'The rapid increase in demand for energy in OECD Member countries and recent developments in the energy situation . . . make the security of supplies a priority aspect of energy policy'.[53] In light of this situation, however, purely importing and consuming countries, such as West Germany, Italy and Japan, came to fundamentally different conclusions from those that were also important producing countries, such as the United States, the United Kingdom, France and the Netherlands.[54] The UK in particular, but also the Netherlands and the US, called for the oil companies to be supported in their negotiations with the consuming countries, while those countries in which no major oil firms were headquartered were more non-committal and, like West Germany, underlined that their influence on the producing countries was negligible in any case.[55] In the summer of 1972, the French accused the Americans of needlessly dramatizing the situation and overestimating the risks of supply disruptions, but could not bring themselves to put forward a positive assessment of the situation either: 'When other delegates started referring to the "black Akins picture" and the "rosy Vaillaud picture", Mr. Vaillaud objected, saying he is in no way optimistic, only that he was less pessimistic than Mr. Akins'.[56]

In October 1972, the agenda of the High Level Group included the question of whether, and if so in what way, the non-European OECD member states, in other words the United States, Canada, Japan and Australia, ought to participate in an emergency oil distribution mechanism ('oil sharing'). The European member states were not guided by altruism – that is, the desire to support their allies in case of emergency – but were instead thinking about what would most benefit them. For example, the West German government was keen to keep the portion of oil to be supplied to the worst affected countries in case of crisis as small as possible relative to the amount distributed on the basis of pre-crisis levels, because it believed it stood to benefit most from this.[57] This conflict overlapped with the issue of the extent to which energy policy ought to be coordinated within the OECD framework or whether it was legitimate to sign bilateral agreements with producing countries. On behalf of the United States, Deputy Secretary of State John Irwin took a markedly multilateral position, calling on the Europeans to avoid vying for Middle Eastern oil should the anticipated crisis occur. In this spirit, he declared, the United States itself had turned down Saudi Arabia's offer of a 'special relationship', but would not hesitate to sign bilateral agreements were the Europeans to opt to do so.[58] In the subsequent debate, James Akins, a well-regarded figure among his European colleagues, was even clearer, declaring that the United States stood ready to compete with other consuming countries for worldwide oil reserves. Its economic power, he underlined, would allow the US to prevail in such a struggle. This harsh threat, as noted with much satisfaction in the United States, had the intended effect on many Europeans.[59] As Ulf Lantzke reported to the minister for economics, 'Mr. Akins made it quite clear that the United States feels strong enough to make the best offer in case of possible competition between consuming countries'.[60] In reality, US government experts started from the premise that it would be 'dangerous, highly divisive, and ultimately more costly' for consuming countries to compete to strike the best bilateral deals with producing countries rather than cooperate. They thus pushed for participation in oil sharing.[61] The latter was considered disadvantageous for the US only under specific conditions. Were an embargo to be imposed exclusively on the United States, US oil experts believed, it might be of benefit. In any case, these experts assumed that in case of crisis there would be massive pressure on the United States to help its allies anyway. As a result, in the summer of 1973, the US declared its willingness to participate in oil sharing, as long as it did not apply to domestic production and would be activated even if just one country was affected.[62]

In significant part, by opting to participate in oil sharing, the Americans were trying to mitigate the effect of Irwin's and Akins' statements made the year before. They were also hoping to improve the climate on the OECD Oil Committee in an attempt to smooth the way for cooperation among consuming countries. In view of a surging oil price, the nationalization of foreign oil companies in Libya, which threatened to set a precedent, and fears of politically motivated supply shortages, communication within the High Level Group had become more difficult.[63] In their chairing role, the British delegation repeatedly expressed their disappointment that participants were no longer speaking openly and it had become virtually impossible to deduce their allies' intentions from what they said.[64] Immediately before the announcement of the embargo and production cutbacks in September 1973, the High Level Group and the Oil Committee were still busy assessing member states' crisis planning, while also ensuring that sufficient stockpiles were in place and that a range of emergency legislation had been enacted, from voluntary consumption restrictions through supply cutbacks to rationing.[65]

In the wake of the nationalization of foreign companies, what worried the OECD states most were developments in Libya and their possible appeal to other countries, yet as late as September 1973, the High Level Group did not believe oil supplies to be at immediate risk from this quarter. Ulf Lantzke and Hansheinrich Kruse, a petroleum expert at the West German Foreign Ministry, reported to Bonn that while there was cause for neither hysteria nor an atmosphere of crisis, it was doubtful that production in Libya and other Arab producing countries would expand to the degree necessary over the next few years.[66]

There is no evidence that the High Level Group and the Oil Policy Committee of the OECD anticipated the specific timing of the oil crisis, and in the 1960s their forecasts were often wrong. Yet by constantly insisting on the need for oil stockpiles and legally enshrined emergency measures in case of supply shortfalls, and by stimulating the debates on oil sharing, they did help to raise awareness of possible supply disruptions and price increases. In the early 1970s, the OECD countries began to simultaneously restructure their energy policies because they shared the perception of a new threatening politics of energy following the loss of US surplus production capacity. The concrete designs of national energy programmes were also inspired by debates in the OECD. In many respects – from the diversification of energy sources and countries of origin to the fostering of energy research – its guidelines read like blueprints for later national schemes. So the oil crisis was not as unexpected – and the measures with which countries responded to it were not as improvised – as is often claimed. Governments, and those sections of the public sphere with an interest in oil, had already begun to worry about the future of the oil supply.

Oil Imports and National Security in the United States

Until the early 1970s, the United States was the largest oil-producing country but after the Second World War oil imports played an ever greater role there. The import of oil was essentially discussed from the vantage point of national security. In the immediate postwar period, oil imports counted as a means of enhancing national security, because they saved the country's own reserves for use in a crisis. In the second half of the 1950s, experts defined the growing dependence on imports as a security risk, prompting the Eisenhower administration to introduce voluntary and later mandatory import quotas. In significant part this was done to protect the US oil industry from cheaper foreign oil.[67] As late as 1968, the Office of Oil and Gas, part of the Department of the Interior, seemed fundamentally optimistic about the American oil economy, believing it to be stronger than its foreign rivals and to be keeping prices under control. It was also convinced that of all the oil in the territory of the United States, only a small proportion had been extracted, ensuring a reliable supply of oil for many years to come. The crucial question, however, was 'whether they [the oil fields] can be located and produced at costs which permit them to compete with other energy sources'.[68] But the Office, which included geologists from the US Geological Survey, was alarmed that US oil reserves were growing more slowly than oil consumption. The geologists responded with proposed technological improvements in exploration and production and advocated shielding the US oil industry against cheaper imported oil in order to boost both reserves and production.[69]

Within two years, the Task Force on Oil Import Control, set up by Nixon, which was to investigate the effectiveness of import controls, came to a different conclusion as energy supply problems began to make themselves felt in the United States.[70] The Task Force, under the leadership of George P. Shultz, argued that the import restrictions had not enhanced national security but had imposed significant additional costs on consumers and, moreover, constituted unacceptable government intervention in the economy.[71] In any case, the Task Force argued, given the currently negligible quantity of oil imports, the only risk to the US oil supply was a lengthy, general, non-nuclear war or an embargo – if it were imposed by all the countries of Africa and Middle East.[72] Were the import quota system to be abolished, oil imports would certainly increase, so that by around 1980 supply disruptions would represent a significant threat to national security, but 'relaxation of import controls over time, coupled with appropriate western hemisphere preferences and a "security adjustment" to prevent undue Eastern Hemisphere imports, would – if adequately monitored by systematic management surveillance – satisfactorily protect security of supply'.[73] In view of these manageable risks – only Secretary of Defense Melvin R. Laird considered them more serious – and the easing in the national energy market that would follow the abolition of import quotas, the Task Force advocated replacing the quota system with import tariffs.

The changes in the international oil market in the early 1970s, faster than expected growth in oil consumption in the industrialized countries, price increases, and intensifying calls for producing countries to enjoy a greater share of oil revenues, quickly rendered the Task Force's assessment obsolete and prompted ever higher levels of government to examine the issue of oil. In the early 1970s, the National Security Council produced two National Security Study Memoranda (NSSM) on oil and energy policy: NSSM 114 on the 'World Oil Situation' of January 1971 and NSSM 174 on 'National Security and US Energy Policy', which appeared in the spring of 1973.[74] NSSM 114 assessed the impact on US security and economic interests of changes in the oil economy, the increasing price of oil and the OPEC countries' aspiration to take control of their oil. It analysed the consequences for NATO, the Middle East conflict, relations with the European allies and Japan, national and international economic development and the leading Western balance of payments and competitive position.[75] In addition to the Departments of the Interior, State, Treasury and Defense, the Council of Economic Advisors and the Office of Emergency Preparedness, the Departments of Justice and Commerce and the Office of Management and Budget were also tasked with developing action plans on oil and energy policy.

The analysis in NSSM 114 began by stating that an abundance of oil had long been available at a low price and Western industrialized countries had begun to take this for granted – but then oil consumption increased dramatically. As a result, higher prices were now likely and supply restrictions possible. Both, the memorandum asserted, would have a negative influence on economic development in the United States, Western Europe and Japan and must therefore be avoided. Three key events were believed to have had a negative impact on the international oil market: the closure of the Suez Canal as a consequence of the Six-Day War, Gaddafi's seizure of power in Libya and the closure of the Trans-Arabian Pipeline.[76] The various ministries, however, had differing views of the threat these developments posed to the energy supply in the United States, Western Europe and Japan. Some believed the increased dependency on oil from the Middle East and North Africa to be a grave security problem, one that must be countered by import restrictions and ample oil stockpiles. Beyond the ninety days' oil stockpiles now available in the OECD countries, this group asserted, there was little hope of keeping the Western European economies going, particularly given that the United States could no longer help out its allies.[77] Apart from these consequences, however, the Pentagon estimated that neither the US war effort in Southeast Asia nor its military capacities in general would suffer from supply shortfalls. Another group considered even this scenario overblown, convinced that there would be no embargo given the producing countries' economic interest in selling their oil to the West.[78] Ultimately, this group believed, the producing countries' sole concern was with setting the oil price, and here the United States could play the role of honest broker between them and the oil companies. Produced under the guidance of the State Department, however, NSSM 114 did discuss the political consequences of the first, more pessimistic view. Over the longer term, it averred, dependence on Middle Eastern oil would increase further, but the major oil companies would become less important to the producing countries.[79] The United States government should therefore begin to draw up emergency plans for any oil supply shortages and foster alternative energy sources.[80]

For State Department oil expert James Akins, the risk assessment produced by the interministerial NSSM 114 did not go far enough. On his initiative, just over a year later, the State Department presented the president with another detailed document on the worldwide oil market and US energy policies with the words: 'our conclusions to date are as clear as they are disturbing'.[81] The report on 'The US and the Impending Energy Crisis' was the product of eighteen months of consultations with representatives of the leading international oil companies, financial experts at major banks and oil experts active within and outside of the government of the United States and allied countries. Essentially, its diagnosis was that – due to unexpectedly rapid consumption increases, particularly in the United States – the international oil market would turn from a buyer's to a seller's market by 1975 at the latest. One or a number of the major producing countries could spark off a supply crisis.[82] Were present trends to continue, the United States would lose its comfortable position and by 1980 it would have to import around 50 per cent of its oil, because production capacity would lag behind consumption.[83] To avert these security risks, consumption must be reduced and the security of oil imports enhanced: 'These decisions ... will be as unpopular as they will be costly'.[84] Over sixteen pages, the report develops what seems with hindsight a motley catalogue of domestic and foreign policy measures, including improving investment conditions for oil firms, diplomatic initiatives vis-à-vis producing and consuming countries, augmenting emergency stockpiles, boosting nuclear energy and new forms of energy, and reducing consumption through instruments such as an increased tax on gasoline.[85] Though no precise calculations were provided to back this up, the report asserted that by 1980 these measures, along with the national 'save-a-watt' campaign and advertising bans in other areas, could reduce oil demand to 22 million barrels a day and increase domestic production to 15 million barrels, so that just 1 to 2 million barrels would have to be imported from the eastern hemisphere.[86]

Daniel Yergin's *The Prize*, drawing on James Akins' own narratives, popularized the notion that the warning memoranda produced by the State Department had no effect on the administration.[87] This is true, however, only in the sense that its demands were not turned directly into political action. The memorandum on the looming energy crisis was noted in the National Security Council, which paid more attention to energy issues as a result.[88] Chester A. Crocker, Council expert on the Middle East and North Africa, contended that while the report contained a number of 'extreme' and 'imperfect' conclusions, overall it was a fascinating piece of work and deserved to be taken seriously.[89] After an internal debate, in July 1972 Henry A. Kissinger was informed of his staff's assessment that the National Security Council must continue to examine the energy supply as a major priority.[90] Akins' memorandum on the 'impending energy crisis', Kissinger was informed, was overly technical and its analysis of prevailing political conditions unconvincing, but there was no doubt that the problem of oil would loom increasingly large in US foreign policy over the years to come.[91] The power shift in the international oil market diagnosed by the State Department, away from the oil companies towards the producing countries, would entail significant risks: 'The growing financial reserves of Middle East producers have made oil a weapon for coercion or blackmail that we can no longer dismiss'.[92] This would have grave consequences for US national security that could not be offset by increasing domestic production, as this would reduce emergency stockpiles.[93] The National Security Council must therefore examine the political ramifications of oil more closely, evaluate oil policy strategies and determine what was in the national interest of the United States.

In March 1973, Kissinger thus commissioned a new NSSM to examine the connection between energy and national security.[94] This time, along with the CIA, the Departments of State, Defense and Treasury were to assess the consequences of varying degrees of oil import dependence on US national security up to 1985. They were also tasked with developing strategies to break the power of OPEC and evaluate implications for the conflict with the Soviet Union. In light of the particularly delicate nature of the subject, once again Kissinger explicitly highlighted the need for secrecy.[95] Alongside the report produced by the Task Force on Oil Imports, the resulting NSSM 174, which was finally completed in August 1973, was the most comprehensive government analysis of US energy policies in the early 1970s. In one of the scenarios it contained, it even anticipated the embargo and outlined a number of ways of responding to it.[96]

While underlining the uncertainty surrounding all energy forecasts, NSSM 174 worked on the assumption that global oil demand would increase by 1985 and that this growth would be largely satisfied by Middle Eastern sources. This, it claimed, would lead to oil price rises of 50 or even 100 per cent, massively burdening the industrialized countries' balance of payments. In 1972, the United States imported 29 per cent of the oil it consumed, which covered just 14 per cent of total energy demand, and only a small proportion of imported oil came from the Middle East. But this would change in future.[97] As a result, the memorandum stated, there would be increased vulnerability to supply disruptions from three possible sources: a non-nuclear war that cut the western hemisphere off from oil supplies, a war in the Middle East and an embargo. A further three possibilities were considered with respect to the latter, namely an embargo supported by all Arab countries; by Iran and Iraq; and by Saudi Arabia. In view of varying production capacities, the memorandum expressed its authors' firm conviction that only a Saudi oil embargo would have serious consequences, which could be mitigated but not entirely offset through the deployment of oil stockpiles and voluntary consumption restrictions.

Though the Western European countries and Japan would be hit significantly harder by an embargo, and once it had begun the United States would have around one year to adjust its energy policies, the NSSM made concrete proposals as to how energy security could be enhanced and energy vulnerability reduced. Due to the key position of Saudi Arabia, to achieve security of supply it was vital to increase that country's interest in maintaining an adequate production rate, diversify oil and gas sources, and support while also monitoring the oil companies in their negotiations with the producing countries. To counter short-term supply disruptions,

NSSM 174 mainly envisaged larger stockpiles, emergency programmes, international distributive schemes and diversification of countries of origin. In order to reduce the country's dependence on oil imports, meanwhile, it was vital to expand domestic coal and nuclear energy, exploit nonconventional sources of oil and, over the long term, reduce consumption. Finally, there must be discussions with other consuming countries on emergency allocation plans, consultation mechanisms, harmonization of research and development and possible sources of oil outside the Arab world. Due to increased oil consumption, as NSSM 174 recognized in its conclusion, energy supply and energy security had become crucial political issues: 'The energy question does not stand in isolation from our major monetary, trade, environmental and national security issues facing this country. It is intrinsically related to these issues'.[98] On the eve of the oil embargo, then, the highest circles of the US government were engaged in intensive discussion of such an eventuality.

West Germany's Dependence on Oil Imports within the Western European Context

In West Germany, energy policy initially meant coal policy, or to be more precise bituminous coal policy. After the Second World War, domestic coal was the most important source of energy in West Germany, but by the late 1950s competition from cheaper energy sources meant that in the absence of state support it would soon decline.[99] As early as 1959, the West German Bundestag responded to the so-called Ruhr mining crisis (*Ruhrbergbaukrise*) by commissioning the Working Group of Economic Research Institutes (Arbeitsgemeinschaft wirtschaftswissenschaftlicher Forschungsinstitute)[100] to produce an expert report on 'trends in the present and future structure of supply and demand in the West German energy economy with special reference to coal mining'. Eighteen months later, the Working Group presented its report, in which, in addition to seventy staff at the various institutes, a further thirty-five experts had been involved.[101] The report estimated both total energy demand and the share covered by various energy sources for 1975.[102] The experts worked on the assumption that gross national product would double by 1975 but total energy consumption would increase by just 60 per cent. Due to its price advantages over coal, oil's share of energy supply would greatly increase. Ultimately, however, there were limits to this increase, so coal would still be required to fill the 'demand gap' arising from strong consumption increases from 1975 onwards. Due to its high costs, however, domestic coal could play this role only with the help of massive state intervention and support.[103]

Not only did the increase in total energy consumption in the 1960s surpass the experts' expectations – forecast consumption by households and small-scale consumers for 1975 was already exceeded in 1963, and for the transport sector by 1966 – but the increase in oil consumption was also markedly higher and increased West Germany's dependence on energy imports.[104] The correction of the energy forecasts made in 1961, carried out in 1966, was also too low.[105] Far from being unusual, during the postwar economic boom it was par for the course for both national and international experts to underestimate increases in energy use and especially in oil consumption.[106] In the United Kingdom, with a single exception, from the report of the Ridley Commission in 1951–52 until the early 1970s, every energy forecast overestimated the future demand for coal while underestimating oil consumption.[107] After the Suez crisis, one report on energy predicted that by 1970 the United Kingdom would require twice as much oil as in 1957, but in fact it used four times as much. In the early 1960s, a committee estimated that in 1970 the country would consume 170 million tonnes of coal and 130 million tonnes of oil, but in fact the figures were 154 and 146 million tonnes respectively. In 1971, the newly established Central Policy Review Staff, headed by Lord Rothschild, clearly recognized the pattern of failure afflicting previous energy forecasts, yet it too underestimated the oil consumption increases for subsequent years.[108] Even the oil firms were surprised by the rates of increase during the 1960s. ESSO AG's 1961 estimate of West German heating oil consumption for 1967 was exceeded by 84 per cent.[109] Only when growth rates fell during the 1970s as a result of the economic crisis and energy policies did this pattern change, with energy consumption forecasts tending to be too high.[110]

Because oil from the Middle East and North Africa was present in abundance and thus available at a low price, West Germany's energy supply initially gave little cause for concern. More worrying were the problems of domestic coal mining, though these were essentially of a regional, economic and social nature. But due to its dependence on oil imports, West Germany seemed particularly and increasingly susceptible to supply disruptions, with more than three-quarters of the German market being supplied by foreign oil companies. Experts feared that these would favour their home countries in case of crisis. As a result, as early as 1967 the Ministry of Economics deployed targeted subsidies to foster the pooling of the exploration activities of German firms that could not compete alone on the world market and had thus joined forces in the German Petroleum Exploration Company (Deutsche Mineralölexplorationsgesellschaft mbH or DEMINEX).[111]

It took the above-quoted declaration by the US delegation to the High Level Group Oil of January 1970 regarding the shortfall in US domestic reserve production capacity to convince the West German government of the gravity of the problem. This announcement triggered the restructuring of West German energy policy, culminating in the first attempt to formulate a comprehensive energy programme in the late summer of 1973. The restructuring process thus reached a peak prior to the so-called oil crisis. The various threads of this process converged in the person of Ulf Lantzke. Born in 1927 and educated as a lawyer, Lantzke had initially headed the Division for Competition in the ECSC (Abteilung für Wettbewerbsfragen in der EGKS), taking over leadership of the Energy Policy and Raw Materials Division (Abteilung für Energiepolitik und Grundstoffe) within the Ministry of Economics in 1968. In the early 1970s, he was mainly occupied with the changes in the international oil market and he was well regarded in international oil-related bodies. In May 1974, Lantzke initially became special advisor on energy issues to the secretary general of the OECD and, in November of the same year, founding director of the International Energy Agency (IEA), which was established in response to the crisis (see chapter 6).[112] Lantzke's assessment of West German energy security changed as a result of the US declaration of January 1970, or in any event he used it to justify the need to restructure energy policy to the West German government. Immediately after the meeting, he reported to undersecretary Detlev Karsten Rohwedder that the measures in place to limit the risk of German oil import dependency – namely a crisis mechanism, maintenance of stockpiles and the planned use of oil from the western hemisphere – were no longer adequate.[113] Disruptions in oil supplies from the Middle East, he stated, would mainly affect the Europeans, and West Germany was at particular risk because it had the smallest oil stockpiles; this should be mitigated by the establishment of a federal crude oil stockpile.[114]

The debate on US reserve production capacity was not limited to oil and energy experts but also reached the West German Bundestag and a broader public.[115] On 21 April, a group of CDU deputies addressed an inquiry to the West German government. Prompted by a press release from Rohwedder, in which he declared that in case of a new supply shortfall the United States could no longer supply West Germany with additional oil, they wanted to establish whether this was correct and how the government planned to respond.[116] The government answered the first part of the question in the affirmative and stated that it was taking steps to implement joint precautionary measures within the OECD and increase oil stockpiles. In late May, the CDU/CSU parliamentary group asked about the specific risks facing the West German energy supply and possible counterstrategies.[117] In a detailed response, the government underlined that in principle global oil reserves were sufficient and that the only problem was one of distribution, but this could be resolved through stockpiling, supply agreements and improved international cooperation.[118] In September 1970, the CDU/CSU parliamentary group again submitted a request for information, in which they alleged that the government was failing to take the changes in the global energy market seriously enough. Their main concern here was with the consequences for policies on coal and nuclear energy arising from these changes.[119]

In view of the increased governmental awareness and broad acceptance of Lantzke's risk assessment, in the early summer of 1970 the Ministry of Economics began to pay more attention to energy and oil policies. Lantzke's report on the meeting of the High Level Group in May 1970 reached the minister of economics himself. The US delegation had focused on damage limitation at this meeting but made no significant retractions, prompting Lantzke to propose that West Germany must take steps to ensure the development of effective crisis mechanisms in the OECD and EEC, improve its relations with the producing countries, and above all increase its own stockpiles.[120] At the same time, a report produced by the Ministry of Economics on the West German energy supply came to the disquieting conclusion that, due to the dominant position of oil for the foreseeable future, there would be no increase in energy security. From 1960 to 1969, crude oil imports had almost quadrupled, with around 45 per cent coming from Libya and almost 90 per cent from countries affected by the Middle East conflict.[121] The expert report also concluded that 'in the case of supply disruptions the potential to substitute for the missing petroleum imports by switching to other energy sources is very limited. A crisis would have a serious impact'.[122] Towards the end of 1970, officials in the Ministry of Economics were convinced that the supply of petroleum was secure for the winter, as long as there were no extremely cold periods or supply disruptions. As the energy production and distribution system was rather inflexible and was running at full capacity, however, the situation was 'highly problematic over the medium term, as even a minor incident could seriously disrupt supply'.[123]

At the beginning of the next year, prompted by the Tehran and Tripoli Agreements, the view increasingly took hold that the producing countries were becoming more powerful and would both wrest control over production from the multinational companies and inject political considerations into their production and supply decisions.[124] In a report on a meeting of undersecretaries compiled for Egon Bahr, minister for special tasks and close adviser of Willy Brandt, Rohwedder concluded that the 'quantitative supply of Western Europe [could be] significantly reduced solely as a result of restrictive measures imposed by Libya and Algeria'. He thus proposed an action plan to expand oil tanker capacity, increase contingency reserves, improve relations with the producing countries, import crude oil from a wider range of sources with the help of DEMINEX and create the legal and organizational prerequisites for effective crisis management.[125] In order to more accurately assess the impact of possible supply shortfalls and implement countermeasures, by January 1971 the government had asked the DIW, RWI and EWI to develop a crisis simulation model. In addition, in the spring a small energy policy working group was established, which included industry representatives along with ministerial officials and staff of economic research institutes.[126] On the basis of a preliminary study produced by the Ministry of Economics, on 26 May 1971 the working group discussed an 'emergency programme to ensure optimal coverage of energy needs in case of a civilian petroleum supply crisis', in other words a situation 'in which, as a result of external supply disruptions, the overall amount of petroleum in West Germany is reduced'.[127] The crisis mechanism of the OECD, then, should be supplemented by national crisis management.

The preliminary study outlined three scenarios involving shortfalls of 15 to 20, 50 and 80 per cent in the supply of crude oil and developed a catalogue of measures, ranging from the deployment of the mandatory stockpiles and voluntary cuts in consumption through weekend travel bans to rationing by coupons. But now the experts advising the ministry in the working group called for more precise modelling of varying levels of shortage and to this end they were keen to harness the talents of the Society for Mathematics and Data Processing (Gesellschaft für Mathematik und Datenverarbeitung) in Bilinghoven.[128] The report on securing the West German energy supply that the DIW, EWI and RWI were asked to produce in September 1971, which was compiled under the leadership of Manfred Liebruck on the basis of surveys carried out in the petroleum industry, failed to provide the kind of detail they had in mind and there was no collaboration with the institution in Bilinghoven. With a marked lack of precision, the institutes assumed oil shortages of up to 50 per cent for a maximum of twelve months, arguing that various combinations of stockpiles, substitute energy sources and consumption restrictions would be sufficient to overcome any crisis.[129] In addition to a catalogue of specific measures, ranging from energy-saving campaigns through the tapping of mandatory stockpiles to the issuing of petrol vouchers and heating oil coupons, the institutes highlighted the fundamental problems involved in obtaining and providing information. In future it would be vital to ensure that 'in case of crisis the decision-making bodies of the West German government [can] take action on the basis of constantly updated data'.[130]

When the Small Working Group presented an interim report in June 1972, the computer-based numerical modelling of various crisis scenarios was still in the pipeline. Nonetheless, the working group put forward detailed recommendations on crisis management. On the supply side, the mandatory stockpiles could be deployed and other energy sources could substitute for oil; alternatively, on the demand side, voluntary or imposed consumption restrictions could play a role.[131] Because these experts believed voluntary measures would have a negligible impact, they called for compulsory consumption restrictions to be placed on a firm legal basis, but at the same time they viewed efforts to increase the mandatory stockpiles as the 'backbone' of supply crisis management. As long as stockpiles were augmented and the government 'empowered' to impose emergency measures without undue delay, they believed West Germany's prospects of overcoming a supply crisis of up to one year to be 'quite favourable'.[132]

When it became clear that there would be new elections, in autumn 1972 Ulf Lantzke was tasked, on the basis of the preliminary work already done, with developing an overall energy plan for the seventh legislative period.[133] In one of his first memoranda, Lantzke explained the need for an energy programme by underlining that the world energy market – particularly when it came to the crucial energy source of oil – was being increasingly influenced by interventions by both producing and consuming countries. If the West German government continued to be the only one to forego interventions in the oil market, it risked losing its autonomy.[134] Despite the fact that past energy forecasts had mostly turned out to be wrong, for Lantzke they were important tools of policymaking on energy and investment planning, so forecasting work had to be intensified and adopt a longer-term perspective. What worried him most was West Germany's weak position in an uncertain global oil market. Only through cooperation within the OECD and EEC could the government exercise an influence in this regard, and thus might have to accept a transfer of sovereignty to supranational bodies. He also called again for the mandatory stockpiles to be increased, the establishment of a federal crude oil reserve and the development of a crisis mechanism. Finally, he mentioned the 'special problem of environmental protection'.[135]

The sixteenth meeting of the OECD's High Level Group Oil on 24 and 25 October 1972 in Paris, provided Lantzke with new arguments that underlined the urgent need to fundamentally restructure West German energy policy. At this meeting, John Irwin had first expressed his expectation that a supply bottleneck would occur, second, warned the United States' allies that in case of interallied conflict the US would get its way, and third, should Nixon be re-elected, announced that the US government would fundamentally restructure its energy policy over the coming year.[136] Against this backdrop and in view of the lack of consensus in the High Level Group, in a 'highly confidential' memorandum to the economics minister, Lantzke stated that the West German government too must get to grips 'as soon as possible with the problem as a whole' and change its energy policy:

> the changed global situation and the American initiative will force us to fundamentally examine our position with respect to petroleum, with enormous consequences for petroleum policy. . . . In light of present trends I believe that securing the energy supply must be given very high priority in any new government programme, as it is now finally becoming clear that the oil supply will not follow the general rules of a free world market in coming years but will instead be largely determined by the political influence not just of the petroleum producing countries but also the major consuming countries.[137]

As Lantzke saw it, the politicization of the oil economy – as a result of intervention by the OPEC governments but also the steps taken by the US, British and French governments and those of other industrialized countries – meant that the West German government must abandon its hands-off approach to economic policy and intervene in the energy sector.

Three months later, in January 1973, when Willy Brandt turned to economic policy in his government declaration for the new legislative period, he did in fact announce that the West German government would prioritize energy policy. He explained that 'if our national economy is to continue to develop well, the energy supply must be secured on a long-term basis'.[138] After numerous interventions by representatives of the coal mining industry over the preceding years, with the Ruhr area in mind he gave a clear assurance that 'German coal, as the most important domestic source of energy [will continue to play] an appropriate role in our country's energy supply'.[139] In the following months, partly due to ever clearer warnings of production restrictions emanating from the Arab world (chapter 3), the West German government had a team headed by Ulf Lantzke begin to work out an energy programme. The working groups tasked with preparing this programme focused a great deal of their attention on oil policies.[140] The participating oil experts agreed that the producing countries' influence on oil production had increased and that they could now cope with the loss of revenue associated with reduced production. As a result, they believed, the risk of economically or politically motivated supply cutbacks had increased, and there was a tendency for consuming countries to conclude bilateral treaties to secure their supply of oil. Due to its weak position, they contended, it was vital for the West German government to take steps to counter this tendency and work towards a common EC energy policy in order to pave the way for a joint strategy with the other major consumers, namely the United States and Japan. Lantzke and his colleagues saw the only realistic alternative to European cooperation as a West German oil and energy policy highly dependent on the United States, but they preferred the European solution.[141] The energy programme that emerged from these deliberations, which was intended to end 'West Germany's role as mere object of the forces of the global oil market' and make the 'supply of petroleum more secure', was discussed in the federal cabinet in late August 1973 and published in early October, a few days before the historic decisions by OPEC and OAPEC.[142]

The West German government's energy programme assumed that the economy would grow at an annual rate of 4.7 per cent and energy consumption by 4.3 per cent a year until 1985. Even if the significance of natural gas and nuclear energy grew during the forecast period, the dominance of oil would continue unabated. The risks arising from changes in the world oil market, the programme went on – with reference to supply problems in the United States and price increases and power outages in Europe – were not 'abstract possibilities' but 'genuine risk factors' that required immediate government action.[143] The first priority was to secure West Germany's long-term supply of oil and energy, and, second, to prevent short-term supply disruptions. Ultimately, both would require cooperation within the European Communities, but also intensified international cooperation: 'This applies both to cooperation with the crude oil producing countries and with the major consuming regions and centrally planned economies, particularly the USSR'.[144] Concrete goals over the long term included minimization of risks with respect to oil, expansion of natural gas, nuclear energy and brown coal, the use of bituminous coal as 'a factor in the stability and elasticity of electricity production', striking a balance between environmental protection and energy security, expanding refinery and oil tanker capacity, fostering research and energy-saving measures.[145] To prevent short-term supply disruptions, the obligatory stockpiles must be increased to ninety days' worth of consumption, a federal crude oil reserve must be established by 1974–75 and crisis provisions must be enshrined in law as rapidly as possible.[146]

In parallel to the West German government, the German states also began to formulate energy programmes, though their analyses of the problem were much the same, not least because they drew on studies from the same economic research institutes.[147] So while it was impossible to predict the exact timing of the oil crisis, supply restrictions or price increases, and precisely what form they would take, energy experts had been considering a constellation such as the oil crisis since the 1960s and with renewed vigour since 1970.[148] In West Germany, the energy programme developed to prevent and overcome these problems – to which the government referred proudly throughout the oil crisis, while the opposition criticized it as inadequate – was henceforth the fulcrum of debates on energy policy and efforts to restructure it. At the same time, West Germany was integrated into European energy structures, within which key actors were also seeking to formulate an apt response to the transformation of the oil and energy economy.

At the beginning of European integration after the Second World War stood the Schumann Plan and the foundation of the European Coal and Steel Community (ECSC) in 1952, in which France, West Germany, Italy and the Benelux countries placed their coal and steel production under the supervision of a supranational authority. In the 1950s, coal was still by far the most important energy source in Western Europe, and in 1957, in addition to the ECSC and the newly established European Economic Community (EEC), the treaties of Rome also gave rise to the European Atomic Energy Community (Euratom), another supranational organization. Thus, even before the oil crisis, significant energy policy competencies no longer lay exclusively in member states' hands. Initially, despite a successful coal policy and less successful nuclear policy, the European Communities (EC), created in 1965 by fusing together the ECSC, Euratom and the EEC, did not attempt to formulate a more comprehensive common energy policy integrating all energy sources. This changed only in the 1960s, when oil ousted coal as the most important energy source in every EC country with the exception of Luxembourg and experts increasingly perceived Europe's energy import dependence as a problem.[149]

In December 1968, the Council of the EC issued initial guidelines on a common energy policy and obligated EEC member states to maintain certain minimal stockpiles of petroleum and/or petroleum products.[150] In view of the key role now played by oil and oil-based products in the Community's energy supply, the Council argued: 'Any problem, even of a temporary nature, that diminishes the supply of these products from third countries, may cause serious disruption to economic activity in the Community; were this to occur, the Community must therefore be in a position to offset or at least mitigate the adverse effects'.[151] Since a supply crisis might occur unexpectedly, every member state should immediately establish minimum stockpiles equivalent to sixty-five days of the previous year's consumption. Given the constant increase in oil imports and changing power relations in the world oil market as a result of the agreements of Tehran and Tripoli, in the early 1970s EC governments stepped up their efforts to establish a common energy policy. This occurred at a time when they were also discussing the possibility of European Political Cooperation – in other words, agreement on a common foreign policy – and debating the admittance of Denmark, Ireland and the United Kingdom, which joined in 1973.[152]

By 1971, the EC was examining the effectiveness of the measures taken to secure the energy supply in short-term supply disruption scenarios of varying gravity.[153] While the Commission still seemed very confident that the EC could cope with supply shortfalls of less than three months, in the following year its longer-term assessment of energy supply in the EC up to 1985 was more sceptical. While the initial guidelines produced in 1968 were concerned with achieving a secure and cheap supply of energy, the price issue was now placed on the back burner as the focus on supply security intensified.[154] In view of the transformation from a buyer's to a seller's market, the Commission stated, everything indicated that 'the unproblematic supply situation of the 1960s [was] highly unlikely to continue', particularly given that energy consumption would at least double by 1985.[155] In these circumstances, by that year supply would depend not just on technological and economic factors but also on political ones that were very hard to predict.[156]

The EC Commission rejected a radical approach to reducing oil and thus import dependency and opposed efforts to pursue autarky.[157] Its view was that only intensive international trade could secure the energy supply over the medium and long term, and for better or worse oil would initially remain dominant, its price and quantity determining the supply of other energy sources. The Commission's proposal, based on this analysis, concerning 'necessary progress towards a common energy policy', also assumed that contemporary problems of energy supply stood 'in a global context, to such an extent that national attempts to solve the problem [seemed] doomed to failure from the outset'.[158] The Commission considered the next ten to fifteen years the most problematic period and expected things to ease up only when nuclear power began to meet a significant portion of energy demand. In the meantime, it argued, given the global nature of the energy issue, what mattered most was to strengthen relations between importing countries and, above all, coordinate political strategies with the United States and Japan within the framework of the OECD. Relations with the producing countries must also be improved through intensified joint efforts on economic issues and long-term cooperation treaties. In May, the Council issued a decree on information about the import of petroleum products, the aim being to eventually expand this into a common import policy.[159] In order to prepare for a crisis, the Commission underlined the need to establish whether it was necessary to increase oil stockpiles to cover 120 days of the previous year's consumption.

In view of what seemed like an increasingly urgent situation, just over six months later the EC published 'guidelines and priority measures with respect to the common energy policy', which again justified these measures, augmented them slightly and outlined them in more detail. In addition to concerns – anchored, over the short and medium term, in political and economic fears rather than material ones – about a sufficient supply of carbohydrates, the EC also pointed out that 'over the longer term . . . the magnitude of the energy sources that must be discovered and developed will necessitate efforts of an unprecedented character'. Ultimately, what this meant was the 'transition from carbohydrates to other energy sources'.[150] This would require massive support for research and development. Nuclear energy in particular appeared to be the environment-friendly energy of the future, but over the medium term coal would also have to be used, as long as this remained economically justifiable. Though the member states agreed on this risk analysis, the development of a common energy policy proved difficult. In the spring of 1973, negotiations initially foundered due to very different national views on energy policy, from France's energy dirigisme to West Germany's general unwillingness to intervene in the economy.[161] While some politicians may have viewed the EC on the eve of the oil crisis, to quote Detlev Karsten Rohwedder's incisive phrase, as a 'community of risk', when it came to energy policy they could only bring themselves to agree on a common programme of action when national interests converged.[162]

Interim Conclusion

In light of the unexpectedly rapid rise in oil consumption in the 1960s and growing dependence on oil imports from the Middle East and North Africa, there were mounting fears over the security of the Western European and US oil supply, not least because oil was viewed as increasingly important to the stability of the Western economic and social orders. There was wide acceptance of the geologists' optimistic assessment that worldwide oil reserves would be sufficient into the foreseeable future, but after the Suez crisis, Six-Day War and the agreements of Tehran and Tripoli, the risk of politically motivated oil supply disruptions loomed ever larger. The Oil Committee of the OECD and its High Level Group, as well as EC bodies and national governments, contemplated how supply shortfalls might play themselves out and how best to deal with them. So, contrary to many later assertions, the actions taken by OPEC and OAPEC in October 1973 were no bolt from the blue for any Western country. Particularly after the United States informed its OECD allies, in January 1970, of the impending loss of American surplus production capacity, experts expected a supply crisis in one form or another. Communication among governments ensured that risk assessments were synchronized and efforts made to coordinate strategic responses. National, international and transnational expectations of future supply crises prompted the first steps to restructure energy policy in Western Europe and the United States. Reorganization had, therefore, already begun when OAPEC announced supply cutbacks. Reflection on these structures of expectation is thus key to understanding the oil crisis, an event that accelerated processes of transformation that had already begun but whose exact timing, despite all the warnings, could not be predicted (see chapter 3).

Notes

1. Yergin, *The Prize*, 588; Frank Umbach, *Globale Energiesicherheit: Strategische Herausforderungen für die europäische und deutsche Außenpolitik* (Munich, 2003), 36; Jeremy Rifkin, *The Third Industrial Revolution: How Lateral Power Is Transforming Energy, the Economy, and the World* (New York, 2011), 10: 'The jolt to our national pride came without warning'. Armelle Demagny-Van Eyseren, 'The French Presidency, the National Companies and the First Oil Shock', in Alain Beltran (ed.), *Oil Producing Countries and Oil Companies: From the Nineteenth Century to the Twenty-First Century* (Bern/Oxford, 2011), 51–63; for a more nuanced picture, see Frank Bösch and Rüdiger Graf (eds), 'The Energy Crises of the 1970s', *Historical Social Research* 39(4) (2014), Special Issue.

2. T.M. Rybczynski (ed.), *The Economics of the Oil Crisis* (New York, 1976), xi: 'True, few foretold the precise date of the outbreak of the War of Yom Kippur, but the possibility of an oil shortage arising for one reason or another had been foreseen for an appreciable period'.

3. Anne-Marie Slaughter, *A New World Order* (Princeton, NJ, 2004), 1.

4. Akira Iriye, *Global Community: The Role of International Organizations in the Making of the Contemporary World* (Berkeley, CA, 2002).

5. Robért Wolfe, 'From Reconstructing Europe to Constructing Globalization: The OECD in Historical Perspective', in Rianne Mahon and Stephen McBride (eds), *The OECD and Transnational Governance* (Vancouver, 2008), 25–42; Richard Woodward, *The Organization for Economic Co-operation and Development (OECD)* (London/New York, 2009); Matthias Schmelzer, *The Hegemony of Growth: The OECD and the Making of the Economic Growth Paradigm* (Cambridge, 2016).

6. Woodward, *The Organization for Economic Co-operation and Development*, 7.

7. Tony Porter and Michael Webb, 'Role of the OECD in the Orchestration of Global Knowledge Networks', in Rianne Mahon and Stephen McBride (eds), *The OECD and Transnational Governance* (Vancouver, 2008), 43–59; Rianne Mahon and Stephen McBride, 'Introduction', in *The OECD and Transnational Governance* (Vancouver, 2008), 3–23, here 6, 9; Peter M. Haas, 'Introduction: Epistemic Communities and International Policy Coordination', *International Organization* 46(1) (1992), 1–35.

8. OECD, High Level Group of the Special Committee for Oil: Draft Preliminary Report on the 1967 Oil Emergency, 28.8.1968, National Archives of the United Kingdom, Kew (henceforth NA UK), POWE 63/280; OEEC Oil Committee, *Europe's Need for Oil: Implications and Lessons of the Suez Crisis* (Paris, 1958).

9. Ulf Lantzke, 'The Role of International Cooperation', in Alvin L. Alm and Robert J. Weiner (eds), *Oil Shock: Policy Response and Implementation* (Cambridge, MA, 1984), 77–96.

10. OEEC Wirtschaftsrat, *Europas Energie-Bedarf: Sein Anwachsen – seine Deckung* (Bonn, 1956).

11. Ethan B. Kapstein, *The Insecure Alliance: Energy Crises and Western Politics since 1944* (Oxford, 1990), 97–125; Simon C. Smith, *Reassessing Suez 1956: New Perspectives on the Crisis and Its Aftermath* (Aldershot/Burlington, VT, 2008); on the impact of the crisis, see also Martin Chick, 'The Risks, Costs and Benefits of Importing Oil: Fuel Import Policy in Britain, France and the United States since 1945', in Alain Beltran (ed.), *Oil Producing Countries and Oil Companies: From the Nineteenth Century to the Twenty-First Century* (Bern/Oxford, 2011), 65–83, here 75f.

12. OEEC Oil Committee, *Europe's Need for Oil*, 18.
13. OECD. Oil Committee: Report to the Council on the Stockpiling Programme, 18.6.1962, NA UK, POWE 63/642; see also OEEC Oil Committee, *Oil, Recent Developments in the OEEC Area* (Paris, 1961), 11.
14. OEEC. Oil Committee, *Europe's Need for Oil*, 44f.
15. OECD. Council: Recommendation of the Council Concerning the Apportionment of Oil Supplies in an Emergency, 6.5.1960, NA UK, POWE 63/642.
16. OECD. Council: Apportionment of Oil Supplies in an Emergency. Report by the Oil Committee, 11.7.1960, NA UK, POWE 63/642.
17. OEEC Oil Committee, *Oil, Recent Developments in the OEEC Area*, 13.
18. OECD Oil Committee, *Oil Today* (Paris, 1964), 9.
19. OEEC Oil Committee, *Oil, Recent Developments in the OEEC Area*.
20. OECD. Oil Committee: Report to the Council on the Stockpiling Programme, 18.6.1962, NA UK, POWE 63/642.
21. OECD. Council: Report to the Council on Plans European Member Countries Have Prepared to Put into Effect in the Event of an Oil Supply Emergency, 31.7.1963; or OECD. Oil Section. Summary of National Plans that OECD European Member Countries Have Prepared to Put into Effect in the Event of an Oil Supply Emergency, 17.8.1966, NA UK, POWE 63/642.
22. See the similar analysis of the peer review procedure used by the Economic and Development Review Committee, in Porter and Webb, 'Role of the OECD'.
23. Meeting of the OECD High Level Group, Minutes, 14/15 June 1965, NA UK, POWE 63/112; British motives become explicit in: Consultation, 21 May 1971, NA UK, POWE 63/868.
24. Meeting of OECD High Level Oil Group, Minutes, 7.12.1965; Action Memorandum following the 4th Meeting of the Small High Level Group of the Special Committee for Oil. 7.12.1965, NA UK, POWE 63/112.
25. OECD. Special Committee for Oil: Report on Oil Supply and Demand Prospects to 1970/75, 25 May 1967, NA UK, POWE 63/112.
26. Ibid.
27. Ibid., 20–22. A metric tonne is about 7.3 barrels.
28. Ibid., 3.
29. Ibid., 4–6.
30. Ibid., 10.
31. M.S. Daoudi and M.S. Dajani, 'The 1967 Oil Embargo Revisited', *Journal of Palestine Studies* 13(2) (1984), 65–90; Keir Thorpe, 'The Forgotten Shortage: Britain's Handling of the 1967 Oil Embargo', *Contemporary British History* 21(2) (2007), 201–22.
32. OECD Council: Minutes of the 145th Meeting, 4 July 1967, NA UK, POWE 63/111.
33. AL II: Dem Herrn Bundeskanzler vorzulegen: Energiepolitik. hier: Energiebericht der OECD, Bonn 8. Juni 1967, Bundesarchiv, Koblenz (henceforth BArch), B 136/8026.
34. Special Committee for Oil. Summary Record, 11th Session, 12/13 June 1967; OECD Council: Report of the Oil Committee, 13 June 1967; Special Committee for Oil, 13th Session, 20/21 July 1967; Special Committee for Oil, General Working Group, 12th Session, 21 July 1967, NA UK, POWE 63/111.
35. OECD, High Level Group of the Special Committee for Oil: Draft Preliminary Report on the 1967 Oil Emergency, 28.8.1968, NA UK, POWE 63/280.
36. OECD. Council: Prospects for Oil Supply and Demand. Report by the Special Committee for Oil, Paris, 3 July 1970; Supplementary Report by the Special Committee for Oil on Oil Supply and Demand Prospects to 1975, NA UK, POWE 63/280, 1.
37. OECD. Oil Section: An Oil Supply/Demand Simulation Model for the OECD Member Countries, 22 May 1969, BArch, B 102/131404.

38. Kling (III D 2) an: Abteilungsleiter III: Sitzung der High Level Group des Öl-Ausschusses der OECD am 2.6.1969, 28.5.1969; OECD: Summary Record of the 8th Session of the High Level Group, 2.7.1969, 9.7.1969, BArch, B 102/131404.

39. Kling (OECD): Kurzbericht Nr. 14 über die Sitzung der High Level Group des Mineralölausschusses der OECD am 8.1.1970, BArch, B 102/131405; Ulf Lantzke an StS Dr. Rohwedder: Sicherung der Rohölversorgung Europas in Krisenzeiten, 19.1.1970, BArch, B 102/131404.

40. Greenwald (US Mission OECD): Meeting of High Level Group of OECD Oil Committee, 16 January 1970, NARA, RG 59, Box 1481 PET 1 to PET 3 OECD; Kling (OECD): Kurzbericht Nr. 14 über die Sitzung der High Level Group des Mineralölausschusses der OECD am 8.1.1970, BArch, B 102/131405.

41. Beckett (Ministry of Technology, GB) an Kling: High Level Group of the OECD Oil Committee, 25.3.1970, BArch, B 102/131405; Lantzke (Abt. III) an BM [gesehen] über Rohwedder: Sicherung der Rohölversorgung Europas in Krisenzeiten, Bericht über Sitzung der High Level Group am 27./28. Mai 1970, 2. Juni 1970, B 102/131405.

42. Greenwald (US Mission OECD): German Oil Company Interest in US Reserve Capacity, 5 February 1970; Rogers (Dept. of State) to US Mission OECD, 9 March 1970; Rush (Amembassy Bonn) to Dept. of State: FRG Reaction to US Declaration on Reserve Oil Capacity, 13 May 1970; Rush (Amembassy Bonn) to Dept. of State: FRG Reaction to US Declaration on Reserve Oil Capacity, 20 May 1970, NARA, RG 59, Box 1481 PET 1 to PET 3 OECD.

43. With reference to an interview with Ulf Lantzke, Daniel Yergin proposes that the Europeans grasped the risks facing them in 1968. This is backed up by Lantzke's retrospective statements (Ulf Lantzke, 'The OECD and Its International Energy Agency', *Daedalus* 104(4) (1975), 217–27, here 218: 'By 1968, the United States could no longer be regarded as a secure supplier for Europe and Japan, since it was consuming domestically all that it produced'), but the documents concerning the meeting of January 1970 suggest otherwise. Daniel Yergin, *Der Preis: Die Jagd nach Öl, Geld und Macht* (Frankfurt am Main, 1991), 724. Hohensee adopts Yergin's dates; Hohensee, *Der erste Ölpreisschock 1973/74*, 109. While we cannot rule out the possibility that Lantzke perceived the problem earlier, this insight prompted no action from the West German government before 1970.

44. Rogers (Dept. of State) to US Mission OECD, 2 April 1970; Rogers (Dept. of State) to US Mission OECD, 25 April 1970; Greenwald (US Mission OECD): High Level Group Meeting, OECD Oil Committee, 28 May 1970, NARA, RG 59, Box 1481 PET 1 to PET 3 OECD.

45. Greenwald (US Mission OECD): High Level Group Meeting, OECD Oil Committee, 28 May 1970, NARA, RG 59, Box 1481 PET 1 to PET 3 OECD.

46. Lantzke (Abt. III) an BM [gesehen] über Rohwedder: Sicherung der Rohölversorgung Europas in Krisenzeiten, Bericht über Sitzung der High Level Group am 27./28. Mai 1970, 2. Juni 1970, BArch, B 102/131405; Rush (Amembassy Bonn) to Dept. of State: US Declaration on Reserve Oil Capacity, 9 June 1970, NARA, RG 59, Box 1481 PET 1 to PET 3 OECD.

47. OECD. Remarks by Dr. Wilson M. Laird. Director – Office of Oil and Gas. US Dept. of the Interior, 8 September 1970, NA UK, POWE 63/642; on the loss of additional production capacity, see also Richard H. Vietor, *Energy Policy in America since 1945: A Study of Business-Government Relations* (Cambridge, 1984), 199.

48. OECD. Oil Section: Review of the Plans which the European Countries Have Ready to Put into Effect in an Oil Supply Emergency, 23 November 1970, NA UK, POWE 63/642.

49. OECD. Council: Prospects for Oil Supply and Demand. Report by the Special Committee for Oil, Paris, 3 July 1970; Supplementary Report by the Special Committee for Oil on Oil Supply and Demand Prospects to 1975, NA UK, POWE 63/280, 27.

50. Lantzke an BM über Rohwedder: Sitzung der High Level Group am 20.1.1971, 21.1.1971 [hat Minister vorgelegen], BArch, B 102/131405.

51. Organization of the Petroleum Exporting Countries, 'Resolutions of the Twenty-Second (Extraordinary) Conference in Teheran, February 3 and 4, 1971', in OPEC, *Official Resolutions and Press Releases: 1960–1980*, 105f.; Jack E. Hartsborn, 'Erdöl als Faktor wirtschaftlicher und politischer Macht: Die Verhandlungen von Tripolis und Teheran zwischen den OPEC-Staaten und den internationalen Ölgesellschaften', *Europa-Archiv* 26 (1971), 443–55; James Bamberg, *The History of the British Petroleum Company*, vol. 3, *British Petroleum and Global Oil 1950–1975: The Challenge of Nationalism* (Cambridge, 2000), 450–66; US Congress. Senate. Committee on Foreign Relations. Subcommittee on Multinational Corporations, *Chronology of the Libyan Oil Negotiations, 1970–1971* (Washington, DC, 1974). On oil price trends, see Richard Chadbourn Weisberg, *The Politics of Crude Oil Pricing in the Middle East: 1970–1975* (Berkeley, CA, 1977).

52. James Akins, 'The Oil Crisis: This Time the Wolf Is Here', *Foreign Affairs* 51 (April 1973), 462–90, here 469.

53. OECD. Energy Committee: Security and Flexibility of Energy Supplies and the Rational Use of Energy, 4.11.1971, NA UK, POWE 14/2503.

54. Lantzke an BM über Rohwedder: Sitzung der High Level Group am 20.1.1971, 21.1.1971 [hat Minister vorgelegen], BArch, B 102/131405.

55. III D 2: Vermerk: Sitzung High-Level-Group, Ölausschuß und Arbeitsgemeinschaft vom 12.–15. Juni 1972 in Paris, 28. Juni 1972, BArch, B 102/131405; A Review of Plans for Consultation and Joint Action in an Emergency, 31.5.1973, NA UK, POWE 63/642; Lantzke an Rohwedder: Ergebnis der gestrigen Aussprache der Mineralölgruppe der OECD, 11.1.1972, BArch, B 102/131405; III C 2: Vermerk. Sitzung der High-Level-Group des Ölausschusses der OECD am 11. September 1973, 13.9.1973, BArch, B 102/183432; III C 2: Notiz: Gespräch mit Mister Benski über Förderländer, 4.9.1973, BArch, B 102/183432.

56. Dept. of State to all OECD Capitals: Highlights of Meeting of High Level Group of OECD Oil Committee, Paris, 13 June 1972, NARA, RG 59, Box 1481 PET 1 to PET 3 OECD.

57. Kling (III D 2) an: Abteilungsleiter III: Sitzung der High Level Group des Öl-Ausschusses der OECD am 2.6.1969, 28.5.1969, BArch, B 102/131404; OECD. Oil Committee: Review of Methods of Apportionment of Available Oil Supplies in an Emergency in the OECD European Area, 26 June 1972; OECD. Council: Apportionment of Oil Supplies in an Emergency in the OECD European Area, Paris, 23 June 1972, NA UK, POWE 63/642.

58. Statement by Deputy Sec. of State John Irwin to the OECD High Level Group of the Oil Committee, Paris, 24 October 1972, NARA, Nixon Library, Yorba Linda/Cal., WHCF, SMOF, EPO 61.

59. Memo: John Schaefer to Peter Flanigan: OECD Oil Meeting, 24 October 1972, 22 November 1972, NARA, Nixon Library, WHCF, SMOF, EPO 61.

60. Lantzke an BM [sehr vertraulich]: Ergebnisse der Sitzung der High Level Group und des Mineralölausschusses der OECD am 24 und 25.10.1972 in Paris, 26.10.1972, BArch, B 102/131405.

61. Dept. of State to US Mission OECD Paris: Instructions for US Delegation, 13/14 June 1973, NARA, RG 59, Box 1482 PET 3 OECD to PET 3 OPEC 1/6/71.

62. Memo: DiBona to Schultz: OECD Meetings, 5 June 1973, NARA, Nixon Library, WHCF, SMOF, EPO 28; Dept. of State to US Mission OECD Paris: Instructions for US Delegation, 13/14 June 1973, NARA, RG 59, Box 1482 PET 3 OECD to PET 3 OPEC 1/6/71.

63. OECD. Oil Section. Topics for Discussion Emanating from the Report on Oil Supply and Demand Problems and Prospects to 1980, Paris, 3.8.1973, BArch, B 102/183432.

64. Note for the Record: OECD Oil Committee, 25/26 May 1971, NA UK, POWE 63/868: 'as discussion was so inhibited it was difficult to judge if national representatives held to different beliefs in private'. Minutes of other meetings point to the same problem; see also A Review of Plans for Consultation and Joint Action in an Emergency, 31.5.1973, NA UK, POWE 63/642.

65. OECD Oil Section: Control of Oil in an Emergency, 3.9.1973, NA UK, POWE 63/869. There were also informal discussions on oil sharing. See Compte-rendu des réunions OCDE relatives à l'étude d'un schema mondial de répartition du pétrole brut en cas de crise [Septembre 1973], Archives Nationales de France, Fontainbleau (henceforth ANF), Service du Premier Ministre. Comite interministériel pour les questions de coopération économique européenne, versement 19900644, art. 2.

66. Hansheinrich Kruse: Bericht über Sitzung der High Level Group Oil am 11.9.1973, 13.9.1973, PA AA, B 71 (Referat 405), 113927; III C 2: Vermerk. Sitzung der High-Level-Group des Ölausschusses der OECD am 11. September 1973, 13.9.1973, BArch, B 102/183432.

67. Grossman, US Energy Policy, 92f.; Chick, Electricity and Energy Policy, 13, 15f.; see also 'A Staff Analysis Prepared at the Request of Henry M. Jackson, Chairman, Committee on Interior and Insular Affairs, United States Senate. Pursuant to S. Res. 45, a National Fuels and Energy Policy Study, Serial No. 93-19 (92-54), Washington 1973', in Howard Gordon and Roy Meador (eds), Perspectives on the Energy Crisis, 2 vols (Ann Arbor, MI, 1977), 149–64.

68. US Department of the Interior. Office of Oil and Gas, United States Petroleum through 1980 (Washington, DC, 1968), vii.

69. Ibid., ix.

70. See chapter 4.

71. US Cabinet Task Force on Oil Import Control, The Oil Import Question: A Report on the Relationship of Oil Imports to the National Security (Washington, DC, 1970), 121, 128.

72. Ibid., 125f.

73. Ibid., 129.

74. NARA, Nixon Library, NSC, Inst. Files ('H-Files'), Box H-180 and Box H-197.

75. Henry A. Kissinger to Secretaries of State, Treasury, Defense, Interior, Chairman Council of Economic Advisers, Chairman Office of Military Preparedness, 15 January 1971, NARA, Nixon Library, NSC, Inst. Files ('H-Files'), Box H-180.

76. NSSM 114: World Oil Situation, 24 January 1971, NARA, Nixon Library, NSC, Inst. Files ('H-Files'), Box H-180, 1–5.

77. Ibid., 39f.

78. Ibid., 42f.

79. Ibid., 85–87.

80. Ibid., 88f.

81. William P. Rogers: Memo to the President: Petroleum Developments and the Impending Energy Crisis, 10 March 1972, NARA, Nixon Library, NSC, Inst. Files ('H-Files'), Box H-197; Yergin, The Prize, 572f.; T. Rees Shapiro 'James Akins, 83, Dies: Energy Expert Presaged Danger of Relying on Mideast Oil', Washington Post, 27 July 2010.

82. Department of State: The US and the Impending Energy Crisis, 9 March 1972, NARA, Nixon Library, NSC, Subject Files, Box 321, i.

83. Ibid., 1, 8.

84. Ibid., ii.

85. Ibid., 70–86.

86. Ibid., 82, 85.

87. Yergin, The Prize, 572f.

88. Phil Odeen/Andy Marshall/Bob Hormats: Memo to Kissinger: National Security and Energy Needs, 4 January 1972, NARA, Nixon Library, NSC, Inst. Files ('H-Files'), Box H-197.

89. C.A. Crocker: Memo to Colonel Kennedy: State Paper on the Energy Crisis, 21 March 1972, NARA, Nixon Library, NSC, Inst. Files ('H-Files'), Box H-197.

90. John B. Walsh: Memo to Chet Crocker: State's Recommendations Concerning the Impending Energy Crisis, 18 May 1972; Ashley C. Hewitt: Memo to Chet Crocker: State's Recommendations Concerning the Impending Energy Crisis, 19 May 1972; John Ferriter: Memo to Chet Crocker: State's Recommendations Concerning the Impending Energy Crisis,

24 May 1972; Harold H. Saunders: Memo to Chester Crocker: Comments on State Department Oil Recommendation, 20 June 1972, all in NARA, Nixon Library, NSC, Inst. Files ('H-Files'), Box H-197.

91. Robert D. Hormats/Richard T. Kennedy/John D. Walsh: Memo to Mr. Kissinger: Foreign Policy Ramifications of US Oil Policy, 11 July 1972, NARA, Nixon Library, NSC, Inst. Files ('H-Files'), Box H-197.

92. Ibid.

93. Ibid.; John B. Walsh in particular argued against a strategy of 'draining America first'; Memo John B. Walsh to Chet Crocker: State's Recommendations Concerning the Impending Energy Crisis, 18 May 1972, NARA, Nixon Library, NSC, Inst. Files ('H-Files'), Box H-197.

94. Jonathan E. Colby: Memo to Mr. Kennedy: Proposed NSSM/CIEPSM on US Energy Policy, 8 December 1972; Henry A. Kissinger: Memo to Peter M. Flanigan: US International Oil Policy; Henry A. Kissinger/Peter M. Flanigan: Memo to Secretaries of State, Defense, Commerce, Treasury, Interior, Directors of CIA, Emergency Preparedness, Atomic Energy Commission: US Energy Policy and National Security; Andy Marshall/Philip Odeen/Robert D. Hormats: Memo on Proposed NSSM on the National Security Aspects of the Energy Crisis, 20 February 1973, NARA, Nixon Library, NSC, Inst. Files ('H-Files'), Box H-197.

95. Henry Kissinger to Secretaries of State, Defense, Treasury, and Director of Central Intelligence, 8 March 1973, NARA, Nixon Library, NSC, Inst. Files ('H-Files'), Box H-197.

96. NSSM 174: National Security and US Energy Policy, August 1974, NARA, Nixon Library, NSC, Inst. Files ('H-Files'), Box H-197.

97. Ibid., 4, 16.

98. Ibid., 57.

99. Falk Illing. *Energiepolitik in Deutschland: Die energiepolitischen Maßnahmen der Bundesregierung 1949–2013* (Baden-Baden, 2012); Dieter Schmitt, 'West German Energy Policy', in Wilfrid L. Kohl (ed.), *After the Second Oil Crisis: Energy Policies in Europe, America, and Japan* (Lexington, MA, 1982), 137–58; Christoph Nonn, *Die Ruhrbergbaukrise: Entindustrialisierung und Politik 1958–1969* (Göttingen, 2001); BArch, B 102/200602: Energiepolitische Fragen aus der Sicht des Bundeskanzleramts, Bd. 1 1958–74.

100. The German Institute for Economic Research (Deutsches Institut für Wirtschaftsforschung or DIW), Berlin, Cologne University's Institute of Energy Economics (Energiewirtschaftliches Institut or EWI), the Rhineland-Westphalia Institute for Economic Research (Rheinisch-Westfälisches Institut für Wirtschaftsforschung or RWI), Essen, the Institute for the Global Economy (Institut für Weltwirtschaft) at the University of Kiel, the Ifo Institute for Economic Research (Ifo-Institut für Wirtschaftsforschung) in Munich and the Hamburg Global Economic Archive (Hamburgisches Welt-Wirtschafts-Archiv).

101. Arbeitsgemeinschaft deutscher wirtschaftswissenschaftlicher Forschungsinstitute e.V., *Untersuchung über die Entwicklung der gegenwärtigen und zukünftigen Struktur von Angebot und Nachfrage in der Energiewirtschaft der Bundesrepublik unter besonderer Berücksichtigung des Steinkohlebergbaus. Auf Beschluß des Deutschen Bundestages vom 12. Juni 1959 durchgeführt, abgeschlossen und vorgelegt 1961* [Conducted on the basis of a decision of the German Parliament, 12 June 1959, completed in 1961] (Berlin, 1962). For an introductory account of energy forecasts in West Germany, see Hans Diefenbacher and Jeffrey Johnson, 'Energy Forecasting in West Germany: Confrontation and Convergence', in Thomas Baumgartner and Atle Midttun (eds), *The Politics of Energy Forecasting: A Comparative Study of Energy Forecasting in Western Europe and North America* (Oxford/New York, 1987), 61–84.

102. Arbeitsgemeinschaft, *Untersuchung über die Entwicklung*, 295–300; Energiewirtschaftliches Institut der Universität Köln (ed.), *Die Energie-Enquete. Ergebnisse und wirtschaftspolitische Konsequenzen. Vorträge und Diskussionsbeiträge der 12. Arbeitstagung am 14. und 15. Juni 1962 in der Universität Köln* (Munich, 1962).

103. Arbeitsgemeinschaft, *Untersuchung über die Entwicklung*; see also the summary by Theodor Wessels, 'Die Struktur und Entwicklungstendenzen der deutschen Energiewirtschaft

in der Sicht der Enquete-Ergebnisse', in Energiewirtschaftliches Institut der Universität Köln, *Die Energie-Enquete*, 12–25. On the so-called energy gap of 1975 to 2000, see Diefenbacher and Johnson, 'Energy Forecasting in West Germany', 63.

104. See the criticisms made by one of the report's authors: Julius Kruse, *Energiewirtschaft* (Berlin, 1972), 261–65.

105. 'Corrigendum zum Energiegutachten von 1961', *Vierteljahrsheft des Deutschen Instituts für Wirtschaftsforschung* (1966), 179–99.

106. Norbert Sandner, 'Die Grenzen der mittel- und langfristigen Prognosen des Energieverbrauchs', *Glückauf. Zeitschrift für Technik und Wirtschaft des Bergbaus* 23(11) (1972), 1147–60; Jürgen Meinert *Strukturwandlungen der westdeutschen Energiewirtschaft* (Frankfurt am Main, 1980), 136–46.

107. Lord Rothschild to R.T. Armstrong: Report on Energy Policy Reviews, 28.4.1971, NA UK, PREM 15/1144. Rothschild had previously been head of the research division at Royal Dutch Shell; see Tessa Blackstone and William Plowden, *Inside the Think Tank: Advising the Cabinet 1971–1983* (London, 1988), v.

108. Rothschild to Armstrong: Report on Energy Policy Reviews, 28.4.1971, NA UK, PREM 15/1144.

109. Uwe Jönck (ESSO AG): Richtige und falsche Ölprognosen, Auszüge aus einem Vortrag anläßlich des Journalisten-Treffens in Travemünde, 27.–29. Oktober 1968, BArch, B 102/200770, Bd. 7 1968–76; see also Diefenbacher and Johnson, 'Energy Forecasting in West Germany', 62: 'Forecasting mistakes have been in no area as drastic as in the energy area'.

110. Michael Kraus, 'Über die Kritik an Energieprognosen und ihre Berechtigung', in Fritz Lücke (ed.), *Ölkrise: 10 Jahre danach* (Cologne, 1984), 253–68, here 253; Kraus, 'Bundesdeutsche Energieprognosen der letzten 30 Jahre. Eine Fehlerursachenanalyse', in Manfred Härter (ed.), *Energieprognostik auf dem Prüfstand* (Cologne, 1988), 89–117; Hendrik Ehrhardt, 'Energiebedarfsprognosen. Kontinuität und Wandel energiewirtschaftlicher Problemlagen in den 1970er und 1980er Jahren', in Hendrik Ehrhardt and Thomas Kroll (eds), *Energie in der modernen Gesellschaft: Zeithistorische Perspektiven* (Göttingen, 2012), 193–222, here 198.

111. 'Unterrichtung durch die Bundesregierung: Die Energiepolitik der Bundesregierung', in *Deutscher Bundestag. Drucksachen. 7. Wahlperiode 1972–1976.* No. 1057, 3 October 1973. On the establishment of DEMINEX, see Karlsch and Stokes, *'Faktor Öl'*, 359–68; Herbert Lötgers, 'Die Deutsche Erdölversorgungsgesellschaft – DEMINEX: Ziele und Aufgaben im Rahmen der deutschen Rohölversorgung', in Institut für Bilanzanalysen (ed.), *Die Mineralölindustrie in der Bundesrepublik Deutschland* (Frankfurt, 1972), 39–44.

112. Ulf Lantzke, in Munzinger Online/Personen – Internationales Biographisches Archiv: http://www.munzinger.de/document/00000016093 (accessed 10 January 2012); 'Mister Energy', *Frankfurter Allgemeine Zeitung*, 8 December 1973; Manfred Horn, *Die Energiepolitik der Bundesregierung von 1958 bis 1972: Zur Bedeutung der Penetration ausländischer Ölkonzerne in die Energiewirtschaft der BRD für die Abhängigkeit interner Strukturen und Entwicklungen* (Berlin, 1977), 280f.

113. Ulf Lantzke an StS Dr. Rohwedder: Sicherung der Rohölversorgung Europas in Krisenzeiten, 19.1.1970, BArch, B 102/131404, Bd. 1 1966–70.

114. Ibid.; and Kling: Vermerk: Rohölversorgung Europas, 17.2.1970, BArch, B 102/131404, Bd. 1 1966–70.

115. On the expert discussion, see, for example, Schieweck, 'Die kommende Welterdöl- und Energiekrise'; Lötgers, 'Die Deutsche Erdölversorgungsgesellschaft'; references to widespread public awareness can be found in Rush (Amembassy Bonn) to Dept. of State: FRG Reaction to US Declaration on Reserve Oil Capacity, 13 May 1970; Rush (Amembassy Bonn) to Dept. of State: FRG Reaction to US Declaration on Reserve Oil Capacity, 20 May 1970, NARA, RG 59, Box 1481 PET 1 to PET 3 OECD.

116. Kleine Anfrage der Abgeordneten Springorum, Lampersbach, Luda, Russe und Genossen, 21.4.1970, Deutscher Bundestag. 6. Wahlperiode. Drucksache VI/654.

117. Der Parlamentarische Staatssekretär des Bundesministers für Wirtschaft an den Herrn Präsidenten des Deutschen Bundestages: Zusätzliche Öllieferungen aus den USA im Falle einer neuen Nahostkrise, 6.5.1970, Deutscher Bundestag. 6. Wahlperiode. Drucksache VI/756; Kleine Anfrage der Abgeordneten Springorum, Dr. Burgbacher, Russe und der Fraktion der CDU/CSU, 26.5.1970, Deutscher Bundestag. 6. Wahlperiode, Drucksache VI/819.

118. Der Parlamentarische Staatssekretär des Bundesministers für Wirtschaft an den Herrn Präsidenten des Deutschen Bundestages: Energiepolitik, 11.6.1970, Deutscher Bundestag. 6. Wahlperiode. Drucksache VI/941.

119. Deutscher Bundestag. 6. Wahlperiode. Drucksache VI/756; Kleine Anfrage der Abgeordneten Springorum, Dr. Burgbacher, Russe und der Fraktion der CDU/CSU, 26.5.1970, Deutscher Bundestag. 6. Wahlperiode, Drucksache VI/819.

120. Lantzke (Abt. III) an BM [gesehen] über Rohwedder: Sicherung der Rohölversorgung Europas in Krisenzeiten, Bericht über Sitzung der High Level Group am 27./28. Mai 1970, 2. Juni 1970, BArch, B 102/131405, Bd. 2 1970–72.

121. Quantitative und qualitative Daten zur Frage der Versorgungskontinuität, 1.6.1970, BArch, B 102/282309, Bd. 2 1970–73.

122. Ibid., 15.

123. III D 2 (Koch) Vermerk: Sitzung der High Level Group des OECD Mineralölausschusses am 30. November 1970, 7.12.1970, BArch, B 102/131405, Bd. 2 1970–72; III D 2 (Koch) an Abteilungsleiter III: Sitzung der High Level Group am 30. November, 27.11.1970, ibid.

124. Lantzke an BM über Rohwedder: Sitzung der High Level Group am 20.1.1971, 21.1.1971 [hat Minister vorgelegen], BArch, B 102/131405, Bd. 2 1970–72.

125. Rohwedder an Bahr, Aufzeichnung für die Staatssekretärsbesprechung über die Versorgung der BRD mit Rohöl, 2.2.1971, BArch, B 136/7520.

126. BArch, B 102/282265, Bd. 3 1971. W. Petersen (Mineralölwirtschaftsverband), Enno Schubert (Gelsenberg), Walter Bauer (Deutsche Shell AG), Hans-Jürgen Knell (Esso AG Hamburg) und Hans-Joachim Burchard (BP AG, Hamburg).

127. Ergebnisbericht über die 1. Sitzung der Arbeitsgruppe für Beratungen über eine optimale Energiebedarfsdeckung im Falle einer Mineralölversorgungsstörung am 26. Mai 1971, 8. Juni 1971, BArch, B 102/282265, Bd. 3 1971.

128. Ibid.; III D 2: Vermerk: Vorläufige Grundzüge des Aufbaus eines Krisenmechanismus; hier: Vorschläge für eine optimale Deckung des Energiebedarfs im Falle einer zivilen Mineralölversorgungskrise (Sofortprogramm), 5. März 1971, BArch, B 102/282265, Bd. 3 1971; Ergebnisbericht über die Sitzung 'Übernahme von EDV Arbeiten' am 16. Juni 1971, ibid.

129. Manfred Liebrucks, H.W. Schmidt and D. Schmitt, *Sicherung der Energieversorgung für die Bundesrepublik Deutschland: Gemeinschaftsgutachten der Institute DIW, EWI und RWE* (Berlin, 1972).

130. Ibid., 78.

131. W/III D: Zwischenbericht über den Aufbau eines 'Krisenmanagements' zur Sicherung einer optimalen Energieversorgung im Falle einer Mineralölversorgungsstörung, 10. Juli 1972, BArch, B 102/282309, Bd. 2 1970–73; see also the report on the proceedings: BMWi: Niederschrift über die Sitzung des Länderausschusses Mineralöl am 8.12.1971 im BMWF, 17.1.1972, BArch, B 102/282309, Bd. 2 1970–73.

132. W/III D: Zwischenbericht über den Aufbau eines 'Krisenmanagements' zur Sicherung einer optimalen Energieversorgung im Falle einer Mineralölversorgungsstörung, 10. Juli 1972, BArch, B 102/282309 Bd. 2 1970–73.

133. Weiß an Abteilungsleiter IV: Energiepolitisches Gesamtkonzept, 2.10.1972, BArch, B 136/7667.

134. Abt. III (Lantzke) an Minister: Gegenwärtiger Stand der Überlegungen zur Weiterentwicklung der Energiepolitik, 20.10.1972, BArch, B 136/7667.

135. Ibid.; see also Energiepolitische Aufgabenstellung und sonstige Fragen im Bereich der Abteilung III, 16.12.1972, BArch, B 102/200515, Bd. 15 1972/73; Abt. III: Aufzeichnung: Vorhaben in der 7. Legislaturperiode aus dem Bereich der Abteilung III, 29.1.1973, ibid.
136. Statement by Deputy Sec. of State John Irwin to the OECD High Level Group of the Oil Committee, Paris, 24 October 1972, NARA, Nixon Library, WHCF, SMOF, EPO 61: 'We intend to take the necessary actions which will be costly and which in many cases will be unpopular. We have little choice'.
137. Lantzke an BM [sehr vertraulich]: Ergebnisse der Sitzung der High Level Group und des Mineralölausschusses der OECD am 24. und 25.10.1972 in Paris, 26.10.1972, BArch, B 102/131405.
138. Willy Brandt: Regierungserklärung, in *Verhandlungen des Deutschen Bundestages. 7. Wahlperiode 1972–1976. Stenographische Berichte*, Bd. 81 (Bonn, 1972/73), 121–34.
139. Ibid.; on these interventions, see, for example, Chef des Bundeskanzleramtes an Bundesminister für Wirtschaft und Finanzen [z.H. MD Dr. Lantzke], 7. Juli 1972: Schreiben des deutschen Steinkohlenbergbaus vom 28. Juni 1972; Rohwedder: Antwortschreiben an Gesamtverband des Deutschen Steinkohlenbergbaus und Steinkohlenbergbauverein, 10.8.1972, BArch, B 136/7667.
140. BArch, B 102/108464; see above all the reports produced by AG 3: Mineralöl – Internationale Verflechtungen, 27.2.1973, AG 4 Öl – deutscher Markt, AG 3: Gemeinsame Mineralölpolitik der EG, 27.2.1973.
141. Ibid.; III: Ergebnisprotokoll. Gespräch über das Energieprogramm bei Herrn Minister am 8. Februar 1973, 9.2.1973, BArch, B 102/200515, Bd. 15 1972/73; Weiß an Chef des Bundeskanzleramtes: Deutsche Mineralölpolitik, 16.1.1973, BArch, B 136/7705.
142. BMWi: Entscheidungsvorlage zum Entwurf des Energieprogramms der Bundesregierung, 22.8.1973; Abt. III: Sprechzettel für die Einführung des Energieprogramms in der Kabinettsberatung am 29. August 1973, BArch, B 102/108470; Auszug aus dem Kurzprotokoll über die 28. Kabinettssitzung der Bundesregierung am 22. August 1973 (7.9.1973), PA AA, B 71 (Referat 405), 113924; 'Unterrichtung durch die Bundesregierung: Die Energiepolitik der Bundesregierung'.
143. 'Unterrichtung durch die Bundesregierung: Die Energiepolitik der Bundesregierung', 5.
144. Ibid., 6.
145. Ibid.
146. Anton Jaumann, 'Bayern bereitet ein Landes-Energieprogramm vor', *Bayerische Staatszeitung*, 20 October 1972; 'Unterrichtung durch die Bundesregierung: Die Energiepolitik der Bundesregierung', 8.
147. See, for example, Bayerisches Staatsministerium für Wirtschaft und Verkehr, *Energieprogramm I: Grundlinien zu einem Energieprogramm für Bayern* (Munich, 1973).
148. Martin Czakainski also divides the history of energy policy in West Germany into three phases, namely 1957–71, when oil ousted coal, 1971–80, when attempts were made to reduce the country's dependency on OPEC, and 1981–89, when the emphasis lay on environmental protection; Martin Czakainski, 'Energiepolitik in der Bundesrepublik Deutschland 1960 bis 1980 im Kontext der außenwirtschaftlichen und außenpolitischen Verflechtungen', in Jens Hohensee and Michael Salewski (eds), *Energie – Politik – Geschichte: Nationale und internationale Energiepolitik seit 1945* (Stuttgart, 1993), 17–34.
149. Albrecht Mulfinger, *Auf dem Weg zur gemeinsamen Mineralölpolitik* (Berlin, 1972), 14; see also Communauté Économique Européenne. Commission. Direction Générale des Affaires Economiques et Financières: Note préliminaire sur les réserves de capacité de production disponibles, 9.7.1964; Communauté Économique Européenne. Commission. Direction Générale des Affaires Economiques et Financières: Note sur la sécurité de l'approvisionnement pétrolier dans la C.E.E., 2.8.1966, ANF, Service du Premier Ministre. Commissariat Général du Plan, versement 19900644, art. 22.

150. Amtsblatt der Europäischen Gemeinschaften 1968, Nr. L 308, 14, reprinted in Hans R. Krämer, *Die Europäische Gemeinschaft und die Ölkrise* (Baden-Baden, 1974), 123–28.

151. Ibid., 123.

152. On EPC, see Daniel Möckli, *European Foreign Policy during the Cold War: Heath, Brandt, Pompidou and the Dream of Political Unity* (London/New York, 2009).

153. Quante an Unterabteilung IIID: Untersuchung der EG Kommission über die Auswirkungen von Unterbrechungen der Ölversorgung aus Nordafrika und aus dem Mittleren Osten auf die Ölvorräte Westeuropas (EG-Dok. XVII-C-2/RDB-JVD/ir vom 23.4.1971), 13.5.1971; EG-Dokument: Beurteilung der Auswirkung evtl. Unterbrechungen der Ölversorgung von Westeuropa auf die Ölversorgung, 23.4.1971, BArch, B 102/282265, Bd. 3 1971.

154. Kommission der Europäischen Gemeinschaft: Probleme und Mittel der Energiepolitik für den Zeitraum 1975/85, Brüssel, 4.10.1972, BArch, B 136/7706.

155. Ibid., 42.

156. Ibid., 49.

157. Ibid., 61: 'Despite the risks to the energy supply that may be posed by import dependence, under no circumstances must autarky be considered a goal of energy policy'.

158. Kommission der Europäischen Gemeinschaft: Notwendige Fortschritte auf dem Gebiet der gemeinschaftlichen Energiepolitik, Brüssel, 4.10.1972, BArch, B 136/7706.

159. Ibid., 17, 22; Kommission der Europäischen Gemeinschaft: Vorschlag für eine Verordnung des Rates. Zur Festlegung einer gemeinsamen Regelung für die Einfuhren von Kohlenwasserstoffen aus dritten Ländern, Brüssel, 4.10.1972, BArch, B 136/7706.

160. Kommission der Europäischen Gemeinschaften: Orientierungen und vordringliche Maßnahmen auf dem Gebiet der gemeinschaftlichen Energiepolitik, Brüssel 19.4.1973, 1, BArch, B 136/7667.

161. Bundesminister für Wirtschaft: Aufzeichnung für die Sitzung der Europa-Staatssekretäre am 10.5.1973; Boemcke: Fernschreiben: 244. Tagung des Rates, 22., 23.5.1973, BArch, B 136/7667.

162. Boemcke: Fernschreiben: 244. Tagung des Rates, 22., 23.5.1973, BArch, B 136/7667.

Chapter 3

THE GLOBAL COMMUNICATION OF THE 'ARAB OIL WEAPON'

In addition to general shifts in the global oil market, OECD governments had more concrete reasons to gear up for sudden supply disruptions. Long before the start of the oil crisis in October 1973, the Western European countries and the United States had noted Arab warnings of production cutbacks. It is inherent in the logic of embargoes that their potential to threaten ought to be exhausted before they are imposed. So the 'Arab oil weapon', to quote the martial terminology adopted by many contemporaries, was already having an effect before it had been fired.[1] An 'embargo' is a prohibition on the export of certain goods in order to force a government to change political course or punish it for a particular stance.[2] Like economic sanctions, imposed by groups of countries in an attempt to prompt other states to meet certain international demands or obligations, embargoes too are intended to convert economic strength into political power.[3]

Seeking to appraise embargoes' success as a policy instrument, political scientists have traditionally worked with a sender-target model. A sender – in other words a state or group of states – prohibits the export of certain goods to a target country or group of target countries with the declared goal of compelling it or them to make specific policy changes. Though the declared goal is only rarely achieved, since the end of the Second World War the number of economic sanctions and embargoes has increased.[4] We can resolve this seeming paradox if we measure the success of an embargo in light not just of its declared goal but of the array of functions it may have. For example, second-order goals may relate to 'the status, behavior and expectations of the government(s) imposing the sanctions', while third-order objectives may be linked with more general international considerations.[5] Furthermore, embargoes always have a performative aspect that is part and parcel of their announcement and is virtually impossible to measure.[6] Even embargoes that fail to compel the affected countries to change course politically may still be significant as symbolic acts domestically or internationally.[7] Ultimately, determining the success of an embargo is always a speculative, contentious matter because it depends on counterfactual reflection on what would have happened had it not been imposed.

Furthermore, simple sender-target models present those countries that impose the embargo as the active party while those affected appear in a passive role. Once the former have settled on their goals and methods, the latter can seemingly only opt to meet the associated demands or suffer the consequences.[8] But the symbolic and expressive aspect of the embargo in particular may be moulded not just by the countries imposing the sanctions but also those affected by them. In view of their multiple goals and functions, embargoes are complex communicative constellations, and both the sanctioning and sanctioned countries contribute to their configuration and determine their course.[9] Through the destruction of communicative routines, a situation of contingency emerges in which all actors try to anticipate the others' moves in order to take appropriate steps. Until new routines have taken hold, participants are plagued by tremendous uncertainty, which they seek to offset by obtaining more information and stepping up their knowledge production. When an embargo is imposed, its consequences cannot be foreseen; it is an open, essentially communicative process in which those affected also negotiate the embargo's content, configuration, effectiveness and meaning. It is through this process that the embargo is constituted and defined in the first place. An embargo's failure to achieve a material effect does not necessarily mean it has made no symbolic impact.

The political and political-scientific discussion of the Arab oil embargo, which began immediately after its imposition, largely neglects its communicative aspect. For example, Roy Licklider interprets the use of the 'oil weapon' as a failure because it did not compel the affected countries to change their policies on the Middle East. The Netherlands, Canada, Japan, the United Kingdom and the United States, he points out, did not immediately adopt a new approach towards the Arab world And Licklider contends that longer-term policy changes were due not to the embargo but to the new Arab prosperity generated by oil price increases.[10] Canadian historian Stephen Duguid criticizes this view, asserting that the embargo cannot be assessed separately from the oil price increases, while its success cannot be measured solely in light of the initially declared goal.[11] In contrast to Licklider, M.S. Daoudi and M.S. Dajani argue that the embargo achieved a number of goals: the restoration of Arab self-esteem, battered by defeat in the Six-Day War, the speedy conclusion of peace between the warring parties and a general shift in Western countries' attitudes towards the Arab world.¹² In line with this, in his study of Arab oil policies, Abdulaziz Al-Sowayegh concludes: 'During 1973 the members of OAPEC successfully demonstrated their ability to use oil as an instrument of international relations to articulate Arab interests and to achieve Arab objectives'.¹³

According to a view widespread at the time, the oil embargo was ineffective on a material level because oil from Arab countries continued to be shipped to the affected states and the oil companies evenly distributed the impact of the production cutbacks.¹⁴ Yet other observers argued that the 'oil weapon' was highly effective. They contended that the combination of production and supply cutbacks, in addition to price increases, had enduringly altered power relations within the international oil economy, prompting Western countries to gradually modify their stance towards the Arab world.¹⁵ Endorsing this perspective, Daniel Yergin describes the consequences of the 'oil weapon' as 'not merely convincing, but overwhelming, and far greater than even its proponents might have dared to expect. It had recast the alignments in the Middle East and the entire world. It had transformed world oil and the relations between producers and consumers, and it had remade the international economy'.¹⁶ As in more sceptical assessments contending that the embargo brought about no fundamental changes in the global political economy,¹⁷ Yergin decouples his assessment of the embargo's success from the intentions and actions of the actors involved in its construction. In contrast, in what follows I analyse the discourse on the embargo's content and terms, a discourse through which the embargo was constituted in the first place. Here I initially focus on the Arab camp, while in the following chapters I take a closer look at the responses of the countries affected and scrutinize the global communicative interplay between the two.

In order to define and instrumentalize the embargo or the production cutbacks, Western governments used classic diplomatic channels: their foreign ministries and embassies sought to fathom the intentions of the producing states and influence them to their own benefit, sending high-ranking delegations to the Arab countries. Concurrently, as OAPEC delegates, Saudi Arabian oil minister Sheikh Zaki Yamani and his Algerian colleague Belaid Abdessalam visited the capitals of the major consuming countries to explain the production and supply cutbacks to both governments and the general public. Because the embargo was in part an act of symbolic politics, much of its communication was carried on in public. Press conferences and press releases, interviews and newspaper articles were key means of presenting others' actions as illegitimate, emphasizing the legitimacy of one's own standpoint and thus, ultimately, determining the meaning of the embargo. Publication venues such as the *Petroleum Press Service*, *Middle*

East Economic Survey and *Petroleum Intelligence Weekly* did much to facilitate the global flow of communication about the embargo,[18] ensuring that statements reported in Arab or Japanese newspapers were publicized in the West. As well as being read by political actors, they were also quoted in Western newspaper reports on the oil market.[19]

Warnings and Threats

As a tool of symbolic communication, the so-called oil weapon had been deployed long before October 1973. In 1972 alone, State Department oil expert James Akins counted fifteen threats made by representatives of Arab countries to deploy oil as a weapon against their 'enemies' – above all the United States.[20] As long as the Saudi Arabian government did not participate, however, these were empty threats; due to its production capacity, it could subvert any embargo or attempts to increase prices by upping its own production. Without Saudi Arabia, the non-Western producing countries could pursue no effective production and price policy. In contrast to the more radical forces within OAPEC – particularly Libya and Iraq – that were keen to instrumentalize oil to strike against the West, however, King Faisal had repeatedly emphasized, most recently in the summer of 1972, that oil and politics must not be mixed. Yet he evidently changed his mind about this over the course of the next year.[21]

In the early 1970s, Saudi Arabia's oil policies were decisively shaped by Sheikh Zaki Yamani. Unlike most other representatives of the Saudi Arabian government, Yamani was not a member of the royal house. The son of an Islamic legal scholar who sent him to study in Cairo, Yamani later studied law at New York University and Harvard Law School before being appointed, at the age of twenty-nine, Saudi Arabia's oil minister in 1962. Along with Prince Saud, who headed the Supreme Petroleum Council, Yamani not only influenced the fate of Saudi Arabian oil policy but rose to become the leading figure in OPEC as well. On its behalf, in 1972 he negotiated the participation agreement with the international oil companies, which set out a timetable for the producing countries to take control of all production on their territory.[22] On 30 September 1972, Yamani gave a lecture at the Middle East Institute in Beirut, which was directed chiefly at the United States. He expressed concern that in the not too distant future the world would have to cope with energy shortfalls, and proposed that the United States and Saudi Arabia cooperate more closely through a 'special relationship'. Saudi Arabia would increase its production in line with US needs if the United States would lower its tariffs and facilitate Saudi Arabian investment in the country in return.[23] Though Yamani repeated this suggestion in the following months in various locations, underlining that it would not necessarily require a formal agreement, the US government failed to take him up on the offer as it was eager to avoid negative reactions from the other consuming countries and feared a 'scramble for Saudi oil'.[24]

Yamani's proposal having come to nothing, in the spring of 1973 the tone of his statements changed. During a visit to Washington, DC, he declared on 16 and 17 April in meetings with both William Casey, undersecretary of state for economic affairs, and Henry Kissinger, national security adviser, that in view of the prospective global oil shortage, Saudi Arabia could not further increase production as long as there were no viable options for investing oil revenues.[25] In addition, he complained that due to its good relations with the pro-Israeli United States, the Saudi Arabian government was coming under increasing pressure from the Arab world.[26] In these conversations, however, Yamani did not make his interlocutors feel that he was making a threat. Instead they had the impression that he was presenting them with the dilemma of Saudi Arabian politics, a personally injurious plight he was at a loss to remedy.[27] But the report of an interview with Yamani that appeared around the same time in the *Washington Post* struck a rather different tone. For the first time in a public statement, he made a connection between oil exports and US policy towards the Middle East: 'Saudi Arabia has told the United States that it will not significantly expand its present oil production unless Washington changes its pro-Israeli stance in the Middle East'.[28] The *Washington Post* averred that Yamani's threat was rooted in frustration over the US government's failure to embrace his proposed special relationship, a proposal for which he had taken a great deal of flak in the Arab world.

Yamani was to be no lone voice in the wilderness. On 3 May, King Faisal himself declared to Frank Jungers, president of Aramco, that he was facing mounting pressure and, in view of the US stance on the Middle East conflict, was uncertain how long he could maintain his pro-American policies. He urged Jungers to pass this message on to Aramco's US parent companies so they would put pressure on the US government. According to the *Washington Post*, they did just that: 'Abandoning their previous low profile, American oilmen have been doing just what Faisal asked – offering to testify before Congressional committees, buttonholing State Department policy makers, even taking their case to the White House'.[29] On 21 June, Mobil Oil took out a full-page advertisement in the *New York Times* calling on the American people to brace themselves for new energy policies and urging the government to take steps to achieve peace in the Middle East.

> If our country's relations with the Arab world (Iran is not an Arab state) continue to deteriorate, Saudi Arabia may conclude it is not in its interest to look favorably on US requests for increased petroleum supplies. The government of

that country has the power to decide how much oil is to be produced within its borders. And to what countries that oil can be shipped. . . . We will need the oil more than Saudi Arabia will need the money. That country could reduce oil exports 3 million barrels a day below present levels and, with its small population, still finance its domestic development programs with a comfortable margin for reserves.[30]

Around a month later, the chairman of Socal responded as well, sending a letter to all shareholders. His appeal to the government to cultivate better relations with the Arab world and pursue peace in the Middle East prompted sharp attacks on the company from Jewish organizations.[31] On 19 September, in a lecture to the Independent National Gas Association, Maurice Granville, president of Texaco, then called for a rethinking of US policy towards the Middle East 'in order to take into account America's growing need for imported oil'.[32]

Having tried to build up pressure via the oil industry, in early July, in a conversation with media representatives at his summer palace in Taif near Mecca, for the first time Faisal publicly declared that it might be difficult to maintain Saudi Arabia's close cooperation with the United States if the latter maintained its strong support for Israel. It might prove necessary to freeze oil production at current levels.[33] The 'oil weapon' rhetoric deployed by the more radical Arab producing countries intensified in parallel: 'For the second time in two months, Colonel Mu'ammar al-Qadhafi . . . has warned that oil may ultimately be used as a weapon in connection with the Arab-Israeli conflict', reported the *Middle East Economic Survey* on 13 July, referring to an interview with Gaddafi on French television that also made waves in the Arab world.[34] While Iraq celebrated a national holiday on 16 July, the Iraqi president called on the Arab countries to deploy their oil and financial reserves to advance the battle against 'Zionism and imperialism'.[35] Three days later, Saddam Hussein, vice president of the Revolutionary Command Council and deputy general secretary of the Ba'ath Party, declared that Iraq was prepared to be the first country to use the oil weapon and nationalize the oil companies active in the country.[36] The summer brought no let-up in this clamour – quite the opposite. In early September, in the *Middle East Economic Survey*, David Hirst took stock: 'With the growth of anti-American feeling, agitation for the use of the oil weapon, and theorizing about the best way of going about it, has also continued unabated. Every week an Arab leader, press pundit or trade union conference takes up the call'.[37]

Compared with these views, Saudi Arabian government spokesmen struck a far more moderate tone. Within the Arab public sphere, they warned that – if at all – the oil weapon must be deployed with caution and prudence. In the influential Beirut weekly newspaper *al-Hawadith*, for example, the commander of the National Guard justified Saudi Arabia's cautious approach: 'In order to maximize the use of oil in the service of the Arab cause we should first study the full implications of this terrible weapon which we hold'. Drawing on orientalist stereotypes – while simultaneously refuting them – he expanded on the political instrumentalization of oil: 'We should act rationally, unhampered by emotions, and be ready to take calculated risks . . . we should insulate this debate from bazaar bargaining and random influences'.[38] To avoid enraging the whole world, he stated, it was vital to calculate precisely when, where, how, against whom and under what conditions oil might be deployed as a weapon. While these statements sounded far more cautious and moderate than the competitively harsh rhetoric emanating from Libya and Iraq, they embodied a much greater risk to the Western oil supply. In late August 1973, attentive observers began to discern the exact conditions under which Saudi Arabia would be prepared to instrumentalize its oil production to political ends. This time, in an interview with *al-Hawadith*, Prince Saud revealed that the Saudi Arabian government would prefer 'progressively increasing curbs on rates of production' to the total cessation of production and was also keen on a discriminatory mechanism that distinguished between the United States, as Israel's main supporter, on the one hand and Europe and Japan on the other. The latter, he explained, had proved significantly more open to Arab concerns.[39] In early September, OAPEC foreign ministries then met in Kuwait to discuss – on the basis of a Saudi Arabian-Egyptian working paper – the potential use of the 'oil weapon' in the context of the Middle East conflict, a meeting that was widely reported internationally.[40] Though no concrete decisions were taken there, shortly afterwards, in an interview with *Newsweek*, for the first time King Faisal declared that Saudi Arabia was open not just to freezing production at present levels but also to cutbacks.[41]

While the threats of an embargo from more radical OAPEC countries were dismissed as insignificant in the United States, particularly given that it was impossible to influence their policies anyway, key American actors took a keen interest in the Saudi Arabian pronouncements.[42] For oil experts such as James Akins, Saudi Arabia was 'the only country that really counts'.[43] In the April issue of *Foreign Affairs*, under the sensation-seeking title 'The Oil Crisis: This Time the Wolf Is Here', Akins published an essay that took up key elements of his internal position paper and argued that the risk of Arab supply cutbacks was now real.[44] The OPEC states, he explained, had recognized that their oil reserves were finite and had begun to tailor their producing policies to this fact. OPEC economists too had studied at first-class Western universities and were therefore quite capable of grasping the relationship between supply and demand. It was short-sighted and insufficient for Western economists to constantly highlight the counterproductive effects of a full embargo; even with smaller production cutbacks, OPEC could make a major impact and the organization was quite aware of this.⁴⁵ On 30 May, J. William Fulbright initiated the Senate hearings on the energy problem by stating that the Arab countries were obviously considering how they might use the 'oil weapon' in the conflict with Israel, the *New York Times* having predicted one day earlier: 'The United States and Western Europe are soon to face their first major diplomatic test of the oil-rich Arab bloc's power to exercise blackmail in respect to the energy shortage'.⁴⁶

In view of the ever more openly expressed threats, which also appeared in the US media, in the summer of 1973 the US government attempted to accommodate Saudi Arabian needs in the fields of economy and security.⁴⁷ In early September, meanwhile, President Nixon publicly responded to the threats. At a press conference on 5 September, he began by rejecting the Arab allegation that US policy towards the Middle East was skewed towards the interests of Israel: US policy was neither 'pro-Israel' nor 'pro-Arab', but merely 'pro-peace'.⁴⁸ At the same time, referring explicitly to the Western reaction to Mossadegh's nationalization of the Anglo-Iranian Oil Company, he threatened to boycott Arab oil, underlining the potential longer-term consequences of an embargo: 'If they continue to up the price, if they continue to expropriate, if they do expropriate without fair compensation, the inevitable result is that they will lose their markets, and other sources will be developed'.⁴⁹ Three days later, in a speech on US energy policy, he repeated that the United States would not have its foreign policy dictated to it and would assert its national sovereignty: 'No nation, and particularly no industrial nation, must be in the position of lying at the mercy of any other nation by having its energy supplies suddenly cut off'.⁵⁰

Warnings from both Western observers and Arab spokesmen about the use of the 'oil weapon' proliferated after the start of the Yom Kippur War on 6 October, when Egypt attacked Israel, catching the West by surprise; but these warnings initially remained contradictory. In early October, James Akins explained on several occasions that Saudi Arabia would not expand its production as long as the United States failed to adopt a more unbiased approach to the Middle East conflict, but said nothing about the fact that OAPEC now had larger goals in mind.⁵¹ The Yom Kippur War also prompted key Arab actors to ramp up their calls not only for there to be no increases in production but for cutbacks.⁵² On 12 October, for example, Nadim al-Pachachi, the Iraqi former secretary general of OPEC, declared that his calls for the use of the 'oil weapon' since May had had no effect. But the war was changing things: 'It is essential that the heroic efforts of the Arab armies . . . should be backed and supplemented by the international weight of the oil weapon'.⁵³ At the same time, the international oil companies were negotiating oil prices with OPEC representatives in Vienna, though they were unable to reach agreement. On 14 October, OPEC unilaterally terminated these talks while concurrently arranging a special conference in Kuwait to be held two days later.[54] At this point in time, the possibility of an embargo and of production cutbacks was subject to intense discussion in the Arab press and beyond, but the overall information flow was contradictory and heterogeneous.[55]

This is evident in the ambassadorial reports submitted to the West German Foreign Ministry, often several times a day. Since the spring, West Germany's representatives at the international organizations in Vienna had reported on numerous occasions that OPEC was discussing supply cuts at its conferences but that its members were unlikely to reach agreement due to opposing interests.[56] By mid October, however, there were increasing signs that a decision would be taken soon – but it was unclear what it would be. The ambassadors reported that in Kuwait and Iraq the 'oil weapon' was constantly being discussed, Gaddafi had recently been avoiding the topic, Iran was determined to maintain its oil production at present levels and Saudi Arabia was attempting to prevent supply cutbacks as long as possible.[57] In view of this range of divergent stances, German diplomats initially expected no serious steps to emerge from the conference in Kuwait on 16 October, not least because, like the Americans, they assumed that Saudi Arabia would continue to reject the approach advocated by Iraq and Libya.[58]

While some American observers believed that the Yom Kippur War had increased the probability of production cuts,[59] others contended that, despite radical OAPEC members' frequent calls for an embargo, it had paradoxically made them less likely for now. This was because the Israeli bombardment of the Mediterranean port facilities at Baniyas and Tartus had already reduced the flow of oil to Europe. Furthermore, the Egyptian army's initial successes made the use of the 'oil weapon' seem unnecessary. On 12 October, the *Middle East Economic Survey* suggested that the consequences of the port bombardments might easily be overshadowed by use of the oil weapon. Arab military successes had made its deployment less likely, but 'the pressure is still there and may well coalesce into a definite plan of action against the principal target, the US, particularly if Washington steps up its supplies of warplanes and military equipment to Israel'.[60] The Arab states might then opt to pursue nationalization, a supply embargo against specific countries or production cutbacks, with a combination of such cutbacks and an embargo being the most likely outcome.

On 16 October, when German diplomats still believed decisive measures to be unlikely, Yamani had already informed the oil companies in Vienna 'that King Faisal may order production cut from 9 million to 7.2 million barrels a day to be followed by further reductions of 5% a month until the Israelis withdraw from occupied Arab territory', if the United States supported Israel – a statement the oil firms passed on to the US government.[61] Before its official announcement, the impending use of the oil weapon was leaked – by sources either in the State Department or in the oil companies – to the *New York Times,* which on 16 October carried detailed reports of the above statement and the probable steps in the offing.[62] While the US administration denied that Saudi Arabia had made official threats of this kind, members of the Senior Review Group, the Washington Special Actions Group and the National Security Council were already discussing how best to respond to a diminished oil supply on the basis of 'Contingency Papers' produced in parallel by the Energy Policy Office and Treasury.[63] But against the background of National Security Study Memorandum (NSSM) 174, analysed in chapter 2, the members of these forums took a sanguine view of the 'Yamani formula – a ceiling on production which could progressively be lowered', because while it would affect the Europeans and Japanese, it would have little impact on the United States.[64] On 17 October, when Arab oil ministers had already announced the first production cutbacks, the Washington Special Actions Group – in addition to reflecting on the possible sources of the reports in the *New York Times* – discussed energy czar John A. Love's (see chapter 4) energy policy proposals, but assumed that, in view of the overall state of energy policy, these measures were necessary in any case and ought to be announced when the current crisis was over.[65] Before the meeting was over, Kissinger seemed convinced that there would be no full embargo against the United States because the Saudi Arabian foreign minister had assured him of this just a few days before, with the same message emerging from Nixon's conversations with the foreign ministers of Saudi Arabia, Algeria, Kuwait and Libya that morning.[66]

A number of White House staff had come to the same conclusion. Even after the start of the Yom Kippur War, they believed that 'for the moment' there would be no embargo against the United States. Only in the event of an Israeli victory was one likely to be imposed. They asked the CIA whether it had obtained information that clashed with this and whether it was technically possible to enforce an oil embargo against the United States.[67] In any case, they simultaneously prepared for such an outcome, with a number of their colleagues in other parts of the administration assuming that visible and massive US support for Israel would make an embargo probable.[68] According to an assessment by one State Department employee, similar expectations and much the same state of readiness could be found in Europe: 'All European countries could be expected to react with comparable vigor to a cut off of Middle East oil. No knowledgeable officials in Western Europe would be surprised, since this is a contingency they have contemplated for some time'.[69] So in view of repeated, increasingly trenchant and realistic warnings over a period of six months, and the concurrent, comprehensive preparations made by key governmental bodies to deal with an embargo, the one imposed in October 1973 was not as sudden and unexpected as has often been claimed. Its precise timing, however, was unclear to the last, with public announcements seeking to alleviate fears and a number of commentators believing, down to the wire, that there would be no embargo.

Communicating the Production Cutbacks

On 16 and 17 October the oil ministers of the Arab producing countries and Iran met in Kuwait, in varying combinations, first to discuss the consequences of the failed negotiations with the oil companies over the price of oil, and second to address the possibility of supporting Egypt and Syria in the Yom Kippur War. The five Arab Gulf states and Iran initially set the price of a barrel of 'Light Arabian' crude oil at 3.65 USD, which equated to a real-terms price increase of 70 per cent.[70] On 17 October, the oil ministers of the Arab producing countries organized in OAPEC, namely Saudi Arabia, Kuwait, Libya, Algeria, Egypt, Syria, Abu Dhabi, Bahrain and Qatar, then announced a gradual reduction in oil production, which had been in the offing for several months. To quote the *Middle East Economic Survey*, the 'long-dormant oil weapon' had finally been fired.[71]

The regime of production and supply cutbacks – and its announcement – had clearly been carefully thought through and subject to painstaking preparation. Henceforth, the countries involved committed to cutting their production every month by at least 5 per cent 'until such time as total evacuation of Israeli forces from all Arab territory occupied during the June 1967 war is completed, and the legitimate rights of the Palestinian people are restored'.[72] Only friendly states or those that opted to support the Arab countries in future would be excepted from the production cutbacks. The justification put forward for these measures was both economic and political. Hitherto, OAPEC claimed, the Arab countries had acted against their own interests. In an attempt to advance general prosperity and international cooperation, they had increased their oil production beyond their economic needs, disregarding the fact that oil reserves would dwindle in the long run. Yet the international community refused to return the favour by responding adequately to Israel's aggression towards the Palestinian people and implementing UN Resolution 242. Some countries were even going so far as to support Israel's struggle against its neighbours. OAPEC thus felt compelled to respond:

> The Arabs have therefore been induced to take a decision to discontinue their economic sacrifices in producing quantities of their wasting oil assets in excess of what would be justified by domestic economic considerations, unless the international community hastens to rectify matters by compelling Israel to withdraw from our occupied territory, as well as letting the US know the heavy price which the big industrial countries are having to pay as a result of America's blind and unlimited support for Israel.[73]

So the message inherent in the production cutbacks was chiefly addressed to the United States, though it was primarily the Western European countries and Japan that would be affected. For the latter, these measures could quickly become a major headache, as the *Middle East Economic Survey* predicted: 'Every oilman will be aware that the West could not endure such escalating reductions in oil supply for very long'.[74]

This resolution did not yet refer to an embargo as such. By 18 October, however, the Saudi Arabian government had issued a declaration stating that it would cease oil exports to the United States if the initial measures failed to prompt a policy shift, as Faisal had warned Nixon in a letter shortly before.[75] The more radical OAPEC members acted even more quickly, announcing, in rapid succession, the suspension of their oil shipments to the United States. It was not until Nixon submitted a 2.2 billion dollar aid package for Israel to Congress on 19 October that Saudi Arabia imposed a ban on oil exports.[76] This was followed by embargo declarations against the Netherlands, which was also regarded as excessively pro-Israeli. Contemporary 'guesstimates' assumed a 20 per cent reduction in oil exports from the Middle East. There were three reasons for this: the 5 per cent reduction was merely a minimum requirement; Saudi Arabia had imposed an initial cutback of 20 per cent and a number of other countries 10 per cent; and the effects of the embargo had to be factored in on top of these cutbacks.[77]

The announcements of OAPEC and its member states, which were open to varying interpretations, caused great uncertainty in the affected countries. How would the measures be implemented? Which countries counted as friendly states and would be spared? How large would reductions actually be? How and when would they make an impact? And what was the best way to respond? Spurred to frantic activity, Western government officials with responsibility for oil and energy rushed to find answers to these questions and minimize the impact of the measures on their countries. In a week full of confusion and uncertainty, the producing countries set out their terms in more detail. Saudi Arabia declared that, like other countries, it would allow no more shipments of oil to the Netherlands, while the Arab countries as a whole warned the countries of the European Communities that supporting the Netherlands would lead to their inclusion in the embargo regime. A list now clarified that the United States, the Netherlands and South Africa would be subject to a full embargo, while there would be no change in oil shipments to the friendly countries of France, Spain, the United Kingdom, Jordan, Lebanon, Malaysia, Pakistan, Tunisia and Egypt. All other countries would be subject to the cutbacks.[78] At the same time, the governments of the producing countries explained to the international oil companies active on their territories how they should go about implementing the embargo and the production cutbacks if they wished to escape total nationalization.[79] All in all, the producing countries attempted to control the terms, meaning and effects of the production cutbacks, but by announcing them they had triggered a communicative process in which other actors were also involved.

The Arab camp was no monolithic block, though it was often presented as such in the Western press. We can distinguish at least four different actors that sought to use the embargo to their own ends, interpreting the regime of production cutbacks in varying ways: OAPEC with its official pronouncements; the moderate forces within OAPEC – above all Saudi Arabia – which decisively shaped the content of the joint declarations; more radical countries that distanced themselves from the production cutbacks and, like Iraq, called for harsher measures; and those who, like Houari Boumedienne, Algerian head of state and leader of the Group of 77, tried to instrumentalize the embargo to fundamentally restructure international economic relations between 'North' and 'South'.

In their public pronouncements, OAPEC and its more moderate members used a language of passivity and regret. Rather than acknowledging that they had actively imposed the embargo and production cutbacks, their declarations tended to give the impression that they had been forced to take action against their will. Previously, they asserted, out of friendship with the West they had produced too much oil, thus exhausting their own reserves too quickly and failing to use them economically. This was because the scarcity of oil inevitably caused its price to increase, and the resulting profit was higher than what might have been obtained by investing current revenues in other areas. In other words, the embargo and cutbacks were described as the cessation of an overly obliging attitude rather than an act of aggression. It was others' aggression that had 'induced' or 'obliged' OAPEC to take this action, to quote, respectively, the original declaration and Prince Saud al Faisal on 13 November in the Beirut newspaper *al-Anwar*. The basic idea here was that the 'oil weapon' was a means of raising awareness of the Arabs' plight in the West.[80]

For example, like many of his colleagues, the Kuwaiti oil and finance minister refused to use the term 'oil weapon' at all, instead underlining the economic function of the production cutbacks.

We are not using a weapon; we are only trying to tell the world that we possess an exhaustible resource and we have been producing this resource in order to satisfy the world's growing demand for it and to enable others to live a comfortable life, while for 25 years we have suffered from backwardness because we devoted our wealth to buying arms instead of using it for development.[81]

If the term 'oil weapon' was used, emphasis was usually placed on its dual character. At the Middle East Conference in Toronto of January 1974, OPEC secretary general Ali Attiga stated: 'The Arab governments are not using oil as a weapon intended for destruction. On the contrary, they are using oil as a strategic commodity in a positive way by saying that we will sell such a vital and constructive commodity only to nations that recognize our rightful claims and cooperate with us to protect our legitimate interest and regain occupied territories'.[82] More casually, Yamani referred to a 'strategy of stick and carrot' and, in common with all other OAPEC representatives, rejected the term 'blackmail'.[83]

OAPEC's politics of language – that is, its efforts to define the terms applied to its measures internationally – attest to a profound understanding that, in addition to the production restrictions' material effects, their discursive framing and public interpretation were crucial to their success. Yamani and other OAPEC representatives repeatedly underlined that their objective was to create a more pro-Arab atmosphere in the West in order to ensure the implementation of UN Resolution 242. To this end, it was vital to avoid coming across as an aggressor.[84] When the editor of the *Petroleum Press Service*, Stanley Tucker, published an article referring to the embargo as a 'dangerous weapon', through which a number of governments had taken the liberty of harming millions of people, the OPEC secretary general responded with an open letter. Attiga declared that attempts to identify causes could not stop at the Arab announcement of the embargo but must also consider the preceding injustice. This was an act of self-defence, he claimed, to which there had been no alternative. According to him, the 'immediate cause' of the oil shortages in Europe, Japan and the United States was the Israeli occupation of Arab territories.[85]

While this debate failed to reach a broader public, by taking out full-page advertisements in the *Washington Post* and *The Guardian*, OAPEC sought to influence public opinion in the countries affected by the production cutbacks and retain discursive sovereignty over their interpretation. As with the embargo declaration, they argued that the Arab countries had been compelled to implement these measures. The cuts, it was stated, neither affected countries with a positive stance towards the Arabs, nor were they aimed at the American people as such, but solely at the US government, which was continuing to supply Israel with weapons. As soon as the terms of the embargo were met, these measures would come to an end. Against those who argued that the embargo was wrong in principle, OAPEC highlighted that in international conflicts the United States had frequently adopted similar measures and had even imposed food embargoes.[86] The advertisement in *The Guardian* was tailored more specifically to the British public, which was assured that 'friendly countries, especially those who helped or are helping the Arabs in their just cause effectively shall not be made to suffer from the Arab oil cut'.[87] In both advertisements, OAPEC countered the allegation that it was committing an illegitimate act of aggression against innocent people, presenting itself as a victim that was merely attempting to restore the legitimate rights of the 'Arab nation', which was imagined as a unified entity. In line with this, OAPEC's actions were subject to intense debate, not just from a moral but also from a legal perspective.[88]

Within the Arab camp, Libya and Iraq did not participate in the production cutbacks but used them, first, to distinguish themselves from the moderate forces by demanding stronger action and, second, at least rhetorically, to further escalate the conflict with the United States. The Iraqi government criticized the general production cutbacks for failing to distinguish clearly enough between friend and foe. By lumping together the more pro-Arab Europeans with the United States, it claimed, they were ultimately playing into the hands of the latter. Iraq called instead for the nationalization of oil company subsidiaries from countries that supported Israel and the imposition of a full embargo on these states while fully supplying friendly states and withdrawing money invested in the United States.[89] In late December, Saddam Hussein reiterated this stance in the Iraqi daily newspaper *al-Thaura*, and in martial tones he declared of the production cutbacks: 'This mistaken policy gives imperialism and Zionism the excuse it has been looking for to commit hideous crimes against the rights of the Arab people under the pretext of defending the world and human civilization. . . . The true and successful way to use oil as a weapon against America and the Zionist enemy is to nationalize American oil interests and the interests of any country standing by the enemy'.[90] Only the statements released by the Libyan government, which had gradually nationalized the foreign oil firms operating in the country, reached the same level of aggressiveness.[91] Unlike Iraq, Gaddafi also threatened the countries of Western Europe directly with an embargo as a way of hitting the United States.[92] Libyan threats mainly related to West Germany, which obtained 25 per cent of its oil from Libya. In an interview with the weekly magazine *Der Spiegel*, Libyan Prime Minister Abdessalam Jalloud gave the production cutbacks or a possible embargo an entirely new twist, geared towards Libyan interests, by linking it with European weapons sales: 'The Europeans must finally lift their weapons embargo and stop depriving me of an important weapon to fight my aggressors with. . . . If we provide the

Europeans with strategically important crude oil, they ought to provide us with strategically important weapons as well'.[93] This was a 'warning, a final warning, before it [was] all too late' and there was no choice left but to subject Europe to the full embargo.[94]

Within OAPEC, however, it was not the radical forces but the moderate ones close to Saudi Arabia that got their way. In order to avoid a deeper confrontation with Western Europe and the United States, spare the global economy serious harm and avoid losing market share, they gradually watered down the regime of production cutbacks and adapted its objective to changed circumstances. In response to declarations by the European countries and Japan on the Middle East conflict, and following intensive negotiations with them, in December OAPEC suspended its monthly 5 per cent production cuts (chapter 5). In November, Saudi Arabian government spokesmen had still been insisting that the embargo would be lifted only after total Israeli withdrawal from the occupied territories and restoration of the Palestinians' legitimate rights, but by early December they had apparently abandoned this position.[95] As the Arab oil ministers declared at their meeting of 8 December, as soon as agreement had been reached on a concrete timetable for withdrawal, an analogous timetable for the full resumption of oil shipments would be forthcoming.[96] Initially, however, the United States was to be subject to the production cutbacks in the same way as a neutral nation. On 24–25 December, OAPEC classified Japan and Belgium as friendly states and raised production to 85 per cent of the level of September.[97] It was keen to present these measures as the next logical step after the October declaration rather than its softening: 'It should be noted that the easing of the Arab oil cutbacks is fully in keeping with the philosophy of the nine Arab countries concerned ... to use oil as an instrument of flexible persuasion rather than as a bludgeon to inflict irreversible damage on the economies of friendly or neutral states'.[98] This tendency to modify its objectives while at the same time emphasizing the coherence of its approach continued to typify OAPEC's pronouncements in 1974.[99]

By mid February, a mini-summit of the heads of state of Egypt, Algeria, Saudi Arabia and Syria – namely Anwar Sadat, Boumedienne, Faisal and Hafez al-Assad – resolved that the embargo ought to be lifted at the next meeting of the oil ministers two weeks later, as long as US efforts resulted in military disengagement on the Syrian-Israeli front.[100] Not until just over a month later, on 18 March 1974, however, were Germany and Italy declared friendly states, while the embargo against the United States was lifted, at least temporarily.[101] In the run-up to this announcement, Yamani had already declared that a possible lifting of the embargo was 'completely in line with our previous actions', which had always been intended to gain friends and bolster pro-Arab sentiment.[102] The communiqué released by the Arab oil ministers also underlined the positive role of the 'oil weapon', namely as a means of influencing public opinion and prompting governments to act in the Arab interest. The decision to temporarily lift the embargo had been made, it was stated, after assessing developments in light of the original objective, which was 'to draw world attention to the Arab question in order to create an atmosphere conducive to the implementation of UN Security Council Resolution 242'.[103] The goal of an Israeli withdrawal from the occupied territories had thus been transformed into the significantly weaker aim of increasing awareness and creating an atmosphere favourable to the implementation of the UN Resolution. At the same time, however, OAPEC strove to mask this changed objective by asserting the coherence of the measures taken and underlining their success.

In addition to its use in the Middle East conflict, a number of actors tried to deploy the 'oil weapon' within the more general conflict between the so-called First and Third worlds.[104] After the Organisation for African Unity had in mid November called on the oil-producing countries to impose a full embargo on Israel, Portugal, South Africa and Rhodesia as an 'effective weapon in the struggle against colonialism',[105] the sixth Arab summit of 26–28 November addressed this issue. The participants (Iraq, Libya and Jordan had sent no representatives) assured the African countries of their full support in the 'struggle for national liberation and economic progress and in their struggle against imperialism and racial discrimination'.[106] Those that had not done so already thus broke off relations with South Africa, Rhodesia and Portugal while concurrently stopping all oil exports to those countries. They also resolved to establish a special bank for the development of Africa, to be furnished in the first instance with at least 125 million USD.[107]

The Saudi Arabian government was unwilling to gear its oil policies towards more general developmental demands to any great extent, and it was chiefly Algerian head of state Houari Boumedienne who pushed this objective as head of the Group of 77. By convening a special session of the United Nations General Assembly on the relationship between natural resources and development issues, he tried to utilize the momentum of the oil crisis to promote longstanding demands for permanent sovereignty over such resources. He also pushed for the kind of global economic order advocated by the developing countries within the framework of the United Nations Conference on Trade and Development (UNCTAD) (chapter 6). These attempts to give the oil embargo paradigmatic significance, to use it as an argument and as a lever to transform the global economic order, generated fear and defensive reactions in the industrialized countries of the West (chapter 7).

Yamani and Abdessalam on Tour

The new economic power of Third World countries was also evident in the diplomatic and public treatment of their emissaries, whose status was bolstered in the wake of the oil crisis. Even before the embargo, Saudi Arabian oil minister Sheikh Zaki Yamani had become known, beyond the world of oil experts, as Faisal's mouthpiece and a key voice within OPEC. But the oil crisis eventually made him the key representative of the new Arab oil policy in the media, and he became the public face of this policy in the West. This was largely because in November the Arab producing countries sent Yamani, along with the less charismatic Algerian industry and energy minister Belaid Abdessalam, to the capitals of the leading consuming countries to explain the reasons for the oil embargo, production cutbacks and price increases.[108] Communication about the embargo took place both face to face and via the mass media. Yamani and Abdessalam set out the producing countries' position through diplomatic talks while also underlining publicly – at press conferences and in newspaper and television interviews – the intention underlying the Arab measures and the conditions under which they would be rescinded. In this way, they achieved a high level of public attention in the various countries they visited, and their statements were also paid close attention by the governments and publics of the other consuming countries.

Their journey to Western capitals began on 27 November in Paris, where they were received for an eighty-minute talk by Minister for Industrial and Scientific Development Jean Charbonnel, Foreign Minister Michel Jobert and President Georges Pompidou.[109] On several occasions, Yamani and Abdessalam explained the mechanism of the supply restrictions and the classification of friendly, neutral and hostile states, urging their interlocutors to assert their influence on the United States and the other European countries.[110] The crucial factor in ending the regime of production cutbacks, they explained, was not a peace settlement as such but implementation of UN Resolution 242. At the same time, they gave reassurances that France, as a friendly state, would continue to receive oil. Yamani rejected a French request for an increase in Saudi Arabian production, however, arguing that his country already had more money than it could spend and the government was rather contemplating a long-term production cut in order to secure oil revenues over a longer period.[111] At a press conference, Yamani called on the other Europeans to put concrete pressure on Israel rather than just making declarations, and warned them, and Willy Brandt in particular, against acts of solidarity with the Netherlands, to which the full embargo applied. If they helped out the Dutch, they might receive no more oil at all. His warning that countermeasures would be a grave error was also addressed to the United States: 'If I were in Mr. Kissinger's shoes, I would never think of counter-measures. I would devote all my efforts towards peace and bring peace to the area. Because if we enter into measures and counter-measures, I think the result will be very disastrous'.[112] By adding the de facto unnecessary comment that the consequences of any escalation would be disastrous, particularly for Europe and Japan, Yamani assured himself of further international attention. From the beginning of his European trip at the latest, Yamani's statements on the regime of production cutbacks – which always had multiple addressees and often sought to play them off against one another – were carefully noted in the affected countries, often triggering debates and disputes.[113]

After their successful visit to Paris, Yamani's and Abdessalam's ensuing trip to London received even greater attention in both the public sphere and diplomatic circles. In the UK, too, the upper echelons of the government received the emissaries. In lengthy talks, Minister for Industry Tom Boardman, Foreign Secretary Alec Douglas-Home and Prime Minister Edward Heath respectively attempted to persuade them that oil shipments to the United Kingdom ought to be increased. As a friendly state, the UK government claimed, it should continue to receive as much oil as in the first nine months of 1973. Boardman in particular explained to the envoys the United Kingdom's precarious position, as it was suffering from a 'substantial shortfall' of 400,000 barrels of crude oil per day and had also lost a further approximately 180,000 barrels of refined products that would normally have passed through Rotterdam.[114] Yamani pointed out to his interlocutors that the United Kingdom was still in a privileged position compared with the Netherlands, Japan or West Germany, but left them with the feeling that the UK's problems had made an impression on him. Despite this, he was only prepared to increase shipments if these came not from a Saudi Arabian production increase but from the oil that would otherwise have been shipped to neutral countries, putting the British government in a difficult position.[115] In France, Yamani's tone had seemed to his interlocutors gentle and almost lachrymose, as he explained that, regretfully, he had been forced to withhold oil from Europe as a result of the hostile policies being pursued by both the United States and Europe. Their British counterparts, in contrast, perceived him as friendly but 'straightforward'.[116] He flattered Tom Boardman by telling him that he was very keen on meeting him in the near future for a long conversation on an appropriate oil price. Douglas-Home had the impression that Yamani was merely looking for a reason to justify ending the embargo and production cutbacks.[117] Nonetheless, British government circles were frustrated at the lack of progress on the key negotiating aims, and were thus keen to send emissaries directly to King Faisal, whom they believed to be open-minded and who held ultimate authority.[118]

Before the UK visit, the Dutch government had asked its British counterpart to point out to Yamani and Abdessalam that it had co-signed the EC declaration of 6 November (chapter 5), which was considered pro-Arab, and had implemented no countermeasures against the embargo. Given this, the Dutch were bewildered by the envoys' failure to pay them a visit. But the British were highly reticent about supporting the Netherlands and repeatedly fell back on joint European positions. Yamani and Abdessalam made no change to their travel plans and only met representatives of the Dutch government at their next stop in Brussels, where, in addition to the Belgian government, they also conferred with the EC.[119] The OAPEC emissaries underlined once again that their aim was not to damage the Europeans, but that in future the Arab producing countries would be unwilling to make economic sacrifices for countries that displayed an – at best – neutral attitude towards them. The Europeans perceived the atmosphere at the talks as gloomy, not least because they had the (not unjustified) impression that one of the emissaries' main objectives was to drive a wedge between them.[120] Even in public, Yamani and Abdessalam repeatedly stated that the EC and European unity meant nothing to them.[121]

The in-depth talks that Yamani and Abdessalam had held with top French and British government representatives, and the increasing attention they were receiving in the press, seem to have bolstered their self-confidence and raised their expectations about future visits. At short notice they cancelled the visit to West Germany planned for early December, officially because they first had to meet Kissinger in the United States. Exchanges with West German officials, meanwhile, reveal that they blamed the chancellor's tight schedule.[122] While the Germans took steps, following the high-profile visits to France and the United Kingdom, to ensure that Yamani and Abdessalam could meet Willy Brandt, the official programme for their visit only included meetings with the ministers Walter Scheel, Egon Bahr, Erhard Eppler and Hans Friderichs.[123] Following a preliminary meeting with the chargé d'affaires of the Algerian Embassy on 28 November, Hansheinrich Kruse, head of the Unit on Foreign Trade Policy and Oil Policy (Referat für Grundsatzfragen der Außenwirtschaftspolitik und Erdölpolitik) in the Foreign Ministry, who was responsible for organizing the visit, reported that his Algerian interlocutor was 'agreeable to the German proposals, but, as he had been instructed, must strongly insist [*insister beaucoup*], that the two ministers be received for "at least an hour" by the chancellor'.[124] The delegation was also dissatisfied with the choice of hotel, informing Kruse a day later that the visit had now been postponed for an unspecified period. The Algerian official 'expressed his government's desire that the visit ought to be more political than economic in character. It should also have the grandeur and authority [*l'éclat et l'autorité*] that had characterized the visits to France and the United Kingdom. . . . He again suggested that the talks proceed in the following order: foreign minister, economics minister, minister for economic cooperation, and finally a meeting with the chancellor, though he remarked that an hour was inadequate for such a talk. . . . Mr. Machou then urgently requested that the ministers be accommodated in a suite in the Hotel Königshof. He described the Hotel Tulpenfeld as not of the same status'.[125] The Arab emissaries' enhanced self-confidence – as a result of the oil weapon and their visits to Paris and London – clearly left a nasty taste in the mouths of Kruse's superiors, who had been accustomed to a different kind of communication with Arab officials prior to the production cutbacks. In the margin of his report, they noted: 'This arrogance is going too far for my taste', prompting the response 'Yes!'. Responsibility for planning the visit now passed to the Foreign Ministry's Political Division (Politische Abteilung).[126]

Before it took place in January 1974, however, Yamani and Abdessalam travelled to the United States, where their visit again made a major splash in the media. The main change in the embargo's interpretation that the two ministers brought with them to Washington, or announced there, was the concession that as soon as a timetable for Israeli withdrawal from the occupied territories had been drawn up, they would in turn provide a clear plan for the resumption of oil shipments. In the talks Yamani again gave the impression that he was only looking for a reason to end the unfortunate and unpleasant reality of the embargo.[127] More remarkable than the visit's concrete results was the way in which, during a week of shuttling between Washington and New York, Yamani was received in US political and economic circles and celebrated in the press.[128]

During his visit, in the unanimous judgement of the press, the 'Arabs' Kissinger', as Yamani was christened by the *New York Times* and *Los Angeles Times*, became an 'instant international celebrity' and the 'star of Washington's diplomatic cocktail circuit'.[129] A reporter for the *Washington Post* gave a vivid account of Yamani's arrival at one of the various receptions held in his honour:

> Yamani, as he greeted the long line of diplomatic and other guests (many representing oil interests), held a small string of red beads in his left hand and quietly and unobtrusively fingered them through the evening. His deep, soft brown eyes seemed to win over women quicker than candy or, for that matter, diamonds; and his path through the embassy seemed lined – casually and by accident, of course – with virtually every woman at the party.[130]

The Global Communication of the 'Arab Oil Weapon'

Figure 3.1. 'Yamani leaves Kennedy Airport, 3 December 1973', *New York Daily News*. © Getty Images.

However, reports on Yamani focused less on the stereotype of the Oriental with an eye for the ladies than on the assurance with which he mastered the twin roles of Bedouin and Western Ivy League graduate, switching between them with aplomb. Virtually every media portrait referred to Yamani's dapper appearance and exquisite clothes, his expensive Western designer suits and shoes, his characteristic goatee and mellifluous voice, often described as flattering.[131] In photographs and on television, Yamani generally clashed with the visual stereotype of the sheikh or Bedouin, a cliché on which caricaturists repeatedly drew during the oil crisis as they sought to visualize the conflict between the Western and Arab worlds. On the contrary, for example in a photograph accompanying his interview with Walter Knips and Hans Hielscher in *Spiegel* magazine, Yamani's high-class and thoroughly proper Western clothing was in marked contrast to Knips' ill-fitting suit and Hielscher's leather jacket and long hair.[132]

In addition to a lengthy report on Arab oil policies, which had been moulded in significant part by Yamani himself, an interview and a two-page biographical portrait, the Christmas edition of *Newsweek* magazine also bore his likeness on its title page. Yamani was presented as the 'man of the moment to a Western industrialized world facing the bleak prospects of imminent fuel starvation'.[133] The potted biography, which was paradigmatic of Yamani's portrayal in the Anglo-American world and beyond, presented him as a border-crosser between the Arab and Western worlds, and it was his hybrid character that was identified as the source of his negotiating clout. Whenever one asked oil industry representatives about Yamani, the article began, they inevitably reached for adjectives such as 'brilliant', 'tough' and 'awesome'. 'And when such comments are passed on to Yamani himself, he is apt to respond with his best nonplussed look. Flashing a Mona Lisa-like smile, his arms spread wide in mock supplication, he protests mildly: "But I'm merely a simple Bedouin"'.[134] While the article was accompanied by photographs showing Yamani swathed in traditional Arab garb, the text underlined that his invariably expensive clothing, which marked him out as an 'international sophisticate', should fool no one into thinking that this 'slick oil expert' and 'tough negotiator' was any kind of Arab playboy. In the final analysis, Yamani was 'an improbable blend of Western drive and Eastern cool'.[135] Yamani's extraordinary ability to move back and forth between the Western and Arab worlds was not limited to his clothing:

> A man who is equally comfortable wearing Western clothes or the flowing *dishdasha* robes and *Kaffiyeh* headdress of Araby, he feels right at home in almost every situation – whether it involves making small talk in the most fashionable salons in London, Paris, Rome or New York or squatting in a Bedouin tent in the desert chatting with illiterate camel herders. Though he is a good Muslim who almost always clutches a string of worry beads in his hand, he has never found any compelling reason to avoid all sybaritic pleasures. . . . He writes Arabic poetry in his spare time, enjoys Western classical music and is considered a lay authority on Islamic law.[136]

Yamani's statements during his many interviews give us a good idea of the source of his special impact in the West. In contrast to the more aggressive and at times, to Western ears, seemingly hysterical voices of Gaddafi in Libya and Saddam Hussein in Iraq, Yamani not only espoused more moderate views. Even when provoked, he always remained calm, underlining just how sorry he was, particularly as a friend of the West, to have to withhold from the Europeans and Americans the oil they so desperately needed. But regrettably, due to their hostile policies, the Arab countries felt compelled to cease doing them the favour they had done them hitherto through irresponsibly high production rates.[137] Certain of the importance of Arab oil until the late 1980s if not until the end of the millennium, he responded calmly when Western governments announced their determination to find alternative energy sources, emphasizing that one day the producing countries would need them too.[138]

Yamani's media portrayal in the West was due, first, to the skilful self-promotion of a man described by his biographer as 'perhaps the most Western-media-savvy Arab ever'.[139] Second, however, this portrayal met the Western need to avoid making a supposed adversary within a global conflict over oil appear nothing but fundamentally Other. Instead it presented him simultaneously as someone who had been educated in the West and had availed himself of Western knowledge and customs. Because Orientalist stereotypes of Arabs as irrational and captive to political and religious fanaticism continued to prevail in Western Europe and the United States, Western observers often struggled to understand how industrialized Western countries could have come to face such pressure from Arab oil policies.[140] A figure like Yamani alleviated the sense of grievance. Educated in law at the best universities in the United States and well versed in all oil-related issues as a result of his negotiations with the multinational oil companies, he ultimately appeared, in part, as a product of the West. From this perspective, then, the West was being challenged by forces it itself had conjured up rather than by 'the Arabs', the radical Others depicted in orientalist stereotypes.

On 25 February 1974, a cartoon in the *New Yorker* captured the idea that the West was being beaten at its own game. In it, two men, fitting the visual stereotype of the Arab sheikh, are sitting in a manifestly luxurious car. One declares: 'As Adam Smith so aptly put it. . .'. The viewer is left to complete this sentence, which recalls the most famous proposition formulated by the Scots moral philosopher in the *Inquiry into the Nature and Causes of the Wealth of Nations,* namely that supply and demand regulate prices and that the market, as long as it is free of restrictions, will be steered as by an invisible hand. The cartoon speaks to a number of issues. First, in 1973 it was *not* the invisible hand that regulated prices via the free play of supply and demand, but the highly visible hand of the producing countries. Second, though, from the perspective of Western governments the notion of the invisible hand was fitting in that the actions of the Arab producing countries did in fact seem like uncontrollable interventions. Ultimately, however, the cartoon's very simple point was that here are two Arabs who know the work of Adam Smith and are deploying his theories against the Western consuming countries.

Yamani and Abdessalam had no scheduled meetings over Christmas or New Year, but returned to Europe in January. During their first stopovers in Madrid and Rome, once again Yamani's statements were addressed at least as much to the other European countries and the United States as to his current hosts. While in Madrid, he had refused to comment on the American government's plans to hold a conference of the consuming countries in Washington, DC. But in Rome, he warned against moves that might worsen the international confrontation by creating blocs, suggesting to the Europeans that the conference was an American attempt to undermine an independent European policy.[141]

The West Germans had clearly learned from the postponement of the talks planned for December and were evidently at pains to give the visit at least as much 'grandeur and authority' as in France and the United Kingdom. The guests were now accommodated in the Hotel Königshof. Over two and a half days, from 15 to 17 January, they were scheduled to meet for talks with Erhard Eppler, minister for economic cooperation, Economics Minister Hans Friderichs, Foreign Minister Walter Scheel and Chancellor Brandt, with the length of the meeting with Brandt increased from forty-five to ninety minutes in order to avoid causing offence.[142] Press reports underlined that this was the most comprehensive programme laid on for foreign guests in recent years.[143] Even the *Los Angeles Times* was impressed by the ceremonial in Bonn, with the Mercedes limousines and police escorts provided not, as one might have expected, for a head of state or government, but for 'Superman. Not the Henry A. Kissinger version; the Saudi Arabian'.[144] In the *Frankfurter Allgemeine Zeitung*, Adelbert Weinstein wrote a biographical portrait of Yamani, taking up many of the elements present in the accounts described above. He quoted reports from Yamani's negotiating partners to the effect that his 'negotiating style, which is almost brutal when it comes to the pursuit of objectives, [is] moderated over the course of long rounds of talks by an overwhelming personal charm'.[145] But Weinstein also emphasized that Yamani and Prince Saud were distinguished by 'unconditional loyalty, comprehensive knowledge of the issues at hand, successful negotiating and boundless diligence'.[146] Having thus attributed to Yamani the supposedly German virtues of diligence, thoroughness and loyalty, and presented him as an equal and worthy opponent, however, Weinstein finally chose to conclude with some rigorous othering: 'Above all else, despite his Western education, he is still essentially an Oriental; a diplomatic nomad whose Bedouin character is unconventional but unmistakable'.[147]

The character of the talks with the West German government was influenced by advance indications from the Algerian camp that moves were afoot to categorize West Germany as a hostile state. Also at issue was the interpretation of the declaration on the Middle East conflict issued by the nine EC foreign ministers of 6 November 1973, which did not specify whether Israel must withdraw from all occupied territory or only some. Chiefly because a statement by Willy Brandt at the EC summit in Copenhagen in December had been understood in the second sense, Yamani and Abdessalam requested clarification (chapter 5).[148] During the talks with Brandt, Yamani then also demanded that, as the British and French governments had already done, the West German government issue an unambiguous statement calling for Israel's withdrawal from all occupied territories. Listening to his advisors, Brandt stuck to the line that 'end the territorial occupation' could only mean that 'the occupation must come to an end, unless there was a failure to agree on minor points, in other words, as long as the Arab side was willing to accept appropriate amendments'.[149] But Brandt refused to issue a more substantial statement. In Copenhagen, he explained, he had merely wished to avoid making neo-colonialist demands, because it must always be possible for sovereign states to change their borders by mutual consent, as set out, for example, in West Germany's treaties with certain Eastern Bloc countries (the *Ostverträge*). Rather than attempting to meet Yamani halfway on this point, Brandt tried to establish common ground by agreeing with Yamani's statements that the era of thoughtless oil consumption was over and that it was imperative to find alternatives.

Despite the pomp and ceremony, then, the visit achieved nothing concrete. In the *Süddeutsche Zeitung*, Martin Süskind remarked, with some justification, that since November Yamani's and Abdessalam's negotiating position had markedly worsened because there had been progress in the Middle East peace process and the issue of oil no longer appeared insurmountable.[150] The aptness of the West German refusal to issue a statement clarifying the meaning of the 6 November declaration also seemed confirmed by a meeting of the Political Committee on European Political Cooperation that took place shortly after the emissaries' visit to Bonn. There the French and British representatives denied having issued a statement to the Arab countries elucidating the common European position. They also voted against a joint confidential declaration, because this would either fail to satisfy the Arabs or be made public by them.[151] Instead it was agreed to step up efforts to enhance European-Arab dialogue, as explained to Yamani and Abdessalam by Walter Scheel in his role as Council president.[152]

Yamani and Abdessalam were again afforded a grand reception during their final stopover in Japan. They were even granted an audience with the emperor, an honour normally reserved for heads of state.[153] Yamani's first four visits to Japan having gone virtually unnoticed, this time the whole country was on its knees, as the *Washington Post* correspondent noted.[154] Not since Henry Kissinger's visit following his trip to China in 1972, he went on, had a guest enjoyed the kind of public attention lavished on Yamani, whose press conference was attended by no fewer than 280 journalists.[155] Once again, Yamani spoke out against agreements between consuming countries that risked intensifying the confrontation with the producing countries. This was scarcely credible, however: since late January, he had spent much of his time defining Arab attempts to mitigate the production cutbacks not as a defeat but as a consequence of their success.[156]

After this final leg of his itinerant diplomacy, Yamani used the provisional lifting of the embargo against the United States and the categorizing of Germany and Italy as friendly states on 18 March 1973 to make another major public splash, as reported in the Austrian daily newspaper *Die Presse*: 'At exactly 6.24 p.m. – fittingly late for a star – Yamani appears. Smiling, he fiddles with something red, which at first glance resembles a rosary but turns out to be his glasses chain. Once again nodding graciously in every direction, he takes his seat to the right of Abdessalam, quickly passing him a note on which he has scribbled some Arab words, before the camera operators and journalists are asked to leave the room'.[157] The article went on to describe how, after Abdessalam had left the room at 9 p.m., declaring that the meeting was over and there was nothing further to report, a number of journalists stayed on because they 'speculated that before the first light of dawn one person in particular would fail to honour the general precept of confidentiality, and Sheikh Yamani was not to disappoint them'. He could not wait, the article explains, to tell the world of his 'new pro-American position' and announced without authorization that the embargo would end, though he provided no further detail.[158]

Interim Conclusion

In contrast to what some authors have maintained, the oil embargo and production cutbacks imposed by the Arab countries of OPEC in October 1973 were not historically significant because the impact of the oil shortage was so severe and the associated objectives were achieved. Neither is it the case that they were insignificant because oil was never truly scarce and the real aims were not achieved, as others have suggested. From a historiographical perspective, the production cutbacks were significant because they destroyed the established communicative and interactional routines of the international oil economy, thus creating a moment of contingency and uncertainty. This engendered a process of communication and negotiation in which an array of actors sought to define and instrumentalize, to their own ends, the content, terms and significance of the embargo. Strictly speaking, the instrumentalization of the embargo began long before its actual imposition. From the spring of 1973 onwards, it was no longer just radical OPEC countries such as Libya or Iraq that were threatening to deploy the 'oil weapon'; Saudi Arabia, so crucial to the enforcement of production cutbacks, made similar statements. So, in view of the numerous threats issued, it would be quite wrong to suggest that the regime of production cutbacks descended upon Western Europe and the United States suddenly and without warning.

The production cuts were communicated both through classic diplomatic channels and the press, with the oil-focused press services doing much to guarantee their global impact. The interplay between diplomatic communication through letters or conversations on the one hand and mass media communication on the other enabled the actors involved to endow the measures with whatever symbolic significance best served their interests and instrumentalize them in a variety of ways. Contrary to their portrayal in many Western accounts, the Arab producing countries were no monolithic bloc. In fact, each pursued its own interests, which differed markedly, as exemplified by Gaddafi, Boumedienne and King Faisal. This range of views, together with the (often intentional) vagueness of official pronouncements, intensified the sense of insecurity triggered by the measures themselves. Most important to the perception of the Arab position in the West was Sheikh Zaki Yamani, whose tour through the capitals of the affected countries attracted a great deal of attention in the media. The fact that Yamani was making demands of the Western Europe countries and the United States – and the way he went about it – called their sovereignty into question. They responded both on the national level, by setting out a comprehensive catalogue of measures, and internationally, through a number of strategies that I scrutinize in the following chapters.

Notes

1. Ian Seymour, 'The Oil Weapon', *Middle East Economic Survey* 16(52) (19 October 1973), 2–4; Hanns W. Maull, *Oil and Influence: The Oil Weapon Examined* (London, 1975); Fuad Itayim, 'Strengths and Weaknesses of the Oil Weapon', in International Institute for Strategic Studies (ed.), *The Middle East and the International System*, vol. 2, *Security and the Energy Crisis* (London, 1975), 1–7; Jordan J. Paust and Albert Paul Blaustein (eds), *The Arab Oil Weapon* (Dobbs Ferry, NY, 1977); initial reflections on the themes explored in this chapter were published as Rüdiger Graf, 'Making Use of the Oil Weapon: Western Industrial Nations and Arab Petropolitics in 1973/74', *Diplomatic History* 36(1) (2012), 185–208.

2. M.S. Daoudi and M.S. Dajani, *Economic Sanctions, Ideals and Experience* (London/Boston, 1983), 8; Alan P. Dobson, *US Economic Statecraft for Survival, 1933–1991: Of Sanctions, Embargoes, and Economic Warfare* (London, 2002); David A. Baldwin, *Economic Statecraft* (Princeton, NJ, 1985); James Barber, 'Economic Sanctions as a Policy Instrument', *International Affairs* 55 (1979), 367–84; Diane B. Kunz, 'When Money Counts and Doesn't: Economic Power and Diplomatic Objectives', *Diplomatic History* 18 (1994), 451–62; R.T. Naylor, *Economic Warfare: Sanctions, Embargo Busting, and Their Human Cost* (Boston, MA, 2001).

3. Margaret P. Doxey, *International Sanctions in Contemporary Perspective* (Basingstoke, 1987), 9.

4. Dean Lacy, 'A Theory of Economic Sanctions and Issue Linkage: The Roles of Preferences, Information, and Threats', *Journal of Politics* 66 (2004), 25–42, here 27; Robert A. Doughty and Harold E. Raugh, Jr., 'Embargoes in Historical Perspective', *Parameters* 21(1)

(1991), 21–30; R.T. Naylor, *Patriots and Profiteers: On Economic Warfare, Embargo Busting and State-Sponsored Crime* (Toronto, 1999), ix; Marc V. Simon, 'When Sanctions Can Work: Economic Sanctions and the Theory of Moves', *International Interactions* 21 (1996), 203–28, here 203; George Tsebelis, 'Are Sanctions Effective? A Game-Theoretic Analysis', *Journal of Conflict Resolution* 34 (1990), 3–28; Kunz, 'When Money Counts and Doesn't'.

5. Barber, 'Economic Sanctions as a Policy Instrument', 369, 373; Adrian U-Jin Ang and Dursun Peksen, 'When Do Economic Sanctions Work? Asymmetric Perceptions, Issue Salience, and Outcomes', *Political Research Quarterly* 60 (2007), 135–45, here 136.

6. Dobson, *US Economic Statecraft*, 287; see also Dobson, 'From Instrumental to Expressive: The Changing Goals of the US Cold War Strategic Embargo', *Journal of Cold War Studies* 12(1) (2010), 98–119.

7. James M. Lindsay, 'Trade Sanctions as Policy Instruments: A Re-examination', *International Studies Quarterly* 30 (1986), 153–73, here 153.

8. Lacy, 'A Theory of Economic Sanctions'.

9. Ang and Peksen, 'When Do Economic Sanctions Work?', 136.

10. Roy Licklider, *Political Power and the Arab Oil Weapon: The Experience of Five Industrial Nations* (Berkeley, 1988), 2f.

11. Stephen Duguid, 'Review of Licklider, *Political Power and the Arab Oil Weapon*', *International History Review* 11 (1989), 403–5.

12. Daoudi and Dajani, *Economic Sanctions*, 107f.

13. Al-Sowayegh, *Arab Petropolitics*.

14. Grossman, *US Energy Policy*, 43.

15. Maull, *Oil and Influence*, 6, 10; Maull, *Ölmacht: Ursachen, Perspektiven* (Frankfurt am Main/Cologne, 1975); Jens Hohensee, 'Böswillige Erpressung oder bewußte Energiepolitik? Der Einsatz der Ölwaffe 1973/74 aus arabischer Sicht', in Jens Hohensee and Michael Salewski (eds), *Energie – Politik – Geschichte: Nationale und internationale Energiepolitik seit 1945* (Stuttgart, 1993), 153–76.

16. Yergin, *The Prize*, 632; see also Merrill, *The Oil Crisis of 1973–1974*, 22.

17. Venn, *The Oil Crisis*.

18. With respect to France from 1969 onwards, see also the bi-weekly *Orient-Petrole*, edited by Jean-Jacques Berreby, which reported chiefly on OPEC and OAPEC.

19. See, for example, Edward Townsend, 'Shaik Yamani Tells of Saudi Arabian Scheme for Cheaper Oil', *The Times*, 28 January 1974.

20. Akins, 'The Oil Crisis', 467.

21. See the interview with Nicholas C. Proffitt, 'Faisal's Threat', *Newsweek*, 10 September 1973, 35–37; MEES 16(46) (7 September 1973), i–ii.

22. Geoffrey Jones, *The Evolution of International Business* (London, 1996), 159f.; on Yamani's biography, see Jeffrey Robinson, *Yamani: The Inside Story* (London, 1989).

23. Speech delivered by Shaykh Ahmed Zaki Yamani before the 26th Annual Conference of the Middle East Institute on 30 September 1972, Lafayette College Libraries, Easton, PA (henceforth LCL) William E. Simon Papers (WSP), Series IIIA, Drawer 17, Folder 13.

24. Memo: Saunders/Knubel/Hormats/Quandt to Scowcroft: US-Saudi Economic Relations and European Economic Policy, Meeting at 2:30 p.m. Wednesday, 9 May, 8 May 1973, Annex A, NARA, Nixon Library, Mandatory Review Opening 2007: Temporary Box Folder, Box 8; Memo: Saunders to Kissinger: Your talk with Prince Saud Faisal – 24, 23 February 1973, NARA, Nixon Library, Mandatory Review Opening 2007: Temporary Box Folder, Box 7.

25. Memo: Saunders/Knubel/Hormats/Quandt to Scowcroft: US-Saudi Economic Relations and European Economic Policy, Meeting at 2:30 p.m. Wednesday, 9 May, 8 May 1973, Annex A, NARA, Nixon Library, Mandatory Review Opening 2007: Temporary Box Folder, Box 8.

26. Saunders to Kissinger: Memorandum of Conversation with Yamani [17 April 1973, 5 p.m.], 2 May 1973, NARA, Nixon Library, Mandatory Review Opening 2007: Temporary Box Folder, Box 8.

27. Ibid.; Memo: Saunders/Quandt to Kissinger: Your Meeting with Saudi Minister Yamani and Prince Saud – Tuesday, 7 April at 5:00 p.m., 17 April 1973, NARA, Nixon Library, Mandatory Review Opening 2007: Temporary Box Folder, Box 7: 'We understand that Yamani states this fact not as a threat, but out of real concern about the vulnerability of Saudi Arabia itself. One person who spent the day yesterday with Yamani describes it as a statement of desperation rather than of threat'.

28. David B. Ottaway and Ronald Koven, 'Saudis Tie Oil to US Policy on Israel', *Washington Post*, 19 April 1973.

29. Ronald Koven and David B. Ottoway, 'US Oil Nightmare: Worldwide Shortage', *Washington Post*, 17 June 1973.

30. 'Mobil Oil: The US Stake in Middle East Peace: I', *New York Times*, 21 June 1973.

31. MEES 16(42) (10 August 1973), 8–10.

32. MEES 16(48) (21 September 1973), 11.

33. Jim Hoagland, 'Faisal Warns US on Israel', *Washington Post*, 6 July 1973.

34. MEES 16(38) (13 July 1973).

35. MEES 16(39) (20 July 1973), 2.

36. MEES 16(40) (27 July 1973), 6; for another threat, see also MEES 16(45) (31 August 1973), 4f.: 'The Ruler of Abu Dhabi, Shaikh Zayid ibn Sultan Al Nuhayyan, has stated that Abu Dhabi will join any coordinated Arab plan to use oil as a weapon, and has called for an Arab summit to discuss oil affairs'; or the interview with the Libyan oil minister in MEES 16(45) (31 August 1973), 6f.

37. David Hirst, 'Israel – America's Wasting Asset', *Middle East Economic Survey* 16(47) (14 September 1973), i–vii. This article was rejected by the *New York Times Magazine* and then published on 6 September in abbreviated form in *The Guardian*.

38. MEES 16(43) (17 August 1973), 8f.

39. MEES 16(45) (31 August 1973), 2.

40. Dilger: Bericht über die außerordentliche Ministerratssitzung der Organisation der arabischen Ölexportierenden Länder (OAPEC), 6.9.1973, PA AA, B 36 (Referat 310), 104991.

41. Proffitt, 'Faisal's Threat'; 'A Fresh Arabian Blend of Oil and Politics', *Newsweek*, 10 September 1973, 36; on perceptions, see MEES 16(44) (24 August 1973), 8; MEES 16(46) (7 September 1973), i–ii. On 31 August on NBC Faisal had already warned: 'We do not wish to place any restrictions on our oil exports to the United States, but America's complete support of Zionism against Arabs makes it extremely difficult for us to continue to supply United States petroleum needs and even to maintain our friendly relations with the United States', MEES 16(46) (7 September 1973), ii.

42. An example being Richard Nixon at a press conference on 5 September 1973; MEES 16(46) (7 September 1973), iii.

43. Interview with *US News and World Report*, MEES 16(50) (5 October 1973), iii.

44. Akins, 'The Oil Crisis'.

45. Ibid., 475, 482f.

46. US Congress. Senate. Committee on Foreign Relations, *Energy and Foreign Policy: The Implications of the Current Energy Problem for United States Foreign Policy, May 30 and 31 1973* (Washington, 1973), 1; 'Looming Blackmail', *New York Times*, 29 May 197.

47. Memo Theodore L. Eliot, Jr. to Kissinger: Meeting of the Committee on International Aspects of Energy, 19 June 1973, NARA, Nixon Library, Mandatory Review Opening 2007: Temporary Box Folder, Box 8.

48. Quoted in MEES 16(46) (7 September 1973), iii.

49. Ibid.

50. Office of the White House Press Secretary: Remarks of the President on the Nation's Energy Policy, 8 September 1973, NARA, Nixon Library, WHCF, SMOF, EPO, Box 24.

51. Akins, 'Saudis Serious on Using Oil Exports to Alter US Policy', *Oil and Gas Journal* 71(41) (1973), 37.

52. See the list of demands from Iraq, Kuwait and the PLO: 'Oil and the Battle', *Middle East Economic Survey* 16(51) (12 October 1973), 3–6.

53. 'Pachachi Calls for Immediate Use of Oil Weapon', *Middle East Economic Survey* 16(51) (12 October 1973), 4–5, here 5.

54. Yergin, *Der Preis*, 732–38.

55. Eickhoff, [Ekkehard]: Telegramm zur irakischen Haltung, 21.10.1973, PA AA, B 36 (Referat 310), 104991.

56. Ungerer, [Werner]: Bericht zur bevorstehenden außerordentlichen Generalkonferenz der OPEC am 16.3.1973, 6.3.1973, PA AA, B 36 (Referat 310), 104991; Fernschreiben zur 32. Generalkonferenz der OPEC vom 16. und 17.3.1973 in Wien, 19.3.1973; Kurth: Fernschreiben über die 33. ausserordentliche Generalkonferenz der OPEC in Wien vom 26.5.1973, 29.5.1973; Ungerer, [Werner]: Schreiben über 'Contingency-Plan' der OPEC, 11.9.1973, PA AA, B 71 (Referat 405), 113907.

57. Dilger: Fernschreiben zur kuwaitischen Haltung im Nahostkrieg, 13.10.1973; Eickhoff, [Ekkehard]: Telegramm zur möglichen Verwendung des Öls als Waffe, 13.10.1973; Werner, [Günter Franz]: Fernschreiben zu Libyens Teilnahme an der Kuwait-Konferenz, 15.10.1973; Lilienfeld, [Georg von]: Fernschreiben zur arabischen Erdölpolitik, 13.10.1973; Metzger, [Peter]: Fernschreiben zur saudischen Erdölpolitik, 17.10.1973, PA AA, B 36 (Referat 310), 104991.

58. Dilger: Fernschreiben zur kuwaitischen Haltung im Nahostkrieg, 15.10.1973; Lankes, [Georg Christian]: Fernschreiben über Auswirkungen der Kriegshandlungen auf Erdölversorgung, 16.10.1973, PA AA, B 36 (Referat 310), 104991.

59. 'US Fields Unable to Fill Gap if Arab Oil is Cut Off', *Oil and Gas Journal* 71(42) (1973), 39–42, here 39: 'Chances of a shutoff of Arab oil shipments to the West have moved from a faint possibility to a definite danger with the fresh outbreak of an Arab-Israel war'.

60. MEES 16(51) (12 October 1973), 1.

61. Memorandum for Mr. Harold Saunders, Subject: Status of Oil Negotiations in Vienna, 10 October 1973, CIA, Doc No/ESDN: 51112a4b993247d4d83944fe; Memo: The Arab War and Oil, 15 October 1973, NARA, Nixon Library, NSC, Inst. Files, WSAG Meetings, Box H-093. So it is not the case that the oil companies in Vienna were left entirely in the dark about what was to come; Yergin, *The Prize*, 602. For the German perception see Hermes, [Peter]: Vorlage für Staatssekretär und Minister zur Kabinettsitzung am 17.10.1973, 16.10.1973, PA AA, B 71 (Referat 405), 113924.

62. Edward Cowan, 'A Saudi Threat on Oil Reported: Minister Is Said to Predict Production Slash if US Resupplies Israel', *New York Times*, 16 October 1973.

63. NARA, Nixon Library, NSC, Inst. Files, WSAG Meetings, Box H-093; The White House: Oil Contingency Paper, 7 October 1973, CIA, Doc No/ESDN: 51112a4a993247d4d83944a0; Memorandum for Mr. Harold Saunders, Subject: Status of Oil Negotiations in Vienna, 10 October 1973, CIA, Doc No/ESDN: 51112a4b993247d4d83944fe.

64. Armstrong and Sutterlin to Casey: SRG Meeting on International Petroleum Situation, Monday, 15 October, 10.00 a.m., NARA, Nixon Library, NSC, Inst. Files, WSAG Meetings, Box H-093.

65. Washington Special Actions Group Meeting: Middle East, Minutes, 17 October 1973, Digital National Security Archive (henceforth DNSA), KT00854.

66. Ibid.; Current Middle East Situation, Memorandum of Conversation, 12 October 1973, DNSA, KT00845: 'Saqqaf affirmed that the Saudis had no intention of "hanging themselves" by cutting off oil and bringing further trouble to the Middle East'.

67. William Quandt/Donald Stukel: Memo to Sec. Kissinger: WSAG Meeting – Middle East, Saturday, 6 October 1973, 3.00 p.m., NARA, Nixon Library, NSC, Inst. Files, WSAG Meetings, Box H-094; Memo to Kissinger: WSAG Meeting, 8 October 1973, NARA, Nixon Library, NSC, Inst. Files, WSAG Meetings, Box H-093.

68. Walter Stoessel: Memo to Kissinger: Actions in the Event of an Arab Oil Embargo against the United States, Western Europe and Japan, 14 October 1973, NARA, Nixon Library, NSC, Inst. Files, WSAG Meetings, Box H-093; Armstrong/Sutterlin: Memo to Casey: SRG Meeting on International Petroleum Situation, Monday, 15 October 10.00 a.m., NARA, Nixon Library, NSC, Inst. Files, WSAG Meetings, Box H-093.

69. Willis C. Armstrong: Memo to the Secretary: European Vulnerability to Arab Embargo, 13 October 1973, NARA, Nixon Library, NSC, Inst. Files, WSAG Meetings, Box H-093.

70. Declarations in MEES 16(52) (19 October 1973), i–ii.

71. Ibid., 1.

72. Ibid., iii.

73. Ibid.

74. Ibid., 4.

75. Ibid., iv; Faysal Letter to Nixon Threatens Oil Halt, Diplomatic Break, 13 October 1973, CIA, Doc No/ESDN: 51112a4b993247d4d8394544.

76. MEES 17(1) (26 October 1973), 3.

77. Ibid., 1.

78. MEES 17(2) (2 November 1973), 1f.

79. US Congress. Senate. Committee on Foreign Relations. Subcommittee on Multinational Corporations, *US Oil Companies and the Arab Oil Embargo: The International Allocation of Constricted Supplies* (Washington, DC, 1975), 1.

80. Quoted in MEES 17(4) (16 November 1973), 6.

81. In the Kuwait daily *al-Siyasah*, 8 November 1973, quoted in MEES 17(4) (16 November 1973), 8.

82. MEES 17(18) (22 February 1974), i–iii, here ii.

83. MEES 17(21) (15 March 1974), 10; see also the statement by Nadim Pachachi in MEES 17(4) (16 November 1973), iii: 'We are not practicing blackmail in using the oil weapon. We are using it in order to draw the attention of the world community to our just and legitimate rights and to defend our civilization and inheritance, which existed before oil was discovered in our lands'.

84. Quoted in MEES 17(2) (2 November 1973), 6.

85. Quoted in MEES 17(10) (28 December 1973), iv.

86. 'Ministry of Finance and Petroleum Kuwait: An Open Letter to the American People', *Washington Post*, 14 November 1973.

87. Reprinted in MEES 17(4) (16 November 1973), 17f.

88. Jordan J. Paust and Albert Paul Blaustein, 'The Arab Oil Weapon: A Threat to International Peace', *American Journal of International Law* 68 (1974), 410–39; Ibrahim F.I. Shihata, 'Destination Embargo of Arab Oil: Its Legality und International Law', *American Journal of International Law* 68 (1974), 591–627; Shihata, *The Case for the Arab Oil Embargo: A Legal Analysis of Arab Oil Measures with a Full Text of Relevant Resolutions and Communiqués* (Beirut, 1975); Richard B. Lillich, 'Economic Coercion and the International Legal Order', *International Affairs* 51 (1975), 358–71; Timothy Stanley, 'Some Politic-Legal Aspects of Resource Scarcity', *American University Law Review* 24 (1975), 1106–21.

89. MEES 17(3) (9 November 1973), 1–3.

90. See MEES 17(10) (28 December 1973), 16; on the position of Iraq, see Eickhoff, [Ekkehard]: Fernschreiben zur irakischen Reaktion auf Kuwait-Konferenz, 18.10.1973; Eickhoff: Telegramm zur irakischen Haltung, 21.10.1973; Löschner, Bericht über die irakische Sicht auf die Ölwaffe, 22.12.1973, PA AA, B 36 (Referat 310), 104991.

91. US Congress. Senate. Committee on Foreign Relations. Subcommittee on Multinational Corporations, *Chronology of the Libyan Oil Negotiations, 1970–1971.*
92. See MEES 17(1) (26 October 1973), 11.
93. 'Europa muß den Arabern Waffen liefern: Der libysche Regierungschef Abd el-Salam Dschallud über Erdöl und Israel', *Der Spiegel,* 12 November 1973, 120–28; partially reprinted in MEES 17(4) (16 November 1973), 8. Libya's message was aimed not just at the European but also at the Arab public; the next day the newspaper *al-Anwar* carried an interview with Jalloud with the same content.
94. 'Europa muß den Arabern Waffen liefern', 127.
95. See, for example, Prince Saud on 13 November in *al-Anwar,* MEES 17(4) (16 November 1973), 6; Yamani on Danish television on 22 November, MEES 17(5) (23 November 1973), 11; or King Faisal the same day in *al-Anwar* and the Cairo newspaper *al-Jumhuriyah,* MEES 17(6) (30 November 1973), 10. Signs of this softening of approach had already been perceived in November; see Using Oil as a Weapon: Implications and Prospects for the Arab Oil Producing States, 23 November 1973, CIA, Nixon Intelligence, Doc No/ESDN: 51112a4a993247d4d8394476: 'We judge there will be no relief from the oil squeeze without real progress on the negotiations [handwritten:] but there is a prospect for movement on the oil problem short of a final peace settlement'.
96. CIA: Memorandum for the Record, Subject: Analysis of Recent Statements by Saudi Arabian Oil Minister Yamani, 11 December 1973, CIA, Nixon Intelligence, Doc No/ESDN: 51112a4b993247d4d8394552; MEES 17(8) (14 December 1973), 4.
97. MEES 17(10) (28 December 1973), 8, 11.
98. Ibid., 10.
99. 'Operation of Arab Oil Measures Clarified', *Middle East Economic Survey* 16(11) (4 January 1974), 1.
100. Memorandum of Conversation: Meeting with Egyptian and Saudi Foreign Ministers and Vice President Ford, 18 February 1974, DNSA, KT01032; see also the well-informed report in MEES 17(22) (22 March 1974), 4.
101. 'Text of Arab Statement in Vienna on End of Embargo', *New York Times,* 19 March 1974.
102. MEES 17(21) (15 March 1974), 10f.
103. Quoted in MEES 17(25) (17 April 1974), 6f.
104. Giuliano Garavini, 'Completing Decolonization: The 1973 "Oil Shock" and the Struggle for Economic Rights', *International History Review* 33(3) (2011), 473–87; Garavini, *After Empires: European Integration, Decolonization, and the Challenge from the Global South 1957-1986* (Oxford, 2012), 162-200.
105. MEES 17(5) (23 November 1973), 15.
106. MEES 17(6) (30 November 1973), 4–9.
107. Ibid., 1; see also 'The Algiers Summit Conference', *MERIP Reports* 23 (December 1973), 13–16.
108. MEES 17(2) (2 November 1973), 4. See Sampson, *The Seven Sisters,* 249; Yergin, *The Prize,* 599–609.
109. Braun, [Sigismund Freiherr von] (28.11.1973): Bericht über den Besuch von Abdessalam und Yamani in Frankreich, PA AA, B 36 (Referat 310), 104992.
110. FM Paris 281200Z: Oil: Visit of Arab Ministers from Algeria and Saudi Arabia, 28 November 1973, NA UK, PREM 15/1842: '"You have leverage" Yamani kept saying'.
111. Ibid.
112. Quoted in MEES 17(6) (30 November 1973), 13.
113. CIA: Memorandum for the Record, Subject: Analysis of Recent Statements by Saudi Arabian Oil Minister Yamani, 11 December 1973, CIA, Nixon Intelligence, Doc No/ESDN: 51112a4b993247d4d8394552.

114. Note of the Minister for Industry's Meeting with Shaikh Yamani and M. Abdessalam, at 10.30 a.m. on Thursday 29 November 1973, NA UK, PREM 15/1842.
115. Ibid.; Record of a Conversation between the Prime Minister and the Saudi Arabian Minister of Petroleum, 29 November 1973, 4.30 p.m., NA UK, PREM 15/1842.
116. A.D. Pearsons: Arab Oil, 29 November 1973, NA UK, PREM 15/1842.
117. DTI to PMO: Situation after Yamani Visit, 30 November 1973; Douglas-Home to PM, 29 November 1973, NA UK, PREM 15/1842.
118. Antony Acland to Tom Bridges: Emissary to Saudi Arabia, 30 November 1973; Mumford: Brief for Lord Carrington: Meeting with Yamani, 28 November 1973, NA UK, PREM 15/1842; Hase, [Karl-Günther v.] (30.11.1973): Bericht über den Besuch Abdessalams und Yamanis in London, PA AA, B 36 (Referat 310), 104992.
119. Brief for Douglas-Home: Meeting with Yamani and Abdessalam, 29 November 1973; Alexander: Supplementary Brief for Douglas-Home: Meeting with Yamani, 28 November 1973, NA UK, PREM 15/1842.
120. Limbourg, [Peter]: Fernschreiben über den Besuch von Yamani und Abdessalam in Brüssel, 30.11.1973, PA AA, B 71 (Referat 405), 113907; Limbourg: Fernschreiben über Besuch von Yamani und Abdessalam in Brüssel, 1.12.1973, BArch, B 136/6342; Limbourg: Besuch von Abdessalam und Yamani in Brüssel, 4.12.1973, PA AA, B 36 (Referat 310), 104992.
121. MEES 17(7) (7 December 1973), 4.
122. Hase, [Karl-Günther v.] (30.11.1973): Fernschreiben zu Gründen der Verschiebung des Besuchs von Yamani und Abdessalam; Limbourg, [Peter] (30.11.1973): Fernschreiben zum Besuch von Abdessalam und Yamani, PA AA, B 36 (Referat 310), 104992; Sprechzettel für die Kabinettsitzung am 5.12.1973: Punkte außerhalb der Tagesordnung: Verschiebung des Besuchs der für Erdölfragen zuständigen Minister Algeriens und Saudi Arabiens, 3.12.1973. PA AA, B 71 (Referat 405), 113906.
123. RD Schröder (402) über Herrn Abteilungsleiter II, den Herrn Chef BK, den Herrn Bundesminister, dem Bundeskanzler: Besuch Yamani und Abdessalam, Bonn, 28.11.1973, BArch, B 136/6342; Programm für den Besuch Ihrer Exzellenzen ... Belaid Abdessalam ... und ... Sheikh Dr. Ahmed Zaki Yamani vom 2. bis 4. Dezember 1973, 29.11.1973, PA AA, B 36 (Referat 310), 104992.
124. Kruse an Staatssekretär: Besuch des algerischen Industrie- und Energieministers Belaid Abdessalam und des saudi-arabischen Erdölministers Yamani in Bonn, 28.11.1973, PA AA, B 71 (Referat 405), 113906.
125. Kruse, [Hansheinrich]: Schreiben an den Staatssekretär zur Verschiebung des Besuchs von Abdessalam und Yamani, 29.11.1973, PA AA, B 36 (Referat 310), 104992.
126. Ibid.
127. William D. Smith, 'Saudi, Here, Links Oil to a Pullout. Meeting with Kissinger: Comment by Iranian', *New York Times*, 5 December 1973; Bernard Gwertzmann, 'Saudi Minister, in Capital, Is Optimistic about Peace. Talk Is Lengthened. US Officials Pleased Israel's Existence "Not an Issue"', *New York Times*, 6 December 1973; on the Saudi Arabian-American negotiations, see chapter 4.
128. Leslie H. Gelb, '2 Aides Underline Arab-Israeli Gap: Yamani and Dayan, in US TV Talks, Differ Sharply on Mideast Peace Terms', *New York Times*, 10 December 1973.
129. 'Personality in the News: Saudi Oil Minister – The Arabs' Kissinger', *Los Angeles Times*, 3 December 1973; 'Merely a Simple Bedouin', *Newsweek*, 24 December 1973, 28–29.
130. Henry Mitchell, 'Table Talk of Oil Talks: Scene', *Washington Post*, 13 December 1973.
131. Ibid.; 'Personality in the News'; 'Merely a Simple Bedouin'.
132. '"Auf König Feisal können Sie sich verlassen": Saudi-Arabiens Ölminister Ahmed Saki el-Jamani über die arabische Ölstrategie', *Der Spiegel*, 3 December 1973, 35–44.
133. 'Merely a Simple Bedouin', 28.
134. Ibid.

135. Ibid.
136. Ibid.
137. 'We are Very Flexible People, I Assure You: Interview with Sheikh Zaki Yamani', *Newsweek*, 24 December 1973, 27; '"Auf König Feisal können Sie sich verlassen"'.
138. 'We are Very Flexible People, I Assure You'.
139. Robinson, *Yamani*, 102.
140. Douglas J. Little, *American Orientalism: The United States and the Middle East since 1945* (Chapel Hill, 2002), 27; for a positively framed example, see Raphael Patai, *The Arab Mind* (New York, 1973).
141. 'Saudi Warns against Bloc of Oil Users: Zionist Attack Renewed', *New York Times*, 13 January 1974; Meyer-Lindenberg: Besuch der Erdölminister Saudi Arabiens und Algeriens in Madrid, 15.1.1974, PA AA, B 36 (Referat 310), 104993.
142. Programm für den Besuch Ihrer Exzellenzen, 14.1.1974; RD Dehmel und RD Thiele an Herrn PR/BK über Abteilungsleiter IV: Besuch Yamani Abdessalam, 8.1.1974, BArch, B 136/6342.
143. 'Großaufgebot für Ölminister', *Frankfurter Rundschau*, 15 January 1974; 'Erdölminister in Bonn', *Frankfurter Allgemeine Zeitung*, 15 January 1974.
144. Joe Morris, 'Mercedes for "Superman": Bonn Gives Oil Sheik High-Octane Welcome', *Los Angeles Times*, 21 January 1974.
145. Adelbert Weinstein, 'Jamani: Wächter über des Königs Öl', *Frankfurter Allgemeine Zeitung*, 15 January 1974.
146. Ibid.
147. Ibid.
148. Bericht von Dr. Meyer, Direktor der DIAG, über ein Treffen mit Belaid Abdessalam am 15.12.1973; Moltmann (Algier) an AA Bonn: Besuch des algerischen Industrie- und Energieministers Abdessalam in Bonn, 17.1.1974; Schauer an Bundeskanzler: Ihr Gespräch mit Yamani und Abdessalam, 14.1.1974; GL II/1 an Bundeskanzler: Ihr Gespräch mit Yamani und Abdessalam. Zusammenfassung der Gespräche mit BM Friderichs und BM Eppler, 16.1.1974; GL II/1 an Bundeskanzler: Ihr Gespräch mit Yamani und Abdessalam. Zusammenfassung des Gesprächs mit StS Frank, 16.1.1974, BArch, B 136/6342.
149. AL II dem Herrn Bundeskanzler: Vermerk über das Gespräch des Bundeskanzlers mit dem algerischen Industrie- und Energieminister Abdessalam und dem saudi-arabischen Erdölminister Yamani am 16. Januar 1974 in Bonn, 17.1.1974, BArch, B 136/6342.
150. Martin E. Süskind, 'Feilschen mit arabischen Zwillingen', *Süddeutsche Zeitung*, 18 January 1974.
151. Niemöller: Sitzung der Arbeitsgemeinschaft Nahost des Politischen Komitees der EPZ am 18.1., 22.1., VS.Bd.9995, PA AA, B 150, 297.
152. Plurex: Schreiben von Scheel an Yamani und Abdessalam vom 30.11. [Wortlaut], 13.2., VS.Bd. 9989, PA AA, B 150, 298; Scheel an Yamani und Abdessalam, Nahost Situation, 12.2.1974, BArch, B 136/6342.
153. Fox Butterfield, 'Saudi Says Oil-Price Cut Must Be Joint Arab Step', *New York Times*, 29 January 1974.
154. Don Oberdorfer, 'Japanese Policy of Aid to Arabs Pays Off in Oil', *Washington Post*, 3 February 1974.
155. Crocker Snow, 'Wooing Saudi', *Boston Globe*, 9 February 1974.
156. Vertrauliche Aufzeichnung über den Besuch von Yamani und Abdessalam in Tokio, Ende Januar 1974, 11.2.1974, PA AA, B 36 (Referat 310), 104993; Graf, 'Making Use of the Oil Weapon'.
157. Herbert Hutar, Andreas Unterberger and Senta Ziegler, 'Lyrik zwischen Embargo und Ölpreis', *Die Presse*, 19 March 1974.
158. Ibid.

Chapter 4

THE POLITICS OF SOVEREIGNTY IN THE ENERGY CRISIS

The United States

When OPEC raised the oil price and OAPEC announced its regime of production and supply cuts in October 1973, the United States was less affected than the Western European countries. Its resilience was due to its still substantial domestic production, its low level of dependence on imports from the Arab world and the multinational oil companies' oil allocation system. Yet nowhere was the challenge to national sovereignty greater; forcing changes in US policy was the embargo's declared goal and the country was already facing an energy crisis. Furthermore, nowhere did an abundant flow of oil possess the same symbolic significance as in the homeland of the oil industry, where it had laid the foundation for prosperity, mass consumption and thus the American way of life. Within the fraught framework of the Cold War, every American president after the Second World War had promised to protect and foster this way of life. Since Franklin D. Roosevelt's presidency, meanwhile, the president's powers had been extended at the expense of Congress, a process perpetuated under Harry S. Truman with respect to foreign policy and then Lyndon B. Johnson on the domestic front.[1] As the presidency grew more powerful, Americans came to expect more of those elected to it and it received greater media attention and scrutiny. The president's path was strewn with snares that might ultimately erode his power – a trend reinforced by his growing role as moral role model and leader who must live up to the standards he himself had set.[2] During the oil crisis, Richard Nixon was already facing challenges to his authority as president as a result of the escalating Watergate scandal and media coverage of atrocities in Vietnam. The US had failed to win the war, global economic interdependencies were intensifying and the Nixon administration had suspended the Gold Standard. Western commentators no longer took US hegemony for granted as they had done just a few years before, and more openly discussed the future of national sovereignty and independence.[3]

Like the governments of other countries affected by the high oil prices and production cuts, the Nixon administration tried to enhance its ability to pursue an effective energy policy. At least equally important given the uncertainty caused by the oil crisis, it also sought to demonstrate this capacity to the US public and abroad. To secure legitimacy and sovereignty, the administration pursued four key strategies: centralization of power over energy policy; the development of governmental expertise on oil and energy; communication with the American public; and diplomatic communication with both the producing and other consuming countries. It was this process of the assertion of sovereignty that turned 'energy' into the autonomous policy field we know today. As set out in chapter 2, this process was preceded by the politicization of energy for several years prior to the oil crisis. It is vital to grasp this point if we want to understand the US government's reactions to the steps taken by OPEC and OAPEC in October 1973.

The Politicization of Energy and the Institutionalization of Energy Policy

The Energy Crisis before the Oil Crisis

The United States' energy supply problems did not begin with the oil crisis of 1973–74.[4] There had been major difficulties during the winter of the preceding year. In November 1972, the Joint Board on Fuel Supply and Fuel Transport described the supply situation as 'fair',[5] but it worsened over the following months due to unexpectedly cold weather in the Northeast and Midwest. In early March, when the city of Boston tried to find a contractor to supply it with petrol for its municipal vehicles from 1 April, not a single firm put in a bid. Its previous supplier, Mobil Oil, indicated that it would be unable to provide petrol even at a higher price.[6] Some regions had run out of petrol or heating oil; Maine and Virginia were suffering a lack of kerosene; and Iowa was low on natural gas and propane, which rapidly led to acute heating problems in many homes.[7] The anxious heads of agricultural cooperatives warned the relevant ministers that even if the nation faced a serious energy crisis, agriculture must have a secure supply of fuel if threats to food production were to be avoided.[8]

By January, George A. Lincoln, director of the Office of Emergency Preparedness, which oversaw the supply situation, had drawn President Nixon's attention to fuel problems in the Midwest. He warned of the risk of justified complaints and petitions from members of Congress, governors and communities.[9] Through appeals to industry and consumers, the Office tried to alleviate the supply bottlenecks. In a speech before the National Petroleum Council, Lincoln called for increased production: 'The administration expects an all-out effort from the oil industry to keep the nation warm this winter'.[10] He also called on the governors, mayors and local authorities to monitor the supply of energy and take remedial action in case of shortfalls. In addition to a catalogue of possible measures, the Office of Emergency Preparedness provided local authorities with concrete suggestions on energy saving. The cover of the *Outline Plan for Energy Conservation by State Local Facilities* featured a humanoid thermometer showing zero, wrapped in a scarf and folding its arms against the cold. The *Plan* stated: 'Our nation is now consuming more gas and oil than it produces, making us dependent upon foreign countries for these energy supplies'.[11] This publication underlined that it was imperative to save energy, and that it was especially incumbent on public authorities and institutions to set a good example. Richard Fairbanks, deputy director of the Domestic Council, forecast that in some areas petrol supplies might reach critical levels in the summer: 'We are faced with potential breakdown of our traditional supply and distribution systems in a few key areas in the domestic energy market over the next nine months'.[12]

As indicated in chapter 2, the problems afflicting the US energy supply were the result of the dramatic increase in energy and oil consumption in the preceding years, with which domestic energy production and the exploitation of oil reserves had failed to keep pace. Again and again in the 1950s and 1960s the rise in oil consumption outstripped forecasts. As late as February 1970, Nixon's Task Force on Oil Imports estimated that, in view of consumption growth, by 1980 the United States would have to import five million barrels of oil a day. In fact, oil imports had already exceeded six million barrels a day by 1973.[13] Oil production in the contiguous United States not only failed to keep pace with these consumption increases, but reached its peak in the early 1970s, as Marion King Hubbert had predicted in the late 1950s. Furthermore, the combination of the domestic regulation of production through the Texas Railroad Commission and oil import controls had hampered the development of the energy infrastructure. Only when import controls had been eliminated was there a surge in the construction of new refineries, but this took time.[14] The energy market, moreover, did not develop autonomously. Through the economic stabilization programme of August 1971, Nixon not only abandoned the

Gold Standard but also introduced wage and price controls. The oil market was therefore highly regulated. It was not until the Carter administration that price controls for oil products were removed.[15]

One of the results of this set of interventions was that the small refineries in the middle of the country, which did not belong to the big oil companies, received no more crude oil for processing.[16] Under the import quota system, these independents, which had no access to the world market, had sold their import licences to the majors, the multinational and vertically integrated oil companies. In return, the latter supplied them with oil, making a profit out of the difference between the price in the United States and on the world market. When this difference diminished as a result of OPEC price increases while the price in the United States could not rise, the majors lost interest in this procedure, as diagnosed by Nixon's energy advisor Charles DiBona.[17] He thus considered it difficult to estimate how large the oil shortage actually was: 'It is not clear from the evidence in the memo whether we have a serious emerging overall shortage or whether there are serious local shortages developing (especially for small refineries and their customers in the Midwest) [continues in longhand:] or whether it is a "crisis" at all in either area'.[18] DiBona, too, saw the existing oil supply situation in the United States as beset by major uncertainty. The Office of Emergency Preparedness was just as anxious about the future, concluding that there would be a need for highly professional, day-to-day management for some time to come.[19]

The supply situation had not improved by the spring or summer of 1973 and it became a key topic of domestic politics. In March and April, the *St. Louis Post-Dispatch* published a series of articles on the 'Crisis in Energy' with dramatic-sounding titles: 'Major Energy Crunch Lies Ahead', 'Petroleum Industry Lags in Finding New Oil and Gas', 'Southern California Facing Energy Crisis', 'Oil Industry Calls for Help To Meet US Energy Demands' and 'Dwindling Fuel Supplies May Alter US Lifestyle'.[20] In mid May, *Time Magazine* reported that almost two thousand petrol stations throughout the country had either run out of petrol entirely or could operate only on an ad hoc basis depending on deliveries.[21] Particularly at the start of the holiday season, when millions of Americans normally made trips, often of several thousand miles, the nation found itself confronted, according to the *Financial Times*, with the first real 'energy crisis' in its history.[22] While the government tried to avoid the rhetoric of crisis, it was on everyone's lips in the summer of 1973. In a Gallup survey of June that year, 83 per cent of respondents stated that they had heard about the energy crisis, and 51 per cent supported lowering the maximum speed limit on motorways to save petrol.[23] Contrary to what is often implied,[24] all this occurred before the beginning of the true oil crisis in October 1973. Even in the winter of

1972–73, the basic problem of energy supply was anything but new or surprising to the American public. By January 1972, staff of the Committee on Interior and Insular Affairs had collated more than seventy articles from magazines and newspapers from 1970 and 1971, with titles such as 'The Coming Power Crisis', 'A Crisis in Fossil Fuels', 'National Energy Crisis' and 'Man Made Fuel Crisis', which diagnosed energy supply problems and made gloomy predictions about future energy security.[25] Committee chair Wayne N. Aspinall painted a desolate picture: the electricity supply was unstable, leading to brownouts and blackouts; coal deliveries were inadequate, while gas was virtually rationed in many parts of the country; there was a shortage of petrol and heating oil on the regional level; the country was increasingly dependent on OPEC for its oil; and so far nuclear energy had failed to live up to its promise. All of this posed serious risks to the economic, political and social order of the United States:

> A country that has developed and grown because of abundant and economic fuel and energy resources today faces the prospect of crippling shortages, rising costs, dependence on foreign sources of supply, and resulting industrial and social chaos unless the problem is understood and dealt with effectively. The strength and efficient operation of our economy, our standard of living, and our national and political security are all dependent on a continuous and adequate flow of environmentally acceptable energy fuels.[26]

In light of brownouts, oil supply shortfalls and rising prices, by August 1970 Richard Nixon had already set up a Committee of the Domestic Council to Study the National Energy Situation. On 4 June 1971, he delivered a speech on energy policy before Congress based on its report.[27] As he himself underlined, this made him the first US president to devote an entire speech to the topic of energy and to call for the development of a comprehensive energy programme.[28] A year after the National Environmental Protection Act had been passed, this speech was written with much input from David Freeman who then worked at the White House's Office of Science and Technology. The speech evoked the dual challenge of solving the energy problem while also protecting the environment, because 'a sufficient supply of clean energy is essential if we are to sustain healthy economic growth and improve the quality of our national life'.[29] While it would be mainly down to industry to achieve this goal, Nixon saw a need for state action in several areas. Research and development on alternative energies, above all nuclear power and coal gasification, must be facilitated and fostered, oil production must be allowed on the Outer Continental Shelf and other federal territories, while construction of nuclear power stations must be speeded up, sulphur dioxide emissions reduced and energy used 'more wisely'. In addition to these energy policy steps, changes must also be made on the administrative level. Because new institutions had been created to deal with each new energy source, the president stated, energy policy competencies were now fragmented. To effectively pursue an energy policy, what was needed was 'a single agency which can execute and modify policies in a comprehensive and unified manner'.[30] Prior to the establishment of such a Department of Natural Resources, the Energy Subcommittee of the Domestic Council was to coordinate energy policy. Energy was now defined more clearly as an autonomous policy field that could not be tackled by a range of different institutions devoted to its separate aspects.

Institutional Restructuring

In early 1973, the reorganization and centralization of energy policy announced by Nixon picked up pace, influencing how the US government acted, and was able to act, in the oil crisis.[31] Nixon himself repeatedly intervened in this process of change. While his agency was circumscribed by the mounting Watergate scandal, which broke in 1973, and his moral authority was publicly questioned, energy policy was a field in which he tried to demonstrate his capacity for effective action and sought to restore his authority.[32] Nixon's approach stood to reason in that the reorganization of energy policy was considered necessary beyond the walls of the White House. The National Science Foundation had called for action on this front as early as 1971, as had the State Department in 1972.[33] In addition, in a widely circulated letter of June 1972, Democratic senator Henry M. Jackson had urged Nixon to come up with a coherent energy strategy in view of the high degree of US dependence on Middle Eastern oil. Jackson contended that the powers over energy currently distributed across the Departments of Defense, State and the Interior as well as the Federal Power Commission, Office of Emergency Preparedness and Energy Policy Subcommittee of the Domestic Council must be brought together in a single authority.[34] The analysis prepared by the Committee on Interior and Insular Affairs, commissioned by Jackson, came to the same conclusion: 'There has never been, nor is there now, a national energy policy in any meaningful sense. Rather, the Federal Government pursues uncoordinated and complex national security; research and development; water, land, and mineral resources; environmental, health and safety, and economic policies which as a byproduct have profound energy consequences'.[35] According to the report, this structure was one of the root causes of the energy crisis.

Proposals on the centralization of energy policy came from all quarters. Following a trip to study other countries' energy policies, Republican congressman Keith Hastings proposed the establishment of a Council on Energy Policy to coordinate this policy field over the short, medium and long term. In late 1972, the National Petroleum Council, in which oil industry representatives advised the government, also underlined the need 'to develop a comprehensive national energy policy and a coordinated, consistent program to accomplish national energy goals'.[36] In May 1973, when the Senate Committee on Foreign Relations, chaired by James William Fulbright, studied the implications of the energy problem for American foreign policy, this demand cropped up once again. Senators repeatedly asked who was responsible for energy policy on the national level, and suggested that it would be better coordinated higher up the chain of government.[37] State Department oil expert James Akins openly admitted that the current division of responsibilities was far from optimal.

Within public debate, the unstructured nature of energy policy was linked directly with the Watergate scandal. One commentator in the *Washington Post* opined that while Nixon was preoccupied with Watergate, consumers were getting the impression that the management of the supply shortfalls was being left to second-rank government staff who lacked the requisite competencies. For him, there were fundamental doubts as to the government's capacity to take effective action: 'Politics is the business of responding to this kind of public anxiety. The ability to respond is the ability to govern, and that is the element now falling into doubt'.[38] From the outset, then, the Nixon administration sought to do more than merely cope with the challenges of energy policy – it tried to use them to demonstrate its overall efficacy.[39] During the Senate hearings of May 1973, the restructuring of energy policy responsibilities was already underway. Partly in anticipation of legislative initiatives by Congress, Charles DiBona – who had studied economics at Oxford as a Rhodes Scholar after graduating from the US Naval Academy – was appointed Nixon's Special Assistant on Energy, with a staff of six, in February 1973.[40] In parallel to this, James Akins, Nixon's 'de facto energy advisor' in the White House, had already been drawing up an energy programme since November 1972. In May 1973, however, when his conclusions proved unpopular, Akins was sent back to the State Department, and he was later appointed ambassador to Saudi Arabia.[41] DiBona was tasked with advising the president on all energy policy matters and also with coordinating the work of the National Energy Office, established on 18 April 1973; its leading members included John D. Ehrlichman, one of Nixon's key advisors, Henry A. Kissinger, the national security adviser, and Treasury Secretary George P. Shultz, who was in overall charge of finance, economic and international economic policies. The task of the National Energy Office was to coordinate the activities of the various government agencies and develop a comprehensive energy strategy.⁴² Ehrlichman was occupied with Watergate, however, and was soon dismissed in the wake of the developing scandal; Kissinger had very little interest in energy issues; and even Shultz delegated the topic, so there was soon a need for a new wave of restructuring.⁴³

Just over two months later, on 29 June 1973, the National Energy Office had already been replaced by the Energy Policy Office, now headed by John A. Love, former Republican governor of Colorado, whom Nixon introduced to the American public as the 'energy czar'.⁴⁴ In the United States, the term 'czar' was used to describe government appointees endowed with virtually unlimited powers over a particular policy field. Previously, 'czars' had mostly been appointed in wartime. That Nixon now drew on this conceptual tradition reflects the scale of the challenge he wanted to convey to the nation. Along with his deputy Charles DiBona and a small team of staff, through the Energy Policy Office Love took over not only the energy-related responsibilities formerly held by the National Energy Office but also those of various ministries such as the Departments of Interior, Agriculture and Commerce, the Army Corps of Engineers and other agencies. Nixon justified this new round of restructuring by asserting that 'the acquisition, distribution, and consumption of energy resources have become increasingly complex and increasingly critical to the functioning of our economy and our society'.⁴⁵ The Energy Policy Office was to take account of this and centralize the government's energy-related competencies at the highest level.⁴⁶ Love and the Energy Policy Office were responsible for dealing with the consequences of the oil embargo and oil price increases, so they started out in the public spotlight.

When the decision taken by OPEC and OAPEC in mid October 1973 made oil a key focus of international politics and national security, in addition to the cabinet the National Security Council was involved in formulating US energy policy. Meetings of the ancillary Senior Review Group and the more implementation-focused Washington Special Actions Group discussed reports by the Energy Policy Office, with Love and DiBona in attendance as appropriate. In addition, an interministerial Emergency Energy Action Group was established in mid November, during the crisis, when the existing structures of the Energy Policy Office no longer seemed capable of producing crisis response strategies.⁴⁷ This body, however, largely bypassed Love. This epitomized the decentralization process of 1973, in which responsibilities and powers overlapped and were marked by a pronounced lack of clarity.

To advance long-term reorganization, plans had already been drawn up for a Department of Energy and Natural Resources. To support the National Energy Office, three divisions had been established within the Department of the Interior, which were dedicated to data collection, energy saving, and research and development: the Office of Energy Data and Analysis, the Office of Energy Conservation and the Office of Research and Development, with a total of thirty-four staff.[48] Initially, the Oil Committee, in which the secretaries of state, interior, defense and commerce, together with the chairs of the Councils of Economic Advisers, had supervised the oil import control programme, continued to exist. At almost the same time as DiBona's appointment as Nixon's energy advisor, it received a new head in the shape of William E. Simon. The latter had become Shultz's deputy at the Treasury Department only in January 1973, which now had responsibility for the oil import controls emanating from the Office of Emergency Preparedness.[49] Previously, Simon had been a senior partner at Salomon Brothers, where his work had not involved oil or energy policy, as he candidly conceded on the occasion of his appointment.[50] In order to acquire the necessary expertise, he established an informal working group consisting of State Department energy expert James Akins; Peter Flanigan and Stephen Wakefield from the Department of the Interior, Duke Ligon and William Johnson from the Treasury Department and Jack Bennett, who worked for Exxon.[51] Equipped with their knowledge and evidently keen to lead and make a public impact, over the next few months Simon rose to become one of the key figures in US oil policy; his ascent then accelerated within the framework of the Energy Emergency Action Group.[52]

These overlapping competences, the blurry division of responsibilities, and diverging views on how much state intervention was required with respect to energy, led to conflicts between Shultz and Simon on one side and Love and DiBona on the other.[53] In early December 1973, when Simon was provided with his own administrative apparatus, Love and DiBona resigned from their posts.[54] Simon was put in charge of the Federal Energy Office, which now replaced the Energy Policy Office as hub for the formulation of energy policy and was endowed with significantly greater powers and resources.[55] Nixon felt that Simon would make a better, more effective energy czar: 'I told the Emergency Energy group yesterday that Bill Simon is a hardcharger, as rough and tough as they come, and that's just the way I want him to be. He may be the first czar to survive a revolution'.[56] In a cabinet meeting, Nixon supposedly went so far as to compare the powers Simon now enjoyed with those of Albert Speer as minister for armaments and ammunition during the Third Reich.[57] Shortly before, Nixon had emphasized that he was personally and regularly involved in the work of his energy advisers and that this would continue so he could quickly and effectively implement the measures needed to overcome the energy crisis.[58]

Nixon identified the reason for this restructuring as the worsening energy situation caused by the oil embargo. In addition to its 'policy-making role', the government must now intervene directly in 'operational matters'.[59] It could do this on the basis of the Emergency Petroleum Allocation Act, quickly passed and signed in late November with cross-party consent. By April 1973, shortly after the oil import restrictions had been eliminated and replaced by a taxation system, the government had already instructed the oil firms to supply their products on the same scale as the previous year, initially to certain priority customers such as farmers, food manufacturers, health services and the police.[60] The Emergency Petroleum Allocation Act turned a voluntary allocation system into a compulsory, complex system of oil distribution intended to ensure access to oil products for end users and independent market players.[61] The allocations were to be made on the basis of 1972 consumption levels, meaning reductions for almost all market participants. Paradoxically, none other than William Simon – who projected an image of himself as anti-bureaucrat and the quintessential economic liberal in his later autobiographical writings, and actively disseminated free market ideas through the Olin Foundation – called for a compulsory allocation system, which he sought to distinguish rhetorically from rationing.[62] To determine the allocations, a vast bureaucracy was necessary. This Simon built up with lightning speed. Nonetheless, it came to grief due to the complexity of the task, so that – in combination with price controls – the allocation regime tended to worsen rather than alleviate supply problems.

Right from the start, the Federal Energy Office was conceived as a stopgap solution that would be required only until the establishment of a Department of Energy and Natural Resources. In addition to administering the allocation system, Simon and his deputy John Sawhill – an economist previously responsible for natural resources, energy and science at the Office of Management and Budget – were also tasked with gathering data on the United States' short- and long-term energy supply.[63] The Federal Energy Office not only took over the work previously done by the energy divisions in the Department of the Interior, the Cost of Living Councils and other agencies, but also absorbed select members of staff.[64] Under Simon's leadership, by January the agency had grown to include around one hundred employees. The in-house view was that, including subordinate regional offices, it should eventually have well over a thousand.[65] Nonetheless, there continued to be areas of overlapping authority, even after the Federal Energy Administration replaced the Federal Energy Office in June 1974, taking over its responsibilities, personnel and equipment, and the Oil Committee was abolished.[66] A Committee on Energy was thus established on the ministerial level to divide responsibility between the Federal Energy Administration, the Energy Research and Development Administration (also newly established) and the energy divisions in the Departments of the Interior, State and the Treasury, and to lay down the basic structures of energy policy.[67] The committee was headed by Simon, now elevated to the post of treasury secretary, while his former deputy John Sawhill was put in charge of the Federal Energy Administration.[68] In November, Simon's former colleague, Frank Zarb, took over the leadership. The restructuring process only came to an end with the creation of the Department of Energy by Jimmy Carter, though even this failed to unite all energy-related powers.

Within just one year, the framework of US policymaking on energy had changed fundamentally. Until 1973, the staff of ministries and agencies had been responsible for energy issues in different contexts, as determined by the various energy sources. But acute supply problems and growing oil imports engendered the perception of an energy crisis, one that could seemingly be dealt with only by a central institution endowed with a wider range of powers. In particular, price controls and the allocation system triggered a surge of bureaucratization that in turn necessitated ever greater state intervention.[69] The rapid name changes, the restructuring, and the transfer and overlap of powers during 1973–74 attest to the flurry of activity through which the White House sought to get a handle on the energy crisis – and this is corroborated by interviews with staff at the Federal Energy Office.[70] The degree of confusion in the administration is evident in the fact that while the Energy Policy Office was stripped of all responsibilities after the resignation of Love and DiBona – with the exception that its director was to head the now defunct Oil Committee – it continued to exist, with four staff members and seven secretaries. It was not until February 1974 that the Office of Management and Budget and White House administrative staff noticed that the leaderless and defunct unit was still there, when a member of staff applied for promotion. Dave Hoopes, adviser to Nixon and responsible for White House administration, was immediately asked to remedy this as rapidly as possible: 'Governor Love and all the senior staff left or have been transferred from EPO, but technically the office is still alive and, in fact, eleven people are carried on its payroll, plus about 6 consultants. . . . I believe that these actions should be taken as quickly as possible to avoid any further embarrassment caused by the expenditure of government funds by an agency that has ceased to function and has no designated head'.[71] But it was to be another month before the Energy Policy Office was finally disbanded, on 26 March 1974. Apparently, its staff still had time to organize its correspondence, neatly filing away thousands of letters received during the first few months of the oil crisis.[72]

Petro-Knowledge: On the Reduction and Production of Uncertainty

On 1 October 1973, against the background of intense debate on the energy crisis, the editors of the *Oil and Gas Journal* came to the conclusion that by now all influential figures in government, Congress and industry ought to be familiar with the basic realities of the US energy problem.[73] Nine days later, however, it emerged that this was not the case. Energy czar John Love, chair of the Atomic Energy Commission Dixy Lee Ray, director of the National Science Foundation H. Guyford Stever, and William T. McCormick, secretary of the advisory committee on research and development in the Energy Policy Office, held a press conference on the ten billion dollar programme of investment in energy-related research and development announced by President Nixon. When asked, none of them could say how much of the oil consumed in the United States came from the Middle East. An incredulous journalist broached the subject again: 'Can someone tell us what share, first of oil, and secondly of energy use as a whole, comes from Middle Eastern oil?' Silence reigned once again until Guyford Stever admitted: 'No, I do not know exactly'.[74] Just a week before the start of the oil embargo, even key figures in US energy policy were clearly unaware of basic facts about the oil and energy supply. This is likely to have changed over the next few weeks. The embargo generated an 'urgency for data' that was considered vital to reducing the uncertainty caused by OPEC and OAPEC and to pursuing a competent energy policy.[75] As a result, state and nonstate expert bodies vied to provide the information on energy policy needed to make decisions. But three factors placed strict limits on this project, namely contingency, structural problems of information and clashing forms of expertise.

The decision made by OPEC and OAPEC in mid October 1973, which destroyed entrenched communicative and interactional routines, threw up a number of imponderables. How severe would the production cutbacks be? Five per cent was just the minimum cut required, while it soon became clear that some countries were secretly willing to supply more oil.[76] Would it be possible for the producing countries to enforce the restrictions and embargo rules in a highly targeted way or would the oil companies manage to evenly distribute the smaller quantity of available oil? Under what conditions – other than the publicly declared ones – would the producing countries revoke their production cuts? 'We have no idea yet just how much crude oil and product will be denied us by Arab action and the aftereffects of the war', concluded the generally well-informed *Oil and Gas Journal* in late October 1973.[77] Other factors of importance to policymaking on energy were also unclear. Given the oil tankers' often long travel times, at what point would the restrictions hit home, and where? How harsh would the winter be, and how much energy would be saved by voluntary and compulsory measures? There were no simple, clear-cut answers to any of these crucial questions. Contingent and characterized by a high degree of uncertainty, they opened up broad scope for speculation and heated debate.

As set out earlier, powers over energy policy were split between a number of mid-level government bodies. In 1973, the United States lacked a central institution that could have collected and competently analysed relevant data.[78] The oil firms reported monthly to the American Petroleum Institute, which they had founded, on imports and refinery activity. But after the majors had been accused – even before the embargo – of orchestrating the energy crisis to enhance their own market position, the API's figures were increasingly viewed as unreliable. The United States' lack of an independent system of energy reporting began to seem scandalous. In early December, CBS reported that the government was relying entirely on the data provided by industry. The report contrasted the firms' assurances that they were releasing all relevant information with the news that in California Exxon, Mobil and Union Oil were suing a state committee that was trying to compel them to disclose data.[79] This loss of trust in industry-provided data led to the introduction of obligatory reporting for firms and an attempt to develop a reporting system within the Federal Energy Office. According to Simon, 'As I've said on many occasions, this is the most – probably the greatest imperfection. For years there was a totally inadequate reporting system in the petroleum industry'.[80] The Federal Energy Office thus duplicated the API's data collection, but soon stopped again as its figures differed only marginally from those of the latter.[81] Furthermore, doubts were already being raised as to whether it was even possible to achieve accurate and complete energy reporting on which the government could then base its policy response to the crisis. The *Washington Post*, for example, argued that the collation of import, distribution and consumption data was so complicated that figures were soon out of date: 'The biggest mistake that anyone could make, in oil policy, is to assume that he has accurate and complete figures on fuel supply and demand. The second biggest mistake is to assume that anybody else has accurate and current figures'.[82]

The Department of the Interior and Federal Energy Office tried to remedy informational shortcomings and the resulting uncertainty by publishing a weekly *Petroleum Situation Report*. This provided detailed reports on the supply situation and estimated the prospective import reductions and falls in consumption. But the impact of these efforts was the opposite of that intended.[83] Due to the mass of confusing data, these estimates changed rapidly and thus tended to increase rather than decrease uncertainty. For the *Washington Post*, these reports were in any case '90 per cent hokum and 10 per cent best wishes for the New Year'. Simon conceded self-critically: 'Maybe we have just been a little too ambitious in our desire to attempt to settle all the facts in front of you in these days of credibility crises and problems. And the result has been some confusion'.[84] Adding to the confusion, other government agencies and energy experts also made statements about the supply situation, throwing up a whole range of different figures. The attempt to legitimize policy by anchoring it in accurate data was thrown into turmoil when the data itself proved contradictory.

On 14 December 1973, Henry M. Jackson opened the hearings of the Senate Committee on Government Operations, which aimed to determine the scale of the supply shortfalls and evaluate the government's response. Jackson began by stating that far from being well informed, the public was confused by contradictory information. Senators such as Abraham Ribicoff, a Democrat from Connecticut, told of distraught voters and journalists in their constituencies who were no longer sure which information they could trust.[85] When John Sawhill testified before the committee that the oil deficit would amount to 3.27 million barrels a day in the first quarter of 1974, Jackson exposed the government's polyphony. Since early October, he declared, various government agencies had produced supply shortage estimates of between 1.6 and 3.27 million barrels of oil a day: 'Do you feel now that you have any more accurate means of making these estimates than we had earlier?'[86] If the supply shortages themselves were hard to predict, this applied even more to their effects on the US economy. Herbert Stein of the Council of Economic Advisers candidly admitted that his calculation that the embargo would increase unemployment by between 0.3 and 0.6 per cent, was 'a very speculative and "iffy" thing'.[87]

Despite tremendous efforts, it proved impossible to make good on the aspiration of formulating policy on a firm scientific foundation. In fact, the sense of confusion deepened, fuelling conspiracy theories that the oil firms had orchestrated the supply problems. Surveys showed that few Americans blamed the Arab countries for their problems, with far more identifying the government or oil firms as the culprit.[88] Convening the committee tasked with investigating the conduct of the international oil companies, Henry M. Jackson alluded to these theories while recapitulating the need to anchor effective energy policy in accurate data:

> We meet here this morning in an effort to get the facts about the energy crisis. The facts are – we do not have the facts. We are not here to get anyone. We are here to get the facts so that Congress can legislate effectively. The American people want to know if there is an oil shortage. The American people want to know why the prices of home heating oil and gasoline have doubled when the companies report record high inventories of these stocks. The American people want to know whether oil tankers are anchored offshore waiting for a price increase or available storage before they unload. The American people want to know whether major oil companies are sitting on shut-in wells and hoarding production in hidden tanks and at abandoned service stations.[89]

Time and again the meetings of the investigative committee reinforced awareness of a problem it could do nothing to resolve. After three days of testimony from the oil companies, Jackson concluded that neither the government nor anyone else had reliable data on oil reserves, stocks, consumption or imports.[90] In the Senate hearings, the Democrat Jackson, who had presidential ambitions himself, may have been less concerned with tackling the energy crisis than with making the Nixon administration look incompetent and ineffective.[91] Despite this political interest, however, his assessments of the informational situation cannot be dismissed out of hand. At the very least, they reflect a widespread public sentiment.

Due to a widely shared scientized conception of policy, during the oil crisis missing or contradictory information on energy caused many to question the government's sovereignty and legitimacy. Experts within and outside the administration were keen to help out. Indeed, the government considered their input vital, envisaging that they would collect and analyse the necessary data and estimate future trends in order to facilitate a competent energy policy. Consultation with experts, the administration believed, would enhance its ability to take effective action, while at the same time demonstrating publicly that it was acting on the best possible informational basis. But this strategy was largely unsuccessful, in significant part because the experts' petro-knowledge was bound up with their particular disciplines, heterogeneous and contradictory. At most, they could agree on the fact that there was a problem with the oil and energy supply, and perhaps on its scale. But when it came to the question of how it had come about or might be remedied, their views diverged greatly.

Causal Analysis: Geology, Economy and Politics

Petro-knowledge was produced chiefly by three groups of experts, most of whom worked in the oil industry or science, but also in government agencies. Petroleum geologists and petroleum engineers in industry, at universities and at the US Geological Survey had spent more time than anyone else attempting to determine where oil might be found, in what quantity, and how it might be extracted and used.[92] Due to oil's growing economic importance, however, economists too increasingly explored the special problems of resource management, which they sought to elucidate via general economic principles of supply, demand and price. In the 1970s, social and political scientists also began to offer specialist knowledge for policymaking on oil and energy. They maintained that political and social questions about the organization of society were crucial to the level of energy consumption. Given the increasing relevance of the Middle East as a producing region and the growing strength of OPEC and OAPEC, political factors also seemed more and more important to securing the energy supply.

The three groups of experts viewed the future availability of oil from very different disciplinary standpoints. They thus produced heterogeneous forms of petro-knowledge that were only partially compatible and suggested different economic and political strategies. This applied above all to the question of whether the oil crisis was underpinned by a genuine scarcity of this natural resource – at present or likely in the near future – or whether it had merely been generated by a producer cartel while oil was actually available in sufficient quantities.[93] The supposition of scarcity would mean that it was vital to use oil sparingly and embrace other energy sources over the medium term. Conversely, if one assumed that physical realities would place no limits on oil consumption in the foreseeable future, and that the difficulties were due solely to interventions in the oil market by the US government, or by OPEC and OAPEC, the imperative was to pursue economic or political countermeasures. Energy experts within and outside the administration disagreed on these issues. In the conflict over the purpose of US energy policy, this disagreement was, and is still, central to a vigorous debate.

Geologists and engineers were not only the actors most concretely involved in determining the availability of oil. For a long time, they had been just about the only experts who had made competent statements on the topic. Over the course of the twentieth century, they had succeeded in finding and exploiting new oil deposits. This caused oil reserves and oil production to grow steadily across the world, while oil became increasingly important to the functioning of modern industrial societies. Their success had generated a pronounced professional consciousness in the 1960s.[94] But they found themselves on the defensive when oil production in the United States peaked in the early 1970s. A growing environmental awareness began to cast doubt on the wisdom of burning fossil fuels and their career prospects seemed less rosy.[95] Geologists faced a new situation. On the one hand, their expert insights into the exploitation of new oil reserves seemed more important than ever during the energy crisis. On the other hand, an ever larger number of eloquent experts, without proven geological knowledge, were asserting themselves as providers of energy-related expertise. Certainly, government spokesmen addressed conferences of geologists and engineers, underlining their indispensable role in securing the energy supply. 'You will have to act as guides in some of the most important aspects of our approach to the energy challenge. It is now up to you geologists to find the resources that are as yet undiscovered or undeveloped. Those of you who are petroleum engineers must find new and better ways to produce the fuels we need', declared Charles DiBona in May 1973 to a gathering of petroleum engineers. He continued the flattery by reassuring his audience that when it came to energy matters, too many 'simplifiers' were currently putting in their two pennies' worth, and it was crucial that this be countered by engineers, who were by nature 'complexifiers'.[96] However, most of the key posts in energy policymaking in the White House and the ministries were occupied by economists. Along with political and social scientists, they increasingly dominated the public discourse on oil and energy issues.

This shift in discursive hegemony due to the politicization and economization of oil was noted in the American Association of Petroleum Geologists. Its presidents called on geologists to do more to project their expertise into the public sphere. They must gen up on the international scene, rather than focusing solely on their work on oil deposits.[97] In April 1974, Merrill W. Haas called for the government to withdraw from energy policy and leave the field to the oil companies and thus to the geologists and engineers. A robust energy policy, he contended, was achievable only on the basis of correct geological data. Geologists must therefore play a more important role not just in the production of resources, but also in the formulation of energy policy.[98] The US Geological Survey welcomed the increased interest in raw material reserves, but lamented the economization of the public and political debate on this core field of geology:

> The almost universal tendency ... is to discuss mineral resources principally from the perspective of economic availability under a given set of circumstances, thereby overlooking the vital fact that reserves are but a part of resources. The results are, we feel, disturbing. Evaluations predicated only on knowledge (or estimates) of current reserves can easily lead to forecasts of the death of the industrial society in a short time. On the other hand, evaluations based on another kind of assumption suggest that a rise in prices will increase the reserves and bring much more material to market economically ... This reasoning too is fallacious because elements are available in the earth's crust in very finite amounts. But in both instances, the reasoning leads to serious misinterpretations because it does not give adequate consideration to the single factor that ultimately determines all levels and degrees of mineral potential: geologic availability.[99]

On this view, then, geological expertise was indispensable to economic and political action, because there could be no economic availability without geological availability.[100]

Faced with studies such as the report commissioned by the Club of Rome, the US Geological Survey tried to shape public discourse and familiarize a broad swathe of the American citizenry with the geological realities of commodity production. This project never had much chance of success. In this specific case, its product was a large-format volume consisting of seventy articles. Over more than seven hundred closely printed pages, featuring a large number of graphs and statistics, this volume provided information on production trends and estimated the reserves of the most important natural resources.[101] Even the introduction was unable to boil this mixed batch of contributions down to a workable set of clear-cut propositions. Its public impact was therefore substantially less than that of texts produced by non-geological energy experts. Economists, political scientists and social scientists repudiated an overly materialistic view of oil reserves, a perspective they ascribed, among others, to geologists. They claimed that it was not the quantity of oil available in the earth that was the key variable for policymaking on energy. Instead, what mattered was its future availability at a specific price.[102] This in turn depended not primarily on the physical quantity but on production costs, demand trends, available alternative energy sources and even political developments.

Apart from the geological quantity of oil, how different actors interpreted the oil crisis and its lessons depended on whether they believed the future availability of oil was determined essentially by political factors or by economic processes. The antithetical nature of these perspectives was evident at the time in the conflict between State Department oil expert James Akins and the influential, eloquent MIT economist Morris Adelman.[103] While the views of neither were capable of attracting majority support among policymakers, they represented the two poles within the political debate on the future availability of oil. They were therefore important reference points in the discussion of energy strategies. Akins is often viewed as a figure who gave early warning of the risk of an oil embargo, but whose policy proposals were marginalized.[104] Adelman, in contrast, was not involved in making energy policy, but his often controversial and radical analyses influenced the energy-focused economists within the administration, such as Charles DiBona, and he was frequently invited to hearings on energy policy.[105]

Akins' first key assumption was that worldwide oil reserves would diminish, while consumption would rise. Second, in view of conditions in the Middle East and the strength of OPEC, he believed political factors would determine the future availability of oil. By 1972, in an article for the *Journal of Petroleum Technology*, he had already declared that the energy crisis marked the end of the brief era of cheap, hydrocarbon-based energy. Just like the Western world's growing dependency on oil supplies from the Middle East, he asserted, this was being overlooked both by scientists and politicians, who displayed astonishing ignorance of current political developments.[106] In a speech to the Institute of Gas Technology in November 1972, Akins was even more blunt, declaring that 'only a few disgruntled and by now largely discredited academics still maintain that supplies of hydrocarbons are nearly infinite; that competition will bring down prices world wide and that there can never be a danger of restriction in supplies for economic or political reasons'.[107]

Akins produced an internal memorandum warning of the risk of an embargo and calling for a fundamental change of course in oil and energy policy. In early 1973, he addressed the foreign policy elite with essays published in *Foreign Affairs* and the *Annals of the American Academy of Political and Social Science*. Akins contended that, according to the present state of knowledge, physical oil reserves would last only until the mid 1980s. Even for this period, it was not just the quantity of geological reserves and production costs that were key to the availability of oil because oil was distributed unevenly across the world.[108] The largest share of reserves was in the OPEC countries, who had now understood that even these were exhaustible. They were beginning to gear their production policies towards the higher price they would be able to charge for their oil in future. Particularly in light of the Middle East conflict, he went on, it was impossible to foresee whether the Arab producing countries would continue to increase their production in accordance with Western consumption or would restrict it: 'In the last analysis, whether Saudi Arabia or any other OPEC country with large reserves would act to disrupt the market is a question of the behavior of men in control of national governments, affected by political factors as much as by theoretical economics'.[109]

Akins worked on the assumption that the oil price would rise because of shifts in Arab producing policies. In fact, he welcomed this development due to his fundamental supposition of scarcity. In a speech to the American Petroleum Institute in April 1973, he declared that the generally accepted view – that competition between OPEC countries would push the oil price down – was wrong, and that in fact a lower price was not even desirable.[110] 'The world must have the supply of energy it needs, and the supply of hydrocarbons must rise to meet the demand until alternative sources of energy are available. Hydrocarbon prices must be allowed to rise, but not to exceed substantially the cost of alternative sources'.[111] In order to achieve this difficult goal, the government must pursue a more active energy policy. Above all, it must strive to improve international cooperation between consuming and producing countries.

Just as Akins opposed a view he claimed was accepted 'almost universally as a revealed truth', namely that the oil price would fall due to differences within OPEC, in his publications Morris Adelman also liked to pose as an outsider. His 1972 study, *The World Petroleum Market*, thus began: 'The official truth in the capitalist, communist, and third world is that crude oil is becoming ever more scarce, special measures are needed to assure its provision, and prices will rise. But the conclusions of this study are that crude oil prices will decline because supply will far exceed demand even at lower prices, and because – a separate issue – there will continue to be enough competition to make price gravitate toward cost, however slowly'.[112] Evidently, in the early 1970s the discourse on the future of the oil supply and the oil price was so broad and heterogeneous that both opponents and exponents of the thesis of scarcity could claim to be swimming against the tide.

Adelman soon had to acknowledge the falsification of his forecast – derived from economic principles – that the oil price would fall until it reached a level close to production costs. But he rubbished the idea that the price increase or production cutbacks could be put down to any genuine scarcity of oil. 'The world "energy crisis" or "energy shortage" is a fiction', as he never tired of repeating, 'but belief in the fiction is a fact'.[113] The US government, he contended, apparently believed the energy shortage fiction, which explained its support for the producers' cartel – aided and abetted by the major oil companies – in their drive to push up prices. Here Adelman launched an all-out attack on Akins: 'The most important player in the game is the American State Department. This agency is deplorably poorly informed in mineral resource economics, the oil industry, the history of oil crises and the participation therein of Arabs with whom it is obsessed'.[114] He claimed that it was the constant talk of steep increases in US oil consumption and future energy scarcity that gave the Arab producing countries the idea of cutting production and raising the oil price. Ultimately, the belief that oil was becoming more scarce and that prices would rise had been a self-fulfilling prophecy.[115] For Adelman, price increase was no indicator of scarcity but was due solely to the conduct of the cartel. This was pursuing economic rather than political interests. As Adelman asserted again in 1975 at Senate hearings on the political and financial consequences of the oil price increase – much to the senators' joy – economic principles were sufficient to understand the oil crisis:

> High world prices are due neither to scarcity, nor politics, but to the cartel of governments. To explain prices by 'political factors' is superfluous nonsense. When a seller raises prices and increases revenues, he is acting reasonably. Whatever King Faisal really wants, money is the royal road to it, and more money is what he seeks. Giving him political favors only proves that money buys power, and whets his appetite for more money. The cartel governments use the multinational companies to maintain prices, limit production, and divide markets.[116]

In the battle for discursive hegemony, Adelman declared in numerous articles that neither geological knowledge nor political expertise on the Middle East were necessary to understanding what was happening. Both were in fact obstructing a solution. The reasons for publicly expressed fears of oil scarcity, emanating from the likes of James Akins, were 'a well kept secret which the economist cannot penetrate'.[117] The oil price was several times greater than production costs because a cartel, encouraged by the

US government, was driving it up and not because OPEC had recognized the finite nature of its oil reserves. Even if this was the case, he opined, according to Hotelling's rule it was only rational for them to limit production if the increased value of oil in the ground exceeded the increased value of money obtained through sales and subsequent investments.[118] The artificially high prices were not only damaging consumers but also leading to the misallocation of resources because the government was now seeking and fostering more expensive energy sources. Adelman's proposed solution, which he repeated on a number of occasions, was that the oil firms must be ousted from their role – an often exclusive one thanks to their licences – as intermediaries in the oil business. This would compel the producing countries to offer their oil in a competitive market.[119] If market conditions were restored in this way, allowing the price mechanism to function, there would be no more need to worry about the exhaustion of oil reserves: 'Oil and other minerals will never be exhausted. If and when consumers will not pay enough to induce investment in new reserves and capacity, the producing industry will dwindle and disappear'.[120] One day, then, oil consumption would fall even though lots of oil would still be in the ground: 'A mineral industry runs out of customers before it can run out of mineral'.[121]

Adelman's theory conceptualizes oil reserves as constructs that can only be meaningfully defined in relation to demand and price. In all its economic rigour, this perspective still has many supporters, not least because it empowers economists to make forecasts about resources. Hendrik S. Houthakker, a member of Nixon's Task Force on Oil Imports and his Council of Economic Advisers, for example, took the same view. As late as 2002, he was still repeating the claim that, despite what many geologists believe, one cannot infer the eventual exhaustion of natural resources from their finite nature. As long as 'market forces' are at work, a rising price will in fact prevent total exhaustion.[122] Even at the time, however, the disputatious Adelman came in for plenty of criticism. On the one hand, economists criticized him for focusing too much on production costs while neglecting processing and failing to consider other energy sources.[123] On the other hand, non-economists assailed his neglect of the political and social influences on the international oil economy, which, they claimed, were crucial to the future availability of oil.[124]

Adelman seemed to hold James Akins personally responsible for the Arab embargo and rising oil price – and thus, we might add, for falsifying Adelman's forecasts. A key target of Adelman's invective, Akins responded to his claims.[125] At the hearings of the Senate Committee on Foreign Relations in May 1973, Akins initially showed irritation when Senator Fulbright asked him whether he was familiar with Adelman's theories: 'Everybody seems to quote him to me'. He then cast doubt on Adelman's credibility when it came to energy forecasts: 'Professor Adelman does not have a terribly good record of predictions on international or even domestic oil matters. He has consistently talked of the imminent demise of OPEC and world oil prices. He is trying to find explanations for the fact that he has been wrong'.[126] Having nonetheless reluctantly provided the senators with a summary of Adelman's theory, he criticized it for assuming that oil was distributed evenly across the world and equally accessible to all: 'It totally ignores the geographic distribution of the oil; it totally ignores the political aspirations of the oil producers; it totally ignores any desires to save oil for future use'.[127]

In the spring of 1973, energy policymakers of a more economic bent prevailed over Akins within the government. He felt sidelined by disciples of Adelman in the Energy Policy Office and crowed over the departure of Love and DiBona in early December in the wake of their conflict with Simon: 'Vice is overthrown! Virtue triumphs! Praise the Lord! . . . I would have thought that Adelman and his disciples (including d[i] B[ona]) would now be crawling into their holes and hoping people would forget them. But I've just received a copy of a recent Adelman speech in which he says he was right all along, or would have been if it hadn't been for my advising OPEC on what to do. Oh well, you can't win them all'.[128] Yet Simon too mostly brought economists from the Treasury and the Department of the Interior into the Federal Energy Office. His appointment thus tended to strengthen the economic perspective within the administration. Few shared Adelman's radical views and, crucially, no steps were taken to strip the oil firms of their power as he recommended. The Federal Energy Office analysed OPEC's behaviour as if it were just another economic cartel, neglecting to seek advice from experts on the Arab world.[129]

Strategies: Increasing Production vs. Reducing Consumption

What conclusions did US policymakers come to in light of the various, discipline-bound interpretations of the energy crisis? There were essentially two ways of responding to the sharp growth in consumption combined with negligible production growth. The first was to increase domestic production of oil and other energy sources such as natural gas, coal and uranium (or imports from 'secure' regions with which the US enjoyed good relations). The second was to reduce the consumption of oil and energy. Under the conditions of the embargo, only energy-saving measures or attempts to prompt the Arab countries to resume production – or other nations to increase theirs – had any prospect of making an immediate impact. Over the medium and long term, however, key actors began to ask whether the focus should be on consumption or production. The answer depended on whether or not one accepted the assumption of scarcity. This was clearly apparent in the influential studies by the National Petroleum Council and the Ford Foundation's Energy Policy Project. Both had been commissioned prior to the embargo, but gained in significance as a result of it.

The National Petroleum Council was a product of the close cooperation between the US government and the oil industry during the Second World War and had been incorporated into the Department of the Interior by President Truman as an advisory body. It consisted of representatives of the multinational oil firms and independents, who were to assess on the government's behalf the security of the oil supply in times of war or crisis.[130] At the beginning of 1970, the Department of the Interior asked the National Petroleum Council how recent trends in the oil economy would influence 'the future availability of petroleum supplies to the United States ... as near to the end of the century as feasible'.[131] In December 1972, Council chair John McLean, who was also head of the Continental Oil Company, and Warren B. Davis, chief economist at Gulf Oil, thus presented a report entitled *US Energy Outlook*. This was produced with the input of more than two hundred staff from a number of national and international oil firms as well as US government agencies.[132]

Given that oil consumption in the United States had outstripped production in the preceding years, the report set out three possible strategies: stepping up domestic production, increasing imports or energy-saving measures. Unsurprisingly, the oil industry representatives behind the study favoured the first solution, asserting that increased imports would put national security at risk, while consumption cuts would threaten economic development: 'It is concluded that increasing the availability of domestic energy supplies is the best option available for improving the US energy supply and demand balance. . . . [It] would benefit all segments of society: employment would increase, individual incomes would rise, profit opportunities would improve, government revenues would grow, and the Nation would be more secure'.[133] The report contended that there were no physical limits to domestic energy production because oil and uranium were present in sufficient quantities and coal in abundance.[134] But to intensify the exploitation of these natural resources, the government should create a climate friendlier to the energy industry. To this end, the oil firms' spokesmen proposed such measures as: continued import controls; tax concessions; deregulation of the gas price; easing of environmental standards; facilitation of the extraction of domestic natural resources; faster approval for oil production on the Outer Continental Shelf; improved coordination of national energy policy; and the fostering of a 'national sense of purpose to solve the energy problem'.[135] If these steps were taken, domestic energy production could keep pace with consumption up to 1985, but this would be impossible if environmentalism were to run rampant.

Reading the *US Energy Outlook*'s conclusions, it seems obvious that the National Petroleum Council's expertise was moulded by the economic interests of the firms from which it recruited its staff. But John McLean also adapted his message to the general public. In a November 1973 article in the *Annals of the American Academy of Political and Social Science*, for example, he leavened his call for increased domestic production with recognition of the need for reasonable environmental policy and energy-saving measures.[136] The obvious self-interest of the National Petroleum Council did nothing to reduce its impact. Amid growing signs of an imminent oil embargo in 1973, the Department of the Interior asked the Council how to minimize the consequences of supply disruptions. The oil industry representatives now conceded that in the context of the current crisis, only energy-saving measures could help over the short term, but they reiterated that over the long term 'the best way to minimize the impact of a disruption of imports [is] to develop our domestic energy resources to the maximum extent possible'.[137]

Shortly after the embargo began, Stephen Wakefield of the Department of the Interior again requested a speedy appraisal of the current supply cutbacks' likely effects.[138] In view of the shortfall anticipated by January of up to three million barrels of oil a day, the National Petroleum Council now assumed that consumption cuts would also be required. It even mentioned rationing in this context, but underlined that cutbacks would be possible only within the private sphere, not in industry.[139] There was no potential at all for saving energy in electricity production, it contended, and in other branches of industry the picture would be little different in the near future.[140] The National Petroleum Council always emphasized that when the embargo was over, the state must withdraw from the field of energy and end its regulation.[141] The Council exercised a major influence not least because – even during the oil crisis – there were very few other expert bodies that might have challenged the oil firms' representatives and their knowledge. At the end of the day, it was chiefly the oil industry and its immediate milieu that had generated petro-knowledge. For experts of this background, the oil and energy crisis did not necessitate consideration of ecological limits and environmental interests. Instead, they used it to back up their opposing arguments. Largely due to a burgeoning environmental awareness and the politicization of oil and energy, however, the early 1970s saw the rise of a growing number of competing expert cadres claiming to produce valid petro-knowledge.

Particularly influential was the Ford Foundation's Energy Policy Project (EPP), established in 1971. This was endowed with four million dollars and led by David S. Freeman, who had earlier been responsible for Nixon's first speech on energy policy while working at the White House.[142] Three hundred thousand copies of the EPP's provisional report, *Exploring Energy Choices*, were distributed through the Book of the Month Club, while six thousand copies of the final report, *A Time to Choose*, also published in 1974, were sent to politicians and government agencies. The intensely negative reaction from industry was one of the main reasons the report received so much public attention.[143] The Energy Policy Project shared the view that the cause of the energy crisis lay not in Arab oil policies but in the widening gap between energy production and energy consumption in the United States. Yet it came to diametrically opposite conclusions. 'We believe that the scope and potential energy savings have not yet received their just due in the national energy debate. In this book we hope to demonstrate that slower energy growth than we have recently experienced can work without undermining our standard of living, and can also exert a powerful positive influence on environmental and other problems intertwined with energy'.[144] The energy problem was a result of excessive increases in consumption. It was in this realm, then, that the solution must be found. A pleasant, comfortable and civilized life was quite possible in the present era despite only negligible growth in energy consumption. In the distant future, meanwhile, it would only be possible on this basis.[145]

The Energy Policy Project identified five objectives for future energy policy, namely supply security, a reasonable price, economic and regional balance, environmental sustainability and international security. It went on to distinguish three ideal-typical scenarios for future development: 'historical growth', 'technical fix' and 'zero energy growth'.[146] These scenarios were not intended as forecasts but to provide 'tools for rigorous thinking', facilitating wise decision-making on energy. The 'historical growth' scenario worked on the assumption that energy consumption would continue to grow as it had hitherto, and could be satisfied by fostering and developing new energy sources. This, however, would throw up enormous political, economic and ecological problems. In the 'technical fix' scenario, new energy-saving technologies would enable the same level of economic growth while energy consumption would only increase by half. 'Zero energy growth is different. It represents a real break with our accustomed ways of doing things. Yet it does not represent austerity', the report went on. If the country embraced a new ethic, it would be possible at least to maintain current living standards.[147] According to the Ford Foundation, each of these paths was possible. But there would have to be a conscious decision to pursue one of them and implement corresponding policies, because the market alone was incapable of solving the problems afflicting the field of energy.[148] Ultimately, the report stated, the interests of the energy firms did not coincide with the public interest. Neither environmental pollution nor foreign policy considerations would inevitably be reflected in energy prices. The report's preference was clearly for the zero-growth path, to be achieved through scientific-technological progress: 'It is therefore our recommendation that the new Energy Policy Council, as an undertaking of the highest priority, make an intensive, continuing study of the desirability, feasibility, and necessity of moving to zero energy growth'.[149]

Though they shared the same diagnosis of the energy problem, the National Petroleum Council and the Ford Foundation's Energy Policy Project thus came up with fundamentally different solutions, marking out the two poles of political debate in the United States.[150] Their reports not only outlined a panorama of possible strategies. They also mirrored the state of energy expertise or petro-knowledge in the United States prior to the oil crisis, a body of knowledge that influenced the US government's ability to develop policies. Apart from oil industry representatives, it was mainly think tanks that possessed petro-knowledge. These organizations were mostly sponsored by nonprofit groups and were, to a significant degree, driven by ecological concerns. Both camps competed to influence the government. Prior to 1973, the US administration included only a small number of institutionally scattered expert staff dedicated to oil and energy policy, but no central institution tasked with its long-term planning and formulation. The establishment of the Federal Energy Administration and the creation of an apparatus to implement 'Project Independence', announced by Nixon, were both intended to remedy this.[151]

Governmental Expertise: 'Project Independence'

A year after Nixon's announcement that the United States would seek to achieve independence from oil imports by 1980, and about six months after the associated work had begun, the Federal Energy Administration presented the comprehensive *Project Independence Report* in November 1974.[152] In the preface, project leader John Sawhill proudly declared the report to be the most comprehensive energy analysis ever undertaken.[153] The amount of effort involved and the dimensions of the study were in fact something quite new, not just for an energy study produced by a public agency but for any comparable publication. In the next ten years, Project Independence received more attention than any other attempt to model energy systems.[154]

In addition to the Federal Energy Administration, also involved in drawing up the *Project Independence Report* were staff of the Atomic Energy Commission; the Council on Environmental Quality; the CIA; the Departments of Agriculture, Commerce, Interior, Labor and Transportation;

the Environmental Protection Agency; the Federal Power Commission; the Maritime Administration; the National Science Foundation; the Office of Management and Budget; and the Tennessee Valley Authority. A total of more than four hundred individuals participated in various working groups on Policy Evaluation; International Assessment; Resource Development; Quantitative Analysis; and Conservation, and in 'Task Forces' on coal; oil; gas; plant manufacturing; synthetic petrol; oil shale; geothermal energy; solar energy; nuclear energy; construction; transportation; finance; environment; and water, with the working groups on the various energy sources being the largest.[155] Even at the design stage of Project Independence, in terms of content Sawhill and Eric Zausner deviated from Nixon's political objective of making the US energy supply independent of oil imports by 1980. Most energy experts considered such an endeavour either impossible or, due to the economic and ecological consequences, undesirable.[156] The pair thus defined 'energy independence' not as a situation in which the United States no longer imported any energy, but as one in which the imported amount was small enough to keep political and economic vulnerability through supply disruptions at acceptable levels.[157] The *Project Independence Report*, moreover, rather than delineating a path towards energy independence, sought to provide a comprehensive toolkit for evaluating energy strategies. In addition to carrying out energy-related surveys and collecting data, this was to be achieved through the Project Independence Evaluation System (PIES) developed by William Hogan. The modelling of the national energy system was difficult due to the large number of interacting variables.[158] Forecasting future conditions in the energy system required the integration, in modular form, of the price sensitivity of consumption; competition between energy sources; technological developments; resource limits; side-effects such as ecological consequences; economic impacts; regional differences; and the timescale of possible changes. The interplay of all these elements also had to be rendered amenable to analysis.[159]

In light of the oil embargo and its economic effects, the report began by presenting a scenario called the 'base case'. This extended present trends into the future assuming an absence of political intervention. It then assessed three different political strategies to determine their capacity to reduce vulnerability to supply disruptions: an increase in domestic energy production; the intensification of energy-saving measures; and the development of emergency stockpiles. In view of oil's central role among energy sources, the oil price was the crucial variable in calculating future developments. At the same time, however, it also represented the greatest element of uncertainty. This was because the formation of the oil price, as the report underlined, depended on both economic and political factors that were very difficult to assess in advance.¹⁶⁰ The greatest uncertainty was the price elasticity of consumption. The oil price having been fairly stable for years, there were no studies of whether, and if so how much, an increasing oil price would reduce consumption. When it came to the most crucial variable within the overall energy system, therefore, the report had to rely on estimates and analogies, as its authors conceded: 'While this study uses the most sophisticated set of models and analyses yet applied to energy forecasting, it represents only the best estimate of what is still a highly uncertain situation'.¹⁶¹ Even the key protagonists of the scientization of policymaking, then, recognized the difficulties involved in legitimizing political acts through scientific analysis.

The success of this 'heroic attempt to apply analysis on a grand scale to the energy debate of the seventies' was in fact limited.¹⁶² Project Independence worked on the assumption that a higher oil price would sharply reduce overall consumption and thus also oil imports from the Middle East. At a price of four dollars a barrel, the report asserted, in 1985 worldwide oil consumption would be 58.9 million barrels a day, at seven dollars a day the figure would be 43.5 million and at eleven dollars just 28.3 million.¹⁶³ This assumption of high price sensitivity prompted the conclusion that the oil price would probably even out at seven dollars. This was because, particularly for smaller oil-producing countries, reduced consumption would mean a loss of income that would strain the cohesiveness of OPEC.¹⁶⁴ Nonetheless, with sufficient political motivation, OPEC could enforce a price of eleven dollars. Energy strategies were thus calculated on the basis of an oil price of both seven and eleven dollars for 1977, 1980 and 1985. Essentially, the *Project Independence Report* assumed that the stimulation of domestic energy production would be better able than energy-saving measures to reduce the need for oil imports in 1985. At an oil price of seven dollars, increased production and decreased consumption could not reduce oil imports, but could freeze them at the level of 1974. At eleven dollars a barrel, meanwhile, production increases themselves would be enough to forgo imports entirely while energy-saving measures could bring imports down to a low level.¹⁶⁵ Although the objective of energy independence, the report claimed, was easier to realize if oil prices were higher, this was not in the interest of the United States because it would place a heavy burden on the other industrialized countries.¹⁶⁶ Overall, then, Project Independence backed up calls for domestic production increases and energy source diversification, which constituted the basic template of US energy policy in the 1970s.¹⁶⁷

By developing its own cadre of energy policy experts tasked with formulating specific proposals, the US government intended to enhance its capacity for effective action on energy and secure national sovereignty and independence. In this sense, 'Project Independence' had a telling name. But perhaps even more important during the oil crisis was the symbolic aspect of the expansion of government energy expertise. The tremendous interministerial efforts made on this front were intended to show the public that the government had the situation under control, that it had the necessary know-how to reorganize the energy sector on a secure basis and prevent future energy crises. Project Independence was therefore accompanied by a massive PR campaign. From August to October 1974, public hearings running to several days were held in all ten administrative districts of the Federal Energy Administration. These gave scientists, businesses, interest groups, organizations, local politicians and ordinary citizens the opportunity to express their views on Project Independence and allegedly help to shape energy policy.[168] Television commercials – showing soldiers in historical uniforms marching to the beat of a drum – urged the general public to get involved: 'Today we need a new Project Independence: Energy Independence . . . be there and share in America's Future'.[169] More than a thousand individuals spoke at the hearings. Their statements, along with minutes and discussions, fill ten large-format volumes running to more than 6,700 closely printed pages. While many of the speakers had been invited in advance to air their views on Project Independence, it was possible to register during the hearings. The volumes thus reflect a broad spectrum of opinion, from governors and members of Congress through renowned scientists of various disciplines, chief executives of energy companies, architects and engineers, to environmental and consumer protection activists. In Denver the hearings revolved chiefly around the use of domestic coal, oil shale and synthetic petrol production; in New York the financing and international implications of Project Independence; in Boston the definition of energy independence and the special situation of New England; in Seattle research and development and the exploitation of oil in Alaska; in Chicago nuclear energy; in Kansas City the infrastructure needed to achieve energy independence; in Houston government regulation of energy production; in Atlanta oil production on the Outer Continental Shelf and the construction of ports; in Philadelphia the consequences for environmental policy; and in San Francisco energy-saving measures.

In his opening remarks, John Sawhill underlined the significance of the hearings. They were concerned not with the future of a normal economic good but with 'the future of energy – a central social resource that determines where and how we live, the nature and relationships of our institutions, and the dynamism and direction of our society'.[170] While there was consensus on the need to reduce energy import dependency, he went on, value-based decisions would be required to achieve this goal. The United

States was now in a position to make these decisions, without the pressure of an acute crisis, through informed public debate. In part, then, the hearings were meant to create legitimacy by bringing the political decision-making process out into the open. At the third hearing in Boston, Sawhill thus repudiated an article in the *Boston Globe* claiming that the key decisions had already been taken and that the hearings were just a mise en scène for the public.[171] In fact, he asserted, the citizens of the United States were engaged in a public discussion on the future of the energy system and thus also on the country's independence. There could be no venue more predestined for this than Faneueil Hall in Boston: 'So, I feel well in the shadow of Sam Adams, James Otis, Daniel Webster and the other giants of New England and America's history'.[172]

Sawhill's assurances that the hearings would inform the *Project Independence Report* seem dubious. They generated a huge quantity of material and yet the report was already published on 14 November, despite the fact that the final hearing was only held on 12 October. Most testimony consisted of well-intended and at times even well-informed statements on the revamping of energy policy. Due to its form, however, it was mostly ill-suited to incorporation into the complex energy scenario models found in the PIES. It consisted of general expressions of opinion such as Edward Kennedy's reflections on the international character of the energy crisis and how to solve it;[173] highly specialized statements such as that by Morris Adelman on how to break the power of OPEC and the oil firms;[174] or proposals such as the plan put forward by one citizen to replace the car-based society with a bicycle-based one.[175] Environmental groups and consumer associations also made extensive contributions, advocating enhanced energy saving and putting forward concrete proposals to achieve it. This was quite at variance with the *Project Independence Report*'s clear preference for domestic production increases – another indication that the hearings were merely intended to create the impression that it was possible to influence the political process. Nonetheless, the effort put into the hearings shows that the government was aware of the need to make the general public feel included in policy formulation in order to enhance its own legitimacy. Project Independence thus blended technocratic ideas with a veneer of grassroots democracy. In view of the apparent threat to national energy sovereignty, the government sought to legitimize its actions by underscoring their scientific basis and highlighting the supposedly democratic roots of its sovereignty.

Just over a year after publication of the *Project Independence Report*, the realities of energy in the United States and worldwide already clashed so markedly with its assumptions and projections that the Federal Energy Administration produced a new report. Now that the 'energy crisis' had abated and public interest in energy had waned, however, the government opted to keep the public out of the *National Energy Outlook*. Under the leadership of Eric Zausner and coordinated by William Hogan and Bruce Pasternack, around 150 staff contributed to the new report, which was intended to take account of the changes that had occurred in the energy field since publication of the *Project Independence Report*. The gravest error in the latter, which invalidated many of the scenarios it outlined, was the overestimation of the price sensitivity of oil consumption and the calculation that the OPEC cartel would be in no position to enforce an oil price of more than eleven dollars a barrel, and that the price was likely to even out at seven dollars.

> The events of the past two years have indicated an ability by the oil producing cartel to maintain the high prices of oil established during the embargo, even in the face of substantial declines in world oil demand ... It seems clear that little can be done between now and 1980 to alter the supply and demand relationship between OPEC and consuming nations enough to weaken the cartel's exclusive control over prices. Thus, there is no significant likelihood of a considerably lower price for OPEC oil in this period.[176]

By 1975, a barrel of oil already cost thirteen dollars and the era of prices of three to four dollars seemed over once and for all. The new report now forecast an oil price of between eight and sixteen dollars a barrel for 1985.[177] It had also become clear that a significant part of oil consumption barely reacted to higher prices, necessitating upward correction of projected consumption. It was apparent in retrospect that the government's measures had led to increased exploration. But the growth in the number of boreholes from 26,600 in 1973 to 37,000 had not yet boosted domestic production. This trend, the new report claimed, would only change with the advent of oil from Alaska.[178] The *National Energy Outlook* continued to distinguish between the strategies of increased production and reduced consumption. It endeavoured to include a greater array of factors, though the oil price remained the central element in calculating future energy scenarios.[179]

In the United States, the oil embargo and oil price increases generated a great deal of uncertainty, which the authorities aimed to reduce through scientific expertise and petro-knowledge. By drawing on oil experts outside the government and, above all, creating its own cadre of energy experts, the administration hoped to make the right decisions to lead the country out of the oil crisis. It also hoped to demonstrate to the public that it could act effectively on the basis of the best possible information. But the oil experts and their petro-knowledge were imperfect tools for achieving these goals. Experts made all kinds of fundamental, value-based assumptions, represented a variety of economic interests and were confronted with a novel situation of high contingency. Their opinions thus differed radically both in terms of their diagnoses and proposed solutions. Far from reducing uncertainty, then, they often intensified it. The 'scientization of policymaking' led to the 'politicization of science', which eroded its legitimatory function as a basis for decision-making supposedly located outside the political arena.[180] The inflationary tendencies and polyphony of widely publicized studies – on the future of the energy supply in general and oil in particular – also seem to have spread a good deal of confusion. When the constantly predicted disasters repeatedly failed to occur, Americans increasingly became inured to negative energy forecasts.[181]

Communicating Sovereignty: Government, Media and Public

'Don't Be Fuelish. . .': Energy Speeches

As set out in the introduction, sovereignty, authority and legitimacy are social categories. To a large extent, to be sovereign means to be recognized as such by others. Governments' political authority depends largely on the degree to which the governed view their representatives as legitimately sovereign. Nixon and his colleagues thus repeatedly sought to communicate directly with the general public in order to legitimize their policies. In 1971, Nixon became the first president to give a speech wholly devoted to energy policy. Between April 1973 and January 1974, he subsequently dedicated no fewer than five major speeches before Congress or on television to the topic. He also made energy the centrepiece of his State of the Union Address of January 1974.[182] At a basic level, Nixon's speeches were, first, a means of communicating the revamping of energy policy and publicizing specific measures. Second, they were intended to gain Congress's support for various legislative projects. Third, his television and radio addresses served to motivate the population to save energy. Fourth, they set out to convince Americans that the president was in control of the situation and had what it took to overcome the energy crisis. Fifth, and finally, during the oil embargo his speeches were also addressed to the producing countries and other consuming countries in an attempt to communicate the United States' position within the international politics of oil. They always evoked a challenge to sovereignty, one that ultimately threatened the country's independence, a challenge to which the government and the people must and would rise.

On 18 April, Nixon announced to Congress the establishment of the National Energy Office. He described the present era as an 'age of transition', in which new problems had arisen, particularly in the field of energy.[183] Over the short term, he contended, the United States, which accounted for 30 per cent of global energy consumption despite having just 6 per cent of the world's population, would have to deal with energy shortfalls and rising prices: 'Clearly we are facing a vitally important energy challenge. If present trends continue unchecked, we could face a genuine energy crisis'. But by implementing the right measures, which would have to strike a balance between economy, ecology and national security, the crisis could be averted, because the United States had both adequate energy sources of its own and virtually unlimited ingenuity. Nixon explained that what this meant in concrete terms was fostering the production of all domestic energy sources by deregulating prices, opening up more of the Outer Continental Shelf to oil drilling and building the Alaska Pipeline. Nuclear energy must be developed more rapidly and the country's large coal reserves used more intensively. To this end, environmental regulations must be eased if necessary. Nixon partially rolled back the import quota system established to protect the domestic oil industry against cheaper oil from the Middle East. For a fee, oil firms were now permitted to import unlimited quantities of oil above and beyond their 1973 concessions.

In addition to these measures and increased support for energy-related research and development, Nixon identified energy saving as a key political and social objective: 'We as a nation must develop a national energy conservation ethic'.[184] The president made it clear that the main antidote to energy supply problems was increased domestic production, and statements placing more emphasis on energy saving had been deleted from earlier advisor-prepared drafts.[185] Still, the closing words of the speech foregrounded 'conservation'. Nixon explained: 'But in the final analysis, the ultimate responsibility does not rest merely with the Congress or with this Administration. It rests with all of us – with government, with industry and with the individual citizen'. Energy policy became a national challenge, a way for the nation to prove its greatness and for individuals to demonstrate their morality. So Jimmy Carter was not the first to give the energy crisis a moral twist, declaring it the 'moral equivalent of war' in his famous 'malaise' speech.[186] This moralization and nationalization of the energy crisis, closely reminiscent of Cold War presidential rhetoric in general, exercised an ongoing influence on the energy policy debate.[187] The Watergate scandal, however, raised growing doubts about Nixon's own moral integrity.

In his speech of 29 June 1973, on the establishment of the Energy Policy Office and the appointment of John A. Love as energy czar, the political challenge of meeting near-term energy needs had already turned into 'one of the most critical problems on America's agenda today'.[188] The moral task facing the nation and its citizens expanded accordingly: 'We must not waste our resources, however abundant they may seem. To do otherwise, in a world of finite resources, reflects adversely upon what we are as a people and a Nation'.[189] Here Nixon parenthetically acknowledged the validity of the prevalent discourse of ecological limits. Implicitly utilizing its alarmist rhetoric, he nonetheless went on to call for merely moderate lifestyle changes. Everyone ought to cut their energy consumption by 5 per cent by turning down the air conditioning, flying less often and using more economical cars. The government would set a good example and cut its own energy consumption by 7 per cent. This change in behaviour, Nixon opined, was simply a matter of common sense and individual intelligence. This was an argument that pervaded his subsequent speeches and was central to the energy-saving campaign launched by the Advertising Council, as captured in its slogan, 'Don't be fuelish. . .'. The intention here was to associate wasting energy with irrationality and irresponsibility, while energy-saving conduct connoted intelligence, pragmatism and common sense, particularly considering the financial benefits.[190] A pamphlet published by the Citizens' Advisory Committee on Environmental Quality compiled a catalogue of measures through which every citizen could participate in the overall energy-saving project. The sense of powerlessness many felt about supply shortfalls, it asserted, was as unjustifiable as the assumption that only the government, 'experts' and 'policy-makers' held responsibility and were in a position to change things. Everyone could save energy in a range of ways, thus helping to secure the country's energy supply: 'Many of them actually require little or no change in our basic life-styles. Most of them will save money for the consumer. All they require us to do is to think a little bit before we act, and to plan ahead so that we will be spending our energy – and thus our money – more wisely'.[191]

In order to underline the pleasant aspects of saving energy, Charles M. Shultz's Snoopy was adopted as the symbol of the official 'Savenergy' campaign initiated by the special assistant to the president for consumer affairs. An illustration shows Snoopy lying on his kennel, thinking 'I believe in conserving energy'.[192] Conversely, a pamphlet published by the Department of the Interior about a year earlier placed less emphasis on individual utility. Instead it foregrounded the obligation to show national solidarity in an attempt to motivate Americans to save energy. Under the heading 'Energy, America, and You', it displayed light switches in the on and off positions, urging citizens: 'Let's Clean Up America For Our 200th Birthday' and 'Don't Let America's Future Dim . . . Conserve Energy!'.[193] This national argument was one of Nixon's favourite moves as he concluded his speeches. Time and again, he proclaimed, national challenges had prompted the American nation to demonstrate its true greatness.[194] In 1973–74, then, appeals to Americans to change their energy-related habits always highlighted individual utility and comfort, responsible conduct and national duty in varying admixtures.

How the oil embargo would affect the United States was initially unclear. The general expectation was that the already poor supply situation would worsen over the winter. In addition to specific measures intended to avert shortfalls, Love now evoked the moral dimension of the energy debate and called repeatedly for the president himself to set a visible example of energy saving. He should also address his fellow Americans on television to convince them of the need for the government's measures.[195] In order to address the people directly rather than through the filter of the TV news, Nixon's speechwriter Dave Gergen suggested that he deliver this televised speech not at midday but around 7 p.m. It should be followed by a discussion featuring Nixon's advisers. This would help to avoid panic, while also demonstrating that the president was making a serious effort to solve the problem and surrounding himself with new, respectable advisers.[196] To intensify the speech's impact, Gergen and his colleagues tried to come up with a term that summed up the government's efforts on the energy front, one as memorable as the 'Manhattan' or 'Apollo' projects.[197] The most appealing suggestion came from Herbert Stein. Against the backdrop of preparations for the 200th anniversary of the Declaration of Independence, he proposed 'Project Independence'.[198] While Nixon was generally happy with the draft versions of the speech, and most of the changes he made were stylistic in nature, he heightened the anti-Congress rhetoric, accusing it of inactivity and delaying crucial decisions on energy policy.[199]

The title under which the speech was disseminated to the press underlined the scale of the challenge now facing the country. Nixon's oration to his fellow Americans from the Oval Office on 7 November 1973 was no longer merely a speech on energy. It was an 'energy emergency address'.[200] In this 25-minute speech, Nixon explained that while the energy supply had previously been an important national challenge, the oil embargo had turned it into a serious national problem – a crisis in fact. Over the next few months and years, there would unavoidably be supply problems. Everyone would notice them but they need cause no real suffering as long as every citizen made small sacrifices.[201] These being the most dramatic shortages since the Second World War, the president went on, a number of additional steps were required beyond those the administration had already taken. Power stations would no longer be permitted to convert from coal to oil and would instead be encouraged to do the opposite; less fuel would be allocated for air travel; and the approval of nuclear power stations would be speeded up. Heating oil consumption must be cut by 15 per cent, so every citizen must set their home thermostat six degrees lower, to an average of 68 degrees Fahrenheit. Nixon smilingly added: 'Incidentally my doctor tells me that in a temperature of 66 to 68 degrees you are really more healthy than when it is 75 to 78, if that is any comfort'. He then went on to reassure viewers that he would see to it 'that the daytime temperatures in federal offices be reduced immediately to a level of between 65 and 68 degrees, and that means in this room, too, as in every other room in the White House'.[202] The moral requirement to change one's lifestyle, viewers were given to understand, applied at least as much to the governing as it did to the governed.

Nixon assured his listeners that he would support the states and local authorities in their efforts to save energy, such as with the introduction of speed limits. The measures the White House had implemented so far had been possible due to the Economic Stabilization Act of 1970 and the Defense Production Act of 1950. But the executive would require enhanced powers to deal with the energy crisis. Congress should therefore pass the 'Emergency Energy Act', enabling the president to introduce daylight saving time, modify environmental standards, set speed limits and utilize the Naval Petroleum Reserve, among other things. At a time of growing doubts about Nixon's integrity and authority, then, he addressed the American public and Congress with a demand for enhanced powers. In view of this paradox, Nixon's speech ended with a 'personal message' to those who questioned his integrity, making it clear that he would not be acceding to demands for his resignation.[203] But the true rhetorical apogee of Nixon's speech was his appeal for the country to achieve energy independence in just seven years:

> Let us unite in committing the resources of this Nation to a major new endeavor, an endeavor that in this bicentennial era we can appropriately call 'Project Independence'. Let us set as our national goal, in the spirit of Apollo, with the determination of the Manhattan Project, that by the end of this decade we will have developed the potential to meet our own energy needs without depending on foreign energy sources. Let us pledge that by 1980, under Project Independence, we shall be able to meet America's energy needs from America's own energy resources.[204]

The next day, Nixon again appeared before Congress to court its approval for his legislative proposals. He reiterated that energetic autarky was not isolationist but was crucial to the United States' capacity to pursue an independent foreign policy.[205]

Congress refused to pass the Emergency Energy Act as Nixon demanded, but it still triggered intensive debate in the Senate and House of Representatives. The bill introduced in the Senate by Henry M. Jackson went significantly further than the government's proposals and provided for both rationing and the regulation of refineries. While the Senate was quick to pass it, the House of Representatives made numerous changes and had major reservations about granting the president special powers. A bill that drew on aspects of both proposals, which Nixon and Simon had both sought in vain to influence, passed the Senate but not the House of Representatives. Not until January was a new compromise proposal passed, though Nixon vetoed it in March because it set the maximum prices for domestically produced oil at a level he regarded as excessively low.[206] Despite this failure and the concerns of some members of Congress about special presidential powers on energy, in late 1973 a paradoxical situation emerged. While raising fundamental doubts about Nixon's authority, the Democrat-dominated Congress was willing to strengthen it when it came to energy.[207] In the meantime, it cooperated with Nixon and embraced the White House's proposals with respect to such things as the Emergency Highway Energy Conservation Act and Daylight Saving Time Energy Conservation Act.

In view of the escalating oil crisis, barely three weeks later Nixon addressed the American public from the Oval Office once again, seeking to convey the same basic message. The oil embargo having turned the anticipated supply problems into a 'major energy crisis', further measures were now required.[208] In an attempt to play down the gravity of these new policies, Nixon underlined the global dimension of the oil shortages, which were having a significantly worse effect on other industrialized countries. There was no need for bans on Sunday driving as in some European countries, but other measures would be essential. Petrol stations were to be closed from 9 p.m. on Saturday until the end of Sunday, and a speed limit of 50 or 55 mph for buses and lorries respectively would be introduced on federal highways. Restrictions would be imposed on air traffic, the exterior lighting of buildings and, above all, Christmas lighting. In addition to these largely symbolic measures, he also elaborated on the Emergency Petroleum Allocation Act, which would reduce oil allocations to various sectors according to a staggered scale.[209] Even more starkly than in early November, Nixon linked the objective of these energy initiatives with the character of the American nation:

> Let me conclude by restating our overall objective. It can be summed up in one word that best characterizes this Nation and its essential nature. That word is 'independence'. From its beginning 200 years ago, throughout its history, America has made great sacrifices ... to achieve and maintain its independence. In the last third of this century, our independence will depend on maintaining and achieving self-sufficiency in energy.[210]

By mid January, Nixon was able to give a radio address highlighting some initial successes. In December, petrol consumption had been 9 per cent lower than expected and in New England heating oil consumption had fallen by no less than 16 per cent.[211] He thanked the public for their willingness to make sacrifices, which had made rationing unnecessary. But then he immediately turned to the achievements of the government, which had reduced its energy consumption not by the target of 7 per cent but by 20 per cent. Nixon also had to address certain new themes that had emerged within the public debate. It would be unacceptable for the oil companies to profit inappropriately from price increases, so if necessary the government would prevent this through a 'windfall profit tax'. To maximize transparency, he had submitted to Congress a bill that would require the oil companies to produce more accurate reports on their activities. He also responded to the widespread belief that there was no real supply shortage and that the oil supply was being artificially restricted in order to raise prices. In fact, he explained, the country was facing a dramatic situation. According to calculations by Bill Simon and his colleagues at the Federal Energy Office, the lack of oil during the first quarter of 1974 amounted to at least 2.7 million barrels a day. The comparison he chose to describe the country's plight could scarcely have been more drastic: 'During the Second World War, Winston Churchill was once asked why England was fighting Hitler. He answered, "If we stop, you will find out"'. The same, he suggested, applied to present-day energy saving. Nonetheless, Nixon predicted that the winter of 1973–74 would eventually be followed by the 'spring of energy independence', as long as everyone worked together on Project Independence.[212]

This message was so important to the White House that on 23 January it was disseminated once again in a brief television broadcast. On the same day, in his State of the Union Address, the president called on Congress to rapidly implement his legislative initiatives.[213] He had, he stated, warned of coming energy shortfalls as early as 1971. But in October 1973, the embargo had suddenly been announced and the United States had been plunged into an energy crisis. Here for the first time Nixon performs a discursive shift, which was replicated sooner or later by everyone involved in US energy policy. It also became par for the course within public debate. Nixon had previously underlined the long-term causes of the energy crisis, identifying its roots in the increasing prosperity of the preceding decades. Yet now the earlier energy crisis faded from view, swamped by the drama of the oil embargo and oil price increases from October 1973 onwards. In early January 1974, in a TV interview, William E. Simon was still declaring, 'oh many, many, many, many times we've warned of the emerging energy crisis'.[214] Yet, consciously or unconsciously, after retiring as treasury secretary in 1978, he turned the facts upside down in his confessional book *A Time for Truth*: 'Then, without warning, the unthinkable happened. In October 1973, in the wake of the Yom Kippur War, the Arab countries unanimously decided to place an embargo on their sales. . . . The long-dreaded energy crisis had arrived'.[215] Even this seems contradictory: the energy crisis is described as an unthinkable event that occurred without warning, yet at the same time as long-feared. In subsequent years, however, this ambivalence was lost. The narrative that the energy crisis was a consequence of the unexpected events of October 1973 became entrenched in public discourse and among researchers, relieving key US political actors of responsibility.

'Nixon Doesn't Practice What He Preaches' – 'Simon Says . . .'

During the energy crisis and oil embargo, Nixon's energy speeches were crucial points of reference as the US government sought to assert its legitimacy and sovereignty. But they did not exist in isolation. They were accompanied by press conferences at which energy policy advisers explained the government's strategy. Some of them, such as John A. Love and especially William E. Simon, became prominent public figures themselves, who moulded both the content and the public perception of energy policy. Members of Congress, governors, local politicians and experts of various stripe also communicated their views on energy policy to the public. The TV broadcasters provided introductions to – and thus framed – Nixon's speeches, while the next day's newspapers summed them up for the general population and commented on their content. Finally, while it was moulded by the mass media, this communication did not flow in one direction. In letters to Nixon and his energy czars, national, regional and local politicians, businesses, interest groups and countless citizens responded, commented and made suggestions. Precisely because the czars were intervening ever more deeply in the field of energy, they became the key addressees for all supply problems. As significant as this communicative ensemble is to the constitution of the energy crisis and to its understanding, disentangling it is far from easy. For example, the Federal Energy Office alone received 993 letters addressed to Simon on Friday 25 January and 3,972 on Monday 28 January 1974. Many of them required individual responses, prompting the creation of a large processing system. In the case of the Energy Policy Office, in addition to official correspondence, the documentary record includes several thousand letters from November and December 1973 under the rubric of 'Public Opinion Mail'.[216]

The public discourse – featuring debates, documentary and discussion programmes on TV and radio, and comprehensive press coverage – is at least as complex. From the beginning of 1973 until Nixon's resignation on 8 August the following year, the *New York Times* and *Washington Post* alone published at least 2,172 articles containing the words 'Nixon' and 'energy'.

In English-language publications, the words 'oil' and 'energy' cropped up with increasing frequency over the 1970s, while the use of 'energy crisis' and 'oil crisis' increased even more dramatically.[217] In 1973–74, the energy crisis was on everybody's lips. In early January 1974, according to a Gallup survey, 46 per cent of all Americans considered the energy crisis the most important problem confronting the United States. It thus toppled the high cost of living from the top of the rankings – if only for a very brief period.[218] Coverage of the oil crisis was surprisingly in depth and well grounded, not just in specialist publications dedicated to oil and energy but in the daily press as well.

There was no need to read a newspaper to become aware of and informed about the energy crisis. On 4 September 1973 at 8 p.m., NBC broadcast a three-hour documentary entitled *An American White Paper – The Energy Crisis*. This gives a sense of the quality of the broad public debate on the energy problem in advance of the true oil crisis.[219] While the film was devoted to the problem of energy as a whole, the focus was on oil. It begins with King Faisal of Saudi Arabia declaring that US policy is making it difficult to maintain the close friendship between his country and the United States. The next time he appears, viewers are informed: 'This is King Faisal of Saudi Arabia. He's going to have a great deal to say in the next few years about the way you live'. Having highlighted the central role of oil in the US energy supply and again elaborated on Saudi Arabia's unique importance to the global oil market, the film openly discussed the threat of an embargo and the growing pressure on Saudi Arabia to deploy oil as a weapon against the West. This meant making a direct link between the individual well-being of US citizens and decisions made by the rulers of remote countries, who were portrayed as exotic. Yet the documentary remained balanced, locating the causes of the energy crisis chiefly inside the United States and in the 'American way of life': 'We are a high energy, technological, advanced affluent society – wasteful and polluting'. This was the key factor threatening the nation's greatness and raising the prospect of a premature end to the 'American Century': 'For almost three decades we have been the richest, most powerful nation on earth. Now a nation of six million warns us we must change our foreign policy if we want full gas tanks. This is the world we expect to live in until we produce new fuels to replace the oil we no longer have'. When it came to whether the oil companies had helped to cause the oil crisis, the documentary was ambivalent. Even the concluding remarks offered no simple solutions, instead arguing that only combining energy savings and alternative energy sources could improve things. The greatness of the nation would ultimately depend on whether it managed to do this. *An American White Paper – The Energy Crisis* received rave reviews in the press. When the oil embargo had begun, NBC staff often referred to it in their interactions with key figures in US energy policy.[220]

Very few Americans, then, will have needed the president's energy speeches in October and November to make them aware of the energy problem. But it was around these speeches that the discourse on political legitimacy and sovereignty crystallized during the energy crisis. There were two reasons for this. First, they dealt with issues of sovereign policymaking on energy. Second, Nixon himself had raised energy saving to the status of moral imperative, in light of which the government's conduct too was now judged. After his energy speech in June, US government departments already began to give all staff specific instructions on how to save energy. In the Treasury Department, this advice encompassed behaviour in the workplace, where staff should avoid turning on appliances and lights unnecessarily. But it also extended to the private sphere: employees were urged to buy low-consumption cars and turn down their heating and air conditioners.[221] Secretary of the Interior Rogers B. Morton addressed all staff members with similar suggestions and such basic, practical, everyday advice as to wear light clothing in summer and warm clothing in winter. He reasoned that 'as employees of the Department having the major Federal responsibility for energy conservation, and as citizens, we have an obligation to be actively engaged in conserving our nation's energy resources'.[222] The Department of Defense was responsible for 85 per cent of government energy consumption, so it was a prime candidate for major energy savings. In light of security concerns, however, it was also one of the most sensitive parts of the administration.[223] As the energy crisis spread, the Pentagon, like all other ministries, called on its staff to save energy, for example issuing a detailed 'Commanders' Checklist for Energy Conservation'. It also reduced military air and sea exercises.[224]

From the outset, the question of what Nixon and his government were doing to save energy played a major role in the public perception of his energy speeches. At the press conference on the energy speech of 29 June, a reporter asked John A. Love and Charles DiBona whether the president would cut his air travel to the same degree he expected from the general population. When Love answered that this had not been discussed, the reporter asked whether they had talked about the air conditioners in the White House. But this topic too had been absent from Love's meeting with Nixon.[225] Over the next few months, Love pressed Nixon to make publicly visible efforts to save energy. The president's statements, however, were always accompanied by intense debate on the seriousness of his efforts and his moral integrity.

In the days leading up to Nixon's speech on 7 November, the energy crisis and the Watergate scandal dominated the news, and the issues were often linked. The NBC White House correspondent reported that the decision to make the speech had been taken only after lengthy discussions. Officials feared it might be interpreted as an overly obvious attempt to divert attention away from Watergate.[226] On the day of the speech itself, the broadcasters agreed that the embargo was not the cause of the energy crisis and that the energy-saving initiatives were essentially justified. But they also reported Nixon's afternoon meeting with the governors, in which they had discussed possible rationing. Given the failure of this topic to appear in Nixon's speech, they questioned whether the proposed measures were sufficient.[227] Commentators in the *New York Times* and *Washington Post* raised similar issues. Edward Cowan saw Nixon's decision to give a speech on energy as a 'double opportunity – to tackle the substance of the energy problem and to show himself to the public as a President who has not been rendered politically impotent by the Watergate controversy'.[228] By making this explicit, he robbed the strategy of much of its persuasiveness, but judged it a failure in any case because the voluntary measures were not enough to resolve the energy crisis. This appraisal dovetailed with the basic thrust of the reports in both newspapers. They explicitly welcomed Nixon's energy-saving proposals as a means of securing US sovereignty: 'Sixty-eight degrees is a bit chilly but, in a good cause, it is tolerable. The cause in this case is, in fact, the economic and political independence of the United States. . . . If we have to turn down the thermostat, or raise prices, or ration gasoline to keep our Arab friends from bending our national interests, the President is surely correct in concluding that most Americans will choose to do just that'.[229] The *New York Times* even mustered a number of doctors who confirmed the views of Nixon's physician that lower temperatures in homes were healthier, even if they had no medical studies but merely common sense to back this up.[230]

While the *New York Times* and *Washington Post* were generally supportive of energy saving, they considered it too little and too late to make any difference to the winter of 1973–74.[231] Above all, these papers criticized Nixon's attempt to shift responsibility onto Congress, assailing it as a transparent manoeuvre intended to mask his own 'belated awakening' and inactivity as a result of Watergate.[232] Watergate and energy were closely associated even in the newspapers' layout. Edward Cowan's article on energy policy in the *New York Times* appeared directly below an opinion piece calling for Nixon's removal from office. Though it was meant to be the highlight of Nixon's speech, the press ignored completely his announcement of Project Independence, paying far more attention to issues of political credibility. In light of the unanswered questions about the president's planes at the Love-DiBona press conference, the *New York Times* contended: 'The White House undoubtedly will have to address itself soon to the 2,000 gallons of jet fuel the President's official plane burns each hour of flight from San Clemente or Key Biscayne'.[233] It also published a lengthy article claiming that few drivers were adhering to Nixon's proposed speed limits: 'An automobile driven along Shirley Highway yesterday at 50 miles an hour, the speed recommended by President Nixon in the face of an energy crisis, was passed in a seven-mile stretch by 36 automobiles, two trucks, a Metrobus and a motorcycle'.[234] The nub of the article was that the number plates of some of these cars revealed them to be the official vehicles of various public agencies.

The energy czar's unnecessary car journeys in his official limousine also attracted public attention: 'Love Uses Limousine and Goes Extra Mile' was the headline of an article in the *New York Times* of 9 November. More sardonic still, the *Charlotte Observer* covered the Associated Press report with alliterative panache: 'Guess Who Guzzles Gasoline?' This article so infuriated Vicky H. from Rock Hill, South Carolina, that she cut it out and sent it to John A. Love the same day, along with a handwritten letter: 'If the article is true, then I feel that you and your associates are not being very fair to the American people. Why should we take drastic measures to curtail our fuel consumption when you seem to use more than necessary? ... I would be *more* than willing to try to help this crisis if I knew that government officials were doing their part also'.[235] This chimed with the views of Wilbur M. of Pasco, Washington, upon reading a similar article in the *Oregonian*. As a Republican, he was increasingly disillusioned and disappointed about the country's leadership.[236] In his speeches, Nixon had repeatedly emphasized that all Americans must combat and overcome the energy crisis as individuals. Ordinary Americans now expected those in power to do the same.

On 25 November, this expectation found yet clearer expression. Dan Rather, CBS White House correspondent, introduced Nixon's TV message on energy with the following words: 'The President will speak about the energy crisis after he returned from Camp David Maryland Mountain Retreat by helicopter'.[237] At this point in the energy debate, most Americans already knew how fuel-intensive helicopter flights were. Outraged newspaper articles soon enlightened those who did not. They denounced the fact that 'Nixon doesn't practice what he preaches', to quote the title of an article by Jack Anderson published on 26 November in the *Hamilton Ohio Journal News*: 'The truth is that the President and his aides haven't been practicing the austerity they have been preaching. He drafted his public appeal in balmy Key Biscayne, Fla., where the warm sun kept the temperatures comfortable. His luxury jet burned 8,000 gallons of fuel to make the round trip'.[238] Detailing more of the president's energy offences, the newspaper reported that Nixon's dog disliked helicopter flights and had been driven to Camp David over the weekend. An incensed Ruth S. from Hamilton, Ohio, sent this article to John A. Love, declaring that those in power should not expect the general public to obey laws they themselves ignored.[239] William E. from North Carolina was also outraged after reading a newspaper article claiming that Nixon's helicopter trip to Camp David had used six hundred gallons of petrol. In a letter to Love of 26 November, he asked almost resignedly: 'Is there not some way to get it across to our leadership in Washington that setting the example is a *must* if we are to succeed at all – not only in the energy crisis but in other areas of our American life?' The government, he stated, had a fundamental credibility problem, 'because *so* many do *not* believe in Mr. Nixon's *integrity* which is so basic in any endeavor'.[240]

The *New York Times* and *Washington Post* now began to pose more fundamental questions about Nixon's authority. 'If you liked World War II, you'll love the energy crisis', to quote Russell Baker's summation of Nixon's argument, to which he retorted: 'When we cannot drive to grandmother's for Sunday dinner because the tank is dry and when we must, therefore, sit home and listen to President Nixon who has just used 6,000 gallons of petroleum products to jet down to Florida and back urge us to sacrifice and beat the Nazis once again, we can give him a gentle, sulky Bronx cheer'.[241] For Edward Cowan of the *New York Times*, Nixon's message that the energy problem would remain within reasonable limits was particularly unsettling. He pointed out that many 'thoughtful people' were significantly more sceptical than the president. Even experts in the administration were now advocating the rationing of oil products.[242] What had become of the 'tough, strong action' promised by Nixon at the outset, asked one commentator, discerning a lack of leadership in the White House: 'The present crisis calls for the kind of Presidential leadership that has not been forthcoming. The nation's most critical energy gap today is in the White House'.[243] For Joseph Kraft in the *Washington Post*, Nixon had squandered the opportunity for a political comeback. He had failed to tell the truth about the energy situation and pursue measures capable of achieving energy autarky. Instead, he had merely set out an entirely unrealistic programme.[244] Both newspapers published the views of experts who considered the steps taken by the government insufficient and called for rationing or other drastic measures.[245] Scepticism was fuelled by Love's hints that the government would be announcing radical new measures within a week or two and would perhaps impose rationing after all.[246] When Nixon failed to announce stronger measures, many felt he was vacillating as a result of Watergate, and thus showing political weakness. In this spirit, the *New York Times* quoted Morris Adelman: 'President Nixon is dragging his feet because he knows the necessary measures will be unpopular. He is so unpopular now that he feels he cannot afford to do anything that will alienate more people'.[247]

Essentially, however, both newspapers stuck to their view that it was right to save energy, merely demanding tougher measures.[248] This dovetailed with the TV coverage. While NBC referred to the possibility of a 'dark Christmas', CBS managed to identify a positive side-effect: this year, Americans would have to celebrate Christmas in their hearts rather than by illuminating their houses.[249] The majority of letters sent to the Energy Policy Office reveal an American public surprisingly willing to save energy. Citizens and families described their efforts to do so while also proposing the introduction of compulsory measures to save more.[250] In another attempt to show that the government was communicating with the general public as directly as possible, Nixon commented publicly on these letters. In early December, he declared on TV: 'Each of these families has my personal gratitude and of the entire nation'.[251] The White House tried to ensure there would be no more negative reports on energy-guzzling presidential travel. When Nixon flew to California on holiday after Christmas, he eschewed the presidential plane, which was normally accompanied by a replacement aircraft. Instead, he flew, with a meagre retinue, on an ordinary scheduled flight.[252] White House press releases underlined the president's determination to help save energy and his desire to be close to the people, an experience he had much enjoyed.[253] Alert to possible criticisms, the White House also stated that the plane had not been full, so there was no need to remove passengers to make way for Nixon, his family and staff. Nixon himself was pleased about this public relations coup, though his security team and Henry Kissinger were far from happy about it. For reasons of security, the president flew home on a military aircraft.[254]

Most of the letters received and answered by the Energy Policy Office or Federal Energy Office were addressed either directly to Nixon or to energy czars John A. Love and William E. Simon. Staff made a distinction between letters from members of Congress, businesses and ordinary citizens. Even before Nixon appointed him energy czar, as chair of the Oil Committee Simon was one of the leading recipients of correspondence on energy policy. In his autobiography he recalled: 'No sooner did the rumor get out that I was to chair the Oil Policy Committee than I was bombarded with advice, demands and warnings from an astounding number of constituencies – ranging from the fifty-five federal agencies that had been regulating the oil industry to the industry itself to refiners, brokers, dealers, jobbers, and, of course, the eight major oil companies'.[255] Particularly when Simon took on responsibility for the complex oil distribution system, he became the key addressee for all relevant complaints and requests. Just the congratulatory missives on his appointment as head of the Federal Energy

Office in December 1973 fill several folders.[256] Apart from letters from old friends – including an ironic comment questioning how someone who had never managed to correctly translate a Latin sentence could rise to such heights – most of the congratulations came from individuals active in the oil economy or involved in oil policy. Virtually all of them underlined the gravity of the times in general and of Simon's task in particular, offered him support and courted his help. Francis W. Sargent, governor of Massachusetts, took the opportunity to request talks with Simon on specific energy supply problems: 'Congratulations (and perhaps condolences, too) . . . you are taking on the toughest job in the toughest of times. At your earliest opportunity I'd like to talk with you about the unique problems of Mass. where heating oils for industry + homes are critical + unemployment already frightening'.[257]

The majority of letters Simon received from members of Congress and industry figures referred to problems involved in the – initially voluntary and later mandatory – allocation of oil products. To distinguish here between 'congressional' and 'industry' correspondence, as the Federal Energy Office did, is artificial in as much as many businesses attempted to put pressure on the relevant government agencies via their representatives in Congress. In letters sent in the summer of 1973, many independents highlighted their meagre access to oil and called on the government to do more to help them obtain a sufficient supply.[258] In a detailed letter to Henry M. Jackson, Harry A. Logan, head of the United Refining Company, described the independents' struggle. He declared that he was no supporter of the conspiracy theory that this was a deliberate ploy by the majors to rid themselves of competition. But every mechanism ended up weakening the domestic oil industry.[259] Jackson forwarded this letter to Simon just as James William Fulbright passed on a missive from Neal Williams, head of the Farmers Oil Corporation, who also complained that it was impossible to obtain enough oil under the present system.[260] Williams had previously approached the relevant agency, namely the Office of Oil and Gas in the Department of the Interior, but had got nowhere. The same happened to the president of Sears Oil, who had filled out the complicated 'Fuel Incident Report'. When this had no effect, he urged Donald J. Mitchell, congressman for New York State, to do what he could to ensure that the 'voluntary allocation' became a 'mandatory' one.[261] Mitchell in turn passed the letter on to Simon, as he was 'extremely concerned' that Sears' business was on the brink of collapse and the government must take action to prevent this.[262]

The introduction of 'mandatory allocation' intensified the need for regulation while prompting more and more complaints to the Federal Energy Office. Senators and congressmen declared that allocations to their regions were too low and must be increased.²⁶³ In the press, cartoonists depicted Bill Simon as a highwayman with bow and arrow, stealing from petrol tanks and declaring: 'Simon Hood's the name. I rob from Wisconsin and give to Illinois'.²⁶⁴ It was not just politicians but also numerous businesses and professional groups that felt the allocations were unfair to them. In letters to Simon, they highlighted the importance of their work and the necessity for a sufficient supply of fuel and energy. Airline companies protested, as did the independent lorry drivers. The United Truckers of America lent weight to their demands by erecting roadblocks and organizing a lorry demonstration. The itinerary included a drive past the White House.²⁶⁵ Complaints came from all quarters, including some eyebrow-raising ones. The president of the American Honey Producers Association and American Beekeeping Federation was deeply worried. Around three thousand apiarists had transported their bees south in winter, and would have to bring them back north in the spring of 1974. They were concerned that the oil shortages would impede this already difficult feat of transportation, which should not be interrupted if possible. In response to a survey of apiarists carried out by Glenn Gibson, secretary of the American Honey Producers, Robins Apiaries, who described himself as a 'migratory beekeeper', stated: 'During the months of April thru June we will be transporting these bees back to Missouri. . . . Would you please advise the Federal Energy Office of our needs for fuel'.²⁶⁶ Gibson collated these demands and passed them on to Congressman Tom Steed, requesting urgent assistance: 'approximately 3,000 beemen will move 2 million bee hives from southern winter locations to the honey producing regions of the North . . . Tom, all of this means that we must have fuel waiting for us to buy up and down the highways seven days a week and sometimes during the night. I will not dwell on the importance of our industry to other segments of agriculture since you know the bees' importance. Help us if you can'.²⁶⁷ Morris Weaver, vice president of the American Beekeeping Federation, mailed Tom Steed one of its resolutions, which called for apiarists to receive special petrol coupons to transport their bees.²⁶⁸ All of this came to the attention of William Simon, who seemed quite amused. He responded that there should be no problems as the independent truckers had managed to lay claim to a sufficient supply of petrol.²⁶⁹

Letters from the general public were mostly concerned with specific energy-saving measures that the government was promoting. These they either approved of or rejected, while often proposing additional ways of saving energy, relating chiefly to external lighting and speed limits. A distinct debate arose around the extension of 'daylight saving time' to the entire year in the wake of accidents suffered by children on their way to school in the dark.²⁷⁰ Outraged, Beverly B. from Melvindale, Michigan, wrote to her Congressman John Dingell: 'Even if we were saving an abundant amount of energy, I do not believe any amount worth taking the life of a human being or causing a life to be miserable because of injury'.[271] Dingell conscientiously forwarded the letter to Simon, requesting that he establish whether changing the clocks was doing any good at all.[272] Congressman Don Fuqua of Florida also saw daylight saving time as a mistake: 'Our people have been saddened by the tragic loss of five children, victims of accidents in these early morning hours. . . . Certainly if it is found that energy is not being saved, the tragic consequences of children departing for school in the dark is not worth the price'.[273] Here Nixon's rhetoric of national sacrifice – which would eliminate any real suffering if every citizen did their part – came up against its most palpable limits, though it is remarkable how self-evidently many Americans related individual accidents to a national policy. At the same time, many people were pleased to note that the number of road deaths had fallen because of the new speed limits.[274]

Following his appointment as energy czar, Simon became the face of US energy policy in the media and the key communicator of the energy crisis. This had much to do with his craving for recognition and pronounced awareness of the need for the media-savvy communication of policy. When John A. Love was still in charge of the Energy Policy Office, Simon's staff had closely followed his public appearances and generally felt he did a poor job.[275] The media devoted a lot of attention to Simon's appointment as head of the Federal Energy Office, and he subsequently held weekly press conferences. Here he dispensed detailed information on the supply situation and energy policies.[276] As a fresh young face, the press coverage during the energy crisis virtually elevated Simon to the status of Anti-Nixon, albeit one loyal to the president. According to *Time Magazine*, Simon had been completely unknown just a year earlier but now addressed the general public in press releases and interviews several times a day. He attempted to use his credibility to persuade the people that the oil crisis was real and would not be over even when the embargo was: 'Simon in the past month has become one of the most powerful and visible figures in a Government starved for leadership'.[277] *Time* explained Simon's credibility as a result of his supposedly exceptional diligence, a pleasant contrast with a president in the death throes of his political career. Simon was 'a decisive policymaker and superbly organized administrator'. Almost overnight he had assembled a thousand 'young, eager troubleshooters' in a 'superagency' that worked day and night, on workdays and weekends, to solve the energy crisis.[278] In December he had probably broken the record for TV appearances, coming across as 'self-assured and purposeful' to some but arrogant to others. During one of Simon's numerous appearances before congressional committees, Republican senator Charles H. Percy – tacitly comparing the energy czar with Nixon – welcomed him with the remark that while there might be an energy crisis there was surely no lack of 'human energy'. Whenever he turned on the television, there was Simon, educating the public. Media reports, meanwhile, made Simon seem credible by portraying his private life, or that of his wife and their seven children – in contrast to the president – as an example of appropriate behaviour during the energy crisis: 'At home, on a seven-acre estate in McLean, Va., Simon seeks to set an example of energy conservation. Wife Carol keeps the thermostat down to 64°, and gathers the family in the library.... "I close the door and keep the fire going"', she informed the reporters. Dinner is eaten by candlelight – though father is mostly absent – and having got rid of their jeep the family now use the more economical car owned by Simon's son.[279]

Journalists were happy about the weekly press conferences and pleased that Simon and his staff made the effort to respond to their enquiries immediately, at all hours of the day. In his dealings with the press he was decidedly jovial, often cracking jokes. On 3 January, for example, he kicked off a press conference with the words: 'I am surprised to see so many people here today. We are almost out of announcements. Maybe I can ask you people lots of questions this morning and you can give me some advice about things we ought to be doing that we have not done already'.[280] He self-critically asked himself whether his efforts to lay bare all the facts about energy policy and respond immediately to enquiries was having the opposite effect to that intended. Amid the overall crisis of credibility, he mused, perhaps he had been too ambitious in his attempts at explanation, contributing to the general state of confusion.[281] Simon had a point. After all, the government's credibility could be eroded not just by too little but also by too much information, especially of a contradictory nature. The government's credibility problem was in fact so profound that many Americans doubted the reality of the energy crisis altogether. Half of what Simon had to do, then, as he himself repeatedly complained, was convince people that the oil crisis was real and would not be over even when the embargo had ended.[282] He also had to explain that neither the government nor the oil firms were responsible for the crisis.

In view of his many statements on the reality of the energy crisis, its magnitude and the policies needed to counter it, Simon became a popular subject for political caricaturists. The children's game 'Simon says...', in which every child must obey Simon's instructions, took on a new semantic dimension in this context, with the phrase often introducing Simon's proposed energy-saving behavioural rules.[283] Elliot Chiprut even modified his earlier 1910 Fruitgum Company hit 'Simon Says' for the band The Energizers:

Let's not use too much heat – THAT'S WHAT SIMON SAYS
Let's not drive too fast – THAT'S WHAT SIMON SAYS
SAVE OUR ENERGY – THAT'S WHAT SIMON SAYS
So that it will last . . .
Keep an eye on your speed – THAT'S WHAT SIMON SAYS
Keep an eye on your heat – THAT'S WHAT SIMON SAYS
SAVE OUR ENERGY – THAT'S WHAT SIMON SAYS
Use only what you need . . .
Don't leave on many lights – THAT'S WHAT SIMON SAYS
Don't drive too much about – THAT'S WHAT SIMON SAYS
Do it when Simon says – THAT'S WHAT SIMON SAYS
And you will never be out.[284]

More grist for the caricaturists' mill came from the notion of the energy czar. Henry A. Kissinger himself initiated a joint press conference in the State Department with the words: 'Well, I wanted to welcome His Majesty, the Energy Czar, to the State Department'.[285] Concealed behind this ironic remark, so it seems, was a sense of unease at Simon's popularity, media management skills and rapid ascent in Washington. Time and again during the press conference, Kissinger used irony in an attempt to put Simon in his place. He underlined that Simon's authority was restricted to domestic policy, and that he, Kissinger, ruled the roost in the State Department: 'Mr. Simon is obviously gaining on me and . . . this cannot be permitted in this building', as Kissinger began the concluding part of the joint press conference.[286]

Since Watergate, it was not just the TV broadcasters and daily press that had largely come to distrust Nixon as a person and the White House as an institution, but the American public as well. This was apparent in letters to both the media and the White House. Americans were beginning to doubt their country's sovereignty and their government's political legitimacy. They did so not so much because of what OPEC and OAPEC were doing as because of their own government's conduct with respect to energy and beyond. For Nixon, the oil embargo was a welcome opportunity to demonstrate leadership. But by this point he was so compromised that his efforts mostly came to nothing or were immediately subverted by the media. Within this credibility and leadership vacuum, William Simon then rose to prominence, seeming to embody everything Nixon was believed to lack. Through his omnipresence in the media and by imparting data on energy policy, Simon tried, first, to restore trust in the US government's capacity for effective action. Second, however, in the shape of the Federal Energy Office, he sought to build an apparatus that would enable the government to make competent decisions on energy. This threw up a dilemma for Nixon. On the one hand, it was vital to surround himself with advisers who seemed to possess competence and integrity, Watergate having compromised many of his closest colleagues. On the other hand, direct comparison with such individuals made him look bad.

Showing Strength: Public and Diplomatic Communication on the Embargo

In addition to the three strategies the administration pursued to ensure domestic sovereignty – namely institutional reorganization, the production of petro-knowledge and communication with the general public – the fourth strategy was centred on foreign policy. Ultimately, the demand inherent in the oil embargo – that the United States adopt a more pro-Arab position in the Middle East conflict – amounted to a challenge to the country's international sovereignty. The US sought to meet this challenge by diplomatic means, through negotiations with the producing countries and its European allies. In a complex communicative context, the administration tried to attain interpretive sovereignty over the embargo and establish what it would take for it to be revoked. It pursued these goals, first, through confidential correspondence and talks with representatives of the producing countries and other consuming states and, second, through a media strategy. Here there was a close interplay between personal and mass media communication. Public opinion, or the opinions of other actors, could function as arguments in diplomatic negotiations, just as deliberate indiscretion concerning confidential talks could publicly force the other side's hand. We can distinguish here between a strategy of strength and one of weakness. The former was intended to suggest to the producing countries that an embargo would have no effect, that the United States could withstand it indefinitely and would never allow itself to be blackmailed. The latter, conversely, emphasized the measures' unjust severity and the suffering of the American public in an attempt to create a public perception that OAPEC was in the wrong and prompt it to moderate its policies. There were countless hybrid positions between these two poles.

Beyond the question of whether the United States ought to demonstrate strength or weakness, debates on strategy in the immediate run-up to the embargo revolved mainly around whether a bilateral or multilateral approach was the best way for the country to secure its sovereignty over oil and energy. The views prevalent within National Security Council circles were moulded by NSSM 174, discussed in chapter 2. This inspired the demand that the country achieve energy security and become immune to international pressure with respect to energy, while ensuring its own ability to exert such pressure.[287] Even before the embargo, key governmental actors discussed with remarkable openness to what extent the US might use oil to achieve other diplomatic goals with respect, for example, to the Europeans. Amid the rapidly changing circumstances of the late summer and autumn of 1973, however, the priority was to turn the basic objective of energy security into a concrete plan of action. At Kissinger's request, on 5 October John Knubel submitted a memorandum that was chiefly intended to clarify whether multilateral or bilateral strategies were better suited to achieving energy security.[288] This memorandum was the basis for the deliberations of the Senior Review Group, which in turn laid the ground for the decisions of the National Security Council.[289] In Knubel's assessment, the United States should try to retain oil as a means of exerting diplomatic pressure on the consuming countries. At the same time, it should seek to minimize oil's potential to spark conflicts within the Western alliance. With respect to the producers, the administration should work to ensure production increases and, if possible, separate oil-related issues from the Middle East conflict.[290] According to the memorandum, due to differing interests and a lack of incentives for cooperation, a multilateral strategy would be hard to achieve within the OECD. It would succeed, at best, over the long term. Meanwhile, bilateral negotiations were likely to trigger conflicts between the consumers. The strategy paper thus called for a combination of approaches and for bilateral efforts to focus on Saudi Arabia.[291]

The US government was convinced that its European allies would be hit much harder by Arab production and supply cuts than the US itself, whose import rate was still much lower. On 15 October, the Senior Review Group discussed how the country ought to proceed within the OECD framework in case of an embargo and how it should approach Saudi Arabia.[292] On the same day, the need to define the country's foreign policy objectives in case of an embargo appeared on the National Security Council's agenda. It concluded that it would be vital, first, to restore the flow of oil to the Western world and Japan; second, to maintain the unity of the Western alliance; and, third, to secure the long-term oil interests of the United States and its allies in the Middle East.[293] Following the imposition of the embargo, on 22 October the Senior Review Group then endorsed the catalogue of objectives identified in Knubel's memorandum.[294] Furthermore, the Group concluded, within the framework of the OECD the US should focus on creating an oil-sharing mechanism for times of crisis and push for closer cooperation on research and development.

Beyond this, however, the United States' international strategy also incorporated domestic energy policies, because lower oil consumption would mitigate the impact of the embargo and thus strengthen the US government's negotiating position. In any event, in order to reorganize US energy policy over the longer term, the administration believed it necessary to implement some of the measures identified by the Energy Policy Office, along with some of the competing proposals put forward by the Treasury Department, which were then integrated into Nixon's pronouncements on energy and into Project Independence. Over the short term, however, only energy-saving measures could strengthen the country's negotiating position, but to do so they had to be made public, whether in the shape of appeals for voluntary action or laws. At a meeting on 17 October, however, when the Arab producing countries had announced production restrictions but not yet the full embargo against the United States, the Washington Special Actions Group initially decided that Nixon should not make the new energy policies public until after the crisis. Only then, in Kissinger's words, should the US show the Arabs 'that blackmail is a losing game'.[295]

This cautious approach was not just due to the optimistic belief that the conflict would soon blow over, but also to fears that highlighting the potential to save energy might have the opposite effect to the one intended. The Associated Press circulated a statement from Simon that the United States had great potential to save energy and could easily make do without Arab oil. This angered Love, who still served as energy czar and feared it might prompt the producing countries to impose production restrictions. He called Kissinger, who was just as angry: 'Tell him for Christ's sake we don't need provocative calls right now'.[296] Two of William E. Simon's staff were also concerned – in light of the poor supply situation – about newspaper articles that interpreted the Treasury Department press release on energy-saving measures as a threat to the producing countries: 'Perhaps we have been negligent in not stressing more heavily than we have, in both the press release and the report prepared for the NSC, that unpopular solutions and some changes in life styles will be required to meet expected shortages'.[297] Communication about energy-saving measures was complex, always simultaneously addressing the American people and the producing countries. A tough approach to saving energy could certainly enhance the country's bargaining power, but it might also give the impression of panic, something that must be avoided on the domestic front, to prevent hoarding, and internationally, to enable the country to negotiate from a position of strength.[298] Adopting the strong position that the country was barely affected by the embargo and could easily withstand it, meanwhile, failed to motivate the general public to save energy and might provoke the producing countries into taking even tougher steps. In a telephone call on 18 October, Kissinger thus declared: 'Say we can handle it. I know that is a token thing but if you say it's a token thing, that will force them to escalate it'.[299]

Because Nixon was generally preoccupied with Watergate, in the last few months of 1973 Henry A. Kissinger was the key figure shaping US foreign policy. On many occasions Kissinger candidly conceded that he knew little about oil and energy issues and largely relied on the economic and security policy analyses produced by State Department and White House staff.[300] Their assessment was that, in contrast to the Europeans, the

United States would survive the Arab production restrictions relatively unscathed.³⁰¹ In early November, for example, Charles A. Cooper concluded: 'The economic implications of the Arab oil embargo for us are unlikely to prove so burdensome that an early abandonment of the embargo is vital to our interest'.³⁰² US countermeasures were sufficient, he stated, because for various reasons the Arab countries would soon ease the embargo on their own initiative. Such diagnoses led Kissinger to assign low priority to the international politics of oil. His primary interest was in achieving a peace settlement in the Middle East and, in line with Cold War power politics, minimizing the Soviet Union's influence in the region. He regarded oil and energy issues as secondary and assumed that they would be resolved as part and parcel of a peace settlement. Nonetheless, they played a major role on a symbolic level because they were linked with the demonstration of national sovereignty and strength on the international stage. In his shuttle diplomacy between the opposing camps in the Middle East, talks with representatives of the producing countries and, above all, the Saudi Arabian government – as in negotiations with allied European states – Kissinger always sought to attain interpretive sovereignty over the embargo, limit its influence on international relations and secure US hegemony.

The US government did not pursue a uniform political strategy vis-à-vis the producing countries during the embargo. In view of the balance of power in the international oil economy and political conditions in the Arab world – with Iraqi and Libya striking a highly anti-American tone and thus ruling themselves out as negotiating partners – US diplomatic efforts focused mainly on Saudi Arabia. Though some State Department memoranda still aired the possibility that Iran might satisfy US oil needs, experts largely agreed that only Saudi Arabia really mattered.³⁰³ As British influence dwindled 'east of Suez', US policy in the Middle East focused on a trio of countries – the 'three pillars' – in an attempt to guarantee regional stability and a continuous flow of oil: Israel, Iran and Saudi Arabia.³⁰⁴ Iran having participated in and even pushed for the oil price rises, while condemning the embargo, Saudi Arabia was the country most likely to help bring about a shift of policy. But the Americans approached even Saudi Arabia with Orientalist reservations.³⁰⁵ Kissinger referred repeatedly, sometimes even in the presence of Arab interlocutors, to the Arabs' romanticism, which hampered diplomatic negotiations that could, as he believed, only ever involve small, pragmatic steps.³⁰⁶ More politically relevant was the longstanding tendency to underestimate OPEC and OAPEC as political forces, a tendency long opposed by oil experts such as James Akins and that now demanded revision under the pressure of the embargo.

Due to his limited knowledge of oil issues, in this policy field Kissinger was more than usually dependent on the memoranda of his staff. In late

October he expressed frustration that they had failed to provide him with a concrete plan of action. Kissinger subsequently articulated this in a staff meeting intended to lay the ground for talks with US oil companies. For years, everyone had been saying there would be an energy crisis and he would have to pursue negotiations with the producing and consuming countries and the oil companies. Yet no one knew just what the subject of these negotiations ought to be or what their objective was. 'I don't even know what the problem is. When people tell me we are consuming six million barrels a day, they might just as well say fifty thousand Coke bottles worth of oil. I don't know what that means. And I have no fixed ideas. . . . What I want to know is what the hell we are going to discuss in these negotiations. What do I discuss with these oilmen this afternoon?'[307] In the summer, he stated, he had sought in vain to convince the French foreign minister Michel Jobert that there would be an energy crisis. But if the latter were to accept this analysis and come to him for advice, he would have no idea what to say.[308] While Kissinger had only a vague grasp of oil and energy issues, he had very clear ideas about how to pursue sovereign power politics. He sensed that the US could instrumentalize the oil embargo: 'If it is true that we have more weight than the others . . . then we might even turn this crisis into a certain kind of an asset, if we could take a leadership position'.[309]

In formulating a sovereign foreign policy, Kissinger was unwilling to be disturbed either by the producing countries or the public statements of other actors such as the oil companies. Even before the embargo had been announced, he found the oil firms' advice out of place. To one staff member's assurances that the firms had agreed 'to play in a low key', he merely responded: 'They shouldn't be playing at all. They have an unparalleled record of being wrong'.[310] The oil companies were 'political idiots', and it was ridiculous that they had such power to damage US foreign policy.[311] He declared to the chief executives of Amerade Hess, Atlantic Richfield, Cabot Co., Exxon, Gulf, Mobil, Socal, Sun Oil and Texaco that some of their statements had been an 'unmitigated disaster'. They had undermined his foreign policy efforts and were unacceptable.[312] The firms should tell their 'Arab friends' that the US government was making serious efforts to achieve peace in the Middle East but would never give in to Arab pressure.

The State Department assumed that the Saudi Arabian government had embraced the embargo chiefly due to pressure from other Arab countries and that because the Saudis had to save face vis-à-vis these countries, there was little prospect of a major change of policy. At the same time, it thought there was a good chance they would take practical steps to mitigate the embargo. In preparation for Kissinger's visit to Saudi Arabia, Charles A. Cooper explained to him: 'There is a difference between Arab rhetoric and performance ... there will be both economic and political incentives for them to rely more on words and less on deeds'.³¹³ Cooper developed a strategy for the talks on this basis. Kissinger should inform Faisal that – particularly when it came to crucial matters such as the US approach to the Middle East conflict, in which the Soviet Union was also involved – American foreign policy could not be influenced by an 'illegitimate and unjustified' embargo, not least because the country could easily withstand it economically. But a prolonged embargo might strengthen the Soviet Union's influence in the Middle East and have a negative influence on US public opinion, impeding US efforts to achieve peace. The embargo would strain relations with the United States and would be inimical to Saudi Arabian interests over the long term because the United States would seek alternative energy sources and reduce its oil imports.³¹⁴ Should Faisal prove unwilling to reach an agreement, Kissinger could hold out the threat of economic countermeasures, chiefly on the part of those countries hardest hit by the embargo. To save face, Faisal might offer to alleviate the measures targeting West Germany and Japan. In exchange, the United States would do everything it could to help Saudi Arabia avoid increased pressure from the other Arab countries.³¹⁵ In light of the negligible material effect on the US, then, for the Americans the discussion revolved from the outset around the embargo's symbolic function in the Arab world. This they sought to counter by highlighting its potentially negative material effects on Saudi Arabia.

When Kissinger visited Saudi Arabia in the wake of the Israeli-Egyptian and Israeli-Syrian ceasefires, his argumentational strategy largely reflected Cooper's suggestions. On the evening of 8 November 1973, accompanied by James Akins, now US ambassador to Saudi Arabia, he first met with King Faisal at his palace in Riyadh for more than one and a half hours of talks. This was followed by discussions with Prince Fahd, who was both interior minister and deputy prime minister, and Foreign Minister Umar al-Saqqaf, both of whom had attended the meeting with Faisal as well. Above all, Kissinger underlined to Faisal the risk posed by the Soviet Union, and tried to show that Saudi Arabia and the US had the same interests on this front. The US, he contended, had had no choice but to support Israel and thus put its 'old friend' in a difficult predicament, in order to counter the expansion of the Soviet influence in the region, which would ultimately be to Saudi Arabia's detriment.³¹⁶ He minced no words in outlining the alternative to Saqqaf: 'If Arab radicals win with Soviet arms, you yourself would be threatened'.³¹⁷ It was in fact this shared anti-Soviet stance that the US hoped would provide the foundation for an agreement with Saudi Arabia, whose representatives were explicitly unhappy about the growing Soviet influence.

Kissinger and Faisal having affirmed this common ground several times over, Kissinger turned to a topic 'about which I know nothing and our Ambassador knows a great deal. This is the question of the embargo on oil by certain Arab states'.[318] When he went on to express his understanding for the emotions that had triggered the decision, Faisal interrupted him, articulating his current state of mind vis-à-vis the embargo:

> This is precisely what makes me red hot with anxiety to expedite this as fast as possible, so we can go not only to rescinding the ban but to increase our production. It has almost been calamitous to my nerves to have to take this action with my American friends. My colleagues can confirm that yesterday I nearly was incapacitated because of my nerves, but I controlled myself and was able to receive you. Yesterday I received the credentials of your ambassador, and – parenthetically, these two things are not related – I nearly had a nervous breakdown.[319]

In response, Kissinger made it very plain – though he believed he had proceeded with great subtlety – that the embargo was having no great economic effect on the United States. It was, however, having a tremendous psychological impact, strengthening the anti-Arab forces in the country and thus hampering his efforts to achieve peace.[320] Kissinger was trying to turn the impact of the embargo on its head and use it to enhance his own strategy by referring to possible counterproductive effects. Faisal countered by highlighting the dilemma facing him. He would very much like to rescind the embargo, but due to the pressure coming from the more radical Arab countries, this would only be possible if the United States changed its policy towards the Middle East and ceased its support for Israel.[321]

There seems to have been a general consensus that the embargo's material impact was fairly minor, and its symbolic dimension now moved centre stage. Kissinger was keen to avoid giving the impression that the United States could be forced to alter its foreign policy. Faisal, meanwhile, wished to counter any notion that his country was failing to show solidarity with the other Arab states. Saqqaf too underlined to Kissinger just how painful it was for Faisal to be unable to back the US, but Saudi Arabia would face terrible isolation if he did so. Not just the Arab countries but virtually every African country had expressed opposition to the United States: 'If I look with a microscope, only Rhodesia is with you'.[322] However, several members of the royal house assured Kissinger that Faisal's statements should not be taken too literally, while Prince Fahd also promised to do his best to eliminate the embargo.[323] The atmosphere of the talks having been pleasant overall, Kissinger left Riyadh with the impression that the Saudis would find a way to water down or rescind the production restrictions – at least tacitly, and under conditions other than those stipulated in the original declaration.[324]

Over the next few weeks, a growing number of reports suggested that Faisal would ease the embargo as soon as he saw concrete steps towards a 'just peace' and received a promise that the Israelis would withdraw their forces. Initially, however, there was no public change in Saudi Arabia's position.[325] Kissinger was keen to reassure the Saudi Arabian government of the seriousness of US efforts to achieve peace. In early December, he asked Nixon to write to Faisal explaining that a prolonged embargo might compel the United States to withdraw from the peace process. This, Nixon should underline, would strengthen the Soviet influence in the region.[326] A few days later, representatives of the Saudi Arabian government did in fact publicly distance themselves from the idea of total Israeli withdrawal as a precondition for easing the production restrictions. As explained earlier, the key requirement now was for Israeli forces to begin their withdrawal, as long as its objective was implementation of UN Resolution 242.[327] On 11 December, former Libyan prime minister Mustafa Ben Halim informed Kissinger that the more moderate forces in the Saudi Arabian government were merely waiting for a pretext – in other words, a pro-Arab gesture from the United States – to lift the embargo and restore good relations between the two countries.[328] Three days later, Kissinger pointed out to King Faisal during his visit to Saudi Arabia that for Nixon it was a matter of dignity and principles not to be forced into making a political decision. The king, however, again called on the United States to make a clearer public statement acknowledging Arab objectives because 'it takes two to tango'.[329] In the second half of December, there were again growing signs that Faisal would be prepared to lift the embargo, but on 27 December the Saudis denied this after differences appeared to emerge within the Saudi Arabian government.[330] Nixon's letter to Faisal of 28 December thus adopted a tougher tone. In view of intensive US efforts to achieve peace in the Middle East, Nixon noted with 'great dismay' OAPEC's decision of 25 December to continue the embargo against the United States despite increasing deliveries to Japan and various European countries.[331] If the United States were to continue exercising its influence at the peace negotiations in Geneva, the embargo would have to be lifted.

In January, reports on Saudi attitudes to lifting the embargo remained contradictory, and it became ever clearer that Nixon and Kissinger differed on strategy.[332] Kissinger was chiefly concerned with the foreign policy dimension of the oil embargo and the United States' role in the Middle East. Nixon, meanwhile, as set out above, saw energy policy as a means of demonstrating leadership and diverting attention away from Watergate. The best way to achieve this, he believed, was for him to announce the end of the embargo himself. As early as November, then, he wanted to invite King Faisal to Washington to persuade him to lift the embargo through face-to-face negotiations. After his trip to the Near and Middle East, Kissinger had gained a more complex understanding of the way the embargo worked. He pulled no punches in warning Nixon's chief of staff Alexander Haig and deputy national security adviser Brent Scowcroft against pursuing this idea any further: 'An attempt to set up meeting with Faisal in Washington is total insanity. Every Arab leader I have talked to so far has made it clear that it is far easier for them to ease pressures de facto than as public Arab policy. Only repeat only course that can work is course we are now on. Invitation to Faisal would be interpreted throughout Arab world as collapse. It would magnify, not reduce, Arab incentives to keep pressure on US via oil weapon'.[333] Were Faisal to be agreeable, however, he had nothing against Nixon's idea of announcing the end of the embargo in Washington.

Partly because he had observed Saudi Arabian efforts to ease the terms of the embargo – helping to ensure that the US Sixth Fleet was supplied with oil, for example[334]– Kissinger was increasingly disgruntled about Nixon's insistence on announcing the end of the embargo in the State of the Union Address at the latest. 'Tawdry PR gains' were not beneficial to longer-term US interests in the region, as he wrote to Scowcroft. 'There is no possible way to arrange the lifting of the oil embargo in such a way as to permit the President to make the announcement of its lifting. . . . We have gotten where we have in this exercise by dealing from (or appearing to deal from) a position of strength. Should the president now indicate to the Arabs the vital importance to the US and to him of ending the oil embargo – and ending it with an announcement from Washington – we will give strength to the Arabs in their determination to deal with us harshly'.[335] By taking this approach, the US might perhaps achieve a short-term easing of the embargo, but could assume that the next time conflict flared up with the Arab countries they would immediately impose another one. For Kissinger, then, a consistent politics of strength was indispensable. Acknowledging the symbolic nature of the discourse on the embargo, however, he made no distinction between actual strength and the mere appearance of acting from a position of strength. What mattered most was to maintain the image of US fortitude, so Kissinger tried to prevent the government from making statements that might clash with it. He advised a group of senators hoping to travel to the Middle East in January: 'Don't look soft and pleading – we can't leave the world at the mercy of twenty million Bedouins. We are a great country. They simply happen to have scarce resources'.[336]

At this point in time, Kissinger's efforts were focused on persuading Egypt's president, Anwar Sadat, to lift the embargo. On 19 January, he obtained his assurance that this would be done within a week.[337] As a result, while he continued to warn that public statements by US politicians could put this agreement at risk,[338] he was now more open to Nixon's idea of announcing the end of the embargo in the State of the Union Address. He even suggested to him that he get in touch with Faisal again.[339] Having obtained Faisal's assurance that Nixon could mention in his speech that leading representatives of the producing countries were discussing an end to the embargo, the pair put their heads together to work out how they might 'jazz it [the announcement] up a bit'. In the end they decided to refer to an 'urgent meeting' of Arab ministers, one that gave every reason to believe that the embargo would be lifted in the near future.[340] After trying to make the relevant passage more clearly convey the success of US foreign policy, the next day Nixon again sought assurances from Kissinger that this would not jeopardize the lifting of the embargo. Kissinger reassured him: 'The text we have given you has been cleared in fact suggested by Saudi Arabia and has . . . been approved by Sadat. It would be a hell of a risk for them if they disavowed you'.[341] A day later, however, the Saudi Arabian government retracted its agreement, so the speech merely included an attenuated allusion to the end of the embargo.[342]

This new reversal annoyed Kissinger, who now ceased to make a sharp distinction between diplomatic negotiations and public pronouncements. From the beginning of the embargo, in his public statements Kissinger had sought to show understanding for the emotions at large in the Arab world while presenting the embargo as unwarranted. As he declared at a press conference on 21 November, given the intense US efforts to achieve peace in the Middle East, it was inappropriate to seek to impose economic pressure. He went on to threaten that, if the embargo were prolonged, the United States would contemplate countermeasures.[343] This public warning, which Kissinger failed to corroborate in diplomatic negotiations, immediately escalated the discourse on the embargo. Not just the more radical forces but Yamani too warned Kissinger that if the US were to take military action against Saudi Arabia, it would blow up its oil wells.[344]

It was chiefly Secretary of Defense James Schlesinger who brought the military option into play, often triggering processes of rhetorical escalation. Whether it was the fear of burning oil fields or Cold War geopolitics that ruled out the possibility of military intervention, it was never seriously discussed.[345] In the heat of passion, Kissinger himself frequently declared that in the nineteenth century it would have been unthinkable for a Bedouin kingdom to treat Europeans this way, or contemplated the occupation of Abu Dhabi. Nonetheless, he considered the Pentagon's military simulations 'insane' and 'crazy'.[346] Also unrealistic was the idea of forcing the Saudi Arabian government to change course through a counter-embargo, on foodstuffs for example, freezing Saudi bank accounts in the United States or ending US military cooperation with the country. None of these measures even made it to the planning stage; while they might have irritated Saudi Arabia, they would have made virtually no difference to its security or development.[347] When it came to a food embargo, an analysis by the Congressional Research Service argued that its impact would be far surpassed by that of an oil embargo because the Arab countries could satisfy their meagre need for imports on the world market.[348] Because every demand for tougher countermeasures was carefully noted in the Arab world, in late November Kissinger and Nixon impressed on Democratic and Republican congressional leaders that threats would only make it more difficult to bring the embargo to an end.[349]

Rather than threatening countermeasures whose viability both the Americans and Saudis doubted – and thus escalating the crisis, at least on a rhetorical level – Kissinger preferred to declare that the embargo was unjustified given his efforts to achieve peace in the Middle East. On 25 January, he stated that if the embargo was not rescinded following a troop withdrawal – at this point in time he still assumed this would happen – this would be 'highly inappropriate, and would raise serious questions of confidence in our minds with respect to the Arab nations with whom we have dealt on this issue'.[350] This dovetailed with a point he had always emphasized in confidential negotiations, namely that the successes of his efforts to achieve peace showed the embargo in an ever worse light. When the Arab producing states had still made no effort to ease the embargo in early February, Kissinger went a step further. In a speech to the Harvard-Yale-Princeton Club in Washington, he quoted publicly from his negotiations with the producing countries in an attempt to reinforce the idea that they were behaving unjustly. He expressed understanding for the announcement of the embargo in the heat of battle, but after his intensive efforts to achieve peace, he had been given to understand that it would be revoked. Its perpetuation was now no more than a form of blackmail that would ultimately hamper US efforts to resolve the Middle East conflict.[351] Without mentioning the wording of the original embargo declaration or its modification by OAPEC spokesmen, then, by referring to confidential talks with the producing countries Kissinger sought to redefine the terms of the embargo to his own advantage. His message was that the United States had done its part, and it was now time for the producing countries to lift the embargo.

Kissinger was pleased with his 'blast', though his advisers had urged a wait-and-see approach.[352] Alfred Atherton, State Department expert on the Middle East, to whose advice Kissinger was generally receptive, felt that the latter's conduct had been similar to the kind of behaviour he usually criticized on the Arab side: 'Just the use of the word blackmail when we are trying to work on the quiet side with the Saudis and Faisal, gives it an emotional and as you said romantic attitude'. When Kissinger retorted that the Saudis were 'pretty rough customers and they have to know we are taking it seriously', Atherton contended that it would be a mistake to publicly challenge the Arabs, because they sometimes 'reacted perversely'.[353] Kissinger, meanwhile, worked on the assumption that his new tough stance and, above all, the threat that the US might withdraw entirely from the peace negotiations, would soon produce the desired result.[354] In mid February, the heads of state of Saudi Arabia, Algeria, Egypt and Syria had agreed in principle to revoke the embargo, as long as Israeli troops were withdrawn from the Syrian front, but it was to be another month before they announced its abandonment.[355] Kissinger, meanwhile, had long since resumed a more conciliatory tone. On 2 March, he asked Faisal again whether the embargo should not really have been revoked by now. In line with his original strategy, he went on to state that this was not an economic problem but more of a political and moral one: the United States could not allow itself to be pressured by friends in this way.[356]

Overall, Kissinger's diplomatic activities vis-à-vis the producing countries and his public statements show that nations affected by embargoes do not face a simple choice between meeting the associated demands or bearing the consequences. In fact, the US government was actively involved in the communicative construction of the embargo regime, its interpretation and thus its impact and function. Nixon sought to use the embargo chiefly for domestic political aims. Kissinger's goal, on the other hand, was to demonstrate international sovereignty by attempting to redefine – from a position of strength – the terms of the embargo to the United States' benefit and prompt the producing countries to back down. In order to achieve this, it was also crucial to interact and communicate with the other consuming countries, whose conduct was another significant factor. Before we can examine the instrumentalization of the embargo in the United States' negotiations with these countries, however, we must analyse the effects of the production restrictions on West Germany and Western Europe as a whole.

Interim Conclusion

Due to massively increased consumption in the 1950s and 1960s, energy supply problems in the United States had begun before the oil crisis. In significant part these were the result of legal regulations that created no incentives to increase domestic production or imports or to reduce consumption.[357] In October 1973, when OPEC raised the oil price and Arab producing countries imposed an embargo on the United States, this merely worsened supply problems that were already on everyone's lips in the context of the energy crisis. These difficulties had already spurred the revamping of US energy policies, but the US government accelerated this process in response to the producing countries' measures, which generated tremendous insecurity in October 1973. Battered by the Watergate scandal, Nixon tried to demonstrate his capacity for effective action on energy policy. In 'Project Independence', his message to the American people was that securing energy sovereignty required the nation to show its greatness and individuals to demonstrate their morality. The government pursued four basic strategies, which were always intended to maintain and demonstrate sovereignty and a capacity for effective action. These were the expansion and centralization of the government's powers over energy policy; the production of governmental expertise as a basis for national energy policies; communication with the general public; and diplomatic negotiations with the producing and consuming countries.

These measures were closely intertwined. The centralization and development of an administrative machinery to tackle energy policy was intended to generate petro-knowledge. Governmental, scientific expertise on energy was meant to strengthen the general public's faith in the government's effectiveness. Meanwhile, like the longer-term restructuring of the energy mix, the goal of the successful appeals to save energy was to enhance the United States' negotiating position vis-à-vis the producing countries. Finally, Nixon was fixated on the idea of using the foreign policy achievement of ending the embargo to bolster his domestic political legitimacy. Overall, US strategies to enhance political sovereignty had a mixed outcome. The restructuring of energy policy certainly had an impact over the longer term, albeit not to the degree originally envisaged. During the oil crisis, however, this process was often so hectic and muddled that it reinforced the impression of a disoriented government. Appeals to save energy made a certain impact, but under conditions of fixed prices even this was limited. Nixon's own efforts to save energy did nothing to enhance his legitimacy. Public trust in him as an individual had been so enduringly eroded by Watergate that all attempts to moralize the oil crisis proved counterproductive. Petro-knowledge failed to provide the hoped-for foundation for policy, because it depended on basic assumptions that varied from one discipline to another and could not themselves be scientifically corroborated. Opposing camps continued to debate whether the oil crisis pointed to a genuine scarcity of this natural resource or whether supply problems could be resolved in future by the market, as long as it was free of state intervention. These differing views implied different policy responses. Paradoxically, while the rhetoric of scarcity dominated public discourse and government pronouncements, the energy-saving measures were essentially symbolic. In fact, the government placed its hopes in research and development and the fostering of domestic energy sources.[358] Project Independence was one manifestation of this, fusing together enormous intellectual and material resources while failing to achieve its declared goal of making the United States independent of oil imports. The country's dependence on oil (imports) actually grew, while the administration massively underestimated OPEC's potential to increase prices. Only the strategy of strength vis-à-vis the producing countries was successful in countering the most obvious challenge to sovereignty. But this too was problematic, as evident in the United States' contemporaneous negotiations with its European allies, to which I will turn in the following chapters.

Notes

1. Shirley Anne Warshaw, 'The Presidency: Legitimate Authority and Governance', in Moorhead Kennedy, R. Gordon Hoxie and Brenda Repland (eds), *The Moral Authority of Government: Essays to Commemorate the Centennial of the National Institute of Social Sciences* (New Brunswick, NJ, 2000), 30–36; see the contemporary critique already put forward by Arthur M. Schlesinger, *The Imperial Presidency* (Boston, 1973), x.

2. Richard M. Pious, 'Moral Action and Presidential Leadership', in Moorhead Kennedy, R. Gordon Hoxie and Brenda Repland (eds), *The Moral Authority of Government: Essays to Commemorate the Centennial of the National Institute of Social Sciences* (New Brunswick, NJ, 2000), 7–12; Michael P. Riccards, 'The Moral Talk of American Presidents', in ibid., 19–23.

3. David S. Painter, 'Oil and the American Century', *The Journal of American History* 99(1) (2012), 24–39.

4. David E. Nye, 'The Energy Crisis of the 1970s as a Cultural Crisis', in Cristina Giorcelli and Peter G. Boyle (eds), *Living with America, 1946–1996* (Amsterdam, 1997), 82–102, here 85; Nye, *Consuming Power*; Neil de Marchi, 'Energy Policy under Nixon: Mainly Putting Out Fires', in Craufurd D. Goodwin (ed.), *Energy Policy in Perspective: Today's Problems, Yesterday's Solutions* (Washington, DC, 1981), 395–475, here 395; Vietor, *Energy Policy*.

5. Joint Board on Fuel Supply and Fuel Transport: Fuel and Energy Situation, Winter 1972/73, Office of Emergency Preparedness, November 1972, NARA, Nixon Library, WHCF, SMOF, EPO, Box 24.

6. Joseph Lerner to William Simon: Motor Gasoline Inventories, 22 March 1973, NARA, Nixon Library, WHCF, SMOF, EPO, Box 24.

7. Fuel Shortage Incidents (Distribution Pattern), o.D., NARA, Nixon Library, White House Central Files, SMOF, EPO, Box 24; George A. Lincoln: Memo for the President: Fuel Situation in the Upper Midwest, 7 January 1973, NARA, Nixon Library, WHCF, SMOF, EPO, Box 24.

8. Statement of Farmer Cooperative Officials to Secretary of Agriculture Butz and Mr. Richard Fairbanks, Assistant Director, Domestic Council, 9 February 1973, NARA, Nixon Library, WHCF, SMOF, EPO, Box 24.

9. George A. Lincoln: Memo for the President: Fuel Situation in the Upper Midwest, 7 January 1973, NARA, Nixon Library, WHCF, SMOF, EPO, Box 24.

10. 'There's No Other Choice, Churn Out the Heating Oil (Editorial)', *Oil and Gas Journal* 71(52) (1972).

11. Ibid.; *Outline Plan for Energy Conservation by State Local Facilities*, January 1973, NARA, Nixon Library, WHCF, SMOF, EPO, Box 24.

12. Dick [Richard] Fairbanks: Memo for John Ehrlichman: Near-Term Energy Crises and Responses, 12 February 1973, NARA, Nixon Library, WHCF, SMOF, EPO, Box 24.

13. Akins, 'The Oil Crisis', 462f.

14. Wildavsky and Tenenbaum, *Politics of Mistrust*, 118; Vietor, *Energy Policy*, 5; Grossman, *US Energy Policy*, 92f., 111.

15. For a concise account of the complex price control system, see Vietor, *Energy Policy*, 236–71; on the debate on deregulation and its effects, see Jacobs, *Panic at the Pump*.

16. Steve Wakefield/Duke Ligon: Memo for Chairman of OPC: Major Oil Import Problems Requiring Immediate Attention, 11 February 1973, NARA, Nixon Library, WHCF, SMOF, EPO, Box 24.

17. DiBona to Richard Fairbanks: Comment on your memo of 12 Feb 1973 entitled 'Near-Term Energy Crises and Responses', 13 February 1973, NARA, Nixon Library, WHCF, SMOF, EPO, Box 24.

18. Ibid.

19. Charles DiBona: Memo for Earl Butz: Possible Fuel Shortages in the Midwest, 24 April 1973, NARA, Nixon Library, WHCF, SMOF, EPO, Box 24; George A. Lincoln: Memo for the President: Fuel Situation in the Upper Midwest, 7 January 1973, NARA, Nixon Library, WHCF, SMOF, EPO, Box 24.

20. *St. Louis Post-Dispatch*, 25.3.1973, 26.3.1973, 30.3.1973, 2.4.1973, 5.4.1973. Ausschnittsammlung in NARA, Nixon Library, WHCF, SMOF, EPO, Box 75.

21. 'Oil: Sharing the Shortage', *Time Magazine*, 21 May 1973; see also John H. Douglas, 'Fuel Shortages in America: The Energy Crisis Comes Home', *Science News* 103(21) (1973), 342–43.

22. Guy de Jonquieres, 'The Great American Energy Disaster', *Financial Times*, 8 June 1973.

23. George Horace Gallup, *The Gallup Poll: Public Opinion, 1972–1977*, 2 vols (Wilmington, DE, 1978), 172.

24. Seifert and Werner, *Schwarzbuch Öl*, 50; James C. Williams, *Energy and the Making of Modern California* (Akron, OH, 1997), 1; Merrill, *The Oil Crisis of 1973–1974*, vii.

25. Henry Cashen II: Memo for John Whitacker: Fuel Shortage, 12 January 1971, NARA, Nixon Library, WHCF, SMOF, Whitaker, Box 54; Office of Emergency Preparedness: Survey of Electric Power Problems, May 1971, NARA, Nixon Library, WHCF, SMOF, Whitaker, Box 57.

26. US Congress. House. Committee on Interior and Insular Affairs (ed.), *Selected Readings on the Fuels and Energy Crisis. 92d Congress, 2d session. Committee Print. Prepared for Members of the House Committee on Interior and Insular Affairs* (Washington, DC, 1972), vii.

27. Office of the White House Press Secretary: The President's Energy Message. Fact Sheet, 4 June 1971, NARA, Nixon Library, WHCF, SMOF, Edward David, Box 101; on the energy supply problems in the United States, see David E. Nye, *When the Lights Went Out: A History of Blackouts in America* (Cambridge, MA, 2010), 105–36.

28. Office of the White House Press Secretary: Nixon's Energy Address to the Congress of the United States, 4 June 1971, NARA, Nixon Library, WHCF, SMOF, John Whitaker, Box 56; Office of the White House Press Secretary: Remarks of the President at Press Conference on the President's Energy Message, 4 June 1971, NARA, Nixon Library, WHCF, SMOF, Edward David, Box 101.

29. Office of the White House Press Secretary: Nixon's Energy Address to the Congress of the United States, 4 June 1971, 1, NARA, Nixon Library, WHCF, SMOF, John Whitaker, Box 56.

30. Ibid., 11.

31. James E. Katz, *Congress and National Energy Policy* (New Brunswick, 1984); Jack M. Holl, 'The Nixon Administration and the 1973 Energy Crisis: A New Departure in Federal Energy Policy', in George H. Daniels and Mark H. Rose (eds), *Energy and Transport: Historical Perspectives on Policy Issues* (Beverly Hills, CA, 1982), 149–58.

32. Nixon's approval ratings sank from 68 per cent (approve) to 25 per cent (disapprove) at the end of January 1973 to 27 per cent and 60 per cent in October 1973 and then fluctuated very little until the end of his time in office. Gallup, *The Gallup Poll*, 95, 206.

33. National Science Foundation, *The US Energy Problem*, vol. I, *Summary Volume* (Washington, DC, 1971); Department of State: The US and the Impending Energy Crisis, 9 March 1972, NARA, Nixon Library, NSC, Subject Files, Box 321, 83.

34. Henry M. Jackson: Letter to the President: Concern about Oil Situation, 13 June 1972, NARA, Nixon Library, NSC, Inst. Files ('H-Files'); NSSM 174, National Security and US Energy Policy, Box H-197.

35. US Senate. Committee on Interior and Insular Affairs, *Federal Energy Organization. A Staff Analysis Prepared at the Request of Henry M. Jackson, Pursuant to S. Res. 45, a National Fuels and Energy Policy Study, Serial No. 93-19 (92-54)* (Washington, DC, 1973); partly reprinted in Howard Gordon and Roy Meador (eds), *Perspectives on the Energy Crisis*, 2 vols (Ann Arbor, MI, 1977), 149–64, here 149; see also 'A Staff Analysis Prepared at the Request of Henry M. Jackson, Chairman, Committee on Interior and Insular Affairs, United States Senate. Pursuant to S. Res. 45, a National Fuels and Energy Policy Study, Serial No. 93-19 (92-54), Washington 1973', in ibid., 149–64; see Wildavsky and Tenenbaum, *Politics of Mistrust*, 119–23.

36. Hastings Keith to John C. Whitaker: Over a Barrel? A Report of a Trip Concerning Energy, 22 June 1972, NARA, Nixon Library, WHCF, SMOF, John Whitaker, Box 56. See other letters in: Nixon Library, WHCF, SMOF, EPO, Box 24, Folder: Energy Policy; John G. McLean, 'The United States Energy Outlook and Its Implications for National Energy Policy', *Annals of the American Academy of Political and Social Science* 410 (November 1973), 97–105.

37. US Congress. Senate. Committee on Foreign Relations, *Energy and Foreign Policy*, 81, 207.

38. 'The Quality of Government', *Washington Post*, 3 June 1973.

39. Grossman, *US Energy Policy*, 18–21 describes this critically as a crisis-induced 'do something' approach, which prompted wrongheaded or pointless decisions.

40. Bruce Kehrli to H.R. Haldeman: White House Staff Man on Energy, 5 February 1973, NARA, Nixon Library, WHSF, SMOF, Staff Secretary, Box 96; on the divergent views on the provision of staff and space, see ibid.

41. Bruce Andre Beaubouef, *The Strategic Petroleum Reserve: US Energy Security and Oil Politics, 1975–2005* (College Station, TX, 2007), 11–12; Yergin, *The Prize*, 591.

42. Executive Order 11712: Special Committee on Energy and National Energy Office, 18 April 1973, NARA, Nixon Library, WHCF, Subject Files, FG 6-23, Box 1.

43. De Marchi, 'Energy Policy under Nixon', 434; Katz, *Congress and National Energy Policy*, 18.

44. De Marchi, 'Energy Policy under Nixon', 435f.

45. Office of the White House Press Secretary: Statement by the President, 29 June 1973, NARA, Nixon Library, WHCF, SMOF, EPO, Box 24, 2f.; similar views are expressed in: John A. Love: Memorandum for Attendees at Roosevelt Room Meeting 2 August 1973: Energy Policy Development. Implementation and Process, NARA, Nixon Library, WHCF, SMOF, EPO, Box 24, Folder: Energy Policy.

46. http://www.nixonlibrary.gov/forresearchers/find/textual/central/smof/epo.php (accessed 16 November 2010); NARA, Nixon Library, WHCF, Subject Files, FG 6-23.

47. NARA, Nixon Library, WHCF, SMOF, EPO, Box 24; de Marchi, 'Energy Policy under Nixon', 449f.

48. See NARA, Nixon Library, WHCF, SMOF, EPO, Box 61; Office of the Secretary, Supplemental Request: Office of Energy Conservation, Office of Energy Data and Analysis, Office

of Research and Development, November 1973, NARA, Nixon Library, WHCF, SMOF, EPO, Box 73. On the plans for the Department of Energy and Natural Resources, see LCL, WSP, Series III A, Drawer 12, Folder 57; for a general account of the restructuring of energy policy, see also Greenberger et al., *Caught Unawares*, 99–106.

49. Executive Order 11703: Assigning Policy Development and Direction Functions with Respect to the Oil Import Control Program, 2 February 1973, NARA, Nixon Library, WHSF, Subject Files, FG 276.

50. Remarks by William E. Simon, Deputy Secretary of the Treasury, Announcing His Appointment as Chairman of the Oil Policy Committee, 26 January 1973; Memo for the Record: Notes of Oil Policy Committee Meeting, 13 February 1973, LCL, WSP, Series III A, Drawer 15, Folder 40.

51. William E. Simon and John M. Caher, *A Time for Reflection: An Autobiography* (Washington, DC/Lanham, MD, 2004), 78.

52. On the Energy Emergency Action Group, see NARA, Nixon Library, WHCF, SMOF, EPO, Box 24.

53. By mid October, the conflict between Love and Simon was already so intense that Brent Scowcroft warned Kissinger to avoid having Simon come to a meeting of the Washington Special Actions Group to which Love had already been invited; Kissinger Telcon with Brent Scowcroft, 13 October 1973, 1725 Local Time, DNSA, KA11224. Kissinger seems to have had a low opinion of Love's abilities, prompting him to insist that Charles DiBona should attend as well; Kissinger Telcon with Brent Scowcroft, 13 October 1973, 1730 Local Time, DNSA, KA11225. See also Greenberger et al., *Caught Unawares*.

54. NARA, Nixon Library, WHSF, SMOF, Ronald Ziegler, Box 51: News Top, 4 December 1973: 'Other major story is the departure of Love and DiBona; both resigned over the shift of power and responsibility to Simon and the new FEA; noted in some cases was Love's sentiment that he would be either superfluous or that he was roughed up – in the in-fighting with Laird-Shultz, and most probably over the issue of raising the price or rationing'. On these conflicts, see also Yanek Mieczkowski, *Gerald Ford and the Challenges of the 1970s* (Lexington, KY, 2005); Grossman, *US Energy Policy*, 27; Jacobs, *Panic at the Pump*, 69.

55. De Marchi, 'Energy Policy under Nixon', 450f.

56. Suggested Energy Statement, 10 AM, 13 December 1973, NARA, Nixon Library, WHSF, Pres. Pers. Files, Box 89.

57. Simon and Caher, *A Time for Reflection*, 84.

58. For example in the energy speech of 25 November 1975. NARA, Nixon Library, WHSF, Pres. Pers. Files, Box 89: 'I pledge to do everything in my power to insure that the decisions I have announced will be carried out swiftly and effectively and fairly . . . I intend to participate personally and on a regular basis, as I have since I last addressed you 3 weeks ago, in the work of my energy advisers'.

59. Noel Koch: Final Draft for Nixon's Announcement of the Creation of a Federal Energy Office, 3 December 1973, NARA, Nixon Library, WHCF, Subject Files, FG 6-26: 'We must now strengthen our ability to make and implement our energy program'.

60. Philip K. Verleger, 'The Role of Petroleum Price and Allocation Regulations in Managing Energy Shortages', *Annual Review of Energy* 6 (1981), 483–528, here 487; Vietor, *Energy Policy in America*, 244; de Marchi, 'Energy Policy under Nixon', 434–41.

61. Verleger, 'The Role of Petroleum Price', 491–93; Beaubouef, *The Strategic Petroleum Reserve*, 18.

62. Grossman, *US Energy Policy*, 27f.; Mieczkowski, *Gerald Ford and the Challenges of the 1970s*, 201f.; Gene T. Kinney, 'Simon Drives Hard to Turn Oil Around', *Oil and Gas Journal* 71 (April 1973): 'When Simon refers to a return to the "free market", he means an oil market remaining under price surveillance required by the oil import proclamation'; on Simon's engagement as neoliberal 'idea broker', see Rodgers, *Age of Fracture*, 7. Meg Jacobs' interpretation of energy policy under Nixon and Ford as paving the way for later neoliberal deregulation cannot

convincingly explain his life as an institution builder; Meg Jacobs, 'Wreaking Havoc from Within: George W. Bush's Energy Policy in Historical Perspective', in Julian E. Zelizer (ed.), *The Presidency of George W. Bush: A First Historical Assessment* (Princeton, NJ, 2010), 139–68; Jacobs, 'The Conservative Struggle and the Energy Crisis', in Bruce J. Schulman and Julian E. Zelizer (eds), *Rightward Bound: Making America Conservative in the 1970s* (Cambridge, MA, 2008), 193–209; Jacobs, *Panic at the Pump*.

63. Establishment of a National Energy Board and Federal Energy Administration, NARA, Nixon Library, WHCF, Subject Files, FG 6-26.

64. In addition to Sawhill, these included Eric Zausner, who had previously developed the new energy divisions in the Department of the Interior and was now responsible for data collection and analysis, John A. Hill, who had assisted the Emergency Energy Action Group, and Duke Ligon, former director of the Office of Oil and Gas. They were joined by Frank Zarb of the Office of Management and Budget. Stephen A. Wakefield from the energy division of the Department of the Interior and John A. Knubel, who had contributed to the National Security Council's studies on energy policy and assisted Kissinger at the start of the embargo, were responsible for international oil policies. NARA, Nixon Library, WHSF, SMOF, Staff Secretary, Box 99, Folder: Energy Reorganization; on the organizational structure of the Federal Energy Office, see LCL, WSP, Series III A, Drawer 14, Folder 4.

65. See Federal Energy Office: Supergrade Summary and Staffing Ceiling, LCL, WSP, Series III A, Drawer 14, Folder 4; Fiscal Year 1974 Supplemental Budget Request for Executive Office of the President. Federal Energy Office. Salaries and Expenses, LCL, WSP, Series III A, Drawer 13, Folder 16.

66. Executive Order 11790: Providing for the Administration of the Federal Energy Administration Act of 1974, 25 June 1974, NARA, Nixon Library, WHCF, Subject Files, FG 377, Box 1.

67. Frank G. Zarb: Memo for Alexander Haig: Coordinating Energy Policy and Programs, 8 May 1974; Office of the White House Press Secretary: Establishment of a Committee on Energy, 14 June 1974, NARA, Nixon Library, WHSF, SMOF, Staff Secretary, Box 98.

68. NARA, Nixon Library, WHCF, Subject Files, FG 377, Box 1; see also Nixon's explanation: http://www.presidency.ucsb.edu/ws/index.php?pid=4199 (accessed 17 November 2010).

69. In the twelve months after the embargo had been imposed, two thousand energy-related bills were introduced to Congress. Most of them, however, came to nothing. In the first twenty-four months of its existence, the Federal Energy Administration contributed around five thousand pages to the Federal Register. Grossman, *US Energy Policy*, 3f.; Vietor, *Energy Policy in America*, 257.

70. Wildavsky and Tenenbaum, *Politics of Mistrust*, 141–65.

71. Robert D. Linder: Memorandum for Dave Hoopes, 23 February 1974, NARA, Nixon Library, WHCF, Subject Files, FG 6-25, Box 2.

72. Executive Order 11775, 26 March 1974, NARA, Nixon Library, WHCF, Subject Files, FG 6-25, Box 2.

73. 'Energy Disaster Might Shock Nation's Leaders into Action (Editorial)', *Oil and Gas Journal* 71(40) (1973), 27.

74. Office of the White House Press Secretary: Press Conference, 11 October 1973, NARA, Nixon Library, WHCF, SMOF, Garmant, Box 83.

75. Wildavsky and Tenenbaum, *Politics of Mistrust*, 112.

76. CIA: The Current State of the Arab Oil Embargo, 5 November 1973, CIA, Doc No/ ESDN: 51112a4b993247d4d8394534.

77. 'Arab Oil Embargo Deserves Consideration (Editorial)', *Oil and Gas Journal* 71(44) (1973), 47.

78. Greenberger et al., *Caught Unawares*, xxi, endorses Craufurd D. Goodwin's conclusion that energy policy in the United States was erratic. What was missing was a 'sizable and capa-

ble body of disinterested and broadgauged specialists competent to deal with complex issues of energy policy'.

79. NARA, Film Archive, 6694, Tape 2: Weekly News Summary of Week 3–9 Dec 73.

80. Issues and Answers: An Interview with William E. Simon, ABC Network, 6 January 1974, LCL, WSP, Series III A, Drawer 13, Folder 39.

81. Wildavsky and Tenenbaum, *Politics of Mistrust*, 145–47.

82. 'The Unknowns in the Oil Shortage', *Washington Post*, 22 December 1973.

83. Scattered examples can be found in NARA, Nixon Library, WHSF, SMOF, Staff Secretary, Box 99.

84. Federal Energy Office: Press Conference, William E. Simon and John C. Sawhill, 3 January 1974, LCL, WSP, Series III A, Drawer 13, Folder 39.

85. US Congress. Senate. Committee on Government Operations, *Conflicting Information on Fuel Shortages. Hearings before the Permanent Subcommittee on Investigations. 93rd Congress* (Washington, DC, 1973), 1, 4.

86. Ibid., 7; see also US Congress. Senate. Committee on Interior and Insular Affairs. *Estimates and Analysis of Fuel Supply Outlook for 1974, Prepared at the Request of Henry M. Jackson* (Washington, DC, 1973).

87. US Congress. Senate. Committee on Government Operations, *Conflicting Information on Fuel Shortages*, 94f.

88. According to a Gallup survey, just 7 per cent of Americans believed that the Arab countries were responsible for the energy crisis. In December 1973, 25 per cent blamed the oil firms, 23 per cent the American government in general, 19 per cent the Nixon administration in particular and 16 per cent US consumers for the supply problems. Gallup, *The Gallup Poll*, 226.

89. US Congress. Senate. Committee on Government Operations, *The Major Oil Companies. Hearings before the Permanent Subcommittee on Investigations. 93rd Congress* (Washington, DC, 1974), 113.

90. US Congress. Senate. Committee on Government Operations, *The Federal Energy Office*, 597.

91. Robert G. Kaufman, *Henry M. Jackson: A Life in Politics* (Seattle, 2000), 301–6.

92. For more detail, see Graf, 'Expert Estimates of Oil-Reserves'; Graf, 'Ressourcenkonflikte als Wissenskonflikte'.

93. Vietor, *Energy Policy in America*, 7, distinguishes in much the same way between a collectivist and individualist perspective on oil reserves, while Wildavsky and Tenenbaum, *Politics of Mistrust*, 20, contrast a resource- and price-oriented perspective.

94. Merrill W. Haas, 'The President's Page', *Bulletin of the American Association of Petroleum Geologists* 50 (1966), 1–2.

95. Sherman A. Wengerd, 'The President's Page: Year in Progress – Organization and Governance of Our Association', *Bulletin of the American Association of Petroleum Geologists* 55 (1971), 1125–27; Wengerd, 'The President's Page: A Single Professional Group – The Sloss Report on AAPD-AIPG Cooperation', *Bulletin of the American Association of Petroleum Geologists* 55 (1971), 1713–14; Wengerd, 'The President's Page: An Allegory on Association', *Bulletin of the American Association of Petroleum Geologists* 56 (1972), 989–90; James E. Wilson, 'The President's Page: Nonprofit, Okay – Deficit, No', *Bulletin of the American Association of Petroleum Geologists* 56 (1972), 837–38.

96. Charles DiBona to American Association of Petroleum Engineers, Anaheim, California, 14 May 1973, 3, 14, NARA, Nixon Library, WHCF, SMOF, EPO, Box 31; here also James E. Akins: New Myths and Old Prejudices, Institute of Gas Technology, 16 November 1972; Charles J. DiBona: National Energy Situation. Policy and Technical Implications [Martin Marietta Corporate R&D Conference], Baltimore, 7 November 1973; Charles DiBona at the 56th Annual Meeting of the National Coal Association, Washington, DC, 18 June 1973; Charles DiBona at the American Mining Congress, Pittsburgh, Pennsylvania, 7 May 1973.

97. Kilkenny, 'The President's Page'; Edd R. Turner, 'The President's Page: Needed – Active Geologists', *Bulletin of the American Association of Petroleum Geologists* 58 (January 1974), 1–2.

98. Merrill W. Haas, 'The President's Page: Elements of National Energy Policy', *Bulletin of the American Association of Petroleum Geologists* 58 (April 1974), 573–74, here 573.

99. Donald A. Brobst and Walden P. Pratt, 'Introduction', in *United States Mineral Resources* (Washington, DC, 1973), 1–8, here 5; on the distinction between 'reserves' and 'resources', see chapter 3.

100. Brobst and Pratt, 'Introduction', 6.

101. Donald A. Brobst and Walden P. Pratt (eds), *United States Mineral Resources* (Washington, DC, 1973).

102. Graf, 'Ressourcenkonflikte als Wissenskonflikte'.

103. Shapiro, 'James Akins, 83, Dies'; Adelman, 'My Education'.

104. Merrill, *The Oil Crisis of 1973–1974*, 20; Ian Rutledge, *Addicted to Oil: America's Relentless Drive for Energy Security* (London, 2005), 46; Yergin, *Der Preis*, 711; Beaubouef, *The Strategic Petroleum Reserve*, 11f.

105. James Akins: Letter to William Simon, 6 December 1973, LCL, WSP, Series III A, Drawer 13, Folder 13. On 27 October 2010 William Hogan also confirmed Adelman's great influence in an interview with me in Cambridge, MA.

106. James E. Akins, 'The Nature of the Crisis in Energy', *Journal of Petroleum Technology* 24 (December 1972), 1479–83, here 1479f.

107. James E. Akins: New Myths and Old Prejudices, Institute of Gas Technology, 16 November 1972, NARA, Nixon Library, WHCF, SMOF, EPO, Box 31.

108. Akins, 'The Oil Crisis', 465.

109. Ibid., 484.

110. James Akins: International Cooperative Efforts in Energy Supply, Paper Delivered at the American Petroleum Institute Meeting, Denver, Colorado, 10 April 1973, LCL, WSP, Series III A, Folder 14, Drawer 3.

111. James E. Akins, 'International Cooperative Efforts in Energy Supply', *Annals of the American Academy of Political and Social Science* 410 (1973), 75–85, here 80.

112. Morris Albert Adelman, *The World Petroleum Market* (Baltimore, MD, 1972), 1.

113. Morris Albert Adelman, 'Is the Oil Shortage Real? Oil Companies as OPEC Tax Collectors', *Foreign Policy* 9 (1972/73), 69–107, here 73.

114. Ibid., 71.

115. Morris Albert Adelman, 'Politics, Economics, and World Oil', *American Economic Review* 64(2) (Papers and Proceedings) (1974), 58–66, here 60.

116. US Congress. Senate. Committee on Foreign Relations, *Political and Financial Consequences of the OPEC Price Increases. Hearings before the Subcommittee on Multinational Corporations. 93rd Congress, 2nd session*, vol. 11 (Washington, DC, 1975), 3; see also Morris Albert Adelman, 'Population Growth and Oil Resources', *Quarterly Journal of Economics* 89(2) (1975), 271–75; Morris Albert Adelman, 'World Oil Production & Prices 1947–2000', *Quarterly Review of Economics and Finance* 42 (2002), 169–91.

117. Adelman, 'Is the Oil Shortage Real?', 91.

118. Adelman, 'Politics, Economics, and World Oil', 59f.

119. Adelman, 'Is the Oil Shortage Real?', 105: 'Get the multinational companies out of crude oil marketing; let them remain as producers under contract and as buyers of crude transport, refine and sell as products. . . . it is a simple and elegant maneuver to destroy the cartel by removing an essential part – the multinational company as crude oil marketers fixing the price on a firm excise tax floor'.

120. Morris Albert Adelman, *The Genie Out of the Bottle: World Oil since 1970* (Cambridge, MA, 1995), 1.

121. Adelman, 'World Oil Production & Prices', 169; Adelman, *The Genie Out of the Bottle*.

122. Hendrik S. Houthakker, 'Are Minerals Exhaustible?', *Quarterly Review of Economics and Finance* 42 (2002), 417–21, here 418; Wildavsky and Tenenbaum, *Politics of Mistrust*, 36.

123. Paul H. Frankel, 'The Oil Industry and Professor Adelman: A Personal View', *Petroleum Review* 27 (September 1973), 347–49; Richard J. Gonzales and Morris Albert Adelman, 'An Exchange on Oil', *Foreign Policy* 11 (1973), 126–33.

124. Jean-Marie Chevalier, *Le nouvel enjeu pétrolier* (Paris, 1973), 13.

125. Adelman, 'Politics, Economics, and World Oil', 59; Adelman repeated these accusations at the hearings on Project Independence and before the Church Committee, adding: 'Our ambassador to Saudi Arabia made wild statements about fuel oil supplies at the US East Coast being critically short by mid or late November if we did not give in immediately. For this appeasement we got what we deserved – a near tripling of prices at the end of 1973, and a further sizeable increase since then'. Federal Energy Administration, *Project Independence Blueprint. Transcript of Second Public Hearing, New York, August 19–22, 1974* (Washington, 1974), 36f.; US Congress. Senate. Committee on Foreign Relations, *Political and Financial Consequences of the OPEC Price Increases*, 12 and passim; though he is not mentioned by name, Adelman's critique of Akins is already evident in Adelman, 'Is the Oil Shortage Real?'.

126. US Congress. Senate. Committee on Foreign Relations, *Energy and Foreign Policy*, 80f.

127. Ibid., 80.

128. James Akins, Letter to William Simon, 6 December 1973, LCL, WSP, Series III A Drawer 13, Folder 13.

129. On the limits of an economic perspective on OPEC's behaviour, see Theodore H. Moran, 'Modeling OPEC Behavior: Economic and Political Alternatives', *International Organization* 35(2) (1981), 241–72.

130. Joseph A. Pratt, William H. Becker and William M. McClenahan, *Voice of the Marketplace: A History of the National Petroleum Council* (College Station, TX, 2002), 3f.

131. National Petroleum Council, *US Energy Outlook: A Summary Report of the National Petroleum Council* (Washington, 1972), 81.

132. Ibid., and John G. McLean and Warren B. Davis, *Guide to National Petroleum Council Report on United States Energy Outlook. Presentation Made to the National Petroleum Council, December 11, 1972* (Washington, DC, 1972).

133. National Petroleum Council, *US Energy Outlook*, 3.

134. Ibid., 4.

135. Ibid., 75–80.

136. McLean, 'The United States Energy Outlook'.

137. National Petroleum Council, Committee on Emergency Preparedness. Coordinating Subcommittee, *Emergency Preparedness for Interruption of Petroleum Imports into the United States. A Supplemental Interim Report of the National Petroleum Council. November 15, 1973* (Washington, DC, 1973), iii, 2.

138. Ibid., 41.

139. Ibid., 8.

140. National Petroleum Council, Committee on Energy Conservation, *Potential for Energy Conservation in the United States: 1974–1978. Electric Utility* (Washington, DC, 1974); National Petroleum Council, Committee on Energy Conservation, *Potential for Energy Conservation in the United States: 1974–1978. Industrial* (Washington, DC, 1974).

141. National Petroleum Council. Committee on Emergency Preparedness. Coordinating Subcommittee, *Emergency Preparedness. Supplemental Interim Report*, 9.

142. Greenberger et al., *Caught Unawares*, 89.

143. Ibid., 86.

144. Ford Foundation, *A Time to Choose: America's Energy Future* (Cambridge, MA, 1974), 2; see also Ford Foundation, *Energy Policy Project: Exploring Energy Choices. A Preliminary Report* (Washington, DC, 1974), 1–8.

145. Ford Foundation, *A Time to Choose*, 6, 11.

146. Ford Foundation, *Energy Policy Project*, 10, 39–41.
147. Ibid., 41.
148. Ford Foundation, *A Time to Choose*, 7.
149. Ibid., 334.
150. William Tavoulareas and Carl Kaysen, *A Debate on A Time to Choose* (Cambridge, MA, 1977).
151. Greenberger et al., *Caught Unawares*, 30.
152. Federal Energy Administration, *Project Independence Report* (Washington, DC, 1974); Greenberger et al., *Caught Unawares*, 108.
153. Federal Energy Administration, *Project Independence Report*, i.
154. Greenberger et al., *Caught Unawares*, 118.
155. Federal Energy Administration, *Project Independence Report*, Appendix 321–44.
156. See, for example, Policy Study Group of the MIT, 'Energy Laboratory: Energy Self-Sufficiency. An Economic Evaluation', *Technology Review* 76 (May 1974), 23–58.
157. Federal Energy Administration, *Project Independence Report*, 18f.
158. Ibid., 199.
159. Ibid., 200f.
160. Ibid., 25; see also OECD, *Energy Prospects to 1985. An Assessment of Long Term Energy Developments and Related Policies: A Report* (Paris, 1975), which set out two scenarios on the basis of oil prices of 3 and 9 USD. On the fundamental problems of oil price forecasts, see Smil, *Energy at the Crossroads*, 149–61.
161. Federal Energy Administration, *Project Independence Report*, 23; for a contemporary look at the price elasticity of oil demand, see also Hans Otto Eglau, 'Ein Spiel ohne Grenzen? Fachleute rechnen, wie hoch die Ölpreise noch steigen können', *Die Zeit*, 11 January 1974.
162. Greenberger et al., *Caught Unawares*, 118; de Marchi, 'Energy Policy under Nixon', 458–66.
163. Federal Energy Administration, *Project Independence Report*, 24.
164. Ibid., 25.
165. Ibid., 34f.
166. Ibid., 14, 43.
167. Paul Sabin, 'Crisis and Continuity in US Oil Politics, 1965–1980', *Journal of American History* 99(1) (2012), 177–86.
168. Federal Energy Administration, *Project Independence Blueprint. Transcripts of Public Hearings*, 10 vols (Washington, DC, 1974–75).
169. 'Project Independence' TV Spots 09/1974, NARA, Film Archive, ARC 88483.
170. Federal Energy Administration, *Project Independence Blueprint. Transcript of First Public Hearing, Denver, Colorado, August 6–9, 1974* (Washington, DC, 1974), 1.
171. Federal Energy Administration, *Project Independence Blueprint. Transcript of Third Public Hearing, Boston/MA, August 26–29, 1974* (Washington, DC, 1974), 3.
172. Ibid.
173. Ibid., 6–9.
174. Federal Energy Administration. *Project Independence Blueprint. Transcript of Second Public Hearing*, 36f.
175. Federal Energy Administration, *Project Independence Blueprint. Transcript of Third Public Hearing*, 591–93.
176. Federal Energy Administration, *National Energy Outlook* (Washington, DC, 1976), 14.
177. Ibid., 15; the oil experts of the OECD and British government produced very similar estimates; see Report of the Working Group on the Planning: Price of Oil. Longer Term Energy Problems, 1975, NA UK, CAB 184/291.
178. Federal Energy Administration, *National Energy Outlook*, 2, 25.
179. Ibid., 14, 18, 30, 32.

180. Peter Weingart, *Die Stunde der Wahrheit? Zum Verhältnis der Wissenschaft zu Politik, Wirtschaft und Medien in der Wissensgesellschaft*, 2nd ed. (Weilerswist, 2005); Sheila Jasanoff, *The Fifth Branch: Science Advisers as Policymakers* (Cambridge, MA, 1990).

181. Thomas E. Fusso, 'The Polls: The Energy Crisis in Perspective', *Public Opinion Quarterly* 42(1) (1978), 127–36.

182. On the 'talking presidency', see Rodgers, *Age of Fracture*, 15–20.

183. Office of the White House Press Secretary: To the Congress of the United States, 13 April 1973, NARA, Nixon Library, WHCF, SMOF, EPO, Box 24.

184. Ibid.

185. Katz, *Congress and National Energy Policy*, 19. The content of the speech drew chiefly on the ideas of Charles DiBona. His more ambitious proposals with respect to research and development, however, were deleted by the Office of Management and Budget at the last moment. Greenberger et al., *Caught Unawares*, 104.

186. Daniel Horowitz, *Jimmy Carter and the Energy Crisis of the 1970s: The 'Crisis of Confidence' Speech of July 15, 1979; a Brief History with Documents* (New York, 2005); Hakes, *A Declaration of Energy Independence*.

187. On the key concepts deployed in presidential speeches, see Rodgers, *Age of Fracture*, 17–20.

188. Office of the White House Press Secretary: Statement by the President, 29 June 1973, NARA, Nixon Library, WHCF, SMOF, EPO, Box 24.

189. Ibid.

190. Office of the White House Press Secretary: Statement by the President, 9 October 1973, NARA, Nixon Library, WHCF, SMOF, EPO, Box 24.

191. *Citizens' Advisory Committee on Environmental Quality: Citizen Action Guide to Energy Conservation* (Washington, DC, 1973), 5f.

192. Office of the White House Press Secretary: Energy Conservation Fact Sheet, 9 October 1973, LCL, WSP, Series III A, Drawer 13, Folder 11; the leaflets in: NARA, Nixon Library, WHCF, SMOF, EPO, Box 1.

193. NARA, Nixon Library, WHCF, SMOF, EPO, Box 1.

194. Office of the White House Press Secretary: To the Congress of the United States, 18 April 1973; Office of the White House Press Secretary: Statement by the President, 29 June 1973, NARA, Nixon Library, WHCF, SMOF, EPO, Box 24.

195. Memo for Kissinger: Emergency Oil Contingency Program, 14 October 1973; John A. Love: Memo for Henry A. Kissinger: Emergency Oil Contingency Action Plan, 15 October 1973, NARA, Nixon Library, NSC, Inst. Files, WSAG Meetings, Box H-093; John A. Love: Memo for Alexander Haig: Administration Response to the Oil Emergency, 1 November 1973; John A. Love: Memo for the President: US Domestic Response to Arab Oil Boycott, 27 October 1973, NARA, Nixon Library, WHCF, SMOF, EPO, Box 35.

196. Dave Gergen: Memo for Alexander Haig and Ronald Ziegler: Recommendation for Energy Presentation, 2 November 1973, NARA, Nixon Library, WHSF, Pres. Pers. Files, Box 102.

197. Dave Gergen: Memo for Haig: Revised Energy Speech, 4 November 1973, NARA, Nixon Library, WHSF, Pres. Pers. Files, Box 102.

198. Alexander Haig: Memo for the President: Draft Energy Speech, 6 November 1973, NARA, Nixon Library, WHSF, Pres. Pers. Files, Box 89. The concept of independence, however, had been introduced into the energy debate earlier; see Caroll L. Wilson, 'A Plan for Energy Independence', *Foreign Affairs* 51 (1973), 657–75. It was attractive in significant part because it could be endorsed by actors on both sides of the political divide; see Hakes, *A Declaration of Energy Independence*; Rifkin, *The Third Industrial Revolution*, 9–12.

199. RN Tape 11/7/73, NARA, Nixon Library, WHSF, Pres. Pers. Files, Box 89.

200. Office of the White House Press Secretary: Fact Sheet: The President's Energy Emergency Address, 7 November 1973, NARA, Nixon Library, WHCF, SMOF, EPO, Box 45;

Memorandum: Energy Meeting with State and Local Officials, 7 November 1973, NARA, Nixon Library, WHSF, Pres. Office Files, Memoranda, Box 93.

201. Office of the White House Press Secretary: Address by the President on the Energy Emergency on Nationwide Radio and Television, 7 November 1973, NARA, Nixon Library, WHCF, SMOF, EPO, Box 45.

202. Ibid.

203. Ibid.

204. Ibid.

205. Office of the White House Press Secretary: Nixon's Address to the Congress of the United States, 8 November 1973, NARA, Nixon Library, WHCF, SMOF, EPO, Box 45.

206. On this complex process, see Katz, *Congress and National Energy Policy*, 22–29, which also provides insights into the atmosphere of the congressional debates.

207. Ibid., 34.

208. Nixon: Energy Speech, 25 November 1973, NARA, Nixon Library, WHSF, Pres. Pers. Files, Box 89.

209. For a critical evaluation of these measures, see Grossman, *US Energy Policy*, 23–27.

210. Nixon: Energy Speech, 25 November 1973, NARA, Nixon Library, WHSF, Pres. Pers. Files, Box 89.

211. Radio Speech on Energy, Nixon, WHSF, Pres. Pers. Files, Box 89.

212. Ibid.

213. Office of the White House Press Secretary: To the Congress of the United States, 23 January 1974, LCL, WSP, Series III A, Drawer 13, Folder 39.

214. Issues and Answers: An Interview with William E. Simon, ABC Network, 6 January 1974, LCL, WSP, Series III A, Drawer 13, Folder 39.

215. William E. Simon and Clare Boothe Luce, *A Time for Truth* (New York, 1978), 54.

216. Golubin Memo to Simon: Administrator's Correspondence, 29 January 1974, LCL, WSP, Series III A, Drawer 14, Folder 4; Flow Chart for Mail Processing, LCL, WSP, Series III A, Drawer 14, Folder 4; NARA, Nixon Library, WHCF, SMOF, EPO, Boxes 6–17: John A. Love Public Opinion Mail 1973.

217. See the Google Ngram Viewer: https://books.google.com/ngrams/.

218. Gallup, *The Gallup Poll*, 230f.; Fusso, 'The Polls'.

219. The writers were Len Giovannitti and Fred Freed, the director was Darold Murray and the narrator was Frank McGee; NARA, Film Archive, VTR# 6523, NBC Reports: An American White Paper – The Energy Crisis, 9/4/1973, 20:00.

220. Peter Kenney (National Broadcasting Company) to William E. Simon, 2 November 1973, LCL, WSP, Series III A, Drawer 16, Folder 16; Peter Kenney (National Broadcasting Company) to Bruce A. Kehrli, 2 November 1973, Nixon, WHSF, SMOF, Staff Secretary, Box 99.

221. Department of Treasury to All Treasury Employees: Conservation Notice, 12 July 1973; Department of Treasury to All Treasury Employees: Conservation Notice, 17 July 1973, LCL, WSP, Series III A, Drawer 13, Folder 11.

222. Department of the Interior: Memo to Employees: Energy Conservation, 31 July 1973, LCL, WSP, Series III A, Drawer 13, Folder 11.

223. Department of the Interior, Office of Energy Conservation: Federal Energy Conservation. An Interim Report, September 1973, LCL, WSP, Series III A, Drawer 13, Folder 11.

224. Memorandum for Brigadier General Richard Lawson, USAF Military Assistant to the President: Petroleum Shortages in the Department of Defense, 30 November 1973; DoD and the Energy Crisis, in: Commanders Digest 14, No. 21, 22 November 1973, NARA, Nixon Library, NSC, Subject Files, Box 321.

225. Office of the White House Press Secretary: Press Conference of John A. Love and Charles DiBona, 29 June 1973, NARA, Nixon Library, WHCF, SMOF, EPO, Box 24.

226. NARA, Film Archive, VTR# 6658, Weekly News Summary, all networks, 5–11 November 1973.
227. Ibid.
228. Edward Cowan, 'Energy Volunteerism', *New York Times*, 9 November 1973.
229. 'The Thermostat, Oil and Independence', *Washington Post*, 9 November 1973; see also Thomas O'Toole, 'President Sets the Pattern', *Washington Post*, 9 November 1973.
230. Lawrence K. Altman, 'Doctors Support Nixon on Cooler Homes', *New York Times*, 9 November 1973.
231. Tim O'Brien, 'Nixon Energy Plan Held Too Late for This Winter', *Washington Post*, 9 November 1973; Gene Smith, 'Industry Acting on Energy Crisis', *New York Times*, 9 November 1973.
232. 'Energy Gap', *New York Times*, 9 November 1973; 'The Thermostat, Oil and Independence'.
233. Cowan, 'Energy Volunteerism'.
234. Donald P. Baker and Cathe Wolhowe, 'Drivers Ignore Fuel-Saving Advice', *Washington Post*, 9 November 1973.
235. NARA, Nixon Library, WHCF, SMOF, EPO, Box 9, Folder 15-43.
236. NARA, Nixon Library, WHCF, SMOF, EPO, Box 8, Folder 10-43.
237. NARA, Film Archive, VTR# 6675, Presidential Energy Speech, 11/25/1973, 19:00, all networks.
238. Jack Anderson, 'Nixon Doesn't Practice What He Preaches', *Hamilton Ohio Journal News*, 26 November 1973.
239. NARA, Nixon Library, WHCF, SMOF, EPO, Box 7, Folder 1-43.
240. NARA, Nixon Library, WHCF, SMOF, EPO, Box 7, Folder 5-43.
241. Russell Baker, 'The Less Oleaginous Life', *New York Times*, 27 November 1973.
242. Edward Cowan, 'Politics and Energy', *New York Times*, 27 November 1973.
243. 'Energy Gap'.
244. Joseph Kraft, 'Mr. Nixon's Energy Program', *Washington Post*, 27 November 1973.
245. Robert McFadden, 'Strategy Described as a "Disaster" by City's Official', *New York Times*, 26 November 1973; William D. Smith, 'Energy Men Find Nixon Plan Weak', *New York Times*, 27 November 1973.
246. Thomas O'Toole, 'Light, Fuel, Auto Speed Curbs Set', *Washington Post*, 26 November 1973.
247. Smith, 'Energy Men Find Nixon Plan Weak'.
248. 'The Latest on Oil', *Washington Post*, 27 November 1973; 'Energy Gap'; Tim O'Brien, 'Some Businesses Protest', *Washington Post*, 27 November 1973.
249. NARA, Film Archive, VTR# 6675, Presidential Energy Speech, 11/25/1973, 19:00, all networks.
250. NARA, Nixon Library, WHCF, SMOF, EPO, Boxes 7-17.
251. NARA, Film Archive, VTR# 6694, Weekly News Summary of Week 3–9, December 1973.
252. Lou Cannon, 'Nixon Flies West on Commercial Jet', *Washington Post*, 27 December 1973; John Herbers, 'Nixon Flies to Coast on Commercial Airliner', *New York Times*, 27 December 1973.
253. 'Nixon Feels Flight to Coast on Commercial Plane "Scored Points" with the Public', *New York Times*, 28 December 1973.
254. Ibid.; Kissinger Telcon with Richard Nixon, 27 December 1973, 1430 Local Time, DNSA, KA11747; Lou Cannon, 'Nixon Returns to Capital in Small Military Jet', *Washington Post*, 13 January 1974.
255. Simon and Caher, *A Time for Reflection*, 77.
256. LCL, WSP, Series III A, Drawer 13, Folder 13-15: Correspondence – Congratulations on Appointment: 1973–1974.

257. Francis W. Sargent to William Simon, 3 December 1973, LCL, WSP, Series III A, Drawer 13, Folder 13.
258. LCL, WSP, Series III A, Drawer 13, Folder 16.
259. Harry A. Logan (United Refining Company) to Henry M. Jackson, 11 July 1973, LCL, WSP, Series III A, Drawer 16, Folder 6.
260. Henry M. Jackson to William Simon, 8 August 1973, LCL, WSP, Series III A, Drawer 16, Folder 6; J.W. Fulbright to William Simon, 30 July 1973; Neal Williams (Farmers Oil Corp.) to J.W. Fulbright, 20 July 1973, LCL, WSP, Series III A, Drawer 16, Folder 5.
261. H.P. Sears to Robert Plett, 20 July 1973; H.P. Sears Oil to Donald J. Mitchell, 24 August 1973, LCL, WSP, Series III A, Drawer 5.
262. Donald J. Mitchell (House, New York) to William E. Simon: Sears Oil, 27 August 1973, LCL, WSP, Series III A, Drawer 16, Folder 5.
263. Clifford P. Case to William Simon, 30 January 1974; John V. Tunney to William Simon, 19 February 1974, LCL, WSP, Series III A, Drawer 13, Folder 17.
264. See, for example, the Wisconsin State Journal, February 1974, LCL, WSP, Series IX, Drawer 50, Folder 3, oversized cartoons.
265. Mike Duval: Memo for Alexander Haig: Truck Drivers Demonstration, Monday, 21 January, 19 January 1974, Nixon, WHCF, Subject Files, FG 6-26; for an in-depth discussion of the political consequences, see Office of the White House Press Secretary: Press Conference: William E. Simon, William J. Usery, 5 February 1974; Office of the White House Press Secretary: Press Conference: William E. Simon, et al., 8 February 1974, LCL, WSP, Series III A, Drawer 13, Folder 40; for a recent, detailed account of the truckers, see Jacobs, *Panic at the Pump*.
266. Robins Apiaries to Glenn Gibson, 31 January 1974, LCL, WSP, Series III A, Drawer 13, Folder 18.
267. Glenn Gibson (Executive Secretary, the American Honey Producers Association) to Tom Steed, 2 February 1974, LCL, WSP, Series III A, Drawer 13, Folder 18.
268. Morris Weaver (Vice President, the American Beekeeping Federation, Inc.) to Tom Steed, 4 February 1974, LCL, WSP, Series III A, Drawer 13, Folder 18.
269. William Simon to Tom Steed, 21 February 1974, LCL, WSP, Series III A, Drawer 13, Folder 18.
270. LCL, WSP, Series III A, Drawer 13, Folder 23.
271. Beverly Bernett from Melvindale to John Dingell, 23 January 1974, LCL, WSP, Series III A, Drawer 13, Folder 19.
272. John Dingell to William Simon, 31 January 1974, LCL, WSP, Series III A, Drawer 13, Folder 19.
273. Don Fuqua to William Simon, 25 January 1974, LCL, WSP, Series III A, Drawer 13, Folder 19.
274. Peter M. Ellis, 'Motor Vehicle Mortality Reductions since the Energy Crisis', *The Journal of Risk and Insurance* 44(3) (1977), 373–81.
275. Bob Nipp: Memo for William E. Simon: Gov. Love's press conference Wed. evening, 7 November 1973, 12 November 1973, LCL, WSP, Series III A, Drawer 16, Folder 22.
276. News Top, 5 December 1973, NARA, Nixon Library, WHSF, SMOF, Ziegler, Box 51.
277. 'The Whirlwind Confronts the Skeptics', *Time Magazine*, 21 January 1974, 24–29, here 24.
278. Ibid., 25.
279. 'A Fitzgerald Hero in Washington', *Time Magazine*, 21 January 1974, 27.
280. Federal Energy Office: Press Conference, William E. Simon and John C. Sawhill, 3 January 1974, LCL, WSP, Series III A, Drawer 13, Folder 39.
281. Ibid.
282. Issues and Answers: An Interview with William E. Simon, ABC Network, 6 January 1974, LCL, WSP, Drawer 13, Folder 39; William E. Simon, 'December 16, 1973', *Face the Nation* 16 (1973), 368–74, here 372.

283. See, for example, the *New Yorker* of 11 February 1974, where a newspaper-reading woman declares to her husband over breakfast: 'William E. Simon says you cannot continue to live your wastrel ways'.

284. LCL, WSP, Series IX, Drawer 50, Folder 3. Album with dedication and photo of the band in LCL, WSP, Series VIII, Drawer 48, Shelf III, Volume II Jan–March.

285. Press Conference by Henry A. Kissinger and William Simon, 10 January 1974, LCL, WSP, Series III A, Drawer 13, Folder 39.

286. Ibid., 37.

287. Philip Odeen: Memo to Kissinger: Energy-Related Foreign Policy Objectives, 15 August 1973, NARA, Nixon Library, NSC, Inst. Files, SRG Meetings, Box H-068.

288. On the genesis of this document, see John Knubel: Memo to Kissinger: SRG Meeting on Energy, 30 October 1973, 29 October 1973, NARA, Nixon Library, NSC, Inst. Files, SRG Meetings, Box H-069.

289. John Knubel: Memo to Kissinger: Alternative Approaches to Oil Problems – A Summary, 5 October 1973; Memo: Oil Supply Arrangements: Alternative Approaches to the Major Producer and Consumer States, 2 October 1973, NARA, Nixon Library, NSC, Inst. Files, SRG Meetings, Box H-069.

290. John Knubel: Memo to Kissinger: Alternative Approaches to Oil Problems – A Summary, 5 October 1973, NARA, Nixon Library, NSC, Inst. Files, SRG Meetings, Box H-069.

291. Ibid.

292. Willis C. Armstrong: Memo to the Secretary: European Vulnerability to Arab Embargo, 13 October 1973; Willis C. Armstrong: Memo to Mr. Casey: US and European Oil Supply Problems, 13 October 1973; Willis C. Armstrong/James S. Sutterlin: Memo to William J. Casey: SRG Meeting on International Petroleum Situation, Monday, 15 October 10.00 a.m., NARA, Nixon Library, NSC, Inst. Files, WSAG Meetings, Box H-093.

293. Talking Points NSC Meeting, 15 October 1973, NARA, Nixon Library, NSC, Inst. Files, WSAG Meetings, Box H-093.

294. John Knubel: Memo to Kissinger: SRG Meeting on Energy 22 October 1973, 18 October 1973, NARA, Nixon Library, NSC, Inst. Files, SRG Meetings, Box H-069, 3.

295. Washington Special Actions Group Meeting: Middle East, Minutes, 17 October 1973, DNSA, KT00854.

296. Telecon Governor Love/Secretary Kissinger, 15 October 1973, 4:05 p.m., DNSA, KA11259.

297. P.L. Essley/W.A. Johnson: Memo to Simon: Seriousness of Possible Disruptions in US Oil Imports, 18 October 1973, LCL, WSP, Series III A, Drawer 15, Folder 37. At the cabinet meeting of 6 November, Secretary of the Interior Rogers Morton still reckoned: 'Our problem is the people don't believe us that a crisis is here – if we dramatize it, we might get more cooperation'. Cabinet Meeting. Minutes, Tuesday, 6 November 1973, NARA, Nixon Library, WHSF, Pres. Office Files, Memoranda, Box 93.

298. Talking Points, 18 October 1973, NARA, Nixon Library, NSC, Inst. Files, WSAG Meetings, Box H-093; Kissinger also warned against panic reactions in: Telcon Jameson/Kissinger, 2 November 1973, 4:00 p.m. and 6:00 p.m., DNSA, KA11587 and KA11585.

299. Telcon, 18 October 1973, 10:07 a.m., Kissinger Telephone Conversation Transcripts, Box 23.

300. 'The Nixon-Kissinger Presidency', in Robert Dallek, *Nixon and Kissinger: Partners in Power* (New York, 2007), 533–66.

301. The White House: Oil Contingency Paper, 7 October 1973, CIA, Doc No/ESDN: 51112a4a993247d4d83944a0; CIA: The Arab Oil Cutback and Higher Prices: Implications and Reactions, 19 October 1973, CIA, Doc No/ESDN: 51112a4b993247d4d8394561; CIA: The Current State of the Arab Oil Embargo: Implications for the Consumers, 24 October 1973, CIA, Doc No/ESDN: 51112a4b993247d4d8394503.

302. Charles A. Cooper: Memo for Secretary Kissinger: Arab Oil Embargo and Production Cutbacks, 3 November 1973, NARA, Nixon, NSC, Subject Files, Box 321.

303. Memo: Oil Supply Arrangements: Alternative Approaches to the Major Producer and Consumer States, 2 October 1973, NARA, Nixon Library, NSC, Inst. Files, SRG Meetings, Box H-069, 2.

304. Little, 'Gideon's Band', 463; Vitalis, *America's Kingdom*.

305. Little, *American Orientalism*; Melani McAlister, *Epic Encounters: Culture, Media, and US Interests in the Middle East, 1945–2000* (Berkeley, CA, 2001).

306. Meeting with Oil Company Executives, Memorandum of Conversation, 26 October 1973, DNSA, KT00872.

307. Secretary's Staff Meeting, Minutes, 26 October 1973, DNSA, KT00871.

308. Ibid., 30.

309. Ibid., 29, 32.

310. Washington Special Actions Group Meeting: Middle East, Minutes, 17 October 1973, DNSA, KT00854.

311. Secretary's Staff Meeting, Minutes, 18 October 1973, DNSA, KT00856.

312. Memorandum of Conversation: Meeting with Oil Company Executives, 26 October 1973, DNSA, KT00872; Memorandum of Conversation [Meeting with British Officials], Secret, 7 July 1974, DNSA, KT01245: 'I never stop being amazed about the political naivete of the oil companies'.

313. Charles A. Cooper: Memo for Secretary Kissinger: Arab Oil Embargo and Production Cutbacks, 3 November 1973, NARA, Nixon Library, NSC, Subject Files, Box 321.

314. Ibid., 1f.

315. Ibid., 3.

316. Memorandum of Conversation between King Faysal and Kissinger, 8 November 1973, NARA, Nixon Library, Mandatory Review 07, Box 34.

317. Memo of Conversation between Umar al-Saqqaf and Kissinger, 8 November 1973, NARA, Nixon Library, Mandatory Review 07, Box 34, 3.

318. Memorandum of Conversation between King Faysal and Kissinger, November 8, 1973, NARA, Nixon Library, Mandatory Review 07, Box 34, 9.

319. Ibid., 9; on Faisal's frame of mind, see also Joseph Albert Kéchichian, *Faysal: Saudi Arabia's King for All Seasons* (Gainesville, FL, 2008), 119–44.

320. Kissinger to General Scowcroft for the President, 16 November 1973 [090850Z NOV 73], NARA, Nixon Library, NSC, HAK Office Files, Trips, Box 41.

321. Memorandum of Conversation between King Faysal and Kissinger, 8 November 1973, NARA, Nixon Library, Mandatory Review 07, Box 34, 10f.

322. Memo of Conversation between Umar al-Saqqaf and Kissinger, 8 November 1973, NARA, Nixon Library, Mandatory Review 07, Box 34, 3.

323. Memo of Conversation: Prince Fahd ibn 'Abd al-'Aziz and Kissinger, 8 November 1973, NARA, Nixon Library, Mandatory Review 07, Box 34, 4; Memorandum of Conversation: Meeting with Oil Company Executives, 20 November 1973, DNSA, KT00915.

324. Kissinger to General Scowcroft for the President, 16 November 1973 [090850Z NOV 73], Kissinger to General Scowcroft for the President, 16 November 1973 [100530Z NOV 73], NARA, Nixon Library, NSC, HAK Office Files, Trips, Box 41.

325. Harold H. Saunders: Memo for Secretary Kissinger: Saudi Position on Lifting the Oil Embargo, 6 February 1974, NARA, Nixon Library, Mandatory Review 07, Box 10.

326. President Nixon to King Faisal, 3 December 1973, NARA, Nixon Library, NSC, Pres. Correspondence 1969–1974, Box 755.

327. Harold H. Saunders: Memo for Secretary Kissinger: Saudi Position on Lifting the Oil Embargo, 6 February 1974, NARA, Nixon Library, Mandatory Review 07, Box 10.

328. Memorandum of Conversation with Former Libyan Prime Minister bin Halim, 11 December 1973, DNSA, KT00947.

329. Memorandum of Conversation with King Faisal of Saudi Arabia, 14 December 1973, DNSA, KT00951.

330. Harold H. Saunders: Memo for Secretary Kissinger: Saudi Position on Lifting the Oil Embargo, 6 February 1974, NARA, Nixon Library, Mandatory Review 07, Box 10.

331. President Nixon to King Faisal, 28 December 1973, NARA, Nixon Library, NSC, Pres. Correspondence 1969–1974, Box 755.

332. Dallek, *Nixon and Kissinger*, 537.

333. Kissinger to General Scowcroft for General Haig, 16 November 1973 [080745Z NOV 73], NARA Nixon Library, NSC, HAK Office Files, Trips, Box 41; Telcon with Alexander Haig, 17 November 1973, 0850 Local Time, DNSA, KA11608.

334. Harold H. Saunders: Memo for Secretary Kissinger: Saudi Position on Lifting the Oil Embargo, 6 February 1974, NARA, Nixon Library, Mandatory Review 07, Box 10.

335. Kissinger to General Scowcroft [200755Z JAN 74], 22 January 1974, NARA, Nixon Library, HAK Office Files, Box 43. The telegram must have been sent between 10 and 19 January.

336. Memorandum of Conversation: Congressional Trip to the Middle East, 10 January 1974, DNSA, KT00988.

337. Kissinger to General Scowcroft [191814Z JAN 74], 19 January 1974; Kissinger to Scowcroft [142015Z JAN 74], 22 January 1974; Kissinger to Scowcroft [112245Z JAN 74], 22 January 1974, NARA, Nixon Library, HAK Office Files, Box 43.

338. Kissinger to General Scowcroft [180846Z JAN 74], 22 January 1974, NARA, Nixon Library, HAK Office Files, Box 43: 'Secretary asks that you emphasize to all in your establishment that there must be no talk of ending the embargo, oil, or related matters, or we will blow the whole deal'.

339. Kissinger Telcon with Nixon, 22 January, DNSA, KA11867.

340. Kissinger, Telcon with Nixon, 28 January 1974, 1123 Local Time, DNSA, KA11913.

341. Kissinger Telcon with Nixon, 28 January 1974, 1910 Local Time, DNSA, KA11919; Kissinger Telcon with Nixon, 29 January 1974, 1325 Local Time, DNSA, KA11921.

342. Kissinger Telcon with Scowcroft, 30 January 1974, 0935 Local Time, DNSA, KA11927; Harold H. Saunders: Memo for Secretary Kissinger: Saudi Position on Lifting the Oil Embargo, 6 February 1974, NARA, Nixon Library, Mandatory Review 07, Box 10.

343. MEES 17(5) (23 November 1973), 8f.

344. Ibid., 11.

345. David S. Painter, 'Oil and Geopolitics: The Oil Crises of the 1970s and the Cold War', *Historical Social Research* 39(4) (2014), 186–208; Congressional Research Service, Library of Congress, *Oil Fields as Military Objectives. A Feasibility Study. Prepared for the Special Subcommittee on Investigations of the House International Relations Committee* (Washington, DC, 1975), 75.

346. See Kissinger's remarks in Secretary's Staff Meeting, 26 October 1973, DNSA, KT00871, 27; for his talks with Jobert, see Secretary's Conversation with Foreign Minister Jobert, Secret, 7401671, 19 December 1973, DNSA, KT00966, and with Sir Alec Douglas-Home, to whom he declared that it was 'intellectually absurd that 8 million Bedouins should hold to ransom the whole of the industrialized West, and at any other time in history this would have been suicide'. Record of Conversation between the Foreign and Commonwealth Secretary and the US Secretary of State, Dr. Henry Kissinger, at the Foreign and Commonwealth Office at 10:30 a.m. on Wednesday, 12 December 1973, Secret, DNSA, KT00948; Memorandum of Conversation with Walter Levy, 26 November 1973, DNSA, KT00923; Kissinger Telcon with Alexander Haig, 27 October 1973, 1228 Local Time, DNSA, KA11497: 'I do not think we can survive with these fellows in there at Defense – they are crazy'. See also Geraint Hughes, 'Britain, the Transatlantic Alliance, and the Arab-Israeli War of 1973', *Journal of Cold War Studies* 10(2) (2008), 3–40, here 33.

347. Responses to the Arab Oil Embargo, 28 November 1973, NARA, Nixon Library, NSC, Inst. Files, WSAG Meetings, Box H-095.

348. US Congress. House. Committee on Foreign Affairs, *Data and Analysis Concerning the Possibility of a US Food Embargo as a Response to the Present Arab Oil Boycott*, prepared by the Foreign Affairs Division, Congressional Research Service, Library of Congress (Washington, DC, 1973), 256; see the similar assessment by Casey in: Secretary's Staff Meeting, Minutes, Thursday, 18 October 1973, DNSA, KT00856, 19.

349. Memorandum of Conversation: Bipartisan Leadership Meeting, 27 November 1973, DNSA, KT00926, 4.

350. MEES 17(14) (25 January 1973), 1.

351. MEES 17(16) (8 February 1974), 3.

352. Kissinger Telcon with Joseph Sisco, 6 February 1974, 1412 Local Time, DNSA, KA11985.

353. Kissinger Telcon with Alfred Atherton, 8 February 1974, 0945 Local Time, DNSA, KA11993.

354. Kissinger Telcon with Alexander Haig, 11 February 1974, 1540 Local Time, DNSA, KA12011: 'The embargo is almost certainly going to be lifted this week or early next week ... result of our threat of stopping all diplomatic efforts ... It proves that the only thing these guys understand is toughness. When we were sucking around them, they kicked us in the teeth'. Kissinger Telcon with Richard Nixon, 14 February 1974, 1815 Local Time, DNSA, KA12032. Akins too was instructed to convey Kissinger's threat to Faisal; Kissinger Telcon with Joseph Sisco, 1 February 1974, 1705 Local Time, DNSA, KA11954.

355. Memorandum of Conversation: Meeting with Egyptian and Saudi Foreign Ministers and Vice President Ford, 18 February 1974, DNSA, KT01032.

356. Memorandum of Conversation with King Faisal, 2 March 1974, DNSA, KT01049, 10.

357. De Marchi, 'Energy Policy under Nixon', 427.

358. Grossman, *US Energy Policy*, 3f.

Chapter 5

WEST GERMANY WITHIN THE WORLD OF OIL

The oil crisis inspired no equivalent of 'Project Independence' in West Germany. This was not because the idea of autarky still had disturbing connotations just under thirty years after the end of Nazi rule, and would have been unacceptable both to the West German public and the country's allies. If US experts were criticizing energy independence as an unrealistic – if not dangerous – objective for the United States, the mere idea that West Germany might consciously pursue autarky would have been laughable in the 1970s. The contrast with the US could hardly have been greater. In the 1960s, petroleum had become West Germany's leading primary energy source. In contrast to its abundant coal, however, the country had to import more than 90 per cent of its oil. The major multinational oil companies provided 75 per cent of this oil, as there were no oil firms of comparable size based in West Germany (though the government attempted to change this in the second half of the 1960s by encouraging and supporting several German oil companies as they created the German Petroleum Exploration Company [Deutsche Mineralölexplorationsgesellschaft mbH or DEMINEX]).[1] In addition, since the foundation of the European Coal and Steel Community (ECSC), West Germany's energy policy had been integrated into supranational structures that constrained the national room for manoeuvre. From the outset, then, limited options for influencing the oil economy and established international commitments primed the West German government to comprehend the oil crisis as an international problem, one that could not be solved on the national level.

Again and again, West German political discourse explicitly underlined that the oil crisis threatened to thwart the legitimization of the democratic system through ever-growing prosperity. The very foundations of the state seemed to be at risk. In the debate on the Energy Security Act in November 1973, liberal Economics Minister Hans Friderichs declared before the Bundestag that the oil crisis was 'a challenge for all of us, because in this society most of us live in prosperity and abundance, even taking this for granted .... In our national economy it is not just a bit more or a bit less comfort that depends on energy. It's not just hot water, watching television or driving a car, but ultimately every job. In other words, to put it bluntly: the lives of the people of this country'.[2] In the Bundestag, Otto Graf Lambsdorff, like the economics minister a member of the Free Democratic Party (Freie Demokratische Partei or FDP), went so far as to refer to the complete cessation of oil supplies as the 'end of the world'. Were this to occur, people would have to brace themselves for 'the end of this economy and social order and an end to growth in this country'.[3] In future, West Germans would have to forego prosperity and consumption and understand that 'hitherto we have lived, worked and earned money on a basis that was probably unrealistic'.[4] The issue of sovereignty took a different form in West Germany than, for example, in the United States, which had its own major oil industry, or France, where the state controlled the energy sector, or the United Kingdom, where energy problems were exacerbated by the miners' strike but where the discovery of North Sea oil held out the prospect of relief.[5] West Germany lacked significant oil production of its own or a strong oil industry and eschewed direct state intervention in the energy sector. However, it possessed a comparatively strong national economy. One of the key questions facing the government was how to position the country within the rapidly changing world of oil in order to guarantee a secure and adequate energy supply and thus safeguard its political sovereignty.

Even regardless of oil and energy issues, the social-liberal coalition, which had been in office since 1969, changed how West Germany positioned itself within the world. It officially abandoned the Hallstein doctrine of rejecting diplomatic relations with countries that recognized the GDR, already watered down under the grand coalition; strove to improve relations with its Eastern European neighbours within the framework of the controversial Ostpolitik; and opened the way for UN membership for both German states.[6] West Germany acceded to the UN on 18 September 1973. Just under two weeks later, before the UN General Assembly, Chancellor Willy Brandt stated that in the present era sovereignty could no longer be guaranteed by the nation state alone, but only within international frameworks. In the first sentence of his speech, he underlined that he was addressing the delegates 'as a German and as a European'.[7] At present, he asserted, Europe was no more than an economic community, but it was on its way to becoming a political one. West Germany had declared its willingness to transfer sovereignty to international organizations and subordinate national to international law because 'the sovereignty of both the individual and of peoples [can] be secured only in larger communities': 'the nation can no longer attain security through isolated sovereignty. In reality, isolation creates dependencies that have nothing in common with enlightened sovereignty'.[8] Because countries and continents had 'moved closer together', conflicts and problems were no longer limited to nations or regions and could, therefore, no longer be solved on these levels. 'Spaceship Earth', Brandt went on – deploying a metaphor popular in the contemporary ecological movement – was coming up against its resource limits.[9] He warned the developing countries, which saw a 'political opportunity of a special kind' in the shortage of natural resources, that they should take no pleasure in the impending shortage. Rather, it should be a cause of concern for everyone.[10] Even before the start of the oil crisis, then, the chancellor believed the problem of oil and energy – in addition to the policy of détente and global economic interconnections – made it vital to conceptualize and secure national sovereignty within an international framework.

Within the world of oil, the West German government had to interact with a large number of national, international and transnational actors in its pursuit of energy security and sovereignty. In addition to the multinational oil companies, these were above all the United States and the international and supranational structures into which West Germany was integrated. Aspects of its energy policy were already being decided on the European level. In addition to the West German government's general effort to deepen European Political Cooperation (EPC), it attempted to develop a common energy policy with its Western European partners. In view of the global transformation of the oil market, it also seemed vital to cooperate with the other major consuming regions – North America and Japan – and this had already taken place within the OECD. Given the tremendous significance of the Middle East and North Africa as suppliers of oil to West Germany, moreover, it was vital to pay special attention to relations with this region. This was complicated by the country's difficult position with respect to the Arab-Israeli conflict. When it came to both the United States and the producing countries, the West German government sought to avoid acting alone, instead proceeding in concert with its European partners. Meanwhile, in an attempt to guarantee an adequate inflow of oil, every oil-importing country tried to improve its relations with the producing countries via bilateral negotiations and sought to utilize multilateral forums of exchange, within the framework of the United Nations for example. Finally, in the early 1970s, the social-liberal coalition negotiated treaties (the Ostverträge) with a number of Eastern Bloc countries. Hence, another priority was to further develop West Germany's relationship with these countries and – above all – the Soviet Union as it had the potential to supply the country with enough oil to reduce its dependency on the Arab states.[11]

Like no other commodity, oil shed light on the global economic web in which West Germany found itself entangled in the early 1970s. It thus pointed up the difficulties involved in sovereign policymaking. The energy programme the government adopted shortly before the oil crisis was intended to enhance its room for manoeuvre with respect to energy policy and guarantee energy security. The price rises and production cutbacks implemented by OPEC and OAPEC in October 1973 then intensified the challenges facing the country. The oil crisis rendered concrete the abstract question of West Germany's position in the world and its relations with Western Europe and the United States, the Arab world and the oil-producing countries, those developing countries lacking significant natural resources, and the Eastern Bloc. This chapter analyses how the West German government positioned the country in the world through specific political decisions. During the oil crisis, how did the government act towards its European partners and the United States, the producing countries, the Arab world, the Third World and the Eastern Bloc? As West Germany was already integrated into international structures through the EC, OECD and United Nations, due consideration must be given to their inherent logics and their influence on West German policymaking.

In order to investigate these international strategies for securing sovereignty, however, we must first reconstruct the effects of the oil crisis on West Germany or, at least, the contemporary perception of these effects. As in the United States, in West Germany the production cutbacks and price hikes generated an element of uncertainty. The West German government was keen to overcome this by obtaining better petro-knowledge, which it believed would allow it to maintain its capacity for effective political action. The increasing importance and inflation of the various types of energy expertise had major consequences for the government's efforts to steer the national economy as a whole. These efforts were to be based on the expert input provided by the Council of Economic Experts (Sachverständigenrat für die gesamtwirtschaftliche Entwicklung), which the government appointed to evaluate overall economic trends. By exploring these developments, in what follows we can examine and add nuance to the common claim that the oil crisis obliterated cherished visions of macroeconomic planning and governance.[12]

Domestic Energy Policy and Shifts in the Political Sphere

Energy Assessments and Responses to Crisis, 1973–74

When the Yom Kippur War began, the West German government was initially uncertain about its consequences for the worldwide and West German energy supply. The Cabinet discussed what to do if supply shortages occurred. It instructed Ulf Lantzke's division in the Ministry of Economics – the ministry that had produced the government's energy programme, adopted just a few weeks before – to provide regular reports on the supply situation and draw up emergency measures in case of shortfalls.[13] In light of its new tasks, over the course of the oil crisis Lantzke's division doubled its staff to more than twenty individuals. It relied on the expertise of the 'Small Working Group', formed in 1971, which included representatives of various firms and the (energy-focused) economic research institutes DIW, RWI and EWI.[14] In quick succession, the Ministry of Economics submitted to the Cabinet a series of reports on the 'Present Situation in the Field of Petroleum' and evaluated the government's options. As in the United States, United Kingdom and most other industrialized countries, politicians who had previously had little or nothing to do with energy issues – but had proceeded on the assumption of an adequate supply of energy – were now confronted with weekly or even daily reports on the supply situation. These reports posed a potential threat to their various political projects.

In West Germany as elsewhere, rapidly changing reports on the energy supply created confusion and hampered consistent policymaking. In late November, during a Bundestag debate on current energy policy, Willy Brandt's exasperation was plain as he responded to the opposition's call for him to tell the truth: 'Anyone with the slightest understanding of developments in recent weeks knows that the truth you are so keen to know has changed on a near-daily basis over the last three or four weeks'.[15] This was an opportunity for one of Brandt's main antagonists, Franz Josef Strauß of the Christian Social Union (Christlich-Soziale Union), to accuse the government of having lost control of the situation. For Strauß, the sometimes rapid changes in the energy situation were no justification for 'speaking of truths that change from day to day'. The government ought to be in a position to present precise and up-to-date data on energy and use it as a basis for policy: 'We want to know the truth. . . . We want a science-based, well-founded analysis of the technological and economic facts and their social consequences. We surely have every right to expect this given how much time your planning staff have devoted to making preparations and so long after the outbreak of the crisis on 6 October'.[16] Representatives of both government and opposition, then, professed a scientized conception of policy, though this was hard to realize under the conditions of the oil crisis. From the beginning of the crisis, the Ministry of Economics tried to provide the government with the kind of information demanded by Strauß, but its numerous reports initially entailed a large number of unknowns. As a result, they were unable to provide the certainty and clarity demanded by the opposition. At the same time, however, they lent the problem of energy a new urgency, elevating it to the upper echelons of governmental decision-making. They thus did much to construct 'energy' as a comprehensive and autonomous policy field.

On 22 October, the Ministry of Economics published its first report after OAPEC's announcement of production cutbacks. It was as yet unable to say much about their effects and restricted itself to calculating the supply shortfalls resulting from the destruction of the ports of Baniyas and Tartus and estimating the reduced flow of oil through the Trans-Arabian Pipeline. The report anticipated a supply cut of 5 per cent. The Small Working Group was to lay the ground for subsequent crisis management and steer developments 'with a light touch (prices, arbitration board)', in other words, 'without legal regulation, in cooperation with the government or, where appropriate, through voluntary consumption cutbacks by the petroleum industry'.[17] Just under two weeks later, the magnitude of the supply restrictions had become clear, but it was still uncertain how they would be implemented and what their impact on Europe would be. The Ministry of Economics now anticipated that West German crude oil imports would fall by 10 to 15 per cent in November.[18] While no serious shortfalls were anticipated before January, the Small Working Group proposed a number of steps to prevent supply problems. During implementation of the OECD's crisis prevention measures, the Group had already prepared a graduated action plan. This the government now aimed to put into effect step by step, subject to supply disruptions. The plan provided for the use of the stockpiles maintained by the oil companies; appeals to the public to make voluntary energy-saving efforts; the use of the mandatory stockpiles based on OECD guidelines; the substitution of oil by other energy sources, primarily coal; and, finally, national cuts in consumption.[19]

In the unanimous view of the energy experts, there were essentially three strategies – in addition to the development and deployment of oil stockpiles – for securing the energy supply, namely energy-saving measures, diversification of energy sources and diversification of source countries. Only energy saving, however, promised to improve things over the short term, whereas diversification could only make an impact over longer timespans.[20] Appeals to the public to save energy were also the simplest step to carry out, though the most difficult to assess in terms of impact. Paradoxically, the major German oil companies promoted the thrifty use of their products in newspaper advertisements. These provided specific energy-saving tips, which the economics minister endorsed in mid November in whole-page advertisements placed in major German dailies. Here he put West German energy problems in the context of a global shortage of raw materials, from which he derived the individual imperative to save energy:

> The days of limitless supplies of energy, especially petroleum, are over. Events in the Middle East have intensified this development. This affects West Germany as well. We can expect oil supply shortages. We must all pull together to alleviate these problems. As consumers, every one of us can make a valuable contribution. The petroleum companies in West Germany recommend that you make economical use of fuel and heating oil. . . . I support the appeals made by the German petroleum industry. There is no cause for alarm at present. Nonetheless, everyone can save energy, in the household, in the car, and at work. Timely energy-saving will guarantee our future energy supply.[21]

As noted above, in case of supply shortfalls, over the short term only energy-saving measures could improve the energy situation and thus the West German government's room for political manoeuvre, and their international negotiating position. Like other countries, then, West Germany put its faith in warnings and appeals or, to put it in more abstract terms, crisis communication, in an attempt to prevent supply problems from reaching serious levels.[22] This involved a precarious communicative tightrope walk. A threatening backdrop was required to motivate the general public to save energy. Yet it was vital to avoid painting an overly dramatic picture that might prompt hoarding.[23] From October 1973 to February 1974, the press was saturated with negative accounts of the current supply situation and gloomy forecasts of its future. These did not reflect real-world shortages.[24] However, to conclude in light of this structural reinforcing of the oil crisis in the media that there was no real crisis – because oil was never truly scarce – is as simplistic as it is beside the point.[25] It is not the things of the world that bring about social and political changes but rather their social and political perception. As Morris Adelman underlined in other contexts, the scarcity of oil may have been a fiction but belief in it was a fact. In the case of the first oil crisis, this fact accelerated the implementation of energy policies drawn up in advance, and at times facilitated the formulation of such measures in the first place.[26]

In contrast to the hard-to-assess effects of the savings appeals, the Small Working Group believed it could more precisely calculate the impact of legally enshrined consumption restrictions such as driving bans. Yet when the oil crisis began, West Germany lacked the legal basis for such measures.[27] The government had introduced the mandatory stockpiles proposed by the OECD, but had as yet passed no law that would have empowered it to impose emergency measures in times of crisis. When the oil crisis became serious, this was changed with impressive speed.[28] On 7 November, a bill on 'securing the energy supply in case of threats to, or disruption of, petroleum or natural gas imports', which had already long been in the pipeline, was discussed in the Cabinet and passed in the Bundestag two days later. This so-called Energy Security Act (Energiesicherungsgesetz) enabled the government to issue decrees on the production, transportation, storage, distribution and consumption of oil and other energy sources, 'in order to cover vital energy needs in case the energy supply is directly threatened or disrupted by threats to, or disruption of, petroleum or natural gas imports and in case these threats or this disruption cannot be remedied, or cannot be remedied in timely fashion, or only through disproportionate means, with the aid of market-compatible measures'.[29] The Energy Security Act augmented the executive's room for manoeuvre, though it granted the Bundesrat and Bundestag extensive rights of scrutiny. It was initially in force for one year, but was made permanent in December 1974. Five years after West Germany had taken over key rights of sovereignty from the Allies through the controversial Emergency Laws (Notstandsgesetze), therefore, state sovereignty was strengthened once again, in order to deal with scenarios that might have put the state order at risk. Having been 'empowered' by the Energy Security Act to intervene massively in the energy economy, and not just in a state of emergency, the Cabinet issued a series of consumption-restricting measures. The four car-free Sundays from 25 November to 16 December in particular triggered a broad public debate, burning itself deeply into the collective memory. To this day, it is often the first thing Germans recall upon mention of the oil crisis.[30]

The Ministry of Economics had anticipated a 15 per cent cut in the oil supply for the month of December, but in mid December Lantzke's division ascertained that it was in fact only 6.2 per cent.[31] Through targeted interventions, it proved possible to avert local threats, for example to the Chancellery's district heating supply – a result of the supply problems facing Bonn's municipal utilities. In general, the government and its ministries tried to save energy or at least to create the impression that they were doing so.[32] However, in view of the highly complex international situation, supply restrictions that were having only a gradual effect due to long oil tanker travel times, and the uncertainty regarding the future conduct of OPEC and OAPEC, for January the West German government continued to assume oil shortfalls of up to 20 per cent and discussed more extensive energy-saving measures.[33] A great deal of mental effort went into evaluating different bans on car use: a last-number system, according to which cars with number plates ending in 2 would be prohibited from travelling on the 2, 12 and 22 of a given month; a badge system allowing every driver to choose their non-driving day; and an alternating weekend travel ban based on even and odd number plates.[34] At a press conference on 19 December, Economics Minister Friderichs and Finance Minister Helmut Schmidt announced that the government had decided to adopt the alternating last-number system on weekends, which was to come into force a month later. On several occasions the journalists in attendance were much amused as the ministers remarked ironically on the detailed issues with which the oil crisis had forced them to grapple. Friderichs was unable to answer when asked whether the system would begin, on 19 January, with even or odd last numbers. To the caustic remark that it would probably depend on the 'whim of some official', he responded that he did not know 'whether it would be down to the division head, the undersecretary or the minister. We will have to look into that'.[35] The amusement intensified with the following verbal exchange:

> Question: Again on the travel ban. You stated that you'll be beginning with the even last numbers. Will they be allowed to travel or prohibited from travelling?
>
> [great amusement]
>
> Chairman Lorenz: Another decision is made before our very eyes.
>
> Minister of Economics Friderichs: Cars with even numbers will not be allowed to travel, cars with odd numbers – because they begin with 1 – will be allowed to travel. Or should we do it the other way round?
>
> [laughter]
>
> I am in a rather difficult position because I don't know the number of my own car off by heart.
>
> Question: What about the number zero?
>
> Minister of Economics Friderichs: We have commissioned a specialist report from a mathematician, so it will depend on what it comes up with.[36]

The West German public, in contrast to the hotel and catering industry, was surprisingly positive about the car-free Sundays. The above exchange during the press conference also indicates a considerable willingness to tackle the consumption restrictions with humour.[37] At the same time, though, as the scientization of policymaking advanced, Friderichs' ironic concluding remark laid bare the evident concerns within the West German government about its increasing dependence on scientific reports and external expertise in all policy fields. Particularly within the field of energy, the rapid changes that occurred in 1973–74 triggered a veritable explosion in knowledge production. Not least due to the long-term effects of decisions made in the energy field, precise data and forecasts seemed essential. Like its US counterpart, the West German government too regarded scientific expertise as a key instrument for maintaining and demonstrating sovereignty.

Energy Forecasts and Energy Policy Planning

In March 1974, in a talk at the University of Chicago, Finance Minister Helmut Schmidt – who, unlike Chancellor Brandt, generally tried to cut an energetic and hands-on figure – spoke with surprising emotion about his experiences during the oil crisis. He had 'felt quite helpless because, for example, there were times during the oil crisis when the information available to the West German government depended entirely on the goodwill of a few oil company directors'.[38] In much the same way, Ulf Lantzke recalled that the information procured by both the government and the oil firms based in West Germany about events in the producing countries was 'incomplete, contradictory and confusing'; only the large multinational companies had had better informational structures at their disposal.[39] In November, the government had begun – too late, in the opinion of Franz Josef Strauß – to obtain current data on the supply situation with the help of a questionnaire sent to the oil companies. The reporting system was then improved in early December. Now the oil firms had to provide regular reports directly to the Ministry of Economics, where they would be examined by independent experts.[40] Concurrently, the relevant ministries – that is, Economics; Transport; Regional Planning, Building and Urban Development; Research and Technology; and Finance – were instructed to draw up 'ancillary measures' intended to improve the energy situation over the long run.[41]

Before, during and after the oil crisis, the West German government received solicited and unsolicited proposals from scientists, industry and self-proclaimed oil and energy experts on how best to safeguard the country's energy supply. In addition to the above-mentioned economic research institutes (DIW, RWI and EWI), in the second half of the 1960s those divisions of the Ministry of Economics concerned with energy policy cooperated with the Association of German Steel Manufacturers (Verein Deutscher Eisenhüttenleute), the Max Planck Institute for Iron Research (Max Planck Institut für Eisenforschung), the IFO Institute (IFO Institut), the German Society for Mineralogy and Coal Chemistry (Deutsche Gesellschaft für Mineralölwissenschaft und Kohlechemie e.V.) and the German Petroleum Institute (Institut für Erdölforschung).[42] The Federation of German Industries (Bundesverband der Deutschen Industrie) also expressed its views on energy policy on a regular basis in detailed reports, chiefly in order to advocate the maintenance of market mechanisms.[43]

The representatives of the various branches of the energy industry engaged in a massive lobbying campaign to enhance the competitive position of their energy sources. The activities of the German coal mining industry in June 1972 provide an example. With reference to the energy crisis already unfolding in the United States and threatening to overwhelm Europe as well, its spokesmen called for the intensification of German coal production. This would help to ensure energy security and avoid balance of payments problems due to the rising cost of oil imports. They argued that the import dependency of both Germany and Europe could only be reduced if coal production at least remained at current levels. But it would be preferable to double output by 1985 given the impossibility of increasing oil, gas or nuclear energy production with sufficient rapidity.[44] In accord with the employers, during the oil crisis the Industrial Union of Mining and Energy (Industriegewerkschaft Bergbau und Energie) also called on Chancellor Brandt to ensure the country made greater use of bituminous and brown coal again.[45]

Predictably, the German Atomic Forum (Deutsches Atomforum) lobbying organization took a fundamentally different view, calling for the accelerated development of nuclear energy in order to overcome the oil crisis. The oil companies, meanwhile – which provided the relevant government agencies with copious amounts of information – still believed that oil would continue to provide the lion's share of the West German energy supply in future.[46] The government took careful note of external forms of expertise and made conscious use of them in many contexts. Exceptions included obscure submissions, such as letters sent by two Spaniards, one who wished to apply his water dowsing skills to oil fields, and the other, an autodidact and semi-invalid, who claimed to have developed a new method of coal hydrogenation.[47] On 7 November, at the expert hearings held by the Bundestag Economic Committee (Wirtschaftsausschuss des Deutschen Bundestages) on 'relevant issues in energy policy', Enno Schubert of Gelsenberg AG and Albert Hallmann of BP AG described to the deputies the situation in the international petroleum market. Two weeks later, Schubert gave members of the government his assessment once again at talks on energy in Münstereifel.[48] The indefatigable Walter Levy, who had already made his expertise available to the US government and had advised British prime minister Edward Heath on the situation in the oil market, also offered the West German government his insights.[49]

As in the United States, over the course of the oil crisis the West German government appointed more staff to tackle energy issues. However, it developed no cadre of experts of its own – comparable to the Federal Energy Administration – that might have forecast future trends or simulated alternative energy paths on the basis of the data collected by the oil firms. This task was still performed by the (energy-focused) economic research institutes, which cooperated with the Ministry of Economics in the Small Working Group. By 1972, the DIW in Berlin, EWI in Cologne and RWI in Essen had already submitted an initial report on how to secure the

West German energy supply against petroleum shortfalls. The Ministry of Economics quickly commissioned a follow-up report, which the institutes worked on during the oil crisis – in parallel to their advisory activities – before presenting it in 1974. The first report had still been vague in many areas. Now, however, the focus of attention lay on the 'use of a simulation model to help guide decisions intended to overcome petroleum supply disruptions in the Federal Republic of Germany'.[50]

On the basis of a yet-to-be-created information system, this simulation model was meant to correlate data on type of crisis, energy consumption, stockpiles, potential substitutes and the effect of possible energy policies. This would provide a foundation for decisions on energy policy. To this end, the institutes established thirty-seven consumer groups and examined the supply and consumption of twelve petroleum products in four regions (north, west, southwest and south).[51] Ultimately, this model was a feedback system, intended to precisely calculate the consequences of disruptions to the normal supply situation and the effects of countermeasures. This would, it was hoped, help to minimize disruptions to the energy supply and economic life. With respect to three exemplary cases of supply disruption, the institutes then showed the model's potential to calculate the effects of different policies, and thus to provide energy policy decisions with a rational basis. At the same time, however, they recognized the limits to the scientific grounding of policy. In case of a lack of energy, they believed it was a political decision whether to deploy stockpiles, substitute oil with other energy sources or introduce consumption restrictions. The government rather than scientists must ultimately make that decision.[52]

During the oil crisis, the institutes were still developing their energy modelling schemes, so the various ministries could not yet make use of them. Nonetheless, the latter worked intensively on a catalogue of measures to alleviate the effects of oil production cutbacks and enhance the long-term security of the West German energy supply. By the end of February, all ministries had responded to the Chancellery's request and put forward proposals concerning energy, transport and structural policy.[53] One of the most important steps taken during the crisis itself was the adoption of the Framework Programme on Energy Research (Rahmenprogramm Energieforschung). Working on the assumption that a sufficient energy supply was the precondition for the 'performance of the entire national economy' and 'individuals' quality of life', the Ministry for Research and Technology (Bundesministerium für Forschung und Technologie) highlighted the risks of focusing on fossil energy sources; the country's growing dependency on the Middle East; and environmental burdens.[54] In light of these factors, it argued, the goal must be to expand nuclear energy, use energy more rationally and frugally and explore the potential of – for example – coal hydrogenation. Together with the government's fourth Nuclear Programme, in the following years the Framework Programme on Energy Research made 1.75 billion deutschmarks available annually for research in these fields.[55]

By the spring of 1974 at the latest, the economic research institutes' forecasts, which had underpinned the energy programme of September 1973, had been overtaken by reality. In view of a highly complex situation and the difficulties involved in forecasting the producing countries' quantitative and pricing policies, however, any attempt to assess future trends seemed beset by major difficulties.[56] Nonetheless, the relevant institutes were tasked with producing a new forecast by May. This would form the basis for the first extension of the energy programme. The four goals of energy policy, or 'goal square' – inspired by the 'magic square' of macroeconomic regulation – namely ensuring an adequate, secure, affordable and environmentally sound energy supply, continued to apply. As Lantzke argued at the closed meeting arranged to discuss the extension of the energy programme, however, these objectives had to be adapted to the new realities.[57] In any case, no fundamental changes could be achieved over the short term – within two to four years – as the programme would take a long time to make an impact. As Shell AG calculated in 1974, for example, the geophysical work involved in finding oilfields required one to three years, drilling a further one to two years and, in the case of offshore drilling, a further six to eighteen months were needed to construct an oil platform. Building a refinery took at least five years and an oil tanker two to three years, while the construction of nuclear power stations took even longer.[58] The general assumption was that over the short and medium term – until 1985 – West Germany's dependence on oil from the Middle East would persist, demand would continue to grow and oil would become scarcer. Only over the long term would it be possible to reduce oil dependency, if the right energy policy decisions were made now.[59] The institutes presented a provisional energy forecast in May 1974, and the Ministry of Economics resolved to present the first extension of the energy programme to the Cabinet by September.[60] By the end of October, the government had put forward the first extension of the energy programme. It justified the revision of a programme that was just one year old by asserting that developments on the world oil market were 'increasingly [being] determined in part by noneconomic factors' and that therefore 'a trouble-free energy supply [can] no longer be taken for granted'.[61] By 1985, the measures in the programme aimed to ensure that oil as a share of the West German energy supply decreased from 55 to 44 per cent, while nuclear energy would increase from 1 to 15 per cent and natural gas from 10 to 18 per cent. Coal would fall from 22 to 14 per cent.[62] These rapid changes were to be achieved through natural gas supply agreements with the Netherlands and the Soviet Union, energy-saving measures, continued production of coal, and the construction of nuclear power stations.

In 1974, nuclear power provided 2,300 megawatts of West German electricity production, equating to around 4 per cent. The energy programme drawn up the year before already provided for its expansion to 18,000 megawatts by 1980 and 40,000 by 1985. In view of the oil crisis, these goals were revised upwards to at least 20,000 and 45,000 megawatts respectively, though 50,000 was thought to be ideal. On the basis of the latter figure, nuclear energy would have made up 45 per cent of electricity production by 1985.[63] Nuclear power was viewed as the alternative energy par excellence, and every industrialized country sought to expand it. This was especially true of France, where nuclear reactors had been used to produce electricity since 1963 and nuclear energy was bound up with notions of national renewal and modernization.[64] France's sixth economic development plan for the 1971–75 period still assumed that oil would increasingly dominate the field of energy. But it already announced a substantial expansion of nuclear energy in the seventh plan, not least because the country was considered backward in this respect.[65] By 1985, nuclear energy should cover 50 per cent of the country's electricity needs and thus 15 per cent of its total energy requirements.[66] The impact of the oil embargo and price rises caused these plans to be modified and their implementation speeded up.[67] By 1985, the plan was for oil as a share of France's total energy supply to be reduced from more than 66 to 42 per cent. At the same time, the share of nuclear energy was to increase to 25 per cent.[68] In contrast to West Germany, where the planned expansion of nuclear energy was delayed by massive public protests, it proceeded fairly rapidly in France.[69]

Despite the comprehensive catalogue of measures drawn up in the energy programme and the great hopes placed in nuclear energy at the time, the government considered West Germany too small and powerless to overcome the now acute energy problems: 'The problems of the world energy market can be solved only through international cooperation. The still largely national energy policy framework is no longer sufficient'.[70] The government thus welcomed moves towards multilateral cooperation, within the framework of the International Energy Agency for example (chapter 6). It was also keen to step up the national effort, commissioning precise forecasts on the supply and demand of the various energy sources. The economic research institutes, which had also provided advice on the extension of the energy programme, now had their hands full, not least because the demand for energy expertise was also booming on the state level. The insecurity caused by the oil crisis, which had radically devalued previous energy forecasts, did not convince the key actors that it was impossible to predict or plan for developments in the oil and energy market. Instead it prompted them to try harder.

In addition to the above-mentioned studies on West Germany's energy supply, the German Institute for Economic Research alone produced, in rapid succession, energy reports for Bavaria (1971, 1973, 1974, 1976, 1977, 1979), northern Germany (1972, 1978, 1980–81), North Rhine-Westphalia (1971), Hesse (1973, 1977), Berlin (1981) and Baden-Württemberg (1974, 1979).[71] It also published studies on future trends in energy demand (1978), nuclear energy (1975), the East-West trade in energy (1975), the substitution of oil (1978, 1980), the conflicting objectives of security, affordability and environmental compatibility (1976, 1978) and trends in energy prices (1979).[72] The rapid changes in the energy market quickly rendered forecasts out of date, as numerous commentators noted.[73] Yet clearly, in West Germany, the resulting insecurity did not engender a conviction that it was impossible to predict trends in energy supply and demand. It merely intensified the demand for forecasts. As a result, the number of energy forecasts grew markedly between 1950 and 1980. From 1968 onwards, at least five were published in any given year. Thirty appeared in 1976 and twenty-eight in 1980.[74] Given the erroneous nature of such forecasts, critics argued that they ultimately said more about the forecaster's institutional milieu than the future of the energy supply. Yet a large majority of West German energy experts still considered them indispensable in the 1980s.[75] Even before the oil crisis, energy forecasters had argued that their analyses should not be misunderstood as precise predictions. Instead they were approximate indications of trends.[76] Frequent falsification prompted some forecasters to develop a range of scenarios. Others believed this merely rendered their statements obscure and that their value must be measured not just in light of real-world developments but also in terms of their significance within the policymaking process.[77] The number of energy forecasts not only increased in the 1970s; they also tackled longer timescales. Measures aimed at changing the energy mix or developing specific energy sources took a long time to make an impact, so more and more often forecasts were extended to the year 2000.[78]

This development was not specific to West Germany but applied to other countries as well. In the wake of the oil crisis and anticipating the advent of North Sea oil, British government planners, for example, began to regard short- and medium-term energy forecasts as inadequate for policymaking. In 1975, therefore, the interministerial working group – which had been dedicated to the medium-term development of oil prices – was replaced by a 'Working Group on the Planning'. This was tasked with producing longer-term energy forecasts for the 1980–2000 period.[79] Another working group, operating in parallel, recognized in its report that forecasts for this period were beset by a high degree of uncertainty and could not, therefore, serve as blueprints for government action. But it went on to argue that this did not divest the government of its duty to produce long-term forecasts. Government action, it contended, was always influenced by specific views of the future, so these must be as valid as they could possibly be.[80]

In November 1977, the Körber Foundation's Bergedorf Round Table (Bergedorfer Gesprächskreis der Körber-Stiftung), headed by the director of Cologne University's Institute of Energy Economics (Energiewissenschaftliches Institut), Hans K. Schneider, discussed longer-term energy policy expectations.[81] Klaus M. Meyer-Abich, professor of the philosophy of the natural sciences at the University of Essen and a member of several energy policy advisory bodies, argued that until the mid 1980s there would be sufficient oil and other energy sources. He also believed that around the turn of the millennium all resource problems would be overcome by more or less inexhaustible energy sources such as nuclear energy, nuclear fusion and solar energy. Serious problems were, however, likely to occur in the intervening period.[82] Meyer-Abich was not alone in this. Walter Levy argued that 'we should consider it at least probable that between 1985 and 1990 we will face very serious energy problems. There will be a lack of coal, nuclear energy and solar energy during this period'.[83]

Though it seems fanciful now, most contemporary energy experts endorsed this perspective on the future, which assumed that oil would become scarce. Even prior to the oil crisis, EC energy experts had worked on the assumption that there would be energy supply problems from 1985 onwards.[84] In the United States, both independent research institutes such as the American Association for the Advancement of Science and companies like Shell predicted an 'energy gap' between around 1985 and 2000.[85] In 1977, the second extension of the West German energy programme was drawn up by the research institutes and passed by the government. During the same year, such different bodies as the Central Intelligence Agency, British Petroleum, the International Energy Agency and the Workshop on Alternative Energy Strategies at MIT put forward similarly pessimistic assessments of the future of oil – and thus of the Western industrialized countries' energy supply. The CIA concluded: 'In the absence of greatly increased energy conservation, projected world demand for oil will approach productive capacity by the early 1980s and substantially exceed capacity by 1985'.[86] The OECD and BP most clearly expressed the overall view that energy consumption would continue to increase at a lower rate of growth and that supply shortfalls would occur between 1985 and 2000.[87] The international team of researchers at MIT – under the leadership of Carroll L. Wilson, and with members including Hans Detzer of BASF, Heinrich Mandel of Rheinisch-Westfälische Elektrizitätswerke and Hans K. Schneider of EWI Cologne – also forecast that global oil production would begin to fall around 1985 and that alternative energy sources would play an ever greater role: 'The task for the world will be to manage the transition from dependence on oil to greater reliance on other fuels, nuclear energy and, later, renewable energy systems'.[88]

The West German economic research institutes closely followed these international discussions on future energy shortfalls and came to similar conclusions, lengthening the forecasting period for the second extension of the energy programme.[89] Their conditional forecast was based on the Ministry of Economics guideline that until 1985 economic growth would amount to an average of 4 and subsequently 3.5 per cent, as this was necessary to maintain employment levels and the welfare state.[90] The institutes set out two alternative scenarios of 3.5 and 4.5 per cent economic growth, contending that if suitable measures were taken, the growth of energy consumption could be decoupled from the growth of GNP and could reach 2.8 or 1.6 per cent respectively.[91] The contribution made by oil should be reduced and that of nuclear energy massively increased. Above all, however, the decoupling of economic and energy consumption growth was to be achieved through energy-saving measures. In the shape of the 'away from oil strategy', the first extension of the energy programme had focused chiefly on the development of other energy sources. The second extension, meanwhile, shifted focus to the demand side.[92] In future too, 'growth [will be] impossible without increasing energy consumption', but more rational use of energy could lessen consumption increases over the long term.[93]

Achieving a more rational use of energy with the help of new technologies was one of the issues already identified in the Framework Programme on Energy Research adopted during the oil crisis. This had extended government research funding, previously focused chiefly on nuclear technology, to other energy sources. Though the largest share of the funds went to projects on coal technology (277.1 million deutschmarks), the second largest was made available to those dedicated to the rational use of energy (227.1 million), followed by savings in the fields of energy conversion, transportation and storage (143.6 million), while smaller sums were invested in mining technology and oil production (115.5 and 33.9 million).[94] By the spring of 1977, before the second extension of the energy programme, the West German government adopted a new programme to support energy research and energy technologies for the 1977–80 period. Rational energy use now ranked higher than the other three funding foci: coal and fossil energy sources, new energy sources and nuclear energy.[95] In parallel to this, after the oil crisis the Ministry for Research and Technology commissioned the Working Group on Environment, Society and Energy (Arbeitsgruppe Umwelt, Gesellschaft, Energie or AUGE) at the University of Essen to produce a study on 'Options for Economic Regulation towards Energy-Saving through Alternative Technologies'. The results were presented in 1978 in three substantial volumes. Under the leadership of Klaus Meyer-Abich, the report concluded that saving energy – in addition to fossil energy sources and nuclear energy – would be the third key 'energy source' of the future.[96] In the 1970s, in West Germany as elsewhere, coal, oil and nuclear policies were brought together under the term 'energy'. This illuminated the overall energy problem from a new perspective, one that included consumption so that consumption cuts could be conceptualized in analogy to the classical energy sources.

Radical ecological visions of a fundamental shift away from fossil energy sources often incorporated alternative lifestyles and models of society. These rejected the primacy of economic growth. The AUGE, in contrast, argued that the energy-saving measures it had in mind would require no state dirigisme and would lead neither to a decline in economic growth nor diminishing affluence.[97] Critics of growth could be found even within the SPD, such as Erhard Eppler, who resigned as development aid minister in 1974 after clashing with Helmut Schmidt over the size of the aid budget. Eppler, who played an important role in the debate on the SPD's policies in the 1970s, drew on the critique of growth emanating from the ecological movement, as expressed in the MIT report for the Club of Rome. Rather than defining growth in purely quantitative terms, he advocated a focus on enhancing quality of life, influencing younger SPD members in particular.[98] However, the limits to the critique of growth within German social democracy were only too apparent at a special symposium organized by the SPD on 'Energy, Employment and Quality of Life', held on 28 and 29 April 1977. The debate guidelines drawn up for the conference by Hans Matthöfer, minister of research and technology, already noted that economic growth and rising energy consumption in West Germany had hitherto developed in surprisingly parallel fashion. While the SPD, as set out in 'Orientation Framework '85', wished to see a shift away from quantitative to qualitative growth, it was nonetheless committed to growth itself. It was, the guidelines asserted, still an open question to what extent growth and energy consumption could be decoupled.[99] Right at the start of the conference, Mayor of Bremen Hans Koschnik declared that social democratic policies would be impossible without further growth and thus increasing energy consumption. Erhard Eppler's opening presentation was followed by a talk by the president of the Industrial Union of Mining and Energy on 'Growth as a Goal of Economic Policy'.[100] While Eppler asked what it was exactly that was supposed to grow, Adolf Schmidt underlined: 'Without a sufficient supply of energy we will be unable to achieve either full employment or environmental protection', prompting him to underline the 'inescapable necessity' of 'providing our national economy with more energy in future than is available at present'.[101] In the closing debate, only the vice president of the German League for Nature and Environment (Deutscher Naturschutzring) was clearly on Eppler's side. Most of the speakers agreed that economic growth would continue to be necessary and would be impossible to achieve without rising energy consumption.[102] While welcoming efforts to achieve economic growth with less energy, Chancellor Schmidt too underlined that the government must keep all energy policy options open: 'a national economy that stagnates rather than grows will be unable to provide the unemployed of today and the youth of tomorrow with the necessary jobs. That's why we need growth, and this growth must not be prevented by a lack of energy'.[103]

Within the CDU/CSU, ecological pioneer Herbert Gruhl, who made a major public splash in 1975 with his book *The Plundering of the Planet*, was also marginalized.[104] His scepticism about growth and progress was particularly unwelcome in the party of the economic miracle, in which Franz Josef Strauß asserted that to be conservative in the present meant leading the charge of progress.[105] Following his resignation, Gruhl became one of the founding fathers of the Green Party (Die Grünen), which initially absorbed some conservative growth sceptics but developed in a rather different direction over the medium term.[106] In the late 1970s, the growth paradigm was so strong that it was impossible to question it if one wished to be heard within energy policy debates. In any event, when it came to calculations for the second extension of the energy programme, the government advised the institutes that economic growth must hit at least 4 per cent, as otherwise it would be impossible to go on implementing policies as hitherto. In this climate, even the Institute for Applied Ecology (Öko-Institut) in Freiburg sought to demonstrate that, 'in future, West Germany will be able to meet its energy needs if economic growth increases – but without using nuclear energy and with a dramatic reduction in petroleum consumption'.[107]

The government formulated the third extension of the energy programme in 1981 against the backdrop of what was now an intense societal debate on nuclear energy. This document gave a positive summary of the government's efforts on the energy front: 'The long-standing, close link between overall growth and a near-equal increase in energy consumption [has been] broken. The policy of "away from oil" has chalked up clearer successes'.[108] Nonetheless, it asserted, partly due to the problems involved in expanding nuclear energy, the country would continue to depend on oil imports.[109] This meant ongoing, high risks to supply, as was most clearly evident in the second oil crisis of 1978–79. The government aimed to reduce this energy vulnerability by continuing to promote energy saving and diversification of energy sources. As in other countries, then, the second oil crisis, which was triggered by the revolution in Iran but was essentially a pricing crisis caused by speculation, led not to a fundamental reorientation of West German energy policy but merely intensified existing trends.[110] However, when it came to methodology, the government reflected on the erroneous nature of previous energy forecasts. It therefore decided to free the institutes from previous guidelines, as economic growth, and thus energy consumption, had turned out to be significantly lower than predicted since the second extension of the energy programme. In line with this, the institutes now assumed that by 1995 energy consumption would grow at only half the rate of GNP, by 1 to 1.4 per cent.[111]

Regulation and Planning during the Oil Crisis

In view of the oil price hikes of 1970–72, which seemed marginal only in comparison with the extreme price rises of subsequent years, economists and economy-focused politicians had begun to reflect on the consequences of changes in the oil market for the West German economy. After the start of the oil crisis, meanwhile, the combination of supply restrictions and rising prices placed a question mark over previous economic stabilization policies. This prompted key figures in the Chancellery to argue that the classical stabilization measures, if implemented to prevent a rise in unemployment, would in turn exacerbate the oil shortage and in fact generate unemployment.[112] The Ministry of Labour and Social Order (Bundesministerium für Arbeit und Sozialordnung) used this as an opportunity to end the active recruitment of so-called guest workers (Gastarbeiter).[113] Partly due to Finance Minister Helmut Schmidt's public highlighting of the conflict between employment and energy policy, a debate flared up within the coalition on economic policy under the conditions of the oil crisis.[114]

The consequences of the oil crisis for economic governance came into focus in the debate on the special report published by the Council of Economic Experts on 17 December 1973. Following the adoption of the Stability and Growth Act (Gesetz zur Förderung der Stabilität und des Wachstums der Wirtschaft) in 1967, the Council of Economic Experts, established in 1963, set the course for comprehensive Keynesian economic management. The aim here was to maintain the equilibrium of the so-called magic square of economic growth, full employment, monetary stability and an equilibrated balance of trade.[115] During the composition of the annual report in November 1973, it became clearer from day to day that 'West Germany, like other industrialized countries of the Western world, was threatened by a restricted supply of petroleum that would confront economic policy with unprecedented challenges'. As a result, the Council of Economic Experts decided to publish a special report,[116] because the supply cutbacks and rapid price rises directly and indirectly affected every part of the economy and altered the macroeconomic variables, throwing up a vast number of questions. The experts candidly admitted: 'We cannot say that we have an answer to all these questions that we would consider adequate'. However, they went on, complete and certain knowledge was not a prerequisite for making 'sensible decisions'; often, approximate estimates were a sufficient basis for recognizing problems and pointing the way ahead.[117]

In its forecast, the Council of Economic Experts anticipated that the OAPEC regime of production cutbacks would continue unchanged over the coming year and that West Germany would have 15 to 20 per cent less oil available to it. Under these conditions, the Council stated, the goal of full employment would be particularly difficult to achieve due both to the limited production options and a partial decline in demand. These problems could not be remedied through the classical instruments of economic stimulation; the lack of oil was impeding production, and the rising price was pushing up inflation and hampering job creation.[118] Correcting the 1973 report, the Council of Economic Experts now assumed that the economic downturn would continue in 1974, while unemployment would rise more sharply than forecast.[119] Despite the negative effects, however, the experts expressed opposition to more extensive measures than cessation of guest worker recruitment, such as their repatriation. They concluded by admitting once again the high degree of uncertainty surrounding their forecast. Both milder and more severe economic scenarios were possible, up to and including fundamental risks to economic life. Nonetheless, they expressed optimism that over the long term human ingenuity would facilitate a transition to an alternative energy future and that, one day, oil would serve merely as the basic material for petrochemistry.[120]

Even before the oil crisis, the Council of Economic Experts had begun to move away from Keynesian macroeconomic regulation and control (*Globalsteuerung*); in a monetarist vein, it now made monetary stability its top priority, a move linked with a generational shift among its members.[121] The oil crisis threw the dilemmas of Keynesian economic policy into sharp relief. Against this background, the difficulties involved in dealing with simultaneous economic stagnation and inflation served as a peg on which to hang a fundamental critique of macroeconomic regulation and an open debate on the principles of economic governance.[122] This critique usually came with a pathos of realism and sobriety. The 1960s, key actors contended, had been an era of soaring expectations, limitless hopes and fantasies of economic and social planning, fuelled by a general belief in the malleability of everything. But on this view, the oil crisis had shown these to be illusory and they had had to make way for a sober, pragmatic and realistic crisis-management approach. To this day, many historians adhere to variants of this notion that in 1973–74 a profound shift in mood occurred, as a fundamentally different approach to policymaking gained traction. This interpretation was already voiced when the Bundestag debated the report on the oil crisis submitted by the Council of Economic Experts on 17 January 1974.[123]

In his New Year address, Willy Brandt had declared that the energy crisis raised questions about the future economic order. He asserted that free markets should regulate whatever they could, but that the state must not evade its responsibilities.[124] However, Economics Minister Friderichs' address on both energy policy and the special report produced by the Council of Economic Experts struck a markedly more market-oriented tone. His speech, which had been agreed in the Cabinet and was based on a draft by Ulf Lantzke, began with a general report on the supply situation in the country, before tackling the question of whether the government's earlier energy policy measures were sufficient, or whether, and if so to what extent, they ought to be augmented.[125] While West Germany's quantitative oil supply situation had eased, Friderichs explained, the government now saw rising oil prices as the main cause for concern; here too, however, uncertainty reigned in view of a constantly changing situation in which no one could 'seriously claim to know what will happen on the world petroleum market over the next few months, what the oil countries will actually do and what the response will be'. Therefore, the time was not as yet ripe for an extension of the energy programme, whose basic approach was still correct.[126] In his draft document, Lantzke had already highlighted the fact that the oil crisis was having two key effects. First, it showed that 'supplying our national economy with sufficient energy [must be] a high priority' by revealing that even small shortages would place restrictions on everyone's lives. Second, the oil crisis made it clear that the energy supply was not exclusively a problem of economic policy but affected the core of the state order and sovereignty: 'Our overall freedom of action domestically and vis-à-vis the rest of the world depends [on it]'.[127] In the Bundestag too, Friderichs emphasized that the burdens and dangers imposed on the Western economies by the oil crisis were unprecedented in the history of West Germany: 'The foundations of our economy are under threat from outside'.[128] Nonetheless, he continued, the country must continue to trust in the liberal economic order and there must be no state regulation of the energy sector, particularly given that the current system had prevented any serious energy shortage. With an emphasis at variance with Brandt's rhetoric, he stated: 'Not everything must or can be done by the state'.[129] With respect to economic consequences and policy responses, Friderichs largely endorsed the report produced by the Council of Economic Experts.

But he also emphasized the international dimension of the crisis and the resulting need to cooperate more closely, and more effectively, with both industrialized, producing and developing countries.[130]

During the debate, other representatives of the governing coalition aligned themselves with Friderichs' assessments, but sometimes presented them in starker terms. FDP deputies Werner Zywietz and Otto Graf Lambsdorff believed that West Germany was on the cusp of a 'new energy era'. From now on, the oil-producing countries would exercise a greater influence on production, endowing oil with a more important role in both foreign and development policy.[131] Lambsdorff spoke in favour of the state-run DEMINEX, but rejected more far-reaching measures; the oil crisis was certainly a challenge to the social market economy, but could be resolved within its framework.[132] During the debate, like their coalition colleagues, SPD deputies always began by thanking the West German public for their willingness to save energy and declared that, in future, there must be a general effort to cut back on energy wastage. However, in contrast to their FDP colleagues, Adolf Schmidt and Herbert Ehrenberg also underlined that energy was not a good like any other. Instead, it was the 'prerequisite for our national economy', because the market economy was 'inconceivable ... without sufficient energy'.[133] With reference to pro-market statements by CDU deputies and energy expert Fritz Burgbacher, Ehrenberg contended that even a 'convinced proponent of the market economy and liberal global trade' must recognize that energy sources could not 'be dealt with solely according to the principles of free competition and the market economy'.[134] In view of their special function, a distinction must be made between energy sources and other goods, because their lack might constitute a threat to national sovereignty.

The response of the CDU/CSU parliamentary group was given by transportation expert Ernst Müller-Hermann. A man with a keen interest in economic governance (*Ordnungspolitik*), he used the debate to launch a head-on attack on the idea of macroeconomic regulation and control (*Globalsteuerung*).[135] He described the report produced by the Council of Economic Experts as rushed and clueless. All it proved, he contended, was that macroeconomic regulation, widely regarded as 'a kind of magic bullet' in 1966, had 'at least so far failed to pass [its] performance test'.[136] On an even more fundamental level, he criticized the 'idea of the malleability of economic processes, which the SPD in particular expounds as a kind of religious creed', but which ignored reality completely, and excoriated 'the constant obsession with forecasting', which was 'particularly pernicious'.[137] There was no reason to assume that the government or some expert possessed 'super-wisdom' and could predict trends over the next year, let alone the next few years. Instead, what was needed was 'data on specific premises for a manageable period of time'. This had now been generally recognized: 'I believe that in 1973, in the entire German public sphere and in every group in our society, a sobering process has set in, which is now being reinforced by the problems of the oil crisis. This sobering process offers a clear opportunity for us to work once again, on new foundations, on developing economic growth while moderating public expectations'.[138] Hermann Josef Russe also considered the trends of the previous few months a 'salutary lesson in the functionality of the social market economy when it comes to economic governance'.[139] Both expressed a view that continues to define historical research on the 1970s, namely that the oil crisis at the very least reinforced and made clear to everyone – if it did not in fact trigger – a fundamental shift in the approach to policymaking in West Germany. However, for Müller-Hermann and others, when it came to economic governance or *Ordnungspolitik*, the wish was father to the thought. We have to ask whether, and if so to what extent, historical analyses of the 1970s share this wishful thinking about a 'sobering' process, which implies a previous lack of realism and suggests that at least a section of the German population or political sphere had entertained illusions and pipe dreams.

On 28 November 1974, the next annual report from the Council of Economic Experts provided an initial summary of the economic and economic policy consequences of the oil crisis. The sections on energy policy had been produced with the collaboration of Hans K. Schneider of EWI Cologne, who was later appointed to the Council of Economic Experts, on which he served from 1982 to 1992, having been made chair in 1985. The sudden increase in the price of oil, this summary asserted, had not brought about but merely worsened the conflict between monetary stability and labour market policy.[140] As a result of the oil crisis, none of the four goals identified in the Stability and Growth Act had been achieved, though the effects were less severe than anticipated at the start of the crisis: the balance of trade remained positive, the economy had continued to grow, albeit at a lower rate, and the consistently restrictive monetary policy – launched by the Bundesbank before the oil crisis – had prevented inflation.[141] The Council of Economic Experts now ascribed tremendous importance to monetary policy, because 'problems that cannot be solved by a stability-oriented monetary policy cannot be solved by a soft monetary policy either'. This understanding, the report contended, was now beginning to take hold even in those countries, such as France and the United Kingdom, which had responded to rising oil prices by increasing the money supply.[142] In order to show that a restrictive monetary and wages policy was still necessary, the Council of Economic Experts produced three conditional forecasts in which monetary policy and wage restraint varied. Five years later, when the Council was required to evaluate the macroeconomic effects of the second oil crisis, it ascertained – with considerable relief – that the burden imposed by the higher oil price was substantially less than in 1974. This was because the prices of export goods from the industrialized countries had reacted by rising sharply.[143] In addition, countries that had responded in 1974 with an expansive monetary policy had learned from this mistake and emulated the German pursuit of monetary stability. What mattered now, then, was to adapt to the higher prices 'without a surge in inflation and without a recession'.[144] In fact, the oil price hike bolstered the government's strategy, which it had been pursuing since the mid 1970s, of reducing the country's dependency on oil to meet its energy needs.[145]

Simplistic accounts often put the paradigm shift in economic theory and policy – the move away from Keynesianism towards monetarism – down to the impact of the oil crisis and the novel phenomenon of stagflation. Yet numerous studies have shown that the transformation actually set in earlier and was merely reinforced by the events of 1973–74.[146] Furthermore, while conservative governments came to power around 1980 in the United States, the United Kingdom, West Germany and other countries, the degree to which economic policy reflected the paradigm shift in economic theory varied greatly.[147] If the idea of macroeconomic regulation and control required one last nail in its coffin, then it may be that the oil crisis provided it. The West German government, however, initially responded with classical Keynesian economic stabilization and special programmes in an attempt to mitigate the effects of the crisis on the labour market, and it regarded these measures as successful.[148] Furthermore, we cannot understand the economic and economic policy transformation that occurred in the context of the oil crisis as a rejection of the culture of planning or the idea of steering economic and societal processes through scientific expertise.[149] This may apply to the idea of the comprehensive planning and steering of economic processes, but within the narrow field of energy policy the opposite was true. By destroying previous expectations about energy, the oil crisis heightened the need for energy expertise. As long as the oil price had remained stable, no one required forecasts of its future development. Only when it became volatile during the oil crisis was there an increased need for forecasts, which countless energy economists have attempted to satisfy up to the present day. Because oil was the most important energy source, the significance and economic potential of coal, gas, nuclear and alternative energy also depended on its price, and numerous models of different energy futures could be produced on the basis of a variety of political and economic assumptions. In this sense, rather than diminishing the horizon of expectation, the oil crisis opened up space for new alternative futures, triggering an intensified production of forecasts and plans.[150]

In contrast to the United States, France and the United Kingdom, in West Germany no central governmental institution took on the task of producing energy forecasts. Instead, the Ministry of Economics delegated this task to three economic research institutes, whose forecasts provided the basis for the government's energy policy. Once again, the trend was not away from the planning of the 1960s to the crisis management of the 1970s. In fact, it was the expectation of the oil crisis that prompted the government to draw up a comprehensive and coordinated energy programme in the first place. Fundamentally, the social-liberal coalition's approach to oil policy remained oriented towards the market economy, like that of its predecessors. However, its targeted support, initially for DEMINEX and nuclear energy, then for coal conversion and energy-saving technologies, was intended – in Ulf Lantzke's words – to steer the development of energy policy with a 'gentle touch'. If anything, far from being compromised by the energy crisis, the political steering of energy policy intensified during it. The crisis, moreover, rather than pointing to a need for shorter-term planning or forecasts, underlined the need for long-term perspectives. Ever more often, energy forecasts now extended up to the year 2000 in order to facilitate long-term planning.

Changes in energy policy, then, contradict the commonplace notion of sobering or disillusionment that tends to pervade historians' accounts of the shifts in culture and mentality in the 1970s. Is it 'more sober' to believe it possible to increase nuclear energy as a proportion of the overall energy mix to 15 per cent, within just a few years, than to rely on ever-gushing oil wells to satisfy a rapidly growing need for energy? The ecological and sociopolitical alternatives extolled by those who purported to have recognized the limits to growth, meanwhile, seem no more sober or realistic than the expectations cherished by the apologists for progress. In any case, in view of the tremendous financial investments required for energy production, and the long periods of time required to make it profitable, the energy economy is probably not the best place for sober and pragmatic crisis managers. There is always something of the long-term vision inherent within it. Who decides, according to what criteria, which energy policy or economic policy ideas were illusory, which visionary and which pragmatic and realistic? This can scarcely be done on a counterfactual basis. The topos of 'sobering' is ill-suited to historiographical accounts in part because its origins lie in a contemporary political debate in which it was deployed to delegitimize opposing views. It may well be that the monetarist believed himself to be more sober and realistic than the Keynesian and that the nuclear lobbyist was convinced that he recognized realities of energy policy that evaded the awareness of those advocating soft energy paths. But this provides no basis for the historian to regard one as more sober than the other.

The institutes' energy expertise and the West German government's energy programme – and its extensions – were intended to lead West Germany 'away from oil', in order to guarantee an adequate energy supply in future and make the country more energy-independent. However, in addition to de facto guaranteeing the government's capacity for effective action, the energy programmes were also intended to demonstrate sovereignty. Yet due to the rapid increase in energy studies whose content diverged considerably, it became more and more difficult to legitimize state action through scientific expertise. It was not just the economic research institutes but also individual energy firms or branches and representatives of the ecological movement that forecast future energy demand and put forward policy proposals. The impression thus arose that one could find an expert to back up every political position.[151] This, however, did not relieve the government of the need to undergird its views scientifically if it was to be seen as both effective and sovereign. But overall, as the relevant energy-focused politicians acknowledged again and again – due to its high dependency on imports – West Germany's sovereignty in energy policy was limited in any case. This made foreign policy strategies aimed at securing sovereignty tremendously important.

The International and Global Contexts of West German Energy Policy

For the debate on current issues in energy policy slated to take place in the Bundestag on 29 November 1973, Willy Brandt's speechwriter presented the chancellor with a draft speech. It began as follows: 'For the first time in the life of the Federal Republic of Germany, we are all confronted with a serious situation of shortage. For the first time, government and opposition, parliament and public are having to get to grips with the psychological, economic, social and political consequences of this shortage'.[152] Brandt was dissatisfied with this lead-in, which alluded to specific experiences of lack over the course of German history and the growing prosperity during the economic boom that followed the establishment of the Federal Republic. He noted in the margin: 'I would like a "more factual" lead-in, which should also be less "national" in character: it's crucial that we emphasize the European and worldwide interconnections from the outset'.[153] Apart from marginal modifications to the text, Brandt's other notes also related to the international dimension of the crisis: the role of the EC, his talks in Paris, and West Germany's relations with the Eastern Bloc. But he was keen to avoid passages that sought only to blame others for recent developments and the resulting economic challenges.[154]

In principle, Brandt, like President Nixon, was quite open to viewing the oil crisis as a national challenge that could and must be overcome through citizens' individual conduct. When he announced the energy-saving measures agreed by the Cabinet on television on 24 November, including the car-free Sundays, he declared this the younger generation's first experience of shortages. If the country was transformed into one great 'pedestrian area' on every Sunday until Christmas, each generation could practise solidarity and demonstrate its 'ingenuity'.[155] The energy crisis, then, provided the opportunity for a new form of community: 'Recent weeks have taught us something that risked being forgotten: that egotism does not even help the egotist, that we are dependent on mutual aid'.[156] However, as Brandt's government declaration before the Bundestag made clear, the international dimension of the crisis was especially important to him. The energy supply, Brandt began, was under threat not just in West Germany and Europe as a whole, but throughout the industrialized world. The 'problems thrown up by the shortage of crude oil' could be solved by none of the consuming countries in isolation – especially not by West Germany – but only through international cooperation, with the European Communities playing a key role.[157] The energy issue would reveal 'the true value of the European Community'.[158] Nonetheless, the chancellor contended, through the energy programme, the natural gas deal with the Soviet Union and his trip to Iran in the spring of 1973, the government had already taken important steps towards enhancing the country's energy security. But the oil crisis was likely to last for a long time and could only be overcome through a new form of cooperation between consuming and producing countries.

With respect to the latter, Brandt tried to strike an appropriate balance between rhetorical strength and accommodation: 'Ladies and gentlemen, I do not make generalizing reference here to "the" Arabs. I repeat: oil and the Middle East are not the same thing, and I would advise against calling for sanctions, particularly in a coarse way, though those involved should know that they are mistaken if they believe us to be weaklings'.[159] Brandt was eager to avoid being seen as too soft and accommodating in international negotiations on the embargo. Again and again, he underlined Germans' willingness to accept sacrifices and privation, if necessary, in order to secure their country's sovereignty. Clearly untroubled by generalizations about 'the Arabs', he declared to the French prime minister, Pierre Messmer, that 'a few days before he – the chancellor – had received the Soviet ambassador and told him to say hello to his Arab friends and remind them that after the war, in a number of European countries, through their peoples' hard work and will to survive, certain processes had been set in motion. The Arab countries should also bear in mind that while it had been decided, a few years ago, not to pursue coal liquefaction as it was considered too expensive at the time, it would be quite easy to fetch the relevant experts back from South Africa'.[160] The message here was not just that West Germany would accept no restrictions on its sovereignty, but that ultimately the producing countries were shooting themselves in the foot, because the production cutbacks would merely prompt the industrialized countries to reduce their dependence on oil.

The debate on Brandt's government declaration in the Bundestag revolved mainly around the specific measures decreed by the coalition on the basis of the Energy Security Act (Energiesicherungsgesetz) and their consequences for the general population.[161] The focus here was on whether the government had responded quickly enough or too slowly, fittingly, excessively or inadequately to the changing energy policy situation. Franz Josef Strauß's immediate response to Willy Brandt, however, initially foregrounded the foreign policy dimension of the oil crisis. In a vehement and confrontational speech, Strauß accused the government of failing to take seriously enough, or ignoring, 'the central issue of the future relationship with the petroleum-producing countries' in the Middle East and Africa. The government, he asserted, was also overlooking the risks involved in the country's growing dependency on oil supplies from the Eastern Bloc and had completely ignored the problems thrown up for the world monetary system by rising oil prices. Strauß's most important criticism of the government, however, was that it had failed to stand shoulder to shoulder with the United States, 'which is virtually the sole guarantor of our security in what [has the potential to be a] life or death crisis for all of us'.[162] According to Strauß, the Europeans must finally demonstrate that, in close collaboration with the United States, they were at least prepared to take on regional responsibility rather than making 'boastful' declarations.[163]

Just under three weeks earlier, on 9 November 1973, the debate on the Energy Security Act had already begun to heat up. The CDU's Rainer Barzel accused the government of having prioritized material oil-related interests over political morality: 'How the chancellor likes to quote the biblical phrase: "Man does not live by bread alone". It would be interesting for this house . . . if the chancellor were to formulate this maxim at some point with respect to oil in light of recent experiences, with a view to the situation of the people here and their experiences in a highly industrialized society and a vulnerable political system'.[164] Through its policies, Barzel claimed, the government had jeopardized West Germany's relationship with Israel and the United States, on which, after all, the country's security and sovereignty crucially depended. Representatives of the social-liberal coalition defended themselves against these attacks and underlined both the balanced nature of their policy towards the Middle East and the dramatic nature of the crisis, which called for decisive government action.[165]

However, they too assailed the EC's inability, due to its member states' nationalism, to formulate a common energy policy and act autonomously vis-à-vis the United States and the producing countries.[166] Beyond the typical polemics flowing between government and opposition, then, the debate revealed fundamentally different views of national security and the geopolitical order. Speakers from the opposition CDU/CSU parliamentary group understood security from a traditional military perspective. They thus viewed it through the prism of the East-West conflict and regarded close alignment with the United States as the core maxim of foreign policy. The governing parties, meanwhile, saw West German security as threatened more by energy-related and economic issues, and here the global lines of division followed a quite different trajectory.

The Foreign Ministry and Relations with the Producing Countries and the Arab World

West Germany's relations with the Arab countries were fraught in the early 1970s, first because of the country's special obligation towards Israel, and second because of the Hallstein doctrine of rejecting diplomatic relations with countries that recognized the GDR.[167] When it emerged that West Germany was supplying Israel with weapons in 1965 and then established diplomatic relations with it, the Arab states withdrew their ambassadors from Bonn.[168] In 1969, the social-liberal coalition then began to normalize relations with the Arab world. Formally abandoning the Hallstein doctrine, West Germany also re-established diplomatic relations with those countries that had recognized the GDR. This process, however, had yet to be concluded at the beginning of the oil embargo, and extended into 1974.[169]

In this delicate situation, tempers and tensions frequently flared whenever the Arab countries felt that West Germany's position on the Middle East conflict, avowedly based on the principle of 'balance', seemed too pro-Israeli. Shortly before the oil crisis, for example, the Arabs criticized the passage on the Middle East in Willy Brandt's speech to the United Nations, accusing the West German government of abandoning its 'balanced' stance shortly after re-establishing relations with most Arab countries.[170] In his speech, Brandt had underlined the West German government's interest in 'a peaceful settlement in the Middle East', along with the importance of the international community's role as mediator. However, he had then gone on to state that it was 'above all direct peace talks between the relevant Arab countries and Israel [that are] capable of striking a balance between both sides' elementary interests'.[171] To the chagrin of the Arab countries, he made no mention of UN Resolution 242, which called for

Israel's withdrawal from the territories occupied during the Six-Day War. He thus seemed to be siding with Israel. The Foreign Ministry felt this had permanently damaged the Arabs' trust in the West German government and urged a return to a consistent official line, namely that UN Resolution 242 embodied the 'foundation for a Middle East peace settlement'; it would be best for Willy Brandt himself to reaffirm this.[172]

Walter Scheel tried to soothe these tensions in direct talks with the ambassadors and heads of mission from Lebanon, Egypt, Libya, Jordan, Tunisia, Morocco, Sudan, Algeria and Saudi Arabia on 8 October 1973. The passage on the Middle East in Brandt's speech 'clearly [having] caused misunderstandings', he affirmed once again that the West German government's stance had not changed.[173] While the Egyptian ambassador responded positively – Egypt having previously felt ignored in its efforts to improve German-Arab relations – the Libyan ambassador called on the West German government to commit itself to the position that Israel must withdraw before negotiations could begin. Sections of Brandt's speech during the debate on the Energy Security Act had also provoked criticism in the Arab world. The Foreign Ministry therefore propagated the official line that on this occasion Brandt had 'had to refer to less pleasing effects of current Arab oil policy'.[174] Not just official government statements but all major public pronouncements in West Germany were closely observed in the Arab world. Due to its use of racist stereotypes, for example, articles on the Middle East in Springer publications were perceived as even worse than the Israeli press. Thus, the German ambassador to Egypt proposed inviting publisher Axel Cäsar Springer for high-level talks; it would be helpful to underline to him the consequences of his articles for West German foreign policy and, potentially, for the country's oil supply.[175]

Another factor problematized the West German government's policy towards the Arab countries: adopting an overly pro-Arab stance might damage relations with Israel. In early November 1973, for example, the Israeli newspaper *Maariv* quipped that Willy Brandt would no doubt soon be photographed repeating his famous Warsaw Genuflection before an oil derrick. The Israeli ambassador, meanwhile, lodged several strongly worded diplomatic protests in response to the government's supposedly biased, pro-Arab policy.[176]

The success of West German strategies to improve relations with the (chiefly Arab) producing countries depended in significant part on the structures within which the Foreign Ministry generated knowledge about the politics of oil and the Arab world. As with the formulation of the government's energy programme, during the oil crisis the various strands of policymaking on energy generally came together in the Economics Ministry – or, to be more precise, in the Energy Policy and Raw Materials Division headed by Ulf Lantzke. Lantzke's division assessed West Germany's position with respect to energy, and the other ministries used these assessments as the basis for their own work. When it came to the international dimensions of the oil crisis, however, the Economics Ministry also relied on the expertise of the Foreign Ministry, whose ambassadors reported on the politics of energy in their various countries of assignment. Even before the acute phase of the oil crisis had begun, duplicates of their reports were always sent directly to Lantzke's division in the Economics Ministry.[177] In addition, much of the West German government's international communication flowed through the Foreign Ministry, which laid the ground for all bilateral and international negotiations and coordinated policy on Europe. All issues relating to the international oil economy were dealt with by the unit on 'Basic Issues in Foreign Trade Policy, Petroleum Policy, Promotion of Foreign Trade, Guarantees in Foreign Trade and Capital Export, and Arms Control' (Referat 403 'Grundsatzfragen der Außenwirtschaftspolitik, Erdölpolitik, Außenhandelsförderung, Gewährleistungen im Außenhandel und Kapitalexport, Rüstungskontrolle'). Petroleum policies were incorporated into the unit's name – during the restructuring of the ministry under the social-liberal coalition – only when changes in the global oil market, from 1970 onwards, had made them crucially important.

In his contribution to the progress report in the *Außenpolitisches Jahrbuch* 1973, unit head Hansheinrich Kruse[178] underlined that 'even without the supply crisis that began in the autumn of 1973, energy policy had an important place in German foreign policy'.[179] Though this is generally correct, the topic of energy did become significantly more important in 1973–74.[180] It was now one of the key foci of Kruse's unit, taking up so much time and effort – as a result of the oil crisis – that part of the unit was hived off and dedicated solely to energy issues.[181] The oil-related structures of knowledge, communication and organization with which the Foreign Ministry entered 1973 left plenty of room for improvement, as its staff often complained. It was not until May 1973, for example, that Kruse requested a subscription to the monthly journal *Öl* and the *Middle East Economic Survey* (MEES).[182] Without the MEES or one of the equivalent news services, it was virtually impossible to keep up with the latest developments in the international politics of oil. In these circumstances, Foreign Ministry staff largely relied on the information provided by the oil firms. So, when ESSO AG sent Kruse's unit the in-house publications *Öldorado 72* and *Gegenwärtige und künftige Probleme der Energieversorgung*, he expressed his sincere gratitude and requested that the company continue to send him 'relevant publications by ESSO A.G.'.[183]

Even before the oil crisis, Kruse's unit was already carefully monitoring changes in the world oil market. It diagnosed four key risks:

1. Competition between the three major consuming regions (the United States, Japan and Europe) in an attempt to create preferential zones. 2. Insufficient investment to satisfy medium-term demand. 3. Politically and economically motivated supply restrictions imposed by the producing countries. 4. Special problem: balance of payments and monetary problems due to the volume of oil imports and the producing countries' surplus capital.[184]

Very much in line with Ulf Lantzke's concurrent problem analysis, Kruse's paper, which he had composed for an ambassadors' conference, also assumed that only the United States was in a position to exercise a formative influence on the global oil market, while West Germany was too weak and Europe too divided. Since bilateral negotiations with just one producing country, such as Iran, were not enough to safeguard the West German oil supply, the country must proceed on the multinational level, working to establish a favourable climate for cooperation between producing and consuming countries. Here, Kruse underlined, the diplomatic service had a key role to play. In fact, energy issues were not discussed at the conference, though the embassies in countries of relevance to the politics of oil constantly complained that they were poorly informed about the issue of energy. On 22 March 1973, for example, Peter Metzger, head of the German mission in Saudi Arabia, requested that the Foreign Ministry provide him with current information on the West German government's energy policies for his talks with Yamani. However, because these policies were being revised and negotiated simultaneously within the EC and OECD, all he received from Kruse, once the latter had conferred with the BMWi, were some notes from the previous year. These were of little use in view of the rapidly changing conditions.[185] In much the same way, in May a request for information from the German mission to the international organizations in Vienna, including OPEC, was declined.[186] A few weeks later, the West German ambassador in Tripoli, Günter Franz Werner, complained that previously the embassy had received regular reports from its counterparts in North Africa and the Middle East on petroleum and natural gas. Recently, however, they turned up only sporadically; above all, there had been no reports from Algeria and Iran. Because these reports were essential not just to the work of the embassy in Tripoli but also to the activities of the petroleum expert based there, who was responsible for Algeria as well, Werner requested a return to former practices.[187] In July, the delegation to OPEC in Vienna was more forceful still. A meeting of the OECD's 'committee of oil experts' had taken place, yet the delegates had as yet received no report on it: 'Only if the delegation is integrated more firmly into the existing flow of information can it keep up-to-date with important developments in the field of petroleum'. Quite rightly, no doubt, the delegation considered this a 'vital prerequisite for talks with the OPEC secretariat'.[188]

The German missions in the relevant countries were required to submit regular reports on changes and decisions of significance to oil. However, they were not always in a position to do so, not least because many embassies in the Arab countries were still under development. As West Germany had re-established relations with Algeria by 1971, reports from the country came in frequently. In Saudi Arabia, by contrast, there was initially just a small German staff based at the Italian embassy in Jeddah. It was not until September 1973 that the countries agreed to resume diplomatic relations, with the formal exchange of ambassadors taking place in January 1974.[189] The West German diplomatic missions in North Africa and the Middle East as a whole included just two oil specialists. These were stationed in Iran and Libya, but tasked with monitoring all the producing countries in the region. In the spring of 1974, Hartwig Berghaus, the oil expert in Tripoli, repeatedly assailed the inadequacy of this staffing structure. As early as December 1973, his ambassador Werner, referring to Arab politicians and American colleagues such as James Akins, had underlined the 'need for a stronger German representation in this region, which is of such importance to our economic development'.[190] Berghaus himself was more specific, demanding that at least one more oil consultant be deployed in the region to cover the Arab Gulf states.[191] In significant part because of the animosities between Teheran and its Arab neighbours, he explained, his colleague in Iran was unable to monitor the latter. Yet these countries were becoming increasingly important to the worldwide and West German oil supply. Though Lebanon was not an oil-producing country, Berghaus suggested that the proposed new consultant be based in Beirut. It was not the flow of oil itself but of oil-related information that determined his choice of location here:

> The three internationally renowned oil journals are headquartered or have an office in Beirut, namely the *Petroleum Intelligence Weekly*, *Middle East Economic Survey* and *Arab Oil and Gas*. As the banking centre of the Middle East, a large amount of information converges in Beirut. Several oil companies are known to send their public relations managers to Beirut now and then for a week to gather information. Some oil companies have offices in Beirut itself, such as Exxon, Continental, Mobil, Aramco and others.[192]

During the months of acute crisis between October 1973 and March 1974, therefore, the Foreign Ministry, and thus the West German government, was largely cut off from this hub of oil-related information. Reports from Lebanon were rarer and played less of a role than those from the regional producing countries. When negotiations between the oil firms and the OPEC countries came to a head and the Yom Kippur War broke out, the Foreign Ministry again contacted the embassies in the Arab countries. Its emphatic request was for 'regular and prompt telegrammed reports on relevant plans or measures being pursued by the governments in the region ... ("oil as weapon") with respect to crisis prevention measures in the field of petroleum that may be required as a result of the Middle East conflict ...'.[193] As hitherto, all reports should also go directly to the energy divisions of the Economics Ministry. Just a week later, Kruse sent out another reminder of the need for reports.[194] A conference of ambassadors in the Middle East, planned for October, was cancelled because they were needed in their various countries of assignment; a number of them did in fact submit a large number of reports, sometimes several a day, on oil-related developments.

Even during the oil crisis, however, the communication between the Foreign Ministry and the embassies was constantly bedevilled by problems. On 19 October, for example, Kruse instructed the embassy in Saudi Arabia to approach the Saudi government at the 'highest possible level' and explain that the West German government had 'always done its best to ensure implementation of UN resolution 242' and took 'no sides in the conflict but [was] keen to see it resolved as envisaged in UN resolution 242'. Not least because diplomatic relations had just been fully restored, Kruse went on, West Germany regarded itself as a friendly country and assumed it would not be affected by the production cuts.[195] But this text, signed by Hans Lautenschlager, did not reach the chargé d'affaires until 24 October, when the politics of oil had already been rocked by new convulsions – prompting the latter to ask whether it still made sense to carry out these instructions.[196] On 3 January 1974, in view of the impending OPEC conference, Lautenschlager directed the German embassies in the OPEC countries to warn their host governments that further price hikes would put global economic development at risk.[197] It proved impossible to do so due to a lack of time in Quito and a holiday in Lagos, while in Jakarta and Baghdad the embassy staff carried out this instruction only on 5 and 6 January respectively.[198] The German ambassador in Kuwait complained that steps such as these could succeed only if the embassy was better supplied with information: 'Therefore suggest compilation of detailed arguments against production curbs and excessive price hikes, which could be used when lodging diplomatic protests but also for other talks. Amid the current euphoria over successful armed encounters with Israel and the apparent success of the "oil weapon", mere appeals to reason and goodwill are having little effect'.[199] Finally, German embassy staff in the producing countries often found themselves facing superbly educated and better-informed counterparts in the relevant host-country ministries, to the detriment of their negotiating position.

Communicational and informational deficiencies were also evident in another hub of worldwide oil-related communication, namely at the Vienna-based OPEC. In contrast to the Foreign Ministry itself, the West German mission to the international organizations in Vienna at least subscribed to the expensive *Petroleum Intelligence Weekly* and was supplied with information directly by OPEC. Beyond this, however, it had little relevant literature at its disposal and received statistics only on an occasional basis, so it relied largely on analyses in daily newspapers.[200] In addition to its negligible stock of information on oil-related issues, the activities of the West German mission were hampered by OPEC's restrained information policy. In January 1973, for example, Werner Ungerer, head of the mission, submitted a detailed report on the impending changes of personnel at OPEC. He regarded new secretary general Abderrahmane Khene as less professionally competent than his predecessor but more accessible, so he anticipated more intensive contact. In order for this to happen, however, Ungerer underlined that he himself must be better 'briefed on German views on the international politics of oil and on energy policies in general': 'Unfortunately, so far the briefing of the delegation has left much to be desired'.[201] Ungerer, however, was soon disappointed by Khene. He reported that OPEC's more open information policy would likely amount to no more than an increase in the number of press releases. It would not extend to interviews and talks.

> This information policy, which is highly restrictive in comparison to other international organizations, also demonstrates the difficulties facing even the small number of diplomatic delegations in Vienna specifically concerned with OPEC when it comes to obtaining 'inside information'. Secretariat members are clearly on strict instructions to behave towards members of diplomatic missions in much the same way as towards representatives of the press. This 'wall' can be partially penetrated only through targeted, personal, social contact with somewhat more open secretariat members, which demands a great deal of time and persistence.[202]

Generally, then, the German mission in Vienna, like the rest of the world, learned of OPEC's decisions only when they were announced. Diplomatic staff certainly speculated in advance about what would be decided at OPEC meetings. Ultimately, however, the organization was something of a 'black box': outside observers registered its output without a detailed knowledge of its inner workings.

The Economics Ministry too was far from optimally informed about OPEC. When the embargo ended in March 1974, the former requested that the Foreign Ministry provide it with a report on the 'political and financial leaders of the cartel of the oil producing countries'. This was compiled by Hansheinrich Kruse's unit and provides a good picture of what German diplomats knew about OPEC.[203] Upon submitting this document on 9 May, Kruse apologized for the delayed response; the report had required input from West Germany's diplomatic missions abroad.²⁰⁴ Essentially, however, it contained generally available knowledge that could have been obtained through newspaper research and certainly by reading the relevant oil journals. The report was clear that the crucial political and financial forces came from 'Iran and the Arab countries, but not from the African, Latin American and Asian members of the OPEC cartel'.²⁰⁵ The leading advocate of price rises was Shah Mohammad Reza Pahlavi, mostly represented by his finance minister, Hushang Ansary, though in making this demand they were supported by Algerian president Houari Boumedienne, another influential figure, and his oil minister Belaid Abdessalam. King Faisal and his oil minister, Ahmed Zaki Yamani, meanwhile, advocated a moderate pricing policy, while other OPEC countries such as Nigeria, Indonesia, Venezuela, Ecuador and Gabon supported decisions on pricing policy to the extent that they advanced their interests. Gaddafi, 'the rulers of Kuwait, the Gulf states and the Iraqi leaders [are . . .] merely followers when it comes to pricing policy. But they are in favour of OPEC and the Arabs pursuing a tough oil policy'.²⁰⁶ They were motivated, the report asserted, first by the risk of the too-rapid exhaustion of their oil reserves and, second, by the experience of colonialism and the Middle East conflict. The Foreign Ministry chiefly blamed Faisal, Boumedienne and Gaddafi for organizing and carrying out the oil embargo. It believed that while Abderrahmane Khene, the Algerian secretary general of OPEC, coordinated the cartel's interests and represented them to the outside world, he had no real influence on policy formulation.

Nonetheless, after Khene's appointment as secretary general in early 1973, the Foreign Ministry closely monitored his public statements. When he attended a lecture in Bonn at the invitation of the Friedrich Ebert Foundation (Friedrich-Ebert-Stiftung) in late September 1973, he met for talks with Detlev Karsten Rohwedder, Ulf Lantzke and Hansheinrich Kruse. Here, as elsewhere, he raised eyebrows with his largely non-economic, profoundly moralistic arguments.²⁰⁷ Like Yamani before him, Khene repeatedly highlighted the finitude of the oil reserves and the resulting need to develop alternative energy sources. German diplomats often regarded this as camouflage for the economic interests underlying the producing countries' oil policies, particularly those of the Arab states, not least because the rhetoric of limits clearly drew on Western interpretations of global oil issues. The German representative at the international organizations in Geneva thus reported that in a talk with Khene, the latter had availed himself of a 'political-moral argument scarcely influenced by insights into economic realities': 'Arguments geared towards the concerns of the "Club of Rome" and the demand for greater economic and social justice in the economic relations between industrialized and developing countries – as the members of OPEC have now learned – are far more useful and more difficult to refute than primitive threats to turn off the oil spigot'.[208] As so often, here again we see Western diplomats surprised to find their Arab interlocutors not only markedly more self-confident, but also in possession of a great deal of information and knowledge, not to mention negotiating acumen.

In contrast to OPEC, about which the German delegation in Vienna submitted regular and detailed reports despite the difficulties involved in compiling them, the West German government was aware of OAPEC only by dint of its statements and via its member countries' embassies. In the second half of October 1973, official reports began to pile up on the basic mood in the various countries' governments and public spheres. These chiefly sought to assess whether West Germany would continue to be categorized as neutral, or be redesignated as friendly or hostile. Few, like the German ambassador in Beirut, noted that there was method in the vagueness of OAPEC's pronouncements: they generated uncertainty and repeatedly compelled the West Germans to make enquiries, produce interpretations and engage in talks.[209] It was in the case of Libya that this applied most clearly and urgently.

Following the overthrow of King Idris and the 1969 revolution, Libya under Muammar Gaddafi was one of the most radical advocates of an oil policy that would prioritize the producing countries' interests. In addition to the nationalization of foreign oil firms, which was easier to achieve in Libya than other countries due to the fragmentation of the production concessions, Gaddafi repeatedly called for oil to be deployed as a weapon to counter the exploitation of the 'Third World' by the 'imperialist powers'.[210] Just a few weeks before the beginning of the oil crisis, Gaddafi had granted *Newsweek* a much-noted interview in which he described the Libyan policy of nationalization merely as a preliminary step towards the use of oil in political conflicts: 'Oil, if properly used, can be more effective than military clashes'.[211] This Libyan verbal radicalism left the US administration relatively unmoved as the United States imported little oil from the region anyway. The West German government, meanwhile, faced a fundamentally different reality. In the autumn of 1973, not only did a significant portion of the German oil firms' international business activities take place in Libya, but West Germany imported more than 25 per cent of its oil from the country, making Libya its largest supplier.[212]

Following the announcement of the supply cutbacks in October 1973, the Economics Ministry initially concluded that short-term oil shortages of one to two weeks would not constitute a serious problem even if they reached 50 per cent. However, if imports remained below current levels over the long term, then even a 20 per cent reduction could cause serious problems.²¹³ Libyan oil was thus essential, and due to the short oil tanker travel times, a Libyan embargo would have had a very rapid impact on the West German energy supply. Foreign Minister Walter Scheel's notes for the Cabinet meeting of 7 November, based on the expertise of the Economics Ministry, stated: 'If Libya, which currently supplies 25 per cent of German petroleum imports, were to take steps against West Germany, the situation would worsen significantly within a week, necessitating drastic cuts in consumption'.²¹⁴ When it emerged in the second half of October that the United States was delivering weapons and military equipment to Israel via bases in Germany, the Arab countries excoriated the West German government for tolerating this. They threatened to include West Germany in the full embargo if it refused to adopt a more pro-Arab stance. In these fraught circumstances, the supposedly abstract issue of West Germany's position in the world took on highly concrete form. Acting to secure sufficient oil supplies meant considering West Germany's special relations with Israel and avoiding excessive strains on its relationship with the United States, while also responding to demands for European solidarity – particularly with the Netherlands, which was subject to the full embargo.

In mid October, expert opinion was divided as to whether massive American military support for Israel would trigger the deployment of the so-called oil weapon. There was, however, no lack of Arab warnings to this effect. Even before the launch of the regime of production cutbacks, the West German Cabinet had noted that the Arab countries were suspicious about 'the possibility of the US supplying Israel with weapons via its units in West Germany'.²¹⁵ On 16 October, Martin J. Hillenbrand, American ambassador to West Germany, had informed Walter Scheel that the United States would supply Israel with weapons from depots on German territory. The next day, the government even received a list of the equipment delivered.²¹⁶ In the second half of October and early November 1973, the West German government worried that these American arms supplies might prompt the Arabs, above all the Libyans, to impose an oil embargo on West Germany. Various Arab statements reinforced these concerns. The head of the Arab League's Bonn office, for example, visited the Foreign Ministry on 25 October to explain that the Arabs had lost all faith in the West German government. While the latter, he stated, might disapprove of the arms shipments, it was still allowing them to take place. The Arabs thus felt West Germany was merely paying lip service to neutrality.²¹⁷

Most disturbing of all, however, were the public statements by Gaddafi. He wrote to Willy Brandt, urging him to unambiguously affirm his support for the Arab cause in the Middle East conflict. In an interview with *Le Monde* on 23 October, he issued the following threat: 'We've made all the preparations – and so have the other Arabs – to deprive Europe completely of oil. We shall ruin your industries as well as your trade with the Arab world.... We are determined to hit America, if necessary by striking Europe'.[218] For Lothar Lahn, head of the Political Division in the Foreign Ministry, this interview, in which Gaddafi had behaved 'with even less self-control than usual', demonstrated an 'alarming extremism'. Regardless of Gaddafi's other 'verbal excesses', he advised Undersecretary Paul Frank to take these statements seriously.[219] Overall, Foreign Ministry staff were unsure what to make of Gaddafi. On the one hand, the German ambassador reported from Tripoli that, after sending his letter to Brandt, Gaddafi had awarded the largest ever contract to German firms in Libya outside the oil sector. Ambassador Werner evaluated this development through classically Orientalist stereotypes. He explained that Gaddafi was trying, 'according to the time-worn customs of the bazaar, to forge close ties with his partner to prevent him from shifting allegiance to his competitors, while not forgetting to make threatening reference to the possibility of breaking off these lucrative business relations'.[220] In Werner's reports, Gaddafi appeared as ultimately driven by economic motives, even if his economic strategies clashed with European norms.[221] On the other hand, Gerhard Müller-Chorus, who was stationed in the German embassy in Libya, did not see Gaddafi as a rational economic actor. It was, he contended, impossible to foresee how a man with Gaddafi's 'mentality and psychological structure' would respond to the experts' unanimous verdict that it would be impossible to enforce an embargo against West Germany. He believed that Gaddafi might be tempted 'to go all out to enforce the embargo ... and get carried away to the point of seeking to "perfect" it. If not before, then when these efforts came to nothing, so much resentment might have built up within him that finally, following the Saudi line – and trumping it in contravention of his own financial interests – he might extend the embargo to include a corresponding production cut, triggering a genuine supply crisis'.[222] Undersecretary Frank also reported that a visit to Tripoli had opened up 'a very different world' to him, 'a world that does not think in the same commercial and economic categories as we do'.[223] In other words, it would be a mistake to assume that because an embargo would ultimately damage their own economic interests, the Arab countries would never go through with it.

Things came to a head on 30 October, when Müller-Chorus was summoned to the Libyan Foreign Ministry. He was instructed to warn the West German government, 'possibly for the last time', to articulate its stance on the Middle East conflict more unambiguously.[224] The Libyan government expected a response within a week. Otherwise, it would initiate steps against West Germany that might include a full embargo, in which the other Arab producing countries would participate as well. Rather than continuing to march in lockstep with the United States, the West German government ought to develop the far more useful relations with the Arab states. Above all, it should know better than to support the Netherlands, which was subject to the full embargo. Due to the diction, after consulting with his American colleagues, Müller-Chorus assumed that this ultimatum had come directly from Gaddafi. It was, he believed, largely motivated by the fact that Libya had interpreted West Germany's insistence on its neutrality, or its recent tendency to distance itself from the United States, as a sign of weakness.[225]

Faced with the choice of giving Gaddafi, who was viewed as unpredictable, a reason to stop supplying West Germany with oil, and risking a conflict with the United States and Israeli protest, the government chose the second option. Through both public pronouncements and diplomatic initiatives, it did everything it could to guarantee a stable oil supply. After the ceasefire, Ambassador Hillenbrand was summoned to the Foreign Ministry on 23 October. He was told that the West German government was working on the assumption that there would be no more US arms shipments from German territory.[226] When ships carrying US munitions continued to leave German ports, the government protested publicly. It also instructed all its ambassadors in the Arab countries to inform their host governments that it had been neither consulted nor informed about this, disapproved of the shipments and was strictly committed to the principle of neutrality with respect to the Middle East conflict.[227] In his letters to Boumedienne and Gaddafi of 26 October 1973, Willy Brandt made no explicit reference to the arms shipments. However, he tried to assure both of them that West Germany would maintain a neutral course when it came to the Middle East conflict and was committed to UN Resolution 242. Here he not only underlined the right of all states to take sovereign action within free and recognized borders, but also explicitly mentioned the 'just resolution of the Palestinian problem' as a precondition for a peace settlement.[228] In public, too, Brandt and Scheel repeatedly expressed West Germany's neutrality with respect to the conflict, irritating the Israelis.[229] Neutrality, as the Israeli ambassador put it to the Foreign Ministry, was not enough because, at the end of the day, this was not a football match but a matter of Israel's survival.[230] Oil and Auschwitz, he reminded his interlocutors, implied very different obligations for the German government. Undersecretary Frank, with whom Ben Horin had lodged his complaint, replied to the ambassador, quite curtly, that neutrality meant non-interference in conflicts and that one could create unnecessary problems for oneself by interpreting words in particular ways. Above all else, the West German government was keen to prevent a third world war, the conditions for which were all in place.[231]

On the same day, Frank received the Libyan ambassador Galal Daghely, with whom he was equally brusque. He began by remarking that the Libyans would be 'well-advised to forget about their warning ("ultimatum") that an answer must be given within a week. This is surely not the right way to speak to one another'.[232] The West German government, Frank went on, was disappointed by the Libyan threats. Ultimately, it had gone further than its allies by risking the ire of the United States, despite its elementary importance to West Germany's security. The West German government had, he contended, always been neutral with respect to the Middle East conflict. Furthermore, a conference in Brussels was presently seeking to formulate a common European position, which, he underlined, West Germany would fully embrace. The West German embassy in Tripoli was also instructed to highlight the country's neutrality and the vital importance of oil to global economic development.[233]

While the news from Libya was contradictory – alongside repeated threats by key political actors, the Libyan press published Willy Brandt's letter and seemed satisfied with its content – West German diplomats in Egypt discerned a promising means of averting the impending embargo.[234] On 2 November, the Egyptian ambassador had declared in the Foreign Ministry that it was wrong to threaten an embargo and that Libya was isolated within the Arab world. At the same time, however, he called on the West German government to adopt a pro-Arab position in order to prevent the embargo.[235] Egypt's President Sadat did in fact seek to dissuade Gaddafi from implementing his plan; Cairo was content with the EC declaration on the Middle East conflict of 6 November and wished to ensure that Willy Brandt did not deviate from this position at the conference of the Socialist International convened by Golda Meir.[236] The next day, Ambassador Werner reported from Tripoli that the Libyan threat of an embargo had now been withdrawn, though Libyan Prime Minister Jalloud was still quoted in the *Spiegel* on 12 November as threatening that, in future, Europe would receive sufficient oil only if it provided the Arabs with weapons.[237]

At their meeting in London, the party and governmental leaders of the Socialist International did in fact decline to endorse Golda Meir's complaint that the Europeans' declaration on the Middle East was too pro-Arab and went beyond UN Resolution 242. Willy Brandt was the first to respond to her criticism. He conceded that in some respects the declaration might have been worded 'better', but Israel should not interpret it to its own disadvantage, and mutual denouncements would only isolate it further.[238] On 16 November, Brandt thanked Sadat for his mediation, having previously told Edward Heath that the West German government's hard line on the Libyan embargo had forced Gaddafi to back down.[239] On a number of occasions during the negotiations with the producing countries and those states involved in the Middle East conflict, it was helpful for the

West German government to be able to refer to a common European position, and the EC declaration of 6 November provided this. How did this collective stance come about and what did it mean for the transatlantic relationship?

European and Transatlantic Cooperation and Conflicts

In the early 1970s, emphatically pro-European governments were in power in the major Western European countries. The Tory government in the UK under Edward Heath, with Sir Alec Douglas-Home as foreign minister, was perhaps its most pro-European government ever (1970–74). In France, President Georges Pompidou (1969–74), and foreign ministers Maurice Schumann (1969–72) and Michel Jobert (1973/74) toned down the country's Gaullist tendencies. The government of Willy Brandt in West Germany, with Walter Scheel as foreign minister, was also decidedly pro-European.[240] During the negotiations on the UK's accession, the countries of the European Communities had already resolved to pursue closer European Political Cooperation (EPC) in parallel with the northern expansion. Despite anticipating supply problems, however, the Europeans failed to agree a common policy on oil and energy that might have gone significantly beyond the crisis prevention mechanisms demanded by the OECD. Nonetheless, during the oil crisis the EC member states no longer pursued a purely national energy policy. Now all energy policy initiatives either had a European component or were reflected upon and discussed in their European contexts.

Even before the oil crisis, in May 1973 the French government had expressed its support for common European regulations on petroleum that would have tallied with French energy policy. However, its efforts came to nothing due to the member states' differing ideas about whether the internal market for oil products ought to be regulated and whether dialogue with the producing countries ought to take priority over solidarity between consuming countries.[241] The oil price hikes and production restrictions of October 1973 raised the stakes in the debate on a common energy policy. For some countries, the oil crisis was a test of the quality of European integration or internal European solidarity and pointed up the need for joint European action. For others, meanwhile, the fear of supply shortfalls engendered national responses. They thus attempted to safeguard their oil supply through unilateral action or bilateral negotiations with the producing countries.[242] To the extent that the production and supply restrictions were triggered by the Yom Kippur War, oil and energy security were closely bound up with the question of whether the EC would manage to agree a common position on the Arab-Israeli conflict. Middle East policy became a litmus test of EPC or a common EC foreign policy independent of the United States.²⁴³

On 13 October, in other words before the deployment of the 'oil weapon', an EC communiqué called for an immediate ceasefire. But just over a week later, EC Middle East experts were unable to agree a common position on UN Resolution 338, which called on the parties to conflict to agree a ceasefire and implement UN Resolution 242.²⁴⁴ The French in particular baulked at any declaration that failed to include condemnation of arms shipments to the combatants. In late October and early November, when the supply restrictions' precise impact on Europe was still very difficult to predict, the EC member states sought to safeguard an adequate supply of oil through bilateral negotiations with the producing countries. But they also tried to agree a common European position on the Middle East conflict. OAPEC's categorization of states into hostile countries, which were to receive no more oil (the Netherlands), friendly ones, which were to receive the same amount of oil as hitherto (the United Kingdom and France), and neutral ones, to which the production restrictions applied, gave rise to profound conflicts of interest.²⁴⁵ While Dutch representatives insisted on European solidarity and were supported in this by the West German government, which feared that it too would be subject to a full embargo, along with Italy, Belgium and Luxembourg, the British and French feared that a declaration of solidarity might endanger their relatively privileged status and their good relations with the Arab world.²⁴⁶

The British government in particular went on the offensive, pursuing a 'Britain first' strategy that attempted 'to safeguard full supplies to the UK even at the expense of our partners'.²⁴⁷ In early November, government officials discussed the possible negative consequences of such conduct for the UK's role in Europe and the world, and looked for ways to remain pro-European at least 'in private and practices'. Nonetheless, British Foreign Secretary Sir Alec Douglas-Home, together with his French counterpart Michel Jobert, rejected European declarations of solidarity, disappointing the Netherlands in particular.²⁴⁸ The French government initially tried to avoid any attempt by the EC to tackle oil and energy issues. When the West German government proposed that the Community ought to express its misgivings about recent developments and declare its intent 'to safeguard the common market against disturbances from outside and ensure that it functions well internally in future',²⁴⁹ Jobert was dismayed at his West German colleagues' failure to keep this initiative secret.²⁵⁰ When the French and British refused to repurpose a foreign ministers' dinner as an 'oil dinner', the West German camp gave assurances that it too was averse to any 'spectacular statement of solidarity'.²⁵¹ Following long negotiations, on 6 November the foreign ministers finally agreed on a minimal text reaffirming that the petroleum supply was a topic of interest to the EC.[252]

The EC declaration on the Middle East, adopted by the foreign ministers the same day following an earlier eighteen-hour debate among the political directors, received greater attention than the above declaration.[253] In it, the EC countries expressed their support for UN Resolutions 338 and 242 and identified the principles that must underpin a future peace settlement: non-violence; an end to the Israeli occupation; respect for sovereignty; and consideration for the legitimate rights of the Palestinians.[254] With this declaration, the Europeans went beyond UN Resolution 242, as the latter had been ambivalent. In its French variant it had called for Israel to withdraw from (all) the territories occupied in 1967, which jibed with the Arab countries' thinking. Its English version, meanwhile, merely demanded withdrawal from territories occupied during the Six-Day War. The EC's declaration on the Middle East eliminated this ambivalence. It was, therefore, generally interpreted as an indication that – in light of the threat of Arab supply cutbacks – the countries of Western Europe had failed to show genuine solidarity with the Netherlands and had abandoned their previous neutrality on the Middle East conflict in favour of a pro-Arab position. In any case, the declaration had been preceded by in-depth discussions with the Arab countries about what they would need to hear in order to ease the production cuts.[255] Ultimately, the declaration was a simple way for the EC to regain an advantage within the debate on oil supplies.[256]

Although this declaration had succeeded, for the first time, in formulating a consistent foreign policy position within the framework of EPC, it could not conceal the massive differences between European governments. All of them viewed possible threats to their countries' oil and energy supply through a national prism.[257] Political observers in many EC countries and the United States generally believed that by issuing the Middle East declaration, the Europeans had caved in completely to Arab pressure. In the German public sphere too, the declaration was rejected as wrong in principle and as a poor strategy for asserting sovereignty. Commentators in the major German daily newspapers were unanimous in their view that the Middle East declaration was an abandonment of the EC's previous neutrality, its pro-Arab character a result of the threatened use of the 'oil weapon'.[258] In the *Süddeutsche Zeitung*, Dieter Schröder called for 'a more cool-headed approach to the oil crisis'. When it came to Israel, he contended, no European country – least of all Germany – could remain neutral, while the Europeans' disunity had virtually provoked the use of the 'oil weapon'.[259] In the *Frankfurter Allgemeine Zeitung*, Günther Gillessen accused the Western European governments of embracing the 'I'm-all-right-Jack' principle: as long as their own house was left intact, the one next door could burn to the ground. Such conduct, however, was short-sighted because 'the European governments' evident fear of oil blackmail makes such extortion more probable, more extensive and repeatable over the long term'. Gillessen thus called for greater solidarity with the Netherlands: 'Freezing for Holland? Let's freeze together and we'll freeze ourselves towards more influence'.[260]

The Foreign Ministry carefully noted the public's dissatisfaction with the government's conduct, which followed a similarly negative response to its stance on American arms shipments to Israel. On the same day the commentaries on the Middle East declaration were published, Undersecretary Paul Frank invited reporters to an off-the-record talk. Clearly incensed, Frank began with a long, emotional and at times aggressive declaration on West Germany's approach to the Middle East conflict and the oil crisis.[261] It is hard to assess whether Frank was truly venting anger that had built up over the previous weeks and months or was merely acting strategically, attempting to intimidate the journalists and encouraging them to write more positive reports. Time and again, the minutes of Frank's conversations with international partners reveal a surprisingly confrontational and at times aggressive communicative style. Referring to negotiations with Kissinger during the oil crisis, Frank retrospectively formulated the following maxim of diplomatic communication: 'When replying to vicious accusations, one must show no trace of fear, because fear is the surest way to provoke the other's aggression'.[262]

Frank declared to the assembled reporters that the commentaries published the day before on the Middle East declaration revealed that at least some of them had failed to understand that this was a matter of war and peace. Furthermore, they had clearly failed to grasp the kind of 'near-apocalyptic' consequences of a significant shortage of oil for a highly industrialized country such as West Germany: 'Just ask the industrialists what 25 per cent less energy would mean for them. Ask the petrochemical industry what would become of it, and ask – bearing in mind that we're far from sure that [the shortfall] would remain at 25 per cent – what the social and economic impact would be in this country and in France and in Holland and in the United Kingdom, if we are stripped of our energy cover, our energy basis'.[263] He claimed that he had not risked a conflict with the United States over its weapons shipments to Israel 'on a whim' or 'to play the tough guy', but in order to protect West Germany's 'vital interests'.[264] In this situation, West German foreign policy must include the right amount of 'self-defensive solidarity' to guarantee the country's 'vital existence'.[265] Contradicting the commentators, Frank emphasized that the EC's Middle East declaration was not a response to the oil crisis, but was in continuity with German and European policy. The 'undignified' juggling with the French- and English-language versions of UN Resolution 242 had to come to an end, even if it had been convenient for the West German government to say 'it's all Greek to me'.[266] Furthermore, the journalists ought to acknowledge that the declaration was the first sign of a newly emerging European political entity and that the crisis provided an opportunity for European unification. Like West Germany, the oil crisis had compelled the EC as a whole to define its place in the world and in relation to other world regions: 'Essentially, Europe has become aware of its interests in this regard, its place in the world and the role it is capable of playing'.[267] The declaration, Frank contended, was not the sum of the member states' nine different positions, but a European position, one the West German government would embrace henceforth. Following his lengthy outburst, there was a ring of truth to Frank's statement that 'personally, [he would have found it] far preferable and more pleasant' had he been able to vent his feelings about these things 'in editorials or other opinion pieces'.[268]

As expected, the Arab countries welcomed the EC's Middle East declaration, which furnished its member states with new diplomatic room for manoeuvre. In line with the communicative logic of the embargo, the ball was no longer in their court. Just a few days after the adoption of the declaration, the British government proposed to its European partners that it might now be used to launch a concerted diplomatic initiative requesting that the Arab countries lift the production restrictions and the embargo: 'It seems desirable that the Community countries should begin to cash the credit which the Declaration has earned them'.[269] In a joint démarche, the Europeans should explain to the Arab countries that European unity would benefit them too; however, the Arab approach to oil was undermining this unity, threatening Europe's economic development and failing to win over public opinion. While most countries welcomed this initiative, France initially rejected it.[270] Nonetheless, on 20 November the EC foreign ministers issued a joint declaration, resolving that it ought to be conveyed to the Arab countries 'confidentially' and 'not as a protest . . . , but as part of the general dialogue between European governments and Arab states concerning the present situation'.[271] The idea was that those ambassadors with the best prospect of selling the declaration – due to their country's relations with the host nation – ought to deliver this message. In Libya, for example, the German and French ambassadors met with the head of the Foreign Ministry's political division for talks in a 'relaxed atmosphere'. They came away with the impression that the Libyans were beginning to comprehend the Europeans as a unified entity and were more likely to espouse easing than intensifying the embargo.[272] OAPEC did in fact abandon the additional 5 per cent reduction in oil supplies to the neutral European countries planned for December, though it left the embargo on the Netherlands in place.

During the oil crisis, then, a bipartite communicative structure developed between the Western European and Arab countries. On the one hand, the West German government and the governments of the other European countries negotiated directly with the producing states in an attempt to safeguard their energy supply. It was above all France and the United Kingdom that sought to achieve bilateral agreements, though West Germany and Japan did so too.[273] On the other hand, however, the EC countries tried to deal with their Arab counterparts as a community, voluntarily relinquishing powers in a core field of sovereign policymaking. However, to view this as a loss of national sovereignty or a fundamental transfer of sovereignty to the supranational level is inadequate. The various governments only allowed the EC to speak on their behalf when they believed this would benefit their national strategies to achieve energy security. The West German government, for example, virtually barricaded itself behind the declaration of the nine in its dealings with the Arab countries, underlining that West Germany, as part of the EC, could neither abandon the Community's declaration nor put its own spin on it. The EPC that had become manifest in the Middle East declaration, then, did not represent a loss of sovereignty on the part of the member states. On the contrary, it expanded the scope of their sovereignty. The member states were too small and powerless to solve the energy problem or play a significant role in the Middle East conflict. It was only by banding together, it seemed, that they could rescue their sovereignty and obtain room for manoeuvre, though this supranational alliance encountered problems whenever it clashed with the interests of any of its members.[274]

The oscillating congruence and tension between national and European energy security continued over the following weeks and was clearly in evidence at the European summit meeting in Copenhagen on 14 and 15 December. At a meeting of the foreign ministers in early December, joint measures proposed chiefly by the Netherlands and Denmark had been scuppered by resistance from France and the United Kingdom, which were keen to avoid provoking the Arabs into escalating the conflict.[275] The British and French governments faced mounting criticism within the EC for their 'sauve qui peut' strategy. In early December, the Planning Committee of the Foreign and Commonwealth Office produced a strategy paper intended to set out the British position at the impending summit meeting. It examined five options: 'a) Increased Saudi Production for Britain . . . b) Arab Preferences without Increased Production . . . c) Accept Equal Misery . . . d) Exploiting the Position of BP . . . e) Restricting Exports to the EEC of Oil and Products'.[276] In view of the complex nature of the regime of production cuts, government experts argued that the UK faced no 'clear-cut choice between a policy of pursuing national advantage and one of European co-operation'.[277] Even were it to be successful, a truly national strategy might lead to a worsening of relations within Europe, whose long-term effects would be even more detrimental than a shortage of oil. They advised the government to initially adopt a wait-and-see approach, particularly given that the oil companies' existing allocation policy had spared even the Netherlands from the worst consequences of the embargo. Drastic action, meanwhile, should be avoided. While it would certainly be possible to intensify cooperation, the UK must avoid any scenario in which Europe would gain access to North Sea oil. In other words, it was vital to retain 'our ability to exploit the North Sea as a national asset'.[278]

As the French government too remained opposed to European declarations of solidarity, it proved impossible to agree a common energy policy at the Copenhagen summit. Ultimately, there were major differences between countries regarding how strongly any common market for petroleum products ought to be regulated and what role the major oil companies ought to play in supplying Europe with oil in future. While France advocated a dirigiste approach and wished to constrain the oil firms' influence in favour of direct communication between the governments of the producing and consuming countries, West Germany favoured a more flexible market and was keen for the multinational companies to continue to guarantee the oil supply.[279] As a result, the heads of state and government in Copenhagen agreed only a very general declaration on energy, which entrusted certain tasks to the Commission and Council.[280]

While the summit's material results were disappointing, the largely symbolic 'Declaration of European Identity', a product of discussions on recasting transatlantic relations, was a significant development. US initiatives had fostered a process of self-understanding within Europe, which now inspired a declaration by the EC countries intended 'to achieve a better definition of their relations with other countries and of their responsibilities and the place which they occupy in world affairs'.[281] The heads of government began by acknowledging the loss of global influence their countries had suffered over the course of the twentieth century. Present-day international problems were so severe that they could only help to solve them by working together. 'Acting as a single entity', Europe must seek accommodation and cooperation with other countries. Interestingly, the list of countries with which Europe was already cooperating and was keen to cooperate in future began with the group 'Africa, Mediterranean countries and the Middle East', followed only in second place by the United States, Japan and Canada. The next priority was cooperation with the Soviet Union in the spirit of détente, followed by the other world regions.²⁸² In the acute phase of the oil crisis, then, the EC countries issued a public declaration that gave relations with North Africa and the Middle East precedence over transatlantic relations, which had been tense since the Middle East declaration, if not earlier. To a significant degree, therefore, Europe defined its role in the world by staking out its differences from the United States with respect to international energy policy. But at the same time, the EC countries remained dependent on cooperation with the United States – not least with respect to energy.

According to Henry A. Kissinger, the year of the oil crisis ought really to have been the year of Europe, one in which transatlantic relations would take on a new form and significance. On 23 April, at the Waldorf-Astoria in New York, he declared that Europe must again move centre-stage within US foreign policy, focused in recent years chiefly on the Soviet Union, China and the war in Vietnam. To the surprise of many Europeans, he proposed the negotiation of a new Atlantic Charter with the United States' European allies by autumn. To a large degree because it coincided with European efforts to achieve political cooperation in Europe, Kissinger's initiative, christened the 'Year of Europe', sparked broad debates.²⁸³ From the outset, European governments responded critically. They felt they had been insufficiently informed about this plan and were displeased that Kissinger sought to grant the United States a global role but Europe merely a regional one.²⁸⁴ In his memoirs, Edward Heath criticized the Americans' failure to factor in European sensitivities in a difficult phase of the unification process: 'For Henry Kissinger to announce a Year of Europe without consulting any of us was rather like my standing between the lions in Trafalgar Square and announcing that we were embarking on a year to save America!'²⁸⁵ Despite what Heath implies here, however, the British government had certainly been consulted about this initiative in advance, though it had different ideas about how best to organize transatlantic cooperation.²⁸⁶

While Kissinger's initiative was intended, among other things, to stabilize US hegemony within the Western Alliance, it had the opposite effect. In fact, it intensified transatlantic tensions, acted as a catalyst for the process of European unification and strengthened the EC countries' efforts to assert themselves vis-à-vis the United States.²⁸⁷ Disagreements emerged chiefly because while Kissinger wished to create a multilateral structure, he initially wanted to negotiate in bilateral and secret talks with the individual European governments, whereas the Europeans were keen to negotiate with the Americans as a single entity.²⁸⁸ The processes of coordination necessary for this delayed the Europeans' response to the Americans' proposals and left them feeling disgruntled. This also applied to the dispatch of European representatives to Washington, such as Danish Foreign Minister Knud Andersen, who were perceived as unsatisfactory in the United States. This was due in significant part to a problem of authority or sovereignty. An EC envoy was authorized to inform the United States about a European decision, but he could not enter into negotiations about it; all he could do was carry out the instructions issued by his superiors in Europe. Kissinger in particular appears to have found this unpalatable.[289] When Richard Nixon told Willy Brandt of his indignation at the Europeans' subdued response to the Year of Europe, the latter tried to reassure the president: the Europe political sphere was presently under construction and was engaged in a learning process, which could be lengthy and at times bothersome. Nonetheless, the United States ought to support European unification and treat Europe as if it had already achieved the desired unity.[290]

While France was fundamentally averse to involving the United States in European affairs and viewed the Year of Europe as an instrument of US hegemony, the British government found itself in a particularly difficult situation. It wanted neither to risk its 'special relationship' with the United States nor to be viewed by the Europeans as a 'Trojan horse' that would allow the United States a covert seat at the European negotiating table.[291] Like the UK's European partners, however, the Heath government opted to give European integration precedence over the special relationship. The external diplomatic pressure generated by the Year of Europe thus led to a strengthening of EPC. Overall, the American plan to give transatlantic relations a new form and structure intensified the conflicts between the United States and its Western European partners as well as the European Communities as a whole. This became particularly plain when the oil embargo and the price hikes laid bare profound transatlantic clashes of interest.

The already tense relationship between the United States and West Germany worsened in the second half of October, when the latter protested against American arms shipments to Israel from depots in West Germany (see above) for fear of a Libyan oil embargo. Even before the embargo had been imposed on the United States, Kissinger and the American ambassador to NATO, Donald Rumsfeld, had responded with irritation to their European allies' failure to support the US in the Middle East crisis, though their criticisms were not focused on West Germany in particular.[292] However, on 24 October, the Foreign Ministry summoned the US ambassador to protest against the departure of Israeli ships loaded with American munitions from Bremerhaven, seriously aggravating the US government. Time and again, both the West German ambassador in Washington, Berndt von Staden, and his American counterpart in West Germany, Martin Hillenbrand, told of the 'wave of resentment over the allies' conduct' and the 'furious response' and 'deep disappointment' in Washington.²⁹³ The Americans' indignation grew all the more intense when the US armed forces were put on red alert in the early hours of 25 October due to a possible confrontation with the Soviet Union.²⁹⁴ The Americans accused the Europeans of leaving them in the lurch during a serious global crisis.

In line with this, the meetings between Undersecretary Frank and American envoy Frank Cash on 24 October and Ambassador Hillenbrand on 25 October were strained and heated. Frank having begun by openly identifying the three troubling aspects of this conflict for West Germany – namely the risk of harming German-American, German-Israeli and German-Arab relations – profound conflicts of interests came to light. These were argued out in blunt terms.²⁹⁵ While Cash claimed, in response to Frank's protest, that the German government had cleared the arms shipments, and while the American envoy repeatedly tried to find a solution that would allow such deliveries in future, Frank dug in his heels and rejected arms shipments of any kind.²⁹⁶ The next day, when Hillenbrand lodged a strong protest on behalf of the US government, Frank assured him that the statements he had made to both Hillenbrand and Cash over the last two days had been carefully considered and approved by the chancellor.²⁹⁷ The West German government's 'balanced policy' on the Middle East conflict was 'dictated by vital German interests'. Frank stated that the United States must find other solutions if it wished to continue to deliver weapons to Israel. He reminded his American partners that an embargo had been imposed on the Netherlands for less valid reasons. Under no circumstances could the West German government risk the same fate.²⁹⁸ When Hillenbrand remarked that the situation was less dramatic than claimed and he was aware West Germany had at least two months' worth of oil stockpiles, Frank replied that, ultimately, oil was not the issue. The West German government was not being weak but attempting to uphold the country's strictly neutral stance on the conflict.²⁹⁹ In a moment of self-criticism, Frank conceded that so far the West German government's strategy had failed to achieve its goals. It had antagonized the Arabs, Israelis and the United States. He was, he added, unsure whether this meant the government had done everything wrong or everything right.³⁰⁰

Within the US government, the conflict over the arms shipments, or between US and European attitudes, was generally interpreted as evidence that 'the United States thinks globally, the Europeans regionally'.³⁰¹ Kissinger and his staff repeatedly declared that the United States' primary goal was to limit the Soviet Union's influence in the Middle East. The Europeans should recognize that over the long term this would serve their interests, rather than worrying about short-term oil supplies.³⁰² Kissinger took the view that, under the conditions of the embargo, only a strategy of strength could secure the long-term flow of oil and curb the Soviet Union's influence in the region (chapter 4). Despite the European allies' significantly greater dependence on oil supplies from the Arab producing countries, he was unwilling to see them adopt a divergent position, as this might undermine his own negotiating strategy. But the hegemonic power's ability to control its allies was limited. The progress of détente in Europe had reduced the perception of threat; the West German government generally, and Willy Brandt specifically, were convinced that the Americans would not significantly reduce their military presence in Europe. Kissinger confirmed this in response to Schlesinger's remarks to the contrary.[303] In any case, the West German government sought to limit the damage to bilateral relations. In a letter to Nixon, Brandt acknowledged the crucial role of the United States and reaffirmed German solidarity.[304] Nonetheless, Brandt maintained his hard line with respect to the issue at hand: 'But it is a quite different matter if American military equipment is transported from the territory of the Federal Republic of Germany – without even correctly informing, let alone asking the West German government about it – for purposes that do not form part of the alliance policy'.[305] On this occasion, Brandt stated, West Germany had been compelled to protest. In his response, Nixon acknowledged the Europeans' different economic interests in the Middle East, but he underlined once again that curbing the Soviet influence in the Middle East did in fact form part of the alliance policy. He also expressed shock at the fact that West Germany's diplomatic protest concerning the arms shipments had become public knowledge before the US government had had a chance to respond.[306] Depending on one's reading, then, either the short-sighted and regionally limited perspective of West German foreign policy or West Germany's 'vital interests' – that is, the necessity of avoiding an Arab embargo – had led to severe conflicts with the American hegemon.[307] Under direct pressure from the oil crisis or uncertainty regarding its future course, the West German government initially tended to act as a European power in concert with its European partners rather than as an ally of the United States. This found its clearest expression in the conflict over the Middle East declaration of 6 November, which attracted strong criticism in the United States.[308]

The tensions between the US and European governments resulted both from their differing degrees of dependency on Middle Eastern oil and their different assessments of the Middle East conflict and its global implications. In the summer of 1973, NSSM 174 had already concluded that the United States would withstand an Arab oil embargo without much trouble, while it would cause the Europeans and the Japanese far greater problems.[309] The US administration was well aware of the country's significantly stronger position with respect to oil and energy in comparison to the Europeans. It proposed to use this as a lever in negotiations, as Philip Odeen suggested to Henry Kissinger:

> Our Western European and Japanese Allies are much more dependent on imported energy than we are. This gives us more leverage in dealing with them on energy matters. We also get leverage from the fact that most major oil companies are American; we have considerable economic and political influence with the two biggest exporters, Saudi Arabia and Iran; and, we lead in most fields of energy-related technology. We must proceed carefully with our Allies in the Year of Europe to ensure that we can use our leverage in energy – for example, in the OECD emergency import sharing discussions – to get concessions in other areas.[310]

From an American perspective, then, the production and supply cuts initially seemed significantly less dramatic. In October 1973, the State Department saw the greatest danger in the potential for the Soviet Union to expand its influence in the Near and Middle East and thus shift global power relations to its advantage. The West German ambassador in Washington, Berndt von Staden, tried repeatedly to bring home to his government the fundamentally different categories and risk assessments characteristic of US foreign policy.[311] In the era of détente, however, European governments tended to see the greatest risks in real and threatened oil shortages rather than in the conflict between East and West.

As set out above, Kissinger considered a peace settlement in the Middle East the only way to safeguard oil supplies over the long term. He believed his strategy of strength was being put at risk by the Europeans' stance, because the producing countries would interpret their Middle East declaration and their pursuit of bilateral deals as signs of weakness. Fundamentally, Kissinger believed, giving into blackmail meant remaining vulnerable to it. Availing himself of Orientalist stereotypes, he explained to British Foreign Minister Sir Alec Douglas-Home that this was especially true of negotiations with Arab leaders, who immediately took the fulfilment of one of their demands as an opportunity to make a new one.[312] Having been presented with a fait accompli by the Europeans in the shape of their Middle East declaration, Kissinger tried to dissuade the Japanese government at least from making a similar pronouncement. He was, however, unsuccessful due to Japan's great dependence on Middle Eastern oil.[313] Kissinger's indignation at what he regarded as the weak posture of the Europeans and Japanese intensified in the face of vociferous criticisms, chiefly emanating from Europe, that the United States saw the embargo and oil price hikes as an opportunity to improve its competitive position vis-à-vis Europe and Japan.[314]

Kissinger left his European interlocutors in no doubt about his disgruntlement. Internally, he was yet more critical and contemptuous of them:

'Europeans are almost impossible right now'.³¹⁵ The British and French seemed particularly keen to use this conflict with the United States to expedite European unification. Just how difficult it was to deal with a peeved Kissinger was evident in a meeting with French Foreign Minister Michel Jobert, for whom the secretary of state had particularly little time. In response to a direct question from Kissinger, Jobert was quick to reassure him that he did not, of course, believe in the 'complex theories' suggesting that the Americans were ultimately out to weaken Europe.³¹⁶ Though the French government was particularly eager to see Europe become more assertive vis-à-vis the United States, and had fundamentally different ideas about international cooperation with respect to oil and energy, this appeared to fade away in the face of Kissinger's rhetorical vehemence. The talks turned out to be surprisingly cooperative. If we can believe the minutes, this also held for Kissinger's meetings with the Western European foreign ministers at – and on the fringes of – a NATO conference on 10 and 11 December in Brussels.³¹⁷ In preparation for his Europe trip, in early December Kissinger was again presented with figures on European supply shortfalls and the resulting foreign policy options. His advisers once again emphasized the United States' superior negotiating position compared with the Europeans: 'We have the power to make their oil situation better or worse'.³¹⁸ This, they underlined, was because only the United States could exercise significant influence on Israel. Due to its negligible import quota and the fact that five of the seven largest oil firms were headquartered in the United States, they went on, it was the only country capable of pursuing a selfish strategy, not least because it could still influence Saudi Arabia and enjoyed an advantage in new energy technologies. The goal of the negotiations must be to help the Netherlands and, by assuring the Europeans of the United States' willingness to cooperate, prompt them to ignore Arab pressure and stop making concessions.

Both at the NATO meeting on 10 December and in talks with the EC foreign ministers the following day, Kissinger was harshly critical of their conduct. He then went on, however, to propose new forms of cooperation on energy.³¹⁹ He fleshed this out on 12 December in a speech to the Pilgrims of Great Britain Society in London, which he had evidently not cleared properly with Nixon.³²⁰ According to Kissinger, the key axioms of any joint US-European policy must be: 'Détente is an imperative. . . . Common defense is a necessity. . . . European unity is a reality. . . . Economic interdependence is a fact'.³²¹ As long as one recognized these precepts, Kissinger contended, the only differences of opinion would arise from whether one interpreted the Middle East conflict as a regional clash or as a global conflict against the backdrop of the Cold War, and whether one regarded the energy crisis as a product of the Yom Kippur War or as a consequence of long-term developments.[322] Kissinger advocated a view of the energy crisis as a long-term problem with global implications, which could only be solved through a collaborative approach. To this end, he proposed the creation of an Energy Action Group, consisting of 'senior and prestigious individuals', which would, in three months, draw up a programme of action to solve the crisis. This approach, he suggested, would turn the oil crisis into an opportunity, functioning as the economic equivalent of the Sputnik Shock of 1957.[323]

Within Europe, it was chiefly the French government that criticized Kissinger's initiative, while the other EC countries welcomed these efforts to advance transatlantic cooperation on energy. Lantzke and Rohwedder, of the West German Economics Ministry, exemplified the latter response: 'Viewed in light of West Germany's energy interests', they informed the chancellor, Kissinger's offer of cooperation must 'in principle [be judged as] highly positive and given support'.[324] At the Copenhagen summit, Brandt thus went all out to ensure that the Community responded positively, though he was unsuccessful. Despite these efforts, during the oil crisis the West German government too initially prioritized the country's relationship with other European states over its relations with the United States. The Europeans as a whole were in fact more concerned with the security of their energy supply than with the stability of the transatlantic alliance. Due to the economic power structure and the conditions of the international oil economy, however, this was merely a brief episode. Most Europeans soon found themselves willing to cooperate closely with the United States once again in order to overcome the oil crisis and prevent future supply disruptions (chapter 6).

Relations with the 'Second' and 'Third' Worlds

The oil crisis changed not just West Germany's relations with those countries from which it imported oil and with its oil-importing European and North American allies. It also influenced the country's relations with the states of the 'Second' and 'Third' worlds, which were not as integrated into the world of oil in which West Germany found itself. In view of the economic threat from oil and energy shortages and higher energy import costs, the country set aside traditional ideological conflicts with the Eastern Bloc, along with more recent, lofty development goals. Above all, it was the pursuit of energy security that determined West German foreign policy.

In addition to the tensions outlined above, the transatlantic relationship was placed under further strain because the energy crisis made the Western Europeans more willing to cooperate economically with the Eastern Bloc. Despite the global Cold War, which was initially focused on Europe, and particularly on the divided Germany, in the early 1960s the Soviet Union already provided a significant share of Western Europe's energy supply. The members of the Council for Mutual Economic Assistance (CMEA or Comecon) were not only self-sufficient in energy. In 1961, oil exports from the Soviet Union accounted for around 35 per cent of Greek, 22 per cent of Italian, 21 per cent of Austrian and 19 per cent of the Swedish oil supply.[325] In West Germany, around 5 per cent of crude oil imports came from the Soviet Union in the early 1960s. These imports initially grew, but fell back again from 1968 onwards. Partly due to rapidly increasing overall energy consumption, they accounted for an ever smaller share of imports.[326] The kind of security considerations one might have expected in view of the Cold War initially played no special role with respect to these supplies; it was assumed that the Soviet Union needed the foreign currency generated by the sale of raw materials at least as urgently as the Western countries needed oil.[327] Initially, it was chiefly the Bavarian state government that advocated the import of Soviet gas, as it was keen to enhance its energy independence vis-à-vis the other West German states.[328] However, the crucial expansion of West German-Soviet energy relations occurred within the framework of the Ostpolitik promoted by Egon Bahr and Willy Brandt. This was intended to achieve 'transformation through rapprochement' with the aid of intensified economic relations.[329] The idea was that forms of economic cooperation of benefit to both sides would intensify cross-border exchanges and promote integration, improving the overall climate between East and West.[330] The most visible sign of economic Ostpolitik and its energy-related elements was the conclusion of the so-called Gas-Pipes Deals (Gas-Röhren-Geschäfte) in 1970 and 1972. Here the Soviet Union declared its willingness to supply a large quantity of natural gas in exchange for 2.4 million tonnes of large-diameter pipes.[331] Even before the oil crisis, the West German government had sought to achieve a three-way gas supply deal with the Soviet Union and Iran. Iran would have delivered gas to the Soviet Union, which would then have delivered it to West Germany, saving on transportation costs (though this plan ultimately came to nothing).[332]

Following the announcement of the production cuts by OAPEC and the associated price hikes, the West German government suddenly became far more interested in oil and gas supplies from the Comecon countries. The experts believed that up to 10 or even 15 per cent of the West German energy supply could come from Eastern European sources, without creating a critical dependency on political adversaries. On the contrary, this would markedly reduce West Germany's dependency on countries like Libya.[333] In fact, achieving a commensurate increase in Soviet production seemed to be the main problem. Serious political consequences seemed less probable against the backdrop of détente, particularly in light of the benefits accruing to both sides, such as the Gas-Pipes Deals.[334] Immediately after the start of the oil crisis, in a letter to Soviet leader Leonid Brezhnev, Brandt complained about the Arab 'politics of blackmail'. He went on: 'Of course, it would all be rather easier if we were less dependent on oil. It would be interesting to contemplate whether, and if so to what extent, the Soviet Union might be willing or able to supply us with oil over the short or medium term. Over the long term, we will make a tremendous effort to reduce our vulnerability to future blackmail'.[335] Two months later, he again asked Brezhnev to use his influence in the Arab world and among the producing countries to promote 'moderation and accommodation'.[336] Brezhnev initially attempted to sow the seeds of discord in the Western Alliance, pointing out that a rapid end to the embargo was against the interests of the United States because it ultimately benefited from the oil price hikes and the weakening of Europe.[337] However, following lengthy negotiations, a new natural gas agreement was concluded in August 1974, within the framework of which the USSR was to provide West Germany with a total of around ten billion cubic metres of gas per year.[338]

Even if growing oil and gas imports from the Soviet Union and the Comecon countries did not result in new dependencies, the United States looked askance at them, interpreting them as a challenge to the transatlantic alliance. The commodity agreements made it quite plain to the global hegemon that its Western European allies were attempting to safeguard their energy security through closer economic ties with the Cold War enemy, because the United States was unable to do so single-handedly.[339] Furthermore, this occurred at a time when tensions between the superpowers had just risen again due to the situation in the Middle East. Yet again, this transatlantic conflict was rooted in the fact that Kissinger viewed the Middle East conflict and the oil crisis primarily from the perspective of the Cold War. Determined to avert any shift in the global balance of power, he tried to prevent an increase in Soviet power in the region. For the Europeans, meanwhile, the focus was on their own energy supply. This pushed ideological considerations into the background. The economic and energy agreements with the Soviet Union had been transformed from an instrument of Ostpolitik into a strategy intended to guarantee West German energy security.[340] In other Western European countries too, energy deals with the Eastern Bloc made a significant contribution to energy security. In the 1980s, their governments thus abided by them despite pressure from the Reagan administration; regardless of Cold War crises, energy imports from the Eastern Bloc had proved stable and reliable.[341]

The oil crisis, then, had made West Germany more responsive to the wishes of the Eastern Bloc states because of its interest in their oil and gas reserves. But it had an adverse effect on its relations with developing countries that lacked significant energy resources. In the early 1970s, West German development policy underwent a process of reorientation. In July 1973, Erhard Eppler, who had been minister for development aid since the grand coalition, produced a paper on the 'goals and principles of German development policy', in which he distinguished it categorically from foreign policy. Development policy, he contended, must be geared towards the interests of the developing countries, while foreign policy pursued national interests. In the Foreign Ministry in particular, the idea that one could make policy in the interest of other countries attracted heavy criticism. But despite all the resistance, in September 1973 Eppler managed to persuade the Cabinet to commit to doubling the country's development aid.[342] In view of the massive oil price hikes of the following months, however, this decision was immediately called into question. In a TV debate in early December, both Erhard Eppler and CDU parliamentary leader Karl Carstens rejected the idea of reducing development aid in response to the oil crisis, as this would be to punish innocent parties. But by this stage the Foreign Ministry was already thinking hard about how it might instrumentalize such aid in the conflict with the producing countries.[343]

By mid November, an official at the Foreign Ministry had produced an overview of UN meetings slated to take place in the near future. Here, in coordination with the other OECD countries, West German delegates should highlight the connection between the oil crisis and development aid. The economic consequences of the supply cutbacks and price increases, they should underline, could impair the industrialized countries' economic performance and thus their willingness to provide aid as well.[344] However, the producing countries were aware that their policies were most detrimental to those developing countries without domestic oil reserves. They thus sought to mitigate the effects and maintain their strong solidarity with these countries, particularly in the fora of the UN. The representatives of the industrialized countries, therefore, tried to weaken this solidarity between the developing countries by making threats. Walter Gehlhoff suggested that it was preferable to avoid general statements and instead to merely hint at the connection between oil and development aid in talks on specific development projects.[345] Peter Hermes too instructed German diplomats to avoid general discussions and confrontations because they might intensify solidarity between Third World countries. They should, however, highlight the factual constraints resulting from the reduced economic activity triggered by the oil crisis. These might 'have detrimental effects not just on the industrialized countries but – directly and indirectly – on the developing countries as well'.[346] To help them argue more effectively, the diplomats were instructed to highlight the following key points. While it was not yet possible to quantify its effects precisely, the oil shortage would undoubtedly lead to a reduction in economic growth, if not a decline in production; the higher energy prices would make capital goods more expensive; necessary investment in new energies also placed a question mark over development aid, as did reduced tax revenues, which would, moreover, diminish the psychological willingness to provide development aid.[347]

To the extent that the developing countries were hit directly by the oil price hikes, the German embassies, like those of other industrialized countries, were required to provide detailed reports on these effects. These reports could then be used to bolster their arguments in negotiations with the producing countries.[348] In the run-up to the UN special session on raw materials and development in 1974 (chapter 6), this information was then compiled systematically. In many countries, it was noted, the higher energy prices were having a direct impact on economic growth, as they lacked potential substitutes and, unlike the industrialized countries, could expect no substantial foreign exchange repatriation. Of the least developed countries, the worst affected were India, Burma, Bangladesh and Pakistan; of the developing countries, South Korea, Thailand and the Philippines; and of the newly industrializing countries, Turkey, Brazil, Taiwan and Jamaica, according to the Foreign Ministry's analysis.[349] On the basis of similar studies by the OECD and the World Bank, the EC Commission distinguished three groups of developing countries. Some profited from the overall increase in the price of raw materials and could therefore cushion the effect of the oil price rise. A second group, which included South Korea, Taiwan and Singapore, could fall back on foreign exchange reserves or take out loans. But the worst affected were those countries that lacked even this option, such as India, Pakistan, Bangladesh and Sri Lanka, the countries of Central America and the Caribbean, those of the Sahel and Senegal, Kenya and Burundi.[350] The Commission thus called for the establishment of a special aid fund to which the EC countries should contribute five hundred million US dollars. When the United Nations instituted the Emergency Aid Fund, however, the West German Cabinet under Helmut Schmidt initially rejected Eppler's request that it approve West Germany's contribution. This was all the more embarrassing for Eppler as he had promoted the fund in the EC Council of Development Ministers, which he chaired. When the decision was made not only to cancel the planned doubling of the development aid budget but to cut it because of the oil crisis, Eppler resigned from his post.[351]

In view of the oil price hikes and production cuts, West German foreign policy focused on the country's relations with the producing countries and the other major consuming countries. By way of contrast, relations with those developing countries that lacked significant oil reserves were of secondary importance and were viewed strategically, in terms of their value in negotiations with the producing countries. In international negotiations, the West German government, like those of other industrialized countries, thus attempted to drive a wedge between the developing countries, seeking to use the fate of those hit hardest by the price increases as a moral argument against the producing countries. This strategy, however, achieved little: the producing countries deftly presented themselves as the avant-garde of the developing world, while taking concrete steps to alleviate its economic problems (chapter 6). Nonetheless, the debt crisis among the least developed countries now gained pace, because they needed credit to cover the higher import costs of energy and other goods and received this on favourable terms due to the simultaneous inflation of petrodollars. Because the material scope for redistribution diminished in the industrialized countries as a result of the oil crisis, in West Germany development aid came under scrutiny and became one of its first political victims. The recasting of West German development policy, launched by Eppler, thus ended before it had truly begun.

Interim Conclusion

In West Germany, fears of a lack of oil and of the economic consequences of a sharp increase in the oil price prompted the reorganization of energy policy; this was already underway by 1970 and reached an initial peak shortly before the oil crisis with the adoption of the Energy Programme. Here the involvement of relevant ministerial staff in transnational networks of experts within the framework of the OECD had a direct impact on national policymaking. Despite the restructuring already in progress, the oil price hikes and production cutbacks posed a challenge to West German sovereignty by seeming to threaten energy security and economic growth. In the 1970s, it was unimaginable for West German politicians to formulate policies in the absence of the economic growth rates of the preceding decades. As late as 1977, for the economic research institutes' forecast concerning the second extension of the Energy Programme, the West German government provided them with guidelines stipulating that economic growth must amount to an average of 4 per cent until 1985 and subsequently 3.5 per cent. Otherwise, the government underlined, it would be impossible to maintain present levels of employment and the welfare state.

The West German government's response to the challenge posed to its political sovereignty by the oil crisis differed from that of its allies. Initially, the Economics Ministry maintained a strong commitment to the free market, objecting to every proposal to step up the regulation of the energy sector. Unlike in France and the United Kingdom, where major governmental institutions were dedicated to governing the energy sector, or the United States, which quickly created such an authority, the West German government made no attempt to develop its own governmental expertise. The expansion of divisions concerned with oil and energy remained moderate and the Economics Ministry relied mainly on the external energy expertise generated by economic research institutes. The need for forecasts on future trends in energy supply and consumption, and related plans, grew rapidly as a result of the changes in the international oil economy. Hence, the hypothesis of a great sobering and the end of planning may perhaps apply to the idea of macroeconomic regulation or *Globalsteuerung*, but it is wide of the mark when it comes to energy-related political practice. Forecasts and plans became more numerous and longer term, and there is absolutely no evidence that the associated euphoric belief in the malleability of economic and social developments diminished.

For the social-liberal government, the oil crisis turned the abstract issue of how West Germany ought to position itself within the world into a very concrete one, compelling it to develop the country's relationship with the various world regions under conditions of perceived or anticipated scarcity of energy. Due to the advancing process of European unification, this applied first and foremost to its relations with its European allies and the formulation of a common foreign policy. In a decade of détente, West Germany and the other European countries signed agreements with the Eastern Bloc to increase oil and gas imports. If it would enhance their energy security, they were willing to risk conflict with the United States and throw ideological ballast overboard. It would, however, be precipitate to view this as the overcoming of the logic of the Cold War or of US hegemony within the Western Alliance. At this point in time, the United States was yet to bring its full economic and political weight to bear in its negotiations with the Europeans and, over the medium term, the fault lines of the Cold War remained just as deep.

While the oil crisis prompted the EC countries to agree a common foreign policy for the first time – in the shape of the Middle East declaration of 6 November 1973 – this does not fit seamlessly into a success story of European unity. In reality, the negotiations on a common energy policy illustrate that the EC member states were only prepared to endorse supranational integration if it enhanced their sovereign room for manoeuvre in other ways. The dominance of economic considerations and energy security was especially evident in relations with those developing countries that lacked significant energy resources. Despite earlier commitments to prioritize the needs of the developing countries, in the face of threats to the country's energy supply the West German government soon found itself contemplating national economic interests. It thus sought to instrumentalize the Third World states in the conflict with the producing countries.

Notes

1. 'Unterrichtung durch die Bundesregierung. Die Energiepolitik der Bundesregierung'; on the foundation of DEMINEX, see Karlsch and Stokes, 'Faktor Öl', 359–68; Lötgers, 'Die Deutsche Erdölversorgungsgesellschaft – DEMINEX'.
2. Hans Friderichs, 'Beitrag zur zweiten und dritten Beratung des Entwurfs eines Gesetzes zur Sicherung der Energieversorgung bei Gefährdung oder Störung der Einfuhren von Mineralöl oder Erdgas', in *Verhandlungen des Deutschen Bundestages*, vol. 85 (Bonn, 1973), 3837–40, here 3838.
3. Otto Graf Lambsdorff, 'Beitrag in der Debatte zur Erklärung der Bundesregierung zu aktuellen Fragen der Wirtschafts- und Energiepolitik', in *Verhandlungen des Deutschen Bundestages*, vol. 85 (Bonn, 1973), 3926–32, here 3927.
4. Ibid., 3930.
5. For an introductory account of France, see Nouschi, *La France et le pétrole*, and the essays in Alain Beltran (ed.), *Oil Producing Countries and Oil Companies: From the Nineteenth Century to the Twenty-First Century* (Bern/Oxford, 2011); on the United Kingdom, see Charles More, *Black Gold: Britain and Oil in the Twentieth Century* (London, 2009); Christopher Harvie, *Fool's Gold: The Story of North Sea Oil* (London, 1994).
6. For the most recent summary, see Bernd Faulenbach, *Das sozialdemokratische Jahrzehnt: Von der Reformeuphorie zur neuen Unübersichtlichkeit; die SPD 1969–1982* (Bonn, 2011); see also Peter Bender, *Die 'Neue Ostpolitik' und ihre Folgen: Vom Mauerbau bis zur Vereinigung* (Munich, 1995); Arne Hofmann, *The Emergence of Detente in Europe: Brandt, Kennedy and the Formation of Ostpolitik* (London, 2007); David C. Geyer and Bernd Schaefer (eds), *American Détente and German Ostpolitik 1969–1972* (Washington, DC, 2004).
7. 'Rede des Bundeskanzlers Brandt vor der Vollversammlung der Vereinten Nationen. 26.9.1973', in Willy Brandt, *Ein Volk der guten Nachbarn: Außen- und Deutschlandpolitik 1966–1974*, edited by Frank Fischer (Bonn, 2005), 498–511.
8. Ibid., 510. For the English translation of Brandt's speech, see Willy Brandt, 'Address to the United Nations General Assembly. 2128th Plenary Meeting, 26 September 1973', in United Nations, General Assembly (ed.), *Twenty-Eighth Session. Plenary Meetings. Verbatim Records of Meetings 18 September-18 December 1973 and 16 September 1974* (New York, 1983), 1–5.
9. Kenneth E. Boulding, 'The Economics of Space-Ship Earth [1966]', in Fred R. Glahe (ed.), *Collected Papers of Kenneth E. Boulding*, vol. 2, *Economics* (Boulder, CO, 1971), 383–94; Sabine Höhler, *Beam Us Up, Boulding! 40 Jahre 'Raumschiff Erde'* (Karlsruhe, 2006).
10. 'Rede des Bundeskanzlers Brandt vor der Vollversammlung der Vereinten Nationen', in Brandt, *Ein Volk der guten Nachbarn*, 504f.
11. See the 'Vorschlag zu einer Methodik der Untersuchung der Energie- und Rohstoffproblematik' vom Dezember 1974, PA AA, B 71 (Referat 405), 113894, which never made it off the drawing board.
12. See Gabriele Metzler, *Konzeptionen politischen Handelns von Adenauer bis Brandt: Politische Planung in der pluralistischen Gesellschaft* (Paderborn, 2005); Jarausch, *Das Ende der Zuversicht?*; Anselm Doering-Manteuffel, 'Nach dem Boom: Brüche und Kontinuitäten der Industriemoderne seit 1970', *Vierteljahrshefte für Zeitgeschichte* 55 (2007), 560–81; Dirk van Laak, 'Planung: Geschichte und Gegenwart des Vorgriffs auf die Zukunft', *Geschichte und Gesellschaft* 34 (2008), 305–26.

13. Übersicht über Regelungen zur Krisenvorsorge im Mineralölbereich, 10.10.1973, PA AA, B 36 (Referat 310), 104991; Tischvorlage für die Kabinettsitzung am 17. Oktober 1973, Bonn, 15.10.1973, BArch, B 136/7706.

14. On the growth of Lantzke's division in the Ministry of Economics, see Wolfgang Hoffmann, 'Bonner Expertenstäbe – Die Verwalter der Krise', *Die Zeit*, 30 November 1973.

15. Willy Brandt, 'Erklärung der Bundesregierung zu aktuellen Fragen der Wirtschafts- und Energiepolitik', in *Verhandlungen des Deutschen Bundestages*, vol. 85 (Bonn, 1973), 3908–13, here 3908.

16. Franz Josef Strauß, 'Beitrag in der Debatte zur Erklärung der Bundesregierung zu aktuellen Fragen der Wirtschafts- und Energiepolitik', in *Verhandlungen des Deutschen Bundestages*, vol. 85 (Bonn, 1973), 3913–23, here 3914.

17. Abteilung III C 1/III C 2 [BMWi]: Aktuelle Situation im Mineralölbereich, 22.10.1973, PA AA, B 71 (Referat 405), 113906.

18. Abteilung III C 1/III C 2 [BMWi]: Aktuelle Situation im Mineralölbereich, 3.11.1973, PA AA, B 36 (Referat 310), 104992.

19. Weiß an Abteilungsleiter IV: Krisenvorsorge im Mineralölbereich; Preisentwicklung im Mineralölbereich, 29.10.1973, BArch, B 136/7708; Quante an Abteilungen im Ministerium: Sitzung der Kleinen Arbeitsgruppe am 31. Oktober 1973, BArch, B 102/282309.

20. Gilford John Ikenberry, 'The Irony of State Strength: Comparative Responses to the Oil Shocks in the 1970s', *International Organization* 40 (1986), 105–37.

21. Hans Friderichs, 'Ein offenes Wort zum Ölverbrauch', *Süddeutsche Zeitung*, 12 November 1973; see, for example, the advertisements taken out by Shell AG in *Die Zeit*: 'Sie sparen bis zu 35% Heizöl mit der richtigen Einstellung', 30 November 1973; 'Erst lüften, dann heizen! Sonst werfen Sie Ihr Geld zum Fenster hinaus', 7 September 1973; 'Wenn Ihr Motor im Stand läuft, verschwenden Sie in 4 Minuten Benzin für 1 km. Stellen Sie ihn ab!', 7 December 1973.

22. On European governments' public communicative efforts during the oil crisis, see also Hohensee, *Der erste Ölpreisschock 1973/74*.

23. For criticism of the West German government from this perspective, see Russe (CDU/CSU), 'Stellungnahme zur Erklärung der Bundesregierung zur Lage der Energieversorgung', in *Verhandlungen des Deutschen Bundestages*, vol. 86 (Bonn, 1974), 4544–50, here 4545.

24. Hans Mathias Kepplinger and Herbert Roth, 'Creating a Crisis: German Mass Media and Oil Supply in 1973–74', *Public Opinion Quarterly* 43 (1979), 285–96.

25. Ibid.; see also Hohensee, *Der erste Ölpreisschock 1973/74*.

26. Adelman, *The Genie Out of the Bottle*, xxii.

27. Quante an Abteilungen im Ministerium: Sitzung der Kleinen Arbeitsgruppe am 31. Oktober 1973, BArch, B 102/282309.

28. Lahnstein an Chef des BK: Mineralölversorgung der BRD, 2.11.1973; Weiß an Chef des BK: Aktuelle Situation im Mineralölbereich, 5.11.1973, BArch, B 136/7708.

29. Sicherung der Energieversorgung bei Gefährdung oder Störung der Einfuhren von Mineralöl oder Erdgas (Energiesicherungsgesetz), *Bundesgesetzblatt* I(89) (10 November 1973).

30. Abteilungsleiter IV an BK: Anwendung des 'Energiesicherungsgesetzes', 14. November 1973, BArch, B 136/7708. On the press discussion of car-free Sundays and of the steps taken by the government, see Hohensee, *Der erste Ölpreisschock 1973/74*, 143–61 and passim. On the use of the term 'enabling' (*Ermächtigung*), see for example W/III D: Zwischenbericht über den Aufbau eines 'Krisenmanagements' zur Sicherung einer optimalen Energieversorgung im Falle einer Mineralölversorgungsstörung, 10. Juli 1972, BArch, B 102/282309.

31. III C 2 Tischvorlage zur aktuellen Situation im Mineralölbereich, 4.12.1973, BArch, B 136/7682; Weiß an BK: Morgige Sitzung des Kabinettsausschusses für Wirtschaft, 16.12.1973, BArch, B 136/7683.

32. Oberstadtdirektor der Stadt Bonn, Dr. Hesse, an Staatssekretär Horst Grabert (BK), 6.12.1973, BArch, B 136/7683; see for example the measures implemented by the Ministry

of Defence, ranging from foregoing exercises to closing swimming pools: Bundesminister der Verteidigung an den Bundeskanzler, 13.12.1973, BArch, B 136/7683.

33. Because the acute supply shortfalls in January and February amounted to only around 15 per cent, however, the voluntary and compulsory energy-saving measures were enough to avert a serious lack of oil; III C 2 Tischvorlage zur aktuellen Situation im Mineralölbereich, 22.1.1974; III C 2: Ergebnisvermerk: Aktuelle Situation im Mineralölbereich, 20.2.1974, BArch, B 136/7708.

34. Weiß an BK: Morgige Sitzung des Kabinettsausschusses für Wirtschaft, 16.12.1973; BMWi: Entscheidungsvorlage zur aktuellen Situation im Mineralölbereich, 17.12.1973; Weiß, Dehmel (Gruppe IV/2): Vermerk für Kabinettsitzung am 19. Dezember 1973, BArch, B 136/7683.

35. Pressekonferenz Nr. 149/73, am Mittwoch, 19. Dezember, 12.15, Pressehaus I, 16, BArch, B 145-I F.

36. Ibid., 18.

37. Ibid., 151f.

38. Helmut Schmidt, 'Die Energiekrise – Eine Herausforderung für die westliche Welt: Vortrag vor der Roosevelt University in Chicago am 13.3.1974', *Bulletin des Presse- und Informationsamts der Bundesregierung* 35 (1974), 325–30, here 329f.

39. Lantzke, 'The OECD and Its International Energy Agency', 219, 225.

40. III C 2 Tischvorlage zur aktuellen Situation im Mineralölbereich, 4.12.1973, BArch, B 136/7682; Strauß, 'Beitrag in der Debatte zur Erklärung der Bundesregierung zu aktuellen Fragen der Wirtschafts- und Energiepolitik', in *Verhandlungen des Deutschen Bundestages*, vol. 85 (Bonn, 1973), 3915.

41. Chef des BKA an alle Bundesminister: Kabinettsitzung vom 19. Dezember: Begleitende Maßnahmen zur Energiesituation, 20.12.1973, BArch, B 136/7682.

42. BArch, B 102/200614, Gutachten des wissenschaftlichen Beirats am BMWi zur Energiepolitik 1967–1980.

43. Siegfried Eichler (BDI) an Lantzke: Stellungnahme des BDI zur Energiepolitik, 24.5.1973; BDI: Memorandum zur Europapolitik, 12. Januar 1974; Stellungnahme des BDI zum Dokument KOM (74)550 der EG Kommission vom 29. Mai 1974, BArch, B 102/200763, Bd. 5: Energiepolitische Vorstellungen der Verbände und Organisationen der Wirtschaft außerhalb der Energiewirtschaft 1972–74.

44. Chef des Bundeskanzleramtes an Bundesminister für Wirtschaft und Finanzen [z.H. MD Dr. Lantzke], 7. Juli 1972: Schreiben des deutschen Steinkohlenbergbaus vom 28. Juni 1972, BArch, B 136/7667. The reply from Undersecretary Rohwedder was rather restrained. It highlighted the fact that the public purse had already done a great deal for the coal mining industry and suggested that now its survival was down to consumers: Rohwedder: Antwortschreiben an Gesamtverband des deutschen Steinkohlenbergbaus und Steinkohlenbergbauverein, 10.8.1972, BArch, B 136/7667.

45. Industriegewerkschaft Bergbau und Energie an Bundeskanzler Willy Brandt, 20.11.1973 BArch, B 102/200539.

46. H. Mandel (Deutsches Atomforum) an Willy Brandt, 7.12.1973, BArch, B 136/7683.

47. Deutsches Generalkonsulat Barcelona an AA: Schreiben des spanischen Staatsangehörigen Vicente Munoz, 10. Juni 1974; Hernández, Rosendo Santana (14.2.1974): Schreiben an den Bundespräsidenten über ein Verfahren der Kohleverflüssigung, PA AA, B 71 (Referat 405), 113905.

48. Unkorrigierte Stenographische Niederschrift über die Anhörung von Sachverständigen in nicht-öffentlicher Sitzung des Ausschusses für Wirtschaft zu relevanten Fragen der Energiepolitik, 7.11.1973, BArch, B 102/200539; Lahnstein an Brandt: Energie-Gespräche in Münstereifel, 21.11.1973, BArch, B 136/7708; see also Schubert's autobiography: Enno Schubert, *Vom Bergmann zum Ölexperten: Stationen einer Karriere; Biografie* (Frankfurt am Main,

2007); Unterlagen zur Anhörung des Sachverständigenrates am 7. Dezember 1973, BArch, B 102/200539.

49. Staden: Gespräch zwischen dem Bundeskanzler und Walter Levi, 27.11.1974, PA AA, B 71 (Referat 405), 113909; Levy is mentioned as an advisor to the Economics Ministry as early as 1970; Der Parlamentarische Staatssekretär des Bundesministers für Wirtschaft an den Herrn Präsidenten des Deutschen Bundestages: Energiepolitik, 11.6.1970, Deutscher Bundestag. 6. Wahlperiode. Drucksache VI/941.

50. Manfred Liebrucks, H.W. Schmidt and D. Schmitt, *Sicherung der Energieversorgung für die Bundesrepublik Deutschland. Teil II: Gemeinschaftsgutachten der Institute DIW, EWI und RWI* (Berlin, 1974), 2.

51. Ibid., 7f.

52. Ibid., 90.

53. Überblick über den Rücklauf aus den Ressorts (Stand 21.2.1974); Chef des Bundeskanzleramtes an die Herren Planungsbeauftragten der Bundesministerien: Synopse der Ressortstellungnahmen zum Schreiben des Chef BK 'Begleitende Maßnahmen zur Energiesituation', 22.3.1974, BArch, B 136/7682.

54. Tischvorlage des BMFT für die 45. Kabinetts-Sitzung am 9.1.1974: Rahmenprogramm Energieforschung 1974–1977, BArch, B 136/7683.

55. Ibid.; 'Unterrichtung durch die Bundesregierung. Erste Fortschreibung des Energieprogramms der Bundesregierung', in *Deutscher Bundestag. Drucksachen. 7. Wahlperiode 1972–1976*, Nr. 2713 (31 October 1974).

56. Quante (III D): Modellrechnungen für die Entwicklung des Energieverbrauchs, 4.3.1974; III D: Diskussionspapier: Thesen zur Energielage und generelle Konsequenzen für die Energiepolitik, 19.3.1974, BArch, B 102/146456.

57. Abt. III: Ergebnisprotokoll: Klausurtagung über die Fortschreibung des Energieprogramms am 25. März 1974 und Vorsitz von Minister Dr. Friderichs bzw. Staatssekretär Rohwedder, 29. März 1974, BArch, B 102/146456; Urs Dolinski and Hans-Joachim Ziesing, *Sicherheits-, Preis- und Umweltaspekte der Energieversorgung* (Deutsches Institut für Wirtschaftsforschung [DIW] Sonderheft, 113) (Berlin, 1976); Urs Dolinski, Hans-Joachim Ziesing and Klaus-Dieter Labahn, *Maßnahmen für eine sichere und umweltverträgliche Energieversorgung* (Berlin, 1978).

58. Shell AG, *The National Energy Outlook* (Houston, TX, 1974), 38.

59. Ibid.; see also III D: Diskussionspapier: Thesen zur Energielage und generelle Konsequenzen für die Energiepolitik, 19.3.1974, BArch, B 102/146456.

60. Lücke (Abt. III): Ergebnisprotokoll: Klausurtagung über die Fortschreibung des Energieprogramms am 9./10. Mai 1974; Arbeitsprogramm der Abteilung III (als Ergebnis der Klausurtagung am 9./10. Mai 1974), 13.5.1974, BArch, B 102/146456.

61. 'Unterrichtung durch die Bundesregierung. Erste Fortschreibung des Energieprogramms', 5.

62. Ibid., 6.

63. Ibid., 15.

64. Guy de Carmoy, 'French Energy Policy', in Wilfrid L. Kohl (ed.), *After the Second Oil Crisis: Energy Policies in Europe, America, and Japan* (Lexington, MA, 1982), 113–36, here 124; Gabrielle Hecht, *The Radiance of France: Nuclear Power and National Identity after World War II* (Cambridge, MA, 1998), 2; see also Sandra Tauer, *Störfall für die gute Nachbarschaft? Deutsche und Franzosen auf der Suche nach einer gemeinsamen Energiepolitik (1973–1980)* (Göttingen, 2012).

65. Vortrag von Yves Bouvier auf der Tagung 'L'Europe et l'énergie', Padua, 18/19 October 2013.

66. *VIe plan de développement économique et social 1971–1975. Rapport général: Les objectifs généraux et les actions prioritaires du VIe plan et annexes au rapport général: Programmes d'actions détaillées* (Paris, 1971), 301; in 1969, French planners were still relying on oil to cover

all necessary growth in energy consumption, but they soon became more sceptical; Comité professionnel du pétrole, *Pétrole 1969. Elements statistiques: Activité de l'industrie pétrolière* (Paris, 1970); for a general account of French 'planification', see Dieter Gosewinkel, 'Zwischen Diktatur und Demokratie. Wirtschaftliches Planungsdenken in Deutschland und Frankreich: Vom Ersten Weltkrieg bis zur Mitte der 1970er Jahre', *Geschichte und Gesellschaft* 34 (2008), 327–59.

67. Commissariat Général du Plan: Rapport d'exécution 1974, 29.7.1974, ANF, Service du Premier Ministre, versement 19890575, art. 204; Commissariat Général du Plan: Crise pétrolière et taux d'actualisation du Plan, 22.5.1975, ANF, versement 19890617, art. 99.

68. Commissariat Général du Plan. Commission de l'Énergie et des Matières Premières du VIIIe Plan: Rapport sur les bilans de la politique énergétique de 1973 à 1978, Paris [1979]; see also Comité professionnel du pétrole, *Pétrole 73. Éléments statistiques. Activité de l'industrie pétrolière* (Paris, 1974); Comité professionnel du pétrole, *Pétrole 74. Éléments statistiques. Activité de l'industrie pétrolière* (Paris, 1975); Horst Mendershausen, *Coping with the Oil Crisis: French and German Experiences* (Baltimore, MD/London, 1976).

69. Joachim Radkau, *Aufstieg und Krise der deutschen Atomwirtschaft 1945–1975: Verdrängte Alternativen in der Kerntechnik und der Ursprung der nuklearen Kontroverse* (Reinbek bei Hamburg, 1983), 434–61.

70. 'Unterrichtung durch die Bundesregierung. Erste Fortschreibung des Energieprogramms', 7.

71. Urs Dolinski and Hans-Joachim Ziesing, *Die regionalen Entwicklungstendenzen des Energieverbrauchs in Baden-Württemberg und seinen Regierungsbezirken bis 1980* (Berlin, 1970); Dolinski and Ziesing, *Die Entwicklungstendenzen des Energieverbrauchs in Nordrhein-Westfalen bis 1980: Untersuchung im Auftrage des Wirtschaftsministeriums von Nordrhein-Westfalen* (Düsseldorf, 1971); Dolinski and Ziesing, *Die regionalen Entwicklungstendenzen des Energieverbrauchs in Bayern und seinen Regierungsbezirken bis 1985* (Berlin, 1971); Manfred Liebrucks and Hildebrand Kummer, *Grundlagen einer regionalwirtschaftlich orientierten Energiepolitik im norddeutschen Raum* (Berlin, 1972); Urs Dolinski and Hans-Joachim Ziesing, *Der Energiemarkt in Bayern im Jahre 1971: Gutachten im Auftrage des Bayerischen Staatsministeriums für Wirtschaft und Verkehr* (Berlin, 1973); Urs Dolinski and Hans-Joachim Ziesing, *Die regionalen Entwicklungstendenzen des Energieverbrauchs in Hessen und seinen fünf Planungsregionen bis 1985: Untersuchung im Auftrage des Hessischen Ministers für Wirtschaft und Technik* (Wiesbaden, 1973); Dolinski and Ziesing, *Die Entwicklung des Energieverbrauches in Baden-Württemberg und seinen 12 Regionalverbänden bis zum Jahre 1990: Gutachten im Auftrage des Ministeriums für Wirtschaft, Mittelstand und Verkehr in Baden-Württemberg* (Stuttgart, 1974); Urs Dolinski, *Der Energiemarkt in Bayern bis zum Jahre 1990 unter Berücksichtigung der Entwicklungstendenzen auf dem Weltenergiemarkt und auf dem Energiemarkt der Bundesrepublik Deutschland* (Berlin, 1974); Urs Dolinski and Hans-Joachim Ziesing, *Ziele für eine bayerische Energiepolitik: Gutachten im Auftrage des Bayerischen Staatsministeriums für Wirtschaft und Verkehr* (Munich, 1975); Dolinski and Ziesing, *Maßnahmen für eine bayerische Energiepolitik. Gutachten im Auftrage des Bayerischen Staatsministeriums für Wirtschaft und Verkehr* (Munich, 1976); Hans-Joachim Ziesing, *Die künftige Entwicklung des Energiemarktes in Bayern bis zum Jahre 1995. Überprüfung und Fortschreibung der Prognose aus dem Jahre 1974. Gutachten im Auftrage des Bayerischen Staatsministeriums für Wirtschaft und Verkehr* (Munich/Berlin, 1977); Ziesing, *Die regionalen Entwicklungstendenzen des Energieverbrauchs in Hessen und seinen Planungsregionen bis 1990: Untersuchung im Auftrage des Hessischen Ministers für Wirtschaft und Technik* (Wiesbaden/Berlin, 1977); Eckhard Casser, *Grundlagen und Ziele für eine gemeinsame Energiepolitik im norddeutschen Raum und Berlin: Gutachten im Auftrage der Konferenz der Wirtschaftsminister/-senatoren der Länder Bremen, Hamburg, Niedersachsen, Schleswig-Holstein und Berlin* (Berlin, 1978); Klaus-Dieter Labahn, *Die künftigen Entwicklungstendenzen der Energiewirtschaft in Baden-Württemberg bis zum Jahre 1990: Gutachten im Auftrage des Ministeriums für Wirtschaft, Mittelstand und Verkehr in Baden-Württemberg* (Berlin, 1979); Urs Dolinski, *Untersuchung zu Fragen regional unterschiedlicher Energiepreise*

innerhalb Bayerns sowie zwischen Bayern und der übrigen Bundesrepublik Deutschland: Gutachten im Auftrage des Bayerischen Staatsministeriums für Wirtschaft und Verkehr (Munich, 1979); *Grundlagen und Ziele für eine gemeinsame Energiepolitik im norddeutschen Raum und Berlin: Gutachten im Auftrage der Konferenz der Wirtschaftsminister/-senatoren der Länder Bremen, Hamburg, Niedersachsen, Schleswig-Holstein und Berlin* (Berlin, 1981); Hans-Joachim Ziesing, *Die Entwicklung des Elektrizitätsverbrauchs im Land Berlin bis zum Jahre 2000: Untersuchung im Auftrage des Senators für Wirtschaft und Verkehr Berlin* (Berlin, 1980).

72. Manfred Liebrucks, *Untersuchung der Möglichkeiten zur Substitution von Mineralöl: Gemeinschaftsgutachten der Institute* (Berlin, 1978); Liebrucks, *Volkswirtschaftliche Auswirkungen bei Verzögerungen des Baus von Kernkraftwerken: Modellrechnungen. Gemeinschaftsgutachten der Institute* (Berlin, 1975); Manfred Liebrucks and Hildebrand Kummer, *Entwicklungstendenzen des Energieeinsatzes in der deutschen Elektrizitätswirtschaft* (Berlin, 1972); Jochen Bethkenhagen, *Bedeutung und Möglichkeiten des Ost-West-Handels mit Energierohstoffen* (Berlin, 1975); Dolinski and Ziesing, *Sicherheits-, Preis- und Umweltaspekte der Energieversorgung*; Dolinski et al., *Maßnahmen für eine sichere und umweltverträgliche Energieversorgung*; Dolinski, *Untersuchung zu Fragen regional unterschiedlicher Energiepreise in der Bundesrepublik Deutschland: Darstellung, Begründung und Auswirkungen am Beispiel ausgewählter Bundesländer* (Berlin, 1979); Dolinski, *Zum Problem der Substitutionsmöglichkeit von Mineralölprodukten durch andere Energieträger: Dargestellt am Beispiel eines Bundeslandes* (Berlin, 1980).

73. Heino Elfert, 'Energieprognosen gestern und heute: Voraussagen sind noch schwieriger geworden', *Die Mineralölwirtschaft* 30(6) (1977), 281.

74. Kraus, 'Über die Kritik'; Kraus, 'Bundesdeutsche Energieprognosen der letzten 30 Jahre, 90; Kraus, *Energieprognosen in der Retrospektive: Analyse von Fehlerursachen der Prognose/ Ist-Abweichungen von Energiebedarfsschätzungen in der Bundesrepublik Deutschland von 1950 bis 1980* (Karlsruhe, 1988).

75. Manfred Härter, 'Diskussion: Energieprognosen', in Fritz Lücke (ed.), *Ölkrise: 10 Jahre danach* (Cologne, 1984), 292–93; Härter, 'Energieprognostik: Kein Fortschritt ohne "Psychologie"?', in *Energieprognostik auf dem Prüfstand* (Cologne, 1988), 3–13.

76. Hans-Joachim Burchard, *Methoden und Grenzen der Energieprognosen* (Hamburg, 1968).

77. Eberhard Jochem, 'Der Ruf der Energiebedarfsprognosen', in Lücke, *Ölkrise*, 269–85; Manfred Härter, 'Einführung in den Problemkreis Energieprognosen', in Lücke, *Ölkrise*, 252–53.

78. 'Unterrichtung durch die Bundesregierung. Zweite Fortschreibung des Energieprogramms der Bundesregierung', in *Deutscher Bundestag. Drucksachen. 7. Wahlperiode 1976–1980*. No. 1357, 19 December 1977, 15; see also Carroll L. Wilson, *Energy: Global Prospects 1985–2000. Report of the Workshop on Alternative Energy Strategies, WAES* (New York, 1977), ix; Smil, *Energy at the Crossroads*, 123.

79. Report of the Working Group on the Planning: Price of Oil. Longer Term Energy Problems, 1975, NA UK, CAB 184/291.

80. Report of the Working Group on Energy Strategy, 9 February 1976, NA UK, POWE 29/917.

81. *Energiekrise – Europa im Belagerungszustand? Politische Konsequenzen aus einer eskalierenden Entwicklung* (Hamburg-Bergedorf, 1977).

82. Ibid., 14.

83. Ibid., 19.

84. Premier Ministre. Comité interministériel pour les questions de coopération économique Européenne. Secrétariat Général: Energie Document de travail pour la réunion du Groupe Energie des 21 et 22 Mars 1973, Paris 15.3.1973, ANF, Service du Premier ministre, versement 19900644, art. 2.

85. Allen L. Hammond, William D. Metz and Thomas H. Maugh, *Energie für die Zukunft: Wege aus dem Engpaß* (Frankfurt am Main, 1974), 158 (translation of *Energy for the Future*, produced at the behest of the Deutsche Forschungsgemeinschaft); Shell AG, *The National*

Energy Outlook; John C. Campbell, Guy de Carmoy and Shinichi Kondo, *Energy: The Imperative for a Trilateral Approach. A Report of the Task Force on the Political and International Implications of the Energy Crisis to the Executive Committee of the Trilateral Commission* (Brussels, 1974).

86. Central Intelligence Agency, *The International Energy Situation: Outlook to 1985* (Washington, DC, 1977), 1.

87. OECD, *Energy Prospects to 1985*; OECD, *World Energy Outlook: A Reassessment of Long Term Energy Developments and Related Policies. A Report by the Secretary-General* (Paris, 1977); BP AG, *Energie 2000: Tendenzen und Perspektiven* (n.p., 1977), 22; see also Shell AG, *Der Beitrag des Mineralöls zur künftigen Energieversorgung: Prognosen erfordern schon heute Entscheidungen* (n.p., 1978); Gerhard Bischoff, 'Einleitung', in Bischoff, Gocht and Adler, *Das Energiehandbuch*, 1–2, 1f.

88. Wilson, *Energy: Global Prospects 1985–2000*, 3; the technical data for the various OECD countries can be found in Paul S. Basile, *Energy Demand Studies, Major Consuming Countries: Analyses of 1972 Demand and Projections of 1985 Demand. First Technical Report of the Workshop on Alternative Energy Strategies (WAES)*, 2nd ed. (Cambridge, MA, 1977); see also the brief summary by Andrew Flower, 'World Oil Production', *Scientific American* 238(3) (1978), 41–49.

89. 'Unterrichtung durch die Bundesregierung. Zweite Fortschreibung des Energieprogramms der Bundesregierung', Anhang III: Ergebnisse von Studien über die Entwicklung der Weltenergiemärkte bis zum Jahr 2000; see also Manfred Liebrucks, H.W. Schmidt and D. Schmitt, *Die künftige Entwicklung der Energienachfrage in der Bundesrepublik Deutschland und deren Deckung: Perspektiven bis zum Jahre 2000* (Essen, 1978), 8.

90. Ibid.; 'Unterrichtung durch die Bundesregierung. Zweite Fortschreibung des Energieprogramms der Bundesregierung', 12.

91. Ibid., 13.

92. See also, from a Marxian perspective, Martin Meyer-Renschhausen, *Das Energieprogramm der Bundesregierung: Ursachen und Probleme staatlicher Planung im Energiesektor in der BRD* (Frankfurt/New York, 1981), 4.

93. 'Unterrichtung durch die Bundesregierung. Zweite Fortschreibung des Energieprogramms der Bundesregierung', 2f.; on the decoupling of economic growth and energy consumption, see also Werner Müller and Bernd Stoy, *Entkopplung Wirtschaftswachstum ohne mehr Energie?* (Stuttgart, 1978); Ehrhardt, 'Energiebedarfsprognosen', 218–20.

94. Projektleitung Energieforschung KFA Jülich, *Rahmenprogramm Energieforschung: Jahresbericht 1976. Im Auftrage des Bundesministers für Forschung und Technologie und des Bundesministers für Wirtschaft* (n.p., n.d).

95. Bundesministerium für Forschung und Technologie, *Programm Energieforschung und Energietechnologien: 1977–1980* (Bonn, 1977), 12f. See also the report, running to almost 1,100 pages, on ways of saving energy in every possible sphere, which had already been produced the following year: Bundesministerium für Forschung und Technologie, *Rationelle Energieverwendung: Statusbericht 1978. Teil 1 und 2* (Bonn, 1978).

96. Klaus Michael Meyer-Abich, *Wirtschaftspolitische Steuerungsmöglichkeiten zur Einsparung von Energie durch alternative Technologien*, vol. 1, *Zusammenfassung* (Essen, 1978), 3. See also the abbreviated version edited for a wider readership: Meyer-Abich (ed.), *Energieeinsparung als neue Energiequelle: Wirtschaftspolitische Möglichkeiten und alternative Technologien* (Munich, 1979). Also involved were Bergbauforschung GmbH Essen, Fichtner Beratende Ingenieure, the Munich Energy Economics Research Centre (Forschungsstelle für Energiewirtschaft München), the Institute for Electrical Facilities and Energy Economics at RWTH Aachen University (Institut für elektrische Anlagen und Energiewirtschaft der RWTH Aachen), Kraftwerk Union AG Erlangen and the Programme Group for Systems Research and Technological Development at the Jülich Nuclear Research Facility (Programmgruppe Systemforschung und Technologische Entwicklung der Kernforschungsanlage Jülich).

97. Meyer-Abich, *Wirtschaftspolitische Steuerungsmöglichkeiten zur Einsparung von Energie durch alternative Technologien*, 2; Meyer-Abich, 'Vorwort', in *Energieeinsparung als neue Energiequelle*, 17–19, here 17.

98. Erhard Eppler, *Ende oder Wende* (Stuttgart/Berlin/Mainz, 1975).

99. Hans Matthöfer, 'Energie: Ein Diskussionsleitfaden', in Wilhelm Dröscher, Klaus-Detlef Funke and Ernst Theilen (eds), *Energie, Beschäftigung, Lebensqualität* (Bonn-Bad Godesberg, 1977), 319–482, here 325f., 331f.

100. Dröscher, Funke and Theilen, *Energie, Beschäftigung, Lebensqualität*.

101. Ibid., 41.

102. Ibid., 271–318.

103. Helmut Schmidt, 'Vorwort: Alle Energie-Optionen offenhalten', in Manfred Krüper (ed.), *Energiepolitik: Kontroversen - Perspektiven* (Cologne, 1977), 7–10, here 8; see also Schmidt's contribution in Dröscher, Funke and Theilen, *Energie, Beschäftigung, Lebensqualität*, 292–305.

104. Herbert Gruhl, *Ein Planet wird geplündert: Die Schreckensbilanz unserer Politik* (Frankfurt am Main, 1975); Silke Mende, *Nicht rechts, nicht links, sondern vorn: Eine Geschichte der Gründungsgrünen* (Munich, 2011), 73–78.

105. Martina Steber, 'A Better Tomorrow: Making Sense of Time in the Conservative Party and the CDU/CSU in the 1960s and 1970s', *Journal of Modern European History* 13(3) (2015), 317–37.

106. For an in-depth account of the intellectual currents prevalent among the early Greens, see Mende, *Nicht rechts, nicht links, sondern vorn*.

107. Florentin Krause, Hartmut Bossel and Karl-Friedrich Müller-Reissmann, *Energie-Wende. Wachstum und Wohlstand ohne Erdöl und Uran: Ein Alternativbericht des Öko-Instituts* (Freiburg, 1980), 9; on similar developments in France, see Michael Bess, *The Light-Green Society: Ecology and Technological Modernity in France, 1960–2000* (Chicago, 2003).

108. 'Unterrichtung durch die Bundesregierung. Dritte Fortschreibung des Energieprogramms der Bundesregierung', in *Deutscher Bundestag. Drucksachen. 9. Wahlperiode 1980–1983*. No. 983, 5 November 1981, 6.

109. On nuclear energy, see 'Unterrichtung (Bericht) Enquete-Kommission. Zukünftige Kernenergie-Politik', in *Deutscher Bundestag. Drucksachen. 8. Wahlperiode 1976–1980*, Nr. 4341, 27 June 1980; on the controversy, see also Cornelia Altenburg, *Kernenergie und Politikberatung: Die Vermessung einer Kontroverse* (Wiesbaden, 2010).

110. A different conclusion is reached by Frank Bösch, 'Umbrüche in die Gegenwart: Globale Ereignisse und Krisenreaktionen um 1979', *Zeithistorische Forschungen/Studies in Contemporary History*, 9(1) (2012) (online); for an introductory account of the second oil crisis anchored in the contemporary political science debate, see Kohl, *After the Second Oil Crisis*; Robert James Lieber, *The Oil Decade* (New York, 1983).

111. 'Unterrichtung durch die Bundesregierung. Dritte Fortschreibung des Energieprogramms der Bundesregierung', 8; on the loss of confidence in forecasts, see also Hans-Joachim Burchard, 'Prognosen und Wirklichkeit', in Dröscher, Funke and Theilen, *Energie, Beschäftigung, Lebensqualität*, 281f.

112. Heick an Chef BK: Konjunkturpolitische Überlegungen zur Erdölkrise, 22.11.1973, BArch, B 136/7708.

113. Bundesminister für Arbeit und Sozialordnung an Präsident der Bundesanstalt für Arbeit: Ausländische Arbeitnehmer, 23.11.1973, BArch, B 149/54458.

114. Hans-Ulrich Spree, 'Ölkrieg in der Bonner Koalition', *Süddeutsche Zeitung*, 28 November 1973.

115. On the Council of Economic Experts and its work, see Tim Schanetzky, *Die große Ernüchterung: Wirtschaftspolitik, Expertise und Gesellschaft in der Bundesrepublik 1966–1982* (Berlin, 2007); Metzler, *Konzeptionen politischen Handelns von Adenauer bis Brandt*.

116. 'Unterrichtung durch die Bundesregierung. Sondergutachten des Sachverständigenrates "Zu den gesamtwirtschaftlichen Auswirkungen der Ölkrise"', in *Deutscher Bundestag. Drucksachen. 7. Wahlperiode 1972–1976.* No. 1456, 19 December 1973, 1.
117. Ibid., 2.
118. Ibid., 3f.
119. Ibid., 9f.
120. Ibid., 16.
121. Schanetzky, *Die große Ernüchterung*, 128–38.
122. Ibid., 161–79; Michael Ruck, 'Ein kurzer Sommer der konkreten Utopie: Zur westdeutschen Planungsgeschichte der langen 60er Jahre', in Axel Schildt (ed.), *Dynamische Zeiten: Die 60er Jahre in den beiden deutschen Gesellschaften* (Hamburg, 2000), 362–401; Michael Ruck, 'Gesellschaft gestalten: Politische Planung in den 1960er und 1970er Jahren', in Sabine Mecking and Janbernd Oebbecke (eds), *Zwischen Effizienz und Legitimität: Kommunale Gebiets- und Funktionalreformen in der Bundesrepublik Deutschland in historischer und aktueller Perspektive* (Paderborn, 2009), 35–47; on the contemporary economic debate, see Hans Karl Schneider et al., *Stabilisierungspolitik in der Marktwirtschaft: Verhandlungen auf der Tagung des Vereins für Socialpolitik, Gesellschaft für Wirtschafts- und Sozialwissenschaften in Zürich 1974*, 2 vols (Berlin, 1975).
123. See, for example, Metzler, *Konzeptionen politischen Handelns von Adenauer bis Brandt*; Schanetzky, *Die große Ernüchterung*; Ruck, 'Ein kurzer Sommer der konkreten Utopie'; Ruck, 'Westdeutsche Planungsdiskurse und Planungspraxis der 1960er Jahre im internationalen Kontext', in Heinz-Gerhard Haupt (ed.), *Aufbruch in die Zukunft: Die 1960er Jahre zwischen Planungseuphorie und kulturellem Wandel; DDR, CSSR und Bundesrepublik Deutschland im Vergleich* (Weilerswist, 2004), 289–325; Faulenbach, *Das sozialdemokratische Jahrzehnt*; Doering-Manteuffel, 'Nach dem Boom'.
124. Willy Brandt, 'Ansprache zum Jahreswechsel 1973/74', *Bulletin des Presse- und Informationsamts der Bundesregierung* 1 (1974), 5–6.
125. Abteilung III: Beitrag Energiepolitik für die Regierungserklärung am 17.1.1974, 12.1.1974; BMWi: Tischvorlage für die Kabinettssitzung am 16. Januar 1974, 15.1.1974, BArch, B 102/200516.
126. Hans Friderichs, 'Erklärung der Bundesregierung zur Lage der Energieversorgung', in *Verhandlungen des Deutschen Bundestages*, vol. 86 (Bonn, 1974), 4539–44, here 4541.
127. Abteilung III: Beitrag Energiepolitik für die Regierungserklärung am 17.1.1974, 12.1.1974, BArch, B 102/200516, 8.
128. Hans Friderichs, 'Erklärung der Bundesregierung zur Lage der Energieversorgung', in *Verhandlungen des Deutschen Bundestages*, vol. 86 (Bonn, 1974), 4539–44, here 4539.
129. Ibid., 4544.
130. Ibid., 4541.
131. Werner Zywietz, 'Stellungnahme zur Erklärung der Bundesregierung zur Lage der Energieversorgung', in *Verhandlungen des Deutschen Bundestages*, vol. 86 (Bonn, 1974), 4571–73.
132. 'Otto Graf Lambsdorff: Stellungnahme zur Erklärung der Bundesregierung zur Lage der Energieversorgung', in *Verhandlungen des Deutschen Bundestages*, vol. 86 (Bonn, 1974), 4556–62.
133. 'Adolf Schmidt: Stellungnahme zur Erklärung der Bundesregierung zur Lage der Energieversorgung', in *Verhandlungen des Deutschen Bundestages*, vol. 86 (Bonn, 1974), 4550–56, here 4552.
134. 'Herbert Ehrenberg: Stellungnahme zur Erklärung der Bundesregierung zur Lage der Energieversorgung', in *Verhandlungen des Deutschen Bundestages*, vol. 86 (Bonn, 1974), 4568–71, here 4570.
135. 'Ernst Müller-Hermann: Stellungnahme zur Erklärung der Bundesregierung zur Lage der Energieversorgung', in *Verhandlungen des Deutschen Bundestages*, vol. 86 (Bonn, 1974),

4564–68; Christiane Reinecke, 'Müller-Hermann, Ernst', in *Biographisches Handbuch der Mitglieder des Deutschen Bundestages 1949–2002*, vol. 1, A-M (Munich, 2002), 589–90.

136. 'Ernst Müller-Hermann: Stellungnahme zur Erklärung der Bundesregierung zur Lage der Energieversorgung', in *Verhandlungen des Deutschen Bundestages*, vol. 86 (Bonn, 1974), here 4565.

137. Ibid., 4566.

138. Ibid., 4565.

139. 'Hermann Josef Russe: Stellungnahme zur Erklärung der Bundesregierung zur Lage der Energieversorgung', in *Verhandlungen des Deutschen Bundestages*, vol. 86 (Bonn, 1974), 4544–50, here 4546.

140. Sachverständigenrat zur Begutachtung der gesamtwirtschaftlichen Entwicklung. 'Jahresgutachten 1974', in *Deutscher Bundestag. Drucksachen. 7. Wahlperiode 1972–1976*, Nr. 2848, 28 November 1974, ii.

141. Ibid., 6.

142. Ibid., 7.

143. Sachverständigenrat zur Begutachtung der gesamtwirtschaftlichen Entwicklung. 'Jahresgutachten 1979/80', in *Deutscher Bundestag. Drucksachen. 8. Wahlperiode 1976–1980*, Nr. 3420, 22 November 1979, 153.

144. Ibid., 156.

145. Ibid., 162–67.

146. John Turner, 'Governors, Governance, and Governed: British Politics since 1945', in Kathleen Burk and Paul Langford (eds), *The British Isles since 1945* (Oxford, 2003), 19–62, here 37; Werner Abelshauser, *Deutsche Wirtschaftsgeschichte seit 1945* (Munich, 2004), 270; Alexander Nützenadel, *Stunde der Ökonomen: Wissenschaft, Politik und Expertenkultur in der Bundesrepublik 1949–1974* (Göttingen, 2005), 22; see esp. Schanetzky, *Die große Ernüchterung*, 128.

147. For an analysis of the oil crisis as a profound caesura, see Martin Werding, 'Gab es eine neoliberale Wende? Wirtschaft und Wirtschaftspolitik in der Bundesrepublik Deutschland ab Mitte der 1970er Jahre', *Vierteljahrshefte für Zeitgeschichte* 56 (2008), 303–21, here 303f.; the thesis of fundamental change can be found in Hobsbawm, *The Age of Extremes*, 286; Doering-Manteuffel, 'Nach dem Boom'; Charles S. Maier, 'Two Sorts of Crises? The "Long" 1970s in the West and the East', in Hans Günter Hockerts (ed.), *Koordinaten deutscher Geschichte in der Epoche des Ost-West-Konflikts* (Munich, 2003), 49–62.

148. 'Unterrichtung durch die Bundesregierung. Erste Fortschreibung des Energieprogramms', 5.

149. See van Laak, 'Planung', 318–20; Gabriele Metzler, 'Am Ende aller Krisen? Politisches Denken und Handeln in der Bundesrepublik der sechziger Jahre', *Historische Zeitschrift* 275 (2002), 57–103; Metzler, *Konzeptionen politischen Handelns von Adenauer bis Brandt*; Nützenadel, *Stunde der Ökonomen*; Winfried Süß, 'Der keynesianische Traum und sein langes Ende: Sozioökonomischer Wandel und Sozialpolitik in den siebziger Jahren', in Jarausch, *Das Ende der Zuversicht*, 120–37; Ruck, 'Gesellschaft gestalten'.

150. On planning in the agricultural sector, see Kiran Klaus Patel, 'The Paradox of Planning: German Agricultural Policy in a European Perspective, 1920s to 1970s', *Past & Present* 212(1) (2011), 239–69.

151. Weingart, *Die Stunde der Wahrheit?*; Jasanoff, *The Fifth Branch*.

152. Erklärung vor dem Deutschen Bundestag, 29.11.1973, BArch, B 136/7683.

153. Ibid.

154. AL IV: Regierungserklärung 29. November 1973 – eine erste Skizze, 23.11.1973, BArch, B 136/7683.

155. 'Erklärung des Bundeskanzlers Brandt im deutschen Fernsehen, 24. November 1973', in Willy Brandt, *Mehr Demokratie wagen: Innen- und Gesellschaftspolitik 1966–1974*, edited by Wolther von Kieseritzky (Bonn, 2001), 467–68, here 467.

156. Ibid., 468; Klaus Harpprecht, *Im Kanzleramt. Tagebuch der Jahre mit Willy Brandt: Januar 1973–Mai 1974* (Reinbek, 2000), 411.
157. Willy Brandt, 'Erklärung der Bundesregierung zu aktuellen Fragen der Wirtschafts- und Energiepolitik (29.11.1973)', in *Verhandlungen des Deutschen Bundestages*, vol. 85 (Bonn, 1973), 3908–13, here 3908, 3911.
158. Ibid., 3911. Here the minutes record applause from every parliamentary group.
159. Ibid., 3911.
160. 'Gespräch des Bundeskanzlers Brandt mit Ministerpräsident Messmer in Paris', in Hans-Peter Schwarz (ed.), *Akten zur Auswärtigen Politik der Bundesrepublik Deutschland 1973*, vol. 3, *1. Oktober bis 31. Dezember*, in collaboration with Ilse Dorothee Pautsch (Munich, 2004), 1909–17, here 1912.
161. Hans Friderichs, 'Beitrag in der Debatte zur Erklärung der Bundesregierung zu aktuellen Fragen der Wirtschafts- und Energiepolitik, 27.11.9173', in *Verhandlungen des Deutschen Bundestages*, vol. 85 (Bonn, 1973), 3932–40.
162. Franz Josef Strauß, 'Beitrag in der Debatte zur Erklärung der Bundesregierung zu aktuellen Fragen der Wirtschafts- und Energiepolitik, 27.11.1973', in *Verhandlungen des Deutschen Bundestages*, vol. 85 (Bonn, 1973), 3913–23, here 3923.
163. Ibid.; on the conflict between the West German government and its US counterpart, see below.
164. Rainer Barzel, 'Beitrag zur zweiten und dritten Beratung des Entwurfs eines Gesetzes zur Sicherung der Energieversorgung bei Gefährdung oder Störung der Einfuhren von Mineralöl oder Erdgas', in *Verhandlungen des Deutschen Bundestages*, vol. 85 (Bonn, 1973), 3841–44, here 3842.
165. See the speeches by 'Apel und Brandt', in *Verhandlungen des Deutschen Bundestages*, vol. 85 (Bonn, 1973), 3845f., 3848–50.
166. Karl Ahrens, 'Beitrag zur zweiten und dritten Beratung des Entwurfs eines Gesetzes zur Sicherung der Energieversorgung bei Gefährdung oder Störung der Einfuhren von Mineralöl oder Erdgas', 9 November 1973, in *Verhandlungen des Deutschen Bundestages*, vol. 85 (Bonn, 1973), 3840–41.
167. William Glenn Gray, *Germany's Cold War: The Global Campaign to Isolate East Germany, 1949–1969* (Chapel Hill, 2003).
168. Peter Hünseler, *Die außenpolitischen Beziehungen der Bundesrepublik Deutschland zu den arabischen Staaten von 1949–1980* (Frankfurt am Main, 1990), 142–56.
169. Ibid., 165.
170. Lahn an Staatssekretär: Arabische Reaktionen auf Nahost Passus in der VN-Rede des Herrn Bundeskanzlers, 4.10.1973, PA AA, B 150, 290.
171. 'Rede des Bundeskanzlers Brandt vor der Vollversammlung der Vereinten Nationen', in Brandt, *Ein Volk der guten Nachbarn*, 508.
172. Lahn an Staatssekretär: Arabische Reaktionen auf Nahost Passus in der VN-Rede des Herrn Bundeskanzlers, 4.10.1973, PA AA, B 150, 290.
173. Vermerk: Treffen Bundesminister Scheel mit Missionschefs von Libanon, Ägypten, Libyen, Jordanien, Tunesien, Marokko, Sudan, Algerien, Saudi Arabien, 8.10.1973, PA AA, Referat 310, 104988; also PA AA, B 150, 290.
174. 1622 Redies an Kairo: Nahost-Konflikt, Ölkrise, 10.11., VS.Bd. 9989, PA AA, B 250, 292.
175. Steltzer Kairo an AA: Deutsch-ägyptisches Verhältnis, 3.11.1973, BArch, B 136/7708.
176. See, for example, Israelische Demarche wegen Haltung der BRD im Nahostkonflikt, 26.3.1974, VS.Bd. 10121, PA AA, B 150, 301; the *Maariv* quotation appears in 'Ölkrise: Kein Verlaß auf Großmütter', *Der Spiegel*, 5 November 1973, 23–27.
177. Heldt: Plurex an Botschaften: Arabische Erdölpolitik, 10.10.1973, PA AA, B 71 (Referat 405), 113906; BMWi an AA (Kruse): Botschafterberichte über Erdölangelegenheiten, 13.6.1973, PA AA, B 71 (Referat 405), 113905.

178. Kruse, born in 1916, was a lawyer and economist by training. Among other things, he had been head of the Economic Division of Germany's Permanent Mission to the United Nations (telephone call with Hans-Stefan Kruse, son of Hansheinrich Kruse, who also worked as a diplomat, on 1 February 2012). His deputy was Hans Lautenschlager, while Peter Hermes became division head in March 1973. In addition, the 'Middle East' Department of the Political Division (headed by Lothar Lahn), under Helmut Redies, also dealt with the relevant producing countries.

179. Die Energieversorgung in der deutschen Außenpolitik, 30.12.1973, PA AA, B 36 (Referat 310), 104935.

180. Peter Hermes, *Meine Zeitgeschichte: 1922–1987* (Paderborn, 2007), 234.

181. Kruse an Diplo Teheran: Berichte über Energiefragen, 12.8.1975, PA AA, B 71 (Referat 405), 113905.

182. Kruse, [Hansheinrich]: Brief zum Bezug von Erdölfachzeitschriften, 8.5.1974, PA AA, B 71 (Referat 405), 113905. In 1976, when the embassy in Kuwait suggested subscribing to the OAPEC News Bulletin, which had evidently not formed part of the holdings of the Foreign Ministry or Economics Ministry, officials were only willing to do so if there were no costs involved. See Dt. Botschaft Kuwait an AA: News Bulletin der Organisation of Arab Petroleum Exporting Countries, 9.2.1976, PA AA, B 71 (Referat 405), 113907.

183. Kruse, Hansheinrich. Brief an Hans Forstmeier (ESSO AG), 20.6.1973, PA AA, B 71 (Referat 405), 113905.

184. Referat 403: Botschafterkonferenz in Djakarta, hier: Internationale Ölpolitik; Kruse, [Hansheinrich]: Aktuelle Erdölpolitik – Stichworte für Vortrag in Jakarta, 18.4.1973, PA AA, B 71 (Referat 405), 113905.

185. Metzger, [Peter]: Schreiben zur Energiepolitik der BRD, 22.3.1973, PA AA, B 71 (Referat 405), 113924; Kruse, [Hansheinrich]: Schreiben an die italienische Botschaft – Schutzmachtvertretung für die Interessen der Bundesrepublik Deutschland in Djidda, 2.4.1973, PA AA, B 36 (Referat 310), 104992.

186. Kruse, [Hansheinrich]: Situationsanalyse des BMWi zur deutschen Energiepolitik an Vertretung der BRD bei den internationalen Organisationen in Wien, 17.5.1973, PA AA, B 71 (Referat 405), 113907.

187. Werner (Tripolis) an AA: Energiepolitische Berichterstattung, 19.6.1973, PA AA, B 71 (Referat 405), 113905.

188. Kurth (Wien) an AA: Sitzung des OECD Ölexpertenausschusses, 24.07.1973, PA AA, B 71 (Referat 405), 113907.

189. AA 303/310 Politische Beziehungen im Verhältnis zu A. Algerien und B. Saudi Arabien, 9.1.1974, BArch, B 136/6342; Algeria and Sudan had played a pioneering role. It was not until 12 March 1972 that the Arab League permitted its members to establish relations with Germany, and Lebanon (30 March 1972), the United Arab Emirates (17 May 1972) and Egypt (8 June 1972) did so. Kuwait (3 February 1973) and Saudi Arabia followed a year later and Iraq (28 February), Syria (7 August) and Yemen (16 September) only in 1974. Hünseler, *Die außenpolitischen Beziehungen der Bundesrepublik Deutschland.*

190. Werner, [Günter Franz]: Bericht über die Nahostreise des Erdölreferenten Berghaus, 22.12.1973, PA AA, B 36 (Referat 310), 104992.

191. Hartwig Berghaus an Kruse: Erdölreferenten in den arabischen Förderländern, Tripolis, 29.5.1974, PA AA, B 71 (Referat 405), 113921.

192. Ibid.

193. Bartels: Schreiben an deutsche Botschaften in arabischen Ländern, 10.10.1973, PA AA, B 36 (Referat 310), 104911.

194. Heldt: Plurex: Arabische Erdölpolitik, 10.10.1973, PA AA, B 71 (Referat 405), 113906; Kruse, [Hansheinrich]: Teilrunderlaß zur Erdölpolitik, 17.10.1973, PA AA, B 36 (Referat 310), 104991.

195. Kruse an Diplogerma Djidda: Saudische Erdölpolitik, 19.10.1973, PA AA, B 71 (Referat 405), 113906.
196. Ibid.
197. Lautenschlager an Botschaften: Bevorstehende OPEC-Sitzung, 3.1.1974, PA AA, B 36 (Referat 310), 104993.
198. See the replies, in PA AA, B 36 (Referat 310), 104993.
199. Freundt (Kuwait) an AA: Bevorstehende OPEC-Sitzung am 7.1.1974, 6.1.1974, PA AA, B 36 (Referat 310), 104993.
200. Ungerer, [Werner]: Aufzeichnung Literatur zur Erdölfrage, 2.9.1974, PA AA, B 71 (Referat 405), 113907.
201. Ungerer, [Werner], OPEC; hier: Neuer Generalsekretär, 7.2.1973, PA AA, B 71 (Referat 405), 113907.
202. Ungerer, [Werner], OPEC; hier: Informationspolitik, 6.3.1973, PA AA, B 71 (Referat 405), 113907.
203. BMWi an AA: Zusammenstellung: Politische und finanzielle Köpfe des Kartells der erdölfördernden Länder, 20.3.1974, PA AA, B 36 (Referat 310), 104993. Just over a year later, the German delegation to OPEC in Vienna also produced a detailed paper on its structure and functioning: Interwien an AA: Organisation der OPEC, 8.7.1975, PA AA, B 71 (Referat 405), 113908.
204. Kruse, [Hansheinrich]: Schreiben an das Bundesministerium für Wirtschaft (Ref. III C 2): Politische und finanzielle Köpfe des Kartells der Erdölproduzierenden Länder, 9.5.1974, PA AA, B 71 (Referat 405), 113906.
205. Ibid.
206. Ibid., 2.
207. Referat 403 an Staatssekretär: Besuch des OPEC Generalsekretärs Khène, 27.9.1973, PA AA, B 71 (Referat 405), 113907; Ungerer, [Werner]: Fernschreiben zum Gespräch Khènes im BMWi, 25.9.1973, PA AA, B 71 (Referat 405), 113907.
208. Herbst: Gespräch mit Khene, 10.1.1974, PA AA, B 71 (Referat 405), 104993.
209. Lankes, [Georg Christian]: Fernschreiben zur arabischen Erdölpolitik, 23.10.1973; Lankes, [Georg Christian]: Nahostkrise, 23.10.1973, PA AA, B 36 (Referat 310), 104991.
210. See chapter 3 and Yergin, *The Prize*, 577–80; for an introduction to German-Libyan relations, see Tim Szatkowski, *Gaddafis Libyen und die Bundesrepublik Deutschland 1969 bis 1982* (Munich, 2013).
211. 'Kaddafi: A New Form of War. Interview', *Newsweek*, 24 September 1973; the Libyan oil minister had already expressed very similar views on 18 August: see MEES 16(45) (31 August 1973), 6f.
212. DiploTripolis an BMWi: Libyen, Erdöl, 1.2.1973; Berghaus: Vermerk: Deutsche Erdölinteressen im Lichte der libyschen Erdölpolitik, 19.12.1972, PA AA, B 36 (Referat 310), 104840; Libya was ahead of Saudi Arabia at 18.5 per cent and Iran, Algeria and Nigeria, which accounted for around 10 per cent each; 'Unterrichtung durch die Bundesregierung. Die Energiepolitik der Bundesregierung', 24f.
213. Kruse, [Hansheinrich]: Herrn Staatssekretär zur Information, 17.10.1973, PA AA, B 36 (Referat 310), 104991; see also Abteilung III C 1/III C 2 [BMWi]: Aktuelle Situation im Mineralölbereich, 22.10.1973, PA AA, B 71 (Referat 405), 113906.
214. Hermes, [Peter]: Sprechzettel für die 39. Kabinettsitzung am 7. November 1973, 6.11.1973, PA AA, B 71 (Referat 405), 113924; [Kruse, Hansheinrich], Bericht zur aktuellen Mineralölsituation. Sachstand, 6.11.1973, PA AA, B 36 (Referat 310), 104992; see also Abteilung III C 1/III C 2 [BMWi]: Aktuelle Situation im Mineralölbereich, 3.11.1973, PA AA, B 36 (Referat 310), 104992; Weiß an Chef des Bundeskanzleramtes: Aktuelle Situation im Mineralölbereich, 5.11.1973, und Weiß: Vermerke für die Kabinettsitzung am 7.11.1973, BArch, B 136/7708.

215. Metzger (Djidda) an AA: Erdölpolitik Saudi Arabiens, 16.10.1973, VS.Bd. 1912 (201), PA AA, B 150, 291; Außenpolitische Unterrichtung des Bundeskabinetts am 17. Oktober 1973, 16.10.1973, PA AA, B 1 (Referat 010), 576.

216. Aufzeichnung über das Gespräch des Herrn Bundesministers mit dem amerikanischen Botschafter am 16.10.1973; Pfeffer: Aufzeichnung Nahostkonflikt, Amerikanische Waffenlieferungen aus der Bundesrepublik Deutschland nach Israel, 17.10.1973, VS.Bd. 1012 (201), PA AA, B 150, 291.

217. Abt. 3 Lahn an Staatssekretär: Besuch des Leiters des Büros der Arabischen Liga Herr Katib, 25.10.1973, PA AA, B 1 (Referat 010), 576; for a more detailed account of the element of fear in the oil crisis, see Rüdiger Graf, 'Gefährdungen der Energiesicherheit und die Angst vor der Angst: Westliche Industrieländer und das arabische Ölembargo 1973/74', in Patrick Bormann, Thomas Freiberger and Judith Michel (eds), *Angst in den Internationalen Beziehungen* (Bonn, 2010), 227–50.

218. Quoted in MEES 17(1) (26 October 1973), 11.

219. Lahn an Staatssekretär: Interview des libyschen Staatspräsidenten mit Le Monde vom 23.10.1973, 25.10.1973, PA AA, B 1 (Referat 010), 576.

220. Werner, [Günter Franz]: Fernschreiben zu Libyens Haltung nach der OPEC-Konferenz vom 17.10. in Kuwait, 20.10.1973, PA AA, B 36 (Referat 310), 104991.

221. Ibid.; see also Werner, [Günter Franz]: Libysche Erdölpolitik, 20.10.1973; Werner, [Günter Franz]: Fernschreiben zur libyschen Erdölpolitik, 23.10.1973, PA AA, B 36 (Referat 310), 104991.

222. Müller-Chorus an AA: Libysche Androhung eines Ölembargos, 1.11.1973, PA AA, B 1 (Referat 010), 576.

223. Hintergrundgespräch mit StS Frank: Nahostdeklaration der Europäischen Gemeinschaft, 7.11.1973, PA AA, B 1 (Referat 010), 576. He recommended that anyone who did not believe this read the Gaddafi interviews in *Le Monde*: 'And this gives you a clear sense of the dimensions, including the psychological dimensions, that we can expect to face in this conflict'.

224. 'Botschaftsrat Müller-Chorus, Tripolis, an das Auswärtige Amt', in Schwarz, *Akten zur Auswärtigen Politik der Bundesrepublik Deutschland 1973*, 1668–89, here 1686.

225. Ibid.; Müller-Chorus an AA: Libysche Androhung eines Ölembargos, 1.11.1973, PA AA, B 1 (Referat 010), 576.

226. Vermerk über Gespräch Frank mit Hillenbrand: Waffenlieferungen, 23.10.1973, PA AA, B 1 (Referat 010), 576; on the conflict with the United States, see also the well-informed article 'Ölkrise: Kein Verlaß auf Großmütter'.

227. Pressemitteilung und Sprachregelungen des Pressereferats (nur zur eigenen Information), 26.10.1973, PA AA, B 1 (Referat 010), 576; see also Jesser/Fiedler an Diplogerma Kairo: Stellungnahme zu Waffenlieferungen, 25.10.1973, PA AA, B 1 (Referat 010), 576.

228. Willy Brandt an Muamar Ghadafi [sic], 26.10.1973; Willy Brandt an Houari Boumediene, 26.10.1973, PA AA, B 1 (Referat 010), 576.

229. Interview mit Bundesaußenminister Scheel für die ZDF-Sendung Bonner Perspektiven, 28.10.1973, PA AA, B 150, 291; the German ambassador in Libya was provided with a selection of Brandt's public statements to help him discuss these issues effectively. See the appendix to Jesser/Fiedler: Libysches Ultimatum, 31.10.1973, PA AA, B 1 (Referat 010), 576.

230. Vermerk über ein Gespräch zwischen Frank und israelischem Botschafter am 5.11.1973, PA AA, B 1 (Referat 010), 576.

231. Ibid.

232. Jesser: Vermerk über ein Gespräch zwischen Staatssekretär Frank und dem libyschen Botschafter Daghely am 5.11.1973, PA AA, B 1 (Referat 010), 576.

233. Jesser/Fiedler: Libysches Ultimatum, 31.10.1973, PA AA, B 1 (Referat 010), 576.

234. Werner (Tripolis) an Bonn: Veröffentlichung des Schreibens des Bundeskanzlers an Ghaddafi vom 26.10., 8.11.1973, BArch, B 136/7708; Werner, [Günter Franz]: Libysche

Erdölpolitik, 5.11.1973; Werner, [Günter Franz]: Libysche Erdölpolitik, 7.11.1973; Werner, [Günter Franz]: Libysche Erdölpolitik, 8.11.1973, PA AA, B 36 (Referat 310), 104992.

235. Redies: Gespräch mit ägyptischem Botschafter Kamel über libysche Boykott-Drohungen am 2.11.1973, 3.11.1973, PA AA, B 150, 292.

236. Steltzer, [Hans Georg]: Fernschreiben zur Nahostkrise, 9.11.1973, PA AA, B 150, 292; AA an Bundeskanzleramt: Ägyptische Unterstützung gegenüber libyschem Ölboykott, 12.11.1973, PA AA, B 1 (Referat 010), 576.

237. Werner, [Günter Franz]: Fernschreiben zur libyschen Ölembargopolitik, 10.11.1973, PA AA, B 36 (Referat 310), 104992; 'Europa muß den Arabern Waffen liefern: Der libysche Regierungschef Abd el-Salam Dschallud über Erdöl und Israel', *Der Spiegel*, 12 November 1973, 120–28.

238. Hase, [Karl-Günther v.]: Bericht über das Treffen der sozialistischen Internationale in London, 12.11.1973, PA AA, B 150, 292.

239. Steltzer, [Hans Georg]: Fernschreiben zur Nahostkrise, 9.11.1973, PA AA, B 150, 292; Gespräch des Bundeskanzlers Brandt mit Premierminister Heath in London, in Schwarz, *Akten zur Auswärtigen Politik der Bundesrepublik Deutschland 1973*, 1807–15, here 1812.

240. Möckli, *European Foreign Policy during the Cold War*, 17–55; for a critical take on Heath, see Catherine Hynes, *The Year That Never Was: Heath, the Nixon Administration and the Year of Europe* (Dublin, 2009); and for critical reflections on France, see Aurélie Elisa Gfeller, 'Imagining European Identity: French Elites and the American Challenge in the Pompidou-Nixon Era', *Contemporary European History* 19(2) (2010), 133–49.

241. Möckli, *European Foreign Policy during the Cold War*, 198; Nigel J.D. Lucas and Dimitri Papaconstantinou, *Western European Energy Policies: A Comparative Study of the Influence of Institutional Structure on Technical Change* (Oxford, 1985), 56; Nigel J.D. Lucas, *Energy and the European Communities* (London, 1977), 56.

242. Tauer, *Störfall für die gute Nachbarschaft?*, 109f.

243. Möckli, *European Foreign Policy during the Cold War*, 198–208.

244. Redies: Gesprächsunterlagen für die Tagung des EG Ministerrates am 5./6. November 1973, 4.11.1973, VS.Bd. 9994, PA AA, B 150, 292.

245. Hellema, Wiebes and Witte, *The Netherlands and the Oil Crisis*; Graf, 'Making Use of the Oil Weapon'; Venn, *The Oil Crisis*.

246. 'Botschafter Lebsanft, Brüssel (EG), an das Auswärtige Amt: Ratstagung, hier: Erdölkrise, 4.12.1973', in Schwarz, *Akten zur Auswärtigen Politik der Bundesrepublik Deutschland 1973*, 1962–65; Lebsanft: Bericht über die EG Tagung vom 6.11.1973, PA AA, B 150, 292.

247. 'Document 356: Fenn to Parsons, 1.11.1973', in Keith Hamilton (ed.), *The Year of Europe: America, Europe and the Energy Crisis, 1972–1974* (London, 2006).

248. 'Document 360: J.E. Cable an J.O. Wright MWE 2/12, 2.11.1973', in Hamilton, *The Year of Europe*; on British-Dutch relations, see Duco Hellema, 'Anglo-Dutch Relations during the Early 1970s: The Oil Crisis', in Nigel John Ashton and Duco Hellema (eds), *Unspoken Allies: Anglo-Dutch Relations since 1780* (Amsterdam, 2001), 255–72; on the communication with the Netherlands in early November, see 'Document 357: Douglas-Home to UKREP Brussels et al.: Netherlands and Arab Oil, November 1973', in Hamilton, *The Year of Europe*; 'Document 358: Douglas Home to Van der Stoel, November 1973', in Hamilton, *The Year of Europe*.

249. Lautenschlager, [Hans]: Vorlage zur Behandlung der Erdölkrise in der EG, 2.11.1973, PA AA, B 36 (Referat 310), 104992.

250. 'Botschafter Lebsanft, Brüssel (EG), an das Auswärtige Amt: Tagung der Europäischen Gemeinschaften am 6.11., 7.11.1973', in Schwarz, *Akten zur Auswärtigen Politik der Bundesrepublik Deutschland 1973*, 1757–60, here 1758; see also 'Botschafter Lebsanft, Brüssel (EG), an das Auswärtige Amt: Ratstagung, hier: Erdölkrise, 4.12.1973', in Schwarz, *Akten zur Auswärtigen Politik der Bundesrepublik Deutschland 1973*, 1965.

251. Lautenschlager, [Hans]: Aufzeichnung über Abendessen der Außenminister der EG in Brüssel, 5.11.1973, PA AA, B 36 (Referat 310), 104992.

252. 'Botschafter Lebsanft, Brüssel (EG), an das Auswärtige Amt: Tagung der Europäischen Gemeinschaften am 6.11., 7.11.1973', in Schwarz, *Akten zur Auswärtigen Politik der Bundesrepublik Deutschland 1973*, 1579; 'Dokument 377: Bericht aus Brüssel, 6.11.1973', in Hamilton, *The Year of Europe*.

253. Hintergrundgespräch II. Teil (Frank und Pachelbel zur Nahostdeklaration der EG am 7. November 1973), PA AA, B 1 (Referat 010), 572.

254. Bulletin published by the Press and Information Office of the Federal Government (Presse- und Informationsamt der Bundesregierung), 14 November 1973, quoted in Hohensee, *Der erste Ölpreisschock 1973/74*, 261f.; French text: 'Déclaration commune des gouvernements de la Communauté économique européenne sur la situation au Proche-Orient 1974', in *La Politique Étrangère de la France: Textes et Documents. 2e semestre 1973* (Paris, n.d.), 171.

255. Metzger, [Peter]: Fernschreiben über saudiarabische Erdölpolitik, 31.10.1973, PA AA, B 36 (Referat 310), 104991; Metzger, [Peter]: Telegramm zur Haltung Saudi-Arabiens zu Freund- und Feindstaaten, 3.11.1973, PA AA, B 36 (Referat 310), 104992.

256. Graf, 'Making Use of the Oil Weapon'.

257. Daniel Möckli adopts the EC's perspective and interprets its declaration on the Middle East as the apogee of EPC; Möckli, *European Foreign Policy during the Cold War*, 185, 204.

258. Erich Hauser, 'Diplomatische Klimmzüge', *Frankfurter Rundschau*, 7 November 1973; Rm, 'Nachgiebigkeit in Brüssel', *Frankfurter Allgemeine Zeitung*, 7 November 1973; Dieter Schröder, 'Mehr Kaltblütigkeit in der Ölkrise', *Süddeutsche Zeitung*, 7 November 1973; see also, months later, the critical assessment of Fritz Ullrich Fack, 'Europa als Restposten', *Frankfurter Allgemeine Zeitung*, 13 February 1974.

259. Schröder, 'Mehr Kaltblütigkeit in der Ölkrise'.

260. Günther Gillessen, 'Frieren für Holland?', *Frankfurter Allgemeine Zeitung*, 7 November 1973.

261. Hintergrundgespräch mit StS Frank: Nahostdeklaration der Europäischen Gemeinschaft, 7.11.1973, PA AA, B 1 (Referat 010), 576.

262. Paul Frank, *Entschlüsselte Botschaft: Ein Diplomat macht Inventur* (Munich, 1985), 271f.

263. Hintergrundgespräch am 7.11.1973 mit StS Frank: Nahostdeklaration der Europäischen Gemeinschaft, PA AA, B 1 (Referat 010), 576, 7.

264. Ibid., 2.

265. Ibid., 8.

266. Ibid., 13.

267. Ibid., 4.

268. Ibid., 16.

269. Lautenschlager: Vermerk: Diplomatische Initiative der Neun in der Erdölfrage, 12.11.1973; Secretary of State (GB): Botschaft an die europäischen Regierungen bezüglich der Aufhebung des Embargos, 10.11.1973, PA AA, B 71 (Referat 405), 113906.

270. 'Document 393: Copenhagen tel 483, MWE 2/12, 15.11.1973: Reports on Meeting of the Political Directors of the Nine and French Veto on Proposed Approach to Arab Oil Producers', in Hamilton, *The Year of Europe*.

271. Redies, [Helmut]: Schritt der 'Neun' bei den arabischen Regierungen, 21.11.1973; Redies: Plurex: Gesprächsführung der EG-Mitgliedstaaten bei den arabischen Ländern, 21.11.1973, VS.Bd. 9994, PA AA, B 150, 293.

272. Werner an AA: Nahostkonflikt – Beziehungen EG arabische Länder, 27.11.1973, VS.Bd. 14059, PA AA, B 150, 293.

273. 'Bilateral Deals: Everybody's Doing It', in MEES 17(13) (18 January 1974), 1; for a listing of bilateral agreements, see 'Document 299: Paper Prepared in the Office of Economic Research, Central Intelligence Agency, Washington, February 4, 1974', in Linda W. Qaimmaqami and Edward C. Keefer (eds), *Energy Crisis, 1969–1974* (Washington, DC, 2012), 840–44; on practices in the United Kingdom, see 'Document 440: Minute: Egerton to Taylor N/B 12/5', in Hamilton, *The Year of Europe*.

274. Milward, *The European Rescue of the Nation-State*, 2f.
275. 'Document 435: UKREP Brussels tel 6054, SMG 12/598/1, 5.12.1973', in Hamilton, *The Year of Europe*; 'Document 445: Tel 764 to Bonn MWE 1/548/25, 10.12.1973', in Hamilton, *The Year of Europe*.
276. Permanent Under-Secretary's Planning Committee: Oil and Europe, 11.12.1973 (PC 73(17)), NA UK, FCO 30/1944.
277. Ibid.
278. 'Document 467: Tel 1551 to UKREP Brussels, SMG 12/598/1, 17. Dezember', in Hamilton, *The Year of Europe*.
279. Lantzke an Friderichs, Behandlung der Energiefragen auf der Gipfelkonferenz am 14./15.Dezember 1973, 7.12.1973, BArch, B 102/201338.
280. The Copenhagen Summit Conference, in *Bulletin of the European Communities* 12 (1973), 6–12.
281. The Declaration of European Identity, in *Bulletin of the European Communities* 12 (1973), http://www.cvce.eu/obj/Declaration_on_European_Identity_Copenhagen_14_December_1973-en-02798dc9-9c69-4b7d-b2c9-f03a8db7da32.html (accessed 20 September 2012); see also Möckli, *European Foreign Policy during the Cold War*, 198–224.
282. For a detailed account, see Aurélie Elisa Gfeller, *Building a European Identity: France, the United States and the Oil Shock, 1973–1974* (New York, 2012).
283. Hynes, *The Year That Never Was*; Möckli, *European Foreign Policy during the Cold War*, 140–83; Gfeller, *Building a European Identity*; Judith Michel, *Willy Brandts Amerikabild und -politik, 1933–1992* (Göttingen/Oxford, 2010), 355 and passim; Alastair Noble, 'Kissinger's Year of Europe, Britain's Year of Choice', in Matthias Schulz and Thomas Alan Schwartz (eds), *The Strained Alliance: US-European Relations from Nixon to Carter* (New York, 2010), 221–35.
284. Keith Hamilton, 'Britain, France, and America's Year of Europe, 1973', *Diplomacy & Statecraft* 17(4) (2006), 871–95, here 876; Gfeller, 'Imagining European Identity', 137.
285. Edward Heath, *The Course of My Life: My Autobiography* (London, 1998), 493.
286. Niklas H. Rossbach, *Heath, Nixon and the Rebirth of the Special Relationship: Britain, the US and the EC, 1969–74* (Basingstoke, 2009), 135–46.
287. Fabian Hilfrich, 'West Germany's Long Year of Europe: Bonn between Europe and the United States', in Matthias Schulz and Thomas Alan Schwartz (eds), *The Strained Alliance: US-European Relations from Nixon to Carter* (New York, 2010), 237–56; see also Daniel Möckli, 'Asserting Europe's Distinct Identity: The EC Nine and Kissinger's Year of Europe', in Schulz and Schwartz, *The Strained Alliance*, 195–220.
288. Möckli, *European Foreign Policy during the Cold War*, 148–51; Keith Hamilton, 'Introduction', in *The Year of Europe*, 1–43, here 36.
289. Henry A. Kissinger, 'The United States and a Unifying Europe: Made before the Pilgrims of Great Britain at London on Dec. 12', *Department of State Bulletin* 69 (31 December 1973), 777–82, here 779.
290. 'Fernschreiben des Präsidenten der Vereinigten Staaten von Amerika, Nixon, an den Bundeskanzler Brandt 30. Juli 1973', in Brandt, *Ein Volk der guten Nachbarn*, 486f.; 'Fernschreiben des Bundeskanzlers Brandt an den Präsidenten der Vereinigten Staaten, Nixon, 4.8.1973', in Brandt, *Ein Volk der guten Nachbarn*, 488–90; see also the talks between Brandt, Scheel, Nixon and Kissinger in late September 1973: Gespräche Brandt/Scheel mit Nixon/Kissinger, 2.10.1973, 240 – 1921/73v, PA AA, B 150, 290.
291. On France, see Gfeller, 'Imagining European Identity', 137; on the United Kingdom, see Noble, 'Kissinger's Year of Europe', 234f.
292. 'Botschafter von Staden, Washington, an Staatssekretär Frank, 20.10.1973', in Schwarz, *Akten zur Auswärtigen Politik der Bundesrepublik Deutschland 1973*, 1627–28; see also the CIA's situation analysis: Memorandum: Troubled Alliance: Western Europe, the US and the Middle East Crisis, 2 November 1973, CIA, Doc No/ESDN: 51112a4b993247d4d8394507.

293. Staden, [Berndt von]: Fernschreiben zum europäisch-amerikanischen Verhältnis, 28.10.1973, PA AA, B 150, 291; 'Gespräch des Staatssekretärs Frank mit dem amerikanischen Botschafter Hillenbrand, 25.10.1973', in Schwarz, *Akten zur Auswärtigen Politik der Bundesrepublik Deutschland 1973*, 1647–53.

294. Asaf Siniver, *Nixon, Kissinger, and US Foreign Policy Making: The Machinery of Crisis* (Cambridge, 2008), 188; Janice Gross-Stein, 'Flawed Strategies and Missed Signals: Crisis Bargaining between the Superpowers, October 1973', in David Warren Lesch (ed.), *The Middle East and the United States: A Historical and Political Reassessment* (Boulder, CO, 1999), 204–26.

295. 'Gespräch des Staatssekretärs Frank mit dem amerikanischen Gesandten Cash, 24.10.1973', in Schwarz, *Akten zur Auswärtigen Politik der Bundesrepublik Deutschland 1973*, 1638–43, here 1640; Paul Frank's memoirs provide us with an impression of the highly charged nature of the (domestic) political debate and of his confrontational debating style. He refers to himself as Caspar Hilzinger: 'Caspar Hilzinger quoted the SPD Bundestag faction's "Foreign Policy" working group . . . . It too had used the unacceptable term "heating oil diplomats". Caspar Hilzinger said this as quietly as he could: "Yes, gentlemen of the SPD parliamentary group, we are oil diplomats. I've got to admit it. We are not responsible for light heating oil but for fuel oil. We do not feel responsible for warm homes but for jobs. . . . Either we get the oil on the basis of good relations with the producing countries, or we have to go and get it, and that would mean war". Caspar Hilzinger could barely make himself heard in the ensuing racket'. Frank, *Entschlüsselte Botschaft*, 270.

296. 'Gespräch des Staatssekretärs Frank mit dem amerikanischen Gesandten Cash, 24.10.1973', in Schwarz, *Akten zur Auswärtigen Politik der Bundesrepublik Deutschland 1973*, 1638–43.

297. 'Gespräch des Staatssekretärs Frank mit dem amerikanischen Botschafter Hillenbrand, 25.10.1973', in Schwarz, *Akten zur Auswärtigen Politik der Bundesrepublik Deutschland 1973*, 1647–53.

298. Ibid., 1651f.

299. Ibid., 1652.

300. Ibid., 1653.

301. Staden, [Berndt von]: Fernschreiben zur Auswirkung des Nahostkrieges auf die amerikanische Haltung bei der KSZE, 27.10.1973, PA AA, B 150, 291.

302. 'Botschafter von Staden, Washington, an Bundesminister Scheel am 26.10.1973', in Schwarz, *Akten zur Auswärtigen Politik der Bundesrepublik Deutschland 1973*, 1662–68; 'Botschafter von Staden, Washington, an Bundesminister Scheel, 17.11.1973', in Schwarz, *Akten zur Auswärtigen Politik der Bundesrepublik Deutschland 1973*, 1943–46; Staden, [Berndt von]: Gespräch mit Secretary of Defense James R. Schlesinger, 31.10.1973, PA AA, B 150, 291; see also Berndt von Staden, *Zwischen Eiszeit und Tauwetter: Diplomatie in einer Epoche des Umbruchs; Erinnerungen* (Berlin, 2005), 138.

303. 'Botschafter von Staden, Washington, an Bundesminister Scheel am 26.10.1973', in Schwarz, *Akten zur Auswärtigen Politik der Bundesrepublik Deutschland 1973*, 1664.

304. 'Gespräch des Staatssekretärs Frank mit dem amerikanischen Botschafter Hillenbrand, 29.10.1973', in Schwarz, *Akten zur Auswärtigen Politik der Bundesrepublik Deutschland 1973*, 1670–77; see also the ex-post account in Frank, *Entschlüsselte Botschaft*, 268; Interview mit Bundesaußenminister Scheel für die ZDF-Sendung Bonner Perspektiven, 28.10.1973, PA AA, B 150, 291.

305. Telegramm Brandt an Nixon, 28.10.1973, PA AA, B 150, 291.

306. 'Fernschreiben des Präsidenten der Vereinigten Staaten von Amerika, Nixon, an den Bundeskanzler Brandt, 30.10.1973', in Brandt, *Ein Volk der guten Nachbarn*, 514–16.

307. With reference to a conversation with Brandt's former speechwriter Klaus Harpprecht, however, Judith Michel reports that the West German government secretly provided

Israel with weapons, getting the transatlantic relationship back onto an even keel. Michel, *Willy Brandts Amerikabild und -politik*, 375f.

308. Walter Laqueur, 'The Idea of Europe Runs Out of Gas', *The Atlantic Community Quarterly* 12 (Spring 1974), 64–75, here 64.

309. On international strategic thinking in the United States see chapter 4.

310. Philip Odeen: Memo for Kissinger: Meeting on Energy, Saturday, 8 September 1973, NARA, Nixon Library, NSC, Subject Files, Box 321.

311. Staden, [Berndt von]: Gespräch mit Secretary of Defense James R. Schlesinger, 31.10.1973, PA AA, B 150, 291. This was also bound up with differing temporal perspectives: 'they [the Americans] regard it as their main task to prevent any shift of equilibrium and ward off any threat to the West's long-term energy supply. . . . they regard European fears of an Arab oil boycott as short-term in nature, and believe they must be put on the back burner in view of the long-term consequences'. Staden, [Berndt von]: Bericht zur amerikanischen Haltung im Nahostkonflikt, 8.11.1973, PA AA, B 150, 292.

312. Record of Conversation between the Foreign and Commonwealth Secretary and the US Secretary of State, Dr. Henry Kissinger, at the Foreign and Commonwealth Office at 10:30 a.m. on Wednesday, 12 December 1973, Secret, DNSA, KT00948; see also Middle East Situation and Prospects [Discussion with Japanese Foreign Minister], Secret, Memorandum of Conversation, 7324413, 14 November 1973, DNSA, KT00911.

313. Middle East Situation and Prospects [Discussion with Japanese Foreign Minister], Secret, Memorandum of Conversation, 7324413, 14 November 1973, DNSA, KT00911; Press Accounts of Secretary Kissinger's Visit to Tokyo, Secret, Memorandum of Conversation, 22 November 1973, DNSA, KT00919. The US government was fully aware of the situation in Japan; see Undersecretary of State for Economic Affairs, Arthur W. Hummel, Memorandum for the Secretary: Arab Oil Cutbacks and Japan, 3 November 1973, NARA, Nixon Library, NSC, Subject Files – Energy Crisis 1973–74, Box 321.

314. Staden, [Berndt von]: Fernschreiben zu atlantischen Beziehungen und Nahostkrise, 23.11.1973, PA AA, B 150, 293.

315. Kissinger Telcon with Donaldson, 3 January 1974, DNSA, KA 11786; Secretary's Staff Meeting, Wednesday, 26 December 1973, 3:10 p.m., DNSA, KT00973.

316. Secretary's Conversation with Foreign Minister Jobert, Secret, 19 December 1973, DNSA, KT00966.

317. Memo: Scowcroft to President: Sec. Kissinger's Address to the NATO Meeting, 12 December 1973, NARA, Nixon Library, NSC, HAK Office Files, Trips, Box 42; Document 447: FM Brussels to FCO: NATO Ministerial Meeting, 10 December 1973, in Hamilton, *The Year of Europe*; Document 449: UKDEL NATO to FCO: NATO Ministerial Meeting Private Session, 11 December 1973, in Hamilton, *The Year of Europe*; Document 450: FCO to UKREF Brussels: EEC – US Declaration, 11 December 1973, in Hamilton, *The Year of Europe*.

318. Memorandum for Secretary Kissinger from Jan Lodal/Helmut Sonnenfeldt, Subject: Next Steps in the European Oil Situation, 4 December 1973, NARA, Nixon Library, NSC, Subject Files – Energy Crisis 1973–74, Box 321.

319. Memo: Scowcroft to President: Sec. Kissinger's Address to the NATO Meeting, 12 December 1973, NARA, Nixon Library, NSC, HAK Office Files, Trips, Box 42; Document 447: FM Brussels to FCO: NATO Ministerial Meeting, 10 December 1973, in Hamilton, *The Year of Europe*; Document 449: UKDEL NATO to FCO: NATO Ministerial Meeting Private Session, 11 December 1973, in Hamilton, *The Year of Europe*; Document 450: FCO to UKREP Brussels: EEC – US Declaration, 11 December 1973, in Hamilton, *The Year of Europe*.

320. Kissinger to Scowcroft [131000Z DEC 73], 23.12.1973, NARA, Nixon Library, NSC, HAK Office Files, Box 42; Kissinger, 'The United States and a Unifying Europe'.

321. Ibid., 779.

322. Ibid., 780.

323. Ibid., 781.
324. Lantzke an Hermes, Entwurf für Schreiben Rohwedder an Grabert, 13.12.1973; Detlev K. Rohwedder an Horst Grabert (BMWi): Gipfelkonferenz am 14./15. Dezember 1973, 13.12.1973, PA AA, B 71 (Referat 405), 113893.
325. David S. Painter, 'Oil, Resources, and the Cold War, 1945–1962', in Melvyn P. Leffler and Odd Arne Westad (eds), *The Cambridge History of the Cold War*, vol. 1 (Cambridge/New York, 2009), 486–507, here 505.
326. 'Unterrichtung durch die Bundesregierung. Die Energiepolitik der Bundesregierung', 24f.; Bethkenhagen, *Bedeutung und Möglichkeiten*, 211 and passim.
327. Hanns-D. Jacobsen, 'Probleme des Ost-West-Handels aus Sicht der Bundesrepublik Deutschland', *German Studies Review* 7(3) (1984), 531–53.
328. Per Högselius, *Red Gas: Russia and the Origins of European Energy Dependence* (Basingstoke, 2013), 87.
329. Gottfried Niedhardt, 'Ostpolitik: Phases, Short-Term Objectives, and Grand Design', in Geyer and Schaefer, *American Détente and German Ostpolitik*, 118–36; Geyer and Schaefer, 'Preface', in *American Détente and German Ostpolitik*, 1–4, here 2.
330. Werner D. Lippert, *The Economic Diplomacy of Ostpolitik: Origins of NATO's Energy Dilemma* (New York, 2011), 20, 34.
331. Bethkenhagen, *Bedeutung und Möglichkeiten*, 202–4.
332. Schauer an Bundeskanzler: Deutsch-iranische Zusammenarbeit auf dem Gebiet der Energieversorgung, 30.4.1973, BArch, B 136/7706; see also BArch, B 136/17572.
333. In light of this, Peter Hermes had already written to Ulf Lantzke by 23 October; see Hermes, [Peter]: Brief an Ulf Lantzke zur Energieimportabhängigkeit vom Ostblock, 23.10.1973, PA AA, B 71 (Referat 405), 113924.
334. Lüders, [Karl Heinz]: Fernschreiben zu Öllieferungen aus der UdSSR, 20.11.1973, PA AA, B 36 (Referat 310), 104992; see also Högselius, *Red Gas*, 155.
335. 'Bundeskanzler Brandt an den Generalsekretär des ZK der KPdSU, Breshnew', in Schwarz, *Akten zur Auswärtigen Politik der Bundesrepublik Deutschland 1973*, 1780–82, here 1781.
336. 'Bundeskanzler Brandt an den Generalsekretär des ZK der KPdSU, Breshnew, am 4. Januar 1974', in Hans-Peter Schwarz (ed.), *Akten zur Auswärtigen Politik der Bundesrepublik Deutschland 1974*, vol. 1, *1. Januar bis 30. Juni 1974*, in collaboration with Ilse Dorothee Pautsch (Munich, 2005), 3–5.
337. 'Egon Bahr: Aufzeichnung des Bundesministers Bahr', in Schwarz, *Akten zur Auswärtigen Politik der Bundesrepublik Deutschland 1973*, 1747–50, here 1748.
338. 'Unterrichtung durch die Bundesregierung. Erste Fortschreibung des Energieprogramms', 11.
339. Manfred Wörner, 'Neue Dimensionen der Sicherheit: Referat bei der XII. Internationalen Wehrkunde-Begegnung, Munich 1.2.1975', in Klaus von Schubert (ed.), *Sicherheitspolitik der Bundesrepublik Deutschland: Dokumentation 1945–1977*, vol. 2 (Cologne, 1979), 590–97.
340. Lippert, *The Economic Diplomacy of Ostpolitik*, 139.
341. Jonathan P. Stern, *Soviet Oil and Gas Exports to the West: Commercial Transaction or Security Threat?* Energy Papers no. 21 (Aldershot, UK/Brookfield, VT, 1987).
342. Peter Hermes, 'Development Policy and Foreign Affairs', *Intereconomics* 9(3) (1974), 91–94; Hermes, *Meine Zeitgeschichte*, 222f.; Bastian Hein, *Die Westdeutschen und die Dritte Welt: Entwicklungspolitik und Entwicklungsdienste zwischen Reform und Revolte 1959–1974* (Munich, 2006), 306.
343. Fernsehdiskussion zwischen Erhard Eppler und Karl Carstens, ARD, 6.12.1973, 21.45, BArch, B 257/34391; see also Erhard Eppler, 'Ölkrise und Entwicklungshilfe', *Die Zeit*, 21 December 1973.
344. Umlauff: Vermerk zu Folgen der Erdölkrise für die Fähigkeit der Industriestaaten, weiterhin Entwicklungshilfe zu geben, 16.11.1973, PA AA, B 71 (Referat 405), 113905; see

also Lautenschlager, [Hans]: Auswirkungen der Erdölpreiserhöhungen und -versorgungsschwierigkeiten auf die internationale Zusammenarbeit, 23.11.1973, PA AA, B 71 (Referat 405), 113905.

345. Gehlhoff, [Walter]: Fernschreiben zu den Auswirkungen der Ölkrise auf die internationale Zusammenarbeit, 4.12.1973, PA AA, B 36 (Referat 310), 104992; see also Dittmann, [Heinz]: Auswirkungen der Erdölpreiserhöhungen auf int. Zusammenarbeit, 7.12.1973, PA AA, B 71 (Referat 405), 113905.

346. Hermes, [Peter]: Plurex an vier Vertretungen zu den Auswirkungen der Erdölpreiserhöhungen auf internationale Zusammenarbeit, 7.12.1973, PA AA, B 71 (Referat 405), 113905.

347. Ibid.

348. 403 an Botschaften: Auswirkungen der Preisentwicklung im Mineralölbereich auf die Entwicklungsländer, 21.2.1974, PA AA, B 36 (Referat 310), 113905.

349. Hermes an den Staatssekretär: Voraussichtliche Auswirkungen der Erdölkrise auf die Entwicklungspolitik der anderen Geberländer, 4.3.1974; Referat 310: Die Auswirkungen der Erdölpreiserhöhungen auf die nicht-erdölproduzierenden außereuropäischen Entwicklungsländer, PA AA, B 36 (Referat 310), 104993; on the public debate on this issue, see 'Entwicklungsländer: Fast vernichtend', *Der Spiegel*, 14 January 1974, 73–74.

350. Kommission der EG: Versuch zur Neutralisierung der Folgen bestimmter internationaler Preisentwicklungen für die am stärksten betroffenen Länder, 20.3.1974, BArch, B 136/8029.

351. Hein, *Die Westdeutschen und die Dritte Welt*, 266f.

Chapter 6

OIL CONFERENCES

Global Interdependence and National Sovereignty

As a result of the actions taken by OPEC and OAPEC in October 1973, the world of oil was out of kilter. For the most part, the governments of the Western industrialized nations did not believe they could guarantee an adequate supply of oil and meet this challenge to their political sovereignty on their own. This finding comes as no surprise in the case of a country such as West Germany. Its (energy) sovereignty was in any case embedded in supranational structures and its representatives had explicitly abandoned traditional notions of isolated sovereignty in the early 1970s. But even the United States, or the European Communities as a collective, could not simply organize the world of oil as they saw fit. While the United States was the strongest player, it did not attempt to achieve energy security unilaterally, instead opting to pursue international cooperation. The very task of collecting the data considered necessary to formulate energy policy, which had already proved troublesome on the national level, was an even greater challenge on a global scale. This too pointed to the need for cooperation.

This was an era in which the Conference on Security and Cooperation in Europe (CSCE) was seeking to restructure the relationship between East and West and reduce antagonisms previously considered insurmountable. What could have been more obvious, then, than to restore order to the world of oil through another international conference? Yet despite this widely shared view, there was little agreement on how best to organize such a conference if it were to effectively reorder the world of oil while guaranteeing the energy security of Western Europe and the United States. Should the leading oil-importing countries initially get together to agree on a joint position, as the United States suggested? Or should they meet immediately with the producing countries, as the French envisaged? Should the conference confine itself to the oil economy or also deal with the establishment of a 'New International Economic Order', as long demanded by the Group of 77? What role would be played by those developing countries lacking significant reserves of raw materials, including oil? Close examination of the competing visions of both the conference and the new order shows that the antagonism between national and international strategies was more apparent than real. In fact, the multiple ways of asserting sovereignty through national, regional, international and supranational structures were closely intertwined.

The United States' Willingness to Cooperate and Pursuit of Hegemony

In his Pilgrim's Speech on 12 December 1973, Henry A. Kissinger proposed the establishment of a new international body to help the major consuming countries better coordinate their oil and energy policies. The Energy Action Group would exist in parallel to the OECD's Oil Committee or represent a higher-level forum, enjoy greater powers and prevent possible confrontations between the three major consuming regions of the United States, Western Europe and Japan, as well as between individual countries. During the acute oil crisis since October, the Oil Committee and its High Level Group Oil had in fact failed, or been unable, to take on any significant coordinating, let alone leadership, role. On 25 October 1973, the High Level Group met for the first time after the decisions made by OPEC and OAPEC. As it was still impossible to estimate the effects of the production cutbacks, it agreed no countermeasures.[1] To avoid worsening the sense of crisis, meanwhile, it decided not to formally activate the International Industry Advisory Board either. The German delegation at least experienced this meeting as simultaneously 'fraught with tension' and pervaded by 'resignation and perplexity' with respect to the producing countries' oil policies.[2] At its next meeting on 19 November, the High Level Group Oil exchanged information on the supply situation in the different OECD countries but again failed to reach agreement on substantive measures. With the exception of the Netherlands, no country was prepared to trigger the OECD's oil-sharing crisis mechanism.[3] Meanwhile, 'in the conversations carried on at the fringes of the meeting', Ulf Lantzke reported, it had become clear 'that [there was] very little hope of a reasonably speedy return to "normal conditions"'.[4]

When the High Level Group next met, on 19 December, Kissinger had already promulgated his proposal for an Energy Action Group. The United

Kingdom and West Germany thought this plan more promising than further cooperation within the framework of the OECD, as favoured by France.[5] With the exception of the French and the Japanese, all the delegations to the High Level Group welcomed the American proposal in principle, while also advocating the inclusion of the producing countries in order to avoid any appearance of confrontation.[6] Under the pressure of the oil crisis, then, the OECD's High Level Group withdrew from the international coordination of energy policy and was prepared to cede its position to an as yet undefined body. Only in January 1974 did Richard Nixon contact the heads of government of France, the United Kingdom, West Germany, the Netherlands, Norway, Canada and Japan, inviting their foreign ministers to a conference of the leading industrialized oil-consuming countries.

Nixon's invitation portrayed the present era as one of dramatic crisis:

> Today the energy situation threatens to unleash political and economic forces that could cause severe and irreparable damage to the prosperity and stability of the world. Two roads lie before us. We can go our own separate ways, with the prospect of progressive division, the erosion of vital interdependence, and increasing political and economic conflict; or we can work in concert, developing enlightened unity and cooperation, for the benefit of all mankind – producer and consumer countries alike.[7]

In order to safeguard economic development, the US administration contended, the leading consuming countries should first meet in Washington to negotiate a reduction in the growth of energy consumption. Concurrently, they must hammer out a common position on how best to reorder the world of oil; this would then be discussed in negotiations with the producing countries. Given the delicate communicative circumstances of the embargo, to avoid escalating the conflict Nixon wrote simultaneously to the leaders of the OPEC countries. He claimed that the goal of the Washington conference was solely to create a structure that would be productive and positive for both producing and consuming countries, one that would be subject to negotiations with them as soon as possible.[8] Despite these reassurances, at least some Arab countries perceived Nixon's invitation as confrontational and criticized it harshly. Such crucial countries as Iran and Saudi Arabia, meanwhile, either expressed no criticisms or voiced merely mild concerns.[9]

In Western Europe too, the responses varied greatly, hampering European Political Cooperation (EPC).[10] Before the invitation had even been sent out, Berndt von Staden, West German ambassador in Washington, 'urgently' advised the government 'to give a basically positive public response to the initiative ... for reasons of political psychology'.[11] In the Economics Ministry, Ulf Lantzke advised Economics Minister Friderichs to urge the Cabinet to embrace the plan.[12] The Foreign Ministry was more critical. Undersecretary Frank in particular aired his suspicions that Kissinger's true goal was to 'get the Europeans and Japanese to fall in line behind the Americans', after his failure to do so the year before.[13] In any case, the government initially informed the United States unofficially of its essentially positive view, but deferred formal acceptance until the next meeting of the EC Council on 14–15 January in light of its commitment to EPC.[14]

In the run-up to the EC Council meeting, three different positions emerged. The representatives of the United Kingdom, West Germany, the Netherlands and Italy were in favour of accepting the invitation to varying degrees. Since Belgium, Ireland and Denmark had received no invitations, their representatives advocated only a common response from the EC rather than individual national responses. The French representative, meanwhile, merely highlighted the problems inherent in the invitation and the potentially negative consequences of such a conference.[15] At the Council meeting itself, the foreign ministers resolved to take part in the conference as long as all EC member states were invited and the EC itself was represented.[16] In their reply, they again emphasized that the conference must only be the first step towards a more fundamental form of co-operation between consumers and producers.[17] The French government in particular repeatedly underlined this aspect, hesitating to accept the invitation. Following the failed Year of Europe initiative, it regarded the Washington conference as a gambit by Kissinger to consolidate US hegemony over energy policy within the Western world. Jobert thus made France's participation dependent on the EC agreeing a common negotiating position – and on its precise character. To avoid confrontation with the Arab producing countries, when the foreign ministers accepted the invitation they simultaneously resolved to expedite European-Arab dialogue, as proposed by the Arab ministers at the Copenhagen summit in December.[18]

Nixon's invitation was now quickly issued to the remaining EC countries, the EC itself and the OECD. This gave rise to a peculiar dual structure: the Washington conference was attended both by representatives of the EC itself and its member states. When the various countries sought to agree a common position for the conference, it was already evident that this joint approach would entail the relinquishment of sovereignty and – at least for some countries – new sovereign room for manoeuvre. When the leading energy officials met on 23 January to thrash out this common position, conflict flared between France, which wished to see a conference of the consuming and producing countries under UN auspices, and the other states.[19] The Commission subsequently advised the Council to avoid confrontation with the producing countries and, at the conference, to seek to identify the most appropriate form of common dialogue. But it also suggested talks on enhanced energy-saving measures and the promotion of new energy sources, the role of the petroleum industry and an allocation system for times of crisis.[20] At the Council meeting on 4 and 5 February, where the common negotiating position was supposed to be agreed, the French government tried to push through a more restrictive proposal. Only in the field of research and development should there be cooperation exclusively between the industrialized countries; all other issues ought to be discussed within existing bodies. Beyond this, the 'Community [must] retain its freedom of action vis-à-vis the producing countries'.[21] The French government feared that the creation of a new institution between 'an as yet disunited Europe and the American leviathan . . . would not produce an equal dialogue', and viewed US policy as 'intrinsically independent and selfish'.[22]

The other EC states were far less convinced that Europe could and should resist the Americans. The United Kingdom rejected the idea of forming a bloc with the United States not for fundamental reasons of power politics, but on purely strategic grounds: it did not wish to provoke the producing countries. In contrast to France's position, Ulf Lantzke took the view that a restrictive negotiating stance would prompt the Europeans to adopt national approaches at the Washington conference, and thus weaken them.[23] As he saw it, the French government's seemingly European strategy was actually intended to preserve national room for manoeuvre and the ability to conclude further bilateral agreements with the producing countries. The West Germans and the British, meanwhile, believed that gaining the support of the United States was a more promising way of retaining their own energy sovereignty. UK experts were convinced that for political, financial and energy-related reasons this would be impossible without the United States. Only the US could put pressure on Israel and the Arab producing countries. In contrast to Europe and Japan, the US was negligibly affected by the crisis economically and would dominate any open contest for oil reserves involving bilateral agreements.[24] The West German Economics Ministry shared this analysis of prevailing power relations. In the run-up to the Energy Conference, Willy Brandt too made it clear to Walter Scheel and Helmut Schmidt that while one of the key goals was to achieve or preserve the 'most united possible stance' on the part of the EC, the West Germans might well face situations 'in which our delegation [must] represent the interests of West Germany in a narrower sense as well'. When it came to security and energy policy, it was vitally important 'to remain in very close contact with the United States'.[25] The British government shared this view. Echoing West German attitudes, British solidarity within the EC hit its limits whenever national interests seemed under threat. At all costs, the British government was determined to retain the potential for bilateral agreements and its authority over the use of the anticipated North Sea oil. Lord Carrington, who was in charge of British energy policy, declared quite openly to EC Commission vice-president Henri Simonet that the United Kingdom would reject any European regulation that restricted British sovereignty over North Sea oil.[26]

In the United States, the State Department, Federal Energy Office and Treasury Department, along with other government departments, were busy preparing for the Washington conference from mid January onwards, yet there was little clarity regarding its objectives and purpose. National Security Council staff member Charles A. Cooper even asked Kissinger what exactly the departments' preparatory efforts were supposed to achieve: 'We need a simple conference to establish a simple political point, not a complex conference which by attempting to resolve a host of technical issues not only fails to make its political point but makes the real problem worse'.[27] All governments, he contended, recognized that the energy crisis had the potential to topple them and thus saw a need for action. But because of the novel character of the crisis, he went on, there was disagreement over how best to respond, not least because solutions that might seem correct domestically could be detrimental from an international perspective. In these circumstances, it would be a mistake to overload the conference with technical issues. Instead it should merely seek to create a framework for cooperation among consuming countries, in order to enhance their bargaining power.

Many observers, including a fair number within the US administration, shared the impression that the conference's agenda was too broad and complex. The plan was for the foreign ministers to form working groups that would discuss relations with the producing countries and the mechanisms of their future cooperation. The finance ministers were to focus on the economic and monetary aspects of the oil crisis, while officials with responsibility for energy would explore how best to limit consumption growth, the development of alternative energy sources and oil sharing. Finally, science and technology experts were to draw up proposals on cooperation in research and development. All this was to culminate in a joint communiqué within two or two-and-a-half days.[28] This overloading of the conference was likely due to Kissinger's lack of expertise on energy issues and his tendency to underestimate their complexity. Kissinger was the world's best-known diplomat in early 1974, and after receiving the Nobel Peace Prize he was also a widely celebrated one. Yet his speciality was bilateral negotiations; this was the first time he had organized an international conference. Partly as a result of Kissinger's monomaniacal working practices, the preparations for the conference took longer than envisaged. His staff, meanwhile, were still unsure what it was meant to achieve.[29]

This lack of communication and strategic clarity had a detrimental impact in the immediate run-up to the conference. At a meeting in the State Department less than two weeks before it was due to start, one member of Kissinger's staff referred to the official position that, rather than seeking to create a bloc of consuming countries, the conference was supposed to take the first step towards a form of cooperation that would include the producing countries. The secretary of state blew his top.

> We have said it a hundred times and it's bull . . . excuse me for using that language. It [the conference] is, of course, designed to create a united front. That's the only purpose of a consumer meeting. And we can waffle around this and we can say elegant things. And, of course, we should say it – but, for God sakes, in a senior group here, let's not kid ourselves. The purpose is to create a consumer group that improves the bargaining position of the consumers.[30]

The industrialized countries, Kissinger declared, must create a united front to avert the revolution that threatened to overtake the global economic and financial order, if they wished to avoid the catastrophe they would face as isolated units. Shortly before the start of the conference, Kissinger set out his objectives in more detail in conversation with Treasury Secretary George P. Shultz and energy czar William E. Simon. First, he wished to create 'some kind of consumer organization', in order to deal more effectively with the producing countries. Second, he explained, French suspicions were quite justified because he was eager to destroy the 'regional autarchy concept' and return to the more cooperative practices of the past. Third, he wished to eliminate the 'sense of panicky impotence' currently driving the Europeans into bilateral agreements.[31] Only the United States, he underlined, could achieve such a united front, as it would gain no direct benefit from it. Kissinger thus aimed to consolidate US hegemony within the Western world over the long term by stepping up cooperation on energy issues, even if this was of no short-term benefit to the United States.

Prior to the conference, Kissinger and his staff tried to ensure its success through bilateral talks with the European countries, particularly the United Kingdom. By the end of January, Kissinger seemed convinced he had the British, and most likely the Germans as well, on his side.[32] In January, Sir Alec Douglas-Home had informed Kissinger of the attitudes of the various European countries, advised him on procedural issues and reassured him that little was likely to come of the European-Arab dialogue before the Americans had concluded their peace efforts in the Middle East.[33] On 31 January, he emphasized the psychological importance of ensuring that the arrangement of the task forces did not look like a fait accompli.

Shortly before the conference, meanwhile, he reaffirmed to Kissinger that the British government would do all it could to ensure that the French were voted down in Europe.[34] In the run-up to the conference, British cooperation was so important to the Americans that Nixon himself approached Edward Heath regarding the delicate matter ('I recognize the sensitivity of this suggestion') of whether a senior British official might help Kissinger prepare for the conference.[35] Though Heath was always keen to avoid appearing as the Americans' 'Trojan horse' within the EC, he immediately dispatched Jack Rampton from the Department of Trade and Industry. He did, however, underline to Kissinger how important it was that 'knowledge of Sir Jack Rampton's mission should not become known to our Community partners'.[36] However, the West German government at least seems likely to have been aware of this mission. On the Wednesday before the start of the conference, Brandt too complied with a request from Nixon to send an experienced official to Washington to help Kissinger's staff with their preparatory work; he too was assured of discretion.[37]

Having sought to prepare the conference in close coordination with the United Kingdom and West Germany, Kissinger was confident it would be a success.[38] Prior to the conference, the CIA concluded that the West German government was increasingly frustrated by French intransigence and, along with the Dutch, would be more likely to risk discord within the EC than accede to French demands.[39] The British ambassador in Paris believed that France would back down at the conference given the pressure it was under. 'Despite Jobert's taunts and tendency to play the mini-Kissinger in reverse, French behavior will also be determined by M Pompidou's wish not to alienate the Americans altogether, his attachment to the Western alliance, and his knowledge of the realities of the world power equation over energy, money and the Middle East conflict.'[40]

Shortly before the conference began, Kissinger met again with Nixon. Shultz and Simon to coordinate the overall American strategy. If the conference was to be a success, Nixon and Kissinger believed, it was essential to limit the role of the foreign ministers as much as possible, as they were overly captive to their national logics of representation. Furthermore, Kissinger had a low opinion of his European colleagues: 'the Foreign Ministers are idiots, except for Home. Moro, Scheel, Jobert – they're all bad'.[41] On a technical level, meanwhile, Nixon believed there was no reason for confrontation; Shultz and Simon must make this clear to their colleagues at the conference by providing a detailed analysis of the consequences of the oil crisis for energy and financial policies. This analysis should be presented in a form that was comprehensible to the foreign ministers as well, if possible. Moreover, Nixon demanded that Shultz and Simon 'talk to the technical types and talk turkey to them – they don't have to posture like the Foreign Ministers'.[42] The Americans, Nixon declared, should not seek confrontation with the Europeans, but if necessary they should make it clear to them that if they failed to cooperate, the US would reduce its military presence in Europe. Kissinger, however, doubted the Europeans would take such a threat seriously. Instead the goal must be to leave them in no doubt that, were they to reject cooperation, the United States would be the strongest player in any competition over scarce oil.

Interdependence and Sovereignty at the Washington Energy Conference

The composition of the delegations from the participating countries gives us a sense of the importance they attached to the conference. In addition to Kissinger and his staff, the United States was represented by Treasury Secretary George P. Shultz, William E. Simon and their advisers. Initially, the British delegation was to be led by Lord Carrington, who bore special responsibility for energy. Foreign Secretary Douglas-Home had only recently returned from a trip to Africa and, as he himself stated, did not feel up to Kissinger-style peripateticism. Nonetheless, at the behest of Kissinger and Nixon, he ended up attending.[43] West Germany sent Foreign Minister Walter Scheel and Finance Minister Helmut Schmidt, with Scheel acting in his role as president of the EC Council. The West German delegation comprised all the key figures involved in the country's policymaking on energy and became so large that it had to request additional space around the conference table.[44] The French delegation, headed by Foreign Minister Michel Jobert, seemed comparatively small next to the German, Canadian and Italian ones, not least due to the absence of the more pro-American Finance Minister Giscard d'Estaing.[45] However, France also dispatched Jean Blancard, the newly appointed general delegate for energy, one of the government's leading energy experts. On behalf of the EC, in addition to Scheel, Commission president François-Xavier Ortoli and vice-presidents Sir Christopher Soames and Henri Simonet attended. The OECD was represented by its secretary-general Émile van Lennep along with Hans K. Schneider, who was in charge of 'long-term energy assessment' and who also advised the West German government as director of the EWI Cologne. When the conference began on 11 February, the State Department's spacious conference hall contained the combined expertise on foreign, energy and financial policy of the major Western industrialized nations and Japan. Compared with the intimate meetings of the High Level Group Oil, where the more junior technical experts from the ministries had dedicated themselves to the same kind of task in the 1960s, this laid bare the upsurge in the political importance of oil and energy within just a few years. The inclusion of the finance ministers reflected the fact that the industrialized countries had begun to evaluate the oil crisis rather differently by this point. Having got through the winter without much trouble so far, they now believed that the greatest short- and medium-term threats did not come from supply shortfalls, but from the dramatic price hikes that were putting such strain on their balance of payments.[46]

At the start of the conference, Kissinger addressed the delegates. He emphasized the magnitude and global character of the energy crisis, which was a threat not just to the industrialized countries' prosperity but to Third World economic development as well. The risks to global economic growth also threatened the stability of the international order.[47] National solutions were impossible; competition between the industrialized countries seeking bilateral agreements with the producing countries would further increase the price of oil and have disastrous consequences for all involved. For their own good, then, they must cooperate and relinquish certain options inherent in sovereign power politics: 'We do not dispute the right of sovereign nations to make individual arrangements. But we believe that it is essential that these arrangements follow agreed rules of conduct. In their absence, unrestrained bilateralism is certain to produce disastrous political and economic consequences'.[48] To reinforce this point, in bilateral talks Kissinger repeatedly underlined that, should it come to a contest between the consuming nations, the United States would be in a superior position given its economic, political and military might, and it would make full use of its power. Consonant with advanced political scientific theories of the day, he explicitly evoked a world of global 'interdependence' in which individual states' isolated efforts to advance their interests would make everyone worse off, a world that demanded international solutions: 'As we look toward the end of this century we know that the energy crisis indicates the birth pains of global interdependence. . . . Will we consume ourselves in nationalistic rivalry which the realities of interdependence make suicidal? Or will we acknowledge our interdependence and shape cooperative solutions?'[49] National sovereignty, Kissinger contended, could only be preserved by relinquishing sovereignty within international frameworks. The conference and the yet-to-be-established successor body, then, must seek to find common solutions on reducing energy consumption; research and development; crisis mechanisms; the international financial order; and relations with the developing and producing countries.

Energy czar Simon related Kissinger's general analysis more specifically to the world of energy and, above all, oil. He identified the causes of the world's present plight, first, in the widespread belief that the era of cheap and unlimited raw materials would go on forever. Second, he contended, the problem lay 'in ourselves – in our own failure to acknowledge our interdependence and plan for it'.[50] Akin to his views as US energy czar, Simon believed the problems of international policymaking on energy had much to do with the prevailing lack of knowledge about energy and particularly oil. This must be rectified if governments were to regain their capacity for effective action.[51] Finally, he explained to the delegates that, despite its name, Nixon's Project Independence was not out to achieve national autarky; rather, by saving energy and fostering research, it would benefit all countries by helping to restore the balance between energy consumption and energy supply.

Treasury Secretary Shultz was given the task of explaining to the delegates the consequences of rising oil prices for both the industrialized and developing countries. Shultz described the present and near future as 'a time of vast new uncertainty'; nothing could be more counterproductive than 'beggar thy neighbor' strategies in which countries sought to obtain advantages at others' expense.[52] Instead, the priority must be to find new means of cooperation on finance and monetary policy. Shultz's message was backed by Walter J. Levy, who was attending as an energy analyst after having advised both the American and British governments. Levy distributed a paper to the delegates in which he estimated that in the years 1972–74 alone, the additional costs of oil imports would amount to 79.3 billion dollars worldwide, with the Europeans accounting for 39.7, the United States 15.9 and Japan 12.8 billion. As a result of his analysis, Levy declared proudly to the *Washington Post*, the ministers in attendance, above all the finance ministers, had become aware of the full magnitude of the problem for the first time.[53] There are solid reasons to doubt this. It was neither the first time the finance ministers had discussed the quadrupling of the oil price, nor is it likely that they now grasped its true scale. The figures and forecasts presented at the conference by the US government, but above all by the OECD, dramatically underestimated the potential for oil price hikes. In their presentations, both Simon and OECD secretary-general van Lennep worked on the assumption that between 1980 and 1985 the oil price would not exceed that of 1973.[54] This assessment was underpinned by the OECD's 'long-term energy assessment', the result of two years of effort by six OECD committees and twelve working groups, in addition to external experts. As its director proudly declared to the delegates, within a few months it would enable modelling of the OECD countries' key energy problems in the 1980s. The first projections of supply and demand were reassuring. Should the price rises persist, Hans K. Schneider explained, then even without new energy policies, in 1980 and 1985 the OECD countries' oil imports would not exceed 1973 levels.[55] According to the OECD secretary-general, this was due to the price mechanism: 'The spectacular rise in the price of imported oil will set in motion powerful forces reducing demand and stimulating alternative sources of supply'.[56] Just like the Federal Energy Office, then, the OECD overestimated the price elasticity of oil consumption while underestimating the cohesion of OPEC. A brief and telling exchange between Nixon and Shultz before the conference began reveals that they shared this supposition:

> Shultz: The price is going down.
> The President: Why?
> Shultz: The price. People respond to price.[57]

At the Washington Energy Conference, almost all foreign and finance ministers underlined the long-term causes of the energy crisis, its global dimensions and the need to come up with international solutions, which must involve the producing countries.[58] Dutch Foreign Minister Max van der Stoel even managed to glean something good from the oil crisis. Over the long term, he averred, oil would have become scarce anyway, and the crisis had compelled the industrialized countries to change course in good time.[59] Norwegian Foreign Minister Knut Frydenlund took much the same view: 'The oil crisis has brought home to us in a dramatic manner that the industrialized countries have been living beyond their means as far as the exploitation of natural resources and raw materials are concerned'.[60] He augmented Simon's diagnosis of a lack of data and information by noting that the oil crisis had laid bare governments' ignorance of – and lack of control over – the multinational oil companies. It was vital that this be remedied in future.

However, in their speeches, the representatives of the EC, France, West Germany and the United Kingdom, so crucial to the success of the conference, paid less attention to the specific problem of energy than to identifying which forms of cooperation among the industrialized countries would be appropriate or inappropriate. As Council president, Scheel presented the EC's position. The global character of the energy problem required international solutions, which must include every group of countries. This conference could only be the first step towards a new, more comprehensive dialogue. Beyond this forum, he went on, bilateral agreements with the producing countries could be to everyone's benefit and pave the way for later multilateral agreements. The Europeans, he explained, did not consider a new institution desirable, instead wishing to entrust the relevant work to the OECD. Scheel explicitly welcomed the French and Algerian proposal to convene a UN conference to thrash out a new world order for oil and raw materials.[61]

However, following this presentation of the European position, Scheel's Cabinet colleague Schmidt, speaking on behalf of the West German government, sided unambiguously with the United States. Schmidt expressed emphatic support for everything the American delegation had said, rejecting what he saw as clichéd protestations of the importance of avoiding confrontation with the producing countries. OPEC and OAPEC had triggered the confrontation and now the industrialized countries must decide whether to cooperate, as proposed by the United States, or attempt to save their own skin. The latter strategy would have disastrous consequences, so Schmidt urged everyone to embrace the American proposals while indirectly threatening his European partners: 'Our reason for advocating co-operation is not that our country would not be able to "go it alone". We do in fact have only little oil and gas in our ground . . . but Germany, speaking frankly, can at least pay its oil bill. We do not foresee any serious balance of payments problems for Germany. Therefore, if everybody tried to go his own way, we would not have to fear competition'.[62] Schmidt concluded his remarks by emphasizing his personal commitment to multilateralism. In recent years, he explained, it had become increasingly clear to him that the problems of security, trade, money and energy were closely intertwined and that resolving them was crucial to everyone's well-being and the equilibrium of the world. It was thus crucial to pursue a collective solution.[63] Sir Alec Douglas-Home's statements were closer to the EC's mandate, underlining that it must still be possible for countries to sign bilateral agreements. He considered existing institutions important, but acknowledged that it would be necessary to create 'follow-up machinery'.[64]

After Douglas-Home had deftly set out the British position, Jobert directed his ire entirely at Scheel, who had allegedly failed to adequately convey the EC's position, and Schmidt, 'who did not have the advantage, or disadvantage, of taking part in our work at Brussels'.[65] The industrialized countries, according to Jobert, must no longer presume to speak for the entire world. Instead, right from the outset, they must seek dialogue with the developing and producing countries on oil and energy. In parallel to the conference, this position was backed by Iraqi president Ahmed Hassan al-Bakr in an open letter to Richard Nixon.[66] Strictly speaking, Jobert went on, the Washington event was not a conference of the consuming countries because the United States and Canada at least, soon to be joined by Norway and the United Kingdom, were also producing countries. Issues of monetary and finance policy would be best dealt with through the OECD, World Bank and International Monetary Fund. Furthermore, Jobert highlighted the Europeans' structural disadvantages compared with the Americans in all energy negotiations. In his critique of the conference and of US foreign policy as a whole, Jobert quoted Democratic senator Edmund Muskie: despite the ubiquitous protestations, the conference's true goal was not to lay the ground for cooperation with the producing countries but rather to create a united front against OPEC in order to drive down the oil price. The United States was pretending to selflessly tackle international issues, yet time and again, 'in the style of our diplomacy' and 'the substance of our actions', it demonstrated that it was in fact pursuing 'narrow nationalistic goals'.[67] The entire design of Project Independence, as Jobert continued to quote Muskie, made it plain that the United States was actually on a path of nationalism, as France had rightly recognized. It would, therefore, be quite wrong to expect the Europeans to embrace the American proposals on cooperation, which merely cast a thin veil over national interests. Jobert concluded by openly calling for economic nationalism at times of crisis: 'I would like to end with an allusion to what Mr. Schmidt said when he stated that everybody did not have to try to save his own hide. Of course when everything is going well, approaches are friendly and completely elegant. But when everything is going badly, everyone tries to save his own hide. I see nothing against this'.[68]

Though Jobert was seemingly the only one to espouse – in its pure form – the EC's position, which he had played a crucial role in formulating, his intransigence placed him outside the consensus now reached by the other Europeans. The following day, in several conversations, they tried in vain to persuade Jobert to back down. The French foreign minister, following President Pompidou's strict instructions, was left unmoved by Scheel's declaration that the Community's survival was threatened by his intransigence, and Schmidt's accusation that he had failed to understand economic realities and the limits to Western Europe's influence in the Middle East.[69] Kissinger too came away with nothing after direct talks with Jobert, which both sides experienced as unpleasant and unproductive.[70] Prior to the conference, both Helmut Schmidt and Douglas-Home were determined, if push came to shove, to prioritize close cooperation with the United States over solidarity with France and the common European position. Nixon's after-dinner speech, in which he explained that 'security and economic considerations are inevitably linked and energy cannot be separated from either', was thus surplus to requirements.[71] This statement could be seen as a straightforward expression of an expanded conception of security, which now encompassed economic security, but it might also be understood as a blatant threat to reduce the American military presence in Europe should the conference fail. There is little reason to suppose that this fear was the crucial element underpinning the pro-American stance of the West Germans or British. Given – apart from anything else – the energy-related balance of power, both had concluded that they could only guarantee energy security and thus national sovereignty in cooperation with the United States.[72]

Prolonged efforts failed to change Jobert's mind. The conference had to be extended by half a day in order to agree a joint communiqué despite this setback, though the French delegation explicitly distanced itself from certain elements of it.[73] In the communiqué, the attending countries acknowledged 'that during the past three decades progress in improving productivity and standards of living was greatly facilitated by the ready availability of increasing supplies at fairly stable prices';[74] the roots of the present crisis lay above all in the dramatic growth of oil and energy consumption and political developments in the producing countries. In order to achieve a 'more equitable and stable international energy relationship', it was vital to develop a comprehensive programme of action while – to quote a crucial compromise formula – 'building on' the work of the OECD. This would require the establishment of a coordinating group to flesh out the programme's approach to saving energy and reducing consumption; crisis response mechanisms; the development of alternative energy sources; and research and development. These were the points to which the French delegation was averse. In addition, however, the countries involved declared that they welcomed initiatives to discuss raw materials issues within the UN framework and were eager to see a joint conference with the producing countries.

In view of this outcome, different actors assessed the conference in widely divergent ways. While still at the airport, Jobert gave a much-noted interview, in which he excoriated the United States for using the conference as a pretext for asserting its political hegemony within the transatlantic alliance. According to Jobert, the Europeans had failed entirely to understand the gravity of the energy problem and had therefore been taken in by Kissinger's political manoeuvres; he had forced them into line by applying massive pressure.[75] Despite this, Jobert had earlier expressed satisfaction with the conference. He meant this, first, in an ironic sense: he had learned a few things about his own conduct and that of his European colleagues. Second, and more seriously, he had managed to preserve 'French independence'.[76] Ultimately, then, Jobert saw the conference as an embodiment of the US pursuit of hegemony, which had compelled him to defend French sovereignty, in conflict with the other Europeans, whom he viewed as 'traitors'.[77]

The West German government regretted the conflict with France and the resulting difficulties for European Political Cooperation. It was, however, fundamentally content with the result of the conference.[78] The furious reactions in certain Arab countries, such as Algeria, did nothing to change this. Abdessalam declared that the United States was attempting to restore its lost hegemony over energy policy.[79] Articles in the Algerian press asserted that 'Germany, Italy and Japan have demonstrated in Washington that they are not independent countries'; France's 'honest, firm and courageous' stance had been the only glimmer of light.[80] The UK's assessment was much like West Germany's, though the British recognized that, through the vehicle of energy policy, the Americans had succeeded in doing what they had failed to do through the Year of Europe.[81] In an attempt to assuage the incensed producing countries, Douglas-Home instructed the British embassies in the OPEC and OAPEC countries to adhere to the following line. The United States' decision to convene the conference had been 'courageous and wise', even if it had shown a lack of sensitivity at times.[82] The UK would have preferred not to choose between France and the United States, but 'when French obduracy obliged us to choose, we had no repeat no hesitation', not least because, during the conference, every delegation had become convinced 'that the French should not get away with it this time'.[83] Given that the French government would no doubt attempt to use the result of the conference to its advantage in negotiations with the producing countries, British diplomats should act to counter this, always underlining the common interests of producers and consumers.

The US administration was extremely pleased with the outcome of the Washington Energy Conference. When Kissinger phoned Nixon to report back on the conference, he began by declaring that he had achieved almost all his goals.[84] As well as getting the EC countries to accept the communiqué, the US had taught them a lesson. Nixon emphatically agreed: 'The point is the European Community, instead of having that silly unanimity rule, learned they can't gang up against us and we can use it now we can use it on trade, security, with everything else'.[85] Kissinger took the same view, adding that the Americans too had recognized a crucial fact: 'It taught us an important lesson: if we really throw our weight around we can have our way'.[86] In public, of course, Kissinger and Nixon struck a quite different tone. On several occasions, Kissinger thanked Douglas-Home for his cooperation at the conference, while Nixon thanked Edward Heath; the conflict at the conference had not been between the United States and France but rather between 'cooperation' and 'ruinous isolation'.[87] Kissinger clothed the pursuit of the United States' national interests in the rhetoric of international cooperation. Only in an interview did he hint that other interpretations might be closer to the truth: '"Sometimes", he said amid laughter, "there are disagreements not because people do not understand each other but because they understand each other only too well"'.[88]

The American press too was overwhelmingly positive about the Energy Conference. Nixon's communicative strategy – of demonstrating strong political leadership on energy policy – had thus proved successful. Prior to the conference, he had already advised Kissinger: 'Give the press something after each session so that we get something positive on TV'.[89] In sum, the *Washington Post* concluded, the Washington Energy Conference amounted to the 'renewal of the Atlantic alliance under American leadership'.⁹⁰ Both the *New York Times* and *Washington Post* explained the concord evident among all the countries, except France, and their willingness to engage in international cooperation, as due chiefly to the compelling economic arguments put forward by Kissinger and Simon.⁹¹ Under the heading 'Two Cheers for France', meanwhile, James Reston described Michel Jobert as the conference's true consensus-builder: 'What Jobert did ... was to dramatize the dangers of nationalism in dealing with the world problems of defense, money, trade and energy ... He made Mr. Nixon look good ... without his eloquent defense of selfish nationalistic interests, we might have never understood how silly they were'.⁹² The spectre of French nationalism, he contended, had made Nixon's Project Independence and Kissinger's international offensive look like an altruistic project of benefit to all. Ultimately, according to Leonard Silk's analysis, the United States' strategy had succeeded for three reasons. Its proposals had been moderate; had entailed a potential threat due to the connection between energy and security; and were underpinned by ample economic power.⁹³

The West German press agreed that, rather than just oil, the Washington Energy Conference had been about the present and future of transatlantic relations, as well as the state of European unity and Europe's role in the world.⁹⁴ The oil crisis, argued Dieter Schröder in the *Süddeutsche Zeitung*, had brought the process of European integration to a 'moment of truth'.⁹⁵ In the face of this existential challenge, the 'veneer of a "common foreign policy"' had been torn away; the Europeans had behaved like castaways, eyeing each other suspiciously and anxious 'to improve their survival prospects by gaining minor advantages', to quote opinion pieces in the *Süddeutsche Zeitung* and *Frankfurter Rundschau* respectively.⁹⁶ The *Frankfurter Allgemeine Zeitung* opined that the Europeans had made a terrible impression or a disgraceful spectacle of themselves. Theatrical metaphors seem to have been the only way to convey these sentiments.⁹⁷ However, most commentators blamed the French for the conflict, excoriating them for failing to recognize the realities of the global oil economy. Even if European governments tried to preserve their and the EC's room for manoeuvre vis-à-vis the United States, they could never be on an equal footing with that country when it came to energy policy.⁹⁸ The United States' proposals on cooperation not only had power but also logic on their side, while the French alternative was a mere chimera, 'a rebellion of irrationalism against Europe's political environment'.⁹⁹ Despite the West German government's assurances that it had not chosen between France and the United States and no such decision was in the offing, the West German press was largely of one mind: if push came to shove, the country must back the US.¹⁰⁰

The International Energy Programme and the International Energy Agency

Having returned to their capitals, the delegations' priority was now to organize the 'follow-up' process and get the 'machinery' up and running that was supposed to reconfigure the world of oil as envisaged in the conference communiqué. Immediately after the Washington Energy Conference, Nixon invited representatives of the participating countries to an initial meeting of the Energy Coordinating Group in Washington on 25 February, in order, as Kissinger explained, 'to maintain [the] momentum' of the conference.[101] A fair number of European commentators were critical of the timing and choice of location. They felt Kissinger had made it de facto impossible for the EC member states to agree a common position while also seeming to hammer home US hegemony within the initiative in a spatial sense. Kissinger was flexible when it came to the location, but insisted on the schedule, believing it vital to quickly sort out procedural issues and allocate tasks. Ultimately, as Kissinger declared to his counterpart Scheel, this was about how the West might best 'preserve its internal order and authority'. In other words, domestic as well as international sovereignty was at stake.[102] In line with the American vision, the Coordinating Group was to tackle a heterogeneous and broad catalogue of topics: energy-saving measures; the accelerated development of conventional energy sources; 'oil sharing'; international cooperation on research and development and uranium enrichment; the economic and financial order; and relations with the producing countries, Third World and international oil companies.[103]

According to the leading members of the West German delegation at the first two meetings of the Coordinating Group in Brussels in February and March, they were productive, and after France had pulled out, proceeded in a pleasant atmosphere.[104] An ad hoc working group chaired by the West Germans was to shed light on research and development issues, an American-led one would consider uranium enrichment, while the Italian delegation would head up a working group dedicated to the role of the international oil companies. The discussion of other topics was outsourced to existing international organizations: the development of conventional energy, oil sharing, energy saving and development aid to the OECD; and monetary and financing problems to the World Bank, International Monetary Fund and OECD. The Coordinating Group itself dealt with relations with other consuming countries, developing countries and producing countries (under UK leadership), possible international institutions to channel the producing countries' long-term investments (West Germany), the development of the international oil market (United States) and the prospects for accelerated socioeconomic development in the producing countries (West Germany).¹⁰⁵

Initially, most of the working groups got stuck into their work and obtained the necessary information from the participating countries. In early May, however, momentum dwindled.¹⁰⁶ The working group considering the role of the oil companies in the international oil economy had been unable to reach agreement. Meanwhile, Dixy Lee Ray, head of the US Atomic Energy Commission, placed tight restrictions on the transfer of US uranium enrichment technology.¹⁰⁷ Differing views on oil price forecasts persisted. While the American delegation adhered to the optimistic analysis produced by Simon's Federal Energy Office, which predicted that the oil price would soon level off at seven dollars a barrel, the other delegations were more sceptical.¹⁰⁸ Early on, the British had advocated direct talks with the producing countries, but by early May, following the Special Session of the UN General Assembly on the problem of raw materials, a consensus emerged that there should be no attempt to communicate with the producing countries until both sides had formulated a coherent position.

In June, these debates regained momentum when the Americans canvassed an Integrated Emergency Programme. While this might not render oil crises such as that of October 1973 impossible, the Americans asserted, it would greatly mitigate their impact. In addition to the general problem of prices and the search for investment options for petrodollars, this crisis prevention mechanism was central to the debates carried on over the next few months, with the Energy Coordinating Group trying to establish a transatlantic oil sharing system. The High Level Group Oil had had something similar in mind as an extension of the purely European allocation system, but this had failed to get off the ground at a time when the industrialized countries had merely anticipated the oil crisis but had yet to actually experience it.¹⁰⁹ While there was general approval for oil sharing in principle, some details required clarification, namely how the mechanism would be triggered and which organization would administer it. The US delegation long resisted the idea that the OECD should administer the programme, considering it overly bureaucratic. Finally, however, it relented in order to make it easier for the Europeans, who had always expressed opposition to a new institution, to give their consent.¹¹⁰

In late September, the foreign ministers signed a draft agreement on an International Energy Programme (IEP). This would be implemented by an International Energy Agency (IEA), to be established within the framework of the OECD. In addition to the countries' agreement, then, this would require a resolution of the OECD Council, which it passed on 15 November 1974, with abstentions from Finland, France and Greece.¹¹¹ In addition to the crisis mechanism, which would 'respond to oil supply crises', the International Energy Programme entailed a set of long-term measures 'to foster a secure oil supply on sensible and fair terms'.[112] The signatory states of Belgium, Denmark, West Germany, Ireland, Japan, Canada, Luxembourg, the Netherlands, Austria, Sweden, Switzerland, Spain, Turkey, the United Kingdom and the United States were 'determined to reduce their dependency on oil imports through long-term efforts to advance cooperation on: the rational use of energy; the accelerated development of alternative energy sources; research and development in the energy field; and uranium enrichment'.[113]

In case of acute supply crises in one or more participating countries, it was agreed that if oil imports declined by more than 7 per cent of normal oil consumption, the affected countries must implement energy-saving measures to cover that amount. In addition, an oil allocation system would evenly distribute the burden of oil shortfalls among participating states, factoring in both required minimum stockpiles and domestic production. To give the crisis mechanism the 'necessary punch', it would be triggered automatically if the Secretariat confirmed the existence of a shortage.[114] This automatic element distinguished the International Energy Programme from the oil sharing already established for the European OECD countries prior to the oil crisis. This could be activated only through a unanimous decision, which proved impossible to achieve under the conditions of the oil crisis.[115] Within the new system, once set in motion, the Administrative Board would require a qualified majority to stop the measures within fifteen days. The member countries' votes were weighted in accordance with oil consumption in such a way that neither the Europeans nor the Americans and Japanese together could outvote the rest. If, to quote Carl Schmitt's classic formula, only those who possess the authority to impose 'a state of emergency [are] sovereign', the automatic activation of the crisis mechanism in emergency situations meant that the nation states had delegated sovereignty to an international authority or abstract mechanism. National governments could regain their freedom of action and deactivate the crisis response mechanism only through cooperation with other participating countries. So, within a specific policy field, under direct pressure from the oil crisis, in which national strategies had exacerbated price increases, governments bound their own hands in order to preserve and safeguard a far more fundamental form of sovereignty over energy.

The establishment of a system of information on the international oil market in general, and the potential to implement emergency measures in particular, was intended to serve the same end. Simon's statement that during the oil crisis the lack of data and knowledge had prevented the US government from pursuing an effective energy policy seemed even more pertinent on the international level. On the work of the High Level Group during the oil crisis, Ulf Lantzke reported: 'It soon became clear that a reliable assessment of the world-market situation was not at all easy to obtain; information available to the governments of the industrialized countries, as well as to the oil companies, concerning events in the oil-producing countries was incomplete, contradictory, and confusing'.[116] In order to reduce this uncertainty, from now on the national governments were to provide the Secretariat with regular reports on the oil firms active on their territory.[117] Given their central position within the international oil economy, both oil sharing and the information system could work only with the cooperation of the multinational oil firms. At an initial meeting, the heads of the major multinational companies seemed willing to cooperate in principle, but expressed reservations about the information system. C.O. Peyton of Exxon, for example, conceded that the era in which the firms controlled the oil market alone was over: 'The new circumstances prevailing in international oil markets indicate both individual governments and inter-governmental organizations must inevitably play a more active role therein'.[118] Highlighting the firms' specific expertise in the production of petro-knowledge, however, he asserted that a general information system would make sense only if the International Energy Programme avoided duplicating the knowledge resources already provided by the firms and, in a first step, acquired a precise knowledge of the oil companies' logistical systems. Only then could the Programme collect and make available relevant information on oil sharing in case of crisis. Along with his colleagues, however, Peyton warned that the new system must be designed in such a way as to preserve 'commercial confidentiality'. Since the firms' expertise and economic potential were indispensable, working groups headed by Exxon and BP developed, respectively, an information system and an oil sharing mechanism as envisaged by the IEP.[119] To a significant extent, the firms' interest in an information system that was formally independent but used their data may have been due to the criticism they faced during and after the oil crisis.[120]

The West German Economics Ministry warmly welcomed the International Energy Programme. It would eliminate the 'lack of information about the international oil companies' activities evident during the last crisis', while also providing an effective crisis mechanism to deal with future supply shortfalls.[121] Though it was regrettable that France was not participating in the IEA, this was balanced out by the integration of the United States into a system of oil sharing.[122] The International Energy Programme, the West Germans contended, was a necessary supplement to the national crisis response measures, whose limits had been laid bare in the months since October 1973. They believed there was no clash between the Programme and EC energy policy, not least because the goals of the latter could only be achieved by including non-European consuming countries.[123] When it came to the problem of oil and energy, then, guaranteeing sovereignty turned out to be too large a task not just for individual states but even for the alliance of Western European countries in the EC.[124]

While in most countries it was the foreign ministries that sent representatives to the IEA, in West Germany the Economics Ministry took on this role, thus shaping the country's stance towards the international politics of energy as a whole. The West German representatives on the Governing Board, the Standing Group on Emergency Questions and Standing Group on the Oil Market were also dispatched by the Economics Ministry. The West German spokesmen in the Standing Group on Long-Term Co-operation and the Committee on Budget and Expenditure came from the Ministry for Research and Technology or Finance Ministry, and only with a great deal of effort did the Foreign Ministry manage to secure the country's seat in the Standing Group on Relations with Producer and other Consumer Countries, despite competition from the Economics Ministry. Thus, the West Germans at least regarded the IEA not so much as a foreign policy organization but more as an economic policy one, in which – as had already occurred within the framework of the OECD – experts from the ministries interacted directly. This shift was expedited and diagnosed by Helmut Schmidt, who had now become chancellor; a few weeks after the establishment of the IEA on 17 January 1975, he opened the SPD's foreign policy conference by observing that 'today, for us, [foreign policy is] not a specialized discipline of well-dressed, well-behaved diplomats with white beards, but [is] at once world economic policy, world materials policy, world agricultural policy, world monetary policy, world development policy and world security policy'.[125] The present era, Schmidt went on, was characterized by 'a universal system of mutual dependencies among nations' and 'total interdependence of political and economic policy developments', which had been both demonstrated and moulded by the oil crisis in particular.[126] It was thus vital to find new ways of organizing international politics. Like Schmidt, many political scientists too considered the oil crisis an indication – and paradigmatic example – of the transformation of international relations. The founding of the International Energy Agency in particular, which C. Fred Bergsten placed within a third wave of international institution-building, was viewed as a prime example of 'transgovernmental coalitions among governmental sub-units with complementary policies and interests'. Robert Keohane and Joseph Nye regarded these coalitions as emblematic of a new era of international or transnational policymaking (chapter 7).[127]

The crisis mechanism developed against the backdrop of the first oil crisis, however, was unable to mitigate the Iranian Revolution's negative effects on the international oil market or prevent the so-called second oil crisis of 1978–79. Because the production shortfalls amounted to less than 7 per cent of the oil supply in the IEA countries, the crisis measures were not triggered. At the same time, due to the high degree of uncertainty, the oil price rose dramatically on the spot markets. Both the second oil crisis and the upheavals in the wake of the Gulf War of 1990–91, however, led to the modification and flexibilization of the crisis mechanism.[128] Nonetheless, the key function of the International Energy Agency consisted neither in crisis prevention nor in long-term energy policy cooperation, though the IEP had begun to consider them and the IEA's Long-Term Cooperation Programme of 1976 and Principles for Energy Policy spelt them out in more detail.[129] Instead, up to the present, the IEA is crucial because it collects and processes oil-related data. Shortly after its establishment, this function was fulfilled by the Crude Oil Import Price Information System, Petroleum Product Price Information System, Crude Oil Cost Information System and Financial Information System.[130]

Like the Oil Committee of the OECD, the IEA monitored its member countries' energy policies and made its reviews public. This put a certain amount of pressure on national governments while also providing them with policy ideas.[131] Beyond this, in addition to many other statistical documents, it periodically published detailed overviews of energy issues in the OECD countries, along with the *World Energy Outlook*.[132] Its first issue in 1977 already highlighted the epochal significance of the oil crisis, after which, as it emphasized, oil prices had risen dramatically but economic growth had slowed in the industrialized countries. Both phenomena, the publication contended, had resulted in greater uncertainty, making forecasts more difficult but also more necessary than ever.[133] Five years later, Ulf Lantzke, who had become the founding director of the IEA, underlined the significance of this development to the social and political order of Western Europe and the United States: 'Over the past decade, we have seen the energy problem strain our economies to an extent which has tested the social consensus on which Western democracies are built'.[134] Despite two oil crises and the energy policy efforts of the previous nine years, the director of the IEA diagnosed a high dependency on oil supplies and a resulting state of vulnerability, prompting him to call for a structural shift 'away from oil'. The IEA aimed to provide the necessary foundation of data and knowledge for the energy policies in the pipeline at the time, and it has remained one of the key producers and distributors of petro-knowledge ever since.

Alternative Ways of Organizing the World of Oil

Cooperation among the leading oil-consuming countries within the International Energy Agency was a way of reordering the world of oil after the experiences of the oil crisis. But this was just one approach within a historically open situation in which others were also discussed. During their negotiations in Washington and Brussels on an International Energy Programme, both the Western European countries and the United States repeatedly underlined that, ultimately, their goal was a more comprehensive form of cooperation that would include the producing and developing countries. Nonetheless, the multilateral communicative forums linking the producing and consuming countries – initiated at the same time by Algeria and France – were unsuccessful. Unlike the cooperation within the International Energy Agency, they neither created new structures for the production of petro-knowledge nor recast sovereignty within the world of oil. Nonetheless, the paths not taken are crucial to understanding developments whose outcome contemporaries could not know. In the mid 1970s, for a time at least, many observers had the impression that the conflict over scarce raw materials in general, and oil in particular, would fundamentally change the geography of global conflict.[135]

In the wave of decolonization after the Second World War, a number of states achieved political sovereignty. But their economies remained dependent on the former colonial powers, who generally benefitted from the structures of the international economic order. As new members of the United Nations, these states attempted to change these structures – which were detrimental to their interests – by means of its constituent organizations. From 1964 onwards, they sought to do this chiefly through the United Nations Conference on Trade and Development (UNCTAD), where the so-called developing countries banded together in the Group of 77 to push their demands in a coordinated way.[136] Having recognized that their political sovereignty was limited under existing economic conditions and could not be converted into true power, their main goal was to attain 'permanent sovereignty over natural resources' on their territory. At a summit in Algiers in September 1973, just a few weeks before the start of the oil crisis, the Non-Aligned Movement had expressed its dissatisfaction at the state of negotiations on a New International Economic Order, and called for a Special Session of the UN General Assembly to examine the issue. The steps taken by OPEC and OAPEC gave new impetus to this ambition, as they seemed to demonstrate the economic power that resource-rich developing countries could wield when they joined forces.[137] At the same time, the oil-producing countries, aware that those developing countries with few natural resources would be hardest hit by the oil price hikes, tried to mitigate their effects and position themselves as the vanguard of the movement for a New International Economic Order.[138] More than anyone else, Algerian head of state Houari Boumedienne emphasized that the 'oil war' had demonstrated the interdependence of countries across the world. This conflict, he contended, was not limited or even limitable to natural resources; it was an element in a global struggle for fairer terms of trade within a New International Economic Order.[139] Because of this – and in order to create an alternative to the Washington conference without limiting discussions to energy issues, as in the concurrent French initiative – on 31 January 1974 he asked UN secretary-general Kurt Waldheim to convene a Special Session of the General Assembly to consider this topic. In mid February, a majority of countries, including West Germany and the other EC countries, expressed their support for this, so from 9 April to 2 May 1974 the Sixth Special Session of the United Nations discussed possible changes to the global economic order.[140]

This Session saw a clash between countries with fundamentally different ideas about what the oil crisis meant for the global economy. Oil and energy were entirely absent from the first third of Houari Boumedienne's opening speech. Instead he presented the Non-Aligned Movement's objective, now that its members had achieved political sovereignty, of advancing their economic development. This, he claimed, could not be achieved within the traditional structures of the global economy because the industrialized countries had a monopoly on the production of industrial goods while also controlling the global commodities markets and the prices of raw materials; Algeria had understood that this was the key to truly sovereign equality within the international system: 'Immediately upon receiving their sovereignty, the Algerian people applied themselves to carrying out the vast undertaking of recovering their natural resources, in order to enable the state and the people to take actual control of the national economy into their own hands'.[141] As the Non-Aligned Movement had concluded at a summit in Algiers in September 1973, without national control of the exploitation of raw materials and their prices, there could be no economic development in the Third World; the actions taken by OPEC and OAPEC were merely a consistent expression of this insight and demonstrated the importance of raw materials to national sovereignty.[142] Boumedienne urged those developing countries that were suffering most from the rising oil price, which had no oil reserves of their own, not to view the oil embargo and oil price hikes as a problem. Instead they should consider them an object lesson and source of hope. The major oil-consuming countries' 'violent reaction' at the Washington Energy Conference merely showed how afraid they were that the steps taken by OPEC and OAPEC might set an example for others to follow.[143] Boumedienne identified the objective of the Special Session as establishing the principles of a new world economic order, which should begin with the transformation of the commodities markets: 'First the developing countries must take over their natural resources, which implies, essentially, nationalizing the exploitation of these resources and controlling the machinery governing the determination of their prices'.[144] Having nationalized key industries, they must form cartels with other countries, helping them to safeguard their sovereignty by surrendering some of it to a collective. By generalizing the problem of oil and energy and including all raw materials, Boumedienne tried to preserve the fragile unity of the Third World, while exploiting the momentum of the oil crisis to advance longstanding demands for change in the global economy.

None of the industrialized countries that had attended the Washington Energy Conference expressed unqualified support for these analyses or the associated demands. In the run-up to the UN Special Session, the US and West German governments were already dubious about its prospects of success.[145] Kissinger still thought it dangerous to enter into a global dialogue before the industrialized countries had united around a common position, fearing this might strengthen the more radical among the developing countries. Meanwhile, Walter Gehlhoff, German ambassador to the United Nations, considered the preliminary documents produced by the Group of 77 an inadequate basis for entering into a serious dialogue. The West German Cabinet thus concluded that the Special Session might well exacerbate rather than ease the North-South conflict.[146]

As expected, at the Special Session it was Henry Kissinger who most clearly expressed opposition to the Group of 77 proposals. He rejected the simple distinction between developed and developing countries as anachronistic; it failed to take account of the tremendous shifts in wealth triggered by the oil price hikes. Furthermore, due to the interdependence of global economic relations, all countries were in the same boat. Neither a single country nor a group of countries could act with total independence or sovereignty.[147] It was not just the industrialized countries but also their developing counterparts that must accept this. Over the long term, gaining sovereignty over raw materials would only benefit them if it occurred with the agreement of the industrialized nations and did not threaten global economic development.[148] Kissinger's catalogue of priorities for the Special Session looked correspondingly different. As he saw it, to foster growth and development for all, the primary prerequisite was a sufficient supply of energy at reasonable prices. This would require a collective effort to enhance expertise on energy and raw materials: 'In the long term, our hopes for world prosperity will depend on our ability to discern the long-range patterns of supply and to forecast future imbalances so as to avert dangerous cycles of surplus and shortage'.[149] In an attempt to sow discord among the developing countries, Kissinger identified the relationship between nutrition and population growth and the situation of the least developed countries without raw materials as the greatest challenges. The contrast between Kissinger and Boumedienne, who seem to have regarded each other's talks as confrontational, could scarcely have been greater, and extended into every detail.[150] Boumedienne justified the oil price hikes in light of the decline in the oil price over the preceding years and the concurrent increase in the cost of finished products, cereals and artificial fertilizer. Kissinger, meanwhile, explained the rising cost of fertilizer, which hit many developing countries hard, as a consequence of oil price increases.

It was not only Boumedienne's speech and the design of the Session — whose driving force he was — that expressed broad common interests of the countries of the so-called Third World; the basic tone of Yamani's and Jamshid Amouzegar's speeches was very similar. The Session also made it clear to the industrialized countries that their common interests boiled down to resolving the problem of energy rather than establishing a new world economic order. As he had done two months earlier in Washington, Walter Scheel again spoke in his dual role. As German foreign minister, like Kissinger he sought to create division within the Third World front. He declared that while the industrialized countries had been affected by the oil crisis, it had not hit their 'nerve centre'; for the many developing countries that could no longer buy fertilizer, on the other hand, this was a matter of sheer survival.[151] Scheel acknowledged the Third World's demand for development, but he emphasized that the realities of the global economy were too complex for it to be rapidly reorganized on the basis of new principles. Reflecting on trends in the energy and financial markets, Scheel also expressed a 'sense of failure, of inadequacy ... of uncertainty and helplessness'. He believed there was a fundamental threat to sovereign policymaking: 'volatility of data, accelerating changes, unpredictability: here governments, or states, come up against the limits. They cannot deal with these problems alone, on an every-man-for-himself basis. . . . All of us have to adapt to a reality whose future course we can no longer determine alone. We are stumbling around in the dark, believing that anonymous forces are holding the reins and manipulating us all'.[152]

When speaking as president of the EC Council, Scheel was more down to earth than Scheel the West German foreign minister. He affirmed the EC's willingness to provide development aid and to consider economic concessions for the developing countries. At the same time, he highlighted that the functioning of the global economy must not be put at risk. Above all, multilateral institutions like General Agreement on Tariffs and Trade must remain in place and be expanded, while any lapse into bilateralism should be avoided.¹⁵³ Jobert shared many of Boumedienne's concerns, but he emphasized that the problem of energy, which was of existential significance to most countries' economies and thus their individual citizens, must form the core of collective efforts. Feeling snubbed, largely because Algeria had managed to arrange the Special Session in parallel or in competition with France's initiative, he argued that sovereignty over energy sources implied a special responsibility:

> In proposing a world energy conference France merely recognized the capital importance of energy raw materials. The development of our nation rests wholly on them. As natural resources, they come of course under the sovereignty of producer States. As a condition of modern economic life, they represent, however, a special responsibility for all those who profit from them – and I naturally include among them the large international companies.¹⁵⁴

The commodities markets, he asserted, must therefore be organized on a global basis; it was also vital to ensure greater transparency, for example when it came to price trends.

The two-week general debate laid bare fundamental differences. Northern governments contended that the focus must be on tackling the oil and energy crisis and its consequences. Their Third World counterparts, meanwhile, wished to use these issues as an opportunity to pursue root-and-branch change in the global economic order. These conflicting interests impeded debates in the ad hoc committee, which was tasked with agreeing a compromise. The committee discussed a declaration and programme of action from the Group of 77 and, from France, a blueprint for regulation of the commodities markets together with a draft aid programme for the least developed countries. Through the brokerage of committee chair and Iranian UN ambassador Fereydoon Hoveyda, a modified version of the Group of 77 proposal attracted broad consent, though no vote was held. In the closing session, therefore, the representatives of the US and West German governments were already distancing themselves from the Declaration on the Establishment of a New International Economic Order.¹⁵⁵

The Declaration, along with the programme of action intended to put it into effect, envisaged an economic order based on 'equity, sovereign equality, interdependence, common interest and cooperation among all States'.¹⁵⁶ In addition to general principles of sovereignty, the New International Economic Order was to be distinguished by 'full permanent sovereignty of every State over its natural resources and all economic activities'. This must include the right to nationalize transnational firms and regulate them by fixing the relationship between the price of commodities and industrial goods, and the right to establish preferential trading areas and producers' associations. In other words, states would attain sovereignty by forgoing sovereignty.[157] It was these points that most concerned West Germany and the other industrialized countries. They took the view that compensation for expropriation must reflect international law, while tying commodities prices to those of finished products would exacerbate inflation, which was already high. Producers' cartels, meanwhile, contravened the principles of open world trade.[158] The West German government considered the Special Session a success for Algeria because it had foiled the West's plan to sow division among the developing countries. It also believed that, while the formal consensus had no legally binding force, it might have a powerful political and moral impact in future negotiations. The fear was that it would strengthen the developing countries' self-confidence and power within the United Nations, where the North-South rather than the East-West conflict would now be played out.[159]

For more than a year, as the developing countries attempted to derive a legally binding framework from the Declaration, the theme of a New International Economic Order and the resulting conflict did in fact occupy various UN bodies.[160] The topic was also on the agenda at the Twenty-Ninth General Assembly of the United Nations, which took place in September 1974 under the chairmanship of the Algerian Abdelaziz Bouteflika. Kissinger now constructed the present era as a time of global decision. The world must choose whether to pursue a path of increasing conflict or develop a new global order, which would require the abandonment of traditional ideas of national sovereignty.[161] In a rare show of unanimity, he, Jobert and the new British foreign minister James Callaghan concluded that the oil price was too high and represented a threat to global economic development.[162] This analysis, however, failed to impress the developing countries. At conferences of the United Nations Environment Programme (UNEP) and UNCTAD in October 1974, they used their voting majority to push through the Declaration on the Establishment of a New International Economic Order, which added ecological perspectives to acknowledgement of the resource problem. The Cocoyoc Declaration fundamentally challenged the growth paradigm and called for the redistribution of global wealth. It also noted, with a certain amount of satisfaction, that when it came to sovereignty, 'in an area critical to the economies of industrialized States, a profound reversal of power exposes them to the condition long familiar in the third world – a lack of control over vital economic decisions'.[163]

In December 1974, in the shape of Resolution 3281 – against the votes of the United States, West Germany, the United Kingdom, Belgium, Luxembourg and Denmark, with ten abstentions – the UN adopted the Charter of Economic Rights and Duties of States, which had been in the pipeline since 1972 within the framework of UNCTAD. The Charter, which was, again, not legally binding, affirmed the key points of the Declaration on the Establishment of a New International Economic Order: permanent sovereignty over natural resources, the right to nationalize in line with national laws and the right to establish consumers' organizations.[164] The conflict over the legal basis for nationalizations continued at the Third General Conference of the United Nations Industrial Development Organization (UNIDO) in March 1975, and at the Seventh Special Session of the UN General Assembly, which passed the Resolution on Development and International Economic Cooperation in September 1975.[165] Within the UN framework, the developing countries or Group of 77 achieved major symbolic successes, turning the changes in the world of oil and energy into an argument for a transformation of the world economic order and pushing through corresponding resolutions, despite objections from the major industrialized countries. Because the United States, Western Europe and Japan rejected the principles of such a new order, however, the declarations had no real effect. Nonetheless, for many observers, at least for a brief time, it seemed as though the oil crisis had altered global power relations and diminished the scope for national sovereignty, in the field of energy and far beyond it. Because a New International Economic Order or the global redistribution of wealth would have meant reduced prosperity in the industrialized countries, the associated debates in these states fuelled anxiety about the stability of the democratic system.[166]

The multilateral conference of the producing, consuming and developing countries on energy issues, which France had envisaged as a competitor to the Washington Energy Conference and the International Energy Agency, made less impact than the UN sessions. Ultimately, this attempt at a collective reordering of the world of oil was wrecked due to the emergence of a consumers' organization and the developing countries' demand that energy issues be discussed only in the context of a more general restructuring of the commodities markets. By January 1974, when President Nixon invited the leading consumer countries to the Washington Energy Conference, the French government had declared that, rather than an association of the consumers, it wanted to see a multilateral dialogue with the producing countries and those developing countries that lacked oil and other raw materials, a position it reiterated during and after the conference. It was not until Giscard d'Estaing had succeeded the late Pompidou as president of France and the other industrialized countries seemed poised to agree the International Energy Programme that the French plans took on more concrete form. On 24 October, Giscard, who was considered more cooperative and pro-American than his predecessor, presented the French plan for ten to twelve countries – half of them exporting and half importing countries – to participate in a conference and look for solutions to the energy problem, which, he contended, was responsible for the current economic crisis.¹⁶⁷ The invitations followed the so-called Yamani formula, that is, they included the EC, the United States, Japan, Brazil, India, Zaire, Iran, Venezuela, Saudi Arabia and Algeria, along with the United Nations, OECD and OPEC as observers. In addition to the nation states, which were to represent the views of the consuming, producing and developing countries, international organizations were supposed to play a significant role.

Both the British and American governments were irked by the French initiative, which added yet another multilateral forum to the existing ones. The West German government was unsure what precisely the conference was supposed to achieve, and fundamentally dubious that the mix of countries involved would facilitate concrete results.¹⁶⁸ The British government in particular considered representation by the EC inadequate and attempted to ensure that at least the United Kingdom, France and West Germany would be represented as well.¹⁶⁹ Another contentious issue was whether the IEA would be granted observer status.¹⁷⁰ Even less clear than the rules of procedure was what exactly the conference was supposed to discuss. As a result, all the relevant governments developed comprehensive but haphazard catalogues of objectives, which did little to facilitate agreement.¹⁷¹ In light of these conflicts, a preliminary conference in Paris – to which the French government invited the various countries in March 1975 on the basis of the Yamani formula – would seek to answer the outstanding questions concerning participants, procedures and agenda.¹⁷²

As the numerous international energy conferences of 1974 had shown, at this point in time there was still great divergence in the major consuming countries' views on energy policy. Like Kissinger, Helmut Schmidt thus considered it inappropriate to enter into dialogue with the producing and developing countries in the absence of a prior agreement among the consumers. By December 1974, therefore, he had already proposed to his colleagues in France, the United States and the United Kingdom that in the first instance a small group of experts should identify common objectives and strategies prior to the preliminary conference in Paris. Here Schmidt – like Nixon during the preparations for the Washington Energy Conference – seemed to assume that it was mostly political considerations that hindered consensus-building on energy, but that this could be rapidly achieved by government-independent experts. He thus suggested to Harold Wilson, Giscard and Gerald Ford that up to fifteen experts, not members of any government but with access to the highest levels of government, should meet unofficially and without public declarations in the anonymity of a major German city. There they should draw up proposed solutions for 'all major problems that have arisen for the world economy as an upshot of the oil price explosion'.[173] After initially pondering whether the kind of people Schmidt envisaged actually existed – competent but not in government – the Wilson government appointed Sir Eric Roll of the Warburg banking house; West Germany sent Wilfried Guth, who was responsible for foreign business on the executive board of Deutsche Bank; the United States dispatched ex-treasury secretary George Shultz; and France sent economist Raymond Barre, EC commissioner for economic and financial affairs from 1967 to 1973.[174] The composition of the group, which met for the first time in early February in Kronberg near Frankfurt, showed that the leading industrialized countries had ceased to view energy issues as such as the main problem. By now they were far more focused on the upheavals in the global financial and monetary system triggered by the oil price hikes.

At the preliminary conference, which took place in Paris in mid April, the representatives of the industrialized countries were remarkably and untypically united. The EC managed to act as a unity; even France only broke ranks briefly at the end of the conference, departing from the common negotiating position in an attempt to obtain the consent of the developing countries.[175] However, the very unity of the EC, the United States and Japan prevented the preliminary conference from reaching a conclusion; the seven developing and producing countries also adopted a common position and, on many points, espoused views diametrically opposed to those of the industrialized countries. While the latter wished to limit the negotiations to energy issues, the developing and producing countries demanded that raw materials and development issues should have equal billing. In view of these antagonisms and both camps' intransigence, the only thing that stopped the preliminary conference from falling apart was its suspension after nine days and no results.[176] The international response to the abortive conference was relaxed.[177] Most industrialized countries had been sceptical about the French initiative and believed it had little chance of success. They therefore felt little disappointment, particularly given that there were other forums available in the shape of the IEA and United Nations.[178] In significant part, it is likely to have been this assessment that had prompted the European countries to allow the EC to represent their interests on a common basis. Nonetheless, the official collapse of the dialogue – to which the industrialized countries had committed themselves so often – seemed to entail incalculable risks. They therefore made a serious effort to resume the talks and ensure their successful conclusion. In early June, the West German government sent Hans-Jürgen Wischnewski, minister of state in the Foreign Ministry, on a 'fact-finding mission' to the seven producing and developing countries in order to get a clearer idea of their intentions.[179] Unsurprisingly, Wischnewski described Algeria as the most radical country; the Saudi Arabian government, he asserted, was the only one to understand global economic realities and had thus adopted a moderate stance.[180] For Zaire, he went on, the increased costs of energy were of minor importance, but they posed serious problems for Brazil and India, the latter being hardest hit by the crisis. Every country, he explained, was prepared to restart the conference, as long as it dealt with issues of energy, raw materials and development on an equal basis.[181] Wischnewski's trip reinforced the West German government's assessment that the conference could only continue with an expanded catalogue of topics, including raw materials and development.[182]

When the preliminary conference reconvened in Paris from 13 to 17 October, the industrialized countries were ready to expand the range of topics and the group of participating states. Beginning in December, the now twenty-seven attending countries, divided into four working groups – each featuring ten developing and producing countries along with five industrialized ones – were to discuss the themes of energy, raw materials, development and financial affairs.[183] Many observers, however, remained sceptical about the conference's prospects of success. It was supposed to uphold the principle of consensus and the negotiating guidelines had been kept highly general. For example, the energy working group was to 'facilitate all arrangements that seem desirable in the field of energy'.[184] At the conference, the EC largely spoke with one voice. However, in addition to France, as the country that had convened the conference, the United Kingdom and Luxembourg demanded speaking rights, the former due to its 'special energy situation' and the latter as the next country to hold the EC Council presidency.[185]

In contrast to the Energy Coordinating Group after the Washington Energy Conference, over the course of 1976 the working groups established at the Paris Conference on International Economic Cooperation – each of them chaired by one industrialized and one developing country – were slow to take up their work. The energy working group certainly addressed all energy-related topics, but it achieved virtually no agreement, due to sharp differences over how the energy problem related to the other topics and what role energy ought to play within the overall framework of the conference. In addition to the United States' proposal for the establishment of an International Energy Institute, the first key item of debate was a paper from the IEA. This asserted that oil was merely a transitional form of energy and must be superseded by other energy sources. There was unanimous support for this basic statement. But it proved impossible to reach agreement regarding its temporal implications. No meaningful consensus was attained on these topics or those addressed by the other committees. The conference thus ended with a communiqué; in addition to a number of vacuous points of agreement, this identified at least as many specific disagreements. For example, it was agreed that oil and gas were exhaustible, and renewable energies and energy saving were therefore necessary. The communiqué put forward general recommendations on national and international energy policies and expressed a desire to improve development aid. But there was – explicitly – no agreement on the level of energy prices, ways of safeguarding the producing countries' purchasing power, the New International Economic Order, the developing countries' debt, the regulation of transnational firms, or anti-inflationary measures.[186]

The relevant UN bodies made no substantial progress on these issues either over the next few years. Instead, the industrialized countries focused on cooperation within the International Energy Agency, while the producing countries reached agreement too, chiefly within OPEC or through bilateral negotiations. Dialogue with the producing countries also receded into the background at the IEA, as Ulf Lantzke noted upon his retirement in 1984.[187] Over the next few years, then, the idea of fundamentally restructuring the world of oil through cooperation between the producing and consuming countries – to which all actors had publicly committed themselves during the oil crisis of 1973–74 – came to grief due to the massive clash of interests between the industrialized and developing countries. The former aimed to ensure a sufficient supply of energy for their economies at stable prices and sought to control the flow of petrodollars. The producing countries, meanwhile, in alliance with those developing countries lacking in oil reserves, sought to achieve a more fundamental restructuring of the world economy to their own benefit.

Studies on specific fields like energy policy (such as the present book) and above all those concerned with foreign policy, all too easily forget that the aspects they privilege from a historical perspective were only ever one element in a much broader mix of issues; contemporary politicians, along with interested members of the public, were concerned with many other things at the same time. In the 1970s, in addition to energy, global finance and North-South relations, which were the focus of the international conferences discussed here, the dominant international theme was the policy of détente between East and West. This was recast at the Conference on Security and Cooperation in Europe (CSCE). Convened in Helsinki in July 1973, just a few months before the oil crisis, the CSCE process reached an initial peak in the Helsinki Final Act, signed on 1 August 1975. The so-called three baskets of the Final Act laid down general tenets of international politics, created a framework for concrete cooperation on economy, science, technology and environment, and underlined the principles of humanitarian cooperation.[188]

At the opening of the CSCE, Soviet Foreign Minister Andrei Gromyko already proposed a follow-up conference devoted to cooperation on energy. After it had finished, Leonid Brezhnev reiterated this proposal at a congress of the Polish Communist Party.[189] In March–April 1976, during a meeting of the UN Economic Commission for Europe, the Soviet Union then officially presented the Western European countries with a proposal for a pan-European conference to consider shared environmental, transport and energy problems. When it came to energy, this would focus chiefly on 'large-scale projects . . . with due regard for available energy resources in Europe' and 'questions [such] as interlinking of the European electrical power and gas-supply systems, and joint construction of large-size fuel-energy enterprises based on coal, brown coal, lignite and natural gas deposits'.[190] Both the European Commission and the West German government believed that the main motives for this initiative were the Soviet interest in capital and technology from the West and the Eastern Bloc countries' exclusion from the comprehensive talks being pursued within the Conference on International Economic Cooperation.

The Western Europeans were, to some degree, interested in closer cooperation on energy with the Eastern European countries, as long as energy and above all gas imports from these states engendered no critical dependency. Nonetheless, as a Commission working paper concluded, this proposal clearly reflected Soviet interests. In the shape of the Economic Commission for Europe, the Conference on International Economic Cooperation and UN and OECD bodies, the paper contended, there were already plenty of multilateral organizations capable of examining these issues. In fact, it went on, when it came to the fields of energy, transportation and environment, the EC member states had scarcely enough qualified individuals to populate the existing bodies. As a result, the EC Commission saw no good reasons either to accept or reject the proposed conference and was, therefore, dilatory in its response. The idea finally fizzled out, not least because, around the same time, the North-South dialogue had achieved virtually nothing, whereas bilateral negotiations had notched up some notable successes. The West German government shared this assessment, in large part because the relevant officials in the Foreign Ministry had serious doubts that there were 'any topics in the field of energy suited to discussion at European conferences'.[191]

Interim Conclusion

The oil crisis not only laid bare the crucial significance of oil to the industrialized countries' economic development. It also showed that energy issues were ultimately global ones. Because the global nature of the oil economy exceeded individual states' capacity for effective action, governments looked for international and transnational solutions. They failed to create – through the United Nations or the Conference on International Economic Cooperation – a truly global body that might have enabled the industrialized, producing and developing countries to jointly address these issues. But the two organizations that survived or emerged from the permanent changes in the global energy landscape of the 1970s, namely OPEC and the IEA, were at least global in their aspirations and reach, and they continued to influence oil and energy policies in the following decades. When it came to energy, both producing and consuming countries concluded that the only way to safeguard their sovereignty was to relinquish some of it to international organizations. Given the global balance of power, the time for an autonomous European energy policy was over before it had truly begun, just as the United States' Project Independence was redefined by the very energy experts who were meant to make it happen.

It would, however, be too simplistic to conclude – in light of the slew of conferences held in the 1970s and the tendency to form international associations – that the key political actors had recognized the increased economic interdependence and thus abandoned unilateral power politics. Despite contemporary claims to the contrary and the historical analyses that buy into them, the category of national sovereignty did not become obsolete in the 1970s. Instead, international organizations and associations served national governments as a means of securing their sovereignty. They used these bodies only to the extent that this strengthened their own sovereignty. The United States relinquished sovereignty to the IEA in order to prevent energy policy structures from emerging in Europe from which it would have been excluded. Most Europeans were willing to forego sovereignty in certain respects because, given the balance of economic power, they wished to avoid an energy policy confrontation with the United States. Much the same goes for the OPEC countries, which managed to agree common strategies chiefly when this served the interests of all. In the 1970s, the national politics of sovereignty persisted, while the leading political actors continued to think in terms of sovereignty. The narrative of a loss of sovereignty as a result of energy interdependence and the forces of globalization is thus inadequate. How, then, might we best fit the oil crisis into the history of sovereignty in the United States and Western Europe in the final third of the twentieth century?

Notes

1. OECD. Oil Section. High Level Group of the Oil Committee, 19th Session 25.10.1973; Abt. III, Lantzke an Bundesminister: Außerordentliche Sitzung der high-level-group am 25. Oktober, 23.10.1973; Schmidt (III C 2): Bericht über die Sitzung der high-level-group und des

OECD Mineralölausschusses, 26.10.1973, BArch, B 102/183432, Bd. 4 1973; Henning Türk, 'The Oil Crisis of 1973 as a Challenge to Multilateral Energy Cooperation among Western Industrialized Countries', *Historical Social Research* 39(4) (2014), 209–30.

2. Emmel, [Egon Heinrich]: Bericht über die Sitzung des Öl-Ausschusses der OECD, 26.10.1973, PA AA, B 36 (Referat 310), 104991; Kruse, [Hansheinrich]: Bericht über die Sitzung der High-Level-Group des Ölausschusses der OECD am 25.10.1973, 26.10.1973, PA AA, B 36 (Referat 310), 104991.

3. III C 2: Sitzung der High Level Group am 19.11.1973: Vorschlag für Stellungnahme, 16.11.1973; Lantzke: Vermerk: Ergebnis der High Level Group in Paris am 19.11.1973, 20.11.1973, BArch, B 102/183433, Bd. 5 1973.

4. Lantzke: Vermerk: Ergebnis der High Level Group in Paris am 19.11.1973, 20.11.1973, BArch, B 102/183433, Bd. 5 1973.

5. Detlev K. Rohwedder an Horst Grabert (BMWi): Gipfelkonferenz am 14./15. Dezember 1973, 13.12.1973, PA AA, B 71 (Referat 405), 113893; Möckli, *European Foreign Policy during the Cold War,* 258.

6. OECD. Oil Section. High Level Group of the Oil Committee, 21st Session 19.12.1973; III C 2: Sitzung der High Level Group am 19.12.1973, 17.12.1973, BArch, B 102/183433, Bd. 5 1973; Vogler: Sitzung von OECD-High-Level-Group und Ölausschuß am 19.12.1973, 22.12.1973, BArch, B 102/183434, Bd. 6 1973–74.

7. 'Document 494: Richard Nixon to Edward Heath, January 9, 1974', in Hamilton, *The Year of Europe*; on the function of diagnoses of crisis, see Rüdiger Graf, 'Either-Or: The Narrative of "Crisis" in Weimar Germany and in Historiography', *Central European History* 43(4) (2010), 592–615.

8. 'Nixon to Heads of OPEC, January 9, 1974', in Hamilton, *The Year of Europe*.

9. Moltmann (Algier) an Bonn: Erdoel als Waffe. hier: Erklaerungen von Minister Abdessalam in Tokyo, 30.1.1974, BArch, B 136/7683.

10. Möckli, *European Foreign Policy during the Cold War,* 253–300.

11. 'Botschafter von Staden, Washington, an das Auswärtige Amt, 5. Januar 1974', in Schwarz, *Akten zur Auswärtigen Politik der Bundesrepublik Deutschland 1974,* vol. 1, 16–18, here 18.

12. Lantzke an Friderichs: Kooperation zwischen Rohölförder- und -verbraucherländern; hier: Initiative von Außenminister Kissinger, 7.1.1974; Geisendörfer an Friderichs, 10.1.1973, BArch, B 102/201371.

13. Frank an Staden: Vorbereitung Gespräch mit Kissinger, Energiekonferenz, 31.1., VS. Bd. 528, PA AA, B 150, 297.

14. Sprechzettel für Kabinettsitzung am 16.1.1974: Vorschau auf Energiekonferenz, 15.1.1974, PA AA, B 71 (Referat 405), 113893.

15. 'Document 503: Palliser, UKREP Brussels tel 168, COREPER Discussion of Energy Conference, January 11, 1974', in Hamilton, *The Year of Europe*.

16. 'Document 509: Tel 120 to Washington: Decision of EC Council of Ministers to Accept Nixon's Conference Invitation, January 17, 1974', in Hamilton, *The Year of Europe*.

17. NARA, Nixon Library, NSC, Subject Files, Energy Crisis 1973–74, Box 321.

18. 'Document 507: Tel 110 to Washington: EC Political Directors Decision to Proceed with Euro-Arab Dialogue, January 16, 1974', in Hamilton, *The Year of Europe*; on the European-Arab dialogue, whose roots lay in a French initiative but which achieved little, see Aurélie Elisa Gfeller, 'A European Voice in the Arab World: France, the Superpowers and the Middle East, 1970–1974', *Cold War History* 11 (2011), 1–18; Tauer, *Störfall für die gute Nachbarschaft,* 155–60.

19. III D I: Vermerk: Vorbereitung der Konferenz über Energiefragen am 11.2. in Washington, 22.1.1974, BArch, B 102/201371; Kittel: Zusammentreffen der Leitenden Energiebeamten der EG-Länder mit Vizepräsident Simonet am 23. Januar 1974; Lautenschlager: Gespräch mit dem französischen Gesandten Morizet über die französischen Vorstellungen zur Einberu-

fung einer Weltenergiekonferenz im Rahmen der UN, 31.1.1974. PA AA, B 71 (Referat 405), 113893.

20. Kommission der EG: Empfehlung der Kommission für eine gemeinschaftliche Haltung für die Washingtoner Konferenz am 11.2.1974, 24.1.1974, BArch, B 102/201371.

21. Lantzke: Aufzeichnung zur Behandlung der Vorbereitung der Washingtoner Konferenz im EG Rat am 5.2.1974, PA AA, B 71 (Referat 405), 113893; for more detail on France's standpoint, see Gfeller, 'Imagining European Identity'; Gfeller, Building a European Identity, 85–113.

22. 'Document 547: Tomkins, Paris tel 185: French Approach to the Energy Conference, February 9, 1974', in Hamilton, The Year of Europe; see also 'Document 544: Paris tel 181: French Desire that Europe Should Not Appear to Be Acting under American Auspices, February 8, 1974', in Hamilton, The Year of Europe.

23. Lantzke: Aufzeichnung zur Behandlung der Vorbereitung der Washingtoner Konferenz im EG Rat am 5.2.1974, PA AA, B 71 (Referat 405), 113893.

24. 'Document 539: Steering Brief for Washington Conference, February 7, 1974', in Hamilton, The Year of Europe.

25. Bundeskanzler Brandt an Walter Scheel: Energiekonferenz, 8.2.1974, PA AA, B 71 (Referat 405), 113893.

26. 'Document 526: Note by Custis: Discussion between Carrington and Simonet, January 31, 1974', in Hamilton, The Year of Europe.

27. 'Document 286: Memorandum from Charles A. Cooper of the National Security Council Staff to Secretary of State Kissinger, Washington, January 21, 1974', in Qaimmaqami and Keefer, Energy Crisis.

28. Non-Paper der amerikanischen Botschaft zur Energiekonferenz am 11.2.1974, 30.1.1974, PA AA, B 71 (Referat 405), 113893.

29. Document 562: FCO Diplomatic Report 192/74 [R.A. Sykes]; 'The Washington Energy Conference, 10–13 February, 1974, 27.2.1974', in Hamilton, The Year of Europe.

30. 'Document 293: Minutes of the Secretary of State's Staff Meeting, Washington, January 31, 1974', in Qaimmaqami and Keefer, Energy Crisis.

31. 'Document 305: Memorandum of Conversation, Energy Conference, Washington, February 6, 1974', in Qaimmaqami and Keefer, Energy Crisis; in retrospect, Kissinger narrowed his goals down to the second point. Möckli adheres to this interpretation, but it fails to capture the complexity of the situation or the difficult international predicament of the oil crisis. Möckli, European Foreign Policy during the Cold War, 262.

32. 'Document 293. Minutes of the Secretary of State's Staff Meeting, Washington, January 31, 1974', in Qaimmaqami and Keefer, Energy Crisis.

33. 'Document 507: Tel 110 to Washington: EC Political Directors Decision to Proceed with Euro-Arab Dialogue'; 'Document 519: Tel 219 to Washington: HMG's Views of the Role of the Energy Conference, January 29, 1974' ; 'Document 520: Washington tel 351: US Preparations for Energy Conference, January 29, 1974'; 'Document 522: Douglas-Home: Tel 237 to Washington: US Paper on the Energy Conference, January 30, 1974', all in Hamilton, The Year of Europe; Memorandum of Conversation: Middle East Disengagement; Washington Energy Conference, Top Secret, 20 January 1974, DNSA, KT01006.

34. 'Document 525: Douglas-Home: Tel 251 to Washington: US Handling of Energy Task Force Proposal, January 31, 1974', in Hamilton, The Year of Europe; Memorandum of Conversation: Energy Conference [Discussion with Alec Douglas-Home] Secret, 10 February 1974, DNSA, KT01026; conversely, Möckli, European Foreign Policy during the Cold War, believes it was not until the conference that the Europeans' united front came undone as a result of Helmut Schmidt changing sides.

35. 'Document 530: Nixon to Heath: Visit from Experienced British Official, February 3, 1974', in Hamilton, The Year of Europe.

36. 'Document 533: Tom Bridges to Michael Alexander: Rampton to Visit Washington for Talks, February 4, 1974', in Hamilton, The Year of Europe.

37. Möckli, *European Foreign Policy during the Cold War*, 270; Nixon an Brandt, 4.2.1974, und Bahr an Kissinger, 4.2.1974, Archiv der Sozialen Demokratie, Nachlass Egon Bahr, EB 439.

38. Staden an AA: Gespräch Bahr-Kissinger, Energiekonferenz, 1.2.1974; Gespräch Scheel – Kissinger: Energiekonferenz, 10.2., VS.Bd. 14066, PA AA, B 150, 298.

39. 'Document 299: Paper Prepared in the Office of Economic Research, Central Intelligence Agency, Washington, February 4, 1974', in Qaimmaqami and Keefer, *Energy Crisis*.

40. 'Document 547: Tomkins, Paris tel 185: French Approach to the Energy Conference, February 9, 1974', in Hamilton, *The Year of Europe*.

41. Memorandum of Conversation: Washington Energy Conference, 9 February 1974, DNSA, KT01025.

42. Ibid.

43. Memorandum of Conversation: Middle East Disengagement; Washington Energy Conference [Talks with British Officials], Top Secret, 20 January 1974, DNSA, KT01006.

44. Among others, the ministers were accompanied by department head Peter Hermes (AA), division heads Helmut Redies and Hansheinrich Kruse (AA) and Undersecretary Karl Otto Pöhl (finances). From the Ministry of Economics, Undersecretary Detlev Karsten Rohwedder and department head Ulf Lantzke took part, along with a deputy department head and head of division from the Ministry of Research and Technology. Heinichen an Scheel: Genehmigung nachstehender Delegationsliste, 28.1.1974; Kruse an Diplogerma Washington; Energiekonferenz in Washington; here: Platzaufteilung, 4.2.1974, PA AA, B 71 (Referat 405), 113893.

45. Möckli, *European Foreign Policy during the Cold War*, 266.

46. CIA: International Oil Developments – Current Overview, 4 January 1974, CIA, Doc No/ESDN: 51112a4b993247d4d8394563; on the public debate, see Hans Roeper, 'Hohe Defizite untergraben die Weltwirtschaft: Die Auswirkungen der Ölverteuerung', *Frankfurter Allgemeine Zeitung*, 14 February 1974.

47. Opening Remarks of the Honorable Henry A. Kissinger, Secretary of State, 11 February 1974, PA AA, B 71 (Referat 405), 113894; 'The Washington Energy Conference: Einladung, Reden, Abschlussdokument', *Atlantic Community Quarterly* 12 (Spring 1974), 22–54.

48. Opening Remarks of the Honorable Henry A. Kissinger, Secretary of State, 11 February 1974, PA AA, B 71 (Referat 405), 113894.

49. Ibid.; on the theoretical edifice, see Nye and Keohane, 'Transnational Relations and World Politics', and chapter 7 for a detailed account. Daniel J. Sargent, *A Superpower Transformed: The Remaking of American Foreign Relations in the 1970s* (New York, 2015); Sargent, 'The United States and Globalization in the 1970s', in Ferguson, *The Shock of the Global*, 49–64. Sargent interprets Kissinger's statements as an expression of his views and de facto guiding principles. Kissinger also instrumentalized the rhetoric of interdependence, however, in order to fortify the United States' hegemonic position; see Möckli, *European Foreign Policy during the Cold War*, 252–79. On the progress of the conference, see also Gfeller, *Building a European Identity*, 114–40; on the German-French relationship, see Claudia Hiepel, *Willy Brandt und Georges Pompidou: Deutsch-französische Europapolitik zwischen Aufbruch und Krise* (Munich, 2012), 292–301.

50. Statement by the Honorable William E. Simon Administrator, Federal Energy Office before the Washington Energy Conference, Washington, DC, 11 February 1974, PA AA, B 71 (Referat 405), 113894.

51. Ibid.

52. Statement by the Honorable George P. Shultz, Secretary of the Treasury, 11 February 1974, PA AA, B 71 (Referat 405), 113894.

53. Hobart Rowen, 'Energy Parley Responds to Economic Facts', *Washington Post*, 17 February 1974. On Levy's position, see Walter J. Levy, 'World Oil Cooperation or International Chaos', *Foreign Affairs* 52 (1974), 690–713.

54. Statement by the Secretary General of the OECD, 11 February 1974, PA AA, B 71 (Referat 405), 113894; on the preparations made for the conference in the High Level Group Oil, see Paris OECD: Sitzung der High Level Group Oil, 4.2.1974, PA AA, B 71 (Referat 405), 113893.

55. Statement by Professor Hans K. Schneider, Director of the OECD L-Term Energy Assessment, 12 February 1974, PA AA, B 71 (Referat 405), 113894.

56. Statement by the Secretary General of the OECD, 11 February 1974, PA AA, B 71 (Referat 405), 113894.

57. Memorandum of Conversation: Washington Energy Conference, Secret, 9 February 1974, DNSA, KT01025; see also 'Schmidt: Der Ölpreis wird sinken', *Frankfurter Allgemeine Zeitung*, 14 February 1974.

58. For a paradigmatic example, see Statement by H.E. Mr. Masayoshi Ohira, Minister for Foreign Affairs of Japan, 11 February 1974, PA AA, B 71 (Referat 405), 113894.

59. Intervention by Max van der Stoel, 11 February 1974, PA AA, B 71 (Referat 405), 113894.

60. Statement by Mr. Knut Frydenlund, Foreign Minister of Norway, 11 February 1974; see also Statement by Mr. Jens Evensen, Minister of Commerce and Shipping of Norway, 12 February 1974, PA AA, B 71 (Referat 405), 113894.

61. Introductory Statement by the President of the Council of the European Communities, 11 February 1974; see also Erklärung des Präsidenten der Kommission der Europäischen Gemeinschaften Francois-Xavier Ortoli, Washington, 11 February 1974, PA AA, B 71 (Referat 405), 113894.

62. Statement by the German Federal Minister of Finance, Helmut Schmidt, 11 February 1974, PA AA, B 71 (Referat 405), 113894.

63. Ibid.

64. Statement by the Right Honorable Sir Alec Douglas Home, K.T., M.F., Secretary of State for Foreign and Commonwealth Affairs, United Kingdom, 11 February 1974, PA AA, B 71 (Referat 405), 113894.

65. Statement by His Excellency Michel Jobert, Minister of Foreign Affairs, Washington, 11 February 1974, PA AA, B 71 (Referat 405), 113894.

66. 'Kissinger warnt vor ruinösem Wettbewerb', *Frankfurter Allgemeine Zeitung*, 12 February 1974.

67. Statement by His Excellency Michel Jobert, Minister of Foreign Affairs, Washington 11 February 1974, PA AA, B 71 (Referat 405), 113894.

68. Ibid.

69. Hiepel, *Willy Brandt und Georges Pompidou*, 300.

70. Hermes, Staden an AA: Energiekonferenz. Delegationsbericht Nr. 1, 12.2.1974; Brunner, Staden an AA: Energiekonferenz. Delegationsbericht Nr. 2, 13.2.1974, PA AA, B 71 (Referat 405), 113893; Möckli, *European Foreign Policy during the Cold War*, 268–79; Peter Hermes reports that during the conference Douglas-Home stated that Jobert was having much the same effect on Kissinger as the IRA had on him. Hermes, *Meine Zeitgeschichte*, 225.

71. Marilyn Berger, 'Nixon Links Security to Fuel', *Washington Post*, 12 February 1974; see also 'Document 555: Sykes, Washington tel 612: Broad Political Consequences of the Energy Conference, February 16, 1974', in Hamilton, *The Year of Europe*; Fiona Venn, 'International Co-operation versus National Self-Interest: The United States and Europe during the 1973–1974 Oil Crisis', in Kathleen Burk and Melvyn Stokes (eds), *The United States and the European Alliance since 1945* (Oxford/New York, 1999), 71–100 here 87.

72. For a different take, see Venn, 'International Co-operation versus National Self-Interest'.

73. 'Document 562: FCO Diplomatic Report 192/74 [R.A. Sykes]; The Washington Energy Conference, 10–13 February, 1974, 27.2.1974', in Hamilton, *The Year of Europe*; Hermes,

Staden an AA: Energiekonferenz. Delegationsbericht Nr. 3, 14.2.1974; Kruse: Ortex Energiekonferenz in Washington am 11.–13.2.1974, 14.2.1974, PA AA, B 71 (Referat 405), 113893.

74. Washington Energy Conference: Communiqué, 13 February 1974, NARA, Nixon Library, NSC, Subject Files, Energy Crisis 1973–74, Box 321.

75. Marilyn Berger, 'Jobert Calls Talks a "Pretext"', *Washington Post,* 14 February 1974.

76. Murrey Marder and Ronald Koven, '12 Nations Agree on Energy Group', *Washington Post,* 14 February 1974; Jan Reifenberg, 'Der tote General hätte Beifall gespendet', *Frankfurter Allgemeine Zeitung,* 15 February 1974; outside France, the response to Jobert's stance was unanimously negative, but mixed and mostly positive in France itself; see 'Lob und Tadel für Jobert', *Frankfurter Allgemeine Zeitung,* 15 February 1974; Gfeller, *Building a European Identity,* 130–33.

77. Hermes, *Meine Zeitgeschichte,* 225 recalls Jobert departing with the words: 'I've been among friends here and now I say goodbye to friends'. See also Möckli, *European Foreign Policy during the Cold War,* 276–78.

78. Hermes, Staden an AA: Energiekonferenz. Delegationsbericht Nr. 3, 14.2.1974, PA AA, B 71 (Referat 405), 113893.

79. Moltmann an AA: Fernschreiben über arabische Reaktion auf Konferenz, 13.2.1974, PA AA, B 71 (Referat 405), 113893.

80. Moltmann: Fernschreiben über arabische Reaktion auf Konferenz, 15.2.1974, PA AA, B 71 (Referat 405), 113893; see also '"Front gegen Ölproduzenten": Scharfe Kritik der OPEC an Washingtoner Energiekonferenz', *Frankfurter Rundschau,* 15 February 1974.

81. 'Document 562: FCO Diplomatic Report 192/74 [R.A. Sykes]; The Washington Energy Conference, 10–13 February, 1974, 27.2.1974', in Hamilton, *The Year of Europe;* 'Document 555: Sykes, Washington tel 612: Broad Political Consequences of the Energy Conference, February 16, 1974', in Hamilton, *The Year of Europe.*

82. 'Document 553: Douglas-Home: Guidance tel 24: Summary: Work of the Energy Conference, February 14, 1974', in Hamilton, *The Year of Europe.*

83. Ibid.

84. Telcon Nixon – Kissinger, 14 February 1974, DNSA, KA12032.

85. Ibid.

86. Ibid.

87. 'Document 556: Nixon to Heath: Douglas Home at Conference, February 18, 1974', in Hamilton, *The Year of Europe.*

88. Marder and Koven, '12 Nations Agree on Energy Group'.

89. Memorandum of Conversation: Washington Energy Conference, Secret, 9 February 1974, DNSA, KT01025.

90. 'An Atlantic Energy Program', *Washington Post,* 14 February 1974, 22.

91. 'Interdependence on Oil', *New York Times,* 13 February 1974; Rowen, 'Energy Parley Responds to Economic Facts'.

92. James Reston, 'Two Cheers for France', *New York Times,* 15 February 1974; a similar critique of the French approach is echoed in André Nouschi, *Pétrole et relations internationales de 1945 à nos jours* (Paris, 1999), 125–27.

93. Leonard Silk, 'Energy Talks: Why US Position Won', *New York Times,* 15 February 1974.

94. G.n., 'Um mehr als Öl', *Frankfurter Allgemeine Zeitung,* 13 February 1974.

95. Dieter Schröder, 'Das europäische Mißverständnis', *Süddeutsche Zeitung,* 15 February 1974.

96. Erich Hauser, 'Abstieg in die Bedeutungslosigkeit', *Frankfurter Rundschau,* 14 February 1974; Schr., '13 in einem Boot', *Süddeutsche Zeitung,* 12 February 1974.

97. Reifenberg, 'Der tote General hätte Beifall gespendet'; Fack, 'Europa als Restposten'; Hans Jürgensen, 'Die europäische Truppe auf Amerika-Tournee', *Frankfurter Allgemeine Zei-*

tung, 14 February 1974; Mom., 'Ohne Frankreich', *Frankfurter Rundschau*, 15 February 1974; Monika Metzner, 'Frankreich und EG tief zerstritten', *Frankfurter Rundschau*, 14 February 1974.

98. Hk., 'Bonn will Entscheidungsspielraum sichern: Geringe Erwartungen der Bundesregierung', *Frankfurter Allgemeine Zeitung*, 11 February 1974; Jan Reifenberg, 'Amerika hat in der Energiepolitik den längeren Atem: Europas Rolle bei der Konferenz von Washington', *Frankfurter Allgemeine Zeitung*, 11 February 1974.

99. G.n., 'Um mehr als Öl'; see also Dieter Schröder, 'Geld fehlt der Weltwirtschaft mehr als Öl', *Süddeutsche Zeitung*, 13 February 1974.

100. Marion Gräfin Dönhoff, 'Allein mit Amerika. . . . wenn Paris weiter mauert', *Die Zeit*, 15 February 1974; Hans Kepper, 'Bonn lehnt Parteinahme ab. Rücksichtnahme auf Kontrahenten bei Energiekonferenz', *Frankfurter Rundschau*, 15 February 1974.

101. Kissinger über Hillenbrand an Scheel über Follow Up zur Energiekonferenz, 21.2.1974, PA AA, B 71 (Referat 405), 113893.

102. Gespräch Scheel Kissinger am 3. März 1974, Energiefragen, 4.3., VS.Bd. 8844, PA AA, B 150, 300.

103. See the documents relating to the meeting on 25 February in PA AA, B 71 (Referat 405), 113894; Sprechzettel für Kabinettsitzung über eventuelle Aussprache über Folgearbeiten der Washingtoner Energiekonferenz, 27.2.1974; Lantzke/Rohwedder: Bericht über die zweite Sitzung der Energie-Koordinierungsgruppe, 14.3.1974, PA AA, B 71 (Referat 405), 113893.

104. Lantzke/Rohwedder: Bericht über die zweite Sitzung der Energie-Koordinierungsgruppe, 14.3.1974, PA AA, B 71 (Referat 405), 113893.

105. Kruse: Bericht über 2. Sitzung der Koordinierungsgruppe, 14.3.1974; Übersicht über Organisationen, die die Folgearbeiten der Washingtoner Energiekonferenz übernommen haben, 27.3.1974, PA AA, B 71 (Referat 405), 113893.

106. Response to Questionnaire from Ad Hoc Group of the Oil Committee on Conserving Energy & Restraining Demand by the United States, 10 April 1974, NARA, Nixon Library, NSC, Subject Files, Energy Crisis 1973–74, Box 321; International Cooperation in OECD on Energy Conservation and Demand Restraint. A Report of the ad hoc Group on Conservation of Energy Resources and Demand Restraint, 9 May 1974, BArch, B 136/8026; John Knubel: United States Response to 'Questionnaire to Participants' from the OECD Group on Accelerated Development of Conventional Energy Resources, 15 April 1974; Group on Accelerated Development of Conventional Energy Resources: Answers to the 'Questionnaire to Participants', by United States, 16 April 1974, NARA, Nixon Library, NSC, Subject Files, Energy Crisis 1973–74, Box 321; Schnellbrief BMWi an Bundeskanzleramt Dr. Thiele, AA Dr. Kruse, Finanzen Dr. Pieske, Zusammenarbeit Herr Stryk: Auswirkungen der jüngsten energiepolitischen Entwicklung auf Weltwirtschaft und Investitionen, 25.3.1974, PA AA, B 36 (Referat 310), 104993; see also PA AA, B 71 (Referat 405), 113895.

107. Kruse an Dg 40: 4. Sitzung der E-K, 2./3.5.1974, 6. Mai 1974, PA AA, B 71 (Referat 405), 113895.

108. Ibid.; see also Memorandum of Conversation: The EC and Energy; the Middle East; Berlin; US-European Relations; SALT [Meeting with British Officials], Secret, 26 February 1974, DNSA KT01035; Memorandum of Conversation: Energy; North Sea Oil; Foreign Assistance; Nuclear Non-proliferation; CSCE; Trade Bill, [Meeting with British Officials], Secret, 7 July 1974, DNSA KT01245.

109. Kruse an Staatssekretär: 5. Sitzung der Energie-Koordinierungsgruppe am 17./18. Juni 1974; Kruse an Staatssekretär: 7. Sitzung der Energiekoordinierungsgruppe, 29./30. Juli, 1.8.1974, PA AA, B 71 (Referat 405), 113895.

110. Kruse an Staatssekretär: 7. Sitzung der Energiekoordinierungsgruppe, 29./30. Juli, 1.8.1974, PA AA, B 71 (Referat 405), 113895; 255 Gespräch Brandt Kissinger, u.a. Energie-

konferenz, 4.3., VS.Bd. 14057, PA AA, B 150, 300; zu Frankreich: BMWi: Aufzeichnung für die deutsch-französischen Konsultationen zur Energiepolitik am 8./9. Juli 1974, 2. Juli 1974, PA AA, B 71 (Referat 405), 113895.

111. OECD, 'Decision of the Council Establishing an International Energy Agency of the Council, 15.11.1974', in Richard Scott, *The History of the International Energy Agency: The First Twenty Years*, vol. 3, *Principle Documents* (Paris, 1994), 27; see Richard Scott, *The History of the International Energy Agency: The First Twenty Years*, vol. 1, *Origins and Structure* (Paris, 1994), 49–54, and with reference to different documents, 'Die Gründung der Internationalen Energieagentur', *Europa-Archiv* 30(2) (1975), D1–30.

112. 'Gesetz zu dem Übereinkommen vom 18. November 1974 über ein Internationales Energieprogramm: Vom 30. April 1975', *Bundesgesetzblatt* 2(31) (1975), 701–42, here 703.

113. Ibid.

114. Ibid., 709–11; Gesprächsführung für einen Besuch des Ministers in Washington am 28. September 1974, 19. September 1974, PA AA, B 71 (Referat 405), 113895.

115. Lantzke, 'The OECD and Its International Energy Agency', 218.

116. Ibid., 219. Elsewhere, Lantzke describes the situation as follows: 'The result was international paralysis, and the OECD Oil Committee was unable to agree even on the formal collection of the information necessary to operate an oil sharing scheme'. Lantzke, 'The Role of International Cooperation', 77f.

117. 'Gesetz zu dem Übereinkommen vom 18. November 1974 über ein Internationales Energieprogramm'.

118. C.O. Peyton (Exxon): International Energy Program, 23.10.1974; Energy Co-ordinating Group: Consultation with the Oil Companies, 23.–24. Oktober 1974, PA AA, B 71 (Referat 405), 113894.

119. Ibid.

120. To quote the assessment of Lantzke, 'The OECD and Its International Energy Agency', 225.

121. BMWi an den Chef des BK: Internationales Energieprogramm (IEP), 14.10.1974, BArch, B 102/200590.

122. Ibid.; Dickas: Vermerk für die Sitzung des Wirtschaftskabinetts am 21.10.1974, 17.10.1974, BArch, B 136/8471.

123. BMWi Denkschrift zum Internationalen Energieprogramm, 11.11.1974, PA AA, B 71 (Referat 405), 113894.

124. Kruse: Überblick über die verschiedenen energiepolitischen Initiativen, 26.11.1974, PA AA, B 71 (Referat 405), 113894.

125. Helmut Schmidt, 'Leitgedanken unserer Außenpolitik', in *Kontinuität und Konzentration* (Bonn-Bad Godesberg, 1975), 226–43, here 227.

126. Ibid., 238.

127. Robert O. Keohane, 'The International Energy Agency: State Influence and Transgovernmental Politics', *International Organization* 32(4) (1978), 929–51, here 931; C. Fred Bergsten, 'Interdependence and the Reform of International Institutions', *International Organization* 30(2) (1976), 361–72; Robert O. Keohane, *After Hegemony* (Princeton, NJ, 1984), 182–240.

128. Lantzke, 'The Role of International Cooperation'; Richard Scott, *The History of the International Energy Agency: The First Twenty Years*, vol. 2, *Major Policies and Actions* (Paris, 1994), 114–19; Gudrun Maass, 'Die Internationale Energieagentur: Lehren aus der Vergangenheit – Herausforderung für die Zukunft', in Jens Hohensee and Michael Salewski (eds), *Energie - Politik - Geschichte: Nationale und internationale Energiepolitik seit 1945* (Stuttgart, 1993), 191–204.

129. Scott, *The History of the International Energy Agency*, vol. 2, 158, 171.

130. Ibid., 304–9.

131. See, for example, International Energy Agency, *IEA Reviews of National Energy Pro-*

grams (Paris, 1978); IEA, *Energy Research, Development and Demonstration in the IEA Countries: 1981 Review of National Programmes* (Paris, 1982).

132. Energy Balances of OECD Countries 1- (1974/76-); World Energy Outlook 1- (1977-).

133. OECD, *World Energy Outlook*.

134. International Energy Agency, *World Energy Outlook* (Paris, 1982); Peter Roggen, *Die Internationale Energie-Agentur: Energiepolitik und wirtschaftliche Sicherheit* (Bonn, 1979).

135. C. Fred Bergsten, 'The Threat from the Third World', *Foreign Policy* 11 (Summer 1973), 102–24; 'One, Two, Many OPECs', *Foreign Policy* 14 (Spring 1974), 56–57.

136. Marc Williams, *Third World Cooperation: The Group of 77 in UNCTAD* (London, 1991); Mahfuzur Rahman, *World Economic Issues at the United Nations: Half a Century of Debate* (Boston, 2002), 146; for an overview of the debates and themes central to the UN and its subconferences, see Waldo Chamberlain, Thomas Hovet and Erica Hovet, *A Chronology and Fact Book of the United Nations 1941–1976* (Dobbs Ferry, NY, 1976).

137. Williams, *Third World Cooperation*; Rahman, *World Economic Issues*, 147.

138. Conference of Sovereigns and Heads of State of OPEC Member Countries, 4–6 March 1975, in OPEC, *OPEC Official Resolutions and Press Releases 1960–1990* (Vienna, 1990), 130–35, 130: 'They also reaffirm that OPEC Member Countries, through the collective, steadfast and cohesive defense of the legitimate rights of their peoples, have served the larger and ultimate interest and progress of the world community and, in doing so, have acted in the direction hoped for by all developing countries, producers of raw materials, in defense of the legitimate rights of their peoples'. On the concrete measures, see Ibrahim Shihata, 'The Opec Special Fund and the North-South Dialogue', *Third World Quarterly* 1(4) (1979), 28–38.

139. Le Monde (5 February 1974), quoted in MEES 17(16) (8 February 1974), x.

140. Dittmann an StS: Algerischer Vorschlag zur Einberufung einer außerordentlichen Tagung der VN-Generalversammlung über Rohstoff- und Entwicklungsfragen, 11.2.1974, PA AA, B 1 (Referat 010), 580.

141. Houari Boumedienne, 'Address to the General Assembly of the UN', in United Nations General Assembly (ed.), *Sixth Special Session. Plenary Meetings. Verbatim Records of Meetings 9 April–2 May 1974, 2208th Plenary Meeting, 10 April 1974* (New York, 1976), 1–11, here 4. For an overall survey of the debate, largely free of analytic perspectives, see Rahman, *World Economic Issues*, 149–60.

142. Boumedienne, 'Address to the General Assembly of the UN', 4.

143. Ibid., 5.

144. Ibid., 6.

145. Lautenschlager: Vermerk über Gespräch mit dem französischen Gesandten Morize über die französischen Vorstellungen zur Einberufung einer Weltenergiekonferenz im Rahmen der UN, 31.1.1974, PA AA, B 36 (Referat 310), 104993.

146. UNO Botschaft an AA: 6. Sondersitzung. Entwurf für Erklärung der Blockfreien 5.3.1974; UNO Botschaft an AA: Sondersitzung VN. Zwischenbilanz der Vorbereitung 8.3.1974; UNOGERMA an AA: Entwurf über die Errichtung einer NIEO, 28.3.1974, PA AA, B 1 (Referat 010), 580; Unterrichtung für die Kabinettsitzung am 20.3.1974 über Sondersitzung der VN, 19.3.1974, PA AA, B 1 (Referat 010), 580.

147. Henry A. Kissinger, 'Address to the UN General Assembly', in *United Nations. General Assembly: Sixth Special Session. Plenary Meetings. Verbatim Records of Meetings 9 April–2 May 1974, 2214th Plenary Meeting, 15 April 1974* (New York, 1976), 3–11, 3.

148. Ibid., 4.

149. Ibid., 5.

150. See the conversation between Kissinger and Boumedienne, Memorandum: Conversation at Dinner at the People's Palace, Algiers, 29 April 1974, Secret, DNSA, KT01124.

151. Rede von BM Scheel auf der 6. Sondersitzung der GV der VN am 10.4.1974, PA AA, B 1 (Referat 010), 580.

152. Ibid.
153. Ibid.; EG. Der Rat. Aufzeichnung Vorbereitung der außerordentlichen VV der VN, 5.4.1974, PA AA, B 1 (Referat 010), 580.
154. Michel Jobert, 'Address to United Nations General Assembly', in *United Nations. General Assembly: Sixth Special Session. Plenary Meetings. Verbatim Records of Meetings 9 April–2 May 1974, 2209th Plenary Meeting, 10 April 1974* (New York, 1976), 5–11, here 7.
155. 'Sondertagung der Vereinten Nationen über Rohstoff- und Entwicklungsprobleme', *Europa-Archiv* 29(2) (1974), 277–300.
156. 'Declaration on the Establishment of a New International Economic Order 1974', in *United Nations. General Assembly: Resolutions Adopted during Its Sixth Special Session 9 April–2 May 1974* (New York, 1974), 3–5.
157. Ibid.; see also 'Programme of Action on the Establishment of a New International Economic Order', in *United Nations. General Assembly: Resolutions Adopted during Its Sixth Special Session 9 April–2 May 1974* (New York, 1974), 5–12.
158. Dohms: Ortex Nr. 48 zur 6. Sondergeneralvers., 3.5.1974, PA AA, B 1 (Referat 010), 580.
159. Ibid.; and Deutsche Haltung zur Erklärung und zum Aktionsprogramm über die Errichtung einer neuen Weltwirtschaftsordnung (6. Sonder-Generalversammlung der VN über Rohstoffe und Entwicklung, 9.4.–2.5.1974 in New York), 21.11.1974, PA AA, B 36 (Referat 310), 113905.
160. Deutsche Haltung zur Erklärung und zum Aktionsprogramm über die Errichtung einer neuen Weltwirtschaftsordnung (6. Sonder-Generalversammlung der VN über Rohstoffe und Entwicklung, 9.4.–2.5.1974 in New York), 21.11.1974, PA AA, B 36 (Referat 310), 113905.
161. Henry A. Kissinger, 'Address to the UN General Assembly', in *United Nations. General Assembly: Twenty-Ninth Session. Plenary Meetings. Verbatim Records of the 2233rd to 2265th Meetings, 17 September–10 October 1974, 2238th Plenary Meeting, 23 September 1974*, vol. 1 (New York, 1974), 59–63, here 59.
162. 'Dokumente zur 29. Generalversammlung der Vereinten Nationen vom 30. August 1974', *Europa-Archiv* 29(2) (1974), 511–38.
163. 'The Cocoyoc Declaration', *International Organization* 29(3) (1975), 893–901, here 895.
164. United Nations. General Assembly, *3281 Charter of Economic Rights and Duties of States*, 1974, http://www.un.org/documents/ga/res/29/ares29.htm (last modified 4 October 2016).
165. United Nations. General Assembly (ed.), *Plenary Meetings. Verbatim Records of the 2336th to the 2349th Meetings, 1–16 September 1975* (New York, 1976); 'Development and International Economic Co-operation 1976', in *United Nations: Resolutions Adopted by the General Assembly during its Seventh Special Session, 1–16 September 1975* (New York, 1976), 3–10.
166. For an account of the new Arab prosperity aimed at a wide readership, see Gerhard Konzelmann, *Die Reichen aus dem Morgenland: Wirtschaftsmacht Arabien* (Munich, 1975).
167. Kruse: Analyse der energiepolitischen Ausführungen des Staatspräsidenten Giscard d'Estaing, 31.10.1974, PA AA, B 2 (Referat 014), 225.
168. Hermes, Abt. 4, an BM: Vorschlag des französischen Staatspräsidenten zur Einberufung einer Konferenz der industrialisierten Verbraucherländer, der Entwicklungsländer und der Erdölexportländer, 6.11.1974, PA AA, B 71 (Referat 405), 113909.
169. Kruse an Staatssekretär: Teilnehmerkreis Vorkonferenz; Verbraucher-Produzenten; 30.1.1975, PA AA, B 71 (Referat 405), 113909.
170. 403–412: Konferenz der erdölverbrauchenden und erdölerzeugenden Länder, 13.2.1975, BArch, B 136/8471.
171. For West Germany, see the 26-page paper produced by the BMWi: Konferenz der Erdölverbraucher- und -erzeugerländer, 26.3.1975, PA AA, B 71 (Referat 405), 113909.

172. AL II an BK: Internationale Energiekonferenz, 4.3.1975, BArch, B 136/8471.
173. Helmut Schmidt an Harold Wilson am 23.12.1974; Armstrong: Schmidt's Proposal of Consumer/Producer Dialogue, 15 January 1975, NA UK, PREM 16/610.
174. Patrick Wright: Schmidt-Proposal, 31.12.1974; Schmidt to Wilson am 14.2.1973; Schmidt to Wilson am 14.2.1973, NA UK, PREM 16/610.
175. Abt. 403: EG-Ratssitzung zu Verbraucher-Produzentenkonferenz. Gesprächsunterlagen; Kurzfassung des Sprechzettels zur Konferenz, 8.4.1975; Kruse an Staatsminister Moersch: Bericht über die Vorkonferenz im Bundeskabinett, 15.4.1975, 11.2.1975, PA AA, B 71 (Referat 405), 113909.
176. Loeck: Vermerk für die Kabinettsitzung am 23. April, Analyse der Ergebnisse der Energievorkonferenz, 22.4.1975; AA 405: Ergebnisse der Vorkonferenz, 24.4.1975, BArch, B 136/8471.
177. Robert (Botschafter z.b.V. für Energiefragen) an BM: Pariser Vorkonferenz der erdölverbrauchenden und -erzeugenden Länder: Gesamtbewertung und Schlussfolgerungen, Bonn, 18.4.1975, PA AA, B 71 (Referat 405), 113905; 405 an D4: internationale Reaktionen nach Unterbrechung der Vorkonferenz, 29.4.1975, PA AA, B 71 (Referat 405), 113910.
178. A precise breakdown of reactions and assessments in the participating countries can be found in: Analyse der Vorkonferenz, 2.5.1975, PA AA, B 71 (Referat 405), 113905.
179. Relevant documents in PA AA, B 71 (Referat 405), 113906; Abt. 4 an BM: Fact Finding Mission eines Vertreters der Bundesregierung in Erdöl- und Entwicklungsländern, 17. Juni 1975, PA AA, B 71 (Referat 405), 113911.
180. Abt. 4: Bericht über die Fact-finding-Mission von StM Wischnewski, 5. August 1975, PA AA, B 71 (Referat 405), 113911; see Hermes, *Meine Zeitgeschichte*, 227.
181. Abt. 4: Bericht über die Fact-finding-Mission von StM Wischnewski, 5. August 1975, PA AA, B 71 (Referat 405), 113911.
182. Grundsätze der Bundesregierung für den Dialog mit den erdölproduzierenden und anderen Entwicklungsländern, 15. August 1975, PA AA, B 1 (MB 010), 178638; Kruse: Bericht über deutsch-französische Konsultationen über Energie- und Rohstofffragen, 2. Juli 1975, PA AA, B 71 (Referat 405), 113910; Helmut Schmidt an Harold Wilson, 2.10.1975, NA UK, PREM 16/612.
183. Ergebnisse der Pariser Vorkonferenz zur Konferenz über internationale wirtschaftliche Zusammenarbeit vom 13.–16. Oktober 1975, PA AA, B 1 (MB 010), 178638; United States Congress, 'Congressional Staff Report on the Conference on International Economic Cooperation', *International Legal Materials* 15(2) (1976), 388–94.
184. Ergebnisse der Pariser Vorkonferenz zur Konferenz über internationale wirtschaftliche Zusammenarbeit vom 13.–16. Oktober 1975, PA AA, B 1 (Referat 010), 178638.
185. Kruse an Minister: Konferenz über die internationale wirtschaftliche Zusammenarbeit (KIWZ). Vertretung der BRD, 9.12.1975; KIWZ, Vorbereitung und Gesprächsführung, 8.12.1975; EG Der Rat: Entwurf der Gesamthaltung der Gemeinschaft auf der KIWZ, 21.11.1975, PA AA, B 1 (Referat 010), 178639.
186. 'United States Congress, 'Congressional Staff Report'.
187. Scott, *The History of the International Energy Agency*, vol. 3, 341.
188. Arie Bloed, *The Conference on Security and Co-operation in Europe: Analysis and Basic Documents, 1972–1993* (Dordrecht, 1993); Bloed, *The Conference on Security and Co-operation in Europe: Basic Documents, 1993–1995* (The Hague, 1997); Oliver Bange and Gottfried Niedhardt (eds), *Helsinki 1975 and the Transformation of Europe* (Oxford/New York, 2008).
189. Working Paper of the Commission Services: Soviet Proposals for Pan-European Conferences in the Fields of Energy, Transport, and the Environment, 1976, PA AA, B 71 (Referat 405), 113892.
190. Ibid.
191. 405–411: Breschnew-Vorschläge für gesamteuropäische Konferenzen; hier: Energie, 24.9.1976; Kruse an Dg 40: Energiekonferenz, 29.9.1976, PA AA, B 71 (Referat 405), 113892.

Chapter 7

PETRO-KNOWLEDGE, THE PERCEPTION OF LIMITS AND SOVEREIGNTY
Creating the Oil Crisis

Today, the 1970s are widely regarded as a turning point in the history of the Western industrialized countries, a time when the postwar economic boom ended and the thorny economic, social and political problems of the present began. As set out in the introduction, the oil crisis plays a key role in this narrative.[1] How did the oil crisis acquire the iconic quality so often ascribed to it in present-day surveys of the 1970s? Or, to put it differently, how and why were the transformations in the world of oil conceptualized as the 'first oil crisis', as we know it or think we know it today?

As we have seen throughout the present work, in the early 1970s, and above all in October 1973, the actions of OPEC and OAPEC destabilized the world of oil. At least in the perception of contemporaries, this posed a fundamental challenge to the Western industrialized countries' sovereignty. The latter responded in a variety of ways: by reorganizing powers over energy and modifying national energy policies; through diplomatic initiatives intended to reorder the world of oil; by drawing on scientific expertise; and through domestic and international communicative strategies. Through this process of asserting sovereignty, energy emerged as the comprehensive, autonomous and vitally important policy field we know today. These changes were accompanied by intensive scientific and public debates, which were directly spawned by the oil crisis and still shape its perception.[2] It was above all political scientists and economists – along with the newly emerging group of energy experts – who asked whether, and if so to what extent, the energy policy constellation laid bare by the oil crisis imposed constraints on state action, both domestically and internationally. Their answers reflected basic disciplinary suppositions, political motives and assumptions about future developments, so we cannot subscribe to any of them as valid analyses of the oil crisis. Instead, we have to scrutinize how these responses shaped the genesis of this crisis and its discursive production.[3]

Many contemporaries viewed the changes that occurred in the world of oil in the early 1970s as a fundamental rupture. By June 1971, in *Foreign Affairs*, Walter J. Levy was already claiming that 'the economic terms of the world trade in oil have been radically altered . . . the winds of change for the oil industry . . . have now risen to hurricane proportions'.[4] Shortly before the oil crisis, French economist Jean-Marie Chevalier argued that 1971 marked a turning point in the history of oil: for the first time, the producing countries had managed to achieve price increases and a larger share of profits in defiance of the oil firms.[5] Unaware of what was to come in the near future, many observers saw developments in the world of oil and energy as fundamental transformations. Within a few months, they seemed like mere harbingers of even greater changes. After the start of the oil embargo and the first price hikes in October 1973, energy experts, political scientists, politicians and political observers all agreed that what was happening constituted a turning point, not just in the history of oil but also in the development of the Western industrialized nations, global processes of economic exchange and international politics. In March 1974 and January 1975, for example, under the aegis of the Harvard Center for International Affairs, influential political scientists and economists gathered in Cambridge, Massachusetts and Turin to discuss the consequences of the oil crisis. In the associated conference proceedings, editor Raymond Vernon reflected on contemporaries' tendency to overestimate the significance of their own era and to view current events, which would later turn out to have been marginal, as major crises. But he went on to state that 'the events in the oil market that drew the world's attention in the months following October 1973 . . . may prove to have a more enduring significance'.[6]

In West Germany, the weekly newspaper *Die Zeit* organized a major debate on the energy crisis in 1974. Its participants included Helmut Schmidt, Ralf Dahrendorf, Carl Friedrich von Weizsäcker, chief executive of Merck AG Hans Joachim Langmann, Carroll Wilson, who led the Workshop on Alternative Energy Strategies (WAES) at MIT, and Hans Karl Schneider, director of the EWI Cologne, who had also contributed to the WAES. Consensus reigned: '"This is no phase, this is the end of an era", . . . we have unanimously concluded that the end of an epoch really has dawned. We are being forced to rethink and look afresh at much to which we have grown accustomed: political decision-making processes, our system of values, our lifestyle'.[7] Around the same time, Franz Josef Strauß articulated his 'firm conviction' that historians 'of the next decade or of later generations [will] very probably regard the year 1973 as a profound turning point in postwar history, as a historical caesura'.[8] Many of the studies of energy produced against the background of the oil crisis also underlined the fundamental rupture it entailed for the industrialized countries and the global economy as a whole. The construction of an epoch-making turning point quickly became a fixed trope in political scientific and economic publications on energy policy.[9] Not limited to a small number of specialists and politicians, these discussions reached a broad public, which came to view the oil crisis as symbolic of a wide variety of anxiety-provoking changes.[10]

Many commentators linked the oil crisis to more general economic or political changes in the industrialized nations, but also to mental or discursive shifts. During the crisis, a growing number of observers expressed fears that the oil price hikes might trigger a global recession and threaten the survival of the affluent societies of Western Europe, the United States and Japan. It thus seemed obvious to trace real-world economic developments back to the oil crisis, or at least to link the two.[11] For Chancellor Helmut Schmidt, 'just a few aspects' of the 'economic world' of 1975 were 'comparable to [the world] of 1973'.[12] Two years later, at the Körber Foundation's Bergedorf Round Table, Guido Brunner stated with respect to energy that things would 'never be as they were before 1973'.[13] In retrospect, many now considered the years of the economic boom a golden age, which was apparently gone forever.[14] Exactly the same assessment of the oil crisis was being articulated on its ten-year anniversary:

> In light of the passage of a decade, October 1973 appears as a virtual continental divide, separating a post-World War II generation of economic recovery, prosperity, and Western unity from an era of stagflation, lost confidence, and disarray. In a sense this date is arbitrary.... Nonetheless, in its scope and endurance as a source of division, the crisis that began in October 1973 marked a new and identifiable era.[15]

Given the globe-spanning structure of the oil economy, key actors also understood the changes wrought by the oil crisis as global in nature. These changes placed national foreign policy within a new set of parameters, which were often regarded as constraints. Concurrently, the newly emerging – and booming – environmental movements argued that, quite apart from the ecological costs of growing energy consumption, the availability of energy resources would place tighter limits on policy in future. The steps taken by OPEC and OAPEC, they contended, had merely expedited this process. In 1976, the first issue of the *Annual Review of Energy* thus regarded their actions as 'the beginning of an era when man first fully realized the magnitude of the energy-resource-environment problem ... which took many years to develop [and] will also take many years to solve'.[16] A similarly unambiguous pathos of crisis and decision emanated from Erhard Eppler's *Ende oder Wende* [End or Turning Point]. This study saw the world standing at a 'historical turning-point', shifting away 'from an age in which humanity overcame limits to one in which it has to determine limits, from an age of unlimited possibilities to one of possible limitations, from an age of partial affluence to one in which we recognize what is superfluous'.[17]

Contemporary assessments like these were often incorporated directly into the writing of environmental history. Political, economic and social scientists, but also activists in the nascent environmental movement, constructed the oil crisis as a fundamental turning point and have continued to expound this interpretation into the present.[18] In both international and domestic political terms, the rise of 'energy' as an important issue seemed to fundamentally alter the conditions for political action and thus to impose tighter limits on sovereignty. In what follows, I aim to show how this contemporary debate structured the world and shaped its perception, while also examining its plausibility in light of both the preceding chapters and subsequent developments. It is crucial to remember that the above-mentioned contemporary interpretations always entailed visions of the future that, from today's perspective, often refer to our past and present. Bearing all this in mind, I seek to illuminate whether, and if so to what extent, the oil crisis represented a turning point in the history of sovereignty.

Transnational Limits to National Sovereignty

Contemporary political scientists intensely debated Western governments' efforts, domestically and internationally, to meet the challenge to their sovereignty mounted by OPEC and OAPEC. They analysed the resulting changes for international politics as a whole, while often attempting to provide policy advice. Issues of sovereignty came into focus here in four main discursive threads. First, oil firms were regarded as the epitome of the multinational company that had largely cast off national constraints.[19] Second, to many observers the changes in the oil market appeared to indicate a fundamental shift in foreign policy priorities and power relations; this, they believed, found expression in the rise of energy security as a key political category. Third, contemporary commentators wondered whether the bipolar order of the Cold War was being superseded by a conflict over resources between 'North' and 'South' or perhaps even the rise of a multipolar world. Fourth and finally, theorists of international relations argued that the oil crisis had revealed the world to be one of complex interdependence, one in which transnational processes and organizations would become increasingly important, while national governments would find it much harder to implement hegemonic policies.

Multinational Oil Firms as Threats to Sovereignty

In response to the oil crisis, on 27 June 1974 the French parliament instructed an investigative committee to report on the activities of the oil firms active in France. Its investigation was to focus not on the state firms Elf-Erap or Compagnie Française des Pétroles (CFP) but on the international companies. The committee reported that the firms had willingly provided it with information but that this had often been very difficult to understand or simply wrong.[20] It was, the committee explained, hard to come to clear-cut conclusions due to the character of multinational companies, which largely evaded the regulatory efforts of individual states and made their decisions in secret. As such, they were incompatible with democratic processes, constituting 'states without territory', whose rulers were appointed by co-optation and then exercised quasi-monarchical power.[21] Hence, if the governments of the Western industrialized countries wished to remain sovereign, they must restrict the companies' power and regulate the oil supply on the state level.[22] As a result of the oil crisis, the debate on multinational companies' restriction of national sovereignty, which had already been fierce, was linked even more closely with the oil firms. Many authors argued that the oil crisis had demonstrated that multinational oil companies constrained sovereignty beyond the countries in which they produced oil. In fact, they contended, since the early 1970s the producing countries had managed to wrest back ever more sovereignty, while the sovereignty of the industrialized countries where the oil firms were based seemed to be at risk from their activities.

It was not just in France that the government examined these issues during and after the oil crisis. In the United States, a variety of Senate committees examined the conduct of the US oil companies. The hearings of the Committee on Government Operations – which took place in January 1974 under the chairmanship of Henry M. Jackson and were discussed in more detail in chapter 4 of the present work – looked at both the Federal Energy Office and the multinational companies. This committee went so far as to ask whether the major oil companies had orchestrated the oil crisis in order to push up prices and drive the independents out of the market.[23] Rumours of oil tankers anchored off the coast with full tanks circulated within the American public sphere. Conspiracy theories of this kind, along with the critique of the oil companies, received new impetus when they notched up record profits in 1973. Before the oil crisis had even begun, the Senate Committee on Foreign Relations, chaired by J. William Fulbright, appointed a subcommittee to scrutinize the role of multinational companies in US foreign policy. This interest had been triggered by the activities of the International Telephone and Telegraph Corporation in the context of the overthrow of the Allende government in Chile. Under the leadership of Frank Church, the committee also began to investigate the multinational oil companies' influence on the formation of US foreign policy since the 1950s.[24] As a result of the oil crisis, a new drama was injected into these hearings – which heard the testimony of company staff, government workers and independent experts – when it emerged that the government depended on the information it received from the oil companies and was, therefore, hardly autonomous when designing its energy policy.[25] The question at issue now, one that attracted a great deal of attention from the American public, was whether, and if so to what extent, the relationship between the oil companies and US foreign policy had helped to bring about the energy crisis. In his opening statement on 30 January 1974, Frank Church asked: 'Can the US Government afford any longer to assume a passive role while private companies negotiate at the international level, with sovereign foreign governments, on questions of petroleum supply?'[26] Church's key goal was to clarify whether the companies' restrictive information policy had limited the government's ability to raise taxes, ensure competition and safeguard the United States' energy supply.[27] The hearings thus focused, first, on the government's inability to adequately monitor the oil companies, which it had granted extensive tax relief, and, second, on the constraints facing the oil companies in negotiations with the producing countries, with respect to which they could bring to bear only economic but not political or military power.

The Committee on Government Operations, chaired once again by Henry M. Jackson, dedicated one of its hearings to an episode that had occurred during the oil crisis, one that epitomized the relationship between multinational oil companies and the American government. In this instance, the oil companies had passed on information to the Saudi Arabian government that enabled it to enhance the effectiveness of the oil embargo.[28] When it had become clear to all those involved that the oil embargo would have no dramatic effect on the United States, the Saudi Arabian government came up with the idea of extending it to those countries from which the globally active US navy obtained its fuel. Yamani thus instructed the president of Aramco, Frank Jungers, to find out within three days from Aramco's American parent companies – in other words from Exxon, Texaco, Socal and Mobil – which countries provided the US fleet with oil.[29] The oil firms complied with this request and clearly had no fundamental reservations about surrendering such data at a point in time when American forces were on high alert due to a possible confrontation with the Soviet Union in the Near and Middle East.

The hearing, which heard testimony from, among others, the president of Exxon, Charles O. Peyton, the head of Texaco's production department, Paul E. Grimm, and Edward F. Kondis of Mobil, saw a clash between the logics privileged by the multinational companies and those cherished by national politicians. Peyton stated that he had considered this new instruction from the Saudi government merely to be the logical continuation – and a more detailed version – of the first embargo declaration, whose content Exxon had immediately conveyed to the US government. Furthermore, his company had been keen to prevent further production cuts, which might have been imposed had it failed to comply and would have had disastrous consequences.[30] It was only shortly before the Saudi deadline that one of Exxon's heads of department phoned the member of staff responsible for the armed forces' energy supply at the Department of Defense, John Nolan. As the latter described so strikingly to the subcommittee, however, this was not an attempt to obtain permission to hand over the data:

> I told Mr. Ward [of Exxon International's Aviation Sales Department] that I could see nothing illegal in releasing data from unclassified government petroleum supply contracts. I also advised Mr. Ward that I was aware of the implications of the Saudi request and I certainly did not encourage EXXON to comply, because of the obvious intent of the Saudi Government to use the information to inhibit the supply of products to US forces around the world. Mr. Ward replied that he had little choice but to comply, and he was only concerned with whether he might 'go to jail' as a result. He added that if I were to provide OSD [Office of the Secretary of Defense] Counsel's view on legality it would have to be forthcoming in 15 minutes if he was to meet his deadline.[31]

In view of the tight deadline, Nolan explained, he did not call again, not least because he had been unable to establish any illegality and Exxon might have interpreted this information as support. This purely economic calculation, entirely devoid of a military or national perspective, which merely examined formal compliance with the law, sent the senators in attendance into a rage. Following his statement, Jackson thus asked Paul E. Grimm: 'Didn't anyone say "Look, boys, we are in the midst of a strategic alert. Shouldn't the Secretary of Defense, the highest people in the government, be advised of the October 31 wire and what do we do about it?" Wouldn't that be the thing an ordinary stiff would understand?'[32] Meekly, and rather unconvincingly, Grimm conceded that in retrospect that was no doubt how it looked. Overall, though, the oil companies' representatives showed little sign of a guilty conscience, emphasizing that they had not in fact broken any laws. Jackson's rhetorical question, however, provides further confirmation that during the oil crisis, hamstrung by a lack of information, even the most senior government officials struggled to act effectively, while the oil companies did whatever they felt to be correct.

The British government had a very similar experience when it asked BP, still mostly state owned, to provide the United Kingdom with oil on a preferential basis and spare the country supply cutbacks. Against the backdrop of the embargo and production cuts of October 1973, senior British government officials met on numerous occasions with BP chairman Sir Eric Drake and director of Shell Transport and Trading Frank MacFadzean. As early as 21 October 1971, Drake warned Prime Minister Heath about potentially dramatic oil supply shortfalls and urged the government to impose rationing. Heath retorted that the ordinary 'man in the street' would find it very difficult to understand such measures as long as a British company such as BP had sufficient oil to safeguard the country's supply. At the very least, BP should sell oil products in the United Kingdom more cheaply than, for example, in Japan.[33] Drake rejected this demand. In talks a few days later with Lord Carrington, who was responsible for British energy policy, he explained that BP was a multinational company that had to deal with eighty-five different governments; all of them wanted preferential treatment and he must at least give them the feeling that they were being treated fairly. He could, he stated, certainly try to provide the United Kingdom with additional oil, but was unable to quantify this in advance.[34] In his memoirs, Edward Heath expressed his anger at BP's refusal to comply with his wishes. He felt the company lacked an adequate sense of national responsibility: 'When I invited the chairmen of Shell and BP to Chequers as my guests, however, I was met with a complete refusal to co-operate. I was deeply ashamed by the obstinate and unyielding reluctance of these magnates to take any action whatever to help our own country in its time of danger'.[35] OAPEC had excepted the United Kingdom from the production cutbacks as a 'friendly nation'. In its negotiations with the oil firms, the British government therefore insisted that they provide the UK with the same amount of oil as before. It rejected the companies' policy of distributing the shortfalls evenly across all importing countries (apart from those subject to the full embargo). However, highlighting possible reprisals in other countries, Shell and BP spokesmen refused to contemplate abandoning the 'equal misery' allocation policy, unless the British government issued an unambiguous and public instruction. 'BP says that unless they are legally compelled to the contrary, they will continue to share out their valuable supplies in a fair and equitable manner among their customers.'[36]

The debate between the oil firms and the British government escalated in the second half of November after ministers publicly declared that BP's oil allocation policy was harming the UK's national interests. In a number of heated discussions, Drake complained about the public pillorying of his company. The decision to provide the UK with oil supplies on a preferential basis was a political one that could only be made by the government, not by BP.[37] Again and again, like MacFadzean, he sought to persuade the ministers that such a policy would not even be in the best interest of the British government. First, he asserted, Germany and Japan would then enter into a tough price war that the United Kingdom could only lose; second, in addition to crude oil imports, the country required refined oil products, supplies of which might be at risk as a result of any economic conflict.[38] Drake seemed 'tense and edgy' to his interlocutors. It was only through strenuous efforts that the ministers could prevent him from making his own public statement to the effect that it was BP rather than the government that was acting in the national interest.[39] The government, meanwhile, shied away from the consequences of publicly instructing BP to violate its supply agreements with other countries and provide the UK with oil on a preferential basis. BP and Shell could thus continue to spread the burdens of the production cutbacks as evenly as possible across all the importing countries.

Thus, it was not governmental agreements between the Western industrialized countries but rather the major oil companies – through autonomous decisions reflecting their own commercial logics – that ensured the equitable allocation of the reduced quantities of oil. This gave new impetus to the debate on the significance of multinational companies to the national sovereignty of the European countries and the United States. As early as 1974, the Center for Science in the Public Interest, a product of the US consumer protection movement, published an information pamphlet entitled *Major Oil: What Citizens Should Know about the Eight Major Oil Companies*. The eight largest oil firms, the introduction stated, were 'world empires', in other words global power structures that crosscut national boundaries; as such, they were becoming ever larger, richer and more powerful. While there were other 'giant corporations' such as Ford and GM, their power did not come close to matching that of the oil industry: 'the Big Eight literally control the life-blood of the modern world. Without oil . . . the technologically advanced nations would be paralyzed. . . . Petroleum is our lifeblood and the Big Eight are the marrow, heart and arteries'.[40] This pamphlet, then, injected further drama into the common metaphor of oil as the blood of modern national economies, by underlining that the firms controlling it evaded all state control. This, readers were informed, meant they could limit nations' sovereign right to safeguard the energy supply and pursue energy policy on a national basis.[41]

The consumer advocates expressed no clear view on whether the oil firms were making positive or negative use of their power. Meanwhile, the parallel critique of these companies intensified. This discourse viewed the power of the multinationals in general and the oil industry in particular as a danger and sometimes took on the traits of a conspiracy theory.[42] New editions of older publications on the oil industry appeared, seemingly trying to outdo one another in their application of superlatives and in ascribing state-like qualities to these firms. For example, in a new edition of his study of the oil industry, first published in 1968, British journalist Christopher Tugendhat described it as 'bigger and more international than any other'. Its representatives negotiated with governments 'on almost equal terms, signing agreements almost as if they were sovereign independent states, and their finances dwarf the national budgets of all but the largest countries'.[43] The work that made the greatest impact within this discursive context was Anthony Sampson's study of the so-called 'Seven Sisters'. This British journalist and economic commentator claimed that he was telling one of the most peculiar stories of his age, namely 'how the world's biggest and most critical industry came to be dominated by seven giant companies; how the Western governments delegated much of the diplomatic function to them'.[44] At the same time, on the basis of conversations with company staff and government representatives, Sampson narrated how these firms, having shaped the economic world of oil over the decades as they saw fit, risked losing their power and market-dominating position during the few months of the oil crisis. Nonetheless, he went on, when the firms equitably allocated the available oil, they functioned once again as a kind of 'temporary world government', even if the company executives themselves would not have seen it that way. When Sampson asked one New York-based oil company chief executive, 'Didn't you feel . . . that you were ruling the world?', he retorted: 'No, the world was ruling us'.[45]

The perception of the oil companies as an unofficial, omnipotent world government jarred with their sudden loss of power and their attempts to obtain state support on a number of occasions during and after the crisis.[46] The oil firms registered record profits during the oil crisis and still mostly controlled downstream operations, in other words the processing of oil and the sale of oil products. Yet their power was eroded both by increased profit-sharing and nationalizations in the producing countries and the industrialized countries' efforts to modify energy policies.[47] In line with this, scholarly discourse took a more nuanced view of the role of globally active companies in general, and the oil firms in particular, than popular publications that assailed the power of the 'multinationals'.[48] Louis Turner declared that it was too soon to come to definitive conclusions about the multinational companies' influence on international politics, but he underlined that in the present era – contrary to classical theories of exploitation – the producing countries had shown themselves to be far from powerless vis-à-vis the oil firms.[49] The oil crisis, he contended, had made it clear that the multinational companies were the agents neither of their home nor host countries. In keeping with this, argued economic historian Mira Wilkins, the firms' activities were not directed against national governments, but exclusively followed their own economic logic.[50] The debate on the relationship between national governments and multinational (especially oil) companies did not fade away in subsequent decades, but has continued into the present. Newspaper and magazine articles on the power of the oil firms, which evades national legal systems, such as Texaco/Chevron in Ecuador or Shell in Nigeria, contrast with publications that – while largely acknowledging the firms' great influence – are less inclined to describe them as criminal.[51]

Did the multinational companies' power render the category of national sovereignty obsolete? According to political scientist Joseph Nye, in light of studies by the International Labour Organization, OECD, EC and the UN Economic and Social Council, the answer had to be a 'qualified "no"'. Certainly, Nye contended, the economic power of the two hundred largest companies was immense, but even weak states were capable of nationalizing their national subsidiaries.[52] However, he went on, the multinational companies' investments had created transnational economic interlinkages that various actors might instrumentalize to political ends; furthermore, this economic interdependence fundamentally altered the concept of national security. Louis Turner too felt it was an exaggeration to describe the oil companies as 'para-governmental bodies', particularly given the growth of political intervention in the fields of oil and energy in the wake of the oil crisis, on both the national and international levels.[53]

The investigative committees of the US Senate had already placed the relationship between oil firms and foreign policy in a historical perspective, a move subsequently emulated by historical researchers. In 1977, Burton I. Kaufmann examined the system through which the oil companies had taken on quasi-foreign policy functions in the 1950s. In the 1980s, David Painter and Fiona Venn scrutinized the changing relationship between oil firms and international relations in the 1940s and 1950s, and during the twentieth century as a whole.[54] While these texts were vastly more nuanced than the more journalistic undertakings that preceded them, they shared similar assumptions; when it came to the multinational oil companies' significance to the politics of sovereignty, the questions they examined departed little from their journalistic counterparts' conceptual framework. Daniel Yergin's history of oil is probably the most influential book in the field. It aimed, first, to tell the history of the 'biggest and most pervasive business' in the world and, second, to investigate the link between oil and both national political strategies and international power politics.[55] Yergin constructed his history as a thriller featuring a cast of hyper-masculine villains and heroes. He thus embraced many of the tropes and narrative elements already central to a key discourse, one that highlighted the oil companies' power and the challenge it posed to the Western industrialized nations' sovereign capacity to pursue energy and foreign policy.[56]

Security, Energy and Energy Security

Security issues affect the core of the state order and national sovereignty. States lay claim to a monopoly on the legitimate use of physical violence; in return, they promise to eliminate threats to the physical and material integrity of their citizens, through a police force domestically and armed forces abroad.[57] The legitimacy of a state largely depends on whether it can guarantee the security of its citizens. Over time, the international preconditions for this security guarantee have changed, as have the general population's demands for security – through, for example, an increased focus on social security. The first oil crisis, or the rise of energy security as a political category and prerequisite for action in the 1970s, played a crucial role in altering the prevailing conception of security.[58] This is evident in an article written by former brigadier general George A. Lincoln, who had been senior planning aide to George Marshall in the Second World War and, following an academic career at West Point, was head of the Office of Emergency Preparedness from 1969 to January 1973. In the year of his retirement, he provided an analysis of energy security in the November issue of *Air Force Magazine*. In light of his experiences in the armed forces and organizing programmes to tackle the US energy crisis prior to the oil crisis, Lincoln argued that the once-significant concern over safeguarding the supply of critical strategic materials, which had never included energy as such, must be superseded by a greater concern for energy security in a broader sense. Having an adequate energy supply, he explained, did not primarily mean meeting military requirements, which made up just 10 per cent of total energy consumption: 'Rather, energy security is a problem area of the heat and light and power for our total economy, together with assurance against coercion by the possessors of those energy resources that make possible our American way of life'.[59]

Influenced by the energy crisis in general and the oil crisis in particular, then, even members of the armed forces began to abandon a narrow and state-centred conception of national security. Classically, and particularly against the backdrop of the Cold War, the term 'national security' had been used to refer to protection from external attacks, and it was chiefly military action that could provide this protection. In this context, raw materials and energy sources were of strategic military importance; their absence could have a direct effect on national security if it limited the armed forces' defensive capabilities. By 1971, for example, Carl Vansant had concluded that, in view of the global distribution of energy sources, the energy supply was of strategic significance: 'Energy is the lifeblood of technical society, and one form of energy – oil – is absolutely essential for modern military mobile operations'.[60] Only with an adequate supply of oil, Vansant continued, could the armed forces guarantee national security. Lincoln, meanwhile, advocated a significantly broader concept of energy security that incorporated the energy supply of the entire economy and society. The idea here was that a lack of energy might threaten the stability of the social and political order.

Even before the oil embargo and the price hikes, certain observers had perceived the energy supply in this broader sense as a security problem for the United States, but especially for Western Europe.[61] Following the debates in the United States on its oil import policy and the OECD's discussions on how to avoid supply disruptions, the connection between energy and security seemed to be even closer and simultaneously more important and comprehensive. In any event, in 1973–74, the governments of the United States and its allies were constantly concerned with the 'security of supplies'. West Germany passed an Energy Security Act, and the focus of debates on the energy supply in that country shifted away from affordability towards security.[62] In the early 1970s, it was above all individuals like Lincoln, who were concerned with the energy supply in a very concrete way, who publicized its importance to national security in a broader sense. A few years later, for example, Philipp Odeen, who had contributed to the National Security Study Memorandum 174 on 'National Security and Energy Policy' in 1973, declared that for too long the United States had failed to recognize the importance of energy to national security and must now make it central to its security policies.[63] The former director of the Federal Energy Administration, John Sawhill, contributed a foreword with much the same content to an anthology edited by Joseph Nye and David A. Deese entitled *Energy and Security*; and Martin Hillenbrand, former US ambassador to Germany, published another multi-authored volume with Daniel Yergin, on the *Global Insecurity* engendered by the energy crises.[64]

While political scientists had published a few contributions on the relationship between energy and national security here and there, they only seriously began to get to grips with it as a result of the oil crisis.[65] They quickly became convinced that 'energy-related foreign policy . . . de facto touches on every essential political sphere: economic growth, the tackling of social conflicts, ensuring the victory of capitalism over communism, the cohesion of the Western alliance, and problems of the global economic and financial system', as Harald Müller elucidated in a 1977 literature review. Particularly in more recent research, he explained, all these aspects were fused together to form a 'new, comprehensive concept of security'.[66] In the newly established journal *International Security*, Linda B. Miller concluded that the oil crisis had rapidly become a paradigm case for political scientists. They were, she claimed, now studying the structural principles of contemporary global politics against this backdrop, much as they had done earlier in light of the Cuban Missile Crisis.[67] The oil crisis, as Miller summed up the mainstream of this new research, had shown that national security could no longer be guaranteed by military means; it had thus broadened the state-centred concept of security by highlighting the significance to security policy of economic developments and entanglements. Furthermore, the oil crisis was not just convulsing international power relations but also the classical analytical parameters of international relations, because scholars could no longer analyse issues of economy and resource supply solely through the 'prism of superpower competition'.[68]

There were a number of different facets to the contemporary debate on the relationship between the oil or energy supply and security, as detailed by Bo Heinebaeck at the behest of the Stockholm International Peace Research Institute. As he contended: oil was essential to military and economic security; attempts to guarantee the flow of oil could lead to conflicts; petrodollars were a threat to economic development in the oil-importing countries and the exporting countries invested a large proportion of them in weapons; furthermore, the transportation of oil entailed risks, while potential oil spills threatened ecological security.[69] While the more general literature on energy and security continued to discuss issues of nuclear proliferation, the political conditions around the Persian Gulf, the geopolitics of scarce resources and, from a classical perspective, the armed forces' energy needs, the key impact of the oil crisis was to expand the concept of security.[70]

There were four aspects to this expansion. First, the topic of national security no longer comprised solely military issues but also economic and thus social and political ones. As Richard N. Cooper set out to the London Institute for Strategic Studies, this meant that in order to guarantee security it was no longer enough to build up oil stockpiles for the armed forces; these must be large enough to handle economic upheavals as well.[71] Second, the key issue was no longer chiefly the security of the state, but rather that of its citizens. In other words, the reference group was significantly expanded. Third, in view of the global character of the oil economy and economic interdependence in general, the security policy perspective underwent a spatial expansion. As a result, the number of possible providers of security increased as well. In a speech to the security policy working group set up by foreign policy think tank the Atlantic Council, for example, Joseph J. Wolf argued that in the present era, security policy must move beyond a regional framework: 'Its ramifications are global'.[72] Finally, there was an expansion in the categorization of threats. Since even minor supply shortfalls could have a major impact, it was vital to eliminate not just acute threats or specific risks, but every form of vulnerability.[73]

This discursive expansion of the concept of security was driven by both political scientists and politicians. It did not reflect the interests of a particular political group. In the wake of the oil crisis and the subsequent economic upheavals, it encompassed the entire political spectrum. For example, President Nixon's statement at the Washington Energy Conference, in the spring of 1974, that energy and security were closely linked and could not be looked at separately, met with widespread approval. At around the same time, Democratic senator and later vice president Walter F. Mondale published an article in *Foreign Affairs*. Here he argued that while the classical security issues – the nuclear arms race, the contest between capitalism and communism and the confrontation between powerful armies or their influence on local conflicts across the world – had not become obsolete, they were ultimately overshadowed by the risk of an uncontrollable economic crisis. His conclusion was that national security policy must change: 'The priority we have accorded for years to traditional political and security concerns must now be given to international economic issues. If we do not resolve them, the security problems that may ensue could dwarf those that now remain'.[74] As late as 1981, Joseph Nye, who had left the academic sphere to join the Carter administration from 1977 to 1979, was still lamenting the fact that while there was a great deal of talk about energy security, the United States was not remotely as well prepared for an energy emergency as it was for a military attack.[75]

In West Germany there was a similarly broad security policy consensus when it came to energy. In October 1977, Chancellor Helmut Schmidt gave a speech at the London Institute for Strategic Studies on 'political and economic aspects of Western security', in which he discerned three new dimensions of security. In the wake of the oil crisis and the destruction of the Bretton Woods system, top of the list for Schmidt was the security of economic development. By this he meant the 'need to safeguard the foundation of our prosperity, guarantee access to energy and raw materials on the premises of free trade and provide ourselves with a monetary system that enables us to achieve these objectives'.[76] Here social and domestic security took a back seat to economic security, for which energy was the most important prerequisite: 'If there is one crucial issue for the economic security of the West, it is the issue of energy', Schmidt declared unambiguously.[77] Manfred Wörner, the CDU's security policy expert, who was touted as a possible minister of defence in the 1972 election campaign, was on much the same page as the chancellor in this regard. In 1975, in a speech to the Munich Security Conference, he had already declared that in view of the oil crisis security should no longer be understood, as it was in the 1960s, as 'synonymous with military strength as organized on a national, regional or international basis'.[78] The energy crisis, he contended, had shown that when it came to the provision of security, NATO was no longer 'autarkic'. As Wörner, following Karl Kaiser, put it, the Allies might 'be able to cover the entire territory of West Germany with a nuclear umbrella, but not with an oil umbrella, let alone a raw materials umbrella'.[79]

In debates on security policy, therefore, the oil crisis was a key reference point; critics were quick to complain that the fixation on oil imports was obscuring the other aspects of the energy supply relevant to security policy.[80] While these debates on security, broadly understood, were chiefly concerned with economic security, which was not solely dependent on oil or energy, oil still played a key role here, no doubt because it was a crucial fuel of modern warfare. Though the majority of authors assumed that the armed forces' energy supply was not at risk, this concern was always hanging in the air. At least since the oil crisis, moreover, predictions of future resource wars had become one of the classical topoi of dystopic visions.[81]

After the oil crisis, the concept of security continued to expand, not least within the United Nations; its most recent manifestation is the concept of human security.[82] Key steps in this expansion were the reports of the so-called Brandt and Palme commissions. In 1980, the Independent Commission on International Development, chaired by Willy Brandt, furnished the UN with a report outlining ways of 'securing' human 'survival' on Planet Earth.[83] The Commission believed the human race faced a significant threat from the structures of the world economy and the prevailing approach to natural resources; oil was thought particularly relevant due to its importance to the development of the world economy as well as the finite nature of oil reserves.[84] The programme of action put forward to enhance humanity's survival prospects was focused on the oil economy, which had also been discussed in the regular UN bodies over the course of the 1970s.

If we consider the makeup of the Brandt Commission, it is no surprise that the oil price and oil supply played a crucial role in its report. In addition to Willy Brandt, many other members of the Commission had occupied senior governmental posts during the oil crisis, such as Edward Heath as British prime minister, Haruki Mori as Japanese ambassador in London, Olof Palme as Swedish prime minister, Layachi Yaker as Algerian trade minister and Jan P. Pronk as Dutch minister for development cooperation. Two years later, in its report *Common Security*, the Independent Commission on Disarmament and Security, chaired by Olof Palme, concluded that countries could not guarantee their national security solely by building up their military strength. 'A secure state is undoubtedly one that neither comes under military attack nor is occupied, nor is subject to any threats of this kind; further, it is one that protects the health and security of its citizens and, very generally, promotes economic prosperity'.[85] Arms policy, the report asserted, was not only unable to guarantee the other aspects of security, but might in fact threaten them, because it tied up financial resources that were no longer available for other policy fields.

What did the expansion of the concept of security mean for ideas about national sovereignty? After the oil crisis, Hans J. Morgenthau, pioneer of the realist analysis of power politics, identified a division between military and economic power, that is, he highlighted the fact that the latter was no longer an emanation of the former.[86] Certainly, during and after the oil crisis and energy crisis there had been public and governmental debates in the United States on the possibility of military intervention in the Persian Gulf. But after the Vietnam War, few authors saw any real prospect of safeguarding the oil supply by military means due to the high risks involved, particularly against the backdrop of the Cold War.[87] The deployment of military force was a sovereign decision for nation states and remained so despite the commitments made by the countries of Europe and North America within the NATO framework. But measures to ensure economic security, for which an adequate supply of energy at a reasonable price was crucial, were not subject to national authority in the same way.[88] Security thus seemed realizable only through enhanced economic and energy policy cooperation with other states. There seemed little prospect of exercising power on a unilateral basis.[89]

This was certainly the hegemonic discourse, but there were those who took a different view, and – as early as the 1970s – wished to achieve energy security by military means. The journal *Commentary*, edited by Norman Podhoretz, was a gathering point for neoconservatives in the 1970s. Here political scientist Robert W. Tucker asserted that the energy crisis by no means necessarily justified calls for increased international cooperation. Against such ideas, he called for greater national 'independence' rather than 'interdependence'.[90] For him, it was nothing less than scandalous that in the face of such an immense challenge to US sovereignty, the use of the armed forces had not even been seriously considered. Tucker believed it quite improbable that the Soviet Union would respond militarily, for example, to a US invasion of Iraq, while European protests could of course be ignored entirely. Failing to intervene and allowing the producing countries to do as they pleased, he went on, would have worse consequences over the long term than military action. This failure to deploy the armed forces, or at least to consider doing so, was the product of 'political incompetence and the failure of will'.[91] On the basis of Tucker's analyses, one 'Miles Ignotus', writing in *Harper's Magazine,* compared the West's stance towards OPEC with its attitude towards Hitler in 1938. Having analysed a number of options, he concluded: 'There remains only force. The only feasible countervailing power to OPEC's control of oil is power itself – military power'.[92] Weighing up all the political and military risks, he contended, it was clearly both possible and vital to intervene: 'For if we do not do it, Project Independence will in fact be Project Isolation, with a somewhat impoverished America surrounded by a world turned into a slum'.[93]

In subsequent years, too, numerous commentators claimed that the consequences of a lack of oil were worse than those of military intervention in the Persian Gulf. In 1981, Robert Tucker still bemoaned the 'decline of the nation's power' in the 1970s. When it came to US policy vis-à-vis the producing countries and above all the political changes in Libya and Iran, he concluded: 'Never before have nations that possessed so great a superiority in power as the Western countries possessed over the Middle East producers placed themselves in so needless and so dangerous a predicament'.[94] In future, the goal of US foreign policy must be to restore a 'more normal political world . . . in which those states possessing the elements of great power again play the independent role their power entitles them to play'.[95] It is not hard to discern a continuity between such statements and recent US policies of intervention in the Persian Gulf, which have gone hand in hand with a new willingness to act unilaterally.[96]

Global Conflicts: North-South Rather than East-West?

In the article in the November 1973 issue of *Air Force Magazine* quoted at the start of the last section, George A. Lincoln predicted that in future, energy issues would become more important: 'Energy issues and policy are likely to replace the now waning cold war as a central policy concern, both domestic and foreign'.[97] During the oil crisis, it seemed to many contemporary observers, partly in view of the advancing process of détente, that the global geography of conflict was changing fundamentally.[98] The policy of détente, many contemporaries concluded, had diminished fears of a military conflict with the Soviet Union; due to the fears of oil scarcity, this had greatly intensified the centrifugal forces within the Western alliance (see chapter 5). For Karl Kaiser, the developments triggered by the crisis had 'shaken the European Community, the Western alliance system and the relationship between the developed and less developed parts of the world to their foundations'.[99] This seemed to have limited the United States' prospects of maintaining its hegemony. Hermann Kahn, head of the Hudson Institute and theorist of 'thermonuclear war', was the epitome of a foreign policy realist and strategist of global power politics. Yet even he forecast the decline of the superpowers and the end of the bipolar world order of the Cold War. Over the medium term, he believed, the economic ascent of Japan, West Germany (or Western Europe) and China would give rise to a multipolar or pentapolar world; military issues would become less important to the structure of international relations.[100] In a report for the Brookings Institution on the *New Forces in World Politics*, Seyom Brown too saw the simple and stable order of the Cold War dissolving.[101] With a rather different thrust, the Trilateral Commission blamed détente for unleashing the potential for conflict within Western societies, which had in turn led to a 'substantial relative decline in American military and economic power' and a 'major absolute decline in American willingness to assume the burdens of leadership'.[102] This, the Commission believed, had eroded the clear-cut bipolar order of the Cold War, while other forces were now influencing international relations, further restricting the established powers' capacity for action.

But what was replacing the East-West conflict? A number of political scientists argued that the global axis of this confrontation had undergone a ninety-degree turn and would be superseded by a conflict between the developed but resource-poor North and the resource-rich but underdeveloped South. These fears were not triggered but reinforced by the attempts of the Group of 77 to instrumentalize the oil crisis in UN negotiations on a New International Economic Order. In international political science journals, many authors from the Third World, such as Iranian Finance Minister Jahangir Amuzegar, constructed a fundamental North-South conflict, viewing the changes in the international oil market against this backdrop.[103] Before the oil crisis had even begun, in an article in *Foreign Policy*, C. Fred Bergsten, who had been Kissinger's advisor on international economic affairs on the National Security Council from 1969 to 1971, had warned of the 'threat from the Third World', triggering a broad public and political science debate.[104] As Bergsten saw it, US foreign policy was taking a major risk if it continued to neglect the Third World and paid less attention to development aid than other industrialized countries. Not only would the developing countries' self-confidence and aspirations grow in future, but so would their economic power, making confrontation with the industrialized countries more likely. This, Bergsten claimed, was reinforced by the fact that 'the security blanket' of the Cold War, which had so far tended to mitigate economic conflicts, was increasingly being cast aside.[105] Particularly when it came to raw materials, he went on, the countries of the Third World could put pressure on the industrialized countries and thus on the United States as well, not least because, after the war in Vietnam, it could no longer be certain of winning a military confrontation. Given the establishment of the producers' cartel, oil policy was merely the prototype for the producing countries' approach to other raw materials.[106] In order to avoid endangering the United States' sovereignty on the international level, then, Bergsten concluded, it was in its national interest to expand its ties with the countries of the Third World and promote their development.

Bergsten's identification of a substantial 'threat from the Third World' seemed to confirm a 'shift of sovereignty with respect to oil' allegedly evident as a result of the oil embargo and production cutbacks.[107] In a series of articles, the journal *Foreign Policy* asked anxiously whether 'one, two, many OPECs' were now likely to emerge.[108] Stephen D. Krasner was particularly sceptical and argued that oil was the exception rather than the rule. Only OPEC and OAPEC, he contended, combined three elements crucial to the enforcement of supply cuts: the multinational companies' tacit toleration; ample revenues, which generated plentiful financial reserves; and an important objective shared by all involved.[109] Furthermore, Krasner claimed, only oil occupied such a central position in the industrialized countries' economies that supply restrictions had any prospect of exercising the required pressure on their governments. He concluded: 'It is not necessary to engage in a futile effort to buy good behavior, or a politically and economically costly form of economic warfare. The Third World is not in a position to squeeze very hard'.[110] Bergsten considered this 'wishful thinking': the economic interests of other raw materials producers were neither as different as Krasner portrayed them, nor were their political commonalities so negligible.[111] Bergsten contended that the confrontation between the superpowers had eased off in the 1970s, while global economic interdependence had intensified over the preceding decades, and he therefore predicted an age of global conflict over resources. He eschewed more precise predictions; the Cold War might return or further dissemination of nuclear weapons might intensify the sense of uncertainty. Still, he believed that in the future, economic developments – and above all relations with the Third World with respect to raw materials – would become more important to guaranteeing national security.[112]

For many authors, then, the oil crisis appeared to have shifted the global geography of conflict. Geoffrey Kemp, who among other things worked for the Pentagon as a security expert, declared that the strategic map of the world had changed as a result of the non-industrialized world's economic power, the growing importance of resources, and changes in maritime law: 'Although the impact of each of the trends is important, taken together the effect is dramatic. For what is emerging is nothing less than a remarkable new strategic map. The practical effects are to resurrect the importance of geography and resources as a factor in military thinking, and to make us more sensitive to the geo-strategic perspectives of regional powers'.[113]

George A. Lincoln had already tried to visualize this altered geography of conflict, depicting the size of the various world regions on a world map in proportion to their oil reserves (see Figure 7.1).

In view of these ratios, in their report on the new geopolitics of energy, which they submitted to the Senate Committee on Interior and Insular Affairs in 1977, Melvin A. Conant and Fern R. Gold backed the idea that the region around the Persian Gulf now demanded greater attention from a security policy perspective.[114] Geographical factors now took on greater importance within strategic military thinking. Around this time, in a new edition of the *Geography of World Affairs*, John Peter Cole stated that the world had changed fundamentally in the just over twenty years since the book was first published. If the world of 1957 had still been largely defined

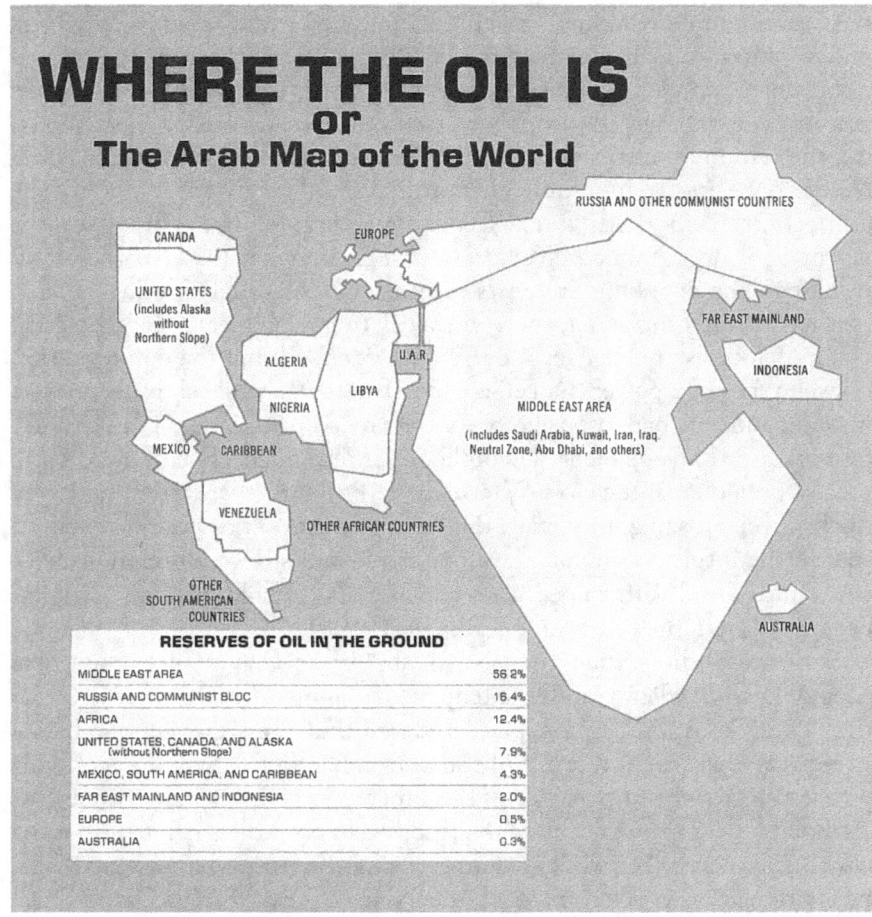

Figure 7.1. George A. Lincoln, 'Energy Security: New Dimension for US Policy', *Air Force Magazine* 56(11) (1973), 49–55, here 51.

by the United States and the Soviet Union, he asserted, it was resources and the limits to growth that now stood centre stage.¹¹⁵

The oil crisis thus seemed to have altered the world's political geography and international order. For Edward Friedland, Paul Seabury and Aaron Wildavsky, this was not an event limited to the narrowly circumscribed field of the international oil economy, or even international economic relations. Instead it amounted to a systematic shift in international relations and global politics. 'Oil is energy; energy is money; money is control; control is power. Oil in the wrong hands is money misspent and control corrupted; control corrupted is power abused; power abused is force misused. With oil out of control, force follows. With force out of control, so may be the world.'¹¹⁶ In light of developments in the field of oil, British political scientist Hedley Bull believed that international politics was excessively tailored towards the United States and the Soviet Union; it should instead pay more attention to the new forces at play. As yet, he averred, OPEC had only limited potential to project its power within the sphere of international politics, merely possessing 'rudimentary military power, the prestige of numbers, the possession of raw materials which others need, and the appeal of ideology'. However, over the longer term their oil revenues would allow its member states to modernize. They would soon enjoy the instruments of power commensurate with this technological and industrial development.¹¹⁷

Hans J. Morgenthau saw a revolution in world politics comparable to the shift from feudalism to the nation state: states lacking the classical instruments of power could exercise power over countries vastly superior to them in military, technological and economic terms.¹¹⁸ As a result of this alleged separation of military and political power, Morgenthau believed, the organizational principles of world politics no longer did justice to prevailing global forces and conditions. For him, it was perverse that oil, 'the lifeblood of an advanced industrial state', was under the control of potentates 'who have no other instrument of power and who are accountable to nobody, morally, politically, or legally'.¹¹⁹ It was already irrational, Morgenthau claimed, to have left nuclear weapons with the potential to destroy humanity in the hands of sovereign nation states. This irrationality had now been surpassed: in the shape of oil, states with a very shaky claim to 'sovereignty' had at their disposal the means to destroy Western civilization – in a less dramatic but equally enduring way. 'The former [the Western nation states] are no longer, and the latter [the producing countries] have never been, capable of performing the functions for which government was established in the first place, that is, to protect and promote the life, liberty and pursuit of happiness of its citizens. Their power is essentially destructive.'¹²⁰

Given these global changes wrought by the oil crisis, the question was: what role would the nation states play in future? For Seyom Brown, the new forces set in motion by the oil crisis undermined not only the Cold War order but the very foundations of the sovereign nation states. They fostered 'other bases of political community – ethnicity, religion, social class, economic function, generation', which would increasingly assert themselves and alter the structure of world politics.[121] This assessment did not go uncontested. Nonetheless, an eloquent group of political scientists around C. Fred Bergsten, Robert Keohane and Joseph Nye perceived a fundamental shift in the principles underpinning global politics, prompting them to formulate a new theory of international relations.[122] The global politics of their era, they believed, was dominated by conflicts not explicable with the conventional tools of political theory.[123]

Transnationalism, Interdependence and International Organizations

Foreign policy realism was a theory of the Cold War in a dual sense. It was a product of that conflict, developed when it began by authors such as Hans J. Morgenthau and George F. Kennan. Furthermore, it served chiefly as a means of analysing and explaining the clash between East and West.[124] Even without the oil crisis, there were ample grounds for a critique of the idea of international relations as a power struggle between sovereign states, one little influenced by economic and domestic political factors. As early as 1954, legal scholar and political scientist Karl Loewenstein pointed out that the idea of sovereign states interacting on an equal footing – a notion characteristic of both international law and the theory of international relations – was a fiction. In light of rapid technological advances, processes of economic and political exchange and growing interdependence, he contended, no country – not even the superpowers – could live in a state of 'isolated sovereignty'.[125] However, Loewenstein asserted, sovereignty and economic cooperation should not be understood in antithetical terms. Especially under Cold War conditions, there was a need for international cooperation that constrained sovereignty in order to preserve it.[126] It was in this spirit, around 1970, that Robert Keohane and Joseph Nye sought to overcome the realist conception of international relations, or at the very least to expand it to more effectively factor in economic interdependencies and transnational processes.

Nye and Keohane knew one another from their time as students of Stanley Hoffmann at Harvard University. They were still at the start of their academic careers when, following a meeting of the editorial board of the journal *International Organization* in 1968, they planned an issue on the theory of international organizations and their role in international relations. Building on the work of Raymond Aron, Philip Jessup, Karl Kaiser, Horst Mendershausen and James Rosenau, the central concept here was to be 'transnationality' or 'transnational relations'. Nye, Keohane and others first put its sustainability to the test in June 1970 at a conference at the Harvard Center for International Affairs. The following year, they edited an issue on 'Transnational Relations and World Politics', which was republished in 1973 as an anthology and remains a key point of reference in the political science debate on transnational relations and nongovernmental actors.[127] Though oil had not provided the stimulus for theory building, following the oil crisis it served as a paradigm, one that theorists could use to illustrate the growing importance of transnational processes and international organizations.[128]

Two years after the oil crisis, Nye and Keohane, in collaboration with C. Fred Bergsten, published an essay that aimed to establish a framework for research on the connection between international economic interdependence and international relations.[129] OPEC and OAPEC having instrumentalized oil to political ends, these authors identified the supply of raw materials as the most important topic for the world economy.[130] As they saw it, the oil crisis had revealed the decline in US hegemony since the end of the Second World War, when the key institutions of the Western world had been created. In a closely integrated world of more than one hundred states, of which at least two dozen were important to global economic development, even the United States was no longer unaffected by other countries' economic problems: 'The oil crisis dramatized the vulnerability of most of the world, including the United States, to supply interruptions of a single key commodity'.[131] While a number of other authors shared this diagnosis, Bergsten went a step further, claiming that the present era was witnessing a new wave of international institution building.[132] For Bergsten, the main goal of the UN Environmental Programme, the World Food Council and the International Energy Agency was 'to make the world safe for interdependence'.[133] Essentially, he argued, world politics could take one of two forms: the hegemony of a single country or cooperative solutions within international organizations. As no country was in a position to exercise hegemony, it was vital to seek cooperation in order to overcome the problems of trade, finance, raw materials, development and security, whose close interconnection the oil crisis had laid bare.

Interdependence within the sphere of energy seemed highly specific and particularly intense, but it also appeared to function as a paradigm for processes of economic exchange as a whole.[134] For those keen to investigate the significance of this interdependence for international relations, the International Energy Agency seemed like the obvious case study.[135] As Robert Keohane saw it, analysing this organization could add nuance to the prevailing doctrine that nation states acted within international organizations not to achieve the good of all but solely to uphold their own interests. International organizations such as the IEA, he averred, created transgovernmental coalitions between governmental subunits, which then influenced policymaking: 'My thesis is that decision making in the IEA Governing Board can be adequately described in interstate terms, but that the politics of policy implementation are only explicable by taking into account transgovernmental as well as state behavior'.[136] James E. Katz also believed that the establishment of the IEA cast new light on the relationship between international organizations and national sovereignty. Even if the IEA had been founded with the goal of protecting and strengthening the nation state, Katz claimed, it had nonetheless led to the crossing of national boundaries and policy coordination on a higher level.[137] Consequently, as Stanley Hoffmann argued, within the IEA the United States had become the Europeans' 'senior partner' rather than a hegemon.[138]

Against this background, in *Power and Interdependence*, published in 1977, Keohane and Nye put forward a comprehensive critique of the realist conception of international relations.[139] For them, complex interdependence was constituted by multiple channels of communication between societies, the absence of clear hierarchies, and the irrelevance of military power in parallel with the growing importance of international organizations. In brief, they argued, this was a state of affairs that classical political scientific theories did not capture adequately.[140] In this context, they repeatedly referred to the oil crisis – or international relations with respect to raw materials as a whole – to show that the United States was no longer capable of maintaining its hegemony.[141] Keohane fleshed out these ideas a few years later in *After Hegemony*. The United States' supremacy, he asserted, had eroded since the 1960s and 'hegemonic leadership is unlikely to be revived in this century for the United States or any other country'.[142] The oil crisis now played a crucial role in Keohane's argument that, first, the categories of 'power' and 'interests' were insufficient to understanding international relations, and, second, the era of the hegemonic powers was over. Abetted by US hegemony, he argued, after 1945 the major oil companies had structured the international oil economy in a way that the loss of this hegemony had made impossible to maintain.[143] Keohane claimed that the destruction of the old oil regime in the early 1970s had revealed the kind of disastrous consequences that might flow from the absence of the hegemon, unless there was a major push to create international structures to regulate processes of economic exchange.[144] Consequently, for Keohane, in the post-hegemonic era, international and transnational organizations such as the IEA had begun to play a crucial role in ensuring the smooth running of these economic processes.[145]

The interpretations put forward by Keohane, Nye, Bergsten and others have influenced both the public and historical perception of the oil crisis into the present. Often, the beginning of the United States' alleged decline as a global power is localized in the 1970s and associated with energy issues.[146] In the same vein as Keohane, and building on his work, Daniel Sargent's recent history of American foreign policy in the 1970s claims that the age of the superpowers ended in the 1970s due to increased economic interdependence.[147] The United States, he asserts, had begun to depend on other world regions, which had become especially clear in the field of energy; this is why, in the shape of the Washington Energy Conference, Kissinger deftly sought to replace unilateral power politics with multilateral cooperation.[148] This transfer of a contemporary interpretation into a historical account is problematic. It depended on specific political preferences and, moreover, had the character of a forecast.[149] Rather than an attempt to explain the present, *After Hegemony* sought to describe the state of a world yet to be created. For those who shared this objective and prognosis, the oil crisis seemed like a crucial turning point in the history of sovereignty, not just for Western industrialized nations but for the world as a whole. In the mid 1980s, for example, American political scientist Richard N. Rosecrance contended that while the Yom Kippur War followed a political and military logic, the oil crisis had laid bare the limits to sovereign power politics imposed by economic interdependence.[150] In view of economic integration, Rosecrance believed, in the present era no state could lay claim to the degree of independence classically implied by the concept of sovereignty.[151] The oil crisis provided crucial stimulus to the debate on the significance of economic interdependence for national strategies, and the debaters referred repeatedly to the oil crisis into the post-Cold War era.[152] In the 1970s, even Stephen D. Krasner, who later wished to save the concept of sovereignty by making it more nuanced, first contemplated US foreign policy in light of the problem of raw materials.[153]

The perception of 'interdependence' as the basic condition of all foreign policy action moulded only some of the theory building on international relations. Likewise, it shaped the perception of the oil crisis only within a section of the political spectrum. Not everyone endorsed the hypothesis that increased interdependence made unilateral power politics impossible and international cooperation essential and would, therefore, diminish national sovereignty in the classical sense.[154] This was at least as much a political demand and hope as it was an analysis of the age; advocates of military intervention in the Persian Gulf were already expressing their opposition in the 1970s. They remained marginal in the 1970s, but organized themselves within the framework of foreign policy think tanks such as the Heritage Foundation, American Enterprise Institute, Hoover Institute, Manhattan

Institute, Center for Strategic and International Studies and Cato Institute, which were partly funded by oil firms.[155] After the Cold War, there were increasingly vociferous calls for the United States to pursue a sovereign, unilateral power politics. The 'New Sovereigntists' associated with the American Enterprise Institute and the Project for a New American Century argued that the United States was not tied down by international legal norms because it had the power to defy them.[156] It was above all Jeremy A. Rabkin who made the *Case for Sovereignty*, according to which it was not just the right but also the duty of the United States to ignore international norms. Ultimately, he contended, all would benefit from a world of independent nation states acting on a sovereign basis.[157] Robert Kagan explained the differences between the US and European assessment of the Iraq War of 2003 in light of the divergent development of theories of power politics and sovereignty on the two continents. On this view, an ever weaker Europe placed its hopes in international agreements, while the United States could act without the consent of the United Nations.[158]

It is ultimately impossible to determine whether the world is moving towards greater economic interdependence, making international cooperation more important, or whether, conversely, unilateral, sovereign power politics remains possible and perhaps even desirable. People's views on this issue depend not just on political preferences but also on particular positions within the historical process. In light of global political conditions, Keohane's *After Hegemony* seemed more plausible when it was published in 1984 than it did ten years later, after the collapse of the Eastern Bloc, or twenty years later, after the invasion of Iraq. This brings out the fundamental problem of contemporary history. It has to take into account the interpretive struggles of the period under examination, while having no way of knowing what will happen in future; yet this would be necessary to assess the validity of contemporary interpretations as they always imply specific future scenarios. To pin down the place of the oil crisis within the history of sovereignty, therefore, is to simultaneously exclude certain interpretive options. Yet these might rapidly come to seem plausible if things turn out differently than expected.[159] No less problematic is the historicization of those contemporary debates that saw the threats to sovereignty emanating from the domestic rather than the international sphere.

The Limited Recognition of Limits: Energy, Politics and Society

From an international perspective, then, many contemporaries viewed the sovereignty of the Western European states and the United States as limited, whether by multinational oil companies, new security policy imperatives, an altered global geography of conflict, growing economic interdependence, or transnational nongovernmental actors. Others, meanwhile, perceived a far more fundamental challenge to nation states' capacity for effective action, both internationally and domestically. They interpreted the producing countries' intentional cutting of the oil supply as a taste of things to come, namely the exhaustion of natural resources, which would spell the end of economic growth. This would place strict limits on states' sovereign room for manoeuvre.

In the 1970s, natural limits to sovereignty were discussed within three discursive contexts. First, a number of academic disciplines had begun to comprehend societies in light of their energy consumption and, consequently, to regard their developmental potential as constrained by the supply of energy. Second, the oil crisis and the energy supply played an important if controversial role in the discourses of ecological limits and in debates on the 'limits to growth', which had attained the status of a catchphrase. Third, the question of whether economic growth was limited by the availability of raw materials was also discussed in energy economics, which was becoming established as a discipline in the 1970s. Its practitioners viewed the resource-based limits to state action more optimistically, but simultaneously placed another type of limit on the state, rejecting intervention in market mechanisms.

Energy as a Medium of Social Reflection

Given the key role played by the energy supply in all economic and social processes, it seems intuitively plausible to describe societies in light of their energy consumption.[160] Hence, many studies of the history of energy published over the last few decades work on the assumption 'that energy might fundamentally drive history'.[161] The thesis that energy is constitutive of society, however, is by no means as self-evident as it appears to be today, but is itself historical. It was first conceived in the nineteenth century, when the laws of thermodynamics were formulated and steamships and railways reconfigured space and its perception.[162] However, until well into the twentieth century, few scholars were interested in grounding the social sciences in the concept of energy, and it was often outsiders within their various subjects who pursued this goal.[163]

Drawing on Hayden White's tropology, David Nye distinguishes five narratives on the connection between energy and society: (1) 'natural abundance'; (2) 'artificial scarcity'; (3) 'human ingenuity'; (4) 'man-made apocalypse'; and (5) 'existential limits'.[164] The narrative of natural abundance, which generally takes the form of a romance, assumes that nature provides us with bountiful treasures there for the taking. Comedies, conversely, foreground the artificial scarcity of resources at the hands of villains (however defined) and the overcoming of scarcity through human ingenuity. The anthropogenic apocalypse due to excessive consumption of fossil energy sources generally takes the form of a tragedy, while the narrative of existential, resource-based limits is typically expressed as satire.[165] Common to all these narratives is the constitutive connection between energy (or transformations of energy) and social processes. However, until the 1970s, this connection was mainly postulated outside the discipline of economics and the social sciences in public, political and even literary discourses, with the PR departments of the major energy firms doing much to propagate it.[166] Partly in an attempt to obtain state support or perks in light of their often enormous expenditure, companies emphasized the power of the energy sources they provided to mould and – always – to improve society; initially, they surrounded new energy forms in particular with a downright utopian aura.[167] It was only when energy resources seemed to become scarcer in the 1970s that the trope of energy's socially constitutive force began to proliferate among economists, sociologists and anthropologists. Frequently basing themselves on retrospective historical accounts and global histories of energy consumption, many scholars now tried to turn 'energy' into a key analytic category of the social sciences.

The *International Encyclopedia of the Social Sciences*, published in 1968, features no entry on 'energy' or related topics, whereas its new edition forty years later has articles on 'energy', the 'energy industry' and the 'energy sector'. Here energy is defined as 'the ability to do work', which is ascribed a decisive role in human cultural evolution, because the formation of ever more complex societies depends on the capacity to master and harness energy.[168] The prosperity of the industrialized countries in the twentieth century, we are informed, rests upon the highly concentrated form of energy found and exploited in fossil energy sources, above all in the easily accessible oil.[169] Again, the sixth, 1958 edition of the German *Staatslexikon* includes only specialized articles on the electricity industry, energy law and the energy economy, but none on the relationship between society and energy as such. It was not until the seventh edition of 1986 that it included an article specifically on energy, which defines it from a physical perspective as the stored capacity for labour.[170] At the same time, however, it also identifies a close connection between energy and the social order: 'The development of human civilization is bound up with the human capacity to harness nonhuman energy on an ever larger scale'.[171] The article sketches an outline civilizational history of growing energy consumption from wood, through coal, to oil. Judging by the encyclopaedias, it appears that between 1968 and 1986 the concept of energy gained greater currency within the social sciences.

Around two years before the oil crisis, *Scientific American* published a special issue on the topic of energy. In a variety of ways, it examined and gave expression to the interrelationships between energy supply and the constitution of society. The articles evinced the belief that 'the artful manipulation of energy has been an essential component of man's ability to survive and to develop socially'.[172] Some of them examined the flow of energy in agrarian or industrial societies and, with the help of complex diagrams, attempted to visualize the supply of energy as a whole, the transformations of energy and the output of energy.[173] This static description of societies in light of their energy budgets was supplemented by a diachronic civilizational history, which identified the increase in energy consumption as a driving force of social development: 'The US industrial societies are based on the use of power . . . . The success of an industrial society, the growth of its economy, the quality of life of its people and its impact on other societies and on the total environment are determined in large part by the quantities and the kinds of energy resources it exploits and by the efficiency of its systems for converting potential energy into work and heat'.[174] In view of the ecological costs of growing energy consumption and the increased entropy anticipated in light of the laws of thermodynamics, the articles also asked what form of social and technological processes were necessary to limit the negative consequences of increased consumption.[175] In addition to an article that explicitly investigated the effects of energy consumption on the anthropogenic geography, full-page aerial photographs of nuclear power stations and transport infrastructure gave visual expression to energy production's profound impact on the planet. Even the ads placed by major energy and electricity firms underlined the message of this issue. For example, the ads commissioned by the Brown Boveri Corporation showed a twilight city illuminated by countless street lamps and other lights. The accompanying text explained that the electricity necessary for lighting was often taken for granted, though it depended entirely on the energy companies. The modern lifestyle, then, would be impossible without them:

> Electricity is twinkling lights. Electricity is downtown streetcars. Chandeliers at the opera . . . . Electricity cooks late suppers. Lets you watch that late show. Keeps you warm or cold. – Electricity turns the wheels of industry. Helping to make things. From spacecraft to bread. Electricity means safety. In the hospital. At the airport. Electricity is essential.[176]

In much the same vein, in an ad featuring a blurred image of people in a sea of lights, Texaco asserted that in a certain sense it was involved in show business. The latter would be impossible without light bulbs, which require electricity to work, while electricity requires transformers and these in turn are enwrapped in an oil-based insulating material produced by Texaco. So there was 'a little bit of Texaco in every light on old Broadway'.[177]

During and after the energy crisis, the power of energy to mould societies was emphasized at every turn, to the point where it became a commonplace. 'Power' was 'all-pervasive', underlined Lawrence Rocks and Richard Runyon;[178] on behalf of the US Geological Survey, Rogers C.B. Morton declared that 'mineral fuels' were 'literally the cornerstones of modern life ... they are the physical source of most of the necessities, conveniences, and comforts of life in the Unites States today'.[179] Time and again, as for example in the reports of the Trilateral Commission, energy was referred to as the 'blood' of economies and societies; this meant that energy supply problems would have a tremendous influence on 'the entire fabric of national and international economic life'.[180] For environmental activist Barry Commoner, the environmental crisis, energy crisis and financial crisis were not separate phenomena, but the outcome of modern societies' basic defect, namely their excessive use of energy.[181] In 1977, the energy report produced for the Committee on Interior and Insular Affairs concluded: 'The development of American society may be traced in the ever increasing use of energy to provide for human wants, to achieve national goals, and to shape a unique life style'.[182] The public valorization of the concept of energy now prompted social scientists to engage with the topic despite their previous lack of interest. In the first edition of Daniel Bell's *The Coming of Post-Industrial Society*, which appeared in 1973, the factor of energy still played virtually no role. In fact, Bell described energy as a raw material characteristic of industrial society, not of its emerging post-industrial counterpart, which he claimed was essentially based on knowledge. In light of the broad discussions on energy that occurred in the interim, in the foreword to the second edition of 1976 Bell then made it plain that a lack of energy might slow the emergence of the new technologies that typified post-industrial society. The new society, he explained, would merely overwrite the old one like a palimpsest, so energy would retain a certain significance.[183]

Within the public discourse on energy, the deterministic 'energy-civilization equation', according to which increased civilization meant greater energy consumption, was increasingly discredited. But even authors who wished to decouple rising energy consumption from increased economic growth continued to assume that societies are constituted by their energy consumption.[184] Amory Lovins thus poked fun at authors who prophesied that falling energy consumption would have disastrous consequences: 'Civilization in this country, according to some, would be inconceivable if we used only, say, half as much electricity as we use now. But that is what we did use in 1963 when we were at least half as civilized as now'.[185] Moreover, he turned the interrelationship between energy and society on its head. If the two were closely but not deterministically linked, then changes in the field of energy, such as Lovins' preferred 'soft energy paths', could bring social changes in their wake.[186] Social scientists eagerly embraced the hypothesis of a close interaction between energy and society because it enabled them to justify their interpretations concerning energy against those of natural scientists and engineers. Many commentators having already expressed scepticism about technological solutions to ecological problems, in the *Proceedings of the Academy of Political Science* Marvin J. Cetron and Vary T. Coates asserted that: 'Any way that the problem of energy is approached, from diplomatic-military contingency plans to solar-energy systems, it has an undeniable relationship with the social environment'.[187] Because energy production always caused moral and political problems, many authors believed the energy crisis could not be solved through purely technical means, but required the competences of other disciplines.[188] Anthropologists Laura Nader and Stephen Beckerman asserted that natural scientists and engineers were about as qualified to solve the energy problem as social psychologists were to build nuclear power stations: 'Technical specialists operating beyond the limits of their competence results in a clouding of human factors'. They claimed that because the provision of energy was always bound up with values, as experts on humanity in general they had an advantage over technical specialists.[189]

The analysis of the energy supply of entire societies was a complex endeavour, requiring consideration of both the various energy sources and the different spheres of consumption. It grew even more complicated in the 1970s, as representatives of such different academic disciplines as petroleum geology, engineering, political science, economics and social science tried to chip in with their expertise. As early as 1970, in the preface to an energy handbook he had edited, Gerhard Bischoff defined the energy supply as one of the most important topics of the present era, before going on to conclude that 'the use of all the Earth's energy sources [is] bound up with such an array of technological and economic problems that no individual [can] gain a complete overview of them'.[190] In view of this complexity, which was intensified by the social dimensions of energy consumption, experts saw a growing need for interdisciplinary exchange, which a number of new journals attempted to satisfy. *Energy Policy*, *Resources Policy* (both founded in 1974) and the *Annual Review of Energy* (1976) aimed to shed light on energy issues, with a strong practical focus but from a variety of scholarly perspectives. These forums played a significant role in defining 'energy' as a new hybrid field of knowledge.

Energy Policy sought to address the economic, ecological, political, planning and social aspects of energy production and consumption facing political decision-makers and businesses. The journal *Resources Policy*, published in the United Kingdom, was dedicated to resource issues more generally, but within this framework energy resources occupied pride of place.[191] The *Annual Review of Energy* also aimed to put forward possible solutions to all the major energy issues. To this end, it explored topics ranging from the technologies of energy production and consumption through regional and global energy systems and their social effects to energy economics and energy policy.[192] In parallel to the establishment of these journals, at the universities a variety of disciplines increasingly offered seminars on energy, creating a need for new, interdisciplinary textbooks. These too began by highlighting the close connection between energy and society or the importance of energy to the history of civilization. 'Nothing influences our living style more than the availability and utilization of energy', as Joseph Priest began the textbook *Energy for a Technological Society*.[193] Priest also reflected on the fact that it was only the sudden, inflationary increase in newspaper and journal articles on energy issues during the oil crisis that had made energy an omnipresent topic of private communication and triggered scholarly interest.[194]

As energy seemed to become scarce and a lack of energy resources seemed to constrain the political room for manoeuvre, the notion that societies are constituted by their energy consumption spread. Many commentators, in other words, discovered the society-constituting force of energy at the very moment when its supply seemed to become critical. Often, the limits of the politically doable seemed set by the energetically possible. Time and again, in a technocratic manner, energy experts of various disciplines sought to assert their ability to gauge the room for political manoeuvre; they also aspired to explain to those in power which decisions could be taken without compromising future energy security. This energetic gauging of the political coincided with a broad discussion on the 'limits to growth' – though far beyond the coterie of the energy experts.

Finiteness? Discourses of Ecological Limits and the Experience of the Oil Crisis

Neither the intentional oil shortage of 1973–74 nor the report for the Club of Rome, which was published worldwide in 1972 under the title *Limits to Growth*, triggered the discourse of ecological limits, within whose framework a variety of commentators called for a fundamental reorientation of policy in the Western industrialized societies. In fact, *Limits to Growth* built on a wave of eco-apocalyptic writings that envisioned disasters to come and proclaimed that states' room for manoeuvre would be severely limited, both by the availability of natural resources and by the environmental consequences of their exploitation.[195] Many studies on the 1970s assume that the impact of the report for the Club of Rome was reinforced by the oil crisis and that a growing number of people began to perceive natural limits to the economic growth they had experienced in the preceding decades.[196] This is quite correct if we consider only the ecological movements that emerged in 'the key decade of environmental history' and their milieu.[197] Beyond the conservative environmental campaigners and *Heimatschützer* and left-liberal, ecological circles, however, the reaction to *Limits to Growth* was mostly negative.[198] In line with this, only certain sections of the political spectrum perceived the oil crisis as confirmation of the claims made by the Club of Rome and concluded that this made environmental policies more urgent. For others, meanwhile, it seemed to lay bare the clashing objectives of environmental and energy policy.[199] It was not in the economic crisis following the oil crisis that economy and ecology first became antagonistic concepts. During the oil crisis itself, there already appeared to be a conflict between the environmental impact of the energy supply and its security. The vast majority of commentators and public opinion privileged the latter over the former.[200]

The influential ecological writings of the early 1970s were united in their tendency to think in terms of complex systems, to extend the ecological perspective to the Earth as a whole – the focus was rarely on anything less than the planet itself – and to expand the analytical perspective, often to the whole of human history.[201] The study for the Club of Rome was underpinned by Jay W. Forrester's theory of system dynamics. From this perspective, the process of industrialization overrode natural feedback mechanisms that inhibit the growth of specific variables, resulting in the exponential growth of, for example, the global population or environmental pollution; since the natural resources of the Earth are limited, within the next century humanity would come up against its absolute limits, unless there was a 'transition from growth to equilibrium'.[202] Many contemporaries believed that this problem was unresolvable under the political conditions of the time. Their reasoning was that, first, environmental threats crossed national boundaries, so individual states lacked the capacity to tackle them, even if they tried to do so. 'Only large regional entities, if not in fact global ones' had any prospect of averting them.[203] Second, as often noted by democratic theorists, the period of time remaining until the predicted disaster exceeded democratically elected governments' horizons, in terms of both their basic conceptual framework and planning practices; but it also extended beyond the lifespan of citizens, who struggled to honour the rights of future generations.[204]

The oil and energy crises fit perfectly into this discursive context: they were global phenomena that could only be modelled through complex systems and required long periods of time to conceptualize and resolve. A symptomatic example is Marion King Hubbert's theory of peak oil, which was growing in popularity. Hubbert often gave this concept visual expression in a diagram depicting worldwide fossil energy use along an extended timeline, which made it seem no more than a brief episode in the history of humanity or the world.[205] Deploying a moralizing language, many commentators, such as West German President Gustav Heinemann in his 1973 Christmas address, assailed the 'overindulgent energy consumption' of the preceding years, which had led to the overly rapid exhaustion of 'vital raw materials', and viewed the oil crisis as a 'salutary shock' that might result in more conscious energy consumption.[206] Figures on both left and right propagated the idea that natural resources might impose limits on the economically possible and that political action must therefore be geared towards these limits, potentially requiring changes in the political system.[207] Despite the trenchant critique of economic growth emanating from the ecological movement, the key political forces, as we saw above in the case of West Germany, remained convinced that it was vital.[208] In the United States in the second half of the 1970s, Jimmy Carter was highly responsive to the ecological movement's ideas on energy policy and contemplated natural limits to the availability of raw materials. Nonetheless, the core principle of his energy policy was still the need for 'healthy economic growth' to continue.[209] Ronald Reagan subsequently purged the US government's public pronouncements of the rhetoric of limits.[210]

Nonetheless, in the 1970s a fundamental critique of growth took hold in the Western industrialized societies, which persists to this day and is the source of the interpretation of the oil crisis quoted at the start of this book.[211] Certainly, the mainstream of both general and energy economists rejected the conclusions of the report for the Club of Rome regarding the limits to growth, contending that it failed to consider the potential for alternative technologies and energies, while also failing to factor in the price mechanism, which would slow the exhaustion of natural resources.[212] But a minority did indeed regard natural resources as limited and argued that their limits placed constraints on the economic and political room for manoeuvre. By the mid 1960s, Kenneth Boulding had attempted to explain to his colleagues that they must modify their economic models to conceive of the world not as an open but as a closed system. Deploying the striking metaphor of 'spaceship Earth', he called for a transition from a 'cowboy' to a 'spaceman economy'.[213] Boulding believed the oil crisis had confirmed key aspects of his analysis.[214] Because he assumed that it was difficult to change habitual ways of life once they had become entrenched, for him the solution lay in the search for new, alternative energy technologies.[215]

In the early 1970s, Nicholas Georgescu-Roegen sought to anchor the notion of the finite nature of fossil energy sources more firmly in economic theory, reformulating the latter in light of the laws of thermodynamics.[216] Rather than the laws of mechanics, Georgescu-Roegen tried to comprehend all economic processes via the law of the conservation of energy and the law of entropy. These, he believed, had a clear consequence: 'A closed system cannot perform work indefinitely at constant rate'.[217] Though he honoured certain predecessors such as John Kenneth Galbraith and Boulding, he asserted that economic theory as a whole had failed to reflect upon the true foundation of the processes of economic growth that had occurred since industrialization, namely 'an extraordinary bonanza of fossil fuels'.[218] It was only through the oil crisis that Georgescu-Roegen's views truly began to find wide resonance. It thus seemed to him ex-post as though the oil crisis had prompted most people, if not everyone, to at least begin to recognize the 'terrestrial origins of human existence'.[219] One student and popularizer of Boulding and Georgescu-Roegen was Herman E. Daly, who gave their theories a practical political thrust by calling for the abandonment of the standard model of economic growth and the establishment of a 'steady-state economy'.[220] The environmental movement certainly took note of Daly's attempt to refound economics, a project he sought to advance with the help of the journal *Ecological Economics*; however, he believed his efforts were 'aggressively ignored by mainstream economists in major universities'.[221]

At least in the 1970s, the ecological movement still included a current highly critical of economic growth. In light of environmental pollution and the predicted lack of resources, its exponents concluded that the industrialized countries must break fundamentally with the growth paradigm. Conservative critics of progress in particular saw the roots of the problem in a purely technical conception of the relationship between human beings and nature. They called for the 'revision of our criteria for measuring value, an economic perspective' that was 'lopsidedly quantitative' and thus a 'regress to survival'.[222] While these views remained marginal on the political right and failed to attract widespread support beyond it, those on the more radical left who had had reservations about the topic of the environment, believing it to be a capitalist ploy, increasingly began to open their minds to it.[223] As the notion of 'environmental protection shifted away from the conservative context towards the progressive left', there were mounting calls, in several political camps but above all within the left-liberal spectrum, for a purely quantitative approach to the measurement of living standards to be at least supplemented by parameters and factors of relevance to the quality of life.[224] This position was reinforced by empirical studies showing that after a certain level of energy consumption there was no clear-cut correlation between energy use and quality of life, and that it is quite possible to improve living standards without rising energy consumption – just as energy consumption may increase without improving standards of living.²²⁵ At the same time, however, the concept of growth was so tremendously powerful that, rather than abandoning it, most of its critics at most sought to redefine it by deploying adjectives such as 'qualitative' or 'moral'.

Among the advocates of resource-preserving economic forms who made the greatest international impact – while continuing to put their faith in technological solutions to energy problems – were Ernst F. Schumacher and Amory Lovins, both of whom contributed key catchphrases to the debate. In the book *Small Is Beautiful*, Schumacher, former chief economic advisor to the UK National Coal Board from 1950 to 1970, envisaged an economy 'as if people mattered'. This was no fantasy of opting out from modern life; Schumacher advocated new technologies and production methods on a smaller scale.²²⁶ The soft energy path proposed by Amory Lovins also continued to assume technological progress, but privileged smaller and more flexible technologies, particularly within the field of renewable energies.²²⁷ The debate, initiated in the 1970s, on the 'limits to growth' in light of ecological factors and resource use – or on the potential to achieve a more ecologically sound and resource-preserving form of growth – has continued into the present with varying degrees of intensity. For example, a 2012 report from the Council of Experts on Environmental Issues (Sachverständigenrat für Umweltfragen), established by the West German government in 1972, stated that there could be 'no unlimited utilization of natural resources . . . in a finite world'. These environmental experts recognize as yet untapped potential to decouple 'welfare and resource use', but they suggest that over the long term there are absolute limits to growth that require social and political adaptation.²²⁸

The Rise of Energy Economics

Why, despite the wide dissemination of the ecological discourse and the intensive debate on alternative economic and social models, has the world failed to embrace the soft energy path envisaged by Amory Lovins or Fritz Schumacher's 'return to the human scale'? Why, in its basic thrust, does the West German Council of Experts' environmental report of 2012 sound like a document out of the 1970s? Why is it that while economic growth and rising energy consumption have in fact been decoupled in many countries, no country has pursued a more radical path towards the protection of resources? The simple answer is: because there was an alternative, and the disaster constantly predicted if nations continued along their well-trodden paths has not yet occurred, at least in the Western industrialized countries. The repeated doom-laden prophecies of impending resource exhaustion may have had a deadening effect here.²²⁹ The rather more complicated answer is bound up with the rise of energy economics as a new academic subdiscipline and the structure of energy firms, in which 'economies of scale' play a major role.

As discussed above in more detail, in the 1970s geologists, engineers, political scientists, social scientists and economists vied to bring their various forms of petro-knowledge to bear on energy policy. In view of the politicization and economization of oil in the 1960s, and especially 1970s, geologists and engineers receded into the background in comparison with their generally more eloquent colleagues from the social sciences and economics. Although, for much of the twentieth century, energy and the economy of exhaustible resources were essentially marginal topics in the discipline of economics, in the 1970s economists began to pay them far greater attention. While the JSTOR database for the years 1960 to 1969 records 339 articles in economic journals bearing the terms 'energy', 'resources' or 'petroleum' in their titles, there were more than six hundred over the next decade.²³⁰ As long as resources were available in abundance, economists did not consider them important, concluded Partha Dasgupta and Geoffrey Heal in the late 1970s. But henceforth, they contended, no general text on economics would be able to ignore resources.²³¹ Conversely, when the first boom in resource economics died down in the mid 1980s, Vince Eagan concluded that theory was clearly just as cyclical as the resource use it sought to describe, always appearing when resources threatened to become scarce.²³²

Though this observation may apply to the publication of economic texts as a whole, the discipline of economics changed enduringly in the 1970s. In the non-economic social and political sciences, energy was an important topic, but beyond the establishment of the hybrid journals described above, it initially underwent no independent institutionalization. In the shape of energy economics, in contrast, a specialized economic subdiscipline emerged. In 1977, at the conference of the American Economics Association, the International Association for Energy Economics was founded. It held its first conference two years later and, from 1980, published the *Energy Journal*.²³³ Offshoots were quickly established in other countries, such as the British Institute for Energy Economics (1980) and the West German Society for Energy Science and Energy Policy (Gesellschaft für Energiewissenschaft und Energiepolitik) (1981). This process of institutionalization also found expression in a growing number of professorships and a mounting need for textbooks and handbooks, a trend still evident today.²³⁴ Right up to the present, energy economists have recognized the formative role of the oil and energy crises of the 1970s in the development of their discipline.²³⁵

As long as oil was available in abundance and the oil price relatively stable, there was a limited need for energy forecasts and the topic of energy attracted little interest. It was only the steps taken by OPEC and OAPEC in the early 1970s and the more active energy policy pursued by the consuming countries that made the oil price volatile. These factors shattered expectations, intensified uncertainties and increased the need for energy forecasts, because it could no longer be taken for granted that the oil price would remain at much the same level over the next few years. As a result of the oil crisis, forecasts of the future oil price and its effects on economic development became a growth area in the discipline of economics, while producing such forecasts emerged as a smart career move for younger economists.[236] The year before the oil crisis, the *Review of Economic Studies* had already published a special issue on the economics of exhaustible resources. This made it plain that the growing uncertainty about the future development of the supply, demand and prices of resources was the driving force behind the growth in economic theory building, while at the same time presenting it with tremendous difficulties. Certainly, it was now possible, on the basis of simple models, to calculate optimal resource exploitation curves, as Geoffrey Heal contended in his foreword. But, he went on, there remained major uncertainties, because it was very difficult to predict technological change over long periods of time.[237] In addition to the optimal exploitation curve, the second question that concerned contemporary economists was whether the market alone would be capable of guaranteeing the best possible form of exploitation or whether it would respond too slowly or too quickly.

The optimal exploitation of natural resources looked different from an energy company's perspective than from that of consumers and was further complicated by attempts to factor in future generations. While the individual firm, in line with Hotelling's 1931 calculations, was out to maximize profit over a given period of time, the societal perspective revolved more around the problem of the security of supply or avoiding shortfalls, a problem that grew worse the longer the period of time involved and, above all, across the generations.[238] This debate saw a clash between optimists and pessimists. The optimists assumed that, due to the price mechanism, the supply of resources would present no fundamental problem: if there were a shortage of raw materials the price would go up. Initially, then, the exploitation of other deposits would become profitable; ultimately, an alternative technology, a so-called 'backstop technology', would emerge that could replace a particular raw material.[239] The pessimists, meanwhile, assumed that the ratio of supply to demand would initially worsen further, which would strengthen OPEC. Since it was impossible to predict technological progress and the discovery of a backstop technology, the pessimists called for greater efforts to preserve natural resources.[240]

The optimists generally put their faith in market forces. For Morris Adelman, every problem and price change in the oil market, into the present era, was the result of interference with market forces, whether at the hands of OPEC, the multinational companies or national governments. 'The oil price is high and unstable because the competitive thermostat has been disconnected. . . . Every price increase, from 1973 through 2001, followed a deliberate output cut or refusal to increase output',[241] as Adelman argued as recently as 2002. Like him, in the 1970s Joseph Stiglitz and many other economists saw no grounds for the assumption that exhaustible raw materials would be used up too quickly or too slowly in a functioning market.[242] Quite the opposite: they argued that artificially slowing the rate of exploitation would result in massive additional costs as a result of investment in more expensive forms of energy.[243] In contrast, the pessimists argued that markets did not ensure optimal exploitation of resources. They claimed either that markets failed to function correctly or were fundamentally incapable of regulating the exploitation of resources, because short-term economic interests conflicted with long-term societal interests. Robert Solow, for example, believed societies could not simply rely on technological progress. Instead, he contended, resource economics must incorporate the concept of 'intergenerational equity', that is, recognize the imperative for the most equitable possible use of resources across generations.[244] Partha Dasgupta and Geoffrey Heal, meanwhile, regarded unclear property rights and economic competition as causes of the overly rapid exhaustion of natural resources. While it was possible, they argued, to eliminate this in a structural sense, when it came to energy the markets were incapable of investing adequately in research and development.[245]

The pessimists certainly had their followers and – along with the above-mentioned economists such as Kenneth Boulding and the more obscure Georgescu-Roegen and Daly – became particularly influential in environmental and resource economics. It was, however, the optimists who tended to dominate the discipline of energy economics.[246] In 1977, for example, an analysis was made of the economic models developed since the oil crisis to investigate the exploitation of exhaustible resources. It concluded that there was no reason to assume that natural resources would be exhausted in the foreseeable future. 'Though stocks are obviously being run down in a physical sense, technical change, economies of scale, and product and factor substitution have largely prevented erosion of the resource base of the economy. On the contrary, it appears that extractive commodities have become less scarce, in terms of the sacrifices to obtain them, over the past hundred years or so.'[247] In this connection, a bet between economist Julian E. Simon and biologist and environmental activist Paul Ehrlich, author of *The Population Bomb,* earned a degree of fame. In 1980 they made a bet on whether five specific raw materials would be more expensive, in other words scarcer, or cheaper by the end of the decade. Despite population growth, Ehrlich the pessimist lost to Simon the optimist.[248] Economists largely understood the increase in raw materials reserves as an effect of market forces, which should be as free as possible from state intervention. In the same vein, when it came to the choice between a market economy and state dirigisme, Hans K. Schneider, probably the West German government's most important energy adviser in the 1970s and 1980s, also came down clearly on the side of the former. It was, he asserted, reliance on the forces of the market that had secured West Germany's energy supply hitherto.[249] These positions on energy policy fit seamlessly into the faith in the market, which was now resurgent in economic theory, as the best means of fostering prosperity for all – as long as the state kept out of the way.[250]

Unsurprisingly, the energy companies too called for their economic sectors to be allowed to develop with as little political intervention as possible. Yet they were far from averse to state support whenever it seemed to benefit them. In any event, there is ample evidence that when it comes to energy the idea of the free market is a fiction. To put it differently: with respect to oil, the results of unregulated, free enterprise have generally been disastrous.[251] In fact, due to the large amount of investment spending and the long periods of time this took to yield a profit, raw materials and energy firms faced particularly great risks, which they attempted to minimize through state support.[252] Once made, companies' decisions on energy have long-term consequences and are hugely expensive to correct. Furthermore, together with the economic risks of alternatives, this inertia or – to use the term rather freely – 'path dependence' makes it difficult to change course; there is a tendency for large energy companies to seek 'more of the same' rather than embrace radical alternatives. In line with this, many of these firms currently seem set on securing the energy supply by tapping unconventional oil and gas deposits. This requires the use of expensive and ecologically questionable but – due to oil price hikes – profitable methods.[253] Given the massive costs involved in changing energy policies, the governments of the Western industrialized nations, which have been struggling with structural fiscal problems since the 1970s, are scarcely capable of pursuing an autonomous energy policy. They require the cooperation of the large energy firms. Once again, the state's capacity for effective action seems limited by the economic logic so central to these companies, which are the only actors capable of guaranteeing an adequate energy supply, under present circumstances.

Notes

1. See the introduction, fn 40.
2. For an initial attempt to survey the upsurge in associated writings, see Alain Beltran, 'Orientation Bibliographique: l'Énergie depuis 1973', *Bulletin de l'Institut d'Histoire du Temps Présent* 45 (1991), 27–54.
3. For an in-depth analysis of this problem, see Graf and Priemel, 'Zeitgeschichte in der Welt der Sozialwissenschaften'.
4. Walter J. Levy, 'Oil Power', *Foreign Affairs* 49 (1971), 652–68.
5. Chevalier, *Le nouvel enjeu pétrolier*, 9; see also Jean-Jacques Berreby, *Le pétrole dans la stratégie mondiale* (Paris, 1974).
6. Raymond Vernon (ed.), *The Oil Crisis* (New York, 1976), vii.
7. *Die Energiekrise. Episode oder Ende einer Ära*, in collaboration with Ralf Dahrendorf et al. (Hamburg, 1974), 11.
8. Franz Josef Strauß, 'Europäische Zäsur', *Zeitbühne* 3(6) (1974), 15–16, here 16.
9. Bayerisches Oberbergamt, *Energiebilanz Bayerns 1973: Daten zur Entwicklung der Energiewirtschaft* (Munich, 1974); Hammond, Metz and Maugh, *Energie für die Zukunft*; Ministère de l'industrie et de la recherche. Delegation générale à l'énergie. Direction Carburants: *Activité de l'industrie pétrolière 1973* (Paris, 1974), 7; Philip Windsor, *Oil: A Plain Man's Guide to the World Energy Crisis* (London, 1975); Energy Systems Program Group International Institute for Applied Systems Analysis, *Energy in a Finite World: A Global Systems Analysis* (Cambridge, MA, 1981); S. Manoharan, *The Oil Crisis: End of an Era* (New Delhi, 1974).
10. Ulf Hansen, 'Begrüßung', in Fritz Lücke (ed.), *Ölkrise: 10 Jahre danach* (Cologne, 1984), 13–16, here 13.
11. See, for example, the *Spiegel* title page of 19 November 1973, 'The Oil Crisis: The End of the Affluent Society?', or Frances Cairncross and Hamish McRae, *The Second Great Crash: How the Oil Crisis Could Destroy the World's Economy* (Bungay, 1975).
12. Schmidt, 'Leitgedanken unserer Außenpolitik', 238.
13. *Energiekrise – Europa im Belagerungszustand?*, 6.
14. Jean Fourastié, *Les trente glorieuses ou la révolution invisible de 1946 à 1975* (Paris, 1979).
15. Lieber, *The Oil Decade*, 1; Joel Darmstadter, Hans H. Landsberg and Herbert C. Morton, *Energy, Today and Tomorrow: Living with Uncertainty* (Englewood Cliffs, NJ, 1983); Lücke, *Ölkrise*; Kohl, *After the Second Oil Crisis*; Antoine Ayoub (ed.), *Le Marché pétrolier international dix ans après la crise de 1973: Bilan et perspectives* (Québec, 1984); Hanns W. Maull, *Raw Materials, Energy, and Western Security* (London/Basingstoke, 1984); Daniel Yergin, 'Crisis and Adjustment. An Overview', in Daniel Yergin and Martin Hillenbrand (eds), *Global Insecurity: A Strategy for Energy and Economic Renewal* (Boston, 1982), 1–28; Klaus Marquardt, *Auf den Spuren der Ölkrise: Eine Weltindustrie verändert ihre Strukturen* (Essen, 1983).
16. Jack M. Hollander, 'Preface', *Annual Review of Energy* 1 (1976), vi–ix, here vi.
17. Eppler, *Ende oder Wende*, 18.
18. Rolf Peter Sieferle, *Epochenwechsel: Die Deutschen an der Schwelle zum 21. Jahrhundert* (Berlin, 1994), 248; Kai F. Hünemörder, *Die Frühgeschichte der globalen Umweltkrise und die Formierung der deutschen Umweltpolitik (1950–1973)* (Stuttgart, 2004), 18; Merrill, *The Oil Crisis of 1973–1974*; and for a more nuanced take, see Patrick Kupper, 'Die "1970er Diagnose": Grundsätzliche Überlegungen zu einem Wendepunkt der Umweltgeschichte', *Archiv für Sozialgeschichte* 43 (2003), 325–48.
19. Louis Turner, 'The Oil Majors in World Politics', *International Affairs* 52 (1976), 368–80, here 368: 'No debate on transnational relations can ignore the issue of the power of the multinational companies (MNCs). No debate on the multinationals can avoid dealing with the Oil Majors'; see also Louis Turner, *Multinational Companies and the Third World* (London, 1973).
20. Commission d'Enquête Parlementaire, *Sur les Sociétés Pétrolières Opérant en France* (Paris, 1974), 12.

21. Ibid., 66.
22. Ibid., 224: 'It is time for states to acquire full sovereignty in the realm of energy; political questions should not be allowed to escape politics'.
23. US Congress. Senate. Committee on Government Operations, *The Major Oil Companies*, 114; US Congress. Senate. Committee on Government Operations, *The Federal Energy Office*.
24. US Congress. Senate. Committee on Foreign Relations, *Multinational Corporations and United States Foreign Policy. Hearings Before the Subcommittee on Multinational Corporations*. 93rd Congress, 2nd session, 15 vols (Washington, DC, 1973–75).
25. US Congress. Senate. Committee on Foreign Relations, *Multinational Petroleum Companies and Foreign Policy. Hearings Before the Subcommittee on Multinational Corporations*. 93rd Congress, 2nd session, vol. 5 (Washington, DC, 1974), 9.
26. US Congress. Senate. Committee on Foreign Relations, *Multinational Petroleum Companies and Foreign Policy. Hearings Before the Subcommittee on Multinational Corporations*. 93rd Congress, 2nd session, vol. 4 (Washington, DC, 1974), 5.
27. Ibid., 8; see also volumes 5 to 8 of the committee report.
28. US Congress. Senate. Committee on Government Operations, *Cutoff of Petroleum Products to U.S. Military Forces. Hearings before the Permanent Subcommittee on Investigations*. 93rd Congress (Washington, DC, 1974), 881.
29. Ibid., 882f.
30. Ibid., 914–18.
31. Ibid., 969–70.
32. Ibid., 900.
33. Note of Discussion Prime Minister with Drake and Fadzean, 21.10.1973, NA UK, PREM 15/1838; see also Eric Drake to Secretary of State for Trade and Industry, 29.10.1973, NA UK, PREM 15/1839; on the relationship between the British government and BP, see Federal Energy Administration, *The Relationship of Oil Companies and Foreign Governments*, 183–88; Bamberg, *The History of the British Petroleum Company*, vol. 3, 481.
34. Mumford: Meeting Drake and Lord Carrington, 24.10.1973, NA UK, PREM 15/1839; BP did in fact try to do so, but sought to prevent it from becoming public; see Mumford to Defence: The Oil Crisis, 25.10.1973, NA UK, PREM 15/1839.
35. Heath, *The Course of My Life*, 503.
36. Report: Secretary of State for Defence saw Eric Drake, Mr. Baxendale and Mr. Pearce, 29.10.1973; Drake in R.T. Armstrong: Commercial: Secret, 23.10.1973, NA UK, PREM 15/1839.
37. Note: Meeting between Secretary of State and Sir Eric Drake, 23.11.1973; Report of a Conversation between the Chancellor of the Duchy of Lancaster John Davis, Eric Drake and McFadzean, 23.11.1973, NA UK, PREM 15/1842.
38. Douglas Allen, Note of Conversation with Drake, 27.11.1973, NA UK, PREM 15/1842; Douglas Allen: Note of Two Meetings with Eric Drake, 22.11.1973, NA UK, CAB 164/1199.
39. Note: Meeting between Secretary of State and Sir Eric Drake, 23.11.1973, NA UK, PREM 15/1842.
40. Fritsch and Gitomer, *Major Oil*, 5; see also US Congress. Senate. Committee on Foreign Relations. Subcommittee on Multinational Corporations., *US Oil Companies and the Arab Oil Embargo: The International Allocation of Constricted Supplies* (Washington, DC, 1975).
41. Fritsch and Gitomer, *Major Oil*, 6.
42. See, for example, Hartmut Elsenhans, *Die Kostensteigerungen für Erdöl vom Juni 1973 bis zum Januar 1974: Berechnung der Kostensteigerung für Erdöl aus den OPEC-Ländern und für die Erdölproduktion der 7 Großkonzerne für Panorama, 4. Febr. 1974, nebst einer Erwiderung der Deutschen Shell AG und deren Widerlegung durch den Autor* (Berlin, 1974); Hartmut Elsenhans

and Gerd Junne, 'Zu den Hintergründen der gegenwärtigen Ölkrise', *Blätter für deutsche und internationale Politik* 18(12) (1973), 1305–17; for a significantly more nuanced account, see Peter R. Odell, 'OPEC und die Multis: Amerikanische Politik und europäische Optionen', in Wolfgang Hager (ed.), *Erdöl und internationale Politik* (Munich, 1975), 41–50.

43. Christopher Tugendhat, *Oil, the Biggest Business*, 2nd ed. (London, 1975), 2. The *New York Times* also described the Saudi Arabian subsidiary, Aramco, as a 'country within a country': Leonard Mosley, 'The Richest Oil Company in the World: Aramco Is Not So Much a Company as It Is a Country within a Country', *New York Times*, 10 March 1974.

44. Sampson, *The Seven Sisters*, ix.

45. Ibid., 262.

46. Robert B. Stobaugh, 'The Oil Companies in the Crisis', *Daedalus* 104(4) (1975), 179–202, here 200.

47. Raymond Vernon, 'An Interpretation', in *The Oil Crisis*, 1–14, here 5–8; Maull, *Ölmacht*.

48. For texts defending them, see Robert B. Krueger, *The United States and International Oil: A Report for the Federal Energy Administration on US Firms and Government Policy* (New York, 1975); Peter F. Drucker, 'Multinationals and Developing Countries: Myths and Realities', *Foreign Affairs* 53 (1974), 121–34; Geoffrey Chandler, 'The Innocence of Oil Companies', *Foreign Policy* 27 (Summer 1977), 52–70.

49. Turner, 'The Oil Majors in World Politics', 370–72.

50. Mira Wilkins, 'The Oil Companies in Perspective', *Daedalus* 104(4) (1975), 159–78; the multinational companies' national links, particularly in the United States, are underlined by Kenneth Neal Waltz, *Theory of International Politics* (Reading, MA, 1979), 151.

51. *Crude*, dir. Joe Berlinger (United States, 2009) [film]; Steve Coll, 'Gusher: The Power of ExxonMobil', *New Yorker*, 9 April 2012, 28–37; Coll, *Private Empire: ExxonMobil and American Power* (New York, 2012).

52. Joseph S. Nye, 'Multinational Corporations in World Politics', *Foreign Affairs* 53(1) (1974), 153–75, here 153; Hans Günter (ed.), *Transnational Industrial Relations: The Impact of Multi-National Corporations and Economic Regionalism on Industrial Relations. A Symposium Held at Geneva by the International Institute for Labour Studies* (London/New York, 1972); United Nations. Department of Economic and Social Affairs, *Impact of Multinational Corporations on Development and on International Relations* (New York, 1974); Nye himself was among the fifty-two 'eminent persons' who produced the study for the UN's ECOSOC.

53. Louis Turner, *Oil Companies in the International System* (London, 1978), 176–99.

54. Burton I. Kaufmann, 'Mideast Multinational Oil, US Foreign Policy and Antitrust: The 1950s', *Journal of American History* 63 (1977), 937–59; David S. Painter, *Private Power and Public Policy: Multinational Oil Companies and US Foreign Policy, 1941–1954* (London, 1986). Fiona Venn, *Oil Diplomacy in the Twentieth Century* (Basingstoke, 1986).

55. Yergin, *The Prize*, 13.

56. Ibid.; Yergin contributed to this discourse before transforming it into a historical narrative; Yergin and Hillenbrand, *Global Insecurity*.

57. Werner Conze, 'Sicherheit, Schutz', in Otto Brunner, Werner Conze and Reinhart Koselleck (eds), *Geschichtliche Grundbegriffe*, vol. 5 (Stuttgart, 1984), 831–62; Franz-Xaver Kaufmann, *Sicherheit als soziologisches und sozialpolitisches Problem: Untersuchungen zu einer Wertidee hochdifferenzierter Gesellschaften* (Stuttgart, 1973); Eckart Conze, 'Sicherheit als Kultur: Überlegungen zu einer "modernen Politikgeschichte" der Bundesrepublik Deutschland', *Vierteljahrshefte für Zeitgeschichte* 53 (2005), 357–80; Nikolaus Werz (ed.), *Sicherheit* (Baden-Baden, 2009).

58. Rüdiger Graf, 'Between National and Human Security: Energy Security in the United States and Western Europe in the 1970s', *Historical Social Research* 35(4) (2010), 329–48.

59. George A. Lincoln, 'Energy Security: New Dimension for US Policy', *Air Force Magazine* 56(11) (1973), 49–55, here 49.

60. Carl Vansant, *Strategic Energy Supply and National Security* (New York, 1971), vii; see also the definitions in Harold J. Barnett, 'The Changing Relation of Natural Resources to National Security', *Economic Geography* 34(3) (1958), 189–201, here 189.

61. Harold Lubell, *Middle East Oil Crises and Western Europe's Energy Supplies* (Baltimore, MD, 1963); Lubell, 'Security of Supply and Energy Policy in Western Europe', *World Politics* 13(3) (1961), 400–422; Levy, 'Oil Power', 662. See chapter 2.

62. See chapter 5 along with Dolinski and Ziesing, *Sicherheits-, Preis- und Umweltaspekte*; Dolinski, Ziesing and Labahn, *Maßnahmen*.

63. Philip A. Odeen, 'Organizing for National Security', *International Security* 5(1) (1980), 111–29, here 115.

64. David A. Deese and Joseph S. Nye (eds), *Energy and Security* (Cambridge, MA, 1981), xvf.; Yergin and Hillenbrand, *Global Insecurity*; see also Martin J. Hillenbrand, 'NATO and Western Security in an Era of Transition', *International Security* 2(2) (1977), 3–24, though here energy plays a merely subordinate role.

65. Samuel Nakasian, 'The Security of Foreign Petroleum Resources', *Political Science Quarterly* 68(2) (1953), 181–202; Theodor Wessels, 'Die Sicherheit der nationalen Versorgung als Ziel der nationalen Wirtschaftspolitik', *Zeitschrift für die gesamte Staatswissenschaft* 120(4) (1964), 602–17; Robert James Lieber, *Oil and the Middle East War* (Cambridge, MA, 1976), 46, 48.

66. Harald Müller, 'Energiepolitik: Ein neuer Bereich der Außenpolitik', *Neue Politische Literatur* 22(4) (1977), 484–502, here 484; see also Michael Stoff, *Oil, War, and National Security: The Search for a National Policy on Foreign Oil, 1941–1947* (New Haven, CT, 1980), ix: 'the crucial link between oil and national security, once solely the concern of military and government officials, has become a matter of public discourse'. Bo Heinebaeck, *Oil and Security* (New York, 1974), 5; Lieber, *Oil and the Middle East War*, 48; Edward N. Krapels, *Oil and Security: Problems and Prospects of Importing Countries* (London, 1977), 29.

67. Linda B. Miller, 'Review: Energy, Security and Foreign Policy: A Review Essay', *International Security* 4(1) (1977), 111–23, here 112. For some, however, the inclusion of energy issues in the security debate did not go far enough; see Melvin A. Conant and Fern R. Gold, *Geopolitics of Energy* (Washington, DC, 1977), 7.

68. Miller, 'Review: Energy, Security and Foreign Policy', 114.

69. Heinebaeck, *Oil and Security*, 12f.; for a discussion of environmental security, see Thorsten Schultz, 'Transatlantic Environmental Security in the 1970s? NATO's "Third Dimension" as an Early Environmental and Human Security Approach', *Historical Social Research* 35(4) (2010), 309–28.

70. David A. Deese, 'Economics, Politics, and Security', *International Security* 4(3) (1979), 140–53, here 142; for examples of classical thinking on military strategy after the oil crisis, see Robert R. Ulin, 'US National Security and Middle Eastern Oil', *Military Review* 59(5) (1979), 39–49; Geoffrey Kemp, 'Military Force and Middle East Oil', In Deese and Nye, *Energy and Security*, 365–90. On the expansion of the concept of security, see Christopher Daase, 'National, Societal, and Human Security: On the Transformation of Political Language', *Historical Social Research* 35(4) (2010), 22–40; Emma Rothschild, 'What is Security?', in Barry Buzan and Lene Hansen (eds), *International Security*, vol. 3, *Widening Security* (Los Angeles, 2007), 1–34. The categories used in the following paragraph follow Daase.

71. Richard N. Cooper, 'Natural Resources and National Security', *Resources Policy* 2 (June 1975), 192–203.

72. Joseph J. Wolf, *The Growing Dimensions of Security: The Atlantic Council's Working Group on Security* (Washington, DC, 1977), 1: 'In the nuclear age, in an increasingly crowded and interdependent world, security is not a matter merely of military strength. Security also involves a combination of many other factors, including domestic as well as foreign ones: political, economic, social and psychological'.

73. Joseph Nye defined energy security as the absence of any threat to the energy supply; Joseph S. Nye, 'Energy Security Strategy', in Samuel P. Huntington (ed.), *The Strategic Imperative: New Policies for American Security* (Cambridge, MA, 1982), 301–29, here 303; see also Richard H. Ullmann, 'Redefining Security', *International Security* 8(1) (1983), 129–53, here 146; Maull, *Raw Materials*, 5; William W. Hogan, 'Import Management and Oil Emergencies', in David A. Deese and Joseph S. Nye (eds), *Energy and Security* (Cambridge, MA, 1981), 261–84; David J. Blair and Paul A. Summerville, *Oil Import Security: The Cases of Japan and Great Britain* (n.p., 1983).

74. Walter F. Mondale, 'Beyond Detente: Toward International Economic Security', *Foreign Affairs* 53(1) (1974), 1–23, here 2.

75. Joseph S. Nye, 'Energy and Security', in David A. Deese and Joseph S. Nye (eds), *Energy and Security* (Cambridge, MA, 1981), 3–22, here 5; Joseph S. Nye, David A. Deese and Alm Alvin, 'Conclusion: A US Strategy for Energy Security', in Deese and Nye, *Energy and Security*, 391–424, here 423.

76. Helmut Schmidt, 'Politische und wirtschaftliche Aspekte der westlichen Sicherheit: Vortrag vor dem International Institute for Strategic Studies, London 28.10.1977', in Klaus von Schubert (ed.), *Sicherheitspolitik der Bundesrepublik Deutschland: Dokumentation 1945–1977, Part 2* (Cologne, 1979), 618–31, here 618.

77. Ibid., 627.

78. Wörner, 'Neue Dimensionen der Sicherheit', 591.

79. Ibid., 593.

80. Amory B. Lovins and L. Hunter Lovins, *Brittle Power: Energy Strategy for National Security* (Andover, MA, 1982), 2f.

81. Ullmann, 'Redefining Security'; Michael T. Klare, *Resource Wars: The New Landscape of Global Conflict* (New York, 2001); Harald Welzer, *Klimakriege: Wofür im 21. Jahrhundert getötet wird* (Frankfurt am Main, 2008).

82. Umbach, *Globale Energiesicherheit*; Cornel Zwierlein and Rüdiger Graf, 'The Production of Human Security in Premodern and Contemporary History', *Historical Social Research* 35(4) (2010), 7–21.

83. Brandt, Willy. *North-South: A Programme for Survival; Report of the Independent Commission on International Development Issues* (London, 1982).

84. Ibid., 160–171.

85. Olof Palme, *Der Palme-Bericht: Bericht der Unabhängigen Kommission für Abrüstung und Sicherheit 'Common Security'* (Berlin, 1982), 20.

86. Morgenthau, 'The New Diplomacy Movement'; see also Klaus Knorr, 'The Limits of Economic and Military Power', in Vernon, *The Oil Crisis*, 229–44.

87. 'Library of Congress Congressional Research Service, Oil Fields as Military Objectives; Document 434: Report by the Joint Intelligence Committee, 5. Dezember 1973', in Hamilton, *The Year of Europe*.

88. Wessels, 'Die Sicherheit der nationalen Versorgung'; Policy Study Group of the MIT, 'Energy Laboratory'. Even for the United Kingdom, North Sea oil did not mean energy independence; see Lawrence Freedman, 'Großbritannien als Erdölproduzent: Die Legende von der Unabhängigkeit', *Europa-Archiv* 15 (1978), 477–87.

89. For the case of Japan, see Saburo Okita, 'Natural Resource Dependency and Japanese Foreign Policy', *Foreign Affairs* 52(4) (1974), 714–24.

90. Robert W. Tucker, 'Oil: The Issue of American Intervention', *Commentary* 59(1) (1975), 21–31. On the refoundation of the right and an overview of its key organs of publication, see Murray Friedman, *The Neoconservative Revolution: Jewish Intellectuals and the Shaping of Public Policy* (Cambridge, MA, 2005), 38, 121; John Ehrmann, *The Rise of Neoconservatism: Intellectuals and Foreign Affairs 1945–1994* (New Haven, CT, 1995), 50; Jacobs, 'The Conservative Struggle and the Energy Crisis'.

91. Tucker, 'Oil', 30.
92. Miles Ignotus, 'Seizing Arab Oil', *Harper's Magazine* 250 (March 1975), 45–62, here 48; this pseudonym has been attributed to both Henry A. Kissinger and Edward Luttwak.
93. Ibid., 62.
94. Robert W. Tucker, *The Purposes of American Power: An Essay on National Security* (New York, 1981), 58f.
95. Ibid., 186; for a critique, see Nye, 'Energy and Security', 15–20.
96. Edward N. Luttwak, 'Intervention and Access to Natural Resources', in Hedley Bull (ed.), *Intervention in World Politics* (New York, 1984), 79–94. The relevant blogs are full of articles that make such connections, sometimes accurately and sometimes in the vein of conspiracy theory; see, for example, Ray McGovern, *Bush, Oil and Moral Bankruptcy*, Counterpunch, http://www.counterpunch.org/2007/09/27/bush-oil-and-moral-bankruptcy/ (accessed 2 October 2016).
97. Lincoln, 'Energy Security', 55.
98. Rüdiger Graf, 'Das Petroknowledge des Kalten Krieges', in Bernd Greiner (ed.), *Macht und Geist im Kalten Krieg* (Hamburg, 2011), 201–22.
99. Karl Kaiser, 'Die Auswirkungen der Energiekrise auf die westliche Allianz', in Wolfgang Hager (ed.), *Erdöl und internationale Politik* (Munich, 1975), 73–86, here 73; Karl Kaiser, 'The Energy Problem and Alliance Systems', in International Institute for Strategic Studies (ed.), *The Middle East and the International System*, vol. 2, *Security and the Energy Crisis* (London, 1975), 17–24; see also Ann-Margret Walton, 'Atlantic Relations: Policy Coordination and Conflict. Atlantic Bargaining over Energy', *International Affairs* 52 (1976), 180–96.
100. Herman Kahn, *Angriff auf die Zukunft. Die 70er und 80er Jahre: So werden wir leben* (Vienna/Munich/Zurich, 1972), 67f.; Kahn, *On Thermonuclear War* (Princeton, NJ, 1960); Morgenthau, 'The New Diplomacy Movement'.
101. See, for example, Kermit Gordon in his foreword to Seyom Brown, *New Forces in World Politics* (Washington, DC, 1974), viif.
102. Crozier, Watanuki and Huntington, *The Crisis of Democracy*, 158.
103. Jahangir Amuzegar, 'The Oil Story: Facts, Fiction, and Fair Play', *Foreign Affairs* 51 (1973), 676–89; Amuzegar, 'OPEC in the Context of the Global Power Equation', *Denver Journal of International Law and Policy* 4 (1974), 221–28; Amuzegar, 'The North-South Dialogue: From Conflict to Compromise', *Foreign Affairs* 54(3) (1976), 547–62; Amuzegar, 'A Requiem for the North-South Conference', *Foreign Affairs* 56(1) (1977), 136–59; Amuzegar, 'Not Much Aid and Not Enough Trade: Cloudy Prospects in North-South Relations', *Third World Quarterly* 1(1) (1979), 50–64; for a bibliographic overview of the debates on the New International Economic Order, see Linus A. Hoskins, 'The New International Economic Order: A Bibliographic Essay', *Third World Quarterly* 3(3) (1981), 506–27; see esp. Richard N. Cooper, 'A New International Economic Order for Mutual Gain', *Foreign Policy* 26 (1977), 66–120; Branislav Gosovic and John Gerard Ruggie, 'On the Creation of a New International Economic Order: Issue Linkage and the Seventh Special Session of the UN General Assembly', *International Organization* 30(2) (1976), 309–45.
104. Bergsten, 'The Threat from the Third World'.
105. Ibid., 107.
106. Ibid., 110.
107. Hans-Joachim Burchard, 'Der Souveränitätswechsel beim Erdöl', *Außenpolitik* 25 (1974), 447–60.
108. 'One, Two, Many OPECs'.
109. Stephen D. Krasner, 'Oil Is the Exception', *Foreign Policy* 14 (Spring 1974), 68–84, here 79; see also Geoffrey Kemp, 'Scarcity and Strategy', *Foreign Affairs* 56 (1978), 396–414; Kemp, 'Military Force and Middle East Oil'.
110. Krasner, 'Oil Is the Exception', 83; for a similar take, see also Richard Löwenthal, 'Committee Discussions on Oil and Strategy: Report to the Conference', in International In-

stitute for Strategic Studies (ed.), *The Middle East and the International System*, vol. 2, *Security and the Energy Crisis* (London, 1975), 38–41; John C. Campbell, 'Oil Power in the Middle East', *Foreign Affairs* 56(1) (1977), 89–110, 90.

111. C. Fred Bergsten, 'The Threat Is Real', *Foreign Policy* 14 (Spring 1974), 84–90, here 86; for a conciliatory approach, see Zuhayr Mikdashi, 'Collusion Could Work', *Foreign Policy* 14 (Spring 1974), 57–68.

112. C. Fred Bergsten, Robert O. Keohane and Joseph S. Nye, 'International Economics and International Politics: A Framework for Analysis', *International Organization* 29(1) (1975), 3–36; see also Conant and Gold, *Geopolitics of Energy*, 5.

113. Geoffrey Kemp, 'The New Strategic Map', *Survival* 19(2) (1977), 50–59, here 52.

114. US Senate Committee on Interior and Insular Affairs. Chair Henry M. Jackson, *Geopolitics of Energy*, in collaboration with Melvin A. Conant and Fern R. Gold (Washington, DC, 1977); for a similar analysis three years later, see US Senate. Committee on Energy and Natural Resources, *The Geopolitics of Oil, Staff Report*.

115. John Peter Cole, *Geography of World Affairs*, 5th ed. (Harmondsworth/New York, 1979), 11, 13, 108, 290.

116. Edward Friedland, Paul Seabury and Aaron Wildavsky, 'Oil and the Decline of Western Power', *Political Science Quarterly* 90(3) (1975), 437–50, here 437.

117. Hedley Bull, 'Arms Control and World Order', *International Security* 1 (1976), 3–16, here 8.

118. Hans J. Morgenthau, 'World Politics and the Politics of Oil', in Gary D. Eppen (ed.), *Energy: The Policy Issues* (Chicago, 1975), 43–51, here 44.

119. Ibid., 50.

120. Ibid.; see also the concurring views of Gary D. Eppen, 'Introduction', in *Energy: The Policy Issues*, xi–xiv, here xi.

121. Brown, *New Forces in World Politics*, 3.

122. Bull, 'Arms Control and World Order', 9; for a similar analysis, see also Campbell, 'Oil Power in the Middle East'.

123. See Bergsten, Keohane and Nye, 'International Economics and International Politics'.

124. Hans J. Morgenthau, *Politics among Nations: The Struggle for Power and Peace* (New York, 1948); George F. Kennan, *American Diplomacy, 1900–1950* (Chicago, 1951).

125. Karl Loewenstein, 'Sovereignty and International Co-operation', *The American Journal of International Law* 48(2) (1954), 222–44, here 223.

126. Ibid.

127. Robert O. Keohane and Joseph S. Nye, 'Preface', *International Organization* 25(3) (1971), v–vi; Robert O. Keohane and Joseph S. Nye (eds), *Transnational Relations and World Politics* (Cambridge, MA, 1973); Thomas Risse-Kappen (ed.), *Bringing Transnational Relations Back In: Non-State Actors, Domestic Structures and International Institutions* (Cambridge, 1995); Thomas Risse, 'Transnational Actors and World Politics', in W. Carlsnaes (ed.), *Handbook of International Relations* (London, 2002), 255–74.

128. This is also evident in Hoffmann, *Primacy or World Order*, 118; see also Stanley H. Hoffmann, *Gulliver's Troubles: Or the Setting of American Foreign Policy* (New York, 1968).

129. Bergsten, Keohane and Nye, 'International Economics and International Politics'.

130. Ibid., 12.

131. Ibid., 23, 35.

132. Bergsten, 'Interdependence and the Reform of International Institutions'; see also Levy, 'World Oil Cooperation or International Chaos'; Harlan Cleveland, 'World Energy and US Leadership', *Atlantic Community Quarterly* 13(1) (1975), 26–45; Wolfgang Hager, 'Die Internationale Energie-Agentur: Problematische Sicherheitsallianz für Europa', in Wolfgang Hager (ed.), *Erdöl und internationale Politik* (Munich, 1975), 87–114; Hoffmann, *Primacy or World Order*, 320f.

133. Bergsten, 'Interdependence and the Reform of International Institutions', 363, 361.

134. Nazli Choucri, *International Politics of Energy Interdependence: The Case of Petroleum* (Lexington, MA, 1976).

135. See, for example, Wilfrid L. Kohl, 'The International Energy Agency: The Political Context', in J.C. Hurewitz (ed.), *Oil, the Arab-Israel Dispute, and the Industrial World: Horizons of Crisis* (Boulder, CO, 1976), 247–57; Mason Willrich and Melvin A. Conant, 'The International Energy Agency: An Interpretation and Assessment', *American Journal of International Law* 71 (1977), 199–223; Bergsten, 'Interdependence and the Reform of International Institutions', 366; Roggen, *Die Internationale Energie-Agentur*.

136. Keohane, 'The International Energy Agency', 932f.

137. James E. Katz: 'The International Energy Agency: Energy Cooperation or Illusion?', *World Affairs* 144(1) (1981), 55–82, here 79.

138. Hoffmann, *Primacy or World Order*, 126; see also ibid., 320f.: 'American hegemony is over. . . . We are, as the globalists tell us, all in the same boat. But it is not clear that all of us know it; there are many different classes and compartments; we do not agree on where it ought to go and who should steer it; and the maneuvers of many of its passengers seem almost calculated to make it sink. We have to learn that although we are the biggest aboard, with belongings in every cabin, we alone cannot set the course. We have to recognize that joint steering may not succeed in saving the ship, but that there is no alternative'.

139. Robert O. Keohane and Joseph S. Nye, *Power and Interdependence: World Politics in Transition* (Boston, 1977).

140. Robert O. Keohane and Joseph S. Nye, *Power and Interdependence*, 3rd ed. (New York, 2004), xv, 30.

141. Ibid., 10f., 13, 31, 37, 204.

142. Robert O. Keohane, *After Hegemony* (Princeton, NJ, 1984), 9.

143. Ibid., 181–90.

144. Ibid., 201–6.

145. Ibid., 237–40; similar ideas can be found in Svante Karlsson, *Oil and the World Order: A Study of American Foreign Oil Policy 1940–1980* (Gothenburg, 1983), 283. For a critique of Keohane that underlines ongoing US hegemony, see, for example, S. Javed Maswood, 'Oil and American Hegemony', *Australian Journal of International Affairs* 44(2) (1990), 131–41.

146. Andrew J. Bacevich, *The Limits of Power: The End of American Exceptionalism* (New York, 2008).

147. Sargent, *A Superpower Transformed*, 5; for a similar analysis, see Wolfram Kaiser and Jan-Henrik Meyer, 'Non-State Actors in European Integration in the 1970s: Towards a Polity of Transnational Contestation', *Comparativ* 20(3) (2010), 7–24; on the growing significance of international organizations, see also Iriye, *Global Community*.

148. Sargent, *A Superpower Transformed*, 155–61.

149. For a more in-depth account, see Graf and Priemel, 'Zeitgeschichte in der Welt der Sozialwissenschaften'.

150. Richard N. Rosecrance, *The Rise of the Trading State: Commerce and Conquest in the Modern World* (New York, 1986), 1–21.

151. Ibid., xi.

152. Camilleri and Falk, *The End of Sovereignty?*, 38; see also Sassen, *Losing Control?*

153. Stephen D. Krasner, *Defending the National Interest* (Princeton, NJ, 1978).

154. Waltz, *Theory of International Politics*, 154: 'We are all constrained but, it appears, not equally. . . . Interdependence, one might think, is a euphemism used to obscure the dependence of most countries'.

155. See examples in Mitchell, *Carbon Democracy*, 197f. On the rebirth of the political right during the oil crisis, see also Jacobs, *Panic at the Pump*.

156. Peter J. Spiro, 'The New Sovereigntists: American Exceptionalism and Its False Prophets', *Foreign Affairs* 79(6) (2000), 9–15.

157. Jeremy A. Rabkin, *The Case for Sovereignty: Why the World Should Welcome American Independence* (Washington, DC, 2004); Rabkin, *Why Sovereignty Matters* (Washington, DC, 1998).

158. Robert Kagan, *Of Paradise and Power: America and Europe in the New World Order* (New York, 2003), 66; for a critique, see, for example, Stephen G. Brooks and William Curti Wohlforth, *World out of Balance: International Relations and the Challenge of American Primacy* (Princeton, NJ, 2008).

159. Graf and Priemel, 'Zeitgeschichte in der Welt der Sozialwissenschaften'.

160. See, for example, the chapter on 'Hydrocarbon Man' in Yergin, *The Prize*, 541–60; the 'Fossil Fuel Age' is also a key concept in Yergin, *The Quest: Energy, Security and the Remaking of the Modern World* (New York, 2011); different intentions are at work in Rifkin, *The Third Industrial Revolution*.

161. Karin Zachmann, 'Past and Present Energy Societies: How Energy Connects Politics, Technologies and Cultures', in Nina Möllers and Karin Zachmann (eds), *Past and Present Energy Societies: How Energy Connects Politics, Technologies and Cultures* (Bielefeld, 2012), 7–41, here 9; see also Hendrik Ehrhardt and Thomas Kroll, 'Einleitung', in *Energie in der modernen Gesellschaft: Zeithistorische Perspektiven* (Göttingen, 2012), 5–11, here 6.

162. David E. Nye, *Narratives and Spaces: Technology and the Construction of American Culture* (New York, 1997), 75.

163. Zachmann, 'Past and Present Energy Societies'; Graf, 'Von der Energievergessenheit zur theoretischen Metonymie'.

164. Nye, *Narratives and Spaces*, 77.

165. Ibid., 77f.

166. Graf, 'Von der Energievergessenheit zur theoretischen Metonymie'; Nye, *Narratives and Spaces*, 75–92.

167. George Basalla, 'Some Persistent Energy Myths', in George H. Daniels and Mark H. Rose (eds), *Energy and Transport: Historical Perspectives on Policy Issues* (n.p., 1982), 27–38.

168. John M. Gowdy, 'Energy', in *International Encyclopedia of the Social Sciences*, vol. 2 (Detroit, 2008), 587–88.

169. Faye Duchin, 'Energy Sector', in *International Encyclopedia of the Social Sciences*, vol. 2 (Detroit, 2008), 591–92; see also David Walls, 'Energy Industry', in *International Encyclopedia of the Social Sciences*, vol. 2 (Detroit, 2008), 588–91.

170. Peter Koslowski, 'Energie', in Görres-Gesellschaft (ed.), *Staatslexikon: Recht, Wirtschaft, Gesellschaft*, 7th ed. (Freiburg/Basel/Vienna, 1986), 247–53.

171. Ibid., 248.

172. Chauncey Starr, 'Energy and Power', *Scientific American* 225(3) (1971), 37–49, here 37.

173. William B. Kemp, 'The Flow of Energy in a Hunting Society', *Scientific American* 225(3) (1971), 104–15; Roy A. Rappaport, 'The Flow of Energy in an Agricultural Society', *Scientific American* 225(3) (1971), 116–32; Earl Cook, 'The Flow of Energy in an Industrial Society', *Scientific American* 225(3) (1971), 134–47.

174. Cook, 'The Flow of Energy in an Industrial Society', 135.

175. Starr, 'Energy and Power', 45; Milton Katz, 'Decision-Making in the Production of Power', *Scientific American* 225(3) (1971), 191–200; Claude M. Summers, 'The Conversion of Energy', *Scientific American* 225(3) (1971), 148–60.

176. *Scientific American* 225(3) (1971), 145.

177. Ibid., 161.

178. Lawrence Rocks and Richard P. Runyon, *The Energy Crisis* (New York, 1972), xii.

179. Rogers C.B. Morton, 'Foreword', in Donald A. Brobst and Walden P. Pratt (eds), *United States Mineral Resources* (Washington, DC, 1973), iii.

180. Campbell, de Carmoy and Kondo, *Energy: A Strategy for International Action*; quotation in Campbell, de Carmoy and Kondo, *Energy: The Imperative for a Trilateral Approach*, 9;

for a similar analysis, see Dieter Stegemann, *Die Energie: Lebensnerv unserer zivilisierten Welt* (Göttingen, 1974).

181. Barry Commoner, *The Poverty of Power: Energy and the Economic Crisis* (New York, 1976), 1–3.

182. 'A Staff Analysis Prepared at the Request of Henry M. Jackson', 149.

183. Daniel Bell, *The Coming of Post-Industrial Society: A Venture in Social Forecasting* (New York, 1976), xiif.

184. On the equation, see Zachmann, 'Past and Present Energy Societies', and for a contemporary critique, see George Basalla, 'Energy and Civilization', in Chauncey Starr and Philip C. Ritterbush (eds), *Science, Technology and the Human Prospect: Proceedings of the Edison Centennial Symposium* (New York, 1980), 39–52. For a historical analysis of the relationship between energy and economic growth in the United States, see Schurr and Netschert, *Energy in the American Economy*; Edward Lawrence Allen, *Energy and Economic Growth in the United States* (Cambridge, MA, 1979), vii.

185. Amory B. Lovins, 'Energy Strategy: The Road Not Taken?', *Foreign Affairs* 55(1) (1976), 65–96, here 94.

186. See Lovins' view, quoted in the introduction, on the social consequences of the soft and hard energy paths. In a sense, of course, this idea is nothing new; it underpinned Lenin's famous dictum that communism was 'Soviet power plus electrification'.

187. Marvin J. Cetron and Vary T. Coates, 'Energy and Society', *Proceedings of the Academy of Political Science* 31(2) (1973), 33–40, here 40; see also Samuel Z. Klausner, 'The Energy Social System', *Annals of the American Academy of Political and Social Science* 444 (July 1979), 1–22; Garrett Hardin, 'The Tragedy of the Commons: The Population Problem Has No Technical Solution; It Requires a Fundamental Extension in Morality', *Science* 162 (December 1968), 1243–48.

188. Lynton K. Caldwell, 'Energy and the Structure of Social Institutions', *Human Ecology* 4(1) (1976), 31–45, here 32, 37; see also Lars Kristoferson, 'Energy in Society', *AMBIO – A Journal of the Human Environment* 2(6) (1973), 178–85, here 178: 'The question of energy supply is, and will always be, the center of all power politics and the base of all economic activity. Therefore, it is self-evident that energy policy is a political problem, and not primarily a technological one'.

189. Laura Nader and Stephen Beckerman, 'Energy as It Relates to the Quality and Style of Life', *Annual Review of Energy* 3 (1978), 1–28, here 2; see also Otis Dudley Duncan, 'Sociologists Should Reconsider Nuclear Energy', *Social Forces* 57(1) (1978), 1–22.

190. Bischoff and Gocht, *Das Energiehandbuch*, Preface.

191. Kingsley Dunham, 'Non-Renewable Mineral Resources', *Resources Policy* 1 (September 1974), 3–13.

192. Hollander, 'Preface', vi.

193. Joseph Priest, *Energy for a Technological Society: Principles/Problems/Alternatives* (Reading, 1975), 2; Hollander, 'Preface', vi; see also Darmstadter, Landsberg and Morton, *Energy, Today and Tomorrow*.

194. Priest, *Energy for a Technological Society*, ix.

195. Kai F. Hünemörder, 'Kassandra im modernen Gewand. Die umweltapokalyptischen Mahnrufe der frühen 1970er Jahre', in Frank Uekötter and Jens Hohensee (eds), *Wird Kassandra heiser? Die Geschichte falscher Ökoalarme* (Stuttgart, 2004), 78–97.

196. Axel Schildt, '"Die Kräfte der Gegenreform sind auf breiter Front angetreten": Zur konservativen Tendenzwende in den Siebzigerjahren', *Archiv für Sozialgeschichte* 44 (2004), 449–78, here 459; Merrill, *The Oil Crisis of 1973–1974*; Elke Seefried, 'Towards the Limits to Growth? The Book and Its Reception in West Germany and Britain 1972–73', *Bulletin of the German Historical Institute* 33(1) (2011), 3–37.

197. Franz-Josef Brüggemeier and Jens Ivo Engels, 'Den Kinderschuhen entwachsen: Einleitende Worte zur Umweltgeschichte der zweiten Hälfte des 20. Jahrhunderts', in *Natur- und*

Umweltschutz nach 1945: Konzepte, Konflikte, Kompetenzen (Frankfurt am Main, 2005), 10–22, here 13; Jens Ivo Engels, Naturpolitik in der Bundesrepublik: Ideenwelt und politische Verhaltensstile in Naturschutz und Umweltbewegung 1950–1980. (Paderborn, 2006); Holger Nehring, 'Genealogies of the Ecological Moment: Planning, Complexity and the Environment of "the Environment" as Politics in West Germany, 1949–1982', in Sverker Sörlin and Paul Warde (eds), Nature's End: History and the Environment (Houndmills/Basingstoke/New York, 2009), 115–38.

198. Friedemann Hahn, Von Unsinn bis Untergang: Rezeption des Club of Rome und der Grenzen des Wachstums in der Bundesrepublik der frühen 1970er Jahre (Freiburg i. Br., 2006); for the critical response, see, for example, 'Weltuntergangs-Vision aus dem Computer', Der Spiegel, 15 May 1972, 126–29; Michael Jungblut, 'Ist Wachstum des Teufels? Der Weltuntergang findet nicht statt: Die Computer des MIT waren falsch programmiert', Die Zeit, 18 August 1972; Sussex University Science Policy Research Unit (ed.), Die Zukunft aus dem Computer? Eine Antwort auf die Grenzen des Wachstums (Neuwied, 1973); Henrich von Nussbaum (ed.), Die Zukunft des Wachstums: Kritische Antworten zum 'Bericht des Club of Rome' (Düsseldorf, 1973); William D. Nordhaus, 'Resources as a Constraint to Growth', The American Economic Review 64 (1974), 22–26.

199. Rüdiger Graf, 'Die Grenzen des Wachstums und die Grenzen des Staates: Konservative und die ökologischen Bedrohungsszenarien der frühen 1970er Jahre', in Jens Hacke and Dominik Geppert (eds), Streit um den Staat (Göttingen, 2008), 207–28.

200. Mende, Nicht rechts, nicht links, sondern vorn, 297.

201. Kupper, 'Die "1970er Diagnose"'; for examples, see H. Liebmann, Ein Planet wird unbewohnbar: Das Sündenregister der Menschheit von der Antike bis zur Gegenwart (Munich, 1971); Gruhl, Ein Planet wird geplündert; Edward Goldsmith and R. Allen, Planspiel zum Überleben: Ein Aktionsprogramm (Stuttgart, 1972); Paul R. Ehrlich and John P. Holdren, 'Impact of Population Growth', Science 171(3977) (1971), 1212–17.

202. Dennis Meadows, Die Grenzen des Wachstums: Bericht des Club of Rome zur Lage der Menschheit (Stuttgart, 1972), 15; Jay Wright Forrester, Der teuflische Regelkreis: Das Globalmodell der Menschheitskrise (Stuttgart, 1972).

203. Forsthoff, Der Staat der Industriegesellschaft, 168.

204. Robert M. Solow, 'Intergenerational Equity and Exhaustible Resources', Review of Economic Studies 41 (1974), 29–45.

205. Hubbert, Energy Resources, 91.

206. Gustav Heinemann, 'Weihnachtsansprache 1973', Bulletin des Presse und Informationsamts der Bundesregierung 1 (1974), 1–3.

207. For West German examples, see Robert Jungk, 'Energie - Krise und Wende', in Meyers Enzyklopädisches Lexikon, 8 vols (Mannheim/Vienna/Zurich, 1973), 771–74; 'Gruppe Ökologie: Ökologisches Manifest', Konservativ heute 4 (1973), 18–19, here 18; 'Bussauer Manifest zur umweltpolitischen Situation', Scheidewege. Vierteljahresschrift für skeptisches Denken 5 (1975), 469–86.

208. From a social democratic perspective that considers the political spectrum as a whole, see Johano Strasser, Die Zukunft der Demokratie: Grenzen des Wachstums, Grenzen der Freiheit? (Reinbek bei Hamburg, 1977).

209. Horowitz, Jimmy Carter and the Energy Crisis of the 1970s, 39f.

210. Rodgers, Age of Fracture, 39.

211. Mende, Nicht rechts, nicht links, sondern vorn, 289–321.

212. Science Policy Research Unit, Sussex University, The Limits to Growth Controversy. World Dynamics Models Described and Evaluated. Resources, Population, Agriculture, Capital, Pollution, Energy (Guildford, 1973).

213. Boulding, 'The Economics of Space-Ship Earth [1966]'; Höhler, Beam Us Up, Boulding!.

214. Kenneth E. Boulding, 'The Social System and the Energy Crisis', Science 184(4134) (1974), 255–57.

215. Ibid., 255.
216. Nicholas Georgescu-Roegen, *The Entropy Law and the Economic Process* (Cambridge, MA, 1971); Nicholas Georgescu-Roegen, *Energy and Economic Myths: Institutional and Analytical Economic Essays* (New York, 1976).
217. Nicholas Georgescu-Roegen, 'Energy, Matter, and Economic Valuation: Where Do We Stand', in Herman E. Daly and Alvaro F. Umana (eds), *Energy, Economics, and the Environment: Conflicting Views of an Essential Relationship* (Boulder, CO, 1981), 43–80, here 59.
218. Ibid., 73.
219. Ibid., 43.
220. Herman E. Daly (ed.), *Toward a Steady-State Economy* (San Francisco, 1973); Daly, *Steady-State Economics: The Economics of Biophysical Equilibrium and Moral Growth* (San Francisco, 1977).
221. Herman E. Daly, *Steady-State economics* (Washington DC) 1991, xii.
222. 'Bussauer Manifest zur umweltpolitischen Situation', 469; Max Himmelheber, 'Rückschritt zum Überleben: Erster Teil', *Scheidewege. Vierteljahresschrift für skeptisches Denken* 4 (1974), 61–92; Himmelheber, 'Rückschritt zum Überleben: Zweiter Teil', *Scheidewege. Vierteljahresschrift für skeptisches Denken* 4 (1974), 369–93.
223. For a classical account, see Hans Magnus Enzensberger, 'Zur Kritik der politischen Ökologie', *Kursbuch* 9(33) (1973), 1–52, and the analysis in Mende, *Nicht rechts, nicht links, sondern vorn*, 304–10.
224. Engels, *Naturpolitik in der Bundesrepublik*, 24; Elke Seefried, 'Rethinking Progress: On the Origin of the Modern Sustainability Discourse, 1970–2000', *Journal of Modern European History* 13(3) (2015), 377–400.
225. A. Mazur and Eugene A. Rosa, 'Energy and Life-Style: Cross-National Comparison of Energy Consumption and Quality of Life Indicators', *Science* 186, no. 4164 (1974), 607–10; Nader and Beckerman, 'Energy as It Relates to the Quality and Style of Life', 25; Frederick H. Buttel, 'Social Structure and Energy Efficiency. A Preliminary Cross-National Analysis', *Human Ecology* 6(2) (1978), 145–64; for a summary of these studies, see Eugene A. Rosa, Gary E. Machlis and Kenneth M. Keating, 'Energy and Society', *Annual Review of Sociology* 14 (1988), 149–72.
226. Ernst Friedrich Schumacher, *Small Is Beautiful: Study of Economics as if People Mattered* (London, 1978); Schumacher, *Die Rückkehr zum menschlichen Maß: Alternativen für Wirtschaft und Technik* (Reinbek bei Hamburg, 1978); see also Geoffrey Kirk (ed.), *Schumacher on Energy: Speeches and Writings of E.F. Schumacher* (London, 1982).
227. Lovins, 'Energy Strategy'; Lovins, *Soft Energy Paths*; Lovins, 'Soft Energy Technologies', *Annual Review of Energy* 3 (1978), 477–518. In Germany, Lovins was viewed as more critical of growth and sceptical about technology. Lovins, *Sanfte Energie: Das Programm für die energie- und industriepolitische Umrüstung unserer Gesellschaft* (Reinbek, 1979); Krause, Bossel and Müller-Reissmann, *Energie-Wende*, 10; but see also Barbara Ruske and Dieter Teufel, *Das sanfte Energie-Handbuch: Wege aus der Unvernunft der Energieplanung in der Bundesrepublik* (Reinbek bei Hamburg, 1982).
228. Sachverständigenrat für Umweltfragen 2012. 'Umweltgutachten 2012: Verantwortung in einer begrenzten Welt'. *Deutscher Bundestag. Drucksachen. 17. Wahlperiode 2009–2013*, Nr. 10285, 5 July 2012.
229. Cf. the contrasting emphasis in Uekötter and Hohensee, *Wird Kassandra heiser?*.
230. Graf, 'Expert Estimates of Oil-Reserves'; Partha Dasgupta and Geoffrey M. Heal, *Economic Theory and Exhaustible Resources* (Welwyn/Cambridge, 1979); and on the 'boom in resource economics in the 1970s and 1980s', Geoffrey M. Heal, 'The Optimal Use of Exhaustible Resources', in Allen V. Kneese and James L. Sweeney (eds), *Handbook of Natural Resource and Energy Economics*, 3 vols (Amsterdam, 1993), 855–80, here 857.
231. Dasgupta and Heal, *Economic Theory and Exhaustible Resources*, 1f.

232. Vince Eagan, 'The Optimal Depletion of the Theory of Exhaustible Resources', *Journal of Post Keynesian Economics* 9 (1987), 565–71.

233. See IAEE, *IAEE-History*, http://www.iaee.org/en/inside/history.aspx (accessed 10 January 2018).

234. Robert A. Meyers, *Handbook of Energy Technology and Economics* (New York, 1983); Allen V. Kneese and James L. Sweeney (eds), *Handbook of Natural Resource and Energy Economics*, 3 vols (Amsterdam, 1993); Jeroen C.J.M. van den Bergh (ed.), *Handbook of Environmental and Resource Economics* (Cheltenham, 1999); Joanne Evans and Lester C. Hunt, *International Handbook on the Economics of Energy* (Cheltenham, 2011); Holger Wacker and Jürgen E. Blank, *Ressourcenökonomik*, vol. 2, *Einführung in die Theorie erschöpfbarer natürlicher Ressourcen* (Munich, 1999).

235. Michael A. Toman, 'The Economics of Energy Security: Theory, Evidence, Policy', in Kneese and Sweeney, *Handbook of Natural Resource and Energy Economics*, 1167–218, here 1167: 'Relatively few events in recent economic history have generated the quantity of scholarly writing, policy analysis, and public debate that have resulted from the "oil shocks" of the 1970s and 1980s. Those events directly stimulated the rapid growth of literature on a number of topics discussed in this volume'.

236. Alan T. Peacock, *The Oil Crisis and the Professional Economist* (York, 1975), 9.

237. Geoffrey M. Heal, 'Symposium on the Economics of Exhaustible Resources: Introduction', *Review of Economic Studies* 41 (1974), 1–2.

238. Hotelling, 'The Economics of Exhaustible Resources'; Partha Dasgupta and Geoffrey M. Heal, 'The Optimal Depletion of Exhaustible Resources', *Review of Economic Studies* 41 (1974), 3–28; Nordhaus, 'Resources as a Constraint to Growth'; Robert M. Solow, 'The Economics of Resources or the Resources of Economics: Richard T. Ely Lecture', *The American Economic Review* 64(2): Papers and Proceedings (1974), 1–14; Solow, 'Intergenerational Equity and Exhaustible Resources'.

239. Adelman, 'Politics, Economics, and World Oil'; Adelman, *The Genie out of the Bottle*, 1; Morris Albert Adelman and Michael C. Lynch, 'Fixed View of Resource Limits Creates Undue Pessimism', *Oil and Gas Journal* 95 (April 1997), 56–60.

240. James W. McKie, 'The Political Economy of World Petroleum', *American Economic Review* 64(2): Papers and Proceedings (1974), 51–57; Dasgupta and Heal, 'The Optimal Depletion of Exhaustible Resources'; on the early history of energy economics before Hotelling and on the distinction between optimists and pessimists, see also T.J.C. Robinson, *Economic Theories of Exhaustible Resources* (London/New York, 1989).

241. Adelman, 'World Oil Production and Prices', 171, 177.

242. Joseph Stiglitz, 'Growth with Exhaustible Natural Resources: Efficient and Optimal Growth Paths', *Review of Economic Studies* 41 (1974), 139–52.

243. Adelman, *The World Petroleum Market*, 9.

244. Solow, 'The Economics of Resources or the Resources of Economics'; Solow, 'Intergenerational Equity and Exhaustible Resources'; see also John M. Hartwick, 'Intergenerational Equity and the Investing of Rents from Exhaustible Resources', *American Economic Review* 67 (1977), 972–74.

245. Dasgupta and Heal, *Economic Theory and Exhaustible Resources*, 471f., 475.

246. For an exception, see Ferdinand E. Banks, *The Political Economy of Oil* (Lexington, MA, 1980); Banks, *Resources and Energy: An Economic Analysis* (Lexington, MA, 1983); Banks, *Energy Economics: A Modern Introduction* (Boston, 2000); Banks, 'Beautiful and Not So Beautiful Minds: An Introductory Essay on Economic Theory and the Supply of Oil', *OPEC Review* (March 2004), 27–62; Banks, *The Political Economy of World Energy*.

247. F.M. Peterson and A.C. Fisher, 'The Optimal Exploitation of Extractive Resources: A Survey', *Economic Journal* 87 (1977), 681–721, here 711.

248. Sabin, *The Bet*.

249. Hans Karl Schneider, 'Marktwirtschaftliche Energiepolitik oder staatlicher Dirigismus? 1978', in *Aufsätze aus drei Jahrzehnten zur Wirtschafts- und Energiepolitik* (Munich, 1990), 162–67.

250. For a summary, see Rodgers, *Age of Fracture*, 41–76; Andreas Wirsching, *Der Preis der Freiheit: Geschichte Europas in unserer Zeit* (Munich, 2012), 226–41.

251. Vietor, *Energy Policy in America*, 1; Sabin, *Crude Politics*; Frank, *Oil Empire*.

252. Horst Siebert, 'The Economics of Resource Ventures', in David William Pearce, Horst Siebert and Ingo Walter (eds), *Risk and the Political Economy of Resource Development* (London, 1984), 11–36, here 13; William W. Hogan and Federico Sturzenegger, *The Natural Resources Trap: Private Investment without Public Commitment* (Cambridge, MA, 2010).

253. Krauss, 'There Will Be Fuel'; Bill McKibben, 'Why Not Frack?', *New York Review of Books* 59(4) (2012), http://www.nybooks.com/articles/archives/2012/mar/08/why-not-frack/ (last modified 2 October 2016); on the controversy over the environmental implications of 'fracking', see also the 2010 documentary *Gasland*, directed by Josh Fox.

Conclusion

SOVEREIGNTY IN CRISIS AND THE OIL CRISIS IN CONTEMPORARY HISTORY

After the Second World War, rising oil consumption increasingly shaped economic and social life in the United States and Western Europe. In the first half of the 1970s, the world of oil changed fundamentally. As we have seen, as this process unfolded, energy policy challenges and debates emerged in Western Europe and the United States with which, for the most part, we are still grappling today. Oil and energy policies received far greater attention on the international level: under pressure from the oil price hikes and supply cutbacks of autumn 1973, the foreign ministers of the leading OECD countries came together the following year at the Washington Energy Conference. The result was the creation of a new international organization in the shape of the International Energy Agency, which was supposed to prevent future supply disruptions and enhance the flow of information on the international oil market. In addition, national governments beefed up their energy-related powers, as in the case of West Germany's Energy Security Act. In the United States, dozens of government agencies had staff dealing with different energy sources in the 1960s. In the wake of the energy crisis, their competencies were bundled together and moved up the hierarchy of government while new staff were appointed; the first body to be established was the Energy Policy Office, which was followed by a number of other institutions, culminating in the creation of the Department of Energy. In West Germany too, the government's 1973 energy programme turned energy into an autonomous policy field. Energy grew in importance each time this programme was revised, though it was never to be institutionalized in its own ministry.

Three crucial discursive shifts received new impetus from the oil crisis, though they had already been present in nascent form. Long before the

– 387 –

1970s, a variety of actors had periodically expressed concern about the security of the oil supply or the energy supply more generally, but until well into the postwar era these concerns focused chiefly on the strategic military consequences of an oil shortage. With the growing economic importance of oil, the concept of security expanded; in addition to military aspects, security increasingly came to encompass economic and social dimensions as well. The example of the oil crisis reinforced the idea that even minor supply disruptions could do tremendous damage to economic, social and political life and thus, ultimately, threaten national security. This idea became ubiquitous and attained the status of common sense. In much the same way, the intensification of global economic interdependence was nothing new, and had long been subject to discussion. But no other good could illustrate worldwide interdependencies as strikingly as oil. It was traded within a complex global system and, with its comprehensive array of products, played a key role in every sphere of the economy and life in general. In the 1970s, the oil crisis thus lent new impetus to debates on economic and political 'interdependence' and its consequences for the assertion of national sovereignty. This culminated in the debate on 'globalization' that is still with us today. In the 1950s and 1960s, a few commentators had already flagged up the risks of the oil running out, but they remained marginal figures, such as Marion King Hubbert with his theory of peak oil. Subsequently, in the 1970s, developments in the field of energy did much to foster the emergence of the environmental movement, which, among other things, sought to make the finiteness of natural resources the basis for political action. However, the fundamental critique of economic growth embraced by sections of the ecological movement in light of the resource problem neither reached the political mainstream nor influenced political practice. The contemporary conviction that there were 'limits to growth' was itself limited. Instead, the core objectives that guided policy were the decoupling of economic growth from rising energy consumption and the development of alternative energy sources, above all nuclear energy. After the experience of the preceding decades, the West German government still regarded continuous economic growth as the vital underpinning of all policies. Among other things, this was evident in the guidelines with which it furnished the economic institutes in order to make their calculations.

Despite these significant changes, it would be wrong to describe the oil crisis as a sudden and unexpected shock that triggered a fundamental shift in the global history of oil and energy, transforming the political, economic and social life of the United States and Western Europe. First, the oil crisis did not descend upon the Western industrialized nations out of a clear blue sky. Second, the idea of a fundamental rupture in the 1970s masks significant continuities in energy consumption and policymaking. Within the framework of the OECD, in the 1960s ministerial officials – crucial to energy policy but often neglected in classical political histories – had already begun to address the security of the energy supply and to make provisions for an event such as the oil crisis. The OECD could pass no binding resolutions and lacked sanctioning mechanisms. Nonetheless, meetings of experts from high up in the national ministerial hierarchies ensured a degree of synchronization, in terms of both the perception of problems and the harmonization of precautionary measures. In no OECD country did the restructuring of energy policy begin with the oil crisis. Across the developed world, this process was already underway when OPEC increased prices in October 1973 and OAPEC imposed the regime of production cuts. This is not an attempt to roll out the standard historical argument that everything began much earlier than generally supposed, but we can only understand the political action taken during the oil crisis by attending to the changes already underway. In the United States, before the oil crisis a home-made energy crisis – the result of the unexpectedly strong growth in oil consumption in the 1960s and various government interventions – was the real trigger for energy policy initiatives. In the other OECD countries, the key impetus for the reworking of national energy policies came from a declaration by the US delegation to the High Level Group Oil in 1970. This stated that the United States would no longer be able to help the Europeans in case of future supply shortfalls, and would in fact compete with them for Middle Eastern oil. The oil crisis thus radicalized and accelerated governments' efforts to implement new energy policies.

While the oil price hikes and the oil embargo – or the supply cutbacks – were not the decisive turning point in the history of energy that historical accounts of the modern world often make them out to be, this does not mean they were insignificant. Those developing countries without oil reserves of their own had to pay more to import oil and oil products, a significant driver of Third World debt. Credit was available on favourable terms, but rather than coming from the United States and Western Europe, loans now ultimately consisted of 'recycled' petrodollars from the producing countries, whose new wealth triggered enormous changes in the international financial markets.[1] Nevertheless, economic historians now believe the oil crisis had less effect on economic developments in the Western industrialized nations in the 1970s than general historical analyses often suggest.[2] They blame structural factors and the ensuing stagflation, which they believe to have been worsened but not caused by the oil price rise. The supply cutbacks, they contend, made little overall impact because during the oil crisis oil was never truly scarce. Nonetheless, for the governments of Western Europe and the United States, the oil crisis was hugely significant symbolically with respect to the politics of sovereignty; over the preceding decades of exceptional economic growth, growing prosperity had increasingly come to underpin Western democracies' political legitimacy. The world of the 1950s and 1960s, with its economic miracles, seemed more and more like a world of oil, one that seemed endangered in October 1973. The seeming threat to the oil supply appeared to put the sovereignty of the Western industrialized nations and Japan at risk as well. Their governments were clearly incapable of guaranteeing a continuous flow of oil, yet this was central to their ability to conduct their policies. They also came under pressure to adopt specific foreign policy positions. Adding insult to injury, this challenge to their sovereignty came from the rulers of far-off lands about which the West knew little and which it was not used to taking seriously. Now, making skilful use of the media, these foreign leaders had started to upend certainties about the future development of Western Europe and the United States.

The Western European countries and the United States sought to preserve and extend their sovereignty through a variety of national and international strategies. The overriding goal of these measures was energy security. This had become vital to governments' capacity for effective action, turning it into a key political category. The concept of energy not only enabled a comprehensive assessment of the different energy sources – oil, coal, gas, nuclear fusion, wind, water and sun – which had previously come under the remit of a number of different agencies. It also made it possible to better integrate consumption into government policies. States thus attempted to reduce their dependence on oil – above all oil imports from the Middle East – both by influencing the composition of primary energy sources and by reducing energy consumption, whenever possible without impairing productivity or living standards. To this end, they reorganized decision-making structures with regard to energy policy, appointed additional staff and stepped up the production of petro-knowledge or, more generally, energy policy expertise. The challenge posed to Western sovereignty by the producing countries was concrete, but it was also symbolic in nature and conveyed through the media. Governments' strategies for maintaining sovereignty were therefore always intended both to enhance their capacity for action and to demonstrate this capacity publicly. The state's room for manoeuvre, which had grown over the decades of the economic boom, had created public expectations and a sense of entitlement that had to be satisfied if states were to uphold their authority. In the world of oil, over the long term, no government felt able to secure their national sovereignty alone, without international cooperation. They thus tried to achieve collective solutions both in collaboration with the producing countries and in opposition to them.

Beyond this basic common ground, however, the strategies pursued to enhance sovereignty differed in line with the initial energy endowments and requirements in the different OECD countries. The United States was the original homeland of industrial oil production, home to five of the seven largest oil firms; it had been the largest producing country into the 1970s and was the hegemonic power within the Western alliance system. Meanwhile, West Germany, a country without significant oil production of its own, was largely dependent on supplies from the multinational oil companies and was integrated into a European alliance. The differences between the two countries, then, could scarcely have been greater. Listing them, as we would have to do in a systematic historical comparison, would produce essentially trivial results. Nonetheless, a number of differences that run counter to present-day expectations are worth noting.

The first surprise is the American impulse to pursue – or at least the rhetoric of – energy autarky. This formed part of the backdrop to Nixon's 'Project Independence' and has been reaffirmed ever since by every American president, though it has never come close to being achieved.[3] The announcement of 'Project Independence' went hand in hand with heavy regulation of the oil market through price controls and an allocation system for oil products; these violated the principles of a free market economy despite being implemented by its fervent devotees, such as William E. Simon. Furthermore, the government expanded its bureaucracy in order to administer this regulatory framework and provide what it saw as the requisite independent expertise on energy policy. Conversely, the social-liberal government in West Germany put more emphasis on the market's regulatory capacity. In the shape of DEMINEX, the government did try to facilitate the establishment of an oil-producing company capable of competing with the large multinational companies, but this project soon proved illusory. Unlike in France or Italy, for example, which had their own national oil companies, West Germany, partly in view of its own economic strength, put its faith in the multinational companies to continue to ensure an adequate supply of oil, even in future crises. Much the same can be said of West German energy policy with respect to the production of knowledge. Though the West German government perceived a lack of petro-knowledge, or insufficient information on energy, as a serious problem during the oil crisis, it sought neither to develop a bespoke energy ministry, as in the United States or the United Kingdom, nor to establish an independent oil-focused research institute along the lines, for example, of the Institut Français du Pétrole.[4] Instead it drew on the expertise of external research institutes such as the EWI Cologne, the RWI in Essen and the DIW Cologne.

The inflation of petro-knowledge and scientific expertise on energy was a response to the contingency and uncertainty unleashed by OPEC and OAPEC in October 1973, which had laid bare the lack of relevant knowledge and information. An increasing number of institutions collected statistical data on the oil and energy supply, while traditional academic disciplines began to consider oil-related issues. In parallel to the development of energy as a policy field, there emerged a hybrid field of knowledge known as 'energy', featuring its own journals and textbooks. This expansion of knowledge was consonant with the basic tendency – often highlighted by scholars in recent years – towards the scientification of society and politics in the twentieth century.[5] Scientification, however, is not best understood as a success story in which scientific knowledge increasingly determined political and social practice. Attempts to ground political action in science quickly threw up serious problems, which contemporaries already began to reflect on. Faced with the challenge to sovereignty posed by the oil crisis, for the US government and its Western European counterparts – accustomed to thinking in terms of legislative periods rather than the long timescales of energy regimes – initially the top priority was to create the impression of acting on the basis of the best possible expertise. However, in an attempt to satisfy the public's burgeoning expectations of government, during the crisis states had to act in the absence of the required expertise, or at least without having established which form of expertise was best. Expert opinions, having proliferated and become politically charged, were notoriously incompatible. So, rather than showcasing the grounding of policy in scientific knowledge, the oil crisis, to quote Sheila Jasanoff, is in fact an example of the forced marriage of science and politics, a result of scientific uncertainty and the pressure on governments to make decisions.[6] As we seek to understand processes of political decision-making, then, it might be more productive to think in terms of 'controlling uncertainty' and 'managing ignorance' rather than foregrounding 'knowledge' – which certainly proliferated but could not provide an adequate basis for decisions.[7]

In foreign policy terms, during the oil crisis the Western European countries and the United States pursued both bilateral and multilateral strategies, though when it came to energy, the latter's potential for an independent foreign policy was incomparably greater than that of West Germany or other European countries. However, rather than focusing on bilateral negotiations with the producing countries, Nixon and Kissinger pursued a multilateral strategy. This distinguished the US from European countries such as France and the United Kingdom, which placed more emphasis on bilateral talks with specific producing countries as a means of safeguarding their energy supply. It would, however, be a mistake to construe the difference between bilateral and multilateral strategies as one between international cooperation and national self-interest, as is often done both by contemporaries and historians.[8] Confronting the threat to their sovereignty posed by the oil crisis, all governments used both these options, in various combinations, in an attempt to achieve their national goals. The French government, as the champion of bilateral negotiations, simultaneously pursued multilateral cooperation within the EC framework; Kissinger, as the leading advocate of international cooperation, concurrently pursued bilateral negotiations with Saudi Arabia. Time and again we find that countries were prepared to forego sovereignty through international cooperation, or organizations such as the International Energy Agency, whenever they expected this to enhance their sovereignty in other ways. At the same time, this engagement was always partly a matter of political symbolism. The concept of sovereignty inevitably entails a social component, because a country can only be sovereign if it is recognized as such by other countries. It was thus crucial to communicate sovereignty through globally networked media ensembles whose inherent logic largely evaded the control of national governments.

The governments of the United States and Western Europe responded to the oil crisis in an ambivalent, flexible way, attempting to secure their energy sovereignty through both national and international structures. It is thus quite impossible to fit the oil crisis into a linear narrative of sovereignty. Contrary to the fears of some contemporaries, the producing countries' success in bolstering their sovereignty over raw materials did not usher in the continuous decline of the West.[9] Neither did the oil crisis foster and demonstrate an irretrievable decline of the nation state – due to increasing economic interdependence – vis-à-vis larger organizational entities, or the triumph of multinational companies over the nation states. One of the key reasons why such hypotheses do little to advance our understanding is that they conceive of the development of sovereignty as the history of a quality that states either have or lack. A more productive approach is to conceptualize sovereignty as a political claim that may be made, recognized, questioned or rejected. From this perspective, the oil crisis was a particularly revealing complex of events, in which the core political and economic conflicts of the era intersected; subsequently, it was the perfect means of legitimizing various claims and opinions about the history of sovereignty.

The oil crisis served economists and company spokesmen as evidence that the state must retreat and focus on ensuring the best possible climate for investment and exploration. The environmental movements saw it as the harbinger of a future scarcity of resources that would place tight limits on state action. Political scientists such as Robert Keohane and Joseph Nye regarded it as a sign that US hegemony was coming to an end, while it prompted Robert W. Tucker and the New Sovereigntists to conclude that, now more than ever, the US must reassert its hegemony. These and other interpretations always implied a variety of conceptions of the future, so their plausibility depended, and depends still, on where we are located within these future horizons. Moreover, to plump for a historical narrative of sovereignty such as the decline or end of sovereignty would fail to do justice to the multiple interpretability of the oil crisis. Yet this is precisely what made it significant and turned it into a key event of the 1970s. Historians and other commentators continue to view it as an episode crucial to understanding the present era, making it a stock component of every historical survey of the last few decades.

As highlighted in the introduction, scholars of contemporary history regard the 1970s as an important time of transformation. On this view, the decades of economic boom – the supposed 'golden age' – came to an end as economies plunged into crisis; a sense of unlimited possibilities was superseded by the recognition of limits; and faith in the power of state planning gave way to pragmatic crisis management. Historians and other commentators generally justify this construction of an era by referring to, among other things, the oil crisis and the problem of energy. But this seems dubious when we consider the changes in energy policy that occurred in the United States and Western Europe. When it came to energy, the oil crisis bolstered rather than diminished the zeal for planning and remaking the world; an ever greater variety of energy futures became conceivable, while plans and forecasts expanded both spatially and temporally. This process is poorly described as 'sobering' or the 'end of confidence'. In fact, a variety of actors deployed the trope of disillusionment within the political debates of the 1970s in an attempt to justify their views and delegitimize other ideas. The critique of growth certainly became more popular, but it remained marginal within societies as a whole and to this day no country has made it the basis for political practice. Instead, at least since the 1970s, the expectation of a coming oil shortage with devastating consequences has stood opposed to the view that there will be enough oil in the foreseeable future as long as market forces are given free rein. Greater attention is paid to exponents of one or the other of these two positions depending on the price of oil. Ulf Lantzke's 1984 assessment still applies: 'Over the past ten years, the public has been presented with an analytical roller coaster where oil crises have alternated with oil gluts'.[10] We are still grappling with the energy policy problems that were laid bare by the oil crisis of 1973–74 and subsequently subject to intensive debate. Climate change has altered the nature of these problems only in the sense that it is no longer the anticipated scarcity of fossil energy sources but rather the predicted consequences of their excessive consumption that serve to justify changes in energy policy. As in many other areas of life, from social security systems through technological development to pop music, here too the 1960s seem like a far distant past, while we tend to perceive the problems and perspectives of the second half of the 1970s as ongoingly relevant. So, while there is undoubtedly a need to supplement and add nuance to previous historical accounts of energetic transformation, it is still quite plausible to identify the first half of the 1970s as the beginning of our era.

Notes

1. Sargent, *A Superpower Transformed*, 139f.
2. Maier, 'Two Sorts of Crises?'; Barry J. Eichengreen, *The European Economy since 1945: Coordinated Capitalism and Beyond* (Princeton, 2007).
3. Michael J. Graetz, *The End of Energy: The Unmaking of America's Environment, Security, and Independence* (Boston, 2011).
4. In the United Kingdom, the Ministry of Fuel and Power was established in 1942, though it was incorporated into the Ministry of Technology in 1969 and the Department of Trade and Industry in 1970. Responsibility for energy policy was transferred to an autonomous Department of Energy in 1974.
5. Raphael, 'Die Verwissenschaftlichung des Sozialen'; Margit Szöllösi-Janze, 'Wissensgesellschaft: Ein neues Konzept zur Erschließung der deutsch-deutschen Zeitgeschichte?', in Hans Günter Hockerts (ed.), *Koordinaten deutscher Geschichte in der Epoche des Ost-West-Konflikts* (Munich, 2003), 277–305; Vogel, 'Von der Wissenschafts- zur Wissensgeschichte'.
6. Jasanoff, *The Fifth Branch*, 8.
7. Jerome R. Ravetz, 'Uncertainty, Ignorance and Policy', in Harvey Brooks and Chester L. Cooper (eds), *Science for Public Policy* (Oxford, 1987), 77–89; Christoph Engel, Jost Halfmann and Martin Schulte (eds), *Wissen – Nichtwissen – unsicheres Wissen* (Baden-Baden, 2002); Wildavsky and Tenenbaum, *Politics of Mistrust*.
8. Venn, 'International Co-operation versus National Self-Interest'.
9. Friedland, Seabury and Wildavsky, 'Oil and the Decline of Western Power'; Walter J. Levy, 'Oil and the Decline of the West', *Foreign Affairs* 58(5) (1980), 999–1015.
10. Ulf Lantzke, 'Energy Policies in Industrialized Countries: An Evaluation of the Past Decade', in Ayoub, *Le Marché pétrolier international*, 15–22, here 15.

BIBLIOGRAPHY

Archival Sources

Archiv der Sozialen Demokratie, Bonn

Archives Nationales de France, Fontainbleau (ANF)
Service du Premier Ministre. Comité interministériel pour les questions de coopération économique européenne
Service du Premier Ministre. Commissariat Général du Plan

Bundesarchiv, Koblenz (BArch)
Bundesministerium für Wirtschaft (B 102)
Bundesministerium für Verkehr (B 108)
Bundesministerium der Finanzen (B 126)
Bundeskanzleramt (B 136)
Bundesministerium für Bildung und Wissenschaft (B 138)
Bundespresseamt (B 145)
Bundesanstalt für Geowissenschaften und Rohstoffe (B 176)
Bundesministerium für Post und Telekommunikation (B 257)

Central Intelligence Agency. Freedom of Information Act Electronic Reading Room (CIA)
President Nixon and the Role of Intelligence in the 1973 Arab-Israeli War (Nixon Intelligence)

Digital National Security Archive (DNSA)
Kissinger Telephone Conversations (KA)
Kissinger Transcripts (KT)

Lafayette College Libraries, Easton, PA (LCL)
William E. Simon Papers (WSP)

The National Archives of the United Kingdom (NA UK)
Cabinet Office Files (CAB)

Records created or inherited by the Department of Energy, 1920–2003 (EG)
Foreign and Commonwealth Office (FCO)
Records created or inherited by the Department of Technical Co-operation, and of successive Overseas Development bodies (OD)
Records created or inherited by the Ministry of Power, and of related bodies (POWE)
Prime Minister's Office (PREM)
Records created or inherited by HM Treasury (T)

National Archives and Records Administration, College Park, MD (NARA)
Department of the Interior (RG 48)
Department of the Treasury (RG 56)
Department of State (RG 59)
Film Archive

Nixon Library, Yorba Linda, CA [formerly College Park] (NARA, Nixon Library)
Henry A. Kissinger, Telephone Conversations (HAK Telcons)
National Security Council, Country Files (NSC, Country Files)
National Security Council, Henry A. Kissinger Office Files (NSC, HAK Office Files)
National Security Council, Institutional Files (NSC, Inst. Files)
National Security Council, Institutional Files, Senior Review Group (NSC, Inst. Files, SRG)
National Security Council, Institutional Files, Washington Special Action Group (NSC, Inst. Files, WSAG)
National Security Council, Presidential Correspondence (NSC, Pres. Correspondence)
National Security Council, Subject Files (NSC, Subject Files)
National Security Council, VIP Visits (NSC, VIP Visits)
White House Central Files, Staff Member and Office Files (WHCF, SMOF)
White House Central Files, Staff Member and Office Files, Energy Policy Office (WHCF, SMOF, EPO)
White House Central Files, Special Files (WHCF, Special Files)
White House Central Files, Subject Files (WHCF, Subject Files)
White House Special Files, President's Office Files (WHSF, Pres. Office Files)
White House Special Files, President's Personal Files (WHSF, Pres. Pers. Files)
White House Special Files, Staff Member and Office Files (WHSF, SMOF)

Politisches Archiv des Auswärtigen Amtes, Berlin (PA AA)
Ministerbüro (B 1)
Büro Staatssekretäre (B 2)
Naher Osten und Nordafrika, Referat 310/311 (B 36)
Internationale Energiepolitik, Referat 405 (B 71)
Dokumente für die Akten zur Auswärtigen Politik der Bundesrepublik Deutschland (B 150)

Published Sources

Abelshauser, Werner. *Deutsche Wirtschaftsgeschichte seit 1945*. Munich, 2004.
Adelman, Morris Albert. *The Genie Out of the Bottle: World Oil since 1970*. Cambridge, MA, 1995.
———. 'Is the Oil Shortage Real? Oil Companies as OPEC Tax Collectors'. *Foreign Policy* 9 (1972/73), 69–107.
———. 'My Education in Mineral (Especially Oil) Economics'. *Annual Review of Energy and the Environment* 22 (1997), 13–46.
———. 'Politics, Economics, and World Oil'. *American Economic Review* 64(2): Papers and Proceedings (1974), 58–66.
———. 'Population Growth and Oil Resources'. *Quarterly Journal of Economics* 89(2) (1975), 271–75.
———. 'World Oil Production and Prices 1947–2000'. *Quarterly Review of Economics and Finance* 42 (2002), 169–91.
———. *The World Petroleum Market*. Baltimore, 1972.
Adelman, Morris Albert, and Michael C. Lynch. 'Fixed View of Resource Limits Creates Undue Pessimism'. *Oil and Gas Journal* 95 (April 1997), 56–60.
Akins, James E. 'International Cooperative Efforts in Energy Supply'. *Annals of the American Academy of Political and Social Science* 410 (1973), 75–85.
———. 'The Nature of the Crisis in Energy'. *Journal of Petroleum Technology* 24 (December 1972), 1479–83.
———. 'The Oil Crisis: This Time the Wolf Is Here'. *Foreign Affairs* 51 (April 1973), 462–90.
———. 'Saudis Serious on Using Oil Exports to Alter US Policy'. *Oil and Gas Journal* 71(41) (1973), 37.
'The Algiers Summit Conference'. *MERIP Reports* 23 (December 1973), 13–16.
Allen, Edward Lawrence. *Energy and Economic Growth in the United States*. Cambridge, MA, 1979 (The Institute for Energy Analysis and the MIT Press Perspectives in Energy Series, 2).
Al-Sowayegh, Abdulaziz. *Arab Petropolitics*. London, 1984.
Altenburg, Cornelia. *Kernenergie und Politikberatung: Die Vermessung einer Kontroverse*. Wiesbaden, 2010.
Altman, Lawrence K. 'Doctors Support Nixon on Cooler Homes'. *New York Times*, 9 November 1973.
American Petroleum Institute. *Facts about Oil*. N.p., 1971.
———. *Petroleum: Facts and Figures*. New York, 1928.
Amuzegar, Jahangir. 'The North-South Dialogue: From Conflict to Compromise'. *Foreign Affairs* 54(3) (1976), 547–62.
———. 'Not Much Aid and Not Enough Trade: Cloudy Prospects in North-South Relations'. *Third World Quarterly* 1(1) (1979), 50–64.
———. 'The Oil Story: Facts, Fiction, and Fair Play'. *Foreign Affairs* 51 (1973), 676–89.
———. 'OPEC in the Context of the Global Power Equation'. *Denver Journal of International Law and Policy* 4 (1974), 221–28.

———. 'A Requiem for the North-South Conference'. *Foreign Affairs* 56(1) (1977), 136–59.
Anderson, Jack. 'Nixon Doesn't Practice What He Preaches'. *Hamilton Ohio Journal News*, 26 November 1973.
Ang, Adrian U-Jin, and Dursun Peksen. 'When Do Economic Sanctions Work? Asymmetric Perceptions, Issue Salience, and Outcomes'. *Political Research Quarterly* 60 (2007), 135–45.
Anghie, Antony. *Imperialism, Sovereignty and the Making of International Law*. Cambridge, 2005.
'Arab Oil Embargo Deserves Consideration (Editorial)'. *Oil and Gas Journal* 71(44) (1973), 47.
Arbeitsgemeinschaft deutscher wirtschaftswissenschaftlicher Forschungsinstitute e.V. *Untersuchung über die Entwicklung der gegenwärtigen und zukünftigen Struktur von Angebot und Nachfrage in der Energiewirtschaft der Bundesrepublik unter besonderer Berücksichtigung des Steinkohlebergbaus*. Auf Beschluß des Deutschen Bundestages vom 12. Juni 1959 durchgeführt, abgeschlossen und vorgelegt 1961 [Conducted on the basis of a decision of the German Parliament, 12 June 1959, completed in 1961]. Berlin, 1962.
'"Auf König Feisal können Sie sich verlassen." Saudi-Arabiens Ölminister Ahmed Saki el-Jamani über die arabische Ölstrategie'. *Der Spiegel*, 3 December 1973, 35–44.
Ayoub, Antoine (ed.). *Le Marché pétrolier international dix ans après la crise de 1973 : Bilan et perspectives*. Québec, 1984 (Groupe de recherche en économie de l'énergie et des ressources naturelles [GREEN]).
Bacevich, Andrew J. *The Limits of Power: The End of American Exceptionalism*. New York, 2008.
Baker, Donald P., and Cathe Wolhowe. 'Drivers Ignore Fuel-Saving Advice'. *Washington Post*, 9 November 1973.
Baker, Russell. 'The Less Oleaginous Life'. *New York Times*, 27 November 1973.
Baldwin, David A. *Economic Statecraft*. Princeton, NJ, 1985.
Bamberg, James. *The History of the British Petroleum Company*. 3 vols. Cambridge, 1983–2000.
———. *The History of the British Petroleum Company*, vol. 3, *British Petroleum and Global Oil 1950–1975: The Challenge of Nationalism*. Cambridge, 2000.
Bange, Oliver, and Gottfried Niedhardt (eds). *Helsinki 1975 and the Transformation of Europe*. Oxford/New York, 2008.
Banks, Ferdinand E. 'Beautiful and Not So Beautiful Minds: An Introductory Essay on Economic Theory and the Supply of Oil'. *OPEC Review* (March 2004), 27–62.
———. *Energy Economics: A Modern Introduction*. Boston, 2000.
———. *The Political Economy of Oil*. Lexington, MA, 1980.
———. *The Political Economy of World Energy: An Introductory Textbook*. New Jersey, 2007.
———. *Resources and Energy: An Economic Analysis*. Lexington, MA, 1983.
Barber, James. 'Economic Sanctions as a Policy Instrument'. *International Affairs* 55 (1979), 367–84.

Barnett, Harold J. 'The Changing Relation of Natural Resources to National Security'. *Economic Geography* 34(3) (1958), 189–201.

Bartoletto, Silvana. 'Patterns of Energy Transitions: The Long-Term Role of Energy in the Economic Growth of Europe', in Nina Möllers and Karin Zachmann (eds), *Past and Present Energy Societies: How Energy Connects Politics, Technologies and Cultures*. Bielefeld, 2012, 305–30.

Basalla, George. 'Energy and Civilization', in Chauncey Starr and Philip C. Ritterbush (eds), *Science, Technology and the Human Prospect: Proceedings of the Edison Centennial Symposium*. New York, 1980, 39–52.

———. 'Some Persistent Energy Myths', in George H. Daniels and Mark H. Rose (eds), *Energy and Transport: Historical Perspectives on Policy Issues*. N.p., 1982, 27–38.

Basile, Paul S. *Energy Demand Studies, Major Consuming Countries. Analyses of 1972 Demand and Projections of 1985 Demand. First Technical Report of the Workshop on Alternative Energy Strategies (WAES)*. 2nd ed. Cambridge, MA, 1977.

Bates, Brainerd S. 'The Crimson Tide'. *Aramco World* 23(2) (1972), 12–14.

Bayerisches Oberbergamt. *Energiebilanz Bayerns 1973: Daten zur Entwicklung der Energiewirtschaft*. Munich, 1974

Bayerisches Staatsministerium für Wirtschaft und Verkehr. *Energieprogramm I: Grundlinien zu einem Energieprogramm für Bayern*. Munich, 1973.

Beaubouef, Bruce Andre. *The Strategic Petroleum Reserve: US Energy Security and Oil Politics, 1975–2005*. College Station, TX, 2007.

Beaudreau, Bernard C. *Energy and the Rise and Fall of Political Economy*. Westport, CT, 1999.

Bell, Daniel. *The Coming of Post-Industrial Society: A Venture in Social Forecasting*. New York, 1976.

Beltran, Alain (ed.). *Oil Producing Countries and Oil Companies: From the Nineteenth Century to the Twenty-First Century*. Bern/Oxford, 2011.

———. 'Orientation Bibliographique: L'Énergie depuis 1973'. *Bulletin de l'Institut d'Histoire du Temps Présent* 45 (1991), 27–54.

Bender, Peter. *Die 'Neue Ostpolitik' und ihre Folgen: Vom Mauerbau bis zur Vereinigung*. Munich, 1995.

Berger, Marilyn. 'Jobert Calls Talks a "Pretext"'. *Washington Post*, 14 February 1974.

———. 'Nixon Links Security to Fuel'. *Washington Post*, 12 February 1974.

Bergsten, C. Fred. 'Interdependence and the Reform of International Institutions'. *International Organization* 30(2) (1976), 361–72.

———. 'The Threat from the Third World'. *Foreign Policy* 11 (Summer 1973), 102–24.

———. 'The Threat Is Real'. *Foreign Policy* 14 (Spring 1974), 84–90.

Bergsten, C. Fred, Robert O. Keohane, and Joseph S. Nye. 'International Economics and International Politics: A Framework for Analysis'. *International Organization* 29(1) (1975), 3–36.

Berreby, Jean-Jacques. *Le pétrole dans la stratégie mondiale*. Paris, 1974.

Bess, Michael. *The Light-Green Society: Ecology and Technological Modernity in France, 1960–2000*. Chicago, 2003.

Bethkenhagen, Jochen. *Bedeutung und Möglichkeiten des Ost-West-Handels mit Energierohstoffen*. Berlin, 1975 (Deutsches Institut für Wirtschaftsforschung [DIW] Sonderheft, 104).

Biersteker, Thomas J., and Cynthia Weber. 'The Social Construction of State Sovereignty', in Thomas J. Biersteker and Cynthia Weber (eds), *State Sovereignty as Social Construct*. Cambridge, 1996, 1–21.

Bischoff, Gerhard, and Werner Gocht (eds). *Das Energiehandbuch*. Braunschweig, 1970.

———. *Das Energiehandbuch*. 2nd ed. Braunschweig, 1976.

Blackstone, Tessa, and William Plowden. *Inside the Think Tank: Advising the Cabinet 1971–1983*. London, 1988.

Blair, David J., and Paul A. Summerville. *Oil Import Security: The Cases of Japan and Great Britain*. N.p., 1983 (PSIS Occasional Papers, 4).

Bloed, Arie. *The Conference on Security and Co-operation in Europe: Analysis and Basic Documents, 1972–1993*. Dordrecht, 1993.

———. *The Conference on Security and Co-operation in Europe: Basic Documents, 1993–1995*. The Hague, 1997.

Blondel, F., and S.G. Lasky. 'Mineral Reserves and Mineral Resources'. *Economic Geology* 51(7) (1956), 686–97.

Böckenförde, Ernst-Wolfgang. 'Die Bedeutung der Unterscheidung von Staat und Gesellschaft im demokratischen Sozialstaat der Gegenwart [1972]', in *Staat, Gesellschaft, Freiheit: Studien zur Staatstheorie und zum Verfassungsrecht*. Frankfurt am Main, 1976, 185–220.

———. 'Die Entstehung des Staates als Vorgang der Säkularisation [1967]', in *Staat, Gesellschaft, Freiheit: Studien zur Staatstheorie und zum Verfassungsrecht*. Frankfurt am Main, 1976, 42–64.

Bösch, Frank. 'Umbrüche in die Gegenwart: Globale Ereignisse und Krisenreaktionen um 1979'. *Zeithistorische Forschungen/Studies in Contemporary History* 9(1) (2012) (online).

Bösch, Frank, and Rüdiger Graf (eds). 'The Energy Crises of the 1970s'. *Historical Social Research* 39(4) (2014). Special issue.

Boulding, Kenneth E. 'The Economics of Space-Ship Earth [1966]'. In Fred R. Glahe (ed.), *Collected Papers of Kenneth E. Boulding*, vol. 2, *Economics*. Boulder, CO, 1971, 383–94.

———. 'The Social System and the Energy Crisis'. *Science* 184(4134) (1974), 255–57.

Boumedienne, Houari. 'Address to the General Assembly of the UN', in United Nations General Assembly (ed.), *Sixth Special Session. Plenary Meetings. Verbatim Records of Meetings 9 April–2 May 1974, 2208th Plenary Meeting, 10 April 1974*. New York, 1976, 1–11.

Bowden, Gary. 'The Social Construction of Validity in Estimates of US Crude Oil Reserves'. *Social Studies of Science* 15 (1985), 207–40.

BP AG. *Buch vom Erdöl: Eine Einführung in die Erdölindustrie*. Hamburg, 1959.

———. *Energie 2000: Tendenzen und Perspektiven*. N.p., 1977.
Brandt, Willy. 'Address to the United Nations General Assembly. 2128th Plenary Meeting, 26 September 1973', in United Nations General Assembly (ed.), *Twenty-Eighth Session. Plenary Meetings. Verbatim Records of Meetings 18 September–18 December 1973 and 16 September 1974*. New York, 1983, 1–5.
———. 'Ansprache zum Jahreswechsel 1973/74'. *Bulletin des Presse- und Informationsamts der Bundesregierung* 1 (1974), 5–6.
———. *Ein Volk der guten Nachbarn: Außen- und Deutschlandpolitik 1966–1974*. Ed. Frank Fischer. Bonn, 2005 (Berliner Ausgabe, 6).
———. *Mehr Demokratie wagen: Innen- und Gesellschaftspolitik 1966–1974*. Ed. Wolther von Kieseritzky. Bonn, 2001 (Berliner Ausgabe, 7).
———. *North-South: A Programme for Survival; Report of the Independent Commission on International Development Issues*. London, 1982.
Brobst, Donald A., and Walden P. Pratt. 'Introduction', in *United States Mineral Resources*. Washington, DC, 1973, 1–8.
———, eds. *United States Mineral Resources*. Washington, DC, 1973 (United States Geological Survey Professional Papers, 820).
Brooks, Stephen G., and William Curti Wohlforth. *World out of Balance: International Relations and the Challenge of American Primacy*. Princeton, NJ, 2008.
Brown, Seyom. *New Forces in World Politics*. Washington, DC, 1974.
Brüggemeier, Franz-Josef, and Jens Ivo Engels. 'Den Kinderschuhen entwachsen: Einleitende Worte zur Umweltgeschichte der zweiten Hälfte des 20. Jahrhunderts', in *Natur- und Umweltschutz nach 1945: Konzepte, Konflikte, Kompetenzen*. Frankfurt am Main, 2005, 10–22.
Bull, Hedley. 'Arms Control and World Order'. *International Security* 1 (1976), 3–16.
Bundesministerium für Forschung und Technologie. *Programm Energieforschung und Energietechnologien: 1977–1980*. Bonn, 1977.
———. *Rationelle Energieverwendung: Statusbericht 1978. Teil 1 und 2*. Bonn, 1978.
Burchard, Hans-Joachim. *Methoden und Grenzen der Energieprognosen*. Hamburg, 1968.
———. 'Prognosen und Wirklichkeit', in Wilhelm Dröscher, Klaus-Detlef Funke, and Ernst Theilen (eds), *Energie, Beschäftigung, Lebensqualität*. Bonn-Bad Godesberg, 1977, 281–82.
———. 'Der Souveränitätswechsel beim Erdöl'. *Außenpolitik* 25 (1974), 447–60.
'Bussauer Manifest zur umweltpolitischen Situation'. *Scheidewege. Vierteljahresschrift für skeptisches Denken* 5 (1975), 469–86.
Buttel, Frederick H. 'Social Structure and Energy Efficiency: A Preliminary Cross-National Analysis'. *Human Ecology* 6(2) (1978), 145–64.
Butterfield, Fox. 'Saudi Says Oil-Price Cut Must Be Joint Arab Step'. *New York Times*, 29 January 1974.
Buzan, Barry, and Lene Hansen (eds). *International Security*, vol. 3, *Widening Security*. Los Angeles, 2007.

Cairncross, Frances, and Hamish McRae. *The Second Great Crash: How the Oil Crisis Could Destroy the World's Economy*. Bungay, 1975.
Caldwell, Lynton K. 'Energy and the Structure of Social Institutions'. *Human Ecology* 4(1) (1976), 31–45.
Camilleri, Joseph A., and Jim Falk. *The End of Sovereignty? The Politics of a Shrinking and Fragmenting World*. Aldershot, 1992.
Campbell, Colin J. *The Coming Oil Crisis*. Essex, 1997.
———. *Oil Crisis*. Brentwood, 2005.
Campbell, John C. 'Oil Power in the Middle East'. *Foreign Affairs* 56(1) (1977), 89–110.
Campbell, John C., Guy de Carmoy, and Shinichi Kondo. *Energy: The Imperative for a Trilateral Approach. A Report of the Task Force on the Political and International Implications of the Energy Crisis to the Executive Committee of the Trilateral Commission*. Brussels, 1974.
———. *Energy: A Strategy for International Action. A Report of the Task Force on the Political and International Implications of the Energy Crisis to the Executive Committee of the Trilateral Commission*. Washington, DC, 1974.
Cannon, Lou. 'Nixon Flies West on Commercial Jet'. *Washington Post*, 27 December 1973.
———. 'Nixon Returns to Capital in Small Military Jet'. *Washington Post*, 13 January 1974.
Carmoy, Guy de. 'French Energy Policy', in Wilfrid L. Kohl (ed.), *After the Second Oil Crisis: Energy Policies in Europe, America, and Japan*. Lexington, MA, 1982, 113–36.
Carter, D.V. (ed.). *The History of Petroleum Engineering*. Dallas, 1961.
Casser, Eckhard. *Grundlagen und Ziele für eine gemeinsame Energiepolitik im norddeutschen Raum und Berlin: Gutachten im Auftrage der Konferenz der Wirtschaftsminister/-senatoren der Länder Bremen, Hamburg, Niedersachsen, Schleswig-Holstein und Berlin*. Berlin, 1978.
Castillo, Greg. 'Domesticating the Cold War: Household Consumption as Propaganda in Marshall Plan Germany'. *Journal of Contemporary History* 40(2) (2005), 261–88.
Central Intelligence Agency. *The International Energy Situation: Outlook to 1985*. Washington, DC, 1977.
Cetron, Marvin J., and Vary T. Coates. 'Energy and Society'. *Proceedings of the Academy of Political Science* 31(2) (1973), 33–40.
Chamberlain, Waldo, Thomas Hovet, and Erica Hovet. *A Chronology and Fact Book of the United Nations 1941–1976*. Dobbs Ferry, NY, 1976.
Chandler, Geoffrey. 'The Innocence of Oil Companies'. *Foreign Policy* 27 (Summer 1977), 52–70.
Chevalier, Jean-Marie. *Le nouvel enjeu pétrolier*. Paris, 1973.
Chick, Martin. *Electricity and Energy Policy in Britain, France and the United States since 1945*. Cheltenham, 2007.
———. 'The Risks, Costs and Benefits of Importing Oil: Fuel Import Policy in Britain, France and the United States since 1945', in Alain Beltran (ed.),

Oil Producing Countries and Oil Companies: From the Nineteenth Century to the Twenty-First Century. Bern/Oxford, 2011, 65–83.

Childs, William R. *The Texas Railroad Commission: Understanding Regulation in America to the Mid-Twentieth Century*. College Station, TX, 2005.

Choucri, Nazli. *International Politics of Energy Interdependence: The Case of Petroleum*. Lexington, MA, 1976.

Citizens' Advisory Committee on Environmental Quality: Citizen Action Guide to Energy Conservation. Washington, DC, 1973.

Clark, James A. 'The Energy Revolution', in D.V. Carter (ed.), *The History of Petroleum Engineering*. Dallas, 1961, 1–14.

Clark, John G. *The Political Economy of World Energy: A Twentieth-Century Perspective*. New York, 1990.

Cleveland, Harlan. 'World Energy and US Leadership'. *Atlantic Community Quarterly* 13(1) (1975), 26–45.

Cochet, Yves. *Pétrole apocalypse*. Paris, 2005.

'The Cocoyoc Declaration'. *International Organization* 29(3) (1975), 893–901.

Cole, John Peter. *Geography of World Affairs*. 5th ed. Harmondsworth/New York, 1979.

Coll, Steve. 'Gusher: The Power of ExxonMobil'. *New Yorker*, 9 April 2012, 28–37.

———. *Private Empire: ExxonMobil and American Power*. New York, 2012.

Comité professionnel du pétrole. *Pétrole 1969. Elements statistiques: Activité de l'industrie pétrolière*. Paris, 1970.

———. *Pétrole 73. Éléments statistiques: Activité de l'industrie pétrolière*. Paris, 1974.

———. *Pétrole 74. Éléments statistiques: Activité de l'industrie pétrolière*. Paris, 1975.

Commissariat Général du plan. Commission de l'Énergie et des Matières Premières du VIIIe Plan. *Rapport sur les bilans de la politique énergétique de 1973 à 1978*. Paris, 1979.

Commission d'Enquête Parlementaire. *Sur les Sociétés Pétrolières Opérant en France*. Paris, 1974.

Commoner, Barry. *The Poverty of Power: Energy and the Economic Crisis*. New York, 1976.

Conant, Melvin A., and Fern R. Gold. *Geopolitics of Energy. Printed at the Request of Henry M. Jackson, Chairman of the Committee on Interior and Insular Affairs, United States Senate*. Washington, DC, 1977.

Congressional Research Service, Library of Congress. *Oil Fields as Military Objectives: A Feasibility Study. Prepared for the Special Subcommittee on Investigations of the House International Relations Committee*. Washington, DC, 1975.

Constant, Edward. 'Cause or Consequence: Science, Technology, and Regulatory Change in the Oil Business in Texas, 1930–1975'. *Technology and Culture* 30 (1989), 426–55.

———. 'Science in Society: Petroleum Engineers and the Oil Fraternity in Texas 1925–65'. *Social Studies of Science* 19 (1989), 439–72.

———. 'State Management of Petroleum Resources: Texas, 1910–1940', in George H. Daniels and Mark H. Rose (eds), *Energy and Transport: Historical Perspectives on Policy Issues*. Beverly Hills, CA, 1982, 157–75.

Conze, Eckart. 'Sicherheit als Kultur: Überlegungen zu einer "modernen Politikgeschichte" der Bundesrepublik Deutschland'. *Vierteljahrshefte für Zeitgeschichte* 53 (2005), 357–80.

Conze, Werner. 'Sicherheit, Schutz', in Otto Brunner, Werner Conze, and Reinhart Koselleck (eds), *Geschichtliche Grundbegriffe*, vol. 5. Stuttgart, 1984, 831–62.

Cook, Earl. 'The Flow of Energy in an Industrial Society'. *Scientific American* 225(3) (1971), 134–47.

———. 'Undiscovered or Undeveloped Crude Oil "Resources" and National Energy Strategies', in John D. Haun (ed.), *Methods of Estimating the Volume of Undiscovered Oil and Gas Resources*. Tulsa, OK, 1975, 97–106.

Cooper, Richard N. 'Natural Resources and National Security'. *Resources Policy* 2 (June 1975), 192–203.

———. 'A New International Economic Order for Mutual Gain'. *Foreign Policy* 26 (1977), 66–120.

'Corrigendum zum Energiegutachten von 1961'. *Vierteljahrsheft des Deutschen Instituts für Wirtschaftsforschung* (1966), 179–99.

Cowan, Edward. 'Energy Volunteerism'. *New York Times*, 9 November 1973.

———. 'Politics and Energy'. *New York Times*, 27 November 1973.

———. 'A Saudi Threat on Oil Reported: Minister Is Said to Predict Production Slash if US Resupplies Israel'. *New York Times*, 16 October 1973.

Craft, Benjamin Cole, and Murray F. Hawkins. *Applied Petroleum Reservoir Engineering*. Englewood Cliffs, NJ, 1959.

Crozier, Michel, Jōji Watanuki, and Samuel P. Huntington. *The Crisis of Democracy: Report on the Governability of Democracies to the Trilateral Commission*. New York, 1975.

Crude. Dir. Joe Berlinger. United States. First Run Features, 2009 (film).

A Crude Awakening: The Oil Crash. Dir. Basil Gelpke and Ray McCormack. Switzerland. Lava Productions AG, 2007 (film).

Czakainski, Martin. 'Energiepolitik in der Bundesrepublik Deutschland 1960 bis 1980 im Kontext der außenwirtschaftlichen und außenpolitischen Verflechtungen', in Jens Hohensee and Michael Salewski (eds), *Energie – Politik – Geschichte: Nationale und internationale Energiepolitik seit 1945*. Stuttgart, 1993, 17–34.

Da Cruz, Daniel. 'How They Find Oil'. *Aramco World* 17(1) (1966), 1–11.

———. 'The Long Steel Shortcut'. *Aramco World* 15(5) (1964), 16–25.

Daase, Christopher. 'National, Societal, and Human Security: On the Transformation of Political Language'. *Historical Social Research* 35(4) (2010), 22–40.

Dallek, Robert. *Nixon and Kissinger: Partners in Power*. New York, 2007.

Daly, Herman E. *Steady-State Economics: The Economics of Biophysical Equilibrium and Moral Growth*. San Francisco, 1977.

———. *Steady-state economics*. Washington DC, 1991
——— (ed.). *Toward a Steady-State Economy*. San Francisco, 1973.
Danielsen, Albert L. *The Evolution of OPEC*. New York, 1982.
Daoudi, M.S., and M.S. Dajani. 'The 1967 Oil Embargo Revisited'. *Journal of Palestine Studies* 13(2) (1984), 65–90.
———. *Economic Sanctions, Ideals and Experience*. London/Boston, 1983.
Darmstadter, Joel, Hans H. Landsberg, and Herbert C. Morton. *Energy, Today and Tomorrow: Living with Uncertainty*. Englewood Cliffs, NJ, 1983.
Dasgupta, Partha, and Geoffrey M. Heal. *Economic Theory and Exhaustible Resources*. Welwyn/Cambridge, 1979.
———. 'The Optimal Depletion of Exhaustible Resources'. *Review of Economic Studies* 41 (1974), 3–28.
de Grazia, Victoria. *Irresistible Empire: America's Advance through Twentieth-Century Europe*. Cambridge, MA, 2005.
de Marchi, Neil. 'Energy Policy under Nixon: Mainly Putting Out Fires', in Craufurd D. Goodwin (ed.), *Energy Policy in Perspective: Today's Problems, Yesterday's Solutions*. Washington, DC, 1981, 395–475.
'Déclaration commune des gouvernements de la Communauté économique européenne sur la situation au Proche-Orient 1974', in *La Politique Étrangère de la France. Textes et Documents. 2e semestre 1973*. Paris, n.d., 171.
'Declaration on the Establishment of a New International Economic Order 1974', in *United Nations. General Assembly: Resolutions Adopted during Its Sixth Special Session 9 April–2 May 1974*. New York, 1974, 3–5.
Deese, David A. 'Economics, Politics, and Security'. *International Security* 4(3) (1979), 140–53.
Deese, David A., and Joseph S. Nye (eds). *Energy and Security*. Cambridge, MA, 1981.
Deffeyes, Kenneth S. *Hubbert's Peak: The Impending World Oil Shortage*, vol. 2. Princeton, NJ, 2003.
Demagny-Van Eyseren, Armelle. 'The French Presidency, the National Companies and the First Oil Shock', in Alain Beltran (ed.), *Oil Producing Countries and Oil Companies: From the Nineteenth Century to the Twenty-First Century*. Bern/Oxford, 2011, 51–63.
'Development and International Economic Co-operation 1976', in *United Nations: Resolutions Adopted by the General Assembly during its Seventh Special Session, 1–16 September 1975*. New York, 1976, 3–10.
Diefenbacher, Hans, and Jeffrey Johnson. 'Energy Forecasting in West Germany: Confrontation and Convergence', in Thomas Baumgartner and Atle Midttun (eds), *The Politics of Energy Forecasting: A Comparative Study of Energy Forecasting in Western Europe and North America*. Oxford/New York, 1987, 61–84.
Dix, C. Hewitt. *Seismic Prospecting for Oil*. New York, 1952.
Dobson, Alan P. 'From Instrumental to Expressive: The Changing Goals of the US Cold War Strategic Embargo'. *Journal of Cold War Studies* 12(1) (2010), 98–119.

———. *US Economic Statecraft for Survival, 1933–1991: Of Sanctions, Embargoes, and Economic Warfare*. London, 2002.

Doering-Manteuffel, Anselm. 'Nach dem Boom: Brüche und Kontinuitäten der Industriemoderne seit 1970'. *Vierteljahrshefte für Zeitgeschichte* 55 (2007), 560–81.

Doering-Manteuffel, Anselm, and Lutz Raphael. *Nach dem Boom: Perspektiven auf die Zeitgeschichte seit 1970*. Göttingen, 2008.

'Dokumente zur 29. Generalversammlung der Vereinten Nationen vom 30. August 1974'. *Europa-Archiv* 29(2) (1974), 511–38.

Dolinski, Urs. *Der Energiemarkt in Bayern bis zum Jahre 1990 unter Berücksichtigung der Entwicklungstendenzen auf dem Weltenergiemarkt und auf dem Energiemarkt der Bundesrepublik Deutschland*. Berlin, 1974.

———. *Untersuchung zu Fragen regional unterschiedlicher Energiepreise in der Bundesrepublik Deutschland: Darstellung, Begründung und Auswirkungen am Beispiel ausgewählter Bundesländer*. Berlin, 1979.

———. *Untersuchung zu Fragen regional unterschiedlicher Energiepreise innerhalb Bayerns sowie zwischen Bayern und der übrigen Bundesrepublik Deutschland: Gutachten im Auftrage des Bayerischen Staatsministeriums für Wirtschaft und Verkehr*. Munich, 1979.

———. *Zum Problem der Substitutionsmöglichkeit von Mineralölprodukten durch andere Energieträger: Dargestellt am Beispiel eines Bundeslandes*. Berlin, 1980.

Dolinski, Urs, and Hans-Joachim Ziesing. *Der Energiemarkt in Bayern im Jahre 1971: Gutachten im Auftrage des Bayerischen Staatsministeriums für Wirtschaft und Verkehr*. Berlin, 1973.

———. *Die Entwicklung des Energieverbrauches in Baden-Württemberg und seinen 12 Regionalverbänden bis zum Jahre 1990: Gutachten im Auftrage des Ministeriums für Wirtschaft, Mittelstand und Verkehr in Baden-Württemberg*. Stuttgart, 1974.

———. *Die Entwicklungstendenzen des Energieverbrauchs in Nordrhein-Westfalen bis 1980: Untersuchung im Auftrage des Wirtschaftsministeriums von Nordrhein-Westfalen*. Düsseldorf, 1971.

———. *Die regionalen Entwicklungstendenzen des Energieverbrauchs in Baden-Württemberg und seinen Regierungsbezirken bis 1980*. Berlin, 1970.

———. *Die regionalen Entwicklungstendenzen des Energieverbrauchs in Bayern und seinen Regierungsbezirken bis 1985*. Berlin, 1971.

———. *Die regionalen Entwicklungstendenzen des Energieverbrauchs in Hessen und seinen fünf Planungsregionen bis 1985: Untersuchung im Auftrage des Hessischen Ministers für Wirtschaft und Technik*. Wiesbaden, 1973.

———. *Maßnahmen für eine bayerische Energiepolitik: Gutachten im Auftrage des Bayerischen Staatsministeriums für Wirtschaft und Verkehr*. Munich, 1976.

———. *Sicherheits-, Preis- und Umweltaspekte der Energieversorgung*. Berlin, 1976 (Deutsches Institut für Wirtschaftsforschung [DIW] Sonderheft, 113).

———. *Ziele für eine bayerische Energiepolitik: Gutachten im Auftrage des Bayerischen Staatsministeriums für Wirtschaft und Verkehr*. Munich, 1975.

Dolinski, Urs, Hans-Joachim Ziesing, and Klaus-Dieter Labahn. *Maßnahmen für eine sichere und umweltverträgliche Energieversorgung*. Berlin, 1978 (Deutsches Institut für Wirtschaftsforschung [DIW] Sonderheft, 125).

Dönhoff, Marion Gräfin. 'Allein mit Amerika. . . . wenn Paris weiter mauert'. *Die Zeit*, 15 February 1974.

Doughty, Robert A., and Harold E. Raugh Jr. 'Embargoes in Historical Perspective'. *Parameters* 21(1) (1991), 21–30.

Douglas, John H. 'Fuel Shortages in America: The Energy Crisis Comes Home'. *Science News* 103(21) (1973), 342–43.

Doxey, Margaret P. *International Sanctions in Contemporary Perspective*. Basingstoke, 1987.

Dröscher, Wilhelm, Klaus-Detlef Funke, and Ernst Theilen (eds). *Energie, Beschäftigung, Lebensqualität*. Bonn-Bad Godesberg, 1977.

Drucker, Peter F. 'Multinationals and Developing Countries: Myths and Realities'. *Foreign Affairs* 53 (1974), 121–34.

Duchin, Faye. 'Energy Sector', in *International Encyclopedia of the Social Sciences*, vol. 2. Detroit, 2008, 591–92.

Duguid, Stephen. 'Review of Licklider, *Political Power and the Arab Oil Weapon*', *International History Review* 11 (1989), 403–5.

Duncan, Otis Dudley. 'Sociologists Should Reconsider Nuclear Energy'. *Social Forces* 57(1) (1978), 1–22.

Dunham, Kingsley. 'Non-Renewable Mineral Resources'. *Resources Policy* 1 (September 1974), 3–13.

Eagan, Vince. 'The Optimal Depletion of the Theory of Exhaustible Resources'. *Journal of Post Keynesian Economics* 9 (1987), 565–71.

Eaton, David J. (ed.). *The End of Sovereignty? A Transatlantic Perspective*. Transatlantic Policy Consortium Colloquium. Hamburg, 2006.

Editors. 'Introduction. Special Issue: Made in . . . the Arab East'. *Aramco World* 25(3) (1974), 3.

Eglau, Hans Otto. 'Ein Spiel ohne Grenzen? Fachleute rechnen, wie hoch die Ölpreise noch steigen können'. *Die Zeit*, 11 January 1974.

Ehrhardt, Hendrik. 'Energiebedarfsprognosen: Kontinuität und Wandel energiewirtschaftlicher Problemlagen in den 1970er und 1980er Jahren', in Hendrik Ehrhardt and Thomas Kroll (eds), *Energie in der modernen Gesellschaft: Zeithistorische Perspektiven*. Göttingen, 2012, 193–222.

Ehrhardt, Hendrik, and Thomas Kroll. 'Einleitung', in Hendrik Ehrhardt and Thomas Kroll (eds), *Energie in der modernen Gesellschaft: Zeithistorische Perspektiven*. Göttingen, 2012, 5–11.

Ehrlich, Paul R., and John P. Holdren. 'Impact of Population Growth'. *Science* 171(3977) (1971), 1212–17.

Ehrmann, John. *The Rise of Neoconservatism: Intellectuals and Foreign Affairs 1945–1994*. New Haven, CT, 1995.

Eichengreen, Barry J. *The European Economy since 1945: Coordinated Capitalism and Beyond*. Princeton, NJ, 2007.

Eichholtz, Dietrich, and Titus Kockel. *Von Krieg zu Krieg: Zwei Studien zur deutschen Erdölpolitik in der Zwischenkriegszeit*. Leipzig, 2008.

Elfert, Heino. 'Energieprognosen gestern und heute: Voraussagen sind noch schwieriger geworden'. *Die Mineralölwirtschaft* 30(6) (1977), 281.

Elkind, Sarah S. 'Oil in the City: The Fall and Rise of Oil Drilling in Los Angeles'. *Journal of American History* 99(1) (2012), 82–90.

Ellis, Peter M. 'Motor Vehicle Mortality Reductions since the Energy Crisis'. *The Journal of Risk and Insurance* 44(3) (1977), 373–81.

Elm, Mostafa. 'Iran's Oil Crisis of 1951–1953: New Documents and Old Realities'. *Harvard Middle Eastern and Islamic Review* 2(2) (1995), 46–61.

Elsenhans, Hartmut. *Die Kostensteigerungen für Erdöl vom Juni 1973 bis zum Januar 1974. Berechnung der Kostensteigerung für Erdöl aus den OPEC-Ländern und für die Erdölproduktion der 7 Großkonzerne für Panorama, 4. Febr. 1974, nebst einer Erwiderung der Deutschen Shell AG und deren Widerlegung durch den Autor*. Berlin, 1974.

Elsenhans, Hartmut, and Gerd Junne. 'Zu den Hintergründen der gegenwärtigen Ölkrise'. *Blätter für deutsche und internationale Politik* 18(12) (1973), 1305–17.

The End of Suburbia: Oil Depletion and the Collapse of the American Dream. Dir. Gregory Greene. Canada. The Electric Wallpaper Co., 2004 (film).

Die Energiekrise: Episode oder Ende einer Ära. In collaboration with Ralf Dahrendorf et al. Hamburg, 1974.

Energiekrise – Europa im Belagerungszustand? Politische Konsequenzen aus einer eskalierenden Entwicklung. Hamburg-Bergedorf, 1977 (Bergedorfer Gesprächskreis zu Fragen der freien industriellen Gesellschaft, 58).

Die Energiepolitik der Bundesregierung', in *Deutscher Bundestag. Drucksachen. 7. Wahlperiode 1972–1976*. No. 1057, 3 October 1973.

Energiewirtschaftliches Institut der Universität Köln (ed.), *Die Energie-Enquete. Ergebnisse und wirtschaftspolitische Konsequenzen. Vorträge und Diskussionsbeiträge der 12. Arbeitstagung am 14. und 15. Juni 1962 in der Universität Köln*. Munich, 1962.

'Energy Disaster Might Shock Nation's Leaders into Action (Editorial)'. *Oil and Gas Journal* 71(40) (1973), 27.

'Energy Gap'. *New York Times*, 9 November 1973.

Energy Systems Program Group International Institute for Applied Systems Analysis. *Energy in a Finite World: A Global Systems Analysis*. Cambridge, MA, 1981.

Engel, Christoph, Jost Halfmann, and Martin Schulte (eds). *Wissen – Nichtwissen – unsicheres Wissen*. Baden-Baden, 2002.

Engels, Jens Ivo. *Naturpolitik in der Bundesrepublik: Ideenwelt und politische Verhaltensstile in Naturschutz und Umweltbewegung 1950–1980*. Paderborn, 2006.

'Entwicklungsländer: Fast vernichtend'. *Der Spiegel*, 14 January 1974, 73–74.

Enzensberger, Hans Magnus. 'Zur Kritik der politischen Ökologie'. *Kursbuch* 9(33) (1973), 1–52.

Eppen, Gary D. 'Introduction', in Gary D. Eppen (ed.), *Energy: The Policy Issues*. Chicago, IL, 1975, xi–xiv.

Eppler, Erhard. *Ende oder Wende*. Stuttgart/Berlin/Mainz, 1975.

———. 'Ölkrise und Entwicklungshilfe'. *Die Zeit*, 21 December 1973.

'Erklärung von Cocoyoc: Verabschiedet von den Teilnehmern des Symposiums des Umweltprogramms der Vereinten Nationen und der Welthandelskonferenz über Modelle der Rohstoffnutzung, des Umweltschutzes und der Entwicklung vom 8. bis zum 12. Oktober 1974'. *Europa-Archiv* 30(2) (1974), 357–64.

'Europa muß den Arabern Waffen liefern: Der libysche Regierungschef Abd el-Salam Dschallud über Erdöl und Israel'. *Der Spiegel*, 12 November 1973, 120–28.

Evans, Joanne, and Lester C. Hunt. *International Handbook on the Economics of Energy*. Cheltenham, 2011.

Fack, Fritz Ullrich. 'Europa als Restposten'. *Frankfurter Allgemeine Zeitung*, 13 February 1974.

Farber, David R. *Taken Hostage: The Iran Hostage Crisis and America's First Encounter with Radical Islam*. Princeton, NJ, 2005.

Faulenbach, Bernd. *Das sozialdemokratische Jahrzehnt: Von der Reformeuphorie zur neuen Unübersichtlichkeit; die SPD 1969–1982*. Bonn, 2011.

Federal Energy Administration. *National Energy Outlook*. Washington, DC, 1976.

———. *Project Independence Blueprint. Transcripts of Public Hearings*, 10 vols plus appendices. Washington, DC, 1974–75.

———. *Project Independence Blueprint. Transcript of First Public Hearing, Denver, Colorado, August 6–9, 1974*. Washington, DC, 1974.

———. *Project Independence Blueprint. Transcript of Second Public Hearing, New York, August 19–22, 1974*. Washington, DC, 1974.

———. *Project Independence Blueprint. Transcript of Third Public Hearing, Boston/ MA, August 26–29, 1974*. Washington, DC, 1974.

———. *Project Independence Report*. Washington, DC, 1974.

———. *The Relationship of Oil Companies and Foreign Governments*. Washington, DC, 1975.

———. *US Oil Companies and the Arab Oil Embargo*. Washington, DC, 1975.

Ferguson, Niall (ed.). *The Shock of the Global: The 1970s in Perspective*. Cambridge, MA, 2010.

Flower, Andrew. 'World Oil Production'. *Scientific American* 238(3) (1978), 41–49.

Ford Foundation. *Energy Policy Project: Exploring Energy Choices. A Preliminary Report*. Washington, DC, 1974.

———. *A Time to Choose: America's Energy Future*. Cambridge, MA, 1974.

Forrester, Jay Wright. *Der teuflische Regelkreis: Das Globalmodell der Menschheitskrise*. Stuttgart, 1972.

Forsthoff, Ernst. *Der Staat der Industriegesellschaft: Dargestellt am Beispiel der Bundesrepublik Deutschland*. Munich, 1971.

Fourastié, Jean. *Les trente glorieuses ou la révolution invisible de 1946 à 1975*. Paris, 1979.

Frank, Alison Fleig. *Oil Empire: Visions of Prosperity in Austrian Galicia*. Cambridge, MA, 2005.
Frank, Paul. *Entschlüsselte Botschaft: Ein Diplomat macht Inventur*. Munich, 1985.
Frankel, Paul H. 'The Oil Industry and Professor Adelman: A Personal View'. *Petroleum Review* 27 (September 1973), 347–49.
Freedman, Lawrence. 'Großbritannien als Erdölproduzent: Die Legende von der Unabhängigkeit'. *Europa-Archiv* 15 (1978), 477–87.
Frick, Thomas C. 'Fossil Fuel Resources in the United States'. *Journal of Petroleum Technology* 18 (February 1966), 155–75.
Friderichs, Hans. 'Ein offenes Wort zum Ölverbrauch'. *Süddeutsche Zeitung*, 12 November 1973.
Friedland, Edward, Paul Seabury, and Aaron Wildavsky. 'Oil and the Decline of Western Power'. *Political Science Quarterly* 90(3) (1975), 437–50.
Friedman, Murray. *The Neoconservative Revolution: Jewish Intellectuals and the Shaping of Public Policy*. Cambridge, MA, 2005.
Fritsch, Albert J., and Ralph Gitomer. *Major Oil: What Citizens Should Know about the Eight Major Oil Companies*. Washington, DC, 1974 (CSPI Energy Series, 4).
Fröhlich, Manuel. 'Lesarten der Souveränität'. *Neue Politische Literatur* 50(4) (2005), 19–42.
Fusso, Thomas E. 'The Polls: The Energy Crisis in Perspective'. *Public Opinion Quarterly* 42(1) (1978), 127–36.
Gallup, George Horace. *The Gallup Poll: Public Opinion, 1972–1977*, 2 vols. Wilmington, DE, 1978.
Garavini, Giuliano. *After Empires: European Integration, Decolonization, and the Challenge from the Global South 1957–1986*. Oxford, 2012.
———. 'Completing Decolonization: The 1973 "Oil Shock" and the Struggle for Economic Rights'. *International History Review* 33(3) (2011), 473–87.
Gasland. Dir. Josh Fox. United States. New Video Group/HBO/International WOW Company, 2010 (film).
Gelb, Leslie H. '2 Aides Underline Arab-Israeli Gap: Yamani and Dayan, in US TV Talks, Differ Sharply on Mideast Peace Terms'. *New York Times*, 10 December 1973.
Georgescu-Roegen, Nicholas. *Energy and Economic Myths: Institutional and Analytical Economic Essays*. New York, 1976.
———. 'Energy, Matter, and Economic Valuation: Where Do We Stand', in Herman E. Daly and Alvaro F. Umana (eds), *Energy, Economics, and the Environment: Conflicting Views of an Essential Relationship*. Boulder, CO, 1981, 43–80 (AAAS selected symposium, 64).
———. *The Entropy Law and the Economic Process*. Cambridge, MA, 1971.
Gerber, Sophie, Nina Lorkowski, and Nina Möllers. *Kabelsalat: Energiekonsum im Haushalt*. [Anlässlich der Ausstellung 'Kabelsalat. Energiekonsum im Haushalt' im Deutschen Museum, Munich, 13 January–15 April 2012]. Munich, 2012.
'Gesetz zu dem Übereinkommen vom 18. November 1974 über ein Internationales Energieprogramm. vom 30. April 1975'. *Bundesgesetzblatt* 2(31) (1975), 701–42.

Geyer, David C., and Bernd Schaefer (eds). *American Détente and German Ostpolitik 1969–1972*. Washington, DC, 2004.

Gfeller, Aurélie Elisa. *Building a European Identity: France, the United States and the Oil Shock, 1973–1974*. New York, 2012.

———. 'A European Voice in the Arab World: France, the Superpowers and the Middle East, 1970–1974'. *Cold War History* 11 (2011), 1–18.

———. 'Imagining European Identity: French Elites and the American Challenge in the Pompidou-Nixon Era'. *Contemporary European History* 19(2) (2010), 133–49.

Giebelhaus, August W. *Business and Government in the Oil Industry: A Case Study of Sun Oil, 1876–1945*. Greenwich, CT, 1980.

Gillessen, Günther. 'Frieren für Holland?' *Frankfurter Allgemeine Zeitung*, 7 November 1973.

Goldsmith, Edward, and R. Allen. *Planspiel zum Überleben: Ein Aktionsprogramm*. Stuttgart, 1972.

Gonzales, Richard J., and Morris Albert Adelman. 'An Exchange on Oil'. *Foreign Policy* 11 (1973), 126–33.

Gordon, Howard, and Roy Meador (eds). *Perspectives on the Energy Crisis*, 2 vols. Ann Arbor, MI, 1977.

Goschler, Constantin, and Rüdiger Graf. *Europäische Zeitgeschichte seit 1945*. Berlin, 2010.

Gosewinkel, Dieter. 'Zwischen Diktatur und Demokratie. Wirtschaftliches Planungsdenken in Deutschland und Frankreich: Vom Ersten Weltkrieg bis zur Mitte der 1970er Jahre'. *Geschichte und Gesellschaft* 34 (2008), 327–59.

Gosovic, Branislav, and John Gerard Ruggie. 'On the Creation of a New International Economic Order: Issue Linkage and the Seventh Special Session of the UN General Assembly'. *International Organization* 30(2) (1976), 309–45.

Govett, G.J.S., and M.H. Govett. 'The Concept and Measurement of Mineral Reserves and Resources'. *Resources Policy* 1 (September 1974), 46–55.

Gowdy, John M. 'Energy', in *International Encyclopedia of the Social Sciences*, vol. 2. Detroit, 2008, 587–88.

Graetz, Michael J. *The End of Energy: The Unmaking of America's Environment, Security, and Independence*. Boston, 2011.

Graf, Rüdiger. 'Between National and Human Security: Energy Security in the United States and Western Europe in the 1970s'. *Historical Social Research* 35(4) (2010), 329–48.

———. 'Either-Or: The Narrative of "Crisis" in Weimar Germany and in Historiography'. *Central European History* 43(4) (2010), 592–615.

———. 'Expert Estimates of Oil-Reserves and the Transformation of "Petroknowledge" in the Western World from the 1950s to the 1970s', in Frank Uekötter and Uwe Lübken (eds), *Managing the Unknown: Essays on Environmental Ignorance*. New York, 2014, 140–67.

———. 'Gefährdungen der Energiesicherheit und die Angst vor der Angst: Westliche Industrieländer und das arabische Ölembargo 1973/74', in

Patrick Bormann, Thomas Freiberger, and Judith Michel (eds), *Angst in den Internationalen Beziehungen*. Bonn, 2010, 227–50.

———. 'Die Grenzen des Wachstums und die Grenzen des Staates: Konservative und die ökologischen Bedrohungsszenarien der frühen 1970er Jahre', in Jens Hacke and Dominik Geppert (eds), *Streit um den Staat*. Göttingen, 2008, 207–28.

———. 'Making Use of the Oil Weapon: Western Industrial Nations and Arab Petropolitics in 1973/74'. *Diplomatic History* 36(1) (2012), 185–208.

———. 'Das Petroknowledge des Kalten Krieges', in Bernd Greiner (ed.), *Macht und Geist im Kalten Krieg*. Hamburg, 2011, 201–22.

———. 'Ressourcenkonflikte als Wissenskonflikte: Ölreserven und Petroknowledge in Wissenschaft und Politik'. *Geschichte in Wissenschaft und Unterricht* 63(9–10) (2012), 582–99.

———. 'Von der Energievergessenheit zur theoretischen Metonymie: Energie als Medium der Gesellschaftsbeschreibung im 20. Jahrhundert', in Hendrik Ehrhardt and Thomas Kroll (eds), *Energie in der modernen Gesellschaft: Zeithistorische Perspektiven*. Göttingen, 2012, 73–92.

Graf, Rüdiger, and Kim Christian Priemel. 'Zeitgeschichte in der Welt der Sozialwissenschaften: Legitimität und Originalität einer Disziplin'. *Vierteljahrshefte für Zeitgeschichte* 59(4) (2011), 1–30.

Gray, William Glenn. *Germany's Cold War: The Global Campaign to Isolate East Germany, 1949–1969*. Chapel Hill, NC, 2003.

Greenberger, Martin. *Caught Unawares: The Energy Decade in Retrospect*. In collaboration with Garry D. Brewer, William W. Hogan, and Milton Russell. Cambridge, MA, 1983.

Grimm, Dieter. *Souveränität: Herkunft und Zukunft eines Schlüsselbegriffs*. Berlin, 2009.

Grossman, Peter Z. *US Energy Policy and the Pursuit of Failure*. Cambridge, 2013.

Gross-Stein, Janice. 'Flawed Strategies and Missed Signals: Crisis Bargaining between the Superpowers, October 1973', in David Warren Lesch (ed.), *The Middle East and the United States: A Historical and Political Reassessment*. Boulder, CO, 1999, 204–26.

Gruhl, Herbert. *Ein Planet wird geplündert: Die Schreckensbilanz unserer Politik*. Frankfurt am Main, 1975.

Grundlagen und Ziele für eine gemeinsame Energiepolitik im norddeutschen Raum und Berlin: Gutachten im Auftrage der Konferenz der Wirtschaftsminister/-senatoren der Länder Bremen, Hamburg, Niedersachsen, Schleswig-Holstein und Berlin. Berlin, 1981.

'Die Gründung der Internationalen Energieagentur'. *Europa-Archiv* 30(2) (1975), D1–30.

'Gruppe Ökologie: Ökologisches Manifest'. *Konservativ heute* 4 (1973), 18–19.

Günter, Hans (ed.). *Transnational Industrial Relations: The Impact of Multi-National Corporations and Economic Regionalism on Industrial Relations. A Symposium Held at Geneva by the International Institute for Labour Studies*. London/New York, 1972.

Gwertzmann, Bernard. 'Saudi Minister, in Capital, Is Optimistic about Peace. Talk Is Lengthened. US Officials Pleased Israel's Existence "Not an Issue"'. *New York Times*, 6 December 1973.

Haas, Merrill W. 'The President's Page'. *Bulletin of the American Association of Petroleum Geologists* 50 (1966), 1–2.

———. 'The President's Page: Elements of National Energy Policy'. *Bulletin of the American Association of Petroleum Geologists* 58 (April 1974), 573–74.

Haas, Peter M. 'Introduction: Epistemic Communities and International Policy Coordination'. *International Organization* 46(1) (1992), 1–35.

Hager, Wolfgang. 'Die Internationale Energie-Agentur: Problematische Sicherheitsallianz für Europa', in *Erdöl und internationale Politik*. Munich, 1975, 87–114.

Hahn, Friedemann. *Von Unsinn bis Untergang: Rezeption des Club of Rome und der Grenzen des Wachstums in der Bundesrepublik der frühen 1970er Jahre*. Freiburg i. Br., 2006.

Hakes, Jay E. *A Declaration of Energy Independence: How Freedom from Foreign Oil Can Improve National Security, Our Economy, and the Environment*. Hoboken, NJ, 2008.

Halliburton advertisement. *Petroleum Panorama: Commemorating 100 Years of Petroleum Progress, Tulsa/Okla. 1959*; *The Oil and Gas Journal* 57(5), inside front cover.

Hamilton, Keith. 'Britain, France, and America's Year of Europe, 1973'. *Diplomacy & Statecraft* 17(4) (2006), 871–95.

———, ed. *The Year of Europe: America, Europe and the Energy Crisis, 1972–1974*. London, 2006 (Documents on British Policy Overseas/Foreign and Commonwealth Office, Ser. 3, Vol. 4).

Hammond, Allen L., William D. Metz, and Thomas H. Maugh. *Energie für die Zukunft: Wege aus dem Engpaß*. Frankfurt am Main, 1974.

Hansen, Ulf. 'Begrüßung', in Fritz Lücke (ed.), *Ölkrise: 10 Jahre danach*. Cologne, 1984, 13–16.

Hardin, Garrett. 'The Tragedy of the Commons: The Population Problem Has No Technical Solution; It Requires a Fundamental Extension in Morality'. *Science* 162 (December 1968), 1243–48.

Harpprecht, Klaus. *Im Kanzleramt: Tagebuch der Jahre mit Willy Brandt: Januar 1973–Mai 1974*. Reinbek, 2000.

Härter, Manfred. 'Diskussion: Energieprognosen'. In Fritz Lücke (ed.), *Ölkrise: 10 Jahre danach*. Cologne, 1984, 292–93.

———. 'Einführung in den Problemkreis Energieprognosen', in Fritz Lücke (ed.), *Ölkrise: 10 Jahre danach*. Cologne, 1984, 252–53.

———. 'Energieprognostik: Kein Fortschritt ohne "Psychologie?"' in *Energieprognostik auf dem Prüfstand*. Cologne, 1988, 3–13.

Hartsborn, Jack E. 'Erdöl als Faktor wirtschaftlicher und politischer Macht: Die Verhandlungen von Tripolis und Teheran zwischen den OPEC-Staaten und den internationalen Ölgesellschaften'. *Europa-Archiv* 26 (1971), 443–55.

Hartwick, John M. 'Intergenerational Equity and the Investing of Rents from Exhaustible Resources'. *The American Economic Review* 67 (1977), 972–74.

Harvie, Christopher. *Fool's Gold: The Story of North Sea Oil*. London, 1994.

Hassan, John A., and Alan Duncan. 'The Role of Energy Supplies during Western Europe's Golden Age, 1950–1972'. *Journal of European Economic History* 18 (1989), 479–508.

Hatfield, C.B. 'Oil Back on the Global Agenda'. *Nature* 387 (1997), 121.

Haun, John D. 'The President's Page: Why Teach Petroleum Geology?' *Bulletin of the American Association of Petroleum Geologists* 53 (1969), 249–50.

Hauser, Erich. 'Abstieg in die Bedeutungslosigkeit'. *Frankfurter Rundschau*, 14 February 1974.

———. 'Diplomatische Klimmzüge'. *Frankfurter Rundschau*, 7 November 1973.

Heal, Geoffrey M. 'The Optimal Use of Exhaustible Resources', in Allen V. Kneese and James L. Sweeney (eds), *Handbook of Natural Resource and Energy Economics*, 3 vols. Amsterdam, 1993, 855–80.

———. 'Symposium on the Economics of Exhaustible Resources: Introduction'. *Review of Economic Studies* 41 (1974), 1–2.

Heath, Edward. *The Course of My Life: My Autobiography*. London, 1998.

Hecht, Gabrielle. *The Radiance of France: Nuclear Power and National Identity after World War II*. Cambridge, MA, 1998.

Hein, Bastian. *Die Westdeutschen und die Dritte Welt: Entwicklungspolitik und Entwicklungsdienste zwischen Reform und Revolte 1959–1974*. Munich, 2006.

Hein, Laura E. *Fueling Growth: The Energy Revolution and Economic Policy in Postwar Japan*. Cambridge, MA, 1990.

Heinebaeck, Bo. *Oil and Security*. New York, 1974.

Heinemann, Gustav. 'Weihnachtsansprache 1973'. *Bulletin des Presse und Informationsamts der Bundesregierung* 1 (1974), 1–3.

Hellema, Duco. 'Anglo-Dutch Relations during the Early 1970s: The Oil Crisis', in Nigel John Ashton and Duco Hellema (eds), *Unspoken Allies: Anglo-Dutch Relations since 1780*. Amsterdam, 2001, 255–72.

Hellema, Duco, Cees Wiebes, and Toby Witte. *The Netherlands and the Oil Crisis: Business as Usual*. Amsterdam, 2004.

Herbers, John. 'Nixon Flies to Coast on Commercial Airliner'. *New York Times*, 27 December 1973.

Hermes, Peter. 'Development Policy and Foreign Affairs'. *Intereconomics* 9(3) (1974), 91–94.

———. *Meine Zeitgeschichte: 1922–1987*. Paderborn, 2007.

Hiepel, Claudia. *Willy Brandt und Georges Pompidou: Deutsch-französische Europapolitik zwischen Aufbruch und Krise*. Munich, 2012.

Hilfrich, Fabian. 'West Germany's Long Year of Europe: Bonn between Europe and the United States', in Matthias Schulz and Thomas Alan Schwartz (eds), *The Strained Alliance: US-European Relations from Nixon to Carter*. New York, 2010, 237–56.

Hillenbrand, Martin J. 'NATO and Western Security in an Era of Transition'. *International Security* 2(2) (1977), 3–24.

Himmelheber, Max. 'Rückschritt zum Überleben: Erster Teil'. *Scheidewege. Vierteljahresschrift für skeptisches Denken* 4 (1974), 61–92.

———. 'Rückschritt zum Überleben: Zweiter Teil'. *Scheidewege. Vierteljahresschrift für skeptisches Denken* 4 (1974), 369–93.

Hinsley, F.H. *Sovereignty*. London, 1966.

Hirst, David. 'Israel – America's Wasting Asset'. *Middle East Economic Survey* 16(47) (14 September 1973), i–vii.

Hk. 'Bonn will Entscheidungsspielraum sichern: Geringe Erwartungen der Bundesregierung'. *Frankfurter Allgemeine Zeitung*, 11 February 1974.

Hoagland, Jim. 'Faisal Warns US on Israel'. *Washington Post*, 6 July 1973.

Hobsbawm, Eric J. *The Age of Extremes: The Short Twentieth Century 1914–1991*. London, 1995.

Hoffmann, Stanley H. *Gulliver's Troubles: Or the Setting of American Foreign Policy*. New York, 1968.

———. *Primacy or World Order: American Foreign Policy since the Cold War*. New York, 1978.

Hoffmann, Wolfgang. 'Bonner Expertenstäbe – Die Verwalter der Krise'. *Die Zeit*, 30 November 1973.

Hofmann, Arne. *The Emergence of Detente in Europe: Brandt, Kennedy and the Formation of Ostpolitik*. London, 2007.

Hogan, William W. 'Import Management and Oil Emergencies', in David A. Deese and Joseph S. Nye (eds), *Energy and Security*. Cambridge, MA, 1981, 261–84.

Hogan, William W., and Federico Sturzenegger. *The Natural Resources Trap: Private Investment without Public Commitment*. Cambridge, MA, 2010.

Högselius, Per. *Red Gas: Russia and the Origins of European Energy Dependence*. Basingstoke, 2013.

Hohensee, Jens. 'Böswillige Erpressung oder bewußte Energiepolitik? Der Einsatz der Ölwaffe 1973/74 aus arabischer Sicht', in Jens Hohensee and Michael Salewski (eds), *Energie – Politik – Geschichte: Nationale und internationale Energiepolitik seit 1945*. Stuttgart, 1993, 153–76.

———. *Der erste Ölpreisschock 1973/74: Die politischen und gesellschaftlichen Auswirkungen der arabischen Erdölpolitik auf die Bundesrepublik Deutschland und Westeuropa*. Stuttgart, 1996.

Höhler, Sabine. *Beam Us Up, Boulding! – 40 Jahre 'Raumschiff Erde'*. Karlsruhe, 2006.

Holl, Jack M. 'The Nixon Administration and the 1973 Energy Crisis: A New Departure in Federal Energy Policy', in George H. Daniels and Mark H. Rose (eds), *Energy and Transport: Historical Perspectives on Policy Issues*. Beverly Hills, CA, 1982, 149–58.

Hollander, Jack M. 'Preface'. *Annual Review of Energy* 1 (1976), vi–ix.

Horn, Manfred. *Die Energiepolitik der Bundesregierung von 1958 bis 1972: Zur Bedeutung der Penetration ausländischer Ölkonzerne in die Energiewirtschaft der BRD für die Abhängigkeit interner Strukturen und Entwicklungen*. Berlin, 1977.

Horowitz, Daniel. *Jimmy Carter and the Energy Crisis of the 1970s: The 'Crisis of Confidence' Speech of July 15, 1979; a Brief History with Documents*. New York, 2005.

Horstmann, Theo, and Regina Weber (eds). 'Hier wirkt Elektrizität': Werbung für Strom 1890 bis 2012. Essen, 2012.

Hoskins, Linus A. 'The New International Economic Order: A Bibliographic Essay'. *Third World Quarterly* 3(3) (1981), 506–27.

Hotelling, Harold. 'The Economics of Exhaustible Resources'. *Journal of Political Economy* 39 (April 1931), 137–75.

Houthakker, Hendrik S. 'Are Minerals Exhaustible?' *Quarterly Review of Economics and Finance* 42 (2002), 417–21.

Howarth, Stephen, Joost Jonker, and Joost Dankers. *The History of Royal Dutch Shell*, 4 vols. Oxford, 2007.

Hoye, Paul F. (ed.). 'Tankers: A Special Issue'. *Aramco World* 17(4) (1966).

Hubbert, Marion King. *Energy Resources: A Report to the Committee on Natural Resources of the National Academy of Sciences – National Research Council*. Washington, DC, 1962 (National Academy of Sciences – National Research Council Publications, 1000 d).

Hughes, Geraint. 'Britain, the Transatlantic Alliance, and the Arab-Israeli War of 1973'. *Journal of Cold War Studies* 10(2) (2008), 3–40.

Hünemörder, Kai F. *Die Frühgeschichte der globalen Umweltkrise und die Formierung der deutschen Umweltpolitik (1950–1973)*. Stuttgart, 2004.

———. 'Kassandra im modernen Gewand: Die umweltapokalyptischen Mahnrufe der frühen 1970er Jahre', in Frank Uekötter and Jens Hohensee (eds), *Wird Kassandra heiser? Die Geschichte falscher Ökoalarme*. Stuttgart, 2004, 78–97.

Hünseler, Peter. *Die außenpolitischen Beziehungen der Bundesrepublik Deutschland zu den arabischen Staaten von 1949–1980*. Frankfurt am Main, 1990.

The Hunt for Black Gold. Dir. Jeff Pohlman. United States. CNBC, 2008 (TV series).

Hutar, Herbert, Andreas Unterberger, and Senta Ziegler. 'Lyrik zwischen Embargo und Ölpreis'. *Die Presse*, 19 March 1974.

Hynes, Catherine. *The Year That Never Was: Heath, the Nixon Administration and the Year of Europe*. Dublin, 2009.

IAEE. *IAEE-History*. http://www.iaee.org/en/inside/history.aspx (accessed 10 January 2018).

Ignotus, Miles. 'Seizing Arab Oil'. *Harper's Magazine* 250 (March 1975), 45–62.

Ikenberry, Gilford John. 'The Irony of State Strength: Comparative Responses to the Oil Shocks in the 1970s'. *International Organization* 40 (1986), 105–37.

Illing, Falk. *Energiepolitik in Deutschland: Die energiepolitischen Maßnahmen der Bundesregierung 1949–2013*. Baden-Baden, 2012.

International Energy Agency. *Energy Research, Development and Demonstration in the IEA Countries: 1981 Review of National Programmes*. Paris, 1982.

———. *IEA Reviews of National Energy Programs*. Paris, 1978.

———. *World Energy Outlook*. Paris, 1982.

Iriye, Akira. *Global Community: The Role of International Organizations in the Making of the Contemporary World*. Berkeley, CA, 2002.

'It Takes Men to Drill Wells'. *Petroleum Panorama: Commemorating 100 Years of Petroleum Progress; The Oil and Gas Journal* 57(5) (1959), 10–11.

Itayim, Fuad. 'Strengths and Weaknesses of the Oil Weapon', in International Institute for Strategic Studies (ed.), *The Middle East and the International System*, vol. 2, *Security and the Energy Crisis*. London, 1975, 1–7.
Jacobs, Matthew F. *Imagining the Middle East: The Building of an American Foreign Policy, 1918–1967*. Chapel Hill, NC, 2011.
Jacobs, Meg. 'The Conservative Struggle and the Energy Crisis', in Bruce J. Schulman and Julian E. Zelizer (eds), *Rightward Bound: Making America Conservative in the 1970s*. Cambridge, MA, 2008, 193–209.
———. *Panic at the Pump: The Energy Crisis and the Transformation of American Politics in the 1970s*. New York, 2016.
———. 'Wreaking Havoc from Within: George W. Bush's Energy Policy in Historical Perspective', in Julian E. Zelizer (ed.), *The Presidency of George W. Bush: A First Historical Assessment*. Princeton, NJ, 2010, 139–68.
Jacobsen, Hanns-D. 'Probleme des Ost-West-Handels aus Sicht der Bundesrepublik Deutschland'. *German Studies Review* 7(3) (1984), 531–53.
Jacobsen, Trudy, C.J.G. Sampford, and Ramesh Chandra Thakur (eds). *Re-envisioning Sovereignty: The End of Westphalia?* Aldershot, 2008.
Jarausch, Konrad H. (ed.). *Das Ende der Zuversicht? Die siebziger Jahre als Geschichte*. Göttingen, 2008.
Jasanoff, Sheila. *The Fifth Branch: Science Advisers as Policymakers*. Cambridge, MA, 1990.
Jaumann, Anton. 'Bayern bereitet ein Landes-Energieprogramm vor'. *Bayerische Staatszeitung*, 20 October 1972.
Jenkins, Gilbert. 'World Oil Reserves Reporting 1948–1996: Political, Economic and Subjective Influences'. *OPEC Review* 21 (1997), 89–111.
Jobert, Michel. 'Address to United Nations General Assembly', in *United Nations. General Assembly: Sixth Special Session. Plenary Meetings. Verbatim Records of Meetings 9 April–2 May 1974, 2209th Plenary Meeting, 10 April 1974*. New York, 1976, 5–11.
Jochem, Eberhard. 'Der Ruf der Energiebedarfsprognosen', in Fritz Lücke (ed.), *Ölkrise: 10 Jahre danach*. Cologne, 1984, 269–85.
Jones, Geoffrey. *The Evolution of International Business*. London, 1996.
Jones, Toby Craig. *Desert Kingdom: How Oil and Water Forged Modern Saudi Arabia*. Cambridge, MA, 2010.
Jonquieres, Guy de. 'The Great American Energy Disaster'. *Financial Times*, 8 June 1973.
Judt, Tony. *Postwar: A History of Europe since 1945*. New York, 2005.
Jungblut, Michael. 'Ist Wachstum des Teufels? Der Weltuntergang findet nicht statt: Die Computer des MIT waren falsch programmiert'. *Die Zeit*, 18 August 1972.
Jungk, Robert. 'Energie - Krise und Wende', in *Meyers Enzyklopädisches Lexikon*, 8 vols. Mannheim/Vienna/Zurich, 1973, 771–74.
Jürgensen, Hans. 'Die europäische Truppe auf Amerika-Tournee'. *Frankfurter Allgemeine Zeitung*, 14 February 1974.
'Kaddafi: A New Form of War. Interview'. *Newsweek*, 24 September 1973.

Kaelble, Hartmut (ed.). *Der Boom 1948–1973: Gesellschaftliche und wirtschaftliche Folgen in der Bundesrepublik Deutschland und in Europa*. Opladen, 1992.
———. *Sozialgeschichte Europas: 1945 bis zur Gegenwart*. Munich, 2007.
Kagan, Robert. *Of Paradise and Power: America and Europe in the New World Order*. New York, 2003.
Kahn, Herman. *Angriff auf die Zukunft. Die 70er und 80er Jahre: So werden wir leben*. Vienna/Munich/Zurich, 1972.
———. *On Thermonuclear War*. Princeton, NJ, 1960.
Kaiser, Karl. 'Die Auswirkungen der Energiekrise auf die westliche Allianz', in Wolfgang Hager (ed.), *Erdöl und internationale Politik*. Munich, 1975, 73–86.
———. 'The Energy Problem and Alliance Systems', in International Institute for Strategic Studies (ed.), *The Middle East and the International System*, vol. 2, *Security and the Energy Crisis*. London, 1975, 17–24.
Kaiser, Wolfram, and Jan-Henrik Meyer. 'Non-State Actors in European Integration in the 1970s: Towards a Polity of Transnational Contestation'. *Comparativ* 20(3) (2010), 7–24.
Kapstein, Ethan B. *The Insecure Alliance: Energy Crises and Western Politics since 1944*. Oxford, 1990.
Karl, Terry Lynn. *The Paradox of Plenty: Oil Booms and Petro-States*. Berkeley, CA 1997.
Karlsch, Rainer, and Raymond G. Stokes. *'Faktor Öl': Die Mineralölwirtschaft in Deutschland 1859–1974*. Munich, 2003.
Karlsson, Svante. *Oil and the World Order: A Study of American Foreign Oil Policy 1940–1980*. Gothenburg, 1983.
Karshenas, Massoud. *Oil, State and Industrialization in Iran*. Cambridge, 1990.
Katz, James E. *Congress and National Energy Policy*. New Brunswick, 1984.
———. 'The International Energy Agency: Energy Cooperation or Illusion?' *World Affairs* 144(1) (1981), 55–82.
Katz, Milton. 'Decision-Making in the Production of Power'. *Scientific American* 225(3) (1971), 191–200.
Kaufman, Robert G. *Henry M. Jackson: A Life in Politics*. Seattle, 2000.
Kaufmann, Burton I. 'Mideast Multinational Oil, US Foreign Policy and Antitrust: The 1950s'. *Journal of American History* 63 (1977), 937–59.
Kaufmann, Franz-Xaver. *Sicherheit als soziologisches und sozialpolitisches Problem: Untersuchungen zu einer Wertidee hochdifferenzierter Gesellschaften*. Stuttgart, 1973.
Kéchichian, Joseph Albert. *Faysal: Saudi Arabia's King for All Seasons*. Gainesville, FL, 2008.
Kemp, Geoffrey. 'Military Force and Middle East Oil', in David A. Deese and Joseph S. Nye (eds), *Energy and Security*. Cambridge, MA, 1981, 365–90.
———. 'The New Strategic Map'. *Survival* 19(2) (1977), 50–59.
———. 'Scarcity and Strategy'. *Foreign Affairs* 56 (1978), 396–414.
Kemp, William B. 'The Flow of Energy in a Hunting Society'. *Scientific American* 225(3) (1971), 104–15.
Kennan, George F. *American Diplomacy, 1900–1950*. Chicago, 1951.

Keohane, Robert O. *After Hegemony*. Princeton, NJ, 1984.
———. 'The International Energy Agency: State Influence and Transgovernmental Politics'. *International Organization* 32(4) (1978), 929–51.
Keohane, Robert O., and Joseph S. Nye. *Power and Interdependence: World Politics in Transition*. Boston, 1977.
———. *Power and Interdependence*. 3rd ed. New York, 2004.
———. 'Preface'. *International Organization* 25(3) (1971), v–vi.
———, eds. *Transnational Relations and World Politics*. Cambridge, MA, 1973.
Kepper, Hans. 'Bonn lehnt Parteinahme ab. Rücksichtnahme auf Kontrahenten bei Energiekonferenz'. *Frankfurter Rundschau*, 15 February 1974.
Kepplinger, Hans Mathias, and Herbert Roth. 'Creating a Crisis: German Mass Media and Oil Supply in 1973–74'. *Public Opinion Quarterly* 43 (1979), 285–96.
Kerr, R.A. 'The Next Oil Crisis Looms Large and Perhaps Close'. *Science* 281(5380) (1998), 1128–31.
Kilkenny, John E. 'The President's Page: AAPG is Global'. *Bulletin of the American Association of Petroleum Geologists* 59 (1975), 1–2.
Kindleberger, Charles P. *American Business Abroad: Six Lectures on Direct Investment*. New Haven, CT, 1969.
Kinney, Gene T. 'Simon Drives Hard to Turn Oil Around'. *Oil and Gas Journal* 71 (April 1973), 60f.
Kinzer, Stephen. *All the Shah's Men: The Hidden Story of the CIA's Coup in Iran*. New York, 2003.
Kipp, Earl. 'The Evolution of Petroleum Engineering as Applied to Oilfield Operations'. *Journal of Petroleum Technology* 23 (January 1971), 107–14.
Kirk, Geoffrey (ed.). *Schumacher on Energy: Speeches and Writings of E.F. Schumacher*. London, 1982.
Kissinger, Henry A. 'Address to the UN General Assembly', in *United Nations. General Assembly: Sixth Special Session. Plenary Meetings. Verbatim Records of Meetings 9 April–2 May 1974, 2214th Plenary Meeting, 15 April 1974*. New York, 1976, 3–11.
———. 'Address to the UN General Assembly', in *United Nations. General Assembly: Twenty-Ninth Session. Plenary Meetings. Verbatim Records of the 2233rd to 2265th Meetings, 17 September–10 October 1974, 2238th Plenary Meeting, 23 September 1974*, vol. 1. New York, 1974, 59–63.
———. 'The United States and a Unifying Europe: Made before the Pilgrims of Great Britain at London on Dec. 12'. *Department of State Bulletin* 69 (31 December 1973), 777–82.
Klare, Michael T. *Blood and Oil: The Dangers and Consequences of America's Growing Dependency on Imported Petroleum*. New York, 2005.
———. *Resource Wars: The New Landscape of Global Conflict*. New York, 2001.
Klausner, Samuel Z. 'The Energy Social System'. *Annals of the American Academy of Political and Social Science* 444 (July 1979), 1–22.
Kneese, Allen V., and James L. Sweeney (eds). *Handbook of Natural Resource and Energy Economics*, 3 vols. Amsterdam, 1993.

Knorr, Klaus. 'The Limits of Economic and Military Power', in Raymond Vernon (ed.), *The Oil Crisis*. New York, 1976, 229–44.
Kohl, Wilfrid L. (ed.). *After the Second Oil Crisis: Energy Policies in Europe, America, and Japan*. Lexington, MA, 1982.
———. 'The International Energy Agency: The Political Context', in J.C. Hurewitz (ed.), *Oil, the Arab-Israel Dispute, and the Industrial World: Horizons of Crisis*. Boulder, CO, 1976, 247–57.
Konzelmann, Gerhard. *Die Reichen aus dem Morgenland: Wirtschaftsmacht Arabien*. Munich, 1975.
Koselleck, Reinhart, 'Staat und Souveränität', in Otto Brunner, Werner Conze, and Reinhart Koselleck (eds), *Geschichtliche Grundbegriffe*, vol. 6. Stuttgart, 1990, 1–154.
Koskenniemi, Martti. *The Gentle Civilizer of Nations: The Rise and Fall of International Law, 1870–1960*. Cambridge, 2002.
Koslowski, Peter. 'Energie', in Görres-Gesellschaft (ed.), *Staatslexikon: Recht, Wirtschaft, Gesellschaft*. 7th ed. Freiburg/Basel/Vienna, 1986, 247–53.
Kotkin, Stephen. 'The Kiss of Debt: The East Bloc Goes Borrowing', in Niall Ferguson (ed.), *The Shock of the Global: The 1970s in Perspective*. Cambridge, MA, 2010, 80–93.
Koven, Ronald, and David B. Ottaway. 'US Oil Nightmare: Worldwide Shortage'. *Washington Post*, 17 June 1973.
Kraemer, M.S. 'Producing Operations of the Future'. *Journal of Petroleum Technology* 23 (1971), 27–32.
Kraft, Joseph. 'Mr. Nixon's Energy Program'. *Washington Post*, 27 November 1973.
Krämer, Hans R. *Die Europäische Gemeinschaft und die Ölkrise*. Baden-Baden, 1974.
Kramer, Martin. *Ivory Towers on Sand: The Failure of Middle Eastern Studies in America*. Washington, DC, 2001.
Krapels, Edward N. *Oil and Security: Problems and Prospects of Importing Countries*. London, 1977.
Krasner, Stephen D. *Defending the National Interest*. Princeton, NJ, 1978.
———. 'Oil Is the Exception'. *Foreign Policy* 14 (Spring 1974), 68–84.
———. *Sovereignty: Organized Hypocrisy*. Princeton, NJ/Chichester, 1999.
Kraus, Michael. 'Bundesdeutsche Energieprognosen der letzten 30 Jahre: Eine Fehlerursachenanalyse', in Manfred Härter (ed.), *Energieprognostik auf dem Prüfstand*. Cologne, 1988, 89–117.
———. *Energieprognosen in der Retrospektive: Analyse von Fehlerursachen der Prognose/Ist-Abweichungen von Energiebedarfsschätzungen in der Bundesrepublik Deutschland von 1950 bis 1980*. Karlsruhe, 1988.
———. 'Über die Kritik an Energieprognosen und ihre Berechtigung', in Fritz Lücke (ed.), *Ölkrise: 10 Jahre danach*. Cologne, 1984, 253–68.
Krause, Florentin, Hartmut Bossel, and Karl-Friedrich Müller-Reissmann. *Energie-Wende. Wachstum und Wohlstand ohne Erdöl und Uran. Ein Alternativbericht des Öko-Instituts*. Freiburg, 1980.
Krauss, Clifford. 'There Will Be Fuel: New Oil and Gas Sources Abound, But They Come With Costs'. *New York Times*, 17 November 2010.

Kristoferson, Lars. 'Energy in Society'. *AMBIO – A Journal of the Human Environment* 2(6) (1973), 178–85.

Krueger, Robert B. *The United States and International Oil: A Report for the Federal Energy Administration on US Firms and Government Policy*. New York, 1975.

Kruse, Julius. *Energiewirtschaft*. Berlin, 1972.

Kunz, Diane B. 'When Money Counts and Doesn't: Economic Power and Diplomatic Objectives'. *Diplomatic History* 18 (1994), 451–62.

Kupper, Patrick. 'Die "1970er Diagnose": Grundsätzliche Überlegungen zu einem Wendepunkt der Umweltgeschichte'. *Archiv für Sozialgeschichte* 43 (2003), 325–48.

Kusmierz, Zoe A. '"The Glitter of Your Kitchen Pans": The Kitchen, Home Appliances, and Politics at the American National Exhibition in Moscow, 1959', in Sebastian M. Herrmann (ed.), *Ambivalent Americanizations: Popular and Consumer Culture in Central and Eastern Europe*. Heidelberg, 2008, 253–72.

Labahn, Klaus-Dieter. *Die künftigen Entwicklungstendenzen der Energiewirtschaft in Baden-Württemberg bis zum Jahre 1990: Gutachten im Auftrage des Ministeriums für Wirtschaft, Mittelstand und Verkehr in Baden-Württemberg*. Berlin, 1979.

Lacy, Dean. 'A Theory of Economic Sanctions and Issue Linkage: The Roles of Preferences, Information, and Threats'. *Journal of Politics* 66 (2004), 25–42.

Lake, David A. 'The New Sovereignty in International Relations'. *International Studies Review* 5 (2003), 303–23.

Lantzke, Ulf. 'Energy Policies in Industrialized Countries: An Evaluation of the Past Decade', in Antoine Ayoub (ed.), *Le Marché pétrolier international dix ans après la crise de 1973: Bilan et perspectives*. Québec, 1984, 15–22.

———. 'The OECD and Its International Energy Agency'. *Daedalus* 104(4) (1975), 217–27.

———. 'The Role of International Cooperation', in Alvin L. Alm and Robert J. Weiner (eds), *Oil Shock: Policy Response and Implementation*. Cambridge, MA, 1984, 77–96.

Laqueur, Walter. 'The Idea of Europe Runs Out of Gas'. *The Atlantic Community Quarterly* 12 (Spring 1974), 64–75.

Levy, Walter J. 'Oil and the Decline of the West'. *Foreign Affairs* 58(5) (1980), 999–1015.

———. 'Oil Power'. *Foreign Affairs* 49 (1971), 652–68.

———. 'World Oil Cooperation or International Chaos'. *Foreign Affairs* 52 (1974), 690–713.

Licklider, Roy. *Political Power and the Arab Oil Weapon: The Experience of Five Industrial Nations*. Berkeley, CA, 1988.

Lieber, Robert James. *Oil and the Middle East War*. Cambridge, MA, 1976.

———. *The Oil Decade*. New York, 1983.

Liebmann, H. *Ein Planet wird unbewohnbar: Das Sündenregister der Menschheit von der Antike bis zur Gegenwart*. Munich, 1971.

Liebrucks, Manfred. *Untersuchung der Möglichkeiten zur Substitution von Mineralöl: Gemeinschaftsgutachten der Institute*. Berlin, 1978.

———. *Volkswirtschaftliche Auswirkungen bei Verzögerungen des Baus von Kernkraftwerken. Modellrechnungen. Gemeinschaftsgutachten der Institute*. Berlin, 1975.

Liebrucks, Manfred, and Hildebrand Kummer. *Entwicklungstendenzen des Energieeinsatzes in der deutschen Elektrizitätswirtschaft*. Berlin, 1972.

———. *Grundlagen einer regionalwirtschaftlich orientierten Energiepolitik im norddeutschen Raum*. Berlin, 1972.

Liebrucks, Manfred, H.W. Schmidt, and D. Schmitt. *Die künftige Entwicklung der Energienachfrage in der Bundesrepublik Deutschland und deren Deckung: Perspektiven bis zum Jahre 2000*. Essen, 1978.

———. *Sicherung der Energieversorgung für die Bundesrepublik Deutschland: Gemeinschaftsgutachten der Institute DIW, EWI und RWE*. Berlin, 1972.

———. *Sicherung der Energieversorgung für die Bundesrepublik Deutschland. Teil II: Gemeinschaftsgutachten der Institute DIW, EWI und RWI*. Berlin, 1974.

Lillich, Richard B. 'Economic Coercion and the International Legal Order'. *International Affairs* 51 (1975), 358–71.

Lincoln, George A. 'Energy Security: New Dimension for US Policy'. *Air Force Magazine* 56(11) (1973), 49–55.

Lindsay, James M. 'Trade Sanctions as Policy Instruments: A Re-examination'. *International Studies Quarterly* 30 (1986), 153–73.

Lippert, Werner D. *The Economic Diplomacy of Ostpolitik: Origins of NATO's Energy Dilemma*. New York, 2011.

Little, Douglas J. *American Orientalism: The United States and the Middle East since 1945*. Chapel Hill, NC, 2002.

———. 'Cold War and Covert Action: The United States and Syria, 1945–1958'. *Middle East Journal* 44 (1990), 55–75.

———. 'Gideon's Band: America and the Middle East since 1945', in Michael J. Hogan (ed.), *America in the World: The Historiography of American Foreign Relations since 1941*. Cambridge, 1995, 462–500.

———. 'Mission Impossible: The CIA and the Cult of Covert Action in the Middle East'. *Diplomatic History* 28 (2004), 663–701.

Loewenstein, Karl. 'Sovereignty and International Co-operation'. *The American Journal of International Law* 48(2) (1954), 222–44.

Lötgers, Herbert. 'Die Deutsche Erdölversorgungsgesellschaft – DEMINEX: Ziele und Aufgaben im Rahmen der deutschen Rohölversorgung', in Institut für Bilanzanalysen (ed.), *Die Mineralölindustrie in der Bundesrepublik Deutschland*. Frankfurt, 1972, 39–44.

Lovejoy, Wallace F., and Paul T. Homan. *Methods of Estimating Reserves of Crude Oil, Natural Gas, and Natural Gas Liquids*. Baltimore, MD, 1965.

Lovins, Amory B. 'Energy Strategy: The Road Not Taken?' *Foreign Affairs* 55(1) (1976), 65–96.

———. *Sanfte Energie: Das Programm für die energie- und industriepolitische Umrüstung unserer Gesellschaft*. Reinbek, 1979.

———. *Soft Energy Paths: Toward a Durable Peace*. Harmondsworth, 1977.

———. 'Soft Energy Technologies'. *Annual Review of Energy* 3 (1978), 477–518.

Lovins, Amory B., and L. Hunter Lovins. *Brittle Power: Energy Strategy for National Security*. Andover, MA, 1982.

Löwenthal, Richard. 'Committee Discussions on Oil and Strategy: Report to the Conference', in International Institute for Strategic Studies (ed.), *The Middle East and the International System*, vol. 2, *Security and the Energy Crisis*. London, 1975, 38–41.

Lubell, Harold. *Middle East Oil Crises and Western Europe's Energy Supplies*. Baltimore, MD, 1963.

———. 'Security of Supply and Energy Policy in Western Europe'. *World Politics* 13(3) (1961), 400–422.

Lucas, Nigel J.D. *Energy and the European Communities*. London, 1977.

Lucas, Nigel J.D., and D. Papaconstantinou. *Western European Energy Policies: A Comparative Study of the Influence of Institutional Structure on Technical Change*. Oxford, 1985.

Lücke, Fritz (ed.). *Ölkrise: 10 Jahre danach*. Cologne, 1984.

Luhmann, Niklas. *Soziale Systeme: Grundriß einer allgemeinen Theorie*. Frankfurt am Main, 2001.

Luttwak, Edward N. 'Intervention and Access to Natural Resources', in Hedley Bull (ed.), *Intervention in World Politics*. New York, 1984, 79–94.

Maachou, Abdelkader. *OAPEC: An International Organization for Economic Cooperation and an Instrument for Regional Integration*. Paris, 1982.

Maass, Gudrun. 'Die Internationale Energieagentur: Lehren aus der Vergangenheit – Herausforderung für die Zukunft', in Jens Hohensee and Michael Salewski (eds), *Energie – Politik – Geschichte: Nationale und internationale Energiepolitik seit 1945*. Stuttgart, 1993, 191–204.

Mahon, Rianne, and Stephen McBride. 'Introduction', in Rianne Mahon and Stephen McBride (eds), *The OECD and Transnational Governance*. Vancouver, 2008, 3–23.

Maier, Charles S. 'Two Sorts of Crises? The "Long" 1970s in the West and the East', in Hans Günter Hockerts (ed.), *Koordinaten deutscher Geschichte in der Epoche des Ost-West-Konflikts*. Munich, 2003, 49–62.

Maier, Hans. 'Fortschrittsoptimismus oder Kulturpessimismus? Die Bundesrepublik Deutschland in den 70er und 80er Jahren'. *Vierteljahrshefte für Zeitgeschichte* 56 (2008), 1–17.

Mallory, William W. 'Accelerated National Oil and Gas Resource Appraisal (ANOGRE)', in John D. Haun (ed.), *Methods of Estimating the Volume of Undiscovered Oil and Gas Resources*. Tulsa, OK, 1975, 23–30.

Manoharan, S. *The Oil Crisis: End of an Era*. New Delhi, 1974.

Marder, Murrey, and Ronald Koven. '12 Nations Agree on Energy Group'. *Washington Post*, 14 February 1974.

Marquardt, Klaus. *Auf den Spuren der Ölkrise: Eine Weltindustrie verändert ihre Strukturen*. Essen, 1983.

Marsh, Steve. 'HMG, AIOC and the Anglo-Iranian Oil Crisis: In Defence of Anglo-Iranian'. *Diplomacy & Statecraft* 12(4) (2001), 143–74.

Martinez, Anibal R. 'Estimation of Petroleum Resources'. *Bulletin of the American Association of Petroleum Geologists* 50 (1966), 2001–08.

Maswood, S. Javed. 'Oil and American Hegemony'. *Australian Journal of International Affairs* 44(2) (1990), 131–41.

Matthöfer, Hans. 'Energie: Ein Diskussionsleitfaden', in Wilhelm Dröscher, Klaus-Detlef Funke, and Ernst Theilen (eds), *Energie, Beschäftigung, Lebensqualität*. Bonn-Bad Godesberg, 1977, 319–482.

Maull, Hanns W. *Oil and Influence: The Oil Weapon Examined*. London, 1975.

———. *Ölmacht: Ursachen, Perspektiven*. Frankfurt am Main/Cologne, 1975.

———. *Raw Materials, Energy, and Western Security*. London/Basingstoke, 1984.

Mayer, Ferdinand. *Erdöl-Weltatlas*. Hamburg/Braunschweig, 1966.

———. *Petro-Atlas*. 3rd ed. Braunschweig, 1982.

———. *Weltatlas Erdöl und Erdgas*. 2nd ed. Braunschweig, 1976.

Mazur, A., and Eugene A. Rosa. 'Energy and Life-Style: Cross-National Comparison of Energy Consumption and Quality of Life Indicators'. *Science* 186(4164) (1974), 607–10.

McAlister, Melani. *Epic Encounters: Culture, Media, and US Interests in the Middle East, 1945–2000*. Berkeley, CA, 2001.

McCaslin, John C. (ed.). *International Petroleum Encyclopedia*. Tulsa, OK, 1977.

McFadden, Robert. 'Strategy Described as a "Disaster" by City's Official'. *New York Times*, 26 November 1973.

McGovern, Ray. *Bush, Oil and Moral Bankruptcy, Counterpunch*. http://www.counterpunch.org/2007/09/27/bush-oil-and-moral-bankruptcy/ (accessed 2 October 2016).

McKelvey, Vincent E. 'Concepts of Reserves and Resources', in John D. Haun (ed.), *Methods of Estimating the Volume of Undiscovered Oil and Gas Resources*. Tulsa, OK, 1975, 11–14.

McKibben, Bill. 'Why Not Frack?' *New York Review of Books* 59(4) (2012). http://www.nybooks.com/articles/archives/2012/mar/08/why-not-frack/ (accessed 2 October 2016).

McKie, James W. 'The Political Economy of World Petroleum'. *The American Economic Review* 64(2): Papers and Proceedings (1974), 51–57.

McLean, John G. 'The United States Energy Outlook and Its Implications for National Energy Policy'. *Annals of the American Academy of Political and Social Science* 410 (November 1973), 97–105.

McLean, John G., and Warren B. Davis. *Guide to National Petroleum Council Report on United States Energy Outlook: Presentation Made to the National Petroleum Council, December 11, 1972*. Washington, DC, 1972.

Meadows, Dennis. *Die Grenzen des Wachstums: Bericht des Club of Rome zur Lage der Menschheit*. Stuttgart, 1972.

Meinert, Jürgen. *Strukturwandlungen der westdeutschen Energiewirtschaft*. Frankfurt am Main, 1980.

Mejcher, Helmut. *Die Politik und das Öl im Nahen Osten*, vol. 1, *Der Kampf der Mächte und Konzerne vor dem Zweiten Weltkrieg*. Stuttgart, 1980.

―――. *Die Politik und das Öl im Nahen Osten*, vol. 2, *Die Teilung der Welt 1938–1950*. Stuttgart, 1990.

'Memorandum of Agreement at San Remo, April 24, 1920', in *Papers Relating to the Foreign Relations of the United States. 1920*, vol. 2. Washington, DC, 1935.

Mende, Silke. *Nicht rechts, nicht links, sondern vorn: Eine Geschichte der Gründungsgrünen*. Munich, 2011.

Mendershausen, Horst. *Coping with the Oil Crisis: French and German Experiences*. Baltimore, MD/London, 1976.

'Merely a Simple Bedouin'. *Newsweek*, 24 December 1973, 28–29.

Merrill, Karen R. *The Oil Crisis of 1973–1974: A Brief History with Documents*. Boston/New York, 2007.

Metzler, Gabriele. 'Am Ende aller Krisen? Politisches Denken und Handeln in der Bundesrepublik der sechziger Jahre'. *Historische Zeitschrift* 275 (2002), 57–103.

―――. *Konzeptionen politischen Handelns von Adenauer bis Brandt: Politische Planung in der pluralistischen Gesellschaft*. Paderborn, 2005.

Metzner, Monika. 'Frankreich und EG tief zerstritten'. *Frankfurter Rundschau*, 14 February 1974.

Meyer-Abich, Klaus Michael (ed.). *Energieeinsparung als neue Energiequelle: Wirtschaftspolitische Möglichkeiten und alternative Technologien*. Munich, 1979.

―――. *Wirtschaftspolitische Steuerungsmöglichkeiten zur Einsparung von Energie durch alternative Technologien*, vol. 1, *Zusammenfassung*. Essen, 1978.

Meyer-Renschhausen, Martin. *Das Energieprogramm der Bundesregierung: Ursachen und Probleme staatlicher Planung im Energiesektor in der BRD*. Frankfurt/New York, 1981.

Meyers, Robert A. *Handbook of Energy Technology and Economics*. New York, 1983.

Michel, Judith. *Willy Brandts Amerikabild und -politik, 1933–1992*. Göttingen/Oxford, 2010.

Mieczkowski, Yanek. *Gerald Ford and the Challenges of the 1970s*. Lexington, KY, 2005.

Mikdashi, Zuhayr. 'Collusion Could Work'. *Foreign Policy* 14 (Spring 1974), 57–68.

Miller, Linda B. 'Review: Energy, Security and Foreign Policy: A Review Essay'. *International Security* 4(1) (1977), 111–23.

Milward, Alan S. *The European Rescue of the Nation-State*, in collaboration with George Brennan and Federico Romero. Berkeley, CA, 1992.

Ministère de l'industrie et de la recherche. Delegation générale à l'énergie. Direction Carburants: *Activité de l'industrie pétrolière 1973*. Paris, 1974.

Mitchell, Henry. 'Table Talk of Oil Talks: Scene'. *Washington Post*, 13 December 1973.

Mitchell, Timothy. 'Carbon Democracy'. *Economy and Society* 38(3) (2007), 399–432.

―――. *Carbon Democracy: Political Power in the Age of Oil*. London/New York, 2011.

———. 'Hydrocarbon Utopia', in Michael D. Gording, Gyan Prakash, and Helen Tilley (eds), *Utopia/Dystopia: Conditions of Historical Possibility*. Princeton, NJ, 2010, 117–47.

———. 'The Resources of Economics: Making the 1973 Oil Crisis'. *Journal of Cultural Economy* 3(2) (2010), 189–204.

Möckli, Daniel. 'Asserting Europe's Distinct Identity: The EC Nine and Kissinger's Year of Europe', in Matthias Schulz and Thomas Alan Schwartz (eds), *The Strained Alliance: US-European Relations from Nixon to Carter*. New York, 2010, 195–220.

———. *European Foreign Policy during the Cold War: Heath, Brandt, Pompidou and the Dream of Political Unity*. London/New York, 2009.

Möllers, Nina. 'Electrifying the World: Representations of Energy and Modern Life at World's Fairs, 1893–1982', in Nina Möllers and Karin Zachmann (eds). *Past and Present Energy Societies: How Energy Connects Politics, Technologies and Cultures*. Bielefeld, 2012, 45–78.

Mom. 'Ohne Frankreich'. *Frankfurter Rundschau*, 15 February 1974.

Mon Oncle. Dir. Jacques Tati. France. Gaumont Distribution, 1958 (film).

Mondale, Walter F. 'Beyond Detente: Toward International Economic Security'. *Foreign Affairs* 53(1) (1974), 1–23.

Moore, T.V. 'Reservoir Engineering Begins Second 25 Years'. *The Oil and Gas Journal* 54(29) (1955), 148.

Moran, Theodore H. 'Modeling OPEC Behavior: Economic and Political Alternatives'. *International Organization* 35(2) (1981), 241–72.

More, Charles. *Black Gold: Britain and Oil in the Twentieth Century*. London, 2009.

Morgenthau, Hans J. 'The New Diplomacy Movement: International Commentary'. *Encounter* (August 1974), 52–57.

———. *Politics among Nations: The Struggle for Power and Peace*. New York, 1948.

———. 'World Politics and the Politics of Oil', in Gary D. Eppen (ed.), *Energy: The Policy Issues*. Chicago, IL, 1975, 43–51.

Morris, Joe. 'Mercedes for "Superman": Bonn Gives Oil Sheik High-Octane Welcome'. *Los Angeles Times*, 21 January 1974.

Morse, Kathryn. 'There Will Be Birds: Images of Oil Disasters in the Nineteenth and Twentieth Centuries'. *The Journal of American History* 99(1) (2012), 124–34.

Morton, Rogers C.B. 'Foreword', in Donald A. Brobst and Walden P. Pratt (eds), *United States Mineral Resources*. Washington, DC, 1973, iii.

Mosley, Leonard. 'The Richest Oil Company in the World: Aramco is Not So Much a Company as It Is a Country within a Country'. *New York Times*, 10 March 1974.

Moyn, Samuel. *The Last Utopia: Human Rights in History*. Cambridge, MA, 2010.

Mulfinger, Albrecht. *Auf dem Weg zur gemeinsamen Mineralölpolitik*. Berlin, 1972.

Müller, Harald. 'Energiepolitik: Ein neuer Bereich der Außenpolitik'. *Neue Politische Literatur* 22(4) (1977), 484–502.

Müller, Werner, and Bernd Stoy. *Entkopplung: Wirtschaftswachstum ohne mehr Energie?* Stuttgart, 1978.

Muskat, Morris. 'The Proved Crude Oil Reserves of the US'. *Journal of Petroleum Technology* 15(9) (1963), 915–21.
N., G. 'Um mehr als Öl'. *Frankfurter Allgemeine Zeitung*, 13 February 1974.
Nader, Laura, and Stephen Beckerman. 'Energy as It Relates to the Quality and Style of Life'. *Annual Review of Energy* 3 (1978), 1–28.
Nakasian, Samuel. 'The Security of Foreign Petroleum Resources'. *Political Science Quarterly* 68(2) (1953), 181–202.
National Petroleum Council. *US Energy Outlook: A Summary Report of the National Petroleum Council*. Washington, DC, 1972.
National Petroleum Council. Committee on Emergency Preparedness. Coordinating Subcommittee. *Emergency Preparedness for Interruption of Petroleum Imports into the United States: An Interim Report of the National Petroleum Council*. Washington, DC, 1973.
———. *Emergency Preparedness for Interruption of Petroleum Imports into the United States: A Supplemental Interim Report of the National Petroleum Council. November 15, 1973*. Washington, DC, 1973.
National Petroleum Council. Committee on Energy Conservation. *Potential for Energy Conservation in the United States: 1974–1978. Electric Utility*. Washington, DC, 1974.
———. *Potential for Energy Conservation in the United States: 1974–1978. Industrial*. Washington, DC, 1974.
National Science Foundation. *The US Energy Problem*, vol. 1, *Summary Volume*. Washington, DC, 1971.
Naylor, R T. *Economic Warfare: Sanctions, Embargo Busting, and Their Human Cost*. Boston, MA, 2001.
———. *Patriots and Profiteers: On Economic Warfare, Embargo Busting and State-Sponsored Crime*. Toronto, 1999.
Nedom, H.A. 'Planning the Energy Years'. *Journal of Petroleum Technology* 23 (January 1971), 13–15.
Nehring, Holger. 'Genealogies of the Ecological Moment: Planning, Complexity and the Environment of "the Environment" as Politics in West Germany, 1949–1982', in Sverker Sörlin and Paul Warde (eds), *Nature's End: History and the Environment*. Houndmills/Basingstoke/New York, 2009, 115–38.
Niedhardt, Gottfried. 'Ostpolitik: Phases, Short-Term Objectives, and Grand Design', in David C. Geyer and Bernd Schaefer (eds), *American Détente and German Ostpolitik 1969–1972*. Washington, DC, 2004, 118–36.
Noble, Alastair. 'Kissinger's Year of Europe, Britain's Year of Choice', in Matthias Schulz and Thomas Alan Schwartz (eds), *The Strained Alliance: US-European Relations from Nixon to Carter*. New York, 2010, 221–35.
Nonn, Christoph. *Die Ruhrbergbaukrise: Entindustrialisierung und Politik 1958–1969*. Göttingen, 2001.
Nordhaus, William D. 'Energy: Friend or Enemy'. *New York Review of Books*, 27 October 2011, 29–31.
———. 'Resources as a Constraint to Growth', *American Economic Review* 64 (1974), 22–26.

Nouschi, André. *La France et le pétrole: De 1924 à nos jours*. Paris, 2001.
———. *Pétrole et relations internationales de 1945 à nos jours*. Paris, 1999.
Nussbaum, Henrich von (ed.). *Die Zukunft des Wachstums: Kritische Antworten zum 'Bericht des Club of Rome'*. Düsseldorf, 1973.
Nützenadel, Alexander. *Stunde der Ökonomen: Wissenschaft, Politik und Expertenkultur in der Bundesrepublik 1949–1974*. Göttingen, 2005.
Nye, David E. *Consuming Power: A Social History of American Energies*. Cambridge, MA, 1998.
———. 'The Energy Crisis of the 1970s as a Cultural Crisis', in Cristina Giorcelli and Peter G. Boyle (eds), *Living with America, 1946–1996*. Amsterdam, 1997, 82–102.
———. *Narratives and Spaces: Technology and the Construction of American Culture*. New York, 1997.
———. *When the Lights Went Out: A History of Blackouts in America*. Cambridge, MA, 2010.
Nye, Joseph S. 'Energy and Security', in David A. Deese and Joseph S. Nye (eds), *Energy and Security*. Cambridge, MA, 1981, 3–22.
———. 'Energy Security Strategy', in Samuel P. Huntington (ed.), *The Strategic Imperative: New Policies for American Security*. Cambridge, MA, 1982, 301–29.
———. 'Multinational Corporations in World Politics'. *Foreign Affairs* 53(1) (1974), 153–75.
Nye, Joseph S., David A. Deese, and Alm Alvin. 'Conclusion: A US Strategy for Energy Security', in Joseph F. Nye and David A. Deese (eds), *Energy and Security*. Cambridge, MA, 1981, 391–424.
Nye, Joseph S., Jr., and Robert O. Keohane. 'Transnational Relations and World Politics: A Conclusion'. *International Organization* 25(3) (1971), 721–48.
Oberdorfer, Don. 'Japanese Policy of Aid to Arabs Pays Off in Oil'. *Washington Post*, 3 February 1974.
O'Brien, Tim. 'Nixon Energy Plan Held Too Late for This Winter'. *Washington Post*, 9 November 1973.
———. 'Some Businesses Protest'. *Washington Post*, 27 November 1973.
Odeen, Philip A. 'Organizing for National Security'. *International Security* 5(1) (1980), 111–29.
Odell, Peter R. 'OPEC und die Multis: Amerikanische Politik und europäische Optionen', in Wolfgang Hager (ed.), *Erdöl und internationale Politik*. Munich, 1975, 41–50.
OECD Oil Committee. *Oil Today*. Paris, 1964.
OECD. 'Decision of the Council Establishing an International Energy Agency of the Council, 15.11.1974', in Richard Scott (ed.), *The History of the International Energy Agency: The First Twenty Years*, vol. 3, *Principle Documents*. Paris, 1994.
———. *Energy Prospects to 1985: An Assessment of Long Term Energy Developments and Related Policies. A Report*. Paris, 1975.
———. *World Energy Outlook: A Reassessment of Long Term Energy Developments and Related Policies. A Report by the Secretary-General*. Paris, 1977.

OEEC Oil Committee. *Europe's Need for Oil: Implications and Lessons of the Suez Crisis*. Paris, 1958.
———. *Oil, Recent Developments in the OEEC Area*. Paris, 1961.
OEEC Wirtschaftsrat. *Europas Energie-Bedarf: Sein Anwachsen – seine Deckung*. Bonn, 1956.
'Oil and the Battle'. *Middle East Economic Survey* 16(51) (12 October 1973), 3–6.
'Oil: Sharing the Shortage'. *Time Magazine*, 21 May 1973.
Okita, Saburo. 'Natural Resource Dependency and Japanese Foreign Policy'. *Foreign Affairs* 52(4) (1974), 714–24.
Oldenziel, Ruth, and Karin Zachmann (eds). *Cold War Kitchen: Americanization, Technology, and European Users*. Cambridge, MA, 2009.
'Ölkrise: Kein Verlaß auf Großmütter'. *Der Spiegel*, 5 November 1973, 23–27.
'One, Two, Many OPECs'. *Foreign Policy* 14, (Spring 1974), 56–57.
OPEC. *OPEC Official Resolutions and Press Releases 1960–1990*. Vienna, 1990.
'Operation of Arab Oil Measures Clarified'. *Middle East Economic Survey* 17(11) (4 January 1974).
Oppenheim, L. *International Law: A Treatise*, vol. 1, *Peace*. New York/Bombay, 1905.
'Organization of Arab Petroleum Exporting Countries', in *The Middle East and North Africa: 1972–73*. 19th ed. London, 1972, 118.
'Organization of Arab Petroleum Exporting Countries', in *The Middle East and North Africa: 1974–75*. 21st ed. London, 1974, 145–46.
Organization of Petroleum Exporting Countries. *OPEC Official Resolutions and Press Releases: 1960–1980*. Oxford, 1980.
Osiander, Andreas. 'Sovereignty, International Relations, and the Westphalian Myth'. *International Organization* 55(2) (2001), 251–87.
O'Toole, Thomas. 'Light, Fuel, Auto Speed Curbs Set'. *Washington Post*, 26 November 1973.
———. 'President Sets the Pattern'. *Washington Post*, 9 November 1973.
Ottaway, David B., and Ronald Koven. 'Saudis Tie Oil to US Policy on Israel'. *Washington Post*, 19 April 1973.
'Over a Barrel: The Truth about Oil'. *ABC News*. ABC, 2009 (TV programme).
Oweiss, Ibrahim. 'Petro-Money: Problems and Prospects', in G.C. Wiegand (ed.), *Inflation and Monetary Crisis*. Washington, DC, 1975, 84–90.
'Pachachi Calls for Immediate Use of Oil Weapon'. *Middle East Economic Survey* 16(51) (12 October 1973), 4–5.
Painter, David S. 'Oil and the American Century'. *The Journal of American History* 99(1) (2012), 24–39.
———. 'Oil and Geopolitics: The Oil Crises of the 1970s and the Cold War'. *Historical Social Research* 39(4) (2014), 186–208.
———. 'Oil and the Marshall Plan'. *Business History Review* 58 (1984), 359–83.
———. 'Oil, Resources, and the Cold War, 1945–1962', in Melvyn P. Leffler and Odd Arne Westad (eds), *The Cambridge History of the Cold War*, vol. 1. Cambridge/New York, 2009, 486–507.

———. *Private Power and Public Policy: Multinational Oil Companies and US Foreign Policy, 1941–1954*. London, 1986.

Palme, Olof. *Der Palme-Bericht: Bericht der Unabhängigen Kommission für Abrüstung und Sicherheit 'Common Security'*. Berlin, 1982.

Papers Relating to the Foreign Relations of the United States: 1920, vol. 2. Washington, DC, 1935.

Parra, Francisco R. *Oil Politics: A Modern History of Petroleum*. London/New York, 2004.

Patai, Raphael. *The Arab Mind*. New York, 1973.

Patel, Kiran Klaus. 'Europäische Integrationsgeschichte auf dem Weg zur doppelten Neuorientierung: Ein Forschungsbericht'. *Archiv für Sozialgeschichte* 50 (2010), 595–642.

———. 'The Paradox of Planning: German Agricultural Policy in a European Perspective, 1920s to 1970s'. *Past and Present* 212(1) (2011), 239–69.

Paust, Jordan J., and Albert Paul Blaustein (eds). *The Arab Oil Weapon*. Dobbs Ferry, NY, 1977.

———. 'The Arab Oil Weapon: A Threat to International Peace'. *American Journal of International Law* 68 (1974), 410–39.

Peacock, Alan T. *The Oil Crisis and the Professional Economist*. York, 1975.

'Personality in the News: Saudi Oil Minister – The Arabs' Kissinger'. *Los Angeles Times*, 3 December 1973.

Peterson, F.M., and A.C. Fisher. 'The Optimal Exploitation of Extractive Resources: A Survey'. *The Economic Journal* 87 (1977), 681–721.

Petersson, Niels P., and Wolfgang M. Schröder. 'Souveränität und politische Legitimation: Analysen zum "geschlossenen" und zum "offenen" Staat'. In Georg Jochum (ed.), *Legitimationsgrundlagen einer europäischen Verfassung: Von der Volkssouveränität zur Völkersouveränität*. Berlin, 2007, 103–50.

Petroleum Panorama. *Commemorating 100 Years of Petroleum Progress*. Tulsa, OK, 1959 (*Oil and Gas Journal* 57[5]).

Pfister, Christian. 'Das "1950er Syndrom": Die umweltgeschichtliche Epochenschwelle zwischen Industriegesellschaft und Konsumgesellschaft', in Christian Pfister and Peter Bär (eds), *Das 1950er Syndrom: Der Weg in die Konsumgesellschaft*, 2nd ed. Bern, 1996, 51–96.

———. 'Das "1950er Syndrom": Zusammenfassung und Synthese'. In Christian Pfister and Peter Bär (eds), *Das 1950er Syndrom: Der Weg in die Konsumgesellschaft*, 2nd ed. Bern, 1996, 21–48.

Philpott, Daniel. *Revolutions in Sovereignty: How Ideas Shaped Modern International Relations*. Princeton, NJ, 2001.

Pious, Richard M. 'Moral Action and Presidential Leadership', in Moorhead Kennedy, R. Gordon Hoxie, and Brenda Repland (eds), *The Moral Authority of Government: Essays to Commemorate the Centennial of the National Institute of Social Sciences*. New Brunswick, NJ, 2000, 7–12.

Policy Study Group of the MIT 'Energy Laboratory: Energy Self-Sufficiency. An Economic Evaluation'. *Technology Review* 76 (May 1974), 23–58.

La Politique Étrangère de la France: Textes et Documents. Paris, 1973–74.

Porter, Tony, and Michael Webb. 'Role of the OECD in the Orchestration of Global Knowledge Networks', in Rianne Mahon and Stephen McBride (eds), *The OECD and Transnational Governance*. Vancouver, 2008, 43–59.

Pratt, Joseph A. *Exxon: Transforming Energy, 1973–2005*. Austin, TX, 2013.

Pratt, Joseph A., William H. Becker, and William M. McClenahan. *Voice of the Marketplace: A History of the National Petroleum Council*. College Station, TX, 2002.

Priest, Joseph. *Energy for a Technological Society: Principles/Problems/Alternatives*. Reading, 1975.

Priest, Tyler. 'Hubbert's Peak: The Great Debate over the End of Oil'. *Historical Studies in the Natural Sciences* 44(1) (2014), 37–79.

Proffitt, Nicholas C. 'Faisal's Threat'. *Newsweek*, 10 September 1973, 35–37.

'Programme of Action on the Establishment of a New International Economic Order', in *United Nations. General Assembly: Resolutions Adopted during Its Sixth Special Session 9 April–2 May 1974*. New York, 1974, 5–12.

Projektleitung Energieforschung KFA Jülich. *Rahmenprogramm Energieforschung. Jahresbericht 1976. Im Auftrage des Bundesministers für Forschung und Technologie und des Bundesministers für Wirtschaft*. N.p., n.d.

Qaimmaqami, Linda W., and Edward C. Keefer (eds). *Energy Crisis, 1969–1974*. Washington, DC, 2012 (Foreign Relations of the United States 1969–1976, 36).

Rabkin, Jeremy A. *The Case for Sovereignty: Why the World Should Welcome American Independence*. Washington, DC, 2004.

———. *Why Sovereignty Matters*. Washington, DC, 1998.

Radkau, Joachim. *Aufstieg und Krise der deutschen Atomwirtschaft 1945–1975: Verdrängte Alternativen in der Kerntechnik und der Ursprung der nuklearen Kontroverse*. Reinbek bei Hamburg, 1983.

Rahman, Mahfuzur. *World Economic Issues at the United Nations: Half a Century of Debate*. Boston, 2002.

Raithel, Thomas, Andreas Rödder, and Andreas Wirsching (eds). *Auf dem Weg in eine neue Moderne? Die Bundesrepublik Deutschland in den siebziger und achtziger Jahren*. Munich, 2009.

Raphael, Lutz. 'Die Verwissenschaftlichung des Sozialen als methodische und konzeptionelle Herausforderung für eine Sozialgeschichte des 20. Jahrhunderts'. *Geschichte und Gesellschaft* 22 (1996), 165–93.

Rappaport, Roy A. 'The Flow of Energy in an Agricultural Society'. *Scientific American* 225(3) (1971), 116–32.

Ravetz, Jerome R. 'Uncertainty, Ignorance and Policy', in Harvey Brooks and Chester L. Cooper (eds), *Science for Public Policy*. Oxford, 1987, 77–89.

Reichow, Hans B. *Die autogerechte Stadt: Ein Weg aus dem Verkehrs-Chaos*. Ravensburg, 1959.

Reifenberg, Jan. 'Amerika hat in der Energiepolitik den längeren Atem: Europas Rolle bei der Konferenz von Washington'. *Frankfurter Allgemeine Zeitung*, 11 February 1974.

———. 'Der tote General hätte Beifall gespendet'. *Frankfurter Allgemeine Zeitung*, 15 February 1974.
Reinecke, Christiane. 'Müller-Hermann, Ernst,' in *Biographisches Handbuch der Mitglieder des Deutschen Bundestages 1949–2002*, vol. 1, A–M. Munich, 2002, 589–90.
Reistle, Carl E. 'Reservoir Engineering', in D.V. Carter (ed.), *The History of Petroleum Engineering*. Dallas, 1961, 811–46.
'Reserves – Tomorrow's Storehouse'. *Petroleum Panorama: Commemorating 100 Years of Petroleum Progress; Oil and Gas Journal* 57(5) (1959), 30–32.
Reston, James. 'Two Cheers for France'. *New York Times*, 15 February 1974.
Riccards, Michael P. 'The Moral Talk of American Presidents', in Moorhead Kennedy, R. Gordon Hoxie, and Brenda Repland (eds), *The Moral Authority of Government: Essays to Commemorate the Centennial of the National Institute of Social Sciences*. New Brunswick, NJ, 2000, 19–23.
Richardson, J.G., and H.L. Stone. 'A Quarter Century of Progress in the Application of Reservoir Engineering'. *Journal of Petroleum Technology* 25 (December 1973), 1371–79.
Rifkin, Jeremy. *The Third Industrial Revolution: How Lateral Power Is Transforming Energy, the Economy, and the World*. New York, 2011.
Risse, Thomas. 'Transnational Actors and World Politics', in W. Carlsnaes (ed.), *Handbook of International Relations*. London, 2002, 255–74.
Risse-Kappen, Thomas (ed.). *Bringing Transnational Relations Back In: Non-State Actors, Domestic Structures and International Institutions*. Cambridge, 1995.
Rm. 'Nachgiebigkeit in Brüssel'. *Frankfurter Allgemeine Zeitung*, 7 November 1973.
Robinson, Jeffrey. *Yamani: The Inside Story*. London, 1989.
Robinson, T.J.C. *Economic Theories of Exhaustible Resources*. London/New York, 1989.
Rocks, Lawrence, and Richard P. Runyon. *The Energy Crisis*. New York, 1972.
Rodgers, Daniel T. *Age of Fracture*. Cambridge, MA, 2011.
Roeper, Hans. 'Hohe Defizite untergraben die Weltwirtschaft: Die Auswirkungen der Ölverteuerung'. *Frankfurter Allgemeine Zeitung*, 14 February 1974.
Roggen, Peter. *Die Internationale Energie-Agentur: Energiepolitik und wirtschaftliche Sicherheit*. Bonn, 1979.
Rosa, Eugene A., Gary E. Machlis, and Kenneth M. Keating. 'Energy and Society'. *Annual Review of Sociology* 14 (1988), 149–72.
Rosecrance, Richard N. *The Rise of the Trading State: Commerce and Conquest in the Modern World*. New York, 1986.
Rossbach, Niklas H. *Heath, Nixon and the Rebirth of the Special Relationship: Britain, the US and the EC, 1969–74*. Basingstoke, 2009.
Roth, Ralf, and Karl Schlögel (eds). *Neue Wege in ein neues Europa: Geschichte und Verkehr im 20. Jahrhundert*. Frankfurt/New York, 2009.
Rothschild, Emma. 'What Is Security?' in Barry Buzan and Lene Hansen (eds), *International Security*, vol. 3, *Widening Security*. Los Angeles, 2007, 1–34.
Rowen, Hobart. 'Energy Parley Responds to Economic Facts'. *Washington Post*, 17 February 1974.

Ruck, Michael. 'Ein kurzer Sommer der konkreten Utopie: Zur westdeutschen Planungsgeschichte der langen 60er Jahre', in Axel Schildt (ed.), *Dynamische Zeiten: Die 60er Jahre in den beiden deutschen Gesellschaften*. Hamburg, 2000, 362–401.

———. 'Gesellschaft gestalten: Politische Planung in den 1960er und 1970er Jahren', in Sabine Mecking and Janbernd Oebbecke (eds), *Zwischen Effizienz und Legitimität: Kommunale Gebiets- und Funktionalreformen in der Bundesrepublik Deutschland in historischer und aktueller Perspektive*. Paderborn, 2009, 35–47.

———. 'Westdeutsche Planungsdiskurse und Planungspraxis der 1960er Jahre im internationalen Kontext', in Heinz-Gerhard Haupt (ed.), *Aufbruch in die Zukunft: Die 1960er Jahre zwischen Planungseuphorie und kulturellem Wandel; DDR, CSSR und Bundesrepublik Deutschland im Vergleich*. Weilerswist, 2004, 289–325.

Rühl, W. 'Erdöl und Erdgas', in Gerhard Bischoff and Werner Gocht (eds), *Das Energiehandbuch*. Braunschweig, 1970, 95–150.

Ruske, Barbara, and Dieter Teufel. *Das sanfte Energie-Handbuch: Wege aus der Unvernunft der Energieplanung in der Bundesrepublik*. Reinbek bei Hamburg, 1982.

Rutledge, Ian. *Addicted to Oil: America's Relentless Drive for Energy Security*. London, 2005.

Ryan, J.M. 'Limitations of Statistical Methods for Predicting Petroleum and Natural Gas Availability'. *Journal of Petroleum Technology* 18 (March 1966), 281–84.

Rybczynski, T.M. (ed.). *The Economics of the Oil Crisis*. New York, 1976.

Sabin, Paul. *The Bet: Paul Ehrlich, Julian Simon, and Our Gamble over Earth's Future*. New Haven, CT, 2013.

———. 'Crisis and Continuity in US Oil Politics, 1965–1980'. *The Journal of American History* 99(1) (2012), 177–86.

———. *Crude Politics: The California Oil Market, 1900–1940*. Berkeley, CA, 2005.

Sabini, John. 'Sea Island Four'. *Aramco World* 24(2) (1973), 6–7.

Sachverständigenrat für Umweltfragen 2012. 'Umweltgutachten 2012: Verantwortung in einer begrenzten Welt'. *Deutscher Bundestag. Drucksachen. 17. Wahlperiode 2009–2013*. No. 10285, 5 July 2012.

Sachverständigenrat zur Begutachtung der gesamtwirtschaftlichen Entwicklung. 'Jahresgutachten 1974'. *Deutscher Bundestag. Drucksachen. 7. Wahlperiode 1972–1976*. No. 2848, 28 November 1974.

———. 'Jahresgutachten 1979/80'. *Deutscher Bundestag. Drucksachen. 8. Wahlperiode 1976–1980*. No. 3420, 22 November 1979.

Sampson, Anthony. *The Seven Sisters: The Great Oil Companies and the World They Made*. London, 1975.

Sandner, Norbert. 'Die Grenzen der mittel- und langfristigen Prognosen des Energieverbrauchs'. *Glückauf. Zeitschrift für Technik und Wirtschaft des Bergbaus* 23(11)(1972), 1147–60.

Sargent, Daniel J. *A Superpower Transformed: The Remaking of American Foreign Relations in the 1970s*. New York, 2015.

———. 'The United States and Globalization in the 1970s', in Niall Ferguson (ed.), *The Shock of the Global: The 1970s in Perspective*. Cambridge, MA, 2010, 49–64.

Sassen, Saskia. *Losing Control? Sovereignty in an Age of Globalization*. New York, 1996.

Schanetzky, Tim. *Die große Ernüchterung: Wirtschaftspolitik, Expertise und Gesellschaft in der Bundesrepublik 1966–1982*. Berlin, 2007.

Schieweck, Erich. 'Die kommende Welterdöl- und Energiekrise'. *Glückauf. Zeitschrift für Technik und Wirtschaft des Bergbaus* 108(9) (1972), 343–55.

Schildt, Axel. '"Die Kräfte der Gegenreform sind auf breiter Front angetreten": Zur konservativen Tendenzwende in den Siebzigerjahren'. *Archiv für Sozialgeschichte* 44 (2004), 449–78.

Schilling, Hans-Dieter, and Rainer Hildebrandt. *Primärenergie, elektrische Energie: Die Entwicklung des Verbrauchs an Primärenergieträgern und an elektrischer Energie in der Welt, in den USA und in Deutschland seit 1860 bzw. 1925*. Essen, 1977.

Schlesinger, Arthur M. *The Imperial Presidency*. Boston, 1973.

Schmelzer, Matthias. *The Hegemony of Growth: The OECD and the Making of the Economic Growth Paradigm*. Cambridge, 2016.

Schmidt, Helmut. 'Die Energiekrise – Eine Herausforderung für die westliche Welt: Vortrag vor der Roosevelt University in Chicago am 13.3.1974'. *Bulletin des Presse- und Informationsamts der Bundesregierung* 35 (1974), 325–30.

———. 'Leitgedanken unserer Außenpolitik', in *Kontinuität und Konzentration*. Bonn-Bad Godesberg, 1975, 226–43.

———. 'Politische und wirtschaftliche Aspekte der westlichen Sicherheit: Vortrag vor dem International Institute for Strategic Studies, London 28.10.1977', in Klaus von Schubert (ed.), *Sicherheitspolitik der Bundesrepublik Deutschland: Dokumentation 1945–1977, Part 2*. Cologne, 1979, 618–31.

———. 'Vorwort: Alle Energie-Optionen offenhalten', in Manfred Krüper (ed.), *Energiepolitik: Kontroversen – Perspektiven*. Cologne, 1977, 7–10.

Schmitt, Dieter. 'West German Energy Policy', in Wilfrid L. Kohl (ed.), *After the Second Oil Crisis: Energy Policies in Europe, America, and Japan*. Lexington, MA, 1982, 137–58.

Schmitz, Silvia. *Energiegeschichten*. Lamspringe, 2007.

Schneider, Hans Karl. 'Marktwirtschaftliche Energiepolitik oder staatlicher Dirigismus? 1978', in *Aufsätze aus drei Jahrzehnten zur Wirtschafts- und Energiepolitik*. Munich, 1990, 162–67.

Schneider, Hans Karl, Monique Dubois, Hans Würgler, Waldemar Wittmann, and Heinz-Dieter Haas. *Stabilisierungspolitik in der Marktwirtschaft: Verhandlungen auf der Tagung des Vereins für Socialpolitik, Gesellschaft für Wirtschafts- und Sozialwissenschaften in Zürich 1974*, 2 vols. Berlin, 1975.

Schr. '13 in einem Boot'. *Süddeutsche Zeitung*, 12 February 1974.

Schröder, Dieter. 'Das europäische Mißverständnis'. *Süddeutsche Zeitung*, 15 February 1974.

———. 'Geld fehlt der Weltwirtschaft mehr als Öl'. *Süddeutsche Zeitung*, 13 February 1974.

———. 'Mehr Kaltblütigkeit in der Ölkrise'. *Süddeutsche Zeitung*, 7 November 1973.

Schubert, Enno. *Vom Bergmann zum Ölexperten: Stationen einer Karriere; Biografie.* Frankfurt am Main, 2007.

Schultz, Thorsten. 'Transatlantic Environmental Security in the 1970s? NATO's "Third Dimension" as an Early Environmental and Human Security Approach'. *Historical Social Research* 35(4) (2010), 309–28.

Schumacher, Ernst F. *Die Rückkehr zum menschlichen Maß: Alternativen für Wirtschaft und Technik.* Reinbek bei Hamburg, 1978.

———. *Small Is Beautiful: Study of Economics as if People Mattered.* London, 1978.

Schurr, Sam H., and Bruce C. Netschert. *Energy in the American Economy, 1850–1975: An Economic Study of Its History and Prospects.* Baltimore, MD, 1960.

Schwarz, Hans-Peter (ed.). *Akten zur Auswärtigen Politik der Bundesrepublik Deutschland 1973*, vol. 3, *1. Oktober bis 31. Dezember*, in collaboration with Ilse Dorothee Pautsch. Munich, 2004.

———. *Akten zur Auswärtigen Politik der Bundesrepublik Deutschland 1974*, vol. 1, *1. Januar bis 30. Juni 1974*, in collaboration with Ilse Dorothee Pautsch. Munich, 2005.

———. *Akten zur Auswärtigen Politik der Bundesrepublik Deutschland 1974*, vol. 2, *1. Juli bis 31. Dezember*, in collaboration with Ilse Dorothee Pautsch. Munich, 2005.

Science Policy Research Unit, Sussex University. *The Limits to Growth Controversy. World Dynamics Models Described and Evaluated. Resources, Population, Agriculture, Capital, Pollution, Energy.* Guildford, 1973.

——— (ed.). *Die Zukunft aus dem Computer? Eine Antwort auf die Grenzen des Wachstums.* Neuwied, 1973.

Scott, Richard. *The History of the International Energy Agency: The First Twenty Years*, vol. 1, *Origins and Structure.* Paris, 1994.

———. *The History of the International Energy Agency: The First Twenty Years*, vol. 2, *Major Policies and Actions.* Paris, 1994.

——— (ed.). *The International Energy Agency: The First Twenty Years*, vol. 3, *Principle Documents.* Paris, 1994.

Seefried, Elke. 'Rethinking Progress: On the Origin of the Modern Sustainability Discourse, 1970–2000'. *Journal of Modern European History* 13(3) (2015), 377–400.

———. 'Towards the Limits to Growth? The Book and Its Reception in West Germany and Britain 1972–73'. *Bulletin of the German Historical Institute* 33(1) (2011), 3–37.

———. *Zukünfte: Eine Geschichte der Zukunftsforschung in den 1960er und 1970er Jahren.* Munich, 2015.

Seifert, Thomas, and Klaus Werner. *Schwarzbuch Öl: Eine Geschichte von Gier, Krieg, Macht und Geld.* Vienna, 2005.

Seymour, Ian. 'The Oil Weapon'. *Middle East Economic Survey* 16(52) (19 October 1973), 2–4.
Shapin, Steven. *The Scientific Life: A Moral History of a Late Modern Vocation*. Chicago, IL, 2008.
Shapiro, T. Rees. 'James Akins, 83, Dies: Energy Expert Presaged Danger of Relying on Mideast Oil'. *Washington Post*, 27 July 2010.
Sheail, John. 'Torrey Canyon: The Political Dimension'. *Journal of Contemporary History* 42 (2007), 485–504.
Sheehan, James J. 'The Problem of Sovereignty in European History'. *American Historical Review* 111(1) (2006), 1–15.
Shell AG. *Der Beitrag des Mineralöls zur künftigen Energieversorgung: Prognosen erfordern schon heute Entscheidungen*. N.p., 1978.
———. *The National Energy Outlook*. Houston, TX, 1974.
Shihata, Ibrahim F.I. *The Case for the Arab Oil Embargo: A Legal Analysis of Arab Oil Measures with a Full Text of Relevant Resolutions and Communiqués*. Beirut, 1975.
———. 'Destination Embargo of Arab Oil: Its Legality und International Law'. *American Journal of International Law* 68 (1974), 591–627.
———. 'The Opec Special Fund and the North-South Dialogue'. *Third World Quarterly* 1(4) (1979), 28–38.
Siebert, Horst. 'The Economics of Resource Ventures', in David William Pearce, Horst Siebert, and Ingo Walter (eds), *Risk and the Political Economy of Resource Development*. London, 1984, 11–36.
Sieferle, Rolf Peter. *Epochenwechsel: Die Deutschen an der Schwelle zum 21. Jahrhundert*. Berlin, 1994.
———. *Der unterirdische Wald: Energiekrise und industrielle Revolution*. Munich, 1982.
Siegenthaler, Hansjörg. 'Zur These des "1950er Syndroms": Die wirtschaftliche Entwicklung der Schweiz nach 1945 und die Bewegung relativer Energiepreise', in Christian Pfister and Peter Bär (eds), *Das 1950er Syndrom: Der Weg in die Konsumgesellschaft*, 2nd ed. Bern, 1996, 97–103.
Silk, Leonard. 'Energy Talks: Why US Position Won'. *New York Times*, 15 February 1974.
Simon, Marc V. 'When Sanctions Can Work: Economic Sanctions and the Theory of Moves'. *International Interactions* 21 (1996), 203–28.
Simon, William E., and Clare Boothe Luce. *A Time for Truth*. New York, 1978.
Simon, William E., and John M. Caher. *A Time for Reflection: An Autobiography*. Washington, DC/Lanham, MD, 2004.
Sinclair, Upton. *Oil!* New York, 1927.
Siniver, Asaf. *Nixon, Kissinger, and US Foreign Policy Making: The Machinery of Crisis*. Cambridge, 2008.
Skeet, Ian. *OPEC Twenty-Five Years of Prices and Politics*. Cambridge, 1988.
Slaughter, Anne-Marie. *A New World Order*. Princeton, NJ, 2004.
Smil, Vaclav. *Energy at the Crossroads: Global Perspectives and Uncertainties*. Cambridge, MA, 2003.

———. 'Energy in the Twentieth Century: Resources, Conversions, Costs, Uses, and Consequences'. *Annual Review of Energy and the Environment* 25 (2000), 21–51.

———. *Energy in World History*. Boulder, CO, 1994.

———. *Transforming the Twentieth Century: Technical Innovations and Their Consequences*. Oxford/New York, 2006.

———. *Two Prime Movers of Globalization: The History and Impact of Diesel Engines and Gas Turbines*. Cambridge, MA, 2010.

Smith, Gene. 'Industry Acting on Energy Crisis'. *New York Times*, 9 November 1973.

Smith, Norman C. 'AAPG Is a Long Time and a Lot of People'. *Bulletin of the American Association of Petroleum Geologists* 56 (1972), 680.

Smith, Simon C. *Reassessing Suez 1956: New Perspectives on the Crisis and Its Aftermath*. Aldershot/Burlington, VT, 2008.

Smith, William D. 'Energy Men Find Nixon Plan Weak'. *New York Times*, 27 November 1973.

———. 'Saudi, Here, Links Oil to a Pullout. Meeting With Kissinger: Comment by Iranian'. *New York Times*, 5 December 1973.

Snow, Crocker. 'Wooing Saudi'. *Boston Globe*, 9 February 1974.

Solow, Robert M. 'The Economics of Resources or the Resources of Economics: Richard T. Ely Lecture'. *The American Economic Review* 64(2): Papers and Proceedings (1974), 1–14.

———. 'Intergenerational Equity and Exhaustible Resources'. *Review of Economic Studies* 41 (1974), 29–45.

'Sondertagung der Vereinten Nationen über Rohstoff- und Entwicklungsprobleme'. *Europa-Archiv* 29(2) (1974), 277–300.

Spiro, Peter J. 'The New Sovereigntists: American Exceptionalism and Its False Prophets'. *Foreign Affairs* 79(6) (2000), 9–15.

Spree, Hans-Ulrich. 'Ölkrieg in der Bonner Koalition'. *Süddeutsche Zeitung*, 28 November 1973.

Staden, Berndt von. *Zwischen Eiszeit und Tauwetter: Diplomatie in einer Epoche des Umbruchs; Erinnerungen*. Berlin, 2005.

'A Staff Analysis Prepared at the Request of Henry M. Jackson, Chairman, Committee on Interior and Insular Affairs, United States Senate. Pursuant to S. Res. 45, a National Fuels and Energy Policy Study, Serial No. 93-19 (92-54), Washington 1973', in Howard Gordon and Roy Meador (eds), *Perspectives on the Energy Crisis*, 2 vols. Ann Arbor, MI, 1977, 149–64.

Stanley, Timothy. 'Some Politic-Legal Aspects of Resource Scarcity'. *American University Law Review* 24 (1975), 1106–21.

Starr, Chauncey. 'Energy and Power'. *Scientific American* 225(3) (1971), 37–49.

Steber, Martina. 'A Better Tomorrow: Making Sense of Time in the Conservative Party and the CDU/CSU in the 1960s and 1970s'. *Journal of Modern European History* 13(3) (2015), 317–37.

Stebinger, Eugene. 'Petroleum in the Ground', in Wallace E. Pratt and Dorothy Good (eds), *World Geography of Petroleum*. Princeton, NJ, 1950, 1–24.

Stegemann, Dieter. *Die Energie: Lebensnerv unserer zivilisierten Welt*. Göttingen, 1974.
Stern, Jonathan P. *Soviet Oil and Gas Exports to the West: Commercial Transaction or Security Threat?* Aldershot/Brookfield, VT, 1987 (Energy Papers no. 21).
Stiglitz, Joseph. 'Growth with Exhaustible Natural Resources: Efficient and Optimal Growth Paths'. *Review of Economic Studies* 41 (1974), 139–52.
Stobaugh, Robert B. 'The Oil Companies in the Crisis'. *Daedalus* 104(4) (1975), 179–202.
Stoff, Michael. *Oil, War, and National Security: The Search for a National Policy on Foreign Oil, 1941–1947*. New Haven, CT, 1980.
Stokes, Raymond G. *Opting for Oil: The Political Economy of Technological Change in the West German Chemical Industry, 1945–1961*. Cambridge, MA, 1994.
Stolleis, Michael. 'Die Idee des souveränen Staates', in *Entstehen und Wandel verfassungsrechtlichen Denkens (Der Staat, Beiheft 11)*. Berlin, 1995, 63–85.
Strasser, Johano. *Die Zukunft der Demokratie: Grenzen des Wachstums, Grenzen der Freiheit?* Reinbek bei Hamburg, 1977.
Strauß, Franz Josef. 'Europäische Zäsur'. *Zeitbühne* 3(6) (1974), 15–16.
Summers, Claude M. 'The Conversion of Energy'. *Scientific American* 225(3) (1971), 148–60.
Süskind, Martin E. 'Feilschen mit arabischen Zwillingen'. *Süddeutsche Zeitung*, 18 January 1974.
Süß, Winfried. 'Der keynesianische Traum und sein langes Ende: Sozioökonomischer Wandel und Sozialpolitik in den siebziger Jahren', in Konrad H. Jarausch (ed.), *Das Ende der Zuversicht? Die siebziger Jahre als Geschichte*. Göttingen, 2008, 120–37.
Swearingen, Wayne E. 'So You Want To Be a Manager'. *Journal of Petroleum Technology* 19(1) (1967), 11–14.
Szatkowski, Tim. *Gaddafis Libyen und die Bundesrepublik Deutschland 1969 bis 1982*. Munich, 2013.
Szöllösi-Janze, Margit. 'Wissensgesellschaft: Ein neues Konzept zur Erschließung der deutsch-deutschen Zeitgeschichte?' in Hans Günter Hockerts (ed.), *Koordinaten deutscher Geschichte in der Epoche des Ost-West-Konflikts*. Munich, 2003, 277–305.
———. 'Wissensgesellschaft in Deutschland: Überlegungen zur Neubestimmung der deutschen Zeitgeschichte über Verwissenschaftlichungsprozesse'. *Geschichte und Gesellschaft* 30 (2004), 277–313.
Tauer, Sandra. *Störfall für die gute Nachbarschaft? Deutsche und Franzosen auf der Suche nach einer gemeinsamen Energiepolitik (1973–1980)*. Göttingen, 2012.
Tavoulareas, William, and Carl Kaysen. *A Debate on A Time to Choose*. Cambridge, MA, 1977.
Therborn, Göran. *Die Gesellschaften Europas 1945–2000*. Frankfurt am Main, 2000.
'There's No Other Choice, Churn Out the Heating Oil (Editorial)'. *Oil and Gas Journal* 71(52) (1972).
'The Thermostat, Oil and Independence', *Washington Post*, 9 November 1973.

Thorpe, Keir. 'The Forgotten Shortage: Britain's Handling of the 1967 Oil Embargo'. *Contemporary British History* 21(2) (2007), 201–22.
Tjetjen, W. Vernon. 'Rig Ahoy!' *Aramco World* 16(2) (1965), 2–7.
Toman, Michael A. 'The Economics of Energy Security: Theory, Evidence, Policy', in Allen V. Kneese and James L. Sweeney (eds), *Handbook of Natural Resource and Energy Economics*, vol. 3. Amsterdam, 1993, 1167–218.
Toprani, Anand. 'The French Connection: A New Perspective on the End of the Red Line Agreement, 1945–1948'. *Diplomatic History* 36(2) (2012), 261–99.
Townsend, Edward. 'Shaik Yamani Tells of Saudi Arabian Scheme for Cheaper Oil'. *The Times*, 28 January 1974.
Tracy, William. 'Island of Steel'. *Aramco World* 17(3) (1966), 1–7.
———. 'A Path to Progress'. *Aramco World* 16(1) (1965), 18–23.
Tsebelis, George. 'Are Sanctions Effective? A Game-Theoretic Analysis'. *Journal of Conflict Resolution* 34 (1990), 3–28.
Tucker, Robert W. 'Oil: The Issue of American Intervention'. *Commentary* 59(1) (1975), 21–31.
———. *The Purposes of American Power: An Essay on National Security*. New York, 1981.
Tugendhat, Christopher. *Oil, the Biggest Business*. 2nd ed. London, 1975.
Türk, Henning. 'The Oil Crisis of 1973 as a Challenge to Multilateral Energy Cooperation among Western Industrialized Countries'. *Historical Social Research* 39(4) (2014), 209–30.
Turner, Edd R. 'The President's Page: Needed – Active Geologists'. *Bulletin of the American Association of Petroleum Geologists* 58 (January 1974), 1–2.
Turner, John. 'Governors, Governance, and Governed: British Politics since 1945', in Kathleen Burk and Paul Langford (eds), *The British Isles since 1945*. Oxford, 2003, 19–62.
Turner, Louis. *Multinational Companies and the Third World*. London, 1973.
———. *Oil Companies in the International System*. London, 1978.
———. 'The Oil Majors in World Politics'. *International Affairs* 52 (1976), 368–80.
Uekötter, Frank, and Jens Hohensee (eds). *Wird Kassandra heiser? Die Geschichte falscher Ökoalarme*. Stuttgart, 2004.
Ulin, Robert R. 'US National Security and Middle Eastern Oil'. *Military Review* 59(5) (1979), 39–49.
Ullmann, Richard H. 'Redefining Security'. *International Security* 8(1) (1983), 129–53.
Umbach, Frank. *Globale Energiesicherheit: Strategische Herausforderungen für die europäische und deutsche Außenpolitik*. Munich, 2003.
United Nations. *General Assembly: Official Records*. New York, 1973–75.
United Nations. Department of Economic and Social Affairs. *Petroleum in the 1970s. Report of the Ad Hoc Panel of Experts on Projections of Demand and Supply of Crude Petroleum and Products. United Nations Headquarters, 9–18 March 1971*. New York, 1974.

———. *Impact of Multinational Corporations on Development and on International Relations*. New York, 1974.

United Nations. General Assembly (ed.). *Plenary Meetings: Verbatim Records of the 2336th to the 2349th Meetings, 1–16 September 1975*. New York, 1976.

United Nations. General Assembly 1974. *3281 Charter of Economic Rights and Duties of States*. http://www.un.org/documents/ga/res/29/ares29.htm (accessed 4 October 2016).

United States Congress. 'Congressional Staff Report on the Conference on International Economic Cooperation'. *International Legal Materials* 15(2) (1976), 388–94.

'Unterrichtung (Bericht) Enquete-Kommission. Zukünftige Kernenergie-Politik', in *Deutscher Bundestag. Drucksachen. 8. Wahlperiode 1976–1980*. No. 4341, 27 June 1980.

'Unterrichtung durch die Bundesregierung. Dritte Fortschreibung des Energieprogramms der Bundesregierung', in *Deutscher Bundestag. Drucksachen. 9. Wahlperiode 1980–1983*. No. 983, 5 November 1981.

'Unterrichtung durch die Bundesregierung. Erste Fortschreibung des Energieprogramms der Bundesregierung', in *Deutscher Bundestag. Drucksachen. 7. Wahlperiode 1972–1976*. No. 2713, 31 October 1974.

'Unterrichtung durch die Bundesregierung. Sondergutachten des Sachverständigenrates "Zu den gesamtwirtschaftlichen Auswirkungen der Ölkrise"', in *Deutscher Bundestag. Drucksachen. 7. Wahlperiode 1972–1976*. No. 1456, 19 December 1973.

'Unterrichtung durch die Bundesregierung. Zweite Fortschreibung des Energieprogramms der Bundesregierung', in *Deutscher Bundestag. Drucksachen 7. Wahlperiode 1976–1980*. No. 1357, 19 December 1977.

Uren, Lester Charles. *Petroleum Production Engineering: Oil Field Exploitation*. 3rd ed. New York/Toronto/London, 1953.

US Cabinet Task Force on Oil Import Control. *The Oil Import Question: A Report on the Relationship of Oil Imports to the National Security*. Washington, DC, 1970.

US Congress. House. Committee on Foreign Affairs. *Data and Analysis Concerning the Possibility of a US Food Embargo as a Response to the Present Arab Oil Boycott, Prepared by the Foreign Affairs Division, Congressional Research Service, Library of Congress*. Washington, DC, 1973.

US Congress. House. Committee on Interior and Insular Affairs (ed.). *Selected Readings on the Fuels and Energy Crisis. 92d Congress, 2d session. Committee Print. Prepared for Members of the House Committee on Interior and Insular Affairs*. Washington, DC, 1972.

US Congress. Senate. Committee on Foreign Relations. *Energy and Foreign Policy: The Implications of the Current Energy Problem for United States Foreign Policy, May 30 and 31 1973*. Washington, DC, 1973.

———. *Multinational Corporations and United States Foreign Policy. Hearings before the Subcommittee on Multinational Corporations. 93rd Congress, 2nd Session*, 15 vols. Washington, DC, 1973–75.

———. *Multinational Petroleum Companies and Foreign Policy. Hearings before the Subcommittee on Multinational Corporations.* 93rd Congress, 2nd Session, vol. 4. Washington, DC, 1974.

———. *Multinational Petroleum Companies and Foreign Policy. Hearings before the Subcommittee on Multinational Corporations.* 93rd Congress, 2nd Session, vol. 5. Washington, DC, 1974.

———. *Political and Financial Consequences of the OPEC Price Increases. Hearings before the Subcommittee on Multinational Corporations.* 93rd Congress, 2nd Session, vol. 11. Washington, DC, 1975.

US Congress. Senate. Committee on Foreign Relations. Subcommittee on Multinational Corporations. *Chronology of the Libyan Oil Negotiations, 1970–1971.* Washington, DC, 1974.

———. *US Oil Companies and the Arab Oil Embargo: The International Allocation of Constricted Supplies.* Washington, DC, 1975.

US Congress. Senate. Committee on Government Operations. *Conflicting Information on Fuel Shortages. Hearings before the Permanent Subcommittee on Investigations.* 93rd Congress. Washington, DC, 1973 (Current Energy Shortages Oversight Series, 1).

———. *Cutoff of Petroleum Products to US Military Forces. Hearings before the Permanent Subcommittee on Investigations.* 93rd Congress. Washington, DC, 1974 (Current Energy Shortages Oversight Series, 8).

———. *The Federal Energy Office: Hearings before the Permanent Subcommittee on Investigations.* Washington, DC, 1974 (Current Energy Shortages Oversight Series, 5).

———. *The Major Oil Companies. Hearings before the Permanent Subcommittee on Investigations.* 93rd Congress. Washington, DC, 1974 (Current Energy Shortages Oversight Series, 2–4).

US Congress. Senate. Committee on Interior and Insular Affairs. *Estimates and Analysis of Fuel Supply Outlook for 1974, Prepared at the Request of Henry M. Jackson.* Washington, DC, 1973.

US Department of the Interior. Office of Oil and Gas. *United States Petroleum through 1980.* Washington, DC, 1968.

'US Fields Unable to Fill Gap if Arab Oil is Cut Off'. *Oil and Gas Journal* 71(42) (1973), 39–42.

US Senate. Committee on Energy and Natural Resources. *The Geopolitics of Oil, Staff Report.* Washington, DC, 1980.

US Senate. Committee on Interior and Insular Affairs. Chair Henry M. Jackson. *Federal Energy Organization: A Staff Analysis Prepared at the Request of Henry M. Jackson, Pursuant to S. Res. 45, a National Fuels and Energy Policy Study, Serial No. 93-19 (92-54).* Washington, DC, 1973.

———. *Geopolitics of Energy.* In collaboration with Melvin A. Conant and Fern R. Gold. Washington, DC, 1977.

van den Bergh, Jeroen C.J.M. (ed.). *Handbook of Environmental and Resource Economics.* Cheltenham, 1999.

van Laak, Dirk. 'Planung: Geschichte und Gegenwart des Vorgriffs auf die Zukunft'. *Geschichte und Gesellschaft* 34 (2008), 305–26.
Vansant, Carl. *Strategic Energy Supply and National Security*. New York, 1971.
Venn, Fiona. 'International Co-operation versus National Self-Interest: The United States and Europe during the 1973–1974 Oil Crisis', in Kathleen Burk and Melvyn Stokes (eds), *The United States and the European Alliance since 1945*. Oxford/New York, 1999, 71–100.
———. *The Oil Crisis*. London, 2002.
———. *Oil Diplomacy in the Twentieth Century*. Basingstoke, 1986.
Verhandlungen des Deutschen Bundestages. 7. Wahlperiode 1972–1976. Stenographische Berichte. Bonn, 1972–76.
Verleger, Philip K. 'The Role of Petroleum Price and Allocation Regulations in Managing Energy Shortages'. *Annual Review of Energy* 6 (1981), 483–528.
Vernon, Raymond (ed.). *The Oil Crisis*. New York, 1976.
———. 'An Interpretation', in *The Oil Crisis*. New York, 1976, 1–14.
———. *Sovereignty at Bay: The Multinational Spread of US Enterprises*. London, 1971.
VIe plan de développement économique et social 1971–1975. Rapport général: Les objectifs généraux et les actions prioritaires du VIe plan et annexes au rapport général: Programmes d'actions détaillées. Paris, 1971.
Vietor, Richard H. *Energy Policy in America since 1945: A Study of Business-Government Relations*. Cambridge, 1984.
Vitalis, Robert. *America's Kingdom: Mythmaking on the Saudi Oil Frontier*. Stanford, CA, 2007.
———. 'Black Gold, White Crude: An Essay on American Exceptionalism, Hierarchy, and Hegemony in the Gulf'. *Diplomatic History* 26(2) (2002), 185–213.
Vogel, Jakob. 'Von der Wissenschafts- zur Wissensgeschichte: Für eine Historisierung der "Wissensgesellschaft"'. *Geschichte und Gesellschaft* 30(4) (2004), 639–60.
Wacker, Holger, and Jürgen E. Blank. *Ressourcenökonomik*, vol. 2, *Einführung in die Theorie erschöpfbarer natürlicher Ressourcen*. Munich, 1999.
Wagenfuehr, Horst. *Report zur Energiekrise: Fakten, Vorschläge und futurologische Aspekte*. Tübingen, 1973.
Walls, David. 'Energy Industry', in *International Encyclopedia of the Social Sciences*, vol. 2 Detroit, 2008, 588–91.
Walton, Ann-Margret. 'Atlantic Relations: Policy Coordination and Conflict. Atlantic Bargaining over Energy'. *International Affairs* 52 (1976), 180–96.
Waltz, Kenneth Neal. *Theory of International Politics*. Reading, MA, 1979.
Warshaw, Shirley Anne. 'The Presidency: Legitimate Authority and Governance', in Moorhead Kennedy, R. Gordon Hoxie, and Brenda Repland (eds), *The Moral Authority of Government: Essays to Commemorate the Centennial of the National Institute of Social Sciences*. New Brunswick, NJ, 2000, 30–36.

'The Washington Energy Conference: Einladung, Reden, Abschlussdokument'. *Atlantic Community Quarterly* 12 (Spring 1974), 22–54.

'We are Very Flexible People, I Assure You: Interview with Sheikh Zaki Yamani'. *Newsweek*, 24 December 1973, 27.

Weeks, Lewis G. 'Estimation of Petroleum Resources: Commentary'. *Bulletin of the American Association of Petroleum Geologists* 50 (1966), 2008–10.

———. 'World Offshore Petroleum Resources'. *Bulletin of the American Association of Petroleum Geologists* 49 (1965), 1680–93.

Weingart, Peter. *Die Stunde der Wahrheit? Zum Verhältnis der Wissenschaft zu Politik, Wirtschaft und Medien in der Wissensgesellschaft.* 2nd ed. Weilerswist, 2005.

Weinstein, Adelbert. 'Jamani: Wächter über des Königs Öl'. *Frankfurter Allgemeine Zeitung*, 15 January 1974.

Weisberg, Richard Chadbourn. *The Politics of Crude Oil Pricing in the Middle East: 1970–1975.* Berkeley, CA, 1977.

'Weltuntergangs-Vision aus dem Computer'. *Der Spiegel*, 15 May 1972, 126–29.

Welzer, Harald. *Klimakriege: Wofür im 21. Jahrhundert getötet wird.* Frankfurt am Main, 2008.

Wengerd, Sherman A. 'The President's Page: A Single Professional Group – The Sloss Report on AAPD-AIPG Cooperation'. *Bulletin of the American Association of Petroleum Geologists* 55 (1971), 1713–14.

———. 'The President's Page: An Allegory on Association'. *Bulletin of the American Association of Petroleum Geologists* 56 (1972), 989–90.

———. 'The President's Page: Year in Progress – Organization and Governance of Our Association'. *Bulletin of the American Association of Petroleum Geologists* 55 (1971), 1125–27.

Werding, Martin. 'Gab es eine neoliberale Wende? Wirtschaft und Wirtschaftspolitik in der Bundesrepublik Deutschland ab Mitte der 1970er Jahre'. *Vierteljahrshefte für Zeitgeschichte* 56 (2008), 303–21.

Werz, Nikolaus (ed.). *Sicherheit.* Baden-Baden, 2009.

Wessel, Horst A. *Das elektrische Jahrhundert. Entwicklung und Wirkungen der Elektrizität im 20. Jahrhundert: Ergebnisse einer Tagung des VDE-Ausschusses 'Geschichte der Elektrotechnik' und des Umspannwerkes Recklinghausen-Museum Strom und Leben, am 24.–25. Oktober 2001 in Recklinghausen.* Essen, 2002.

Wessels, Theodor. 'Die Sicherheit der nationalen Versorgung als Ziel der nationalen Wirtschaftspolitik'. *Zeitschrift für die gesamte Staatswissenschaft* 120(4) (1964), 602–17.

———. 'Die Struktur und Entwicklungstendenzen der deutschen Energiewirtschaft in der Sicht der Enquete-Ergebnisse', in Energiewirtschaftliches Institut der Universität Köln (ed.), *Die Energie-Enquete. Ergebnisse und wirtschaftspolitische Konsequenzen. Vorträge und Diskussionsbeiträge der 12. Arbeitstagung am 14. und 15. Juni 1962 in der Universität Köln.* Munich, 1962, 12–25.

'The Whirlwind Confronts the Skeptics'. *Time Magazine*, 21 January 1974, 24–29.

White, David. 'The Petroleum Resources of the World'. *Annals of the American Academy of Political and Social Science* 89 (May 1920), 111–34.

Wildavsky, Aaron B., and Ellen Tenenbaum. *The Politics of Mistrust: Estimating American Oil and Gas Resources*. Beverly Hills, CA, 1981.

Wilkins, Charles E. 'Learn, Remember and Know'. *Aramco World* 15(6) (1964), 27–28.

Wilkins, Mira. 'The Oil Companies in Perspective'. *Daedalus* 104(4) (1975), 159–78.

William E. Simon. 'December 16, 1973'. *Face the Nation* 16 (1973), 368–74.

Williams, James C. *Energy and the Making of Modern California*. Akron, OH, 1997.

Williams, Marc. *Third World Cooperation: The Group of 77 in UNCTAD*. London, 1991.

Willrich, Mason, and Melvin A. Conant. 'The International Energy Agency: An Interpretation and Assessment'. *American Journal of International Law* 71 (1977), 199–223.

Wilson, Caroll L. *Energy: Global Prospects 1985–2000. Report of the Workshop on Alternative Energy Strategies, WAES*. New York, 1977.

———. 'A Plan for Energy Independence'. *Foreign Affairs* 51 (1973), 657–75.

Wilson, James E. 'The President's Page: Nonprofit, Okay – Deficit, No'. *Bulletin of the American Association of Petroleum Geologists* 56 (1972), 837–38.

Windsor, Philip. *Oil: A Plain Man's Guide to the World Energy Crisis*. London, 1975.

Wirsching, Andreas. *Der Preis der Freiheit: Geschichte Europas in unserer Zeit*. Munich, 2012.

Wolf, Joseph J. *The Growing Dimensions of Security: The Atlantic Council's Working Group on Security*. Washington, DC, 1977.

Wolfe, Robért. 'From Reconstructing Europe to Constructing Globalization: The OECD in Historical Perspective', in Rianne Mahon and Stephen McBride (eds), *The OECD and Transnational Governance*. Vancouver, 2008, 25–42.

Woodward, Richard. *The Organization for Economic Co-operation and Development (OECD)*. London/New York, 2009.

Wörner, Manfred. 'Neue Dimensionen der Sicherheit: Referat bei der XII. Internationalen Wehrkunde-Begegnung, Munich 1.2.1975', in Klaus von Schubert (ed.), *Sicherheitspolitik der Bundesrepublik Deutschland: Dokumentation 1945–1977*, vol 2. Cologne, 1979, 590–97.

Yamani, Ahmed Zaki. 'Oil: Towards a New Producer–Consumer Relationship'. *World Today* 30(11) (1974), 479–486.

Yergin, Daniel. 'Crisis and Adjustment: An Overview', in Daniel Yergin and Martin Hillenbrand (eds), *Global Insecurity: A Strategy for Energy and Economic Renewal*. Boston, 1982, 1–28.

———. *Der Preis: Die Jagd nach Öl, Geld und Macht*. Frankfurt am Main, 1991.

———. *The Prize: The Epic Quest for Oil, Money, and Power*. New York, 1991.

———. *The Quest: Energy, Security and the Remaking of the Modern World*. New York, 2011.

Yergin, Daniel, and Martin Hillenbrand (eds.). *Global Insecurity: A Strategy for Energy and Economic Renewal*. Boston, 1982.

Zachmann, Karin. 'Past and Present Energy Societies: How Energy Connects Politics, Technologies and Cultures', in Nina Möllers and Karin Zachmann (eds), *Past and Present Energy Societies: How Energy Connects Politics, Technologies and Cultures*. Bielefeld, 2012, 7–41.

Zahrani, Mostafa T. 'The Coup that Changed the Middle East: Mossadeq v. the CIA in Retrospect'. *World Policy Journal* 19(2) (2002), 93–99.

Zapp, Alfred. *Future Petroleum Producing Capacity of the United States. Contributions to Economic Geology. A Discussion of the Nature of Certain Petroleum Statistics and Estimates and Their Meaningfulness in Appraising the Outlook for Future Supply*. Washington, DC, 1962 (United States Geological Survey Bulletin, 1142-H).

Ziesing, Hans-Joachim. *Die Entwicklung des Elektrizitätsverbrauchs im Land Berlin bis zum Jahre 2000: Untersuchung im Auftrage des Senators für Wirtschaft und Verkehr Berlin*. Berlin, 1980.

———. *Die künftige Entwicklung des Energiemarktes in Bayern bis zum Jahre 1995. Überprüfung und Fortschreibung der Prognose aus dem Jahre 1974. Gutachten im Auftrage des Bayerischen Staatsministeriums für Wirtschaft und Verkehr*. Munich/Berlin, 1977.

———. *Die regionalen Entwicklungstendenzen des Energieverbrauchs in Hessen und seinen Planungsregionen bis 1990: Untersuchung im Auftrage des Hessischen Ministers für Wirtschaft und Technik*. Wiesbaden/Berlin, 1977.

Zwierlein, Cornel, and Rüdiger Graf. 'The Production of Human Security in Premodern and Contemporary History'. *Historical Social Research* 35(4) (2010), 7–21.

INDEX

A

AAPG. *See* American Association of Petroleum Geologists
Abdessalam, Belaid, 90, 105–14, 239, 300
Achnacarry Agreement, 28
Adelman, Morris, 140–44, 152, 166–67, 192n105, 192n119
    as expert, 371
    in media, 193n125
advertisements
    for energy, 361–62
    by government, 170–71, 199n297
    by OAPEC, 101–2
    by oil industry, 1–2, 33–38, 208–9
    political by oil industry, 92–93
    in West Germany, 25
Africa, 25–28
    diplomacy and, 70–71, 235
    globalization for, 104
    Middle East and, 63, 77–78, 105–14, 205, 231, 233, 310–11, 317–18
    US and, 179
    West Germany and, 314
After Hegemony (Keohane), 356–58
agriculture, 22, 124, 169
AIME. *See* American Institute of Mining and Metallurgical Engineers
AIOC. *See* Anglo-Iranian Oil Company
Air Force Magazine, 351–53
Akins, James, 59–61, 64–65, 91, 94–95, 192n105
    policy and, 129, 131, 140–44, 176, 178, 202n354
    reputation of, 236
Algeria, 26, 30–31, 70, 97–98, 103, 184, 233, 235–36, 300, 309–10, 313–14, 317. *See also* Africa
alternative energy, 127–28, 215–17, 219–20

American Association of Petroleum Geologists (AAPG), 33
American Institute of Mining and Metallurgical Engineers (AIME), 32–33
American Petroleum Institute (API), 24, 37
    politics and, 135
    research by, 39–41
Amouzegar, Jamshid, 312
Amuzegar, Jahangir, 350
Andersen, Knud, 252–53
Anderson, Jack, 165–66
Anglo-Iranian Oil Company (AIOC), 29–30
Annual Review of Energy, 334–35
Ansary, Hushang, 239
API. *See* American Petroleum Institute
Apiaries, Robins, 169
Arabian-American Oil Company (Aramco), 28–29, 31, 92, 236, 337, 357n43
Arab oil weapon, 14
    in diplomacy, 88–114, 119n83, 241–44
    in media, 117n36
    oil embargo as, 14, 184–86, 253–56, 283n311
    politics of, 351–54
    scarcity and, 98–104, 114–15
Arab states. *See* Middle East
Aramco. *See* Arabian-American Oil Company
Al-Assad, Hafez, 103
Atherton, Alfred, 183–84
Attiga, Ali, 101
Austria, 259, 305
automobilization, 21

B

backstop technology, 370–71
Bahr, Egon, 70, 107, 259
Baker, Russell, 166

Index

al-Bakr, Ahmed Hassan, 298
Barre, Raymond, 317
Barzel, Rainer, 231
Beckerman, Stephen, 363
Bell, Daniel, 362
Bennett, Jack, 131
Berghaus, Hartwig, 236
Bergsten, C. Fred, 307, 350–51, 354–55, 357
Bischoff, Gerhard, 363
Blancard, Jean, 294
Boardman, Tom, 106
Böckenförde, Ernst-Wolfgang, 6
Bodin, Jean, 5
Bösch, Frank, 272n110
Boulding, Kenneth, 366, 371
Boumedienne, Houari, 100, 103–4, 115, 239, 243, 310–13
Bouteflika, Abdelaziz, 314
Brandt, Willy, 70, 73, 105–7, 112–13, 207
    diplomacy for, 241–42, 260, 290, 293
    economics for, 259
    in media, 229–33, 243–44, 278n229
    Nixon and, 255
    Ostpolitik, 259–61
    reputation of, 212–13, 224, 245
    sovereignty for, 204–5, 253
    UN Commission, 347–48
Brezhnev, Leonid, 260, 320
British Petroleum, 29, 218, 250, 306, 339–40, 374n34
Brown, Seyom, 350, 354
Brunner, Guido, 334
Bull, Hedley, 353
Burgbacher, Fritz, 225

C

Callaghan, James, 314
Carrington (Lord), 291, 294, 339
Carstens, Karl, 261
Carter, Jimmy, 126, 133, 155, 346, 366
Casey, William, 92
Cash, Frank, 254
Cetron, Marvin J., 363
Charbonnel, Jean, 105
Chevalier, Jean-Marie, 333
Chevron, 23, 42n5, 48n97
Chiprut, Elliot, 171–72
Church, Frank, 337
Churchill, Winston, 33–34
Club of Rome, 364–65
CMEA. *See* Council for Mutual Economic Assistance
coal. *See also* energy
    economics of, 43n14, 214–15
    ECSC, 75
    in Europe, 67–68, 73
    oil compared to, 19–21, 227
    politics of, 212–13, 267n44

Coates, Vary T., 363
Cocoyoc Declaration, 314
Cold War
    diplomacy in, 155
    energy in, 12, 66
    for Europe, 255–58, 320, 349–50
    interdependence and, 335–36
    Middle East compared to, 260–61
    policy in, 74
    politics of, 4, 22, 176, 178, 182, 204–6, 229–30, 264, 344–49, 382n186
    theory of, 354
    for Western Society, 252–53
Cole, John Peter, 352–53
colonialism, 5, 104, 239
Commoner, Barry, 362
Conant, Melvin A., 352
Conference on Security and Cooperation in Europe (CSCE), 319–20
conservation. *See* energy saving
Cooper, Charles A., 176–78, 291
Cooper, Richard N., 345
cooperation. *See* diplomacy; foreign policy; globalization; interdependence
Council for Mutual Economic Assistance (CMEA), 258–59
Cowan, Edward, 164–65
Crocker, Chester A., 65
crude oil
    economics of, 74–75, 192n119
    scarcity of, 54, 71, 138, 141–42, 185, 249, 308, 359–60
CSCE. *See* Conference on Security and Cooperation in Europe
culture
    advertisements and, 33–38
    of energy, 155–60, 267n33, 343, 359–64, 367–68, 387
    of hydrocarbon-based energy systems, 22–23
    of oil, 47n92
    oil shocks for, 385n235
    of policy, 227
    of science, 392
    of Western Society, 111
Czakainski, Martin, 86n148

D

Daghely, Galal, 243–44
Dajani, M. S., 89–90
Daly, Herman E., 367, 371
Daoudi, M. S., 89–90
Dasgupta, Partha, 369, 371
Davis, Warren B., 145
debt crisis, 263
Declaration of European Identity, 251–52
decolonization, 5, 16n12, 309
Deese, David A., 344
Defense Protection Act (1950), 158

Deffeyes, Kenneth, 37
democracy
    economy and, 8–11, 16n6
    in Western Society, 308
détente. *See* Cold War
Detzer, Hans, 218–19
developing nations
    economics of, 389–90
    globalization and, 264–65, 311, 350–54
    Group of 77 for, 309, 311, 315, 350
    oil crisis (1973–74) for, 258–63
    oil for, 303–4
DiBona, Charles, 126, 129–31, 133, 138–39, 163–64
    Kissinger and, 189n53
    Nixon and, 189n54, 195n185
Dingell, John, 169–70
diplomacy
    advertisements for, 92–93
    Africa and, 70–71, 235
    Arab oil weapon in, 91–98, 119n83
    for Brandt, 241–42, 260, 290, 293
    in Cold War, 155
    EC for, 112–13, 245–53, 258
    in economy, 318–20
    in energy crisis, 154–61
    for energy security, 25–31, 55
    for Gaddafi, 277n211, 278n223
    for Iran, 236
    for Kissinger, 325n70
    in Middle East, 264–65, 276n189
    natural resources, 313–14
    by Nixon, 174–75, 189nn58–59
    with OAPEC, 276n182
    OECD in, 64, 205, 208, 294, 296–300, 303–8, 328n116
    for oil, 282n295
    from oil embargo, 89–91, 105–6, 161, 177, 238–39
    by OPEC, 114–15
    politics of, 14–15, 59–62, 89–91, 101
    for UN, 98–99, 104, 248–49
    for US, 120n95, 252–58
    Watergate scandal and, 129–30, 155, 163–64, 172–73, 185
    for Western Society, 184, 286–87, 388–89
    for West Germany, 232–39, 242–45
Douglas-Home, Alec, 106, 201n346, 245–46, 256
    Europe and, 292–93, 298, 300–301
    in politics, 294, 325n70
Drake, Edwin L., 23
Drake, Eric, 339–40

E

Eagan, Vince, 369
Eastern Bloc. *See* Cold War
EC. *See* European Communities
ecological limits. *See* environmentalism

economics. *See also* Organization for Economic Cooperation and Development; scarcity
    API for, 24
    for Brandt, 259
    CMEA for, 258–59
    of coal, 43n14, 214–15
    of crude oil, 74–75, 192n119
    democracy and, 8–11, 16n6
    of developing nations, 389–90
    diplomacy in, 318–20
    education and, 40–42
    EEC for, 75
    of energy, 219, 260–63, 368–72
    of energy crisis, 137–44, 194n160, 343
    of energy policy, 372
    of energy security, 240–41
    environmental, 147–48, 219–21, 394–95
    EPC for, 245–47
    ERP, 21
    of fossil fuels, 19–23, 366–67
    of globalization, 263–64, 355
    for government, 225–26
    of hegemony, 295
    history of, 385n235
    IMF for, 298, 303
    imports in, 149–50
    of industrialism, 248–49
    Lantzke on, 305–6, 319, 328n116
    New International Economic Order, 287, 309–10, 313–15, 319
    for OAPEC, 249–50
    OEEC for, 52–55
    of oil, 31–38, 63–64, 267n33
    of oil crisis (1973–74), 152–53, 206, 213–14, 296
    of oil crisis (1978–79), 308
    of oil production, 30–31, 111
    for OPEC, 46n63, 94–95
    petrodollars in, 45n53
    policy from, 72–74, 388
    politics and, 5–6
    of raw materials, 310
    regulation in, 222–29
    research for, 229
    of scarcity, 124–28
    science and, 39–40
    stagflation in, 227
    in UK, 217–18
    UN and, 276n178, 309
    in Western Society, 334–35
    of West Germany, 6, 346–47
    World Bank for, 298, 303
Economic Stabilization Act (1970), 158
ECSC. *See* European Coal and Steel Community
education
    for petroleum, 29, 32–34, 37
    research and, 71
EEC. *See* European Economic Community
Egypt, 181–82, 244
Ehrenberg, Herbert, 225

– 449 –

Ehrlich, Paul, 371–72
Ehrlichman, John D., 129–30
Emergency Petroleum Allocation Act, 132, 159
The Energizers, 171–72
energy. *See also* International Energy Agency; *specific energies*
    advertisements for, 361–62
    alternative energy, 127–28, 215–17, 219–20
    Annual Review of Energy, 334–35
    in Cold War, 12, 66
    culture of, 155–60, 267n33, 343, 359–64, 367–68, 387
    economics of, 219, 260–63, 368–72
    globalization of, 6–8
    history of, 19–20
    hydrocarbon-based energy systems, 16n6, 22–23
    imports of, 68
    interdependence and, 7–8
    for Jackson, 8–9, 336–39
    for Japan, 4–5
    labor and, 20–21, 282n295
    as national security, 343–44
    oil as, 318–19
    politics of, 3–5, 65–66, 93–98, 374n22, 382n188
    raw materials for, 311–12
    renewable energy, 218–19, 318–19
    solar energy, 218
    Western Society and, 3–5, 9–11, 14–15
energy autarky, 391
energy crisis
    diplomacy in, 154–61
    economics of, 137–44, 194n160, 343
    history of, 123–24
    institutional restructuring in, 128–33
    in media, 126–27, 135, 211, 301–2, 333–35
    national sovereignty in, 195n198
    Nixon in, 163–73, 288–89, 296–97
    oil crisis (1973–74) and, 124–28, 184–86, 233–34
    oil embargo and, 173–84, 242
    petro-knowledge and, 133–37, 332–35
    policy for, 144–48, 304
energy policy
    economics of, 372
    environmentalism as, 155–57
    by EPC, 205–6
    globalization and, 341–42
    High Level Group Oil for, 72–73
    history of, 13–15, 86n148
    labour and, 222–23
    by Nixon, 128–34, 162, 184–86, 188n39, 190n78, 301
    oil and, 370
    petro-knowledge for, 369
    politics of, 332–33
    research for, 12–13, 207, 214–15
    in West Germany, 212–22, 229–32, 263–65
Energy Policy Project (EPP), 145–48

energy resources
    globalization of, 61–62
    nationalization of, 31
energy saving, 271n95
energy security, 11–15, 18n40, 377n73. *See also* energy; oil crisis (1973–74); Organization of Arab Petroleum Exporting Countries (OAPEC); Organization of Petroleum Exporting Countries (OPEC); petro-knowledge
    diplomacy for, 25–31, 55
    economics of, 240–41
    Energy Security Act (West Germany), 344
    for France, 105–6, 216, 245–46
    government and, 148–54, 254–55
    High Level Group Oil for, 53–62, 68–70
    in Japan, 42n7, 113–14, 178
    law for, 209–11
    in media, 90–91
    Middle East for, 4–5
    national sovereignty and, 343–49
    for Nixon, 148–49, 154–61
    oil crisis (1973–74) and, 320–21
    oil in, 387–88
    policy for, 268n66, 345–46, 382n188
    politics of, 241–45, 258–59, 303–4
    renewable energy for, 318–19
    research for, 9–11
    science of, 56, 148–49
    for UK, 106–7, 250–51
    for US, 39–42, 57–58, 97–98, 144–48, 283n311
    in Western Society, 19–23, 51–52, 77–78
    for West Germany, 107–8, 178, 231–32
environmentalism
    Chevron and, 48n97
    economics of, 147–48, 219–21, 394–95
    as energy policy, 155–57
    media and, 35–37
    National Environmental Protection Act, 127
    oil crisis (1973–74) and, 362, 364–68
    politics of, 158–60
    scarcity and, 209, 364–68
    UN and, 314
    in US, 167
EPC. *See* European Political Cooperation
EPP. *See* Energy Policy Project
Eppler, Erhard, 107, 220–21, 261–62, 335
ERP. *See* European Recovery Program
d'Estaing, Giscard, 294, 315–16
Europe. *See also* Organization for Economic Cooperation and Development; Western Society
    CMEA for, 258–59
    coal in, 67–68, 73
    Cold War for, 255–58, 320, 349–50
    CSCE in, 319–20
    Declaration of European Identity, 251–52
    Douglas-Home and, 292–93, 298, 300–301

Index

EC and, 107
Gas-Pipes Deals in, 259–60
history of, 203–6
Middle East and, 245–47
OEEC for, 52–55
oil dependency in, 76–77
policy in, 234
politics in, 54–55, 230–31
Scheel for, 297–98, 312–13
Schmidt, H., and, 323n34
UN and, 243, 247
US and, 58–59, 69–70, 73–74, 80n43, 111–12, 231, 241, 263–64, 344
West Germany and, 306–7
European Coal and Steel Community (ECSC), 75
European Communities (EC), 75–77
for diplomacy, 112–13, 245–53, 258
Europe and, 107
as government, 288–91, 293–94
nationalism and, 231–32
European Economic Community (EEC), 70, 72, 75, 250
European Political Cooperation (EPC), 245–47
energy policy by, 205–6
Western Society and, 288–89
European Recovery Program (ERP), 21
Exxon, 23, 28, 42n5, 131, 135, 177, 236, 306, 337–38
Exxon Valdez (oil tanker), 36

F

Fahd (Prince), 178–79
Fairbanks, Richard, 125
Faisal (King)
as leader, 91–93, 96–97, 99, 103, 239
US and, 117n41, 162, 178–84
bin Faisal, Saud (Prince), 31
Flanigan, Peter, 131
Ford, Gerald, 189n62, 202n355, 316
Ford Foundation. *See* Energy Policy Project
foreign policy
from Cold War, 354
by Kissinger, 174–84, 189n53, 201n338, 201n346, 202n354, 252–58, 300–303, 311–12, 392–93
politics of, 10–11
for US, 18n40, 337
for Western Society, 389–94
for West Germany, 12, 302
Forrester, Jay W., 365
Forsthoff, Ernst, 6
fossil fuels. *See also* energy
economics of, 19–23, 366–67
globalization of, 3–5
France. *See also* Jobert, Michel; Western Society
energy security for, 105–6, 216, 245–46
globalization for, 226, 306, 315–16
Middle East and, 293

oil for, 268n66
regulation and, 313
UK and, 28, 256–57, 299
US and, 289–90
Frank, Paul, 242–44, 248–49, 254, 282n295
Freeman, David, 127, 146–47
Friderichs, Hans, 59, 107, 112
policy for, 204, 211, 224–25
as politician, 288–89
Friedland, Edward, 353
Frydenlund, Knut, 297
Fulbright, J. William, 95, 129, 143–44, 168, 336–37
Fuqua, Don, 170

G

Gaddafi, Muamar, 64, 93, 96, 102, 110, 115
diplomacy for, 277n211, 278n223
in politics, 239–44
gas, 59
Gas-Pipes Deals, 259–60
Gehlhoff, Walter, 261, 311
geography
of national security, 351–53
of oil, 11–12, 25–28
of oil reserves, 262–63
geology, 137–44, 345. *See also* science
geopolitics. *See* globalization; politics
Georgescu-Roegen, Nicholas, 366–67, 371
Geren, Dave, 157
German Atomic Forum, 213
Gibson, Glenn, 169
Gillesen, Günther, 247–48
global interdependence. *See* interdependence
globalization
Achnacarry Agreement in, 28
for Africa, 104
Arab oil weapon in, 88–91, 105–14, 241–44
of automobilization, 21
of Cold War, 258–59
of colonialism, 5
developing nations and, 264–65, 311, 350–54
economics of, 263–64, 355
of energy, 6–8
energy policy and, 341–42
of energy resources, 61–62
EPC in, 245–47
of fossil fuels, 3–5
for France, 226, 306, 315–16
government in, 258
of interdependence, 15
Israel in, 92–99, 101–5, 108, 112–13, 232
of law, 239–40
Middle East in, 13–14, 70
national security and, 376n72
national sovereignty in, 336–43, 349–54
New International Economic Order in, 287, 309–10, 313–15, 319, 350

– 451 –

OAPEC in, 130, 389, 391–92
of oil, 11–15, 23–31, 234
oil conferences in, 286–94, 309–20
of oil crisis (1973–74), 12–15, 64–65, 323n31
oil sharing and, 82n65
OPEC in, 91, 130, 143–44, 389, 391–92
politics in, 41–42, 56–57, 358–59
for Saudi Arabia, 162
scarcity and, 66–67
UK in, 226, 300–301
UNCTAD for, 104, 309, 314
US and, 59–60, 234–35, 244, 262, 314–15
for West Germany, 225, 239–42, 258–63
Gold, Fern R., 352
Goodwin, Craufurd D., 190n78
government
advertisements by, 170–71, 199n297
EC as, 288–91, 293–94
economics for, 225–26
energy security and, 148–54, 254–55
in France, 336
in globalization, 258
Jackson in, 128, 136–37, 158–59, 168
in Japan, 21
OAPEC as, 309–10
OECD and, 88
oil embargo for, 190n69
OPEC as, 309–10
policy and, 154–57, 218–19, 389
research for, 18n40, 228
in UK, 339–40
in US, 128–33, 167–69, 336–39
in West Germany, 268n49
Granville, Maurice, 93
Greece, 259
Grimm, Paul E., 338
Gromyko, Andrei, 319–20
Group of 77
for developing nations, 309, 311, 315, 350
for oil, 100, 104, 287, 313
Gruhl, Herbert, 221
Gulf War (1990–91), 308
Guth, Wilfried, 317

H

Haas, Merrill W., 34, 139
Haig, Alexander, 181, 201n346, 202n354
Halliburton, 1–2, 35
Hallman, Albert, 213
Harpprecht, Klaus, 282n307
Hastings, Keith, 128–29
Heal, Geoffrey, 369–70
Heath, Edward
expert advice, 106, 213, 244–45, 252
as leader, 244–45, 293, 339, 347
hegemony
After Hegemony (Keohane), 356–58

economics of, 295
politics of, 300
for US, 287–94, 302–4, 323n49, 356–58, 380n138, 393–94
Heinebaeck, Bo, 345
Heinemann, Gustav, 366
Helsinki Final Act, 319
Hermes, Peter, 261, 276n178, 325n70
Hielscher, Hans, 109
High Level Group Oil, 53–62, 68–70, 389
for energy policy, 72–73
oil crisis (1973–74) and, 287–88, 294, 304–5
Hill, John A., 190n64
Hillenbrand, Martin J., 241, 243, 253–54, 344
Hilzinger, Caspar. *See* Frank, Paul
Hirst, David, 93
history
of economics, 385n235
of energy, 19–20
of energy crisis, 123–24
of energy policy, 13–15, 86n148
of Europe, 203–6
of interdependence, 323n49
of OAPEC, 30–31
of oil crisis (1973–74), 4, 7, 126–27, 332–35, 387–95
of oil crisis (1978–79), 221–22
of OPEC, 30
research and, 342–43
of scarcity, 371–72
of technology, 359–64
of US, 23–24
Yergin for, 344
Hoffman, Stanley, 1, 356
Hogan, William, 149, 153, 192n105
Homan, Paul T., 39–40
Hoopes, David, 133
Horin, Ben, 243
Houthakker, Hendrik S., 143
Hoveyda, Fereydoon, 313
Hubbert, Marion King, 40–41, 125, 365–66, 388
human rights, 6, 180, 329n138
Hussein, Saddam, 93, 102, 110
hydrocarbon-based energy systems, 16n6, 22–23

I

IEA. *See* International Energy Agency
IEP. *See* International Energy Programme
IMF. *See* International Monetary Fund
imports. *See also* Task Force on Oil Import Control
in economics, 149–50
of energy, 68
Mandatory Oil Import Program (US) in, 24–25
from Middle East, 53–54, 66–67, 93
of oil, 305

Index

politics of, 62–67
    Task Force on Oil Import Control, 62–63, 66, 125–26
    for US, 186
industrialism
    economics of, 248–49
    labor and, 47n80
    of Middle East, 46n57
    policy from, 261–62
    politics and, 200n312
    scarcity and, 54–55
    UNIDO for, 315
    in Western Society, 368–69
institutional restructuring, 128–33
interdependence, 6, 380n154. *See also* globalization
    Cold War and, 335–36
    energy and, 7–8
    globalization of, 15
    history of, 323n49
    for Kissinger, 287–89, 291–95
    for Middle East, 56–57
    national sovereignty and, 286–87, 320–21, 354–58
    sovereignty and, 294–302
International Energy Agency (IEA), 11, 303–8
    for oil crisis (1973–74), 69, 216–17
    OPEC and, 321
    policy and, 355–57
International Energy Programme (IEP), 303–8
international law, 5
International Monetary Fund (IMF), 298, 303
international relations, 354–55
Iran, 66, 92, 96, 98, 176, 222, 230, 235, 239, 256, 259, 277n212, 288, 316, 349. *See also* Middle East
    diplomacy for, 236
    UK and, 29–30
Iraq, 28, 30–31, 66, 91, 93–94, 96, 100, 102, 104, 110, 114, 348, 358
Irwin, John, 60–61, 86n136
Israel, 92–99, 101–5, 108, 112–13, 232
    in media, 117n41
    oil embargo and, 118n59, 180
    US and, 243
    Western Society and, 254, 257–58
    West Germany and, 282n307
Italy, 259

J

Jablonski, Wanda, 25
Jackson, Henry M.
    energy for, 8–9, 336–39
    in government, 128, 136–37, 158–59, 168
Jalloud, Abdessalam, 102–3, 244
Japan. *See also* Western Society
    energy for, 4–5
    energy security in, 42n7, 113–14, 178

    government in, 21
    OAPEC and, 180
    oil embargo for, 66–67
    US and, 256, 283n313
    West Germany and, 80n43
Jasanoff, Sheila, 392
Jobert, Michel, 105, 177, 201n346, 245–46, 257
    as leader, 289, 293–94, 298–300, 313
    reputation of, 301–2, 325n70, 326nn76–77
Johnson, Lyndon B., 123
Johnson, William, 131
Journal of Petroleum Technology, 34
Jungers, Frank, 92, 337

K

Kagan, Robert, 358
Kahn, Hermann, 349–50
Kaiser, Karl, 347, 349
Katz, James E., 356
Kaufmann, Burton I., 342
Kemp, Geoffrey, 351
Kennedy, Edward, 152
Keohane, Robert, 6, 307, 354–58, 393–94
Keynesianism. *See* regulation
Khene, Abderrahmane, 238–39
Khrushchev, Nikita S., 22
Kindleberger, Charles, 6
Kissinger, Henry A., 92, 117n27, 129–30, 167, 172
    diplomacy for, 325n70
    foreign policy by, 174–84, 189n53, 201n338, 201n346, 202n354, 252–58, 300–303, 311–12, 392–93
    interdependence for, 287–89, 291–95
    in Middle East, 65–66
    reputation of, 248, 298–300, 323n31, 3234n49
Knips, Walter, 109
Knubel, John, 174, 190n64
Kondis, Edward F., 338
Koschnik, Hans, 220
Kraft, Joseph, 166
Krasner, Stephen D., 7, 351, 357
Kruse, Hansheinrich, 61, 107–8, 234–35, 237–39, 276n178
Kruse, Hans-Stefan, 276n178
Kuwait, 30, 94, 96–98, 100, 118n52, 119n86, 237, 239, 276n182, 276n189

L

labour
    economics of, 32–33
    energy and, 20–21, 282n295
    energy policy and, 222–23
    industrialism and, 47n80
    national security and, 342
    oil embargo and, 136–37

Index

Lahn, Lothar, 242, 276n178
Laird, Wilson M., 58, 63, 189n54
Lambsdorff, Otto Graf, 204, 225
Lantzke, Ulf, 59–61, 69–70, 72–74, 239, 258
    on economics, 305–6, 319, 328n116
    energy policy, 207, 212, 215, 224, 228, 233–35, 287, 290, 394
Lautenschlager, Hans, 237, 276n178
law
    for energy security, 209–11
    globalization of, 239–40
    international law, 5
    Texas Railroad Commission for, 24
    in US, 31–32
Levy, Walter, 213, 218, 268n49, 296, 333
Libya, 26, 30–31, 58, 61, 70, 91, 94, 96, 98, 102, 104, 114, 176, 233, 236, 240–44, 249, 259, 349. *See also* Africa; Gaddafi, Muamar; Middle East
Licklider, Roy, 89
Liebruck, Manfred, 71
Ligon, Duke, 131, 190n64
limits. *See* globalization; interdependence; policy; regulation
Limits to Growth (report), 364–65
Lincoln, George A., 125, 343, 349, 352
Loewenstein, Karl, 354
Logan, Harry A., 168
Love, John A., 97, 130, 133–34, 155–57, 189n53
    Nixon and, 189n54
    publicity of, 161, 163–67, 170, 175
Lovejoy, Wallace F., 39–40
Lovins, Amory, 3, 362–63, 368, 382n186

M

MacFadzean, Frank, 339–40
Mandatory Oil Import Program, 24–25
Mandel, Heinrich, 218–19
Marshall Plan, 21
mass media, 13
Matthöfer, Hans, 220
McCormick, William T., 134
McKelvey, Vincent E., 38
McLean, John, 145–46
media
    Arab oil weapon in, 117n36
    Brandt in, 229–33, 243–44, 278n229
    energy crisis in, 126–27, 135, 211, 301–2, 333–35
    energy security in, 90–91
    environmentalism and, 35–37
    Israel in, 117n41
    mass media, 13
    Middle East and, 93–94, 100, 115
    OAPEC in, 12
    oil embargo in, 114
    OPEC in, 12
    petro-knowledge in, 10, 363–64
    politics and, 7
    research in, 139–40
    Saudi Arabia in, 118n66
    on scarcity, 109–10
    in US, 94–96, 108–9, 161–72
    Western Society in, 348–49
    Yamani in, 103–4, 115, 117n27, 235
MEES. *See Middle East Economic Survey*
Meir, Golda, 244
Messmer, Pierre, 230–31
Metzger, Pete, 235
Meyer-Abich, Klaus M., 218
Middle East, 4–5, 191n88. *See also* Faisal; oil; oil embargo
    Africa and, 63, 77–78, 105–14, 205, 231, 233, 310–11, 317–18
    Aramco in, 28–29
    Cold War compared to, 260–61
    diplomacy in, 264–65, 276n189
    Europe and, 245–47
    France and, 293
    in globalization, 13–14, 70
    human rights in, 329n138
    imports from, 53–54, 66–67, 93
    industrialism of, 46n57
    interdependence for, 56–57
    Kissinger in, 65–66
    media and, 93–94, 100, 115
    oil crisis (1973–74) for, 51–52
    politics and, 26–31
    Trans-Arabian Pipeline for, 64, 208
    UN and, 232–33
    US and, 99, 134, 173–75
    Western Society and, 11, 31, 90–91, 105–14, 278n223
    West Germany and, 215, 247–52
Middle East Economic Survey (MEES), 25, 234
Miller, Linda B., 345
Mitchell, Donald J., 168
Mitchell, Timothy, 9, 16n6
Mobil Oil, 23, 124, 135
Möckli, Daniel, 280n257, 323n31
Mondale, Walter F., 346
Morgenthau, Hans J., 348, 353
Mori, Haruki, 347
Morton, Robert B., 163
Morton, Rogers, 199n297, 362
Mossadegh, Mohammad, 29–30
Müller, Harald, 344–45
Müller-Chorus, Gerhard, 242–43
Müller-Hermann, Ernst, 225–26
multinational oil firms, 336–43, 373n19
Muskie, Edmund, 298–99

N

Nader, Laura, 363

– 454 –

Index

Nasser, Gamal Abdel, 53
National Environmental Protection Act, 127
nationalism
    EC and, 231–32
    transnationalism, 354–58
nationalization
    of energy resources, 31
    in Iraq, 93
    of oil, 61
National Petroleum Council, 129, 145–46
national security
    energy as, 343–44
    geography of, 351–53
    globalization and, 376n72
    oil and, 376n66
    in US, 62–67
National Security Study Memoranda (NSSM), 63–67, 97, 173
national sovereignty, 15
    in energy crisis, 195n198
    energy security and, 343–49
    in globalization, 336–43, 349–54
    interdependence and, 286–87, 320–21, 354–58
    research on, 335–36
    for US, 150–51
natural gas, 74, 93, 215–16. *See also* energy
Netherlands, 4, 14, 55, 60, 89, 99–100, 105–07, 215, 241, 243, 246–48, 250–51, 254, 257, 287, 288–89, 305. *See also* Europe; Western Society
New International Economic Order, 287, 309–10, 313–15, 319, 350
Nixon, Richard, 22, 62, 95, 195n185
    Brandt and, 255
    diplomacy by, 174–75, 189nn58–59
    for energy autarky, 391
    in energy crisis, 163–73, 288–89, 296–97
    energy policy by, 128–34, 162, 184–86, 188n39, 190n78, 301
    energy security for, 148–49, 154–61
    as leader, 293–94
    in oil crisis (1973–74), 123–27
    policy by, 180–83, 392–93
    reputation of, 188n32, 189n54, 191n88, 253
    Washington energy conference for, 294–302, 315, 346
Nolan, John, 338
North Africa. *See* Africa
North Sea, 251, 290–91, 377n88
NSSM. *See* National Security Study Memoranda
nuclear energy, 59, 74, 376n72
    politics of, 221–22, 228, 304
    scarcity and, 215–16
Nye, Joseph
    as expert, 342, 344, 346, 354–56, 359–60, 377n73
    theory of, 6, 307, 393–94

O

OAPEC. *See* Organization of Arab Petroleum Exporting Countries
Odeen, Philip, 255–56, 344
OECD. *See* Organization for Economic Cooperation and Development
OEEC. *See* Organization for European Economic Cooperation
oil. *See also* energy
    advertisements for, 208–9
    AIOC for, 29–30
    coal compared to, 19–21, 227
    crude oil, 71, 74–75, 192n119, 308
    culture of, 47n92
    for developing nations, 303–4
    diplomacy for, 282n295
    economics of, 31–38, 63–64, 267n33
    as energy, 318–19
    energy policy and, 370
    in energy security, 387–88
    for France, 268n66
    geography of, 11–12, 25–28
    globalization of, 11–15, 23–31, 234
    Group of 77 for, 100, 104, 287, 313
    High Level Group Oil, 53–62, 68–70, 72–73
    imports of, 305
    Limits to Growth (report) on, 364–65
    multinational oil firms for, 336–43
    nationalization of, 61
    national security and, 376n66
    North Sea for, 251, 290–91, 377n88
    peak oil, 365–66, 388
    as raw materials, 262
    research for, 305–6
    from Soviet Union, 258–59
    Suez Canal and, 43n14, 53–54, 56–57, 64
    Task Force on Oil Import Control, 62–63, 66, 125–26
    technology for, 151
    for UK, 176
    Western Society and, 19–23, 340–43
Oil! (Sinclair), 31–32
Oil and Gas Journal, 1–2, 25, 34, 133–34
oil conferences
    in globalization, 286–94, 309–20
    Washington energy conference, 294–302, 315, 346
oil crisis (1973–74), 8–10, 199n297
    for developing nations, 258–63
    economics of, 152–53, 206, 213–14, 296
    energy crisis and, 124–28, 184–86, 233–34
    energy security and, 320–21
    environmentalism and, 362, 364–68
    globalization in, 12–15, 64–65, 323n31
    High Level Group Oil and, 287–88, 294, 304–5
    history of, 126–27, 332–35, 387–95

Index

IEA for, 69, 216–17
for Middle East, 51–52
Nixon in, 123–27
petro-knowledge in, 12–13, 306
policy from, 77–78, 209–10, 225–27, 286–87
politics of, 18n40, 237–45
research from, 212, 223–24, 344–45
scarcity in, 78n2
technology for, 71–72
for UN, 347
for US, 164–65, 171, 260
for West Germany, 207–11, 222–29, 263–65
oil crisis (1978–79), 272n110
economics of, 308
history of, 221–22
oil dependency, 76–77, 86n148, 203–6
oil embargo, 11
as Arab oil weapon, 184–86, 253–56, 283n311
diplomacy from, 89–91, 105–6, 161, 177, 238–39
energy crisis and, 173–84, 242
for government, 190n69
Israel and, 118n59, 180
for Japan, 66–67
labor and, 136–37
in media, 114
for OAPEC, 95–96
for OECD, 174
policy and, 131–32, 149–50, 172–73
politics of, 57–58, 99–104
for Saudi Arabia, 338
Task Force on Oil Import Control and, 66
US and, 88–90, 153–54, 157–58
for Western Society, 242–43
for West Germany, 56–57
oilmen, 31–38
oil production, 30–31, 111
oil reserves
geography of, 262–63
OECD on, 69–70
technology for, 38–42
in US, 49n122
oil rigs, 45n54, 215
oil sharing, 60–62, 82n65
oil shocks, 385n235
OPEC. *See* Organization of Petroleum Exporting Countries
Oppenheim, Lassa Francis Lawrence, 5
Organization for Economic Cooperation and Development (OECD), 8
in diplomacy, 64, 205, 208, 294, 296–300, 303–8, 328n116
government and, 88
Oil Committee for, 14, 51–57, 59, 61, 77
oil embargo for, 174
on oil reserves, 69–70
OPEC and, 235–37
policy from, 263
politics of, 51–52, 81n64

UK and, 194n177
UN and, 12, 261–62
Western Society and, 52–62
Organization for European Economic Cooperation (OEEC), 52–55
Organization of Arab Petroleum Exporting Countries (OAPEC), 4, 14. *See also* Yamani, Zaki
advertisements by, 101–2
diplomacy with, 276n182
economics for, 249–50
in globalization, 130, 389, 391–92
as government, 309–10
history of, 30–31
Japan and, 180
in media, 12
oil embargo for, 95–96
policy for, 123–24, 134, 147, 173
in politics, 7–8, 98–103
West Germany and, 240
Organization of Petroleum Exporting Countries (OPEC), 4, 14
diplomacy by, 114–15
economics for, 46n63, 94–95
in globalization, 91, 130, 143–44, 389, 391–92
as government, 309–10
history of, 30
IEA and, 321
in media, 12
OECD and, 235–37
policy for, 123–24, 134, 184–85
in politics, 7–8, 237–40
politics of, 353
raw materials for, 329n138
West Germany and, 277n203
Ortoli, François-Xavier, 294
Ostpolitik, 259–61

P

Pachachi, Nadim, 119n83
Pahlavi, Mohammad Reza (Shah), 239
Painter, David, 342
Palme, Olof, 347
Pasternack, Bruce, 153
peak oil, 40–41, 365–66, 388
Percy, Charles H., 170–71
petrodollars, 45n53
petro-knowledge, 1–5, 8–11. *See also* research
energy crisis and, 133–37, 332–35
for energy policy, 369
in media, 10, 363–64
in oil crisis (1973–74), 12–13, 306
as research, 391–92
Resources for the Future Inc., for, 39–40
scarcity and, 38–42
petroleum
API for, 24, 37, 39–41, 135

– 456 –

education for, 32–34, 37
Emergency Petroleum Allocation Act (US), 132, 159
Journal of Petroleum Technology, 34
National Petroleum Council (US), 129, 145–46
regulation of, 251
science of, 23, 47n81
SPE for, 33
technology and, 29, 36–37
Petroleum Intelligence Weekly, 25
Petroleum Panorama, 38
Petroleum Press Service, 25
Petromin, 31
Peyton, Charles O., 338
planification, 268n66
planning. *See* policy
Podhoretz, Norman, 348
policy. *See also* energy policy; foreign policy
Akins and, 129, 131, 140–44, 176, 178, 202n354
for British Petroleum, 339–40
in Cold War, 74
culture of, 227
from economics, 72–74, 388
for energy crisis, 144–48, 304
for energy security, 268n66, 345–46, 382n188
in Europe, 234
for Friderichs, 204, 211, 224–25
government and, 154–57, 218–19, 389
IEA and, 355–57
from industrialism, 261–62
for Lantzke, 207, 212, 215, 224, 228, 233–35, 287, 290, 394
by Nixon, 180–83, 392–93
for OAPEC, 123–24, 134, 147, 173
from OECD, 263
from oil crisis (1973–74), 77–78, 209–10, 225–27, 286–87
oil embargo and, 131–32, 149–50, 172–73
for OPEC, 123–24, 134, 184–85
politics and, 307
for pollution, 365
for scarcity, 138, 228–29, 234
in US, 123–24, 126
Watergate scandal and, 180–81, 185
by Yamani, 239, 337–38
political sovereignty, 309–10
politics
API and, 135
of Arab oil weapon, 351–54
of coal, 212–13, 267n44
of Cold War, 4, 22, 176, 178, 182, 204–6, 229–30, 264, 344–49, 382n186
of diplomacy, 14–15, 59–62, 89–91, 101
Douglas-Home in, 294, 325n70
economics and, 5–6
of energy, 3–5, 65–66, 93–98, 374n22, 382n188

of energy policy, 332–33
of energy security, 241–45, 258–59, 303–4
of environmentalism, 158–60
EPC for, 245–47
in Europe, 54–55, 230–31
of foreign policy, 10–11
Gaddafi in, 239–44
in globalization, 41–42, 56–57, 358–59
of hegemony, 300
of imports, 62–67
industrialism and, 200n312
media and, 7
Middle East and, 26–31
of nuclear energy, 221–22, 228, 304
OAPEC in, 7–8, 98–103
of OECD, 51–52, 81n64
of oil crisis (1973–74), 18n40, 237–45
of oil embargo, 57–58, 99–104
of OPEC, 353
OPEC in, 7–8, 237–40
policy and, 307
of Saudi Arabia, 29
of science, 128, 137–44
Simon, William E., in, 295–96
of sovereignty, 387–95
in US, 189n62
Watergate scandal, 129–30, 155, 163–64, 172–73, 180–81, 185
of Yom Kippur War, 98–99, 257–58
pollution, 365
Pompidou, Georges, 105, 245, 299
Priest, Joseph, 364
Project Independence Evaluation System, 149, 152
Project Independence Report, 148–54
Pronk, Jan P., 347

R

Rabkin, Jeremy A., 358
Rampton, Jack, 293
Rather, Dan, 165
raw materials
debt crisis and, 263
economics of, 310
for energy, 311–12
mining for, 267n44
oil as, 262
for OPEC, 329n138
scarcity of, 259–360, 357, 393–94
for UN, 304
for West Germany, 366
Ray, Dixy Lee, 134, 304
Reagan, Ronald, 260, 366
Redies, Helmut, 276n178
regulation, 222–29
France and, 313
of petroleum, 251
renewable energy, 218–19, 318–19

research
   for alternative energy, 127–28, 215–17
   by API, 39–41
   EC for, 75–77
   for economics, 229
   education and, 71
   for energy policy, 12–13, 207, 214–15
   for energy saving, 271n95
   for energy security, 9–11
   for government, 18n40, 228
   history and, 342–43
   Limits to Growth (report), 364–65
   in media, 139–40
   on national sovereignty, 335–36
   NSSM for, 63–67, 97, 173
   for oil, 305–6
   from oil crisis (1973–74), 212, 223–24, 344–45
   petro-knowledge as, 391–92
Resources for the Future Inc., 39–40
Reston, James, 302
Rhodesia, 179
Ribicoff, Abraham, 136
Ridley Commission, 68
Rockefeller, John D., 23
Rocks, Lawrence, 362
Rohwedder, Detlev Karstan, 59, 69–71, 77, 239, 258, 267n44
Roll, Eric, 317
Roosevelt, Franklin D., 123
Rosecrance, Richard N., 357
Rothschild (Lord), 68, 84n107
Royal Dutch Shell, 23, 28, 35, 40, 42n5, 44n35, 84n107, 85n126, 215, 218, 339–340, 342
Rumsfeld, Donald, 253
Runyon, Richard, 362
Russe, Herman Josef, 226

S

Sadat, Anwar, 103, 181–82, 244
Sampson, Anthony, 341
San Remo Conference, 28
al-Saqqaf, Umar, 178–79
Sargent, Daniel, 357
Sargent, Francis W., 168
Saud (King), 28–29
Saud (Prince), 91, 94, 100, 112
Saudi Arabia. *See also* Faisal; Middle East
   globalization for, 162
   in media, 118n66
   oil embargo for, 338
   politics of, 29
   US and, 91–93, 174, 176–81, 183–84
   West Germany and, 236–37
Sawhill, John
   career of, 132–33, 136, 148–49, 151–52, 190n64
   as expert, 344

scarcity
   Arab oil weapon and, 98–104, 114–15
   of crude oil, 54, 71, 138, 141–42, 185, 308, 349, 359–60
   diplomacy for, 142, 230–32
   economics of, 124–28
   environmentalism and, 209, 364–68
   geology and, 137–44, 345
   globalization and, 66–67
   history of, 371–72
   industrialism and, 54–55
   media on, 109–10
   nuclear energy and, 215–16
   in oil crisis (1973–74), 78n2
   petro-knowledge and, 38–42
   policy for, 138, 228–29, 234
   of raw materials, 259–360, 357, 393–94
Scheel, Walter, 107, 113, 233, 241, 243
   for Europe, 297–98, 312–13
   reputation of, 245
   Schmidt, H., and, 290, 294
Schlesinger, James, 182, 255
Schmidt, Adolf, 220–21, 225
Schmidt, Helmut, 211–12, 220–23, 262
   Europe and, 323n34
   as politician, 307, 316–17, 346–47
   reputation of, 298–99
   Scheel and, 290, 294
Schmitt, Carl, 6, 305
Schneider, Hans K., 218–19, 226, 294, 296–97, 372
Schröder, Dieter, 247, 302
Schubert, Enno, 213
Schumacher, Ernst F., 368
Schumann, Maurice, 245
science. *See also* petro-knowledge; research
   AAPG for, 33
   culture of, 392
   economics and, 39–40
   of energy security, 56, 148–49
   of petroleum, 23, 47n81
   politics of, 128, 137–44
   USGS for, 24
Scowcroft, Brent, 181, 189n53, 201n338
Seabury, Paul, 353
Shell. *See* Royal Dutch Shell
Shultz, Charles M., 156
Shultz, George P., 63, 129–31, 189n54, 292–94, 296–97, 317
Silk, Leonard, 302
Simon, Julian E., 371–72
Simon, William E., 131–33, 135, 159–62, 167–72, 189n53
   Kissinger and, 292–94
   in politics, 295–96
   reputation of, 189n62, 199n283, 391
Simonet, Henri, 291, 294
Sinclair, Upton, 31–32
Six-Day War, 56–57, 64, 247
Small Working Group, 71, 207–9, 213

Smith, Adam, 111
Soames, Christopher, 294
social science. *See* culture
Society of Petroleum Engineers (SPE), 33, 47n76, 47n82
solar energy, 218
Solow, Robert, 371
sovereignty. *See also* national sovereignty; *specific topics*
    for Brandt, 204–5, 253
    Case for Sovereignty (Rabkin), 358
    as concept, 5–8
    diplomacy in, 313–14
    interdependence and, 294–302
    oil crisis (1973–74) and, 42
    political sovereignty, 309–10
    politics of, 387–95
Soviet Union. *See also* Cold War
    oil from, 258–59
    Ostpolitik for, 259–61
Al-Sowayegh, Abdulaziz, 90
SPE. *See* Society of Petroleum Engineers
Speer, Albert, 131
Springer, Axel Cäsar, 233
Stability and Growth Act, 226
von Staden, Berndt, 253–54
stagflation, 227
Standard Oil, 23
Steed, Tom, 169
Stein, Herbert, 135, 157
Stever, H. Guyford, 134
Stiglitz, Joseph, 371
van der Stoel, Max, 297
Strauß, Franz Josef, 207–8, 212, 221, 231, 334
Suez Canal, 43n14, 53–54, 56–57, 64
Sun Oil, 34
Süskind, Martin, 113
Sweden, 259
Syria, 30–31, 98, 103, 184. *See also* Middle East

T

Task Force on Oil Import Control, 62–63, 66, 125–26
Tati, Jacques, 36
technology
    backstop technology, 370–71
    Energy for a Technological Society (Priest), 364
    history of, 359–64
    Journal of Petroleum Technology, 34
    for oil, 151
    for oil crisis (1973–74), 71–72
    for oil reserves, 38–42
    petroleum and, 29, 36–37
Texaco, 361–62
Texas Railroad Commission, 24
Third world nations. *See* developing nations
Torrey Canyon (oil tanker), 36
Trans-Arabian Pipeline, 64, 208

transnationalism, 354–58
Truman, Harry S., 123, 145
Tucker, Robert W., 348–49, 393–94
Tucker, Stanley, 101
Tugendhat, Christopher, 341
Turner, Louis, 341–42, 373n19

U

UK. *See* United Kingdom
UN. *See* United Nations
UNCTAD. *See* United Nations Conference on Trade and Development
Ungerer, Werner, 238
UNIDO. *See* United Nations Industrial Development Organization
Union Oil, 135
United Kingdom (UK). *See also* Western Society
    economics in, 217–18
    energy security for, 106–7, 250–51
    France and, 28, 256–57, 299
    in globalization, 226, 300–301
    government in, 339–40
    Iran and, 29–30
    OECD and, 194n177
    oil for, 176
    Petroleum Press Service in, 25
    petrol for, 23
    Ridley Commission for, 68
United Nations (UN)
    diplomacy for, 98–99, 104, 248–49
    economics and, 276n178, 309
    Emergency Aid Fund by, 262
    environmentalism and, 314
    Europe and, 243, 247
    for human rights, 6, 180
    for international law, 5
    Middle East and, 232–33
    OECD and, 12, 261–62
    oil crisis (1973–74) for, 347
    raw materials for, 304
    UNIDO, 315
United Nations Conference on Trade and Development (UNCTAD), 104, 309, 314
United Nations Industrial Development Organization (UNIDO), 315
United States (US). *See also* Cold War; Washington energy conference; Western Society
    Africa and, 179
    Defense Protection Act (1950) in, 158
    diplomacy for, 120n95, 252–58
    Economic Stabilization Act (1970) in, 158
    Egypt and, 181–82
    Emergency Petroleum Allocation Act in, 132, 159
    Energy Policy Project in, 145–48
    energy security for, 39–42, 57–58, 97–98, 144–48, 283n311

Index

environmentalism in, 167
Europe and, 58–59, 69–70, 73–74, 80n43, 111–12, 231, 241, 263–64, 344
Faisal (King) and, 117n41, 162, 178–84
foreign policy for, 18n40, 337
France and, 289–90
globalization and, 59–60, 234–35, 244, 262, 314–15
government in, 128–33, 167–69, 336–39
hegemony for, 287–94, 302–4, 323n49, 356–58, 380n138, 393–94
history of, 23–24
imports for, 186
Israel and, 101, 243
Japan and, 256, 283n313
law in, 31–32
Mandatory Oil Import Program in, 24–25
media in, 94–96, 108–9, 161–72
Middle East and, 99, 134, 173–75
National Environmental Protection Act in, 127
National Petroleum Council in, 129, 145–46
national security in, 62–67
national sovereignty for, 150–51
oil crisis (1973–74) for, 164–65, 171, 260
oil embargo and, 88–90, 153–54, 157–58
oil reserves in, 49n122
policy in, 123–24, 126
politics in, 189n62
Project Independence Report in, 148–54
Saudi Arabia and, 91–93, 174, 176–81, 183–84
Syria and, 30
West Germany and, 252–58, 297–98
United States Geological Survey (USGS), 24
US. *See* United States
USGS. *See* United States Geological Survey

V

Vaillaud, Michel, 60
Vansant, Carl, 344
Venn, Fiona, 18n40
Vernon, Raymond, 6, 333

W

Wakefield, Stephen, 131, 146
Waldheim, Kurt, 310
Washington energy conference, 294–302, 315, 346
Watergate scandal. *See also* Nixon, Richard
diplomacy and, 129–30, 155, 163–64, 172–73, 185
policy and, 180–81, 185
Weaver, Morris, 169
Weinstein, Adelbert, 112
Werner, Günter Franz, 235–36, 242

Western Society, 67–77, 112–13
Cold War for, 252–53
culture of, 111
democracy in, 308
diplomacy for, 184, 286–87, 388–89
economics in, 334–35
energy and, 3–5, 9–11, 14–15
energy security in, 19–23, 51–52, 77–78
EPC and, 288–89
foreign policy for, 389–94
industrialism in, 368–69
Israel and, 254, 257–58
in media, 348–49
Middle East and, 11, 31, 90–91, 105–14, 278n223
OECD and, 52–62
oil and, 19–23, 340–43
oil embargo for, 242–43
West Germany, 67–77, 112–13
advertisements in, 25
Africa and, 314
diplomacy for, 232–39, 242–45
economics of, 6, 346–47
energy policy in, 212–22, 229–32, 263–65
Energy Security Act in, 344
energy security for, 107–8, 178, 231–32
Europe and, 306–7
foreign policy for, 12, 302
globalization for, 225, 239–42, 258–63
government in, 268n49
Israel and, 282n307
Japan and, 80n43
Middle East and, 215, 247–52
OAPEC and, 240
oil crisis (1973–74) for, 207–11, 222–29, 263–65
oil dependency in, 86n148, 203–6
oil embargo for, 56–57
OPEC and, 277n203
raw materials for, 366
Saudi Arabia and, 236–37
Stability and Growth Act in, 226
US and, 252–58, 297–98
White, David, 24, 26–28
Wildavsky, Aaron, 353
Wilkins, Mira, 342
Wilson, Caroll L., 218–19
Wilson, Harold, 316
Wischnewski, Hans-Jürgen, 317–18
Wolf, Joseph J., 345–46
World Bank, 298, 303
Wörner, Manfred, 346–47

Y

Yaker, Layachi, 347
Yamani, Zaki (Sheikh), 31, 90–92, 96–97, 105–14, 182
in media, 103–4, 115, 117n27, 235

policy by, 239, 337–38
reputation of, 312
Yergin, Daniel, 19–20, 22, 34, 65, 90
    for history, 344
    reputation of, 342–43
Yom Kippur War, 95–96, 98–99, 207, 236–37, 257–58

Z

Zarb, Frank, 190n64
Zausner, Eric, 149, 153, 190n64
Zywietz, Werner, 225

www.ingramcontent.com/pod-product-compliance
Lightning Source LLC
Chambersburg PA
CBHW071144070526
44584CB00019B/2652